Museum Objects

Museum Objects creates a distinctive emphasis and perspective on the things that lie at the heart of interpretive practice in museums, material culture studies and further afield. Bringing together diverse, theorised and practice-based articles and extracts from a range of international academic and contextual perspectives, the texts stimulate reflection on the nature and definition of the object, and people's experiences of and relationships to it.

This volume in the Leicester series focuses on the individual object and the nature of human experience of it, and on the application of these ideas to aspects of interpretive practice in museums, anthropology, art practice, management studies, archaeology, art history, and beyond. The book aims to focus, first, on what objects might be and on the nature of their properties and stability (or not); second, on the sensory, emotional and other aspects of how objects are encountered and experienced; third, on the impacts of different settings on such experience; and, fourth, on where the boundaries between objects and persons can be found and how the relationships between the two may be described or imagined.

Museum Objects thus constitutes a very particular, bottom-up perspective on both objects and museums. Its introductory chapter argues that starting with the object, and a fundamental understanding of its nature and of the possibilities in encountering it, can enable both the richest kinds of museum experience and the fullest knowledge of the object's original and later contexts. The overall result is a definitive set of readings that offers a fresh approach to thinking about objects and their place within the museum context and elsewhere. The book will be of value to students of objects and museums and museum practitioners alike.

Sandra H. Dudley is Senior Lecturer in the School of Museum Studies, University of Leicester. Recent books include *Materialising Exile: Material Culture and Embodied Experience Among Karenni Refugees in Thailand* (2010), *Museum Materialities* (ed., Routledge 2010) and *The Thing About Museums* (co-ed., Routledge 2011).

Leicester Readers in Museum Studies
Series Editor: Professor Simon J. Knell

Museum Management and Marketing
Richard Sandell and Robert R. Janes

Museums in the Material World
Simon J. Knell

Museums and their Communities
Sheila Watson

Museums in a Digital Age
Ross Parry

Preventive Conservation
Christopher Caple

Museum

Objects

Experiencing the Properties of Things

Edited by

Sandra H. Dudley

Routledge
Taylor & Francis Group

LONDON AND NEW YORK

First published 2012
by Routledge
2 Park Square, Milton Park, Abingdon, Oxon OX14 4RN

Simultaneously published in the USA and Canada
by Routledge
711 Third Avenue, New York, NY 10017

Routledge is an imprint of the Taylor & Francis Group, an informa business

British Library Cataloguing in Publication Data
A catalogue record for this book is available from the British Library

Library of Congress Cataloging in Publication Data
Museum objects : experiencing the properties of things / edited by Sandra
Dudley.
     p. cm. — (Leicester readers in museum studies)
  "Simultaneously published in the USA and Canada"—T.p. verso.
  Includes bibliographical references and index.
  1. Museums—Social aspects.   2. Museums—Psychological aspects.
  3. Museum exhibits—Social aspects.   4. Museum exhibits—Psychological
  aspects.   5. Material culture—Social aspects.   6. Material culture—
  Psychological aspects.   7. Senses and sensation—Social aspects.
  8. Senses and sensation—Psychological aspects.   I. Dudley, Sandra H.
  AM7.M87255 2012
  069—dc23

                                                        2011042164

ISBN: 978-0-415-58177-6 (hbk)
ISBN: 978-0-415-58178-3 (pbk)

Typeset in Perpetua
by RefineCatch Limited, Bungay, Suffolk

Printed and bound by CPI Group (UK) Ltd, Croydon, CR0 4YY

For Richard Dudley,
with love

Contents

Figures

Contributors

Samuel J. M. M. Alberti is Director of Museums and Archives at the Royal College of Surgeons, where his responsibilities include the Hunterian Museum; previously he held a joint post at the University of Manchester between the Centre for Museology and the Manchester Museum. He has chaired the Museums and Galleries History Group, and retains an interest in the past, present and future of natural history and medical collections. He is author of *Nature and Culture: objects, disciplines and the Manchester Museum* (Manchester University Press, 2009) and *Morbid Curiosities: medical museums in nineteenth-century Britain* (Oxford, 2011) and he edited *The Afterlives of Animals: a museum menagerie* (Virginia, 2011).

Geoffrey Batchen is Professor of Art History at Victoria University of Wellington in New Zealand. His books include *Burning with Desire: the conception of photography* (The MIT Press, 1997); *Each Wild Idea: writing, photography, history* (The MIT Press, 2001); *Forget Me Not: photography and remembrance* (Van Gogh Museum/Princeton Architectural Press, 2004); *William Henry Fox Talbot* (Phaidon, 2008); *Photography Degree Zero: reflections on Roland Barthes's Camera Lucida* (The MIT Press, 2009); and *Suspending Time: life-photography-death* (Izu Photo-Museum, 2010). His next book is a co-edited anthology titled *Picturing Atrocity: photography in crisis* (Reaktion, 2011).

Olga Belova completed her PhD in Management Studies at the University of Essex, researching visual images, experience and perception of advertising materials. She has since lectured at the University of Essex and conducted postdoctoral research into multiple identities of knowledge workers in organisations characterised by diversity. Publications include the book *Visual Images of Organizations* (VDM Verlag, 2009).

Kim Christensen is a Doctoral candidate in the Department of Anthropology at the University of California Berkeley. A historical archaeologist, her research focuses on domestic sites of the nineteenth and twentieth centuries, collaborative archaeology, gender and feminist theory, and the politics of the past.

Jeremy Coote is Curator and Joint Head of Collections at the University of Oxford's Pitt Rivers Museum. Trained as a social anthropologist, in the 1980s and 1990s he drew on his research in Southern Sudan to contribute to debates in the anthropology of art and aesthetics, most notably in *Anthropology, Art, and Aesthetics* (co-edited with Anthony Shelton; Oxford University Press, 1992). Since joining the Pitt Rivers in 1994, he has led a number of externally funded, collections-based research projects, resulting in the publication of the Museum's collections from, for example, South Sudan, Ancient Cyprus, and James Cook's Pacific voyages. He is currently working with Alison Petch on 'Rethinking Pitt-Rivers', a three-year project funded by The Leverhulme Trust (2009–2012); a monograph on Pitt-Rivers's collecting activities is due for publication in 2013. Since 2006 he has also been the Editor of the Museum Ethnographers Group's *Journal of Museum Ethnography*.

Peter de Bolla is Professor of Cultural History and Aesthetics at the University of Cambridge. He has contributed to the study of artworks and aesthetics both theoretically, in *The Discourse of the Sublime* (Blackwell, 1989) and practically in *Art Matters* (Harvard, 2001). He has also published on eighteenth-century landscape, architecture and painting, *The Education of the Eye* (Stanford, 2003), and a book entitled *The Touch of Painting* is in progress.

Caitlin DeSilvey is a Lecturer in Cultural Geography at the University of Exeter. Her research explores the cultural significance of material transience and crafts alternative interpretations of the material past. Current projects include a connective ethnography of copper-mining regions, a network exploring the concept of anticipatory history and a collaborative documentary project on mending and repair practices. She has also carried out research on themes of landscape and memory, adaptive heritage management and the intersection between geography and contemporary arts practice. Publications include *Anticipatory History* (Uniformbooks, 2011, ed. with Simon Naylor and Colin Sackett).

Sandra H. Dudley is Senior Lecturer in the University of Leicester's School of Museum Studies, and was formerly at the Pitt Rivers Museum, University of Oxford. A social anthropologist with an earlier training in aesthetics, she has conducted long-term ethnographic research in mainland Southeast Asia. Her research is reflected in publications on material culture, textiles and dress, museums, Karenni refugees and Burma, including *Textiles from Burma* (co-ed., 2003), *Materialising Exile* (Berghahn, 2010), *Museum Materialities* (Routledge, 2010) and *The Thing about Museums* (co-ed., Routledge, 2011). She is co-editor of the forthcoming annual journal *Museum Worlds: Advances in Research*.

Jan Geisbusch is a researcher at University College London. His research interests centre on popular religion, material culture and the cult of saints, especially within the context of Roman Catholicism in the contemporary age.

Alfred Gell (d. 1997) was a Reader in Anthropology at the London School of Economics and Political Science. He did field research in Melanesia and India. Notable publications other than *Art and Agency* include *Wrapping in Images: tattooing in Polynesia* (Clarendon, 1993), *The Anthropology of Time* (Berg, 1992) and *Metamorphosis of the Cassowaries* (Athlone, 1975).

Anna Gibbs is an Associate Professor in Writing and Society at the University of Western Sydney. Her research interests include affect theory, public emotion, embodiment and corporeality, psychoanalysis and media. Notable articles include 'Writing and Danger: the intercorporeality of affect', in Nigel Krauth and Tess Brady (eds.) *Creative Writing* (Post Pressed, 2006).

Sabrina Gschwandtner is a visual artist who works with photographic and textile media. She has exhibited her work internationally, at institutions including the Victoria and Albert Museum, London; the Contemporary Arts Museum, Houston; Bucharest Biennale; Gustavsbergs Konsthall, Sweden; the Museum of Arts and Design, New York; Contemporary Art Centre, Lithuania; and SculptureCenter, NY. She has lectured on handcraft, craftivism, feminism and fine art extensively, at Harvard University; the Rhode Island School of Design; the Smithsonian American Art Museum; Central Saint Martins College of Art and Design; Bergen National Academy of the Arts, Norway; and the Museum of World Culture, Sweden, among others. From 2002 to 2007 she published *KnitKnit*, a 'zine included in the permanent collections of The Museum of Modern Art, the New York Public Library, and the Fine Arts Library, Fogg Art Museum at Harvard University. She is the author of *KnitKnit: profiles and projects from knitting's new wave* (Stewart, Tabori and Chang, 2007).

Thomas Hardy (1840–1928) was an English novelist and poet. His best-known novels include *Tess of the d'Urbervilles*, *The Mayor of Casterbridge* and *Jude the Obscure*. His first volume of poetry, *Wessex Poems*, was published in 1898.

Anita Herle is Senior Curator for World Anthropology at the Museum of Archaeology and Anthropology (MAA), University of Cambridge. She has coordinated the MPhil course in Social Anthropology and Museums for the Department of Social Anthropology since the early 1990s and also teaches in the anthropology of art and visual media. Her research is concerned with a range of ethnographic and disciplinary contexts for the Museum's collections and their many contemporary resonances. Within the history of British anthropology, her work has explored the intersection between different knowledge systems, the complex intersubjective relations that develop in the anthropological field, and the potency of objects and photographs in relational encounters. Much of her research has resulted in the production of innovative collaborative exhibitions, at MAA and elsewhere. She has regional interests in Canada, Torres Strait, Vanuatu and Fiji.

Steven Hooper is Professor of Visual Arts and Director of the Sainsbury Research Unit for the Arts of Africa, Oceania and the Americas at the University of East Anglia. His research interests include Pacific material culture and society, cultural property, ethnographical museums and the art market. Publications include *Pacific Encounters: art and divinity in Polynesia 1760–1860* (British Museum Press, 2006), and *The Fiji Journals of Baron Anatole von Hügel, 1875–77* (co-ed., The Fiji Museum, 1990).

Tim Ingold is Professor of Social Anthropology at the University of Aberdeen. Current research interests, stemming from earlier work on the perception of the environment, encompass the dynamics of pedestrian movement, the creativity of practice, and the linearity of writing. Publications include *Lines* (Routledge, 2007), *Creativity and Cultural Improvisation* (co-ed., Berg, 2007), *The Perception of the Environment* (Routledge, 2000), and *Key Debates in Anthropology*, 1988–1993 (ed., Routledge, 1996).

Liz James is Professor of Art History at the University of Sussex. Her research centres on Byzantine art history and the ways in which the Byzantines appear to have perceived and used their art. Publications include *Empresses and Power in Early Byzantium* (Leicester, 2001), *Light and Colour in Byzantine Art* (Clarendon, 1996), *Art and Text in Byzantium* (ed., Cambridge, 2007), *Icon and Word* (co-ed., Ashgate, 2003), and *Desire and Denial in Byzantium* (ed., Variorum, 1999).

Simon J. Knell is Professor of Museum Studies, and former Dean of Arts, at the University of Leicester. He researches those disciplinary cultures associated with museums focusing particularly on the relationships between people, objects and practices. His books include *The Great Fossil Enigma* (Indiana, in press), *National Museums* (co-ed., Routledge, 2010), *Museum Revolutions* (co-ed., Routledge, 2007) and *Museums in the Material World* (ed., Routledge, 2007).

Christina F. Kreps is Associate Professor of Anthropology and Director of Museum and Heritage Studies and the Museum of Anthropology at the University of Denver, USA. For nearly twenty years, Dr Kreps has been conducting research on museums and museological behaviour from a comparative cross-cultural perspective, and engaged in museum development and training in the Netherlands, Indonesia, Viet Nam, Thailand, Italy and the United States. Publications include *Liberating Culture: cross-cultural perspectives on museums, curation, and heritage preservation* (Routledge, 2003) and 'Appropriate Museology in Theory and Practice', *Journal of Museum Management and Curatorship*, 2008. Recent projects include her work with the Field School for Intangible Cultural Heritage in Lamphun, Thailand Centre, and the European Commission-sponsored projects: Museums as Places for Intercultural Dialogue (MAPforID) and the Learning Museum (LEM).

Susanne Küchler is Professor of Material Culture in the Department of Social Anthropology at University College London. Research interests include art, material culture, design and social change in the Pacific, and new materials and technologies. Publications include *Malanggan: art, memory and sacrifice* (Berg, 2002), *Pacific Pattern* (with Graeme Were, Thames & Hudson, 2005) and *Tvaivai: the social fabric of the Cook Islands* (with Andrea Eimke, British Museum, 2009).

Anna MacLennan completed her Masters of Research in Social Anthropology at the University of Aberdeen, focusing on traditional fur clothing from the Canadian Eastern Arctic. She has worked as a teaching assistant in a Dehcho Dene community in the Northwest Territories, Canada. She has a long-standing interest in Canadian First Nations and Métis beadwork and the historic links between Canada and Scotland.

Lambros Malafouris is Research Fellow in Creativity at Keble College, Oxford, and was formerly Balzan Post-Doctoral Research Fellow in Cognitive Archaeology, in the McDonald Institute for Archaeological Research at the University of Cambridge. His research interests include the archaeology of mind and the anthropology of the brain–artefact interface. Publications include *The Cognitive Life of Things: recasting the boundaries of the mind* (co-ed. with Colin Renfrew, McDonald Institute Monographs, 2010), and 'Between brains, bodies and things: tectonoetic awareness and the extended self', *Philosophical Transactions of the Royal Society of London B: Biological Sciences*, 2008.

Julie Marcus is Adjunct Senior Research Fellow at the University of South Australia. Her research interests focus on cultural differences, gender, race and sexuality, including in relation to museums and exhibitions. She has conducted field research in Turkey and central Australia. Her book *Indomitable Miss Pink: a life in anthropology* (University of New South Wales, 2002) won the Dobbie Award for the best first published book by an Australian woman writer.

David Morgan is Professor of Religion at Duke University and Director of the Graduate Program in Religion. His research interests encompass the history of religious visual and print culture, art history and critical theory, and religion and media. His books include *The Embodied Eye: religious visual culture and the social life of feeling* (California, 2012), *The Lure of Images: a history of religion and visual media in America* (Routledge, 2007), *Visual Piety* (University of California Press, 1998), and *The Sacred Gaze* (University of California Press, 2005). He is a Life Member of Clare Hall, Cambridge University, co-editor of the journal *Material Religion*, and co-editor of the book series 'Religion, Media and Culture', published by Routledge.

Howard Morphy is Professor and Director of the Research School for Humanities at the Australian National University, Honorary Curator of Pitt Rivers Museum, University of Oxford and Adjunct Curator of the Kluge-Ruhe Research Centre, University of Virginia. His research interests include material culture and the anthropology of art and aesthetics, visual anthropology, and museums. Publications include *Ancestral Connections* (University of Chicago, 1992) and *Becoming Art* (Berg, 2008).

Gabriel Moshenska is a Leverhulme Trust Early Career Research Fellow at UCL Institute of Archaeology, working on the history of public archaeology. His research interests include the historical archaeology of modern conflicts, material cultures of childhood, and public engagement in archaeology. Publications include *Archaeologies of Internment* (co-ed. with Adrian Myers, Springer, 2011) and *Community Archaeology: themes, methods and practices* (co-ed. with Sarah Dhanjal, Oxbow, 2011).

Susan M. Pearce is Professor Emerita in the School of Museum Studies and former Pro-Vice-Chancellor at the University of Leicester, and a former President of the Museums Association. She has published extensively in the fields of museum objects and collections, collecting, material culture, the archaeology of south-west Britain, history of museums, ethnography and curatorship.

Celmara Pocock is Lecturer in Anthropology at the University of Southern Queensland, and former Research Fellow at The University of Queensland. Her research interests include environmental anthropology, cultural history, tourism, and representations of space and place. Publications include 'Sensing Place, Consuming Space', in *Tourism Consumption and Representation* edited by Meethan, Anderson and Miles (CABI, 2006); and *Australian Anthropologies of the Environment* (Special Issue 17 of *The Australian Journal of Anthropology* co-edited with Jane Mulcock and Yann Toussaint, 2005).

Leon Rosenstein is Professor Emeritus in the Department of Philosophy at San Diego State University. A distinguished scholar in aesthetics and the philosophy of art, he has also been an antiques dealer in San Diego for the past twenty-five years. His publications include numerous chapters and articles, and his book *Antiques: the history of an idea* (Cornell University Press, 2008).

Victoria L. Rovine is Associate Professor in the School of Art and Art History and the Center for African Studies at the University of Florida, and was formerly Curator of the Arts of Africa, Oceania, and the Americas at the University of Iowa Museum of Art. Research interests include the revival of traditional textiles in Africa (particularly Mali) and African fashion designers in global markets. Publications include her book *Bogolan: shaping culture through cloth in contemporary Mali* (Indiana, 2008).

M. A. Schaffner has published poetry in *Stand*, the *Beloit Poetry Journal*, *Poet Lore* and *The North*. He is author of the poetry collection *The Good Opinion of Squirrels* (Word Works, 1997) and of a novel, *War Boys* (Welcome Rain, 2002).

Ernst van de Wetering is a trained artist and Professor of the History of Art at the University of Amsterdam. He is Chair of the Rembrandt Research Project and former art historian of Amsterdam's Central Research Laboratory for Restoration. He has published numerous articles on historic painting techniques and on the theory and ethics of conservation and restoration, and wrote the book *Rembrandt: the painter at work* (University of Amsterdam, 2000).

Semir Zeki is Professor of Neuroaesthetics at University College London, and a Fellow of the Royal Society. His research uses imaging and psychophysical techniques to explore the organisation of the visual brain. He has published numerous articles, and books including *A Vision of the Brain* (Blackwell, 1993), *Inner Vision: an exploration of art and the brain* (Oxford University Press, 1999), and *Splendours and Miseries of the Brain* (Blackwell, 2008).

Acknowledgements

The editor is grateful to all those who granted permission for the reproduction of copyright material and thus made this book possible.

M. A. Schaffner, 'Wayward Docents', *Beltway Poetry Quarterly*, Volume 10, Number 1, Winter 2009. Reproduced by kind permission of the author.

1. Objects and their properties

S. Pearce, 1993. Museum objects. From S. Pearce (ed.) *Museums, Objects and Collections*, Washington (DC): Smithsonian Institution Press; pp. 4–6.

L. Rosenstein, 1987. The aesthetic of the antique. *The Journal of Aesthetics and Art Criticism* 45 (4); pp. 393–400. Copyright © 1987 L. Rosenstein. Reproduced by permission of Blackwell Publishing Ltd.

S. Hooper, 2005. On looking at a Tahitian god-house. *Journal of Museum Ethnography*, 17: 89–100. Reproduced by permission of the Museum Ethnographers Group and the author.

A. MacLennan, 2008. Making life beautiful: my experience of doing beadwork. In A. Brown (ed.) *Material Histories*, Aberdeen: Marischal Museum, pp. 77–9. Reproduced by permission of the University of Aberdeen and Anna MacLennan. Full publication available for free download at <http://www.abdn.ac.uk/materialhistories/proceedings.php>.

S. Gschwandtner, 2008. Knitting is . . . *Journal of Modern Craft* 1(2): 271–8. Reproduced by permission of Berg Publishers, an imprint of Bloomsbury Publishing Plc.

S. Küchler, 1988. Malangan: objects, sacrifice and the production of memory. *American Ethnologist* 15(4): 625–37. Reproduced by permission of the American Anthropological Association.

G. Batchen, 2004. Ere the substance fade: photography and hair jewellery. In E. Edwards and J. Hart (eds.) *Photographs Objects Histories*, London: Routledge, pp. 32–46. Reproduced with permission.

S. J. M. M. Alberti, 2009. Preparing and conserving. From Chapter 5 (Practice: technique and the lives of objects in the collection) in his *Nature and Culture: objects, disciplines and the Manchester Museum*, Manchester: Manchester University Press, pp. 124–7. Reproduced with permission.

2. Experiencing objects

D. Morgan, 2008. The materiality of cultural construction. *Material Religion* 4(2): 228–9; p. 228. Reproduced by permission of Berg Publishers, an imprint of Bloomsbury Publishing Plc.

E. van de Wetering, 1996. The surface of objects and museum style. In N. S. Price, M. K. Talley and A. M. Vaccaro (eds) *Historical and Philosophical Issues in the Conservation of Cultural Heritage*, LA: The Getty Conservation Institute: pp. 415–21. Originally presented at the Third International Seminar for Restorers, Veszprém, Hungary, 1981; first published as 'Die Oberfläche der Dinge und der museale Stil', *Maltechnik Restauro* 2 (1982): 98–102; translated by A. Trone. Reproduced by permission of The Getty Conservation Institute and Restauro (Callwey Verlag).

S. Zeki, 1998. Art and the brain. *Daedalus* 127(2): 71–103; pp. 71–5. Reproduced by permission of the MIT Press.

O. Belova, 2006. The event of seeing: a phenomenological perspective on visual sense-making. *Culture and Organization*, 12(2): 93–107. Reproduced by permission of Taylor and Francis.

L. James, 2005. Senses and sensibility in Byzantium. In D. Cherry (ed.) *Art: History: Visual: Culture*, Oxford: Blackwell, pp. 45–59. Reproduced with permission.

A. Gibbs, 2002. Disaffected. *Continuum: Journal of Media and Cultural Studies* 16(3): 335–41. Reproduced by permission of Taylor and Francis.

P. de Bolla, 2001. *Art Matters*. Cambridge (MA): Harvard University Press, pp. 141–5. Reproduced with permission.

S. Dudley, (2010). Sensory exile in the field. From Chapter 1 of *Materialising Exile: material culture and embodied experience among Karenni refugees in Thailand*. Oxford: Berghahn; pp. 4–6. Reproduced with permission.

T. Hardy, 1984 (1914). In the British Museum. From *The Complete Poetical Works of Thomas Hardy. Vol. 2, Satires of Circumstance: moments of vision: late lyrics and earlier*. Oxford: Clarendon Press.

3. Contexts of experiencing objects

K. Christensen, 2011. Ideas versus things: the balancing act of interpreting historic house museums. *International Journal of Heritage Studies*, 17(2): 153–68. Reproduced by permission of Taylor and Francis.

J. Marcus, 2000. Towards an erotics of the museum. In E. Hallam and B. V. Street (eds) *Cultural Encounters: representing 'otherness'*. London: Routledge, pp. 229–44. Reproduced with permission.

J. Geisbusch 2007. For your eyes only? The magic touch of relics. In E. Pye (ed.) *The Power of Touch: handling objects in museum and heritage contexts*. Walnut Creek (CA): Left Coast Press, pp. 73–88. Reproduced with permission.

J. Coote, 1992. 'Marvels of everyday vision': the anthropology of aesthetics and the cattle-keeping Nilotes. In J. Coote and A. Shelton (eds) *Anthropology, Art and Aesthetics*. Oxford: Clarendon, pp. 245–73. Reproduced with permission.

C. Pocock, 2002. Sense matters: aesthetic values of the Great Barrier Reef. *International Journal of Heritage Studies*, 8(4): 365–81. Reproduced by permission of Taylor and Francis.

C. DeSilvey, 2006. Observed decay: telling stories with mutable things. *Journal of Material Culture*, 11(3): 318–38. Reproduced by permission of Sage Journals.

V. L. Rovine, 2007. Handmade textiles: global markets and authenticity. In D. C. Johnson and H. B. Foster (eds) *Dress Sense: emotional and sensory experiences of the body and clothes*, Oxford: Berg, pp. 133–43. Reproduced by permission of Berg Publishers, an imprint of Bloomsbury Publishing Plc.

C. F. Kreps, 2003. Museum Balanga as a site of cultural hybridization. From Chapter 2 of *Liberating Culture: cross-cultural perspectives on museums, curation and heritage preservation*, London: Routledge, pp. 26–34. Reproduced with permission.

4. Object/person distinctions

A. Herle, 2003. Objects, agency and museums: continuing dialogues between the Torres Strait and Cambridge. In L. Peers and A. Brown (eds) *Museums and Source Communities: a Routledge reader*, London: Routledge, pp. 194–207. Reproduced by permission of Crawford House Press.

G. Moshenska, 2009. Resonant materiality and violent remembering: archaeology, memory and bombing. *International Journal of Heritage Studies*, 15(1): 44–56. Reproduced by permission of Taylor and Francis.

A. Gell, 1998. 'Things' as social agents. *Art and Agency: an anthropological theory*. Oxford: Clarendon; pp. 17–24. Reproduced with permission.

H. Morphy, 2009. Art as a mode of action: some problems with Gell's *Art and Agency*. *Journal of Material Culture* 14(1): 5–27. Reproduced by permission of Sage Journals.

L. Malafouris, 2008. Beads for a plastic mind: the 'Blind Man's Stick' (BMS) hypothesis and the active nature of material culture. *Cambridge Archaeological Journal* 18(3): 401–14; pp. 403–5. Reproduced by permission of Cambridge University Press.

T. Ingold, 2000. Making culture and weaving the world. In P. M. Graves-Brown (ed.) *Matter, Materiality and Modern Culture*. New York: Routledge, pp. 50–71. Reproduced with permission.

I also wish to express gratitude to the School of Museum Studies and Catharina Hendrick for assistance with some of the editorial tasks for this reader. Thanks are due too to Simon Knell for asking me to do a reader for the Leicester series, to the anonymous reviewers of the original proposal for their constructive and helpful comments, and to Amy Davis-Poynter and Matthew Gibbons at Routledge for their professionalism and patience.

Series preface

Leicester Readers in Museum Studies provide students of museums – whether employed in the museum, engaged in a museum studies programme or studying in a cognate area – with a selection of focused readings in core areas of museum thought and practice. Each book has been compiled by a specialist in that field, but all share the Leicester School's belief that the development and effectiveness of museums relies upon informed and creative practice. The series as a whole reflects the core Leicester curriculum which is now visible in programmes around the world and which grew, forty years ago, from a desire to train working professionals, and students prior to entry into the museum, in the technical aspects of museum practice. In some respects the curriculum taught then looks similar to that we teach today. The following, for example, was included in the curriculum in 1968: history and development of the museum movement; the purpose of museum; types of museum and their functions; the law as it relates to museums; staff appointments and duties, sources of funding; preparation of estimates; byelaws and regulations; local, regional, etc. bodies; buildings; heating, ventilation and cleaning; lighting; security systems; control of stores, and so on. Some of the language and focus here, however, indicates a very different world. A single component of the course, for example, focused on collections and dealt with collection management, conservation and exhibitions. Another component covered 'museum activities' from enquiry services to lectures, films, and so on. There was also training in specialist areas, such as local history, and many practical classes which included making plaster casts and models. Many museum workers around the world will recognise these kinds of curriculum topics; they certainly resonate with my early experiences of working in museums.

While the skeleton of that curriculum in some respects remains, there has been a fundamental shift in the flesh we hang upon it. One cannot help but think that the museum world has grown remarkably sophisticated: practices are now regulated by equal opportunities, child protection, cultural property and wildlife conservation laws; collections are now exposed to material culture analysis, contemporary documentation projects, digital capture and so on; communication is now multimedia, inclusive, evaluated and theorised. The museum has over that time become intellectually fashionable, technologically advanced and developed a new social relevance. *Leicester Readers in Museum Studies* address this change. They deal with practice as it is relevant to the museum today, but they are also about expanding horizons beyond one's own experiences. They reflect a more professionalised world and one that has thought very deeply about this wonderfully interesting and significant institution. Museum studies remains a vocational subject but it is now very different. It is, however, sobering to think that the Leicester course was founded in the year Michel Foucault published *The Order of Things* – a book that greatly influenced the way we think about the museum today. The writing was on the wall even then.

Simon J. Knell
Series Editor

Preface

In 2010, museum historian Steven Conn published a book entitled *Do Museums Still Need Objects?* While the book might be criticised for its particular focus on the physical, historical, largely nineteenth-century objects one would expect given the author's academic area of expertise and for its lack of transgression of the traditional boundaries of 'the museum object',[1] it is excellent in many ways – not least in its affirmative conclusion that museums do indeed still need objects (whatever, one might add, we might define those objects to be). Museum objects constitute material 'facts' and evidence for stories to be told, and at the same time are now understood, in our postmodern world, within a frame of subjectivity – that is, we know that they mean different things to different people. These perspectives on objects, and the interpretive processes that are integral to both, are well explored through a range of readings in a previous reader in the Leicester series, Simon Knell's *Museums in the Material World* (2007). That publication also positioned museums within the social world of consumption and questioned the process of keeping so central to the very notion of the museum, revealing and critiquing disciplinary practices and their change over time.

This book, *Museum Objects*, sets out to complement *Museums in the Material World* by adding a volume to the series that looks in detail at the individual object and the nature of human experience of it, and enables a specific application of these ideas to aspects of interpretive practice – in museums, and also in other contexts. The aim is to sharpen the focus: first, on what objects might be and on the nature of their properties and stability (or not); second, on the sensory, emotional and other aspects of how objects are encountered and experienced; third, on the impacts of different settings on such experience; and, fourth, on where the boundaries between objects and persons can be found and how the relationships between the two can be described. The book stays within this sharp focus on objects *per se*: it does not seek to be a general material culture reader and thus does not, for example, address the circulation of objects within and to collections (such a subject is addressed in different ways in such volumes as Knell 2004, 2007; Gosden and Knowles 2001; Gosden, Larson and Petch 2007) or the gendering of objects (see for example Strathern 1990, Hoskins 2007).

Instead, this volume maintains a very particular perspective on both objects and museums not found running as a *leitmotif* through any other museum studies or material culture studies collection. This perspective, a bottom-up focus on objects, is based on a profound belief – elaborated in Chapter 1 – that starting with the object and a fundamental understanding of its nature and of the possibilities in encountering it enables both the richest kinds of museum experience and the fullest knowledge of the object's original and later contexts. Through this perspective, this book aims to change and enhance the views and work of students and practitioners by providing a set of readings that together create a distinctive emphasis on the objects at the heart of practice in museums, material culture studies and everyday life. Older and up-to-date texts on the nature and definition of the object itself, the senses and embodied experience of objects, representing a wide disciplinary range, are brought together and arranged thematically rather than as a historical trajectory.

It is important to point out that this book largely addresses the material object, essentially to allow a focus on the sensory and emotional aspects of encounter, and subject–object duality, that the readings highlight. However, objects, including museum objects, need not of course only be physical and discrete; furthermore, many of the embodied and embedded ways in which they are experienced apply too to other kinds of objects, including 'intangibles' and digital objects or 'e-tangibles'. Some of these issues are discussed in Chapter 1. Digital objects, and some of their implications for questions of authenticity and rarity, as well as materiality in the museum, are touched upon in another reader in the Leicester series, Ross Parry's *Museums in a Digital Age* (2007).

Ultimately we might, perhaps, turn Steven Conn's question on its head and ask: *do objects need museums?* Certainly, we have long known that objects in danger of loss or disappearance benefit from museums' traditional role as keeping places. But beyond this if we look closely at the ways in which objects and ideas, objects and experience, and objects and subjects are entwined in the museum space, at what is unique to that space and what happens similarly and dissimilarly in 'real' life outside, we can learn a great deal indeed about objects, their properties, and our experiences of and relationships with them. This is of obvious interest to explorers of museums and material culture alike. And as many of the readings that follow make clear, it is in the interests of both objects themselves and the human subjects with whom they are associated, that those objects be better understood – something which, as this book demonstrates, museums can bring about in uniquely special ways.

Sandra H. Dudley

Note

1   See also Geismar 2010.

References

Geismar, H. (2010) 'Do museums still need objects? Conn, Steven. 2010.' Review. Material World blog, <http://blogs.nyu.edu/projects/materialworld/2010/03/do_museums_still_need_objects.html>, last accessed 28 September 2011.

Gosden, C. and C. Knowles (2001) *Collecting Colonialism: material culture and colonial change*, Oxford: Berg.

Gosden, C., F. Larson and A. Petch (2007) *Knowing Things: exploring the collections at the Pitt Rivers Museum 1884–1945*, Oxford: Oxford University Press.

Hoskins, J. (2007) 'Afterword – gendering religious objects: placing them as agents in matrices of power', *Material Religion* 3(1): 110–19.

Knell, S. J. (ed.) (2004) *Museums and the Future of Collecting*, Farnham: Ashgate.

Knell, S. J. (ed.) (2007) *Museums in the Material World*, London: Routledge.

Parry, R. (ed.) (2007) *Museums in the Digital Age*, London: Routledge.

Strathern, M. (1990) *The Gender of the Gift: problems with women and problems with society in Melanesia*, Berkeley (CA): University of California Press.

Wayward docents

M. A. Schaffner

The fading labels were the museum's
chief attraction. It helped when they fell off.
Then memory or imagination brought
unprecedented interpretations.
A mummy was my great-uncle Clemons.
Tourists stared as my buddy and I talked
of wars and plagues their high schools never taught,
though vital to the progress of mankind.

When I last went through, new labels were there,
with new lighting, sound, and touch-screen movies,
quite frenzied in an interactive way,
and often wrong enough to make me stare.
We were such amateurs, my friend and I,
to love history enough to simply lie.

Chapter 1

Encountering a Chinese horse
Engaging with the thingness of things[1]

Sandra H. Dudley

The horse and the power of object encounter

In 2010, I visited for the first time the art gallery at Compton Verney in Warwickshire, England. As well as notable collections of Neopolitan, British, northern European and folk art, Compton Verney holds one of the top three Chinese collections in Europe,[2] centred on bronze ritual vessels and other objects. I did not know this, however, as my visit began and as I walked into the first room of Chinese artefacts. The room was lined with sparsely filled and elegantly lit cases of bronze vessels, and alone, facing the entrance to the room, on a plinth in the middle of the floor and without any glass around it, stood what to me seemed an extraordinarily beautiful and animated, bronze figure of a horse. The horse was green, over a metre high, and stood considerably higher still as a result of its plinth. I was utterly spellbound by its majestic form, its power, and, as I began to look at it closely, its material details: its greenish colour, its textured surface, the small areas of damage. I wanted to touch it, though of course I could not – but that did not stop me imagining how it would feel to stroke it, or how it would sound if I could tap the metal, or how heavy it would be if I could try to pick it up. I was, in other words, sensorially exploring the object, even though I had to intuit and imagine rather than directly experience most of the encounter. There was no label at all adjacent to the object, only a small number which correlated to the interpretive text on the gallery hand guide that I had not yet picked up. I still knew nothing at all about this artefact, other than that it clearly represented a horse and that I guessed it was made of bronze; nonetheless, its three-dimensionality, tactility and sheer power had literally moved me to tears. I allowed myself considerable time to reflect upon that feeling and upon the object, before I picked up the hand guide.

When eventually I did retrieve the text, I read:

Han Dynasty (206 BC–AD 220): Heavenly Horse, *tian ma*. Bronze. This large horse would have been a funerary offering for the tomb of an élite Chinese man, the intention being for the owner of the tomb to use the horse to pull his chariot in the afterlife. Such large bronze horses were very rare during the Western Han period, becoming more popular during the Eastern Han. It was extremely difficult to produce such large bronze figures in one mould, therefore this stallion is cast in nine close fitting pieces and joined together, an expensive method in terms of labour and material.

I was left breathless all over again. That this wonderful object was so intimately associated with someone's death, that it was so ancient, and that it was so rare, further intensified its power over me. I looked for the joins and counted the pieces, and studied the detail of the surface even more intently than I had before.

My initial response to the horse was a fundamental, emotional, sensory, even visceral, one to its form, materials, colour, scale and texture. Had the information about the horse been displayed next to it in the form of a label or text panel, I am certain it would have interfered with, even prevented altogether, the powerful and moving reaction I had to the object for its own sake: I would have been distracted by the text, would have been drawn to read it first, and would not have had the opportunity to experience and sensorially explore the artefact's physicality for its own sake. That is, I would not have had the powerful experience that I did, had the object been displayed in a way that impeded my ability to encounter it alone, in and of itself, *before* I discovered the crucial, contextual information the gallery had provided for it.

So what, if any, was the significance of that initial, pre-knowledge encounter with the physical object? Was it of no purpose beyond something purely personal to an individual visitor, of no wider relevance to other visitors and the gallery? Or was it a kind of personally transformative event that should be encouraged in museums? Utilising sensory and emotional aspects in the museum environment certainly has an established value in relation to learning and is evident in some contemporary educational activities and exhibition strategies (e.g. Golding 2010, Wehner and Sear 2010). It certainly made a major difference to how I subsequently reacted to the information I read about the object: because I was already emotionally receptive to the artefact, I had an empathic as well as purely cognitive response to, and thus a greater interest in, its history. Furthermore, as the temporal distance between the present moment and my encounter with the horse has increased, I find I can remember a surprising amount about it – something I can only explain by the personal impact it made upon me.

But what about the value of a powerful response to an object just for itself, rather than only because of how it might enhance learning or appreciation of the wider aspects of an exhibition? The opportunity to be moved to tears, tickled pink, shocked or disgusted by a museum object, or simply to reflect upon it, as a result of sensory and emotional engagement with its physicality before necessarily knowing anything at all about it, is itself a powerful component of what a museum experience can offer – not just as a step on the journey towards cognitive understanding of the story the object helps to tell, but as a potent and sometimes transformative phenomenon in its own right. This does not mean that cognitive understanding and stories are unimportant; only that the physicality of the object itself can be too, because it can trigger personal, emotional and sensory responses that may have a significance of their own as well as in enhancing subsequent understanding. This argument has resonances with James Clifford's suggestion that we should 'return to [museum objects] . . . their lost status as fetishes. *Our* fetishes. This tactic, necessarily personal, would accord to things in collections *the power to fixate, rather than simply the capacity to edify or inform*' (1985: 244; emphasis added).[3] The word 'return' is important: museums in the past often displayed some objects at least, principally to captivate or inculcate a sense of wonder rather than or as well as to educate. Indeed, arguably many still do this to some extent with some of their objects, as my experience at Compton Verney or a visit to some of the 'treasures' at national museums and galleries demonstrates.

Many of us would not question this notion of the object's 'power to fixate' if it concerned only the fine and decorative arts, or some genres thereof at least. We can accept, for example, that some conceptual art may set out precisely to move, shock, amuse or puzzle us, just as some products of design may seek to stimulate our acquisitiveness, our desire to possess. We are also familiar with such elemental responses to objects in the consumption practices that run through our daily lives – and of course, such responses are well understood and manipulated in the commercial sector by advertisers and retailers. This is less so in the world of museum practice, however. Yet encounters with objects can, in themselves, serve to enhance wellbeing and have a range of positive impacts, as an increasing array of empirical research is beginning to demonstrate.[4] Objects matter within museum practice, of course – but where once some of them at least would have been used to awe and inspire visitors, today they more often feature as, effectively, grammatical marks punctuating a story being told, rather than as powerful items in their own right. The effort expended by museums to render objects and interpretation accessible, and to enable visitors to identify meaning and context, is laudable and important; yet arguably it may sometimes be the strategies employed in that very effort which prevent or limit the opportunities for directly encountering and responding to objects in and of themselves, prior or in addition to cognitively exploring the stories they have to tell. The challenge lies in producing successful and accessible interpretive interventions which simultaneously do not act to dilute, if not remove altogether, the sense of magic, mystery and excitement that objects can also convey.

The object in material culture studies and museum studies

How best, then, might one begin to explore and understand more about how people and things in museums interact? Eleven years ago, Eilean Hooper-Greenhill wrote that 'material culture studies . . . have very little to say about the relationship between objects and museum visitors' (2000: 107). My contention is that, if material culture studies are broad and flexible enough, the opposite is true and they can make substantial contributions to understanding the relationships between objects and museum visitors, precisely because the links between people and things are, or could be, at their very heart.

Material culture studies comprise a large subject. There are now, for example, many metres of library shelves of texts from an impressively wide range of disciplinary perspectives addressing objects in relation to their role as commodities or gifts and their importance in social and economic relations – indeed their importance *as* arrays of relations (cf. Law 2000). The material nature of objects and how they are perceived and experienced has, with some notable exceptions referred to later in this essay, on the whole been less significant in the literature than discussions of exchange, meaning and value; i.e. the majority of sources tend to emphasise the (equally complex and important) *cultural* rather than the *material* aspects of objects and their roles in the human world. The last two or more decades have, for example, produced many useful studies of the meanings and values imputed to material objects embedded within social life – indeed, credited with having their own 'social life' (Appadurai 1986, Kopytoff 1986). Yet there are far fewer studies looking at the role played by the material actuality of the objects in question – the role of surface, material, density, colour, texture and so on – to the extent that Paul Graves-Brown accused much of the literature as having a tendency to see objects as just a 'world of surfaces on to which we project significance' (2000: 3–4). Instead, the focus has primarily been on human agency, ideology, concepts, signifiers and signifieds (this is true even of most work that addresses what it refers to as 'materiality', as Ingold points out [2007]).

These sorts of material culture studies are highly valuable in the cultural, social and historical insights they provide, but, because their emphasis does not lie primarily on the material *per se*, they are limited in helping us to understand how people actually experience and interact with objects on a physical, sensory or emotional level, whether in a museum or not. Hooper-Greenhill's claim is thus true for many of these studies, useful though they are in other ways. Furthermore, while it may not be the intention, because the focus of this work lies at the cultural rather than the material end of the material cultural continuum, in some of it objects appear at least to be reduced to materialisations of abstract human ideas, instead of rounded elements of a material world that influences our ideas and feelings too, that has and is a 'physicality which resists and enables' in a two-way relationship (Boivin 2004: 64).[5]

In museum studies meanwhile, some notable contributions have focused on the making of meaning, influenced by hermeneutical and reception aesthetics approaches such as those of Stanley Fish (1980; e.g. Hooper-Greenhill 2000), in which meaning and interpretation are primarily in the mind of the viewer and the influence of the object (or text, for Fish) and its qualities are markedly diminished or absent in the analysis. Such postmodernist critiques have been important in illuminating the role of the viewer and the significance of their sociocultural context and pre-existing knowledge in determining how the world – including material objects – is experienced. Indeed, the ontological perspective brought by these studies, and elsewhere by the insights of social and cultural anthropology, is essential to understanding the relationship between the different actors and elements that make up our world and in explaining the situated, contingent and shifting values and meanings objects and people give to each other, in museums and elsewhere.

To augment this perspective further with sensitivity to the real, material qualities of things and to the corporeal, culturally nuanced, sensory modalities through which those qualities are experienced and valued, is something I argue that a truly material, material culture studies approach can bring.[6] It is time to see a materially focused, material culture studies back in the centre of museum practice and museum studies. It has not held such a place since the late nineteenth century and it deserves to return – not in the positivist, static form and role it held in the past, but through a gentle, twenty-first-century revolution in which the object is once more at the heart of the museum, this time as a material focus of experience and opportunity, a subtle and nuanced, constructed, shifting thing, but also physical, ever-present, beating pulse of potential, quickening the institution and all that it is and could be.

Objects and subjects

My emphasis, then, is essentially on objects themselves: things as things, stuff as stuff. It is worthwhile probing a little further what objects are, and how they relate to the perceiving subject. I am using 'object' and 'thing' interchangeably;[7] nonetheless, the reader should be aware that there are some areas of scholarship – particularly literary thing theory (e.g. Brown 2001) and psychological object theory (e.g. Hood and Santos 2009) – in which they have distinct and sometimes opposite meanings.[8] The focus here is on physical objects, primarily in order to make some particular points about sensory experience and its relationship to the material characteristics of things – texture, shape, colour, density, and so on. However, both museums and the category 'material culture' include objects without clear, bounded material form; furthermore, we experience objects without fixed, three-dimensional material form (such as songs, dance performances, digital images, and so on) in multi-sensory ways – indeed, many of the points made in this essay can and should be extended to thinking about other sorts of things in museums and beyond.

The English word 'object' is most often assumed to refer to something tangible, measurable, visible and limited – something that extends through physical space, but is also defined, discrete, bounded.[9] Thus people think naturally of jugs, necklaces, fossils or swords as objects, but often find it hard to conceive similarly of something that is equally physically tangible but spatially far more extensive, such as a landscape. Everyday parlance of the term also tends to imply something man-made, artefactual – hence for most, bowls spring to mind more readily than butterflies – though as with other initial assumptions, there is often a strong and unsurprising influence from particular disciplinary backgrounds, so those with a science background do conceive of pieces of the natural world as objects as easily as they think of handmade and manufactured artefacts. To interrogate and problematise these notions about objects is useful for thinking about practice in museums, ethnography or elsewhere. In relation to museums, it provokes reflection upon how many different kinds of things institutions hold, beyond those traditionally thought of as constituting the stuff of their collections.[10] But it can also initiate some contemplation of the nature of museum practice itself – or at least, consideration of both what it is that museums do, and what it is they do it with and about. If objects can encompass so diverse a gathering of things, from a historical photographic print to a dinosaur tooth, a silver trophy to a digital film, an Iron Age hill fort to an archive sound recording, a live dance performance to a digitally recorded collection of community memories, what can possibly bring all these things together into one category? What, in other words, defines 'the object' in such a setting?

In part, it is interpretation: the object is, or is potentially, interpreted; it is an *object*, in the grammatical sense, of the interpretive process – something acted upon, something influenced by the action of the subject: I hugged *her*; the curator wrote a text panel about *the canoe*. Material and non-material things alike can all be interpreted in museum or other interpretive practice. Indeed, such interpretation goes hand-in-glove with the fundamental role of objects in human social and cultural life: in the Kula gift-exchange in the Trobriand Islands, famously first described by Malinowski (1922), ceremonial *mwali* arm-ornaments and *soulava* necklaces are the central artefacts in a formalised set of ongoing exchange processes that establish and maintain trading and political relationships amongst men within and between islands; thus so long as these items remain in the islands, they are passed around between individuals as the objects at the centre of this ritualised exchange system; then once in the museum, they are *interpreted* so as to explain that former role. The Compton Verney horse was interpreted by the gallery in the text that I eventually read.[11]

But in museums, many such things often end up being used as accessories within the interpretation of something else – as props in the telling of a story rather than as the focus of the story themselves. Thus letters and black-edged calling cards from the archive, and items of Whitby jet jewellery are used to punctuate an exhibition on death in Victorian times, in which the main items are the hearse and the mourning dress; abundant oral histories are edited and run in extract form on an audio guide as background between key points on a coal mining heritage trail; richly woven textiles, cowrie shells and unusual coins are scattered as examples, but unexplored in themselves, throughout a display about trade across cultures and history. Those items' *own* particular epistemological or narrative potential may lie mostly unexplored and unrevealed.

Yet there is still an (often unintended) experiential dimension to the presence of those things, still a possibility to engage with them in surprisingly direct and sensorially and emotionally valid ways. The colours, textures, intricacy and sheer beauty of the textile; the gravelly, flat, yet surprisingly moving voice of a miner now dead, recalling the camaraderie of life in the pits; the sombre power of the now fragile letters of condolence written long ago . . . these objects may be peripheral to the narrative of the exhibitions in which they appear, little more than structural components in a much larger story, yet individually too they have the power to arrest, to captivate, to startle. This capability of things – material or otherwise – to produce experience in the perceiving subject, is also an aspect of what I would argue defines the object: it is an object of *experience*, as well as an object of interpretation. Indeed, in this dimension the passive, grammatical sense of the word 'object' becomes more tenuous. As we shall see, objects begin to seem quite active, and even to blur with subjects, because of the ability of the sensible, material characteristics of objects to trigger our particular sensory experience.

Certainly, as constructivism has shown us, our interpretations of our sense perceptions are socially, culturally, personally and historically situated and contingent; that is, they are heavily influenced by who we are and the prior knowledge, experiences, feelings, and so on, we bring to bear. Yet the sense perceptions we interpret also have a biological reality in our neurological responses to physical stimuli. In other words, we do not entirely invent our experiences, but hear, touch or see what we do partly because of the personal and cultural baggage we carry, and partly because of the physical reality of ourselves and the material world within which we live. We are not only constructivist creatures (though that is an important element); we are also packages of flesh and nerve cells, bodily interacting with other physical things (including other people). We have the sensory experiences we do partly because of an artefact having particular material qualities – bigness, blueness, roundness, smoothness, and so on. Two different people will certainly demonstrate the subjectivity and contingency of experience by responding to the same object in different ways (and they will assess, interpret and attribute meaning and value to bigness, blueness, roundness and smoothness differently); but for both of them, part at least of their engagement with the object will be determined by its material characteristics – *their reactions would not be as they are (whatever they may be), if the object were not what it is*. This experiential step in our engagement with an object is so fundamental and so basic, that it is often missed in exploration of the socioculturally and historically constituted and situated nature of our emotional and cognitive responses to objects. Up to a point this is entirely valid: many studies, as we have seen, emphasise the cultural rather than the material side of the equation and make highly valuable contributions in the process. But if we are fully to probe the processes at work when people encounter things, we need not only to understand the subjectivities involved in human cognitive response, but also to examine what, if any, material, sensory and emotional factors are at work (some studies do attempt both aspects strongly; e.g. Ingold 2000, Keane 2005, Tilley 2004).

An object's actual, material qualities, then, are basic to both what it is and how it is experienced. The quantitative (height, weight, etc.) and qualitative (colour, texture, shape, smell, sound) characteristics of the object, and their internal relations within it (cf. Merleau-Ponty 1962, Tilley 2004), simultaneously physically define the object and inform the sensorially derived data processed in the perceiving subject's mind. Indeed, before we formulate any (socioculturally and historically contingent) ideas about an object, we can and do experience more fundamental physical and emotional responses to it – feelings that can include awe, disgust, hilarity, horror, sadness and much more. Sometimes these effects only transpire through a *combination* of the object's material characteristics and other, culturally and historically situated, associations the viewer already has. They can also, however, be a result simply of reactions to the physical qualities of the thing before us – reactions that can sometimes be very potent, even transformative (cf. Greenblatt's notion of wonder, 1991; see also De Bolla 2005), and can be felt and evidenced physically as well as emotionally. My initial, overwhelming, emotional reaction to the Chinese horse was entirely as a result of its material characteristics. The history and fame across the Trobriand islands of particular Kula objects, and thus the awe inspired by some of them, meanwhile, can be physically seen and felt by all those who handle them as part of the Kula exchange because they are material realities as a result of the wearing away of the shell epidermis over time and the appearance of red striations: '[t]ime is literally inscribed into the shell surface which increases in value with age' (Rowlands 1993: 149, citing Campbell 1983). For islanders to recognise and be awed by a particularly special *mwali* or *soulava* object, is to see and feel such actual, physical qualities and at the same time to interpret them within a particular cultural framework. Such actualities can also be experienced by museum visitors from other parts of the world – but their powerful cultural meanings in the Trobriands, of course, will need to be explained.

It is in the engagement between object and subject, in their very confluence, that sensory responses, emotions and ideas are generated. It is also only in this engagement, I suggest, that subjects and objects come fully into being at all. The process of encounter bridges the two, causing them, at the instant of perception, to exist only in relation to each other. The perceiving subject and the perceived object become real to each other, in that moment (cf. Tilley 2004). The feelings and thoughts initiated during that interaction, not only have the potential to have an ongoing influence on the subject; they may also affect the fate of the object. Indeed, we could say that in that engagement the two *form* each other, in the sense of their new hybrid forms: subject + perception of object + evolving interpretation of object; and perceived + interpreted object. In this mutually constitutive process, and this evolving state of hybridity, the object is as much a part of the totality of the experience as the subject (see also Gell 1998, Gosden 2005, Pearce 1994). To paraphrase Marilyn Strathern, persons and things alike are actualised in the active relationships that connect them to each other (1988, 1999).

In a museum context or elsewhere, then, envisioning the relationships between people and things in a newly material way emphasises, first, the sensory and emotional, pre-cognitive ways in which an object is experienced; second, the mutual embeddedness of the object's physical qualities and the subject's sensory modalities; and third, the materiality of not only the object but also the subject, who experiences the world through a physical body and interprets it with a material mind.[12] Put simply, this is a view that focuses on (i) how people respond to things before they even know or ask anything about them, and the influence on those responses of (ii) the object's often overlooked, particular characteristics (as well as the more conventionally considered matters of exhibition design, object juxtaposition, lighting, textual interpretation, and so on) and (iii) the physicality of the subject themselves. This is an area of research being pursued elsewhere (e.g. Dudley forthcoming; see also Quian Quiroga, Dudley and Binnie 2011), that seeks to move away from a Cartesian view of subject–object duality both theoretically and empirically. To consider the realms of subject and object as not really separate at all may be more than a useful heuristic; it may open up new and creative approaches to understanding people and things, and to enhancing experience in museums.

Exhibited objects

One way in which experience may be enhanced through rethinking the relationships between subjects and objects is as part of an endeavour by the museum to reduce the sense of distance that often seems to be inherent in museum displays, particularly those of social and cultural history and ethnography (cf. Alpers 1991 and Baxandall 1991, both of whom refer to museum displays of cultures as divided from – *other than* – the viewer by either space or time or both). If museums seek to reduce this distance between person and thing, if displays and interpretations are constructed in such a way as to facilitate a wider or deeper sensory and emotional engagement with an object, rather than simply to enable intellectual comprehension of a story or set of facts presented by the museum and merely illustrated or punctuated by the object, might visitors actually be enabled to appreciate more aspects of both the object and its story? Kirsten Wehner and Martha Sear, curators of the new *Australian Journeys* gallery at the National Museum of Australia, have recently attempted to facilitate precisely these kinds of bodily, multi-sensory and emotional – as well as purely cognitive – interactions with the objects chosen for an exhibition which seeks to tell some of the many and diverse stories of migrating to Australia (Wehner and Sear 2010). They sought to connect 'visitors to the richness and detail of others' life worlds', to invite 'visitors to engage imaginatively with others' subjective experiences and understandings', to enable objects to 'connect people . . . to their own historical selves' (2010: 143), as well as to the past of others. They wanted their exhibition to be 'object-centred', rather than a largely text-based, story-telling exercise accessorised by objects – which is how they characterise previous exhibitions at their museum and, indeed, how one might characterise many other exhibitions elsewhere. As they explain, in the latter kind of exhibition objects merely illustrate stories – the actual, real work of communication is done mainly by words, not things. Wehner and Sear wanted to change this, to make a less bland exhibition that allowed visitors to rediscover the capacity of objects to 'inspire that slightly dislocating delight that comes from recognising that an object was "there" at another time and . . . place and is now "here" in this time and . . . place and in our own life'. They wanted to give objects back their 'particularity', their 'power to excite and inspire curiosity' (2010: 145).

Choosing objects with particular aesthetic qualities or resonances and drama because of their association with certain events or persons, the curators of *Australian Journeys* constructed object biographies for their selected artefacts, focusing especially on how objects participated in the movements of people to and from Australia. What they did not want to do, however, was then construct a display in which the objects' stories were relayed through large amounts of text. Rather, they wanted to let the objects and their juxtapositions do much of the communicating. They facilitated this by bringing about what they call an 'intense, interactive' kind of looking that gets visitors first to focus on the physical qualities of the objects, 'to dwell in the process of collecting sensory data', *before* reflecting on what an object might be, what it could be for, and who might have used it for what, when and where (2010: 153). They wanted to stimulate visitors' empathy for and imagination of other lives – but they were sensible enough too to realise that they still needed to provide context. Their strategy involved dividing the exhibition into forty smaller exhibits, and centring each of those on one key object with a number of other objects leading off from it in order to evoke different strands of the stories concerned, encouraging visitors to concentrate primarily on objects and the relationships between them. They worked hard to separate necessary text from the objects themselves, in order not to detract from the artefacts and not to distract the visitor from properly and primarily engaging with the physical things before them – indeed, they tried (though they did not always succeed) to have no interpretive text in the glass cases at all, placing it instead as a 'ribbon' running along one side only of each case. They also installed 'sensory stations' to accompany each exhibit, trying to facilitate not just superficial explorations of objects but more lasting, imaginative and empathic engagements through the stimulation of the bodily senses. Visitors can, for example, smell sea cucumbers when looking at cauldrons used by Indonesian fishermen, or trace with their finger the stitches on an embroidered map that is a copy of the original displayed adjacent to it.

The curators of *Australian Journeys* have tried to engage visitors with objects more directly and sensually, and through those objects to reach a state of deeper and more subtle engagement with the past people, places and events associated with the artefacts. They have indicated historical uses and significances of the objects they used, but avoided creating clear-cut, singular historical contexts for the objects. They felt that to pin 'objects to singular times and places' would 'close down the imaginative possibilities' the objects offered – the chance for visitors simultaneously to attempt to empathise with the sensations of people and in the past, and recognise the subjectivity of their own responses in the present (2010: 159). Instead, through encouraging direct, multi-sensorial engagements with the physical objects and through carefully restricting the extent and position of textual interpretation, they have enabled their visitors to respond to objects in their own way and at the same time to imagine, through those objects, how it felt to be someone in the past. Visitors to *Australian Journeys* thus have the opportunity to encounter objects that are at as little distance from them as possible (literally and metaphorically), and are provided with enough (but not too much) context to be able not only to 'place' and understand an object but also to experience real emotional responses to it. The individual encounters visitors can have are wrapped up in the experiential possibilities of objects that can result from interacting directly – whether physically or emotionally or both – with objects themselves as well as with the context of those objects. The objects can be engaged with directly, rather than simply encountered along the way as mere illustrators or punctuators of stories communicated by other means.

This freeing up of the possibilities of direct encounters with objects contrasts with the manner in which they are so often conceptualised and utilised in museum settings as mere illustrators or punctuators. This is one way in which museums distance objects from visitors and diminish the possibilities for engagement between the two. Information or context, for example, important though it is, can become so central that museums and visitors alike grow so focused on the story *overlying* the physical thing, they may inadvertently close off other, perhaps equally significant potentials *in* things. Specifically, museums often (though not always) close off the potential to produce powerful emotional and other personal responses in individual visitors through physical, real-time, sensory engagement between people and things. Yet to ignore the potential of those interactions, in and of themselves, may be to miss out on something very compelling in the museum experience.

Active, two-way engagements between people and things that are as full, material, and sensory as feasible, on the other hand, are rich with possibility. Partly, this is because they will enrich the ways in which visitors are able to connect with the people, stories and emotions of the past. More radically, as I have tried to argue above, the experiential possibilities of objects are important in themselves. It is through these possibilities that objects can 'speak' to us, even when we know nothing about them at all. This only partially contradicts the established view that objects are mute unless they are enabled to 'speak' through effective interpretation such as exhibition text and design: the latter interpretive strategies reveal the stories that objects represent or help to tell, but objects alone can also, sometimes at least, have a significance, a relevance, a meaning, for visitors, for their experiential value too. It is a suggestion that risks accusations of elitism – accusations that would be justified were one invoking connoisseurial or 'pure, detached, aesthetic' responses to things (O'Neill 2006: 104), as such responses depend or are expected to depend upon a prior set of knowledge and cultivated tastes (cf. Bourdieu 1984). But there is nothing elitist about avoiding the inhibition of individual, subjective, embodied, physical and emotional responses. These are very different sorts of experience from those elicited by either the foregrounding of things as illustrators of information and stories or by a purist, aesthetic focus. They are instead potential reactions that fall into a space somewhere in between, where the thing does not '*dissolve* into meanings' (Hein 2006: 2; emphasis added) and context does not inhibit our opportunities to engage with things, even those we know nothing about.[13]

Museums cannot necessarily predict and effectively enable powerful responses to objects – they will not happen for all of us all of the time, nor even in response to the same artefacts – but they can seek to place the object once more at the heart of the museum endeavour, and work to avoid the inhibition of emotional and sensory interactions wherever possible. They can think a little more closely about what happens and what might happen when people encounter objects on display. They can ponder what it would be like for visitors more often than not to be able properly, bodily, emotionally to engage with an object rather than look at it half-heartedly prior to, or even after, reading a text panel on a wall or a label in a case. Of course, their duty to conserve objects means that museums cannot usually permit visitors to pick up, listen to, lick and sniff the things in their care. But museums would do well to remember that visitors can and do still imagine many of the material qualities of the objects they see. I can see that the oil painting's surface is three-dimensional, and while I may not be allowed to actually touch it, by drawing on my own sense memories of other textured surfaces I can imagine, even feel in my fingertips, what the sensation would be if I did handle it. Yes, I might get it wrong – but equally I might not. And maybe it does not matter, so long as I am not inhibited from engaging with and responding to an object in some way beyond passively looking, reading a label, and moving on, uninspired and unengaged. Yet a museum preference for the informational over the material, and for a narrowly defined learning over a broader and more fundamental conception of enhancing personal experience, may lead to the production of displays that actually inhibit and even preclude emotional and personal response.

To call for a museum return to the material reality of the material, to shift attention back to objects as objects, focusing again on aspects of those things' apparently trivial and obvious material qualities and the possibilities of directly, physically, emotionally engaging with them, is not a faint plea from the back of a nineteenth-century card catalogue drawer. It is an active agenda for creatively enhancing the twenty-first-century museum visit, acknowledging that embodied and emotional engagements with objects should be its fundamental building block. It is not an advocacy for museums to go back to being dusty elitist places that fail to think about multiple audiences and accessibility, or to lose anything they have learned about interpretation and telling stories; but it is a plea to regain something powerful about the magic of things themselves – something that is central to what museums can offer and yet much of which has somehow been lost along the way. It is a manifesto that seeks not to detract from the now established approaches to learning and social inclusion in museums, but to add to them. If museums keep open the space that lies *between* artefacts being either carriers of information or objects of detached contemplation, they also keep open the possibility that visitors can reflect creatively, even transformatively, upon both things and themselves.

Notes

1 I am grateful for helpful comments from Simon Knell and Lisanne Gibson on earlier drafts of this essay. Some sections of the paper appear in an earlier form in a working paper written for the University of Michigan: S. Dudley, 2012. 'Materiality matters: experiencing the displayed object', University of Michigan Working Papers in Museum Studies, No. 8, 2012.
2 http://www.comptonverney.org.uk/collections/chinese.aspx (last accessed 12 March 2011).
3 I explore ideas of the power of the object, and the object as fetish, further elsewhere (Dudley forthcoming).
4 E.g. Kaplan et al. 1993, Noble and Chatterjee 2008, Chatterjee et al. 2009. Ongoing doctoral research by Jennifer Binnie at the University of Leicester, co-sponsored by the Art Fund and the Arts and Humanities Research Council, explores the impact on wellbeing of visual encounters with artworks in the gallery; see Quian Quiroga, Dudley and Binnie 2011.
5 Chris Gosden puts it thus: '[p]eople crystallize out in the interstices between objects, taking up the space allowed them by the object world, with [their] senses and emotions educated by the object world' (2005: 196).
6 Siân Jones makes a not dissimilar argument in relation to heritage studies, our understandings of 'authenticity' and why people like old things, urging a 'return to the materiality of objects, sites and places – an aspect that has been rather neglected by constructivist critiques, and indeed by much of the recent research focusing on the experience of heritage' (2010: 183).
7 Conversely, I avoid use of the term 'materiality' here as it has a range of meanings depending on the context in which it is used, and its academic connotations do not necessarily coincide with its more everyday implications. For an interesting debate on the term and its relationship to materials, see Ingold 2007, Tilley 2007, Knappett 2007, Miller 2007, Nilsson 2007.
8 Other theorists may use yet other terms, in addition or alternatively; hence Heidegger, for example, distinguishes between three kinds of objects: things, works and equipment (2002).

9 The statements made in this section are based largely on observations made during eight years' material culture teaching of an internationally diverse postgraduate student body at the University of Leicester.

10 It also provokes reflection on the conventional distinction between 'tangible' and 'intangible'. Intangibility implies the lack of physical, material presence – literally, there is nothing that can be touched. But depending on the 'intangible' in question, one might still able to hear, smell, see or taste it. And where is the cut-off between the intangible and the tangible? Material objects and places (the 'tangible') are embedded within and embody aspects of culture (the 'intangible'), and terminologically to divide the two does not reflect life as it is lived. Equally, 'intangibility' can be subjective/context-dependent: things considered intangible from one perspective are tangible from another (e.g. nature spirits may be tangible to those who believe in them but intangible to outsiders). See also Kirshenblatt-Gimblett 2004 for further discussion of the problematic nature of the notion of 'intangible heritage'.

11 It was also, of course, interpreted in being selected and in the way in which the gallery had chosen to display it.

12 Cf. Ingold's critique of Renfrew's 'material engagement theory' (e.g. Renfrew 2001), in which, Ingold says, 'the [problem of the] polarity of mind and matter remains. For the engagement of which he speaks does not bring the flesh and blood of human bodies into corporeal contact with materials of other kinds, whether organic or inorganic. Rather, it brings incorporeal minds into contact with a material world' (Ingold 2007: 3).

13 Of course, even if museums work hard not to obscure the object itself and to allow visitors the opportunity for direct experiences of it before they know anything about it, the object cannot 'speak' unhindered and uninfluenced for itself: one's encounter with it is always influenced by the museum, by the fact that it has been selected, by how it has been positioned, lit and juxtaposed with other objects, and so on. In other words, as Susan Vogel and others have pointed out, the object on display always speaks in part of the museum values dominating at the time (Vogel 1991).

References

Alpers, S. (1991) 'The museum as a way of seeing', in I. Karp and S. D. Lavine (eds) *Exhibiting Cultures: the poetics and politics of museum display*, Washington (D.C.): Smithsonian Institution Press.

Appadurai, A. (ed.) (1986) *The Social Life of Things: commodities in cultural perspective*, Cambridge: Cambridge University Press.

Baxandall, M. (1991) 'Exhibiting intention: some preconditions of the visual display of culturally purposeful objects', in I. Karp and S. D. Lavine (eds) *Exhibiting Cultures: the poetics and politics of museum display*, Washington (D.C.): Smithsonian Institution Press.

Boivin, N. (2004) 'Mind over matter? Collapsing the mind-matter dichotomy in material culture studies', in E. DeMarrais, C. Gosden and C. Renfrew (eds) *Rethinking Materiality: the engagement of mind with the material world*, Cambridge: McDonald Institute for Archaeological Research.

Bourdieu, P. (1984) *Distinction: a social critique of the judgement of taste*, London: Routledge & Kegan Paul.

Brown, B. (2001) 'Thing theory', *Critical Inquiry* 28 (1): 1–22.

Campbell, S. F. (1983) 'Kula in Vakuta', in J. Leach and E. Leach (eds) *The Kula: new perspectives on Massim exchange*, Cambridge: Cambridge University Press.

Chatterjee, H. J., S. Vreeland and G. Noble (2009) 'Museopathy: exploring the healing potential of handling museum objects', *Museum and Society* 7 (3): 164–77.

Clifford, J. (1985) 'Objects and selves – an afterword', in G. W. Stocking (ed.) *Objects and Others: essays on museums and material culture*, Madison (WI): The University of Wisconsin Press.

De Bolla, P. (2005) *Art Matters*, Cambridge, MA: Harvard University Press.

Dudley, S. (forthcoming) 'What, or where, is the (museum) object? Fetish and feeling in the gallery and beyond', in A. Witcomb and K. Message (eds) *Museum Theory: an expanded field*, Oxford: Blackwell.

Fish, S. (1980) *Is There a Text in This Class? The authority of interpretive communities*, Cambridge (MA): Harvard University Press.

Gell, A. (1998) *Art and Agency: an anthropological theory*, Oxford: Oxford University Press.

Golding, V. (2010) 'Dreams and wishes: the multi-sensory museum space', in S. Dudley (ed.) *Museum Materialities: objects, interpretations, engagements*, London: Routledge, pp. 224–40.

Gosden, C. (2005) 'What do objects want?', *Journal of Archaeological Method and Theory* 12: 193–211.

Graves-Brown, P. (2000) 'Introduction', in P. Graves-Brown (ed.) *Matter, Materiality and Modern Culture*, London: Routledge.

Greenblatt, S. (1991) 'Resonance and wonder', in I. Karp and S. Lavine (eds) *Exhibiting Cultures: the poetics and politics of museum display*, Washington (D.C.): Smithsonian Institution Press.

Heidegger, M. (2002) *Off the Beaten Track* (tr. J. Young and K. Haynes), Cambridge: Cambridge University Press.

Hein, H. (2006) 'Assuming responsibility: lessons from aesthetics', in H. H. Genoways (ed.) *Museum Philosophy for the Twenty-first Century*, Oxford: AltaMira Press.

Hood, B. and L. Santos (eds) (2009) *The Origins of Object Knowledge*, Oxford: Oxford University Press.

Hooper-Greenhill, E. (2000) *Museums and the Interpretation of Visual Culture*, London: Routledge.

Ingold, T. (2000) 'Making culture and weaving the world', in P. M. Graves-Brown (ed.) *Matter, Materiality and Modern Culture*, London: Routledge.

Ingold, T. (2007) 'Materials against materiality', *Archaeological Dialogues* 14 (1): 1–16.

Jones, S. (2010) 'Negotiating authentic objects and authentic selves: beyond the deconstruction of authenticity', *Journal of Material Culture* 15 (2): 181–203.

Kaplan, S., L. V. Bardwell and D. B. Slakter (1993) 'The museum as a restorative environment', *Environment and Behaviour* 25 (6): 725–42.

Keane, W. 2005. 'Signs are not the garb of meaning. On the social analysis of material things', in D. Miller (ed.) *Materiality*, Durham (N.C.): Duke University Press.

Kirshenblatt-Gimblett, B. (2004) 'Intangible heritage as metacultural production', *Museum International* 56 (1–2): 52–65.

Knappett, C. (2007) 'Materials *with* materiality?', *Archaeological Dialogues* 14 (1): 20–3.

Kopytoff, I. (1986) 'The cultural biography of things: commoditization as process', in A. Appadurai (ed.) *The Social Life of Things*, Cambridge: Cambridge University Press.

Law, J. (2000) 'Objects, spaces and others', Centre for Science Studies, Lancaster University, http://www.comp.lancs.ac.uk/sociology/papers/Law-Objects-Spaces-Others.pdf (last accessed 20 May 2011).

Malinowski, B. (1922) *Argonauts of the Western Pacific*, London: Routledge and Kegan Paul.

Merleau-Ponty, M. (1962) *Phenomenology of Perception*, London: Routledge.

Miller, D. (2007) 'Stone age or plastic age?', *Archaeological Dialogues* 14 (1): 23–7.

Nilsson, B. (2007) 'An archaeology of material stories. Dioramas as illustration and the desire of a thingless archaeology', *Archaeological Dialogues* 14 (1): 27–30.

Noble, G. and H. J. Chatterjee (2008) 'Enrichment programmes in hospitals: using museum loan boxes in University College London Hospital', in H. Chatterjee (ed.) *Touch in Museums: policy and practice in object handling*, Oxford: Berg.

O'Neill, M. (2006) 'Essentialism, adaptation and justice: towards a new epistemology of museums', *Museum Management and Curatorship* 21: 95–116.

Pearce, S. M. (1994) 'Objects as meaning; or narrating the past', in S. M. Pearce (ed.) *Interpreting Objects and Collections*, London: Routledge.

Quian Quiroga, R., S. Dudley and J. Binnie (2011) 'Looking at Ophelia: a comparison of viewing art in the gallery and in the lab', *ACNR* 11 (3): 15–18.

Renfrew, C. (2001) 'Symbol before concept. Material engagement and the early development of society', in I. Hodder (ed.) *Archaeological Theory Today*, Cambridge.

Rowlands, M. (1993) 'The role of memory in the transmission of culture'. *World Archaeology* 25 (2): 141–51.

Strathern, M. (1988) *The Gender of the Gift*, Berkeley: University of California Press.

Strathern, M. (1999) *Property, Substance and Effect: anthropological essays on persons and things*, London: Athlone Press.

Tilley, C. (2004) *The Materiality of Stone.* Oxford: Berg.

Tilley, C. (2007) 'Materiality in materials', *Archaeological Dialogues* 14 (1): 16–20.

Vogel, S. (1991) 'Always true to the object, in our fashion', in I. Karp and S. D. Lavine (eds) *Exhibiting Cultures: the poetics and politics of museum display*, Washington (D.C.): Smithsonian Institution Press.

Wehner, K. and M. Sear (2010) 'Engaging the material world: object knowledge and *Australian Journeys*', in S. Dudley (ed.) *Museum Materialities: objects, engagements, interpretations*, London: Routledge.

PART I

Objects and their properties

Introduction to Part I

Sandra H. Dudley

THIS FIRST PART OF THE BOOK focuses on the nature of those tangible things conventionally thought of as 'objects', in museums and beyond. It examines the nature and significance of objects' material properties – both formal (stylistic, for example) and physical (including such issues as patina and decay). It emphasises the importance – in practice, surprisingly often overlooked in the quest for meaning and social context – of attending closely to the object's fundamental material characteristics as the *starting* point of wider analyses and interpretations. The readings exemplify kinds of examinations of objects' form and its relationship to function and meaning. In the process, this part of the book enables the raising of questions about the linkages between form, function and meaning of objects and how they may change over time or with context, and about the implications for objects in museums. Readings also explore the making of things and the potential for change in, and finiteness of, objects' material properties. In addition, some texts examine questions of object boundedness and authenticity, and touch upon things that have not always been treated as material objects – here, photographs.

The first reading, by a major, long-established figure in the field of museum material culture studies, outlines the definitions and parameters of 'material culture' and related terminology (such as 'artefact', 'thing', 'specimen', etc.). Importantly, it also introduces the notion of selection, particularly in a museum context, and its potential to transform the identity of the object. It starts off this reader just as it did an earlier one (Susan Pearce's *Interpreting Objects and Collections*, 1994), providing us with some sense of continuity with earlier debates – it is important to recognise such shared beginnings, even if we later move in a different direction.

The second article is by a philosopher of art. It begins with a discussion of the antique as a category (and in juxtaposition to the category of art), which is a useful addition to the earlier treatment of terminology in the Pearce extract. It then enables a first foray into the *properties* of objects, by exploring and distinguishing formal characteristics (such as style) and physical ('material', in Rosenstein's terms) properties (such as patina and other aspects of agedness), and the possible reasons for their aesthetic appeal. There is some relatively arcane philosophical discussion in this reading, such as that on the 'translucency' of art objects – but there is also much of real practical application. In particular, Rosenstein's discussion of the signs of agedness – and distinguishing between what he calls formal, or stylistically present, and materially present signs thereof – is both interesting and useful.

Steven Hooper's article discusses aspects of the relationship between an object's form, function and meaning. Written as a tribute to Peter Gathercole, it 'reflects his encouragement of students to *look* at objects – to examine them, appreciate them and, in many cases, be awed by them'. Its purpose is to demonstrate the importance of attending closely and firstly to the formal and physical, material features of an object 'without recourse initially to written or pictorial evidence', and the extent to which such a detailed focus 'can provide a foundation for interpretations of function, significance and meaning'. Focusing on one object – a Tahitian god-house collected in Polynesia in the early nineteenth century and now in the British Museum – it strongly makes the point that to examine properly the materiality of the object should be the fundamental starting point of studying and interpreting material culture, whether in a museum or not.

In the fourth reading, we begin to move on from detailed considerations of object properties in a static sense – the object as a fixed, made, unchanging thing – to think more about their dynamic qualities. Anna MacLennan's brief piece allows reflection on the importance of the production of objects as well as its end result. In particular, it allows consideration of the possibilities of using hands-on experience of making as an interpretive strategy in museum and heritage settings, exemplifying the empathic and imagined understandings it can bring.

Continuing the consideration of making, and through a personal reflection on the author's own artistic knitting practice, Sabrina Gschwandtner's accessible article enables exploration of how important, rich, complex and meaningful the productive process itself can be. Indeed, here the emphasis is primarily on process rather object, as the author reflects on the ways in which knitting has inspired her to make, curate and write about participatory and interdisciplinary artworks. For her, knitting and its end results become sculpture, participation, community, writing, gift, pleasure, home and media.

Change, process and mutability continue to be important themes in the next reading, but here giving us cause to reflect on those processes towards the end rather than the beginning of an object's life. Susanne Küchler's classic article on Malangan funerary carvings, looks at indigenous and museum perspectives on objects treated in museums as 'art' but originally produced for gift giving and, ultimately, for their own destruction. The article thus raises questions on the temporality and materiality of the object, on different frameworks for understanding these, and on the relationships between form, function and meaning.

Geoffrey Batchen's chapter, focusing on a Victorian locket containing a photograph and a lock of hair, examines the interrelated materiality, functions and meanings of the object and their change over time, and also introduces the notion of indexicality. It also focuses on photographs, an example of a category of objects often not treated as such. Batchen considers the photograph both *as* the material object and, with specific reference to the lock of hair, in juxtaposition *to* it.

In the last reading, Samuel Alberti details the technical and material processes undergone by (mainly natural science) objects at the Manchester Museum after they were collected. In so doing, he successfully demonstrates the extent of material change that continues to be undergone by objects *after* the points of museum collection and accession, and shows what the author describes as 'the dynamism of museum objects'. This is a useful note on which to end this first part of the book: through the readings, objects' material qualities have been seen to be myriad and fundamental, mutable and processual; importantly, those principles do not cease to apply when objects enter a museum.

Chapter 2

Museum objects

Susan M. Pearce

IT WILL BE HELPFUL TO CLEAR some paths through the undergrowth by picking out some of the key words relating to museum material, and taking a closer look at them. One group comprises those words which are used to describe an individual piece, or in general terms a number of pieces, and this group includes 'object', 'thing', 'specimen', 'artefact', 'good' usually used in the plural as 'goods', and the term 'material culture' used as a collective noun. All of these terms share common ground in that they all refer to selected lumps of the physical world to which cultural value has been ascribed, a deceptively simple definition which much of this book will be devoted to discussing [see original reading], but each carries a slightly different shade of meaning because each comes from a distinguishably different tradition of study.

One problem common to them all, and one which throws up the characteristic cleft between philosophical speculation and the everyday meanings attached to words, revolves around the scope to be attributed to them. Strictly speaking, the lumps of the physical world to which cultural value is ascribed include not merely those discrete lumps capable of being moved from one place to another, which is what we commonly mean when we say 'thing' or 'artefact', but also the larger physical world of landscape with all the social structure that it carries, the animal and plant species which have been affected by humankind (and most have), the prepared meals which the animals and plants become, and even the manipulation of flesh and air which produces song and speech. As James Deetz has put it in a famous sentence: 'Material culture is that segment of man's physical environment which is purposely shaped by him according to a culturally dictated plan' (Deetz 1977: 7).

This is to say, in effect, that the whole of cultural expression, one way or another, falls within the realm of material culture, and if analytical definition is pushed to its logical conclusion, that is probably true. It is also true that the material culture held today by many museums falls within this broader frame, like the areas of industrial landscape which Ironbridge exhibits. However, for the purposes of study, limits must be set, and this book [see original reading] will concentrate upon those movable pieces, those 'discrete lumps' which have always formed, and still form, the bulk of museum holdings and which museums were, and still are, intended to hold.

This brings us to a point of crucial significance. What distinguishes the 'discrete lumps' from the rest – what makes a 'movable piece' in our sense of the term – is the cultural value it is given, and not primarily the technology which has been used to give it form or content, although this is an important mode of value creation. The crucial idea is that of selection, and it is the act of selection which turns a part of the natural world into an object and a museum piece. This is clearly demonstrated by the sample of moon rock which went on display in the Milestones of Flight hall at the National Air and Space Museum, Washington, DC:

> The moon rock is an actual piece of the moon retrieved by the Apollo 17 mission. There is nothing particularly appealing about the rock; it is a rather standard piece of volcanic basalt some 4 million years old. Yet, unlike many other old rocks, this one comes displayed in an altar-like structure, set in glass, and is complete with full-time guard and an ultrasensitive monitoring device (or so the guards are wont to say). There is a sign above it which reads, 'You may touch it with care.' *Everyone touches it.*
>
> (Meltzer 1981: 121)

The moon rock has been turned into material culture because through its selection and display it has become a part of the world of human values, a part which, evidently, every visitor wants to bring within his own personal value system.

What is true of the moon rock is equally true of the stones which the Book of Joshua tells us Joshua commanded the twelve tribes of Israel to collect from the bed of the River Jordan and set up as a permanent memorial of the crossing of the river, and of all other natural objects deliberately placed within human contexts. It is also equally true of the millions of natural history pieces inside museum collections for which 'specimen', meaning an example selected from a group, is our customary term. It is clear that the acquisition of a natural history specimen involves selection according to contemporary principles, detachment from the natural context, and organization into some kind of relationship (many are possible) with other, or different, material. This process turns a 'natural object' into a humanly defined piece, and means that natural history objects and collections, although like all other collections they have their own proper modes and histories of study, can also be treated as material culture and discussed in these terms. The development of contemporary epistemology suggests that no fact can be read transparently. All apparently 'natural' facts are actually discursive facts, since 'nature' is not something already there but is itself the result of historical and social construction. To call something a natural object, as Laclau and Mouffe say (1987: 84), is a way of conceiving it that depends upon a classificatory system: if there were no human beings on earth, stones would still be there, but they would not be 'stones' because there would be neither mineralogy nor language with which to distinguish and classify them. Natural history specimens are therefore as much social constructs as spears or typewriters, and as susceptible to social analysis.

'Thing' is our most ordinary word for all these pieces, and it is also used in everyday speech for the whole range of non-material matters (a similarly elusive word) which have a bearing on our daily lives. 'Object' shares the same slipperiness both in ordinary speech and in intellectual discourse, where it is generally the term used. The ways in which we use these terms, and the implications of this usage for the ways in which our collective psyche views the material world are very significant, and are further pursued in the next chapter [see original reading]. The term 'artefact' means 'made by art or skill' and so takes a narrow view of what constitutes material objects, concentrating upon that part of their nature which involves the application of human technology to the natural world, a process which plays a part in the creation of many, but by no means all, material pieces. Because it is linked with practical skills, and so with words like 'artisan', 'artefact' is a socially low-value term, and one which is correspondingly applied to material deemed to be humble, like ordinary tables and chairs, rather than paintings and sculptures. In this book [see original reading] 'thing' and 'object', and sometimes 'artefact', will be used to refer to material pieces without any particular distinction being made between them, and 'material culture' will be used in the same general sense.

References

Deetz, J. (1977) *In Small Things Forgotten*, Garden City, New York: Doubleday Natural History Press.

Laclau, E., and Mouffe, C. (1987) 'Post-Marxism without apologies', *New Left Review*, 166: 79–106.

Meltzer, D. J. (1981) 'Ideology and material culture', in R. A. Gould and M. B. Schiffer (eds) *Modern Material Culture: the archaeology of us*, New York: Academic Press.

Chapter 3

The aesthetic of the antique

Leon Rosenstein

I

The antique, as a category, and antiques, as objects which embody this characteristic, have gained considerable attention in the modern world. Little serious thought has yet been given on a philosophical level, however, to what this character is. This essay will therefore address the questions, what is "an antique" and "the antique"? Why is it worthy of critical analysis? How does it function within a broader range of aesthetic categories?

II

Let us deal with the second question above, in a preliminary way, by examining the current appeal of the antique. The source of this appeal and the function it serves are varied, to be sure. Economic investment as a hedge against inflation, acquisition of social status, and decorative service to fill empty spaces come to mind. But these are mainly extraneous to aesthetics. There does seem to be a psychological function as well – viz., escape from the reality of the present.

There is no doubt that a large body of contemporary aesthetic experience is devoted to the antique as the only alternative to nature itself in the struggle against the void of the contemporary fabricated environment. Here the antique is an antidote to the insipidity of mass-produced furnishings. It is an antidote as well to modern anomic art, the art of "the they" (*das Man*), supported by attempts to elevate the undone (one cannot any longer employ the term "shocking" seriously) to the status of the highest criterion and at the same time everywhere to homogenize the already bland. To be sure, the antique has this antidotic function – the escape from vapid "they" art and its attendant "they" art criticism. But this can hardly be all. Certainly it would not be a sufficient explanation of the category itself. Nor would it be a unique means of escape from the inauthenticities of present reality: several stiff drinks would achieve the same end, after all. Yet there is some special significance to the deliberate preference for past reality that the antique satisfies, and certainly the consideration of this aspect of the antique has some respectable parentage.

The antique must be treated in any investigation of renaissances and revivals in style and taste, for instance. All such revivals deliberately choose to re-create the past by fashioning new objects imitating the old, or by incorporating certain traits of the old, or by collecting and analyzing actual old objects with appropriate veneration. Western civilization has seen such recollections often enough and at regular intervals in the past – though in each instance with a difference. The fortitudinous consciousness generated in the Italian Renaissance by reawakening the classicism of Greece and Rome, for example, was not the same as the consciousness generated subsequently by the revival of this past in late eighteenth- and early nineteenth-century England and France. The latter revival was attended by attitudes of nostalgia for the old and the past; e.g., the cult of the ruin and associations with the picturesque, which were perhaps foreshadowings of the Romantic temperament, which Hegel would identify not with "fortitude" but with the "unhappy consciousness." Such references and revivals are not uniquely Western, of course. Japanese and Chinese instances occur. There is, even more appropriately for our present concern, the Japanese appreciation of *sabi* – their general preference for aged objects.

In themselves, revivals and renaissances may tell us where and under what circumstances "the antique" and "antiques" become relevant to a civilization's self-conception. But they cannot explain why and how the antique exerts its special appeal, or furnish appropriate criteria for distinguishing and establishing the antique as an aesthetic category.

III

For the purposes of this inquiry, an antique shall be defined as a primarily handcrafted object of rarity and beauty which, by means of its style and the durability of its materiality, has the capacity to evoke and preserve for us the image of a world now past.

Each component of this definition will be examined for the sake of clarity. This section and the next will deal with the issue of *what kind of thing* an antique is. Section V will address the *means* by which the antique achieves its aesthetic function. [. . .]

We begin by contrasting the antique with the "art object" in general so as to understand more clearly what kind of handcrafted article an antique is. Several years ago I argued in these pages[1] that the existentiality of an art object is unique. Art objects do not reside in the world like other objects, but captivate our attention through the sensuous vehicles of their media, and, tearing through the extra-artistic world of everyday concern, set up their own worked (i.e., "artistic," "artificial") worlds of meaning and reality. Such objects, I said, have ontological integrity (and thus are genuine art objects) insofar as their corporeal nature (i.e., their sensuous vehicle or material medium) exhibits the special property I called "translucence." To have this quality, the art object must avoid the two false and opposite extremes of "transparency" and "opacity." If too transparent in its medium, the art object becomes merely an instrument for communication, as its corporeal nature dissolves and disappears from notice – a special problem often occurring with didactic art. If too opaque, the art object becomes so enmeshed in the reality of its corporeality that it becomes a mere curiosity inhabiting the extra-artistic world – a thing of fancy. It cannot construct or communicate any content, any *worked* world at all, because it is entirely a creature of this one. (This is a special problem which often occurs in contemporary non-representational art and in art objects whose media are incoherently blended into the material elements of the overall environment.) An art object that has ontological integrity is thus "translucent" in its materiality only insofar as we remain captivated by the corporeal structures of its medium and, at the same time, are continuously attuned by them to the forms of the unique worked world which it generates as its content – a world with its own objective givens and its own values and interpretations. This is the illusion of the art object – that it opens up its own space and time and "puts into play" there the creatures of its own reality.

Now certainly not all art objects are antiques and not all antiques are "art objects" as normally understood (i.e., as "fine art"). But each is an object of aesthetic experience. Their similarities and differences are therefore worth noting.

Art objects set up their own uniquely worked artistic world – a timeless and spaceless reality with its own arbitrary extra-artistic associations and its own interpretations – and thus they remain forever at the center of their own stage, referring ultimately to themselves by means of their translucence.

Antiques set up the image of a world of the past – a real world in space and time, with all the associations and interpretations appropriate to it (or at least as we best imagine it to have been). Thus, they are symbols for a context of past possibilities, and are icons potent in transubstantiating the past reality's presence by means of their style and by an appeal to the duration of their materiality. They do this (as we shall see in section V) by relying upon certain constants in the interrelatedness of their forms and contents which are art-historically isolable, and by relying in a certain fashion upon the corporeality of their media so as by both of these means to generate "an image of the past" as their message.

It is probably for these very differences between the two that we normally reserve the term "antique" for works we would classify as craft rather than fine art. Even while recognizing the antique qualities of a Rembrandt painting, we generally prefer to notice only its existence as a fine art object. (Rembrandt's bed or chamber pot we might call antiques – *faute de mieux*, as it were.) We seem to experience some conflict in adjusting ourselves to the equal reality of the painting's fine-art-objectness on the one hand and its antiqueness on the other – or to their equal status. This is, I believe, a serious error, for it deprives us of an important aspect of the total aesthetic experience of art objects such as Rembrandt's paintings. If they contain properties which tell us they are also antiques and tell us they should also be experienced from that perspective, we should be fools to deny ourselves that pleasure simply from a prudish prejudice for experiential purity. As Nelson Goodman has correctly observed, rather:

> The aesthetic properties of a picture plainly include not only those found by looking at it but also those that determine how it is to be looked at.[2]

That we in fact usually do set aside antiqueness in favor of fine-art-ness is probably due, however, not merely to a sense of respect for the work's purely formal properties, but also to a genuine ambiguity (if not antinomy) regarding the "correct" attitude. This occurs, I submit, in great measure due to the conflict arising between the respective worlds they evoke: art objects erecting a new world of their own through the translucence of their media, antiques re-evoking an image of a past world. Crafts, having less (or no) self-subsistent ideational content, and constrained to exist entirely in their own materiality (i.e., opacity), are naturally more disposed to the generation of the past world through the materiality of their media. They can become antiques, then, more easily. They can do this both by displaying the appropriate modifications in the opacity of their media, and by the peculiar modifications, coordinations, and combinations of their corporeal elements which we call "style" (see section V). Moreover, it is precisely because of the divergent world-creating and world-referent characteristics of the art object and the antique respectively that antiques (like all crafts in general) invariably affirm the values of the world they evoke and preserve, and can never critique that world and its values, as can fine art.[3] So, for example, we say that Goya's *The Third of May, 1808* critiques the extra-artistic world of its creator; though perhaps it would be better to say that this painting *as* fine art evokes a worked world which in turn subjects the contemporary real world it represents to criticism, but *as* antique the painting evokes that past real world and seeks to preserve it.

Having developed a clearer notion of the "whatness" of the antique, we shall need to determine *how* the antique functions to evoke an image of past reality. This can be accomplished by examining both *style* (the peculiar coordination of the object's corporeal and contentual elements which are constants discriminable by art-historical analysis) and the *durability of its materiality* (a modification of opacity which we will call "agedness").

First of all, however, two other issues suggested by the definition of antique require clarification. These are the references to rarity and beauty.

IV

While beauty is rare, not all rare things are beautiful. It is this quality of beauty above all others which *should* enable us to distinguish between the antique and other crafted articles which are often associated with it in practice – viz., artifacts, souvenirs, and collectibles. I say "should enable us" because beauty, appearing as a formal property of the object, must remain notoriously indefinable as a quality. We can only here adopt the ancient criterion that beauty is *quod visum placet* – that which is pleasing to the eye.

In view of the indecipherability of the quality of beauty, however, and the consequent absence of certainty in this regard, we may also rely on other appropriate differentia.

The antique is to be distinguished from the mere artifact. Objects encountered in archaeological and art-historical contexts are "artifacts." They are seen as examples and evidences from among other such entities. Such proof objects have only antiquarian reality and a documentary and testimonial value. The stone door jamb, unglazed pot, and arrowhead sort of artifact, moreover, is usually neither sufficiently impressive, unique, or relevant to us so as to generate a *Lebenswelt* of the past — real or imagined. On the other hand, to oppose documentary value to the aesthetic experience of the antique would be a false antinomy, since, in the context of its appreciation, the past world it testifies to is its significant aspect. The only valid question is, "Is it *merely* documentary and thus *merely* an artifact?"

The antique is not a "souvenir," either. The souvenir is an *aide-memoire* to personal experience. Natural objects, e.g., dried flowers pressed in books, may be souvenirs. For me, a Metropolitan Opera program for a performance of *Il Trovatore* would call to mind an event from my childhood when, at the age of four, I saw that performance as my first opera experience. That program, however, is not an antique; and my age alone has no bearing on that fact. Souvenirs have only subjective reality and autobiographical value. Souvenirs may *become* antiques — assuming they fulfill other requisite criteria — only if they obtain objective recognition as icons of the past. Nor is the antique to be identified with the collectible. Collectibles are comprised by a category of things whose forms are primarily dictated by practical function — e.g., Coca Cola signs, campaign buttons, bits of barbed wire, beer cans — which are invariably only one of a series of mass-produced exemplars whose value resides entirely in the fact of their collectibility. Last year's limited edition of numbered plates or commemorative medals by a recognized maker may be instantly "collectible," but they are not antiques. Unlike artifacts which they may in some other respects resemble, collectibles are valued above all for their collectibility — and vice versa. For these reasons they have a tautological reality and economic values established by current peculiarities of their market or psychological values invested in them by the individual accumulator or collector, who himself has a unique mentality. Thus, other considerations, in *addition to beauty*, may serve to distinguish the "antique" from the "collectible," the "artifact," and the "souvenir."

In the antique, "rarity" is not only a function of beauty, for beauty is rare, as we have said. Rareness is also a function of original "fewness" or uniqueness — itself due to its handcraftedness. Thirdly, rareness is a function of the durability of its medium. These last factors are best understood in conjunction with "agedness."

Simply to define an "antique" legally as an "object over 100 years of age" is about as meaningful and reliable as establishing that a person is mature at the age of twenty-one. A somewhat more reasonable stipulation on time would be "pre-1830." This criterion places the antique object prior to the machine age and thus increases or guarantees both its rarity and uniqueness. Furthermore, as the iconic embodiment of the objective spirit of the creator and his age now past, the antique must move us out of our present reality. An unmachined object reflecting a pre-machine world is an assurance of that move to the past. But "pre-1830" is still a false criterion because it remains arbitrary and artificial. The term "machine" is itself vague and arbitrary (a potter's wheel is a machine of sorts) and there are many instances of objects we would call "antiques" without hesitation which are at least in part "machined."

Moreover, the date is far too restrictive in practice. The Gallé vase, the Art Nouveau pewter charger, the Lalique bracelet, the Tiffany window – these are certainly antiques, though all were made c. 1900 and thus fail to meet either the pre-1830 or 100 year criterion. More significant than their years and dates, it is the beauty and rarity of these examples which is important. This is so because they capture our attention and tell us that they are uncommon, not everywhere to be encountered in the everyday world of the present, and hence not of this world.

Age is important. But it is important – as stated in our definition – as an appeal to style and to the durability of the object's materiality, and not as an enumeration of years. This brings us to a consideration of agedness.

V

We must now come to terms with the *how* of the antique's nature. This must be done in conformity with our definition's stipulations of "style" and "durability of materiality," both of which are references to age. It is this quality of the antique which evokes and preserves an image of the past.

An object's age is first of all recognized in style. While we cannot here set forth a fully developed theory of style, suffice it to affirm, first and foremost, that style in art objects generally is a function of both form (the material vehicle) and content (the worked world erected by it).

For example, the Elizabethan style in tragedies is as much a creation of its vehicles of corporeal manifestation (i.e., the particular sounds and pronunciations of English words, sentence structure, method of acting, costumes and stage design, metaphors, and imagery) as it is of its content, the structured, meaningful, worked world it generates for us (i.e., a world wherein power-driven kings are encountered, where tragic flaws and demonic forces work out their bloody solutions). Thus, the style of Elizabethan tragedy could not possibly be mistaken for ancient Greek or French neoclassical or modern tragedies. Similarly, in painting the Impressionist style is as much a matter of subject (peaceful landscapes and domestic scenes of bourgeois or Bohemian daily affairs – no Old Testament patriarchs and prophets, or kings receiving peace terms from the conquered or ensconced in their seraglios) as it is of medium (spectrum palette, optical mixing, avoidance of black "holes," quick brushstroke, mottled lighting effects, small easel canvases, etc.). One does not mistake such a work for a Holbein, a Delacroix, or a Caravaggio. Furthermore, the works of different masters within a given style can be distinguished by using these same two criteria. For example, Van Gogh's heavy impasto, his bold, intense, contrasting colors and gash-like brushstrokes, his brooding interior subjects, crazed portraits, and incendiary landscapes distinguish his style from that of Monet.[4]

Moreover, differences in style result from the unique fine-tuning of these two factors – the material elements and world elements – both internally and externally, each with the other. Thus, internally, the material medium is composed of various subvehicles. In painting, for example, the subvehicles are surface texture, disposition of shapes, clarity of line, contrast and intensity of color, and thinness or type of paint – each of which must be adjusted to the others, some being more or less emphasized, actualized, balanced. Correspondingly, internally the worked world is composed of submeanings or subjects, e.g., the social status of the persons depicted (if any), the expressions and intentions suggested by their dispositions and gestures, the action or the story being told, the emotional atmosphere generated or statements communicated; these, too, must be harmonized. And, finally, the various contents or submeanings of the worked world and the various components or subvehicles of the material medium must each be coordinated externally to the other. Thus, clear line, realistic modeling, formal balance, glassy surface texture may (Raphael) or may not (Dali) – depending upon the entire nexus of adjustments uniquely made on all levels and in all areas – generate a worked world of objective rationality and peaceful normality. Style in painting is the result of the totality of these separate factors and of the distinct manner in which the artist or epoch coordinates them.

Again, noticing differences between the art object *per se* and the antique will prove helpful. Since the antique exists primarily in the direction of the opacity of its medium, the appropriate modifications and coordinations in its corporeal elements will surely determine the antique's particular style as well. But since antiques are usually weak in generating a contentual worked world of their own, but, rather, generate an image of the past world now gone by, we cannot speak here in the same sense of style as a function of an interior worked-world vision and of correspondingly coordinated cognitive elements.

Thus, we would say that we recognize the latter, the contentual or cognitive elements of an art object's worked world, as typical, e.g., of the "Elizabethan style," when, in experiencing a tragedy, we find ghosts crying out for vengeance, just as we would recognize the style's material presence in corpses strewn about the stage, or in its now "archaic" language. We recognize Botticelli's style, similarly, from both its Neo-Platonic images and the interrelative meanings of the idealized reality they construct (part pagan, part Christian, part Renaissance humanist – but uniquely Botticelli) and also recognize the style from the pure, clear, flowing, disembodied line which established itself in the sensuous vehicle through which this worked world shines.

But what of the bronze Ming dynasty temple bell or the Lalique pendant or the Georgian epergne? Surely one cannot speak of the unique worked world of cognitive meaning, independent of space and time, generated by the Georgian epergne. No. For, just as this sort of object is tied ineluctably to the real world in virtue of its corporeality, so this very corporeality evokes an image of the real world, though it is the image of a real world of the *past*.

The Ming dynasty temple bell of course evokes a world – an image of Imperial Ming China, of its long tradition of crafting in bronze, of its religious attitudes and ceremonial commitments. And in this generation of an historically and culturally conditioned image we note its style. Because of this style recognition, moreover, we should immediately detect any "errors" – either errors in our judgment of style or in the thing itself. So, for example, we might suddenly notice that the bell's metal is too thin ever to have been used for its presumed function, or that the manner of stylizing the cloud patterns in its surface decoration is of nineteenth-century origin. In either such instance of "error" we would be noting *stylistic* contradictions, either between material structure and past-world use or between material configuration of design and presumed age. This is also true in the case of the Georgian epergne: the image of the opulence of the dinner tables where it performed its service is evoked, the guests, their clothes and conversations, the flowers and fruits that it held, etc. But suppose, again, that we discover "errors" as we scrutinize it further: the unpolished bottoms of its ruby glass inserts are wrong for this period; however, the overall shape and design is exact for the period, and the sterling silver frame with its engraved and repoussé decoration is the correct material for that design; on the other hand, the size of the whole object seems a bit diminutive for the kind of dinner service we would expect for the society using that material and that design; still, the hallmarks on the silver are absolutely correct; we breathe lightly on the hallmarked area to test and a resulting line of condensation indicates solder has been used to "let in" a genuine hallmark cut from a Georgian spoon. At this point we conclude that it is a deliberate forgery. We have accomplished all this by combining and contrasting the material elements, first one with the next, then with those elements discovered (or not discovered) in the image of the past world that the object generates. In this process we have pursued a dialectic of its *style*.

Style is something we can (and which antique dealers and museum curators must) become keenly, even subconsciously, attuned to. Seeing the past in the antique through its style, by virtue of its consistencies and inconsistencies, is the prime means by which the appraiser/authenticator evaluates a piece. Thus, it is often noted as a truism in the field that deliberate fakes of antiques, hard to spot when they are new, become easy to detect after a generation or so. Whereas the style of the present or immediate past is always too transparent to notice, we can detect clearly, when enough time has passed, an incongruity between two styles of the past colliding in the same object.

In these various ways, then, style enables us to recognize age. Style, as we now see, is the result of a nexus of interrelated elements, of forms and contents which are art-historically isolable and sufficiently constant for us to recognize their congruity and incongruity. By its style, the antique shows its age and thereby evokes the image of an historical world.[5]

There remains now the second consideration in the recognition of an object's age – the durability of its materiality. Age here relates to the modifications in the materiality of the sensuous vehicle noted in section III. It explains how, through this other mode, the antique becomes an icon for the image of a past reality. It also explains how antiques differ from certain artworks which may also be historical (or, better yet, which "exist historically"). Hence musical art objects (as opposed to their books or scores) cannot be antiques. My hearing of the art object called *Le nozze di Figaro*, an event of great "rarity" and "beauty," can certainly by its *style* evoke and preserve an image of a world now gone by. My reading of *War and Peace* re-creates nineteenth-century Russia and makes that world live again for me. But the novel, the literary masterpiece itself; the opera performance, the musical masterpiece itself: these cannot be antiques. These artworks cannot evoke a past world by "appealing to the durability of their own materiality," because their media cannot display that sort of material modification which we call "agedness."

All antiques, we say, should *show their age*. Agedness, however, is made apparent not only through style – as when we recognize that an object's beauty is not presently in vogue, is "old-fashioned," of "another time and place." Style is a formal trait of the object. There remains also the material or corporeal aspect of agedness. This appears in the form of dirt, wear, damage, discoloration, patina, and the like. This materially present agedness has two effects. First, it may increase or decrease the object's formal aesthetic appeal *per se* (i.e., making it more/less beautiful). Second, it increases the object's material aesthetic appeal (i.e., making us experience it as antique).

In the first instance, the purely formal aesthetic response may increase through the effects of agedness. This occurs either by (a) enabling the object's present appearance to coincide with current expectations or preferences, so that, for example, the colorlessness of Classical Greek marble statues now appeals to present taste as tasteful, whereas their original bright pigmentation would appear garish; or by (b) improving surface qualities: either making objects sometimes simpler, as when wear smoothes and obscures irregularities, or patina blends and softens original sharp incongruities (hence, Ruskin: "whatever faults it may have are rapidly disguised . . . whatever virtue it has still shines and steals out in the mellow light"[6]); or, more often, having the contrary effect in making these aged objects more complex, as when, for example, stains, small chips, tiny cracks, or the disappearance of very minor parts creates irregularities and asymmetries which are, in their visual and tactile conditions, more interesting and stimulating to the imagination than uniform regularity (hence, Kant: "all stiff regularity . . . has something in it repugnant to taste; for our entertainment in the contemplation of it lasts for no length of time, but it rather . . . produces weariness"[7]).

But materially present (as opposed to formal, i.e., stylistically present) agedness (patina, and the like) has the second effect of increasing the object's material (as opposed to purely formal) aesthetic appeal. Materially present agedness denotes the object's historicality and stimulates the aesthetic response to its antiqueness. Patina becomes the peculiar modification of the object's corporeal structure (and, in the case of representational or fine art objects – as opposed to crafts – the peculiar modification of the opacity of their sensuous vehicles) in which we recognize the duration of the object's existence through the durability of its materiality. This objective manifestation of endurance in time – agedness – becomes an Ariadne's thread, conducting the mind to the image of a past world, an icon invoking a past reality into the present and preserving it in a transubstantial entity which stands before us. Thus, for example, an Ancient Greek play or a Renaissance madrigal may evoke for us the spirit of their respective ages, but they have not sensuously materialized that time past. The play, the tune, are abstractions and can enjoy only the "intervality" of existence. But the antique wears time like a trophy – like Ahab's White Whale, bearing the scars of experience and the weight of history.

Hence, if it is true (and I think it is), as Trilling claims regarding literature of the past, that "its historicity is a fact in our aesthetic experience,"[8] then, a fortiori, antiques, as physically enduring objects which sensuously display their history in agedness, contribute a unique element in the totality of our aesthetic response.[9] It is one thing to know the age of the work, another to see and feel its palpable presence. In antiques, historicality is patently tactile – we feel, we can hold and caress, the age. The durability of its materiality, which marks of agedness prove, objectifies the duration of the antique's reality and so its "right" to speak for the past.

Hence, it is at least as much in the duration of its materiality, noted by physical signs of agedness we can "touch," as in style, noted by formal coordinations of material elements we observe, that we experience the aesthetic enjoyment of the antique. It is primarily in this corporeal and sensuous mode – in its historicality rather than in its mere history – that we appreciate authenticity in the antique. Authenticity, as Walter Benjamin has noted, is not merely a matter of who made it and when and where; it is a function of the object's entire existence in the world. Authenticity, he writes, is "the essence of all that is transmissible from its beginning, ranging from its substantive duration to its testimony to the history which it has experienced." In the age of mechanical reproduction, therefore, the object's own "time and place" become irrelevant, the "aura" (as he calls it) of the object is eliminated, and consequently it loses its "authority."[10] Thus, to be told of a pocket watch that it was "made for Napoleon" does not serve merely to verify its antiqueness as to date and provenance, but to ascribe to it a life-world which it has lived through and which has earned it the right to speak for and evoke an image of the past.

Notes

1   "The Ontological Integrity of the Art Object from the Ludic Viewpoint," *Journal of Aesthetics and Art Criticism* 34, no. 3 (1976): 323–36.

2   Nelson Goodman, "Art and Authenticity," in *Forgery in Art*, ed. Dennis Dutton (University of California Press, 1983).

3   On this issue and related matters see Herbert Marcuse, *One Dimensional Man* (Boston, 1964), chap. 9; and *The Aesthetic Dimension* (Boston, 1978).

4   To be sure, Van Gogh is classed as a "Post-impressionist." But there is no "Post-impressionist" style *per se*: "Post-impressionist" masters like Van Gogh perform stylistic variations in an "impressionistic" manner.

5   Cf. Joseph Alsop's discussion in "The Faker's Art" (*New York Review of Books*, 33, no. 16: 30) where he points out that we, as creatures of a self-consciously historical civilization, must adopt a purely aesthetic *and* an historical response to works of art; and that, in cases of proven inauthenticity (especially art fakery), the historical response "goes to war with" and "most often" subdues the aesthetic one.

6   John Ruskin, *Modern Painters* (London, n.d.), part 2, sec. 1, chap. 6, p. 97.

7   Immanuel Kant, *Critique of Aesthetic Judgement*, trans. J. H. Bernard (New York, 1953), sec. 22, p. 80.

8   Lionel Trilling, *The Liberal Imagination* (New York, 1953), p. 179.

9   I am indebted, for several of the ideas expressed in the above three paragraphs, to suggestions made by Yuriko Saito in the article "Why Restore Works of Art?" *Journal of Aesthetics and Art Criticism* 44, no. 2 (1985): 141–51.

10 Walter Benjamin, "The Work of Art in the Age of Mechanical Reproduction," in *Illuminations*, ed. Hanna Arendt, trans. Harry Zohn (1968; reprint, Huntington, N.Y., 1973), pp. 222–23.

Chapter 4

On looking at a Tahitian god-house

Steven Hooper

Prologue

This contribution is offered as a personal tribute to Peter Gathercole, and reflects his encouragement of students to *look* at objects – to examine them, appreciate them and, in many cases, be awed by them. I first encountered Peter in 1974 in London, when he gave a lecture on Māori artefacts. He discussed a number of objects, among them a *rei puta* neck-pendant in the British Museum and various Cook Voyage pieces in Cambridge, including the shell and wood trumpet on which he later published a paper (1976). Such, I recall, was the dynamic and motivational nature of Peter's presentation that soon afterwards I visited Cambridge and was encouraged by him to consider postgraduate study. I eventually went to Fiji to do doctoral research, and am now teaching Pacific art and running a research project on Polynesia. I cannot say that Peter can be blamed for this, but I am grateful for his enduring energetic engagement with his subject matter, because without that spark, which reminded me of the inspiring approach of my own grandfather,[1] my life might not have taken the course it did. It seems that by some happy operation of the law of unintended consequences (or perhaps of chaos theory), students would not now be studying Pacific art in my department had Peter not cavorted so enthusiastically on that stage in London some thirty years ago.

This paper derives from some of the initial research of the Polynesian Visual Arts project that is currently underway.[2] It takes as its primary subject a carving regarded as one of the more remarkable of those brought back from Polynesia by the missionaries of the London Missionary Society in the early part of the nineteenth century. It is the wooden god-house with four legs from Tahiti, which is now in the British Museum (figure 4.1). Although it has featured in a number of publications on Pacific art, it has never to my knowledge been the subject of any detailed formal analysis.[3] In the spirit

Fig. 4.1 God-house, Tahiti, wood and coir cord. British Museum, no. LMS 120; length 87 cm. Photograph courtesy of the Trustees of the British Museum.

of Gathercole's analysis of the Māori trumpet in Cambridge, in which he focused 'on one object in order to describe and to seek to explain its material features in an integrated way' (1976: 197), this paper attempts to show how, without recourse initially to written or pictorial evidence, close examination and formal analysis of an object can provide a foundation for interpretations of function, significance and meaning. It is hoped that by taking the reader through a specific case, the potential will be explored for form, materials and techniques to be instructive, and be suggestive of pertinent questions.

An intriguing wooden object

We move to the stores of the British Museum on 27 July 2004. Jill Hasell, Maia Jessop and I have on a table before us a wooden object, museum no. LMS 120, about three feet long.[4] It is composed of an apsidal-ended canopy above a cylinder which stands on four short legs with projecting feet. The rear end of the cylinder (oriented by the legs) is shaped as a flattened hemisphere, while the front end is open, revealing that the cylinder is in fact a hollow tube, tapering very slightly towards the end. The interior length of the tube is 55 cm, and its average width is 14–15 cm. The presence of a stepped flange to the roughly circular mouth, and of four small lugs – three on the outer side of the tube and one (broken) on the underside of the canopy – suggest that formerly a solid 'cap' of some kind was fitted to the aperture. A vestigial piece of coir cord is still attached through a hole in the lug on its proper left side.

Let us now move respectfully closer. Many who have not had the privilege of closely examining this object might assume that the canopy is removable – that it is a large lid for top access to the hollow chamber. But no, the entire piece is made from one solid log of wood, which varies in colour from dark brown to mid-brown. The species is possibly breadfruit, though the wood has not been tested. The canopy is cracked, split and glued in places, with some losses to the back and back-left sides. Written on both upper sides are inscriptions, much faded, in large black letters (of which more later). The upper surface is smoothly finished, as is the underside, though both show evidence of tool marks and rasp abrasions. The line where the underside of the canopy merges into the sides of the cylinder is cleanly finished. This area would have been technically difficult to access with the chisels and adzes – whether of stone, shell or metal – used by Tahitian craftsmen in the late eighteenth and early nineteenth centuries. It was also an area, because of having to work along the grain of the wood, where it would have been difficult to achieve a smooth finish without considerable labour.

A first, technical, observation can be that if the sculpture had been made in two large pieces, as a box with a lid, it would have been a much more straightforward task for the carver(s). However, a clear choice was made not to do that, despite the extra difficulty. It was intended to be in one piece. Why might that be so? Some observations on intentionality and the choices open to carvers of religious objects will be made later, so let us proceed for the moment with the physical examination of the piece, ignoring what might already be known of its purpose.

Inspection of the underside of this object revealed that on the belly of the cylinder, and flush with it, is a rectangular panel, c. 30 × 8.5 cm, neatly fitted in and tightly bound with three-ply plaited coir cords. This panel is plain, appears to be of the same wood species, and is positioned not directly under the cylinder, but angled to the proper right side. It is set towards the closed end of the cylinder and begins 18 cm from the aperture (figure 4.2). Why was it placed there? Jill, Maia and I discussed various hypotheses. Was it to allow special side access to the interior? Was it to cover or replace a damaged section of wood – a kind of repair? The first option would seem technically, if not ritually, redundant because of the existing access to the chamber through the open front end. With respect to the second option, no flaws or tears were detected in the timber around the panel to suggest that it was placed there to cover a large hole, knot or break.

Let us look at the fixing of the panel. It has been so skilfully done as to appear almost watertight, though it is not caulked. The edges of panel and cylinder are precisely butted and present a smooth surface on the exterior. Cords of plaited coir have been threaded and secured through ten pairs of holes, in two groups of two pairs on each of the long sides and a single pair on each short side. A wood tightening-peg has then been driven into each hole and broken off. This manner of fixing would appear to be the work of skilled carpenters familiar with canoe-building techniques. On the inside, the edges of the panel and body do not form a smooth join, as on the outside, but dip towards each other, creating a slight valley where the two edges meet. The inside surface of the panel is also slightly flatter than the cylinder walls around it. A remarkable aspect of the cylinder walls is their thinness, which averages some 5–6 mm. The inside surface, almost as smooth as the outside, is very cleanly finished all the way down to the end of the tube. What became apparent during this examination was how securely the panel was fixed, to the extent that removing it would have proved difficult and risked damage to the body. The panel was likely to have been fitted once and was not intended to be removed, in contrast to the missing cap for the circular front aperture.

Why then, if not as a special side access door, was the panel placed there? My favoured hypothesis, based on experience of living with canoe-building carpenters in eastern Fiji, is a technical one. The panel is there to cover an access hole that had to be made to allow full excavation of the cylinder. Excavation of a tube 14 cm wide to a depth of 55 cm could not have been achieved directly from the front aperture with the tools available. One could conjecture that this implies an absence of drilling tools, such as the European-derived brace and bit, and might thus be construed as evidence of pre-contact manufacture, but let us set those considerations to one side for the moment. Certainly, the adzes and chisels of the kind that we know were in the tool kit of eighteenth-century Tahitian carpenters could not have reached very far into such a narrow tube, so a side access large enough to allow entry of the carver's hand could have been made to permit full and careful excavation. Once the interior was completed to the satisfaction of the maker, the access hole was carefully sealed with a well-wrought panel.

Several things can be proposed if this hypothesis is accepted. First, that a tube of these specific dimensions and proportions was required, because trees certainly existed which could have furnished larger and more easily fashioned tubes – indeed this very log was big enough for a much larger tube if that had been the desire or intention of the maker. Second, it was important to have access from a single end rather than side access, and that the sliding of the tube's contents in and out of the front may have been procedurally appropriate. Excavation from both ends would have been easier and would probably have obviated the need for side access, but this course of action was not chosen. Third, the doing of extra work involving more complex carpentry and a high degree of finish was intentionally chosen by the maker(s), as mentioned above, because a much easier technical solution would have been to make a detachable top lid for a trough that could have been carved out in the manner of a simple canoe hull.

The missing front 'cap' is an enigma. What form it took remains a matter of conjecture, as is the manner of its fixing with cords to the lugs. It could have been a plain bulbous cap, possibly concave on the inside to make the total interior length, once closed, about 58 cm. This would balance with the form of the other end of the tube. Alternatively, it could have been shaped as a humanoid or animal head – this thought is prompted by the presence of legs. The fact that a quadruped appears to be depicted invites speculation that an animal such as a pig may have been represented, with an appropriate head, although depictions of animals are rare, if not absent, in surviving Tahitian carvings of the period. All four feet have been repaired at some stage in the past. The rear proper right foot is a complete replacement in wood from the ankle down – clearly the piece was valued to the extent that someone wanted to 'complete' it, probably for display purposes in the British Museum because the foot is missing in the photograph in the *British Museum Handbook* (BM 1910: 159).

A god-house?

Having concluded an examination of the material artefact, and having made some observations about the manufacturing decisions made by the maker(s), we can now turn to written sources to supplement what has been learned. The first source is the inscription on the canopy. On the proper left side is written in large black ink characters: 'F..re Atua Ta. . . .', with the largest capital letter some 4 cm high. This writing is much faded, but the British Museum catalogue slip for LMS 120 gives the text as: 'Fare Atua Tahiti'. On the proper right side, equally large but faded, is: '44 House for holding smaller idols at the Marae. Tahiti'. *Fare* is the generic Tahitian term for house, *atua* the generic term for a god, and *marae* the term for a temple or religious precinct. The number 44 remains a puzzle at present, because we find that this object is listed in the published catalogue of the London Missionary Society museum (LMS n.d.: 14) as: '4 An idol chest, or house, made to hold the smaller gods. From the marae at Tahiti. – *Presented by the late Mr. Bennet.* 'The British Museum catalogue slip provides further notes in different hands, including a reference to George Bennet, who with Reverend Daniel Tyerman comprised the deputation that made a long tour of LMS mission stations in the 1820s. The published account of their journey reveals the following:

> Oct. 1. [1823] Mr. Bennet obtained a *fare na atua*, or house of a god, the only relic of the kind that we have seen in these islands; so utter was the demolition of such things even when the idols themselves were preserved for transportation to England as trophies of the triumphs of the gospel. This shrine was wrought out of one solid block of timber; in form it resembled a dwelling-house, with roof and sloping ends, and was three feet in length. Underneath there was a cylindrical hole, having a door which closely fitted the opening. This was the depository of the idol. The fabric was supported on four short legs resembling those of a tortoise. The idol itself was of great antiquity – a female fiend, hideously mis-shapen, to mimic humanity. Her name was Tii Vahine, and we were told that she had slain her thousands [*sic*], having been held in the highest veneration and worshipped from time immemorial. At the general overthrow of idolatry, this image and the house in which it was kept were secreted, by some of her priests, in a cave among the mountains, and not produced till lately, when the whole was brought to market and sold, not for its value, but for its curiosity.
>
> (Montgomery 1831, vol. II: 58)

We can learn several things from a critical reading of this account compiled for publication by James Montgomery. The god-house in question is certainly the one described. It emerged for sale some seven years after the 'overthrow of idolatory' which took place in Tahiti in 1815–16 (see Newbury 1961). There was formerly a 'door' for the circular aperture, as suspected (unless this is a reference to the panel). George Bennet was the collector on 1 October 1823 at Papara in south-western Tahiti, although whether the object was made on Tahiti, and is therefore 'Tahitian', is impossible to verify.

The reference to a female idol in the above passage is, however, more problematic. This has led to a subsequent association of the god-house with LMS 98, a small female figure some 10.7 cm high, also in the British Museum. They were illustrated together in a photograph in both editions of the *British Museum Handbook* (BM 1910: 159; BM 1925: 164). However, this association would seem to be at odds with the very precise nature of the tubular shape that we have now established, and it has to be borne in mind that the god-house was acquired in a curiosity 'market' situation where, then as now, a good story was likely to enhance the value of the goods on offer. It is more likely that, after the mass conversions to Christianity on Tahiti, the two items, which may not have belonged together previously, were hidden together and subsequently became associated.

In support of this view, the precise form of the tube would seem to indicate a very specific form of inhabitant of the god-house. Adrienne Kaeppler (2003: 5–6; 1997: 69, 84, fig. 355), prompted by observations in Henry (1928: 136), has proposed that it was intended for a *to'o* image associated with the deity 'Oro. Many of these *to'o* images, for which a formal typology has yet to be done, have a generally cylindrical elongated ovoid form and range from 30–70 cm in length. They are composed of tightly bound coir cordage, sometimes enclosing a wood staff, and several surviving examples still retain bindings of feathered cords and tassels. These images, and the *pa'iatua* rituals in which they featured, have been discussed by Kooijman (1964) and Babadzan (1981; 1993: 89–141), and originally by the LMS missionary Ellis (1829: II: 205–6). A number are in the LMS collection at the British Museum. Some years ago Adrienne Kaeppler requested that the British Museum place one in the aperture of the *fare atua* for a photograph (figure 4.3). That particular *to'o* would seem too large for this *fare atua*, but the point is taken that a smaller example, such as the one in Cambridge, enclosed in a protective wrapping, could easily have been inserted and withdrawn from the *fare* when ritual procedures of consecration and reconsecration required. Certainly, whatever the god-house was intended to contain was unlikely to

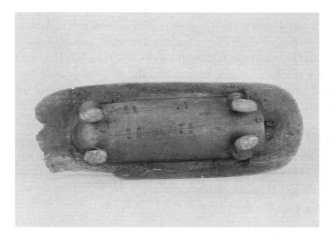

Fig. 4.2 View of underside of LMS 120. Photograph courtesy of the Trustees of the British Museum.

Fig. 4.3 LMS 120 with a large *to'o* image partially inserted into the chamber. Photograph courtesy of the Trustees of the British Museum.

have been inserted via the side panel in the cylinder, nor was it originally likely to have been a small figure 10.7 cm high, although this could subsequently have become the case.

Thus it looks probable that, in manufacture, the tube's dimensions were tailored to the tapering cylindrical form of a wrapped *to'o* image. However, one other possibility can be suggested. The dimensions of the tube could also have admitted the long bones of a human being (the femur, the longest, being some 50 cm long), and some of these, suitably wrapped, could have fitted in neatly. This hypothesis is connected to a statement by Orliac (2000: 106) that this object has been misidentified as a *fare atua*, and is more properly a *fare oromatua* for the preservation of bones and particularly the skull. This attribution is presumably partly based on an account by Joseph Banks, from Cook's First Voyage, of an occasion when he investigated the contents of a god-house on Ra'iatea (in the Leeward group of the Society Islands, west of Tahiti) and found skulls inside (Beaglehole 1962, vol. I: 324). However, there is clearly no way in which a skull, even minus the jawbone, could have fitted into the tube of this god-house, and besides, Banks also gives an account of investigating (and desecrating) another god-house on Ra'iatea. He wrote:

> One of these I examind by putting my hand into it: within was a parsel about 5 feet long and one thick wrappd up in matts, these I tore with my fingers till I came to a covering of mat made of platted Cocoa nut fibres which it was impossible to get through so I was obligd to desist, especially as what I had already done gave much offence to our new friends.
>
> (Beaglehole 1962, vol. I: 318)

What the Ra'iateans made of Banks and his activities need not detain us here, but with respect to the god-house under consideration, the evidence of Banks finding 'platted Cocoa nut fibres' seems to support strongly Kaeppler's contention that it was intended for a *to'o*, from which it has become separated.

There is neither time nor space here to develop further discussions that might be prompted by this intriguing object. Some lines of enquiry will be pursued during the course of the Polynesian visual arts project, such as the relations of equivalence between manufactured god-images and ancestral bones, and the formal connections between this object and other Tahitian and Polynesian containers and reliquaries of various kinds, such as houses, canoes, bodies, boxes, drums and hollow figures, such as the famous image in the British Museum of the Rurutu deity A'a. Questions also arise concerning the relationship between different forms of 'house' in central Polynesia, including *fare atua, fare oromatua* and mortuary structures called *fare tupapa'u*. In addition, the connections between houses and canoes remain unclear. Shrine houses of the *fare atua* kind were portable, and it is probable, on technical grounds, that they were made by canoe-building specialists.[5] Finally, there is also no opportunity here to attempt to disentangle the somewhat inconsistent literature on 'Oro, *to'o* and *fare atua*, or indeed to investigate the nature of *atua*.

However, besides all these unresolved questions, one piece of information from the literature may help us interpret what has been learned from the formal analysis. Henry (1928: 426) records a myth, received from a number of different sources in the 1820s, which states that the original *fare atua* was formed from the body of the major deity Ta'aroa, and that 'it became a model for all other god's houses'. It is also recorded that the god 'Oro was the offspring of Ta'aroa (Ellis 1829, vol. II: 192). In this regard we may recall that specific skilled labour was expended on making a tube with access from one end and not a trough with a lid, which would have been easier. This suggests that the sliding of the contents, most probably a *to'o*, in and out of the aperture was an important ritual procedure. If the *fare atua* is equivalent to the body of Ta'aroa, this would imply that the *to'o* image of 'Oro was periodically disgorged and engorged by Ta'aroa. This is not a birthing procedure in the conventional sense, for the aperture is at the front, nor was a kind of Caesarian section through the side appropriate. This draws our attention to the manner in which creative and productive processes were conceived in ritual, and to the role of the mouth in material representations, a topic that has been discussed by Kaeppler (1982) in relation to Hawaiian images.

A final word may be said about the 'animal' legs. They in fact resemble those on humanoid images from the Society Islands, and a congener for the quadruped form in this part of Polynesia may be found in the large four-legged humanoid figure from Mangareva in the Vatican Museum in Rome (Kaeppler 1997: pl. 41).

Objects, makers and intentionality

Returning to the creative process by which this object was given material form, a few final observations on intentionality will be offered. We know comparatively little about the social and ritual status of eighteenth- and nineteenth-century woodworking specialists in this region, but whoever made this object will have been working in the context of an understanding of the appropriate form which was desired, of the technical procedures for achieving it and of the desirability of a high level of finish. Technical decisions will have been made according to religious requirements and notions of appropriateness; they will have been governed by ideas of efficacy, not ease or speed. Skilled woodworking in the Pacific can be considered as a kind of sacrificial action or worship, designed to please the gods as well as to produce artefacts which would do a job effectively and be fit for their purpose. We have already noted the specific labour- and skill-intensive form of this god-house, and its fine finish, inside and out. The same may be said for many Polynesian objects which are elaborated and finished far in excess of requirements for technical efficiency – they must also satisfy requirements for ritual efficacy. There can be no doubt that this object was intended to be made as it was, and that the difficult and time-consuming excavation to achieve a smooth tubular chamber was important to the eventual efficacy of the artefact in its context of use in religious ritual.

This paper has been an exercise in seeing how far close inspection of a given artefact can produce questions and hypotheses that can assist in a greater understanding of that artefact and of its contexts, especially when combined with written and pictorial sources. If objects are to fulfil their potential in the analysis of social and religious systems, they need to be seen as more than illustrative of culture, but as constitutive of cultural practices. They can be primary data, amenable to informed and rigorous examination, and can be the basis for plausible propositions about the intentions and contexts of the actors who made and used them. Their form, materials, assembly, use and display were key parts of religious practice. If we foreground this we are likely to develop more profound understandings of Polynesian religion, particularly when these formal investigations are allied to oral and written records, and to archaeological data. These objects, many of them housed in museum collections, are important evidential materials whose potential remains largely untapped.

Acknowledgements

I would like here to express my thanks to Lissant Bolton, Jenny Newell and Jill Hasell of the Department of Africa, Oceania and the Americas at the British Museum for their enthusiastic co-operation in our Polynesian project work – and especially to Jill for her assistance, ideas and hospitality when Maia Jessop (the project research student) and I were examining the Tahitian god-house. I also wish to thank Dr Les Jessop of the Hancock Museum, University of Newcastle, for supplying a copy of the London Missionary Society catalogue (LMS n.d.), and Anita Herle and two anonymous readers for *JME* for constructive comments on this paper.

Notes

1   The ethnographical collector James Hooper, proprietor from 1957 to 1963 of 'The Totems Museum' in Arundel, Sussex, where I grew up. See Phelps (1976) for a catalogue of the collection containing a short biography of my grandfather (written under my former name).

2   This three-year project (2003–6), 'Polynesian visual arts; meanings and histories in Pacific and European cultural contexts, 1760–1850', is based at the Sainsbury Research Unit, UEA, and is sponsored by a research grant from the Arts and Humanities Research Board, whose assistance is gratefully acknowledged. For further information on this project, see: <http://www.sru.uea.ac.uk/polynesia/welcome.htm>.

3   Adrienne Kaeppler, in a recent (2003) unpublished paper concerning a large Tuamotuan god-house in the Vatican Museum, and in an earlier publication (1997: 69, 84), has briefly discussed the present piece and its possible function. It has also been illustrated by Edge-Partington (1890: 26), Oliver (1974: I: 102), Barrow (1979: 45) and Orliac (2000: 106).

4   The precise dimensions of LMS 120 are: length 87.0 cm, height 31.5 cm, width 25.5 cm. It arrived at the British Museum in 1890 with other loan material from the London Missionary Society.

5   The twin pairs of bindings which secure the panel on this piece correspond to the technique of canoe-plank binding illustrated by Handy (1932: 50–2), even down to the cord which links each pair of bindings on the inside.

References

Babadzan, A. 1981. 'Les Dépouilles des Dieux: essai sur la symbolique de certaines effigies Polynésiennes', *Res* 1: 8–39.
—— 1993. *Les Dépouilles des Dieux: essai sur la religion tahitienne à l'époque de la découverte.* Paris: Editions de la Maison des Sciences de l'Homme.
Barrow, T. E. 1979. *The Art of Tahiti.* London: Thames and Hudson.
Beaglehole, J. C. (ed.) 1962. *The Endeavour Journal of Joseph Banks 1768–1771*, 2 vols. Sydney: Angus and Robertson.
British Museum [BM] 1910. *Handbook to the Ethnographical Collections.* London: British Museum.
—— 1925. *Handbook to the Ethnographical Collections* (second edition). London: British Museum.
Edge-Partington, J. 1890. *An Album of the Weapons, Tools, Ornaments, Articles of Dress, Etc. of the Natives of the Pacific Islands.* Issued privately. (A facsimile reprint of all three volumes, 1890–8, was published privately in 1969 by John Hewett, London).
Ellis, W. 1829. *Polynesian Researches during a Residence of nearly Six Years in the South Sea Islands*, 2 vols. London: Fisher, Son and Jackson.
Gathercole, P. 1976. 'A Maori Shell Trumpet at Cambridge', in Sieveking, G. de G., Longworth, I. H., and Wilson, K. E. (eds), *Problems in Economic and Social Archaeology.* London: Duckworth.
Handy, E. S. C. 1932. *Houses, Boats and Fishing in the Society Islands.* Honolulu: B. P. Bishop Museum Bulletin 90.
Henry, T. 1928. *Ancient Tahiti.* Honolulu: B. P. Bishop Museum Bulletin 48.
Kaeppler, A. L. 1982. 'Genealogy and disrespect: a study of symbolism in Hawaiian images', *Res* 3: 82–107.
—— 1997. 'Polynesia and Micronesia', in Kaeppler, A. L., Kaufmann, C. and Newton, D. *Oceanic Art.* New York: Abrams.
—— 2003. 'Containers of Divinity' (unpublished typescript).

Kooijman, S. 1964. 'Ancient Tahitian god-figures', *Journal of the Polynesian Society* 73 (2): 110–25.

LMS [London Missionary Society] n.d. (*c.* 1850s). *Catalogue of the Missionary Museum, Blomfield Street, Finsbury*. London: London Missionary Society.

Montgomery, J. (ed.) 1831. *Journal of Voyages and Travels by the Rev. Daniel Tyerman and George Bennet, Esq., deputed from the London Missionary Society to visit their various stations in the South Sea islands, China, India, etc., between the years 1821 and 1829*, 2 vols. London: Westley and Davies.

Newbury, C. W. 1961. *The History of the Tahitian Mission 1799–1830, written by John Davies Missionary to the South Sea Islands*. Cambridge: Hakluyt Society, second series, no. CXVI.

Oliver, D. 1974. *Ancient Tahitian Society*, 3 vols. Honolulu: University Press of Hawai'i.

Orliac, C. 2000. *Fare et Habitat à Tahiti*. Marseille: Editions Parenthèses.

Phelps, S. 1976. *Art and Artefacts of the Pacific, Africa and the Americas: the James Hooper Collection*. London: Hutchinson.

Chapter 5

Making life beautiful
My experience of doing beadwork

Anna MacLennan

THE MATERIAL HISTORIES WORKSHOP HELD ON the 26th and 27th of April 2007 at Marischal Museum in Aberdeen was an opportunity for curators and academics from all over Scotland to meet with First Nations and Métis colleagues, including curators, academics and seamstresses from Manitoba and Saskatchewan, Canada. This interaction enabled a better understanding of the hide garments and beadwork that have found their way to Scotland over the years as a result of Scots' involvement in the fur trade from the seventeenth through to the twentieth centuries. Unlike a conference setting, the Material Histories workshop focused as much on doing as it did on talking. The 'doing' involved beading sessions that formed the core of the two-day event. The participants were split into three groups and, led by Jenny Meyer, Jennine Krauchi and Sherry Farrell Racette, each group was taught to create a simple beaded flower pattern for a pin cushion. The differences in backgrounds, experience and knowledge of sewing that participants brought to the workshop meant that everyone would have taken something different from it, and I can only write from an individual perspective.

Beadwork continues to hold an important place in the public and private lives of many Canadians, and attending the workshop allowed me to develop my understanding of the beadwork seen on the clothing worn nowadays by First Nations and Métis people at public events in Canada, such as powwows. The experience of learning how to do beading has also altered the way I approach and understand historic beadwork found today in museum settings, and my responses to museum 'objects' more broadly. First, my appreciation of the skill and patience of seamstresses was amplified. In order to get my beadwork to lie flat and avoid gaps between beads I had to unpick and redo my stitches on many occasions. Even then, Jenny graciously sorted out a couple of beady messes I managed to create! Unlike some of the sewing I had done previous to the workshop, beading requires much more time for much less progress. Taking my time in an attempt to create neat work meant spending hours huddled over the same few centimetres of beads.

Second, I was encouraged to consider not only the aesthetics of the finished products that were familiar to me from museum settings, but also the story of these objects' creation in the hands of a seamstress. What struck me was that although our finished beadwork may be worlds apart, our experience of beading may not be so totally different. The makers of some of the museum pieces may have sat around in groups sewing, much as we did in the workshop, talking about their families, memories triggered by a certain pattern, or what they were having for dinner. Only through doing, in addition to talking, was this transition in my understanding of beadwork possible.

In the closing discussions, Keith Goulet highlighted the concept of 'appreciation' as a way of summing up the workshop as a whole. Like Keith, I also appreciated the coming together of people from different backgrounds, and the thoughts and action involved in the sewing and beading process. However, what stood out to me through trying beadwork myself was an appreciation of the seamstress's skill. It is often true that an understanding of how difficult a task is cannot be fully grasped until one tries it for oneself. Seamstresses certainly make the process look easy. As a beginner, I felt frustrated that my simple flower design was not always flat against the fabric and was not as neat as I would have liked. This was *despite* the fact that I was beading directly onto a ready-made pattern. Even more than before, when I look at some of the extremely neat, intricate and often perfectly symmetrical beadwork found on garments and other objects, I am left in awe. The time, patience and precision a project must have required, not to mention the years of practice it would take to reach the level of expertise I see in some of the pieces in today's museum collections, amazes me.

I am now drawn to thinking more about the *process* of creating beautiful beadwork, rather than solely the beauty of the beadwork itself. Despite my inability to make the beads do what I wanted them to, having now tried to do beadwork myself, I feel able to empathise more with seamstresses, and I wonder about the stories behind the work they produced. I wonder under what circumstances the beadwork was created. What was their relationship with the person they were making it for? Was it a gift, a favour, or a business venture? What did the patterns and colours they chose mean to them? The list of questions could go on. The beadwork I created was so much *more* than an object of material culture. To me, the beads told a story of where I was when I was making the pin cushion, who taught me what to do, who else was there, who I planned to give it to once I was finished, and the various conversations the production process sparked. As a result, the finished product – my pin cushion – has many stories attached to it that are specific to my experience of making it.

I found beading to be relaxing, and not so demanding that it required my full attention, so conversations were able to develop. As people in my group became more comfortable with the skills required, it was amazing how quickly the beading was accompanied by everyday conversations about our daily lives. It made me more aware of the sorts of conversations seamstresses in Canada may have been having while creating the beadwork we now see in museums. The potential that every object has for a personal story specific to the seamstress that made it, adds a hidden depth that I had not considered prior to this workshop. As a result, the beadwork I now see in museums seems far more complex and rich than objects to be admired solely for their beauty and workmanship. Though these stories are largely unknown, as are the identities of the women who produced much of the work now found in museum collections, for me, this is not the most important thing. Instead, it is my increased awareness of the human experience of making beadwork that has altered my appreciation of it.

Overall, my experience of learning how to do simple beadwork at the Material Histories workshop has changed the way I approach and understand beadwork found in museums, and has resulted in me considering the production process in *addition* to the finish article. I am now much more aware of the skill, patience and practice required to make the beautiful beadwork displayed in many museums. Moreover, I have become more cognisant of the existence of stories, experiences and histories inextricably linked to beadwork that began during the production process. This has added a very rich and interesting layer to the beaded museum exhibits I have seen. In broader terms, this new-found awareness and appreciation of beading and beadwork can be extended to include many other artefacts in museums. What interests me is not just the objects that are on display, but the story of their production, use and how they came to be displayed in that particular museum: their material history.

Chapter 6

Knitting is ...

Sabrina Gschwandtner

WHEN I'M ASKED WHAT I DO I often reply that I'm an artist who works with film, video and textiles. To me the link between the three is instinctive and implicit – media is a textile – and my work expresses why and how I find that to be true. The model for my career as an artist, curator, writer, editor and publisher is knitting.

I started knitting in my final semester of college as an art/semiotics student at Brown University. Two of my roommates were textile students at the Rhode Island School of Design and when they came home late at night, still full of energy, they'd climb onto the yellow stools in our kitchen and chatter and spool yarn toward their needles like addicts. They showed me the basics of knitting and crochet (my mother had taught me when I was eight but I had mostly forgotten) and I was charmed. I started to knit during breaks from the dense theory I was reading for school; stitching, I was completely concentrated on the rhythm of my hands and my frenetic mind would go empty. Within a few months, although I had been rigorously devoted to experimental and avant-garde film during all four years of college, handcraft had become my guiding creative format.

I'd knit or crochet something, leave it, come back, rip it up, fix it, wear it, add some other material, hang it up, leave it, project film onto it, record that, edit it, show it, give it away and start over. Even when I'm not working with knitting as my actual medium or technique I'm still working with it as a single thread out of which emerges a surface, a fabric, a narrative, an outfit, a pattern, a text, a recording, and even, despite my seemingly erratic way of working, a form that encompasses all of these things.

Knitting is sculpture

Stitching was how I first conceived of working with film as a sculptural material. For an early project, I sewed onto 35 mm slides that had come back from the lab blurry

Fig. 6.1 Sabrina Gschwandtner, *Phototactic Behavior in Sewn Slides*, 2007. Dimensions variable. Cotton thread, 35 mm slides, Kodak Ektapro 9020 slide projector. Image courtesy of Sabrina Gschwandtner.

and unusable as the documentation I'd intended. I found that when the sewn slides were projected, the pattern of the thread and the holes left by the sewing needle became the foreground imagery, instead of the photographic image on the slide. The fan of the slide projector blew the loose threads in all directions, which also caused an unusual kind of animation. The slide projector's automatic focus mechanism struggled to focus on the three-dimensional thread hanging in front of and behind the slides and it sometimes gave up, leaving the viewer to inspect a blurry field in between thread and image. I selected a group of eighty slides, put them into the carousel and let them project for ten seconds each in a continual loop. This was the piece; all the ways in which the slide projector abstracted and activated a non-narrative about space. In conceiving of an approach to filmmaking that was in part defined by the craft ethos of mending and recycling but still devoted to the history of avant-garde cinema, I was able to expand on the potential for the projected image, but place it within the context of handcraft.

Knitting is participation

The more I worked with handcraft materials, the more I came to think about the social spaces they implied. I swung from making quiet, sculptural spaces to creating sites of conversation. I realized that knitting had potential to reach out to a different audience and that collective crafting and dialogue could be part of the art experience:

it could catalyze a different kind of exchange, outside of traditional art audience boundaries. This reflected a new interest in the public sphere and in creating artwork with social and political components.

I started thinking about handcraft as a site of resistance – to an oppressively commodity-based art market and to an omnipresent, excessive, and high-speed communicative landscape – but also as a site of empowerment and activism. Knitting has, after all, become popular during every major American war.[1] During wartime, knitters have used their craft for civic participation, protest, therapeutic distraction, and even direct attack.[2]

For my piece *Wartime Knitting Circle*, an interactive installation created for the Museum of Arts & Design's 2007 exhibition "Radical Lace and Subversive Knitting," I wanted to exploit these different uses of wartime knitting in order to incite political conversation between different kinds of people. Knitters represent a diverse audience group in terms of age, race, politics and economics (for every knitter using qiviut, spun copper, or other high-priced yarns there is a knitter making clothes out of economic necessity).

The installation consisted of nine machine-knitted photo blankets – which in 2005 became a popular way for families to honor their relatives who had been deployed to Iraq and Afghanistan – depicting images culled from newspapers, historical societies and library archives that all showed different ways knitting has been and is being used during war. The installation provided a space and materials for knitters to work on wartime knitting projects; it was also a place for them to consider the role their handcraft could play in the Iraq war. Knitters were allowed to bring in their own projects, or they could choose to work on one of four wartime knitting patterns that were provided. The patterns included Lisa Anne Auerbach's Body Count Mittens,[3] which memorialize the number of US soldiers killed at the time the mittens are made; a simple square to be used for blankets, which were either mailed to Afghans for Afghans[4] or to US soldiers recovering in military hospitals; balaclavas to be sent either to troops in Iraq and Afghanistan or to Stitch for Senate, microRevolt. org's war protest project;[5] and *USS Cole* Slippers, sent to troops on ships. Many of these items were knit by several different people; one knitter would cast on, add a few stitches or rows, then put the project down and later another knitter would advance the piece.

I witnessed several heated arguments at the knitting table and I participated in one of them.

A visitor comment book included in the installation recorded some of what happened when I wasn't there:

Political associations made for a more interesting group knitting experience. *Devon Thein*

Added a bit to the helmetliner – Kay worked a square, of course. *Ann Shayne*

Knitting in public is a radical act. *Bonnie Gray*

My earliest memories are the clack of knitting needles (on the therapeutic theme) – my grandmother knitted continuously as we sat in the air-raid shelters in Scotland 1942–45. *S. Holton*

Knitting is community

When I started *KnitKnit* in 2002 it was a very personal format for my thinking through the connections between handcraft and fine art. I had been making one-of-a-kind knit and crochet clothes by hand and selling to boutiques in Manhattan for about two years when I decided that I wanted to return to art making. I interviewed two friends who had come to handcraft, like me, after studying fine art in college and I put that text into a very rough, photocopied and stapled booklet with spray-painted stencils. *KnitKnit* became a biannual 'zine that took different formats each time and included contributions by all kinds of artists, designers, writers and makers: producing *KnitKnit*, distributing it, and organizing *KnitKnit* launch events and art exhibitions were ways to create a far-flung community of people interested in displacing the boundaries between art and craft.

When I initiated a *KnitKnit* book in 2006, I purposely situated it as a craft *and* an art endeavor, working with a craft book editor at Abrams, a publishing house that also makes and distributes art books. With the publisher committed to sending the book to major chains, art bookstores and yarn shops, I chose to profile a mix of knitters making clothing, sculpture, graffiti, therapy, protest and performance, juxtaposing political and conceptual gestures with functional and technical achievements.

Knitting is writing

This is why so many knitters blog; they're dauntingly aware that making a sweater is, in a way, writing history. As Jim Drain told me when I was interviewing him for my book, ". . . knitting is a living tradition – it's physical knowledge of a culture. Knowledge of language dies so quickly. It's awesome to find a sweater and look at the language of it – to see how it's made, what yarn was used, and how problems were solved. A sweater is a form of consciousness."[6]

My 2007 video, *A History of String*, includes a chapter on quipus, which are recording devices from the Inca Empire. Quipus are beautiful bundles of twisted and knotted colored threads that were continuously tied and retied and presumably read by touch and sight. Each part of the quipu – length, color of string, number of knots, and type of knots – is thought to contain meaning. Because the Spanish destroyed as many quipus as they could find during their colonial conquest, only about 600 pre-Columbian examples survive, preserved in private and museum collections. Although quipus are generally believed to contain numerical information, some anthropologists are working to translate them into language, reading them as three-dimensional binary code (similar to the way computers translate eight-bit ASCII into letters and words).[7]

One has to wonder how future generations might read our sweaters if written and photographic records of them are lost.

Knitting is gift

I co-curated (with Sundown Salon founder Fritz Haeg and producer Sara Grady) a salon called the KnitKnit Sundown Salon in 2004. The daylong event included a meeting of the Church of Craft, an exhibition of art and craft works, a film / video screening, a performance and several impromptu fashion shows, among other happenings. It wasn't just the quality of the work inside the geodesic dome where the event was held, nor the abundant activities there that made the salon so memorable; it was the complete reciprocity with which the work was given and received. For eight hours on a cold February day in Los Angeles, the KnitKnit Sundown Salon existed as a utopian, three-tiered marvel of handmade wonders and a communal undertaking that gave me hope for the rise of a new social order.[8]

Knitting is pleasure

As my mentor Leslie Thornton wrote to me by email:

> I know I've told you this, many women my age must tell you the same thing, but making things, sewing, designing all of my own clothes, knitting, even making beads, but that was much later; when the train to Providence was driving me crazy, so anyway, I was saying, in this very long sentence, possibly the longest I've ever written in my life, I made things nearly constantly when I wasn't in school, studying, going to rock concerts or sleeping, playing kickball, or riding my bike or picking flowers in our huge beautiful yard or catching frogs, from the age of three on.

Knitting is home

Through my friend Alysa Nahmias, who had at the time just started her architecture degree at Princeton, I learned of Gottfried Semper, the nineteenth-century architect and theorist who asserted that woven and knitted materials effectively separated inner and outer life to create what we know as "home." After a trip to a library, where I read more of his writings, I ended up reprinting one of his texts in *KnitKnit*'s third issue. Brian Sholis, an art critic, wrote an introduction to the issue that included the following lines: "Semper not only rehabilitates arts and crafts, integrating them more fully with our understanding of architecture and other fine arts; he also smudges the line between 'advanced' and 'barbaric' contributions to culture, reincorporating the contributions of minority citizens to the achievements of ancient Greece, Egypt, and beyond."[9]

At a "Stitch In" at the Jersey City Art Museum in October 2007 I gave a short talk about war and handcraft. It concluded with a recollection of someone telling me that she thought women did housekeeping/homemaking activities with a kind of irony these days. I asked how the audience felt about that. It really got people going – everyone has an opinion about their home. One by one people spoke up and their responses ranged from detailed explanations of 1970s fiber art to Martha Stewart's design influence on the marketplace to the agony of making a decision about whether to hire a housekeeper to ideas about post 9/11 nesting.

Swedish critic Love Jönsson put this forward during a recent lecture: avant-garde art proposes an access to the everyday that craft, through its traditional link to utility and material culture, already has. Young artists working with handcraft do not need an art world seal of approval, he said, and in reevaluating the craft tradition they have emphasized that:

- making things by hand is joyful; and
- "the functional object is the most interesting one."[10]

Whether knitting is high architecture, hip Home Ec, functional art, or a reaction to terrorism, it is helping us think through our notions of domesticity.

Knitting is media

It's true that people pick up crochet hooks as an escape from the computer. In the face of everything fast and glinting, they want something real – a reinjection of the artisanal or some sense of the integrity of labor. But handcraft will usually send them to the web, which is a contemporary Whole Earth Catalog if you know where to look. When crafters go online searching for instruction they usually end up commenting on other crafters' blogs or posting to myriad threads on craft community boards. In contrast to the lifestyle associated with the professional craftsperson of the late twentieth century (which is still the academic craft model), DIY crafters fluidly use technology to market and sell their work and participate in their communities. As artist and knitwear designer Liz Collins has remarked, "putting together a MySpace page is not that different from collaging or quilting. You're using different materials, to different ends, but along the way you're starting with matter and transforming it into something else, using your hands and your brain."[11]

Knitting is a site, and it can and should be used as a form of broadcasting, just like the Internet, television, or any other public media.

Notes

1   Allison Smith, *The Muster* (New York: Public Art Fund, 2007).
2   Anne MacDonald, *No Idle Hands: the Social History of American Knitting* (New York: Ballantine Books, 1990).
3   See www.stealthissweater.com/patterns/mittenpattern.pdf.
4   See www.afghansforafghans.org.
5   See www.stitchforsenate.us.
6   Sabrina Gschwandtner, *KnitKnit: Profiles and Projects from Knitting's New Wave* (New York: Stewart, Tabori and Chang, 2007), p. 52.
7   Sabrina Gschwandtner, "A Brief History of String," *Cabinet* 23 (Winter 2006): 38–41.

8   Fritz Haeg (ed.), *Sundown Salon 2001–06: In Words and Pictures* (New York: Evil Twin Productions, 2008).

9   Brian Sholis, "Writings of Nineteenth Century Architect Gottfried Semper," in Sabrina Gschwandtner (ed.) *KnitKnit* 3 (January 2004): 1.

10 Urban FIELD symposium, University College for the Creative Arts, Farnham, England. November 14, 2007.

11 Julia Bryan-Wilson (ed.), "The Politics of Craft," *Modern Painters* (February/March 2008): 78–83.

Chapter 7

Malangan
Objects, sacrifice and the production of memory

Susanne Küchler

THE DOCUMENTATION OF GIFT EXCHANGE SYSTEMS has an uninterrupted history in Melanesian ethnography. This is because exchange activities in Melanesia have not merely continued, but have effloresced during a period that has been increasingly dominated by a commodity-based economy (Gregory 1982:166). This efflorescence of gift exchange systems took different forms at different times and places with various consequences for society and culture.

Evidence for the escalation of exchange activity derives mostly from ethnographies that show an increase in the frequency and the visibility of ceremonies in which gift objects and valuables circulate. Ethnographic collections tend to be neglected as comparative data, because of the prevailing tendency to classify objects with representational properties as art and as removed from exchange. With the help of the example of Malangan art and data collected during two years' research at the location of its production in northern New Ireland, Papua New Guinea, I want to point out that much can be gained from analyzing certain ethnographic collections as indexes of attitudes, beliefs, and practices surrounding the production of objects as gifts. The material gives evidence of a dynamic relation between a mode of representation and a mode of circulation and suggests the need to reconsider object collections whose representational properties lead to their exclusion from the ethnography of exchange.

The Malangan collections of northern New Ireland are famous for their size, which is comparable with those of the Northwest coast of America or of the Sepik River in mainland New Guinea. The size of these collections, however, is not proof of a vigorous "salvage" anthropology alone, but of gift production for transactions that usually culminated in the destruction of objects.[1] In northern New Ireland, sale has become an alternative to destruction, so that the size of the collections is indicative of a particular kind of exchange system and its efflorescence.

Exchange systems that feature the destruction of gifts are rare but are not restricted to specific cultures.[2] For example, the Melanesian material referred to in this paper could be compared with the potlatch of the Northwest coast. "Gifts to god systems," to use Gregory's term, have flourished and developed under the impact of Western money and Western goods (Gregory 1980:627), and have contributed to the development of new forms of ranking and of regional forms of social organization (cf. Wolf 1982:191). While the theory of gift destruction has tended to emphasize the relation between alienation and capital accumulation, and to focus on gift objects as tokens in an economic transaction (Gregory 1980:627), it has ignored the ephemeral character of gifts and the specificity of their production as a source for the comparative understanding of the difference such "gift to god systems" created in the degree of ranking, in the nature of kinship, and in gender relations.[3]

This paper thus aims to develop a perspective on "gift to god systems" that takes as its starting point the nature of the objects sacrificed in the exchanges. Such objects characteristically feature representational properties that have led us to ignore them in the analysis of exchange systems. The representational properties are argued to be significantly embedded in exchange systems in which not objects, but the images they embody are circulated in transactions. The circulation of imagery is achieved through the destruction of gift objects and is made possible through processes of memory; mnemonically processed and circulated imagery enables the transcendence of kinship-based forms of organization by "ritual confederations" that imply a distinctive territorial mode of ranking (Wolf 1982:191). The ethnography of Malangan art is a particularly clear example of gift production for sacrificial exchange and the concomitant development of both a visual mnemonic system and a regional form of social organization with emerging new forms of ranking. For this reason it is discussed extensively in this paper with the hope of inspiring a fresh look at comparative ethnographies and collections that document the operation of those rare, but anthropologically interesting, exchange systems in which gift objects are produced to be sacrificed.

Collections as data

Collections of objects that were made for destruction have remained an untapped resource of potential data for analysis, because we impose assumptions derived from Western art history on objects with representational properties and overlook the distinctive conceptions under which they are produced. We assume, for example, that the fact of their destruction has no relevance for how they are produced or for the form given to the objects in production. We therefore approach collections disregarding the relation between object and temporality and dismiss as irrelevant the tension between constancy and variation by interpreting this tension as a further reason to leave the responsibility for analysis to those who look at these objects as "art" and as removed from exchange.

Objects produced as gifts, however, confound time in specific and anthropologically interesting ways. In confounding time, they both visually and conceptually create the disinterested character of gift exchange (Bourdieu 1977:171). There are two ways in which the production of gifts can confound time. With gift objects that endure, time is literally inscribed as age into the gift as it continues to be circulated. Time, however, can also be confounded through renewal, which is the principle underlying the destruction of gifts. The sacrifice of the gift creates time not as history, which is visible as age in objects, but as memory, which as imagery is subjected to renewal.

The production of memory is characteristic of systems that feature the destruction of gifts. It is based on a conception of time that emphasizes its renewal and produces imagery subject to retention and recall. Malangan art is a well-documented example of gift objects whose imagery is repeatedly reproduced through deliberate recall from memory for successive gift productions;[4] Malangan objects are sculptures that are both intricately carved and painted and that display a visual and conceptual complexity that is expressed in the tension between constancy and variation in the carved and painted motifs. The motifs and motif combinations are recurrent throughout the collections of Malangan art, with variations being introduced in the painted surface and in the number and selection of motifs. This pattern of constancy and variation is a product of a process of transformation that occurs in the recall of imagery for reembodiment in a gift object; the recall is not random, but is governed by the calculations of exchange. This systemic feature of transformation enables us to use certain of these collections as documentation for the efflorescence of "gift to god systems" and its consequences for political evolution.

Malangan sculptures are produced for transaction in the final ceremony for the dead, are symbolically killed in the exchanges, and are destroyed.[5] What is circulated in the exchanges is not things, but the right to reproduce images that are remembered and recalled for reembodiment in ever new sculptures. The separation of imagery from a sculpture that is serving as a gift is effected through sacrificing the sculpture and releasing, as it is left to rot, what is called its "smell" (musung), which is the most important aspect of memory.

To clarify the distinctive character of objects in "gift to god systems" as exemplified in Malangan art, I want to make a brief comparison with another Melanesian exchange system, the Kula. In the Kula, shell valuables are passed from island to island; as they travel, they produce history that, as it accumulates, increases the fame of the shells and of the transactors (Weiner 1976; Munn 1986). The age of the shell and the path it forms as it is moved around the islands are two manifestations of the time without which there would be no notion of the gift as disinterested exchange. The concern with perpetuating the movement of the shells disguises the calculation of transaction. Transactors of Kula valuables are thus thought of as partners in the cooperative venture of producing the history of shells.[6]

In contrast, Malangan transactions do not create lasting partnerships and there is no sense of "marriages" between images as is said of the meeting of Kula shells. There is indeed no sense of two transactions being linked or separated through time. Malangan transactions are dramatized as sacrifice and the objective is the production of memory. In recounting transactions and relationships based on them, memory is represented as knowledge of how to reembody the Malangan imagery which is in circulation. This knowledge is the basis for ranking clans in expanded and territorially organized units that are activated in ritual situations.

These examples highlight the different ways in which objects that serve as gifts can confound time. Kula shell valuables thus change visibly as they continue on their path around the islands of the Massim. Through the handling of shells, their epidermis is removed and red striations are formed on the shell surface (Campbell 1983:236). Time is literally inscribed into the shells, which increase in value with age (Campbell 1983:237). The Malangan imagery, however, creates during its reembodiment a network of stoppages that freeze the passing of time and allow for the perception of what Bergson called the *durée*.[7] The value ascribed to such objects concerns how much they retain and not how much has been taken away through time.

The complexity of the production of memory in general and its specific articulation in exchange is all too little explored in the anthropological literature. This is because it requires us to rethink our assumptions about objects that, on account of being embedded in memory production, embody imagery of an apparently representational character. For us, they are "art" and thus made to be remnants of individual and cultural creativity. It is not the status of "art" that needs questioning, but the conception of objects as original and nonrecoverable things.

Rethinking Malangan art

Complex visual objects such as Malangan sculptures are problematic for anthropologists, who regard them with a sense of distance that appears appropriate for all things falling within our category of art. This distance is also imposed upon the analysis in that the relation between object and context is seen to be primarily one of representation. The assumptions of such an analysis are so contrary to the assumptions under which the sculptures were produced that hardly anything is known in the present literature about the form given to the objects, or about their relation to exchange in what I will call the *Malangan system*. The sad remark by one of the earliest anthropologists working on Malangan could have been made in the 1980s as well as in 1932, when it was written:

> We have so little information about the Malangan. . . . Their exact significance is still not quite clear. We know that they are to honor the dead, that they are taboo to women, that they are surrounded by very elaborate dances and other ritual, that wealth is necessary to make the feasts accompanying them and that much prestige comes to him who holds Malangan. We know too, that they have come from the distant past (Powdermaker 1932:134).[8]

The Malangan system encompasses assumptions and practices that surround the embodiment of imagery in gifts. As gifts they are governed in production and consumption by conceptions of the relation between persons and things. I use the term "system," because Malangan imagery has been scattered in a manner similar to the dispersal of the clans that now reside in five distinct language areas. The Malangan system thus integrates these language areas into a region that corresponds to the northern New Ireland subgrouping of languages.

New Ireland is located northeast of mainland New Guinea and is one of the islands of the Bismarck Archipelago, placed on the map during several explorations between 1527 and 1761. The island was frequented by traders as early as the late 18th century. Trading companies and plantation sites were established on the island by the 1840s. Reports of missionaries and explorers who followed in the footsteps of the trading companies give evidence of a culture that was, as it were, no longer "untouched." Of large centralized villages in the northern part of the island nothing but their memory and traces in the landscape were left, their inhabitants scattered through warfare across the island or decimated by disease. The culture thus encountered was thought to be doomed and so was its art, which was taken and brought back to Europe, first as treasures of curiosity and later as venerated fragments of a dying culture that had to be preserved at whatever cost.[9]

This assumption of the ancient character of Malangan art, which came to constitute one of the largest collections of non-Western art in the Western world, has never been questioned. The evidence that sculptures were produced in ever greater numbers (in 1930 six sculptures were produced for a single ceremony in Medina village) and at ever shorter intervals has not shaken this assumption. The efflorescence of production was merely interpreted as a sign of decadence and disintegration and thus as symptomatic of a culture in decline.[10]

The Malangan system, as it is known through collections and ethnography, however, is indeed a distinctive development of a period dominated by the imposition of Western trade and commodities. This is suggested first of all by the collections themselves and only secondarily by ethnography.

It is evident from the collections that between 1840 and the end of the 19th century alone, more than 2000 objects were produced for transaction.[11] Due to the inaccessibility of the interior, these objects were collected from a handful of villages situated along the east coast of the island. As the production of sculptures for ceremonies occurred only during the dry and harvest season and was a village affair, the collections indicate a boom in production, with more sculptures being produced for a single ceremony and ceremonies occurring at shorter intervals in the village. From the collections we also know that despite the almost unlimited variety in sculptures, certain elements continually recur with respect to shape, form, and the selection and combination of motifs. Such constancy in the formal properties of sculptures is not limited to particular localities within the region in which they were collected. On the contrary, this constancy is apparent primarily when we look at sculptures collected at different and frequently distant places in the region or at those collected at different times during the period in which sculptures came to reach the West.

The constancy in Malangan art suggests that the ability to retain and recall imagery was given increasing importance with the expansion of the ceremonial exchange system and thus placed constraints on the carving process. Only this interplay between the mnemonic processing of imagery and the technique of art-making can account for the nonrandom transformation of Malangan imagery across the region and for its interpretation in terms of consistent distinctions upon which new forms of ranking came to be based (Bartlett 1932; Küchler 1987).

All sculptures that have been collected on the island are classified by the people who participate in the transactions of Malangan imagery into nine named templates, of which three are recognized in woven sculptures and six in wooden ones. Each template is associated with a stock of named images that are circulated within and between the linguistically distinct localities of the region.[12] The regional distribution of these templates corresponds to the networks of ritual confederations whose members act together in all matters concerning the work for the dead that climaxes in the production and sacrifice of Malangan. These ritual confederations encompass several clans whose relationship is not perceived in terms of a common history of intermarriage, but in terms of the memory of imagery and of the knowledge of how to reembody this imagery into Malangan sculptures. Memory has thus become part of the technology of image-making through activated recall and also governs the generation of new images through forgetting.

The production of memory in the form of mobile and objectifiable imagery documents a historically situated concern with temporality and with confounding it in ways other than its inscription into durable or aging things. With the escalation of warfare, following the imposition of foreign trade and the abandonment of central villages in the mountain, clans shattered into fragments and scattered across the region. Continuity could no longer be perceived in the relation between people and land, but had to be recreated at a place that epitomizes the arrest of movement and of time; this place is the place of burial where memories came to be rooted and shaped into images of Malangan art.

The burial place as the location for gift production constitutes the significant difference in the nature of the gift object and in the mode of its transaction and circulation; this is because it introduces beliefs and practices surrounding immortality into the strategies of exchange. Malangan art reflects not only these beliefs and practices, but is the very means through which they can be ascertained as truth.

The body and the conception of Malangan

The term *malangan* is polysemous, its possible translations ranging from heat and abundance to likeness. It is the latter meaning, that of likeness, which refers to the making and to the form given to the gift object.

To say that Malangan sculptures are figurative and therefore strike a likeness with the human body is not sufficient, as this implies that the likeness is thought to exist between one *thing* and another. Malangan sculptures, however, are conceived to be the product of *processes* that are analogous to those underlying production and bodily reproduction more generally. The term for sculpting is *tetak* (literally, the making of skin), and applies also to the socially induced process of maturation and to the production of gardens. "Skins," or "containers" of a force to which life is attributed, are created through heat (*malangan*). Glowing sticks or irons are thus used for the marking and drilling of holes into wood in the process of carving; newborn infants are held over the smoking and glowing embers of a fire as they are given a name by their father's matriclan, and new gardens are prepared by burning spaces into the secondary forest.[13] Decomposition as a process of rotting (*hasu*, literally, the causing of smell), in turn, is a common treatment for sculptures after the ceremonial transaction of their imagery, for the bodies of deceased persons, and for the crops harvested from a garden that was planted for a ceremony.

Bodily processes of the development of outer form and its decomposition are perceived as inseparable aspects of renewal and as necessary attributes of things that contain life-force, whether it be gardens, sculptures, or people. The analogy between gardens, sculptures and people that is suggested by the sharing of processes of generation and renewal enables the transferability of life-force from one to the other. The transference of life-force from deceased person to sculpture occurs at the place of burial, where it is reactivated and rechanneled to the living. Life-force, however, is not just transferred from the deceased person to the Malangan sculpture and back again to the living, but is significantly transformed in the process. This is because life-force is not only captured, but also freed in a process that follows the scheme of sacrifice; in the form of smell and its associated imagery it is subjected to the force of memory in its recirculation among the living.

Malangan production as sacrifice

Sacrifice and the production of memory are thus intertwined in the New Ireland material.[14] A sculpture is a product of a process of creating a container that can serve as replacement for the decomposed body of the deceased person. The term "ancestor-sculpture," persistently used to characterize Malangan art, is misleading, however, because it ignores the process of capture and transformation whose product is memory. The production of Malangan is patterned not by "tradition" but by the logic of sacrifice; the sculpture is thought to come to life as a result of its production, its "killing," and its decomposition in a manner similar to the three stages that structure the process of sacrifice.

Wooden sculptures are produced in three stages, of which the first and the last articulate the entry and the exit of a life-giving force into the medium. These three stages approximate the stages of the process of sacrifice and culminate in the production of a renewable entity, that is, of an image subjected to memory.[15]

Wood is first cut in the forest and carried into an enclosure situated adjacent to the graveyard, and used as a resting place for the dead prior to burial.[16] Both wood and the bodies of the dead are left to dry in this enclosure. The draining of fluid from the body between pregnancies is also a common practice among women seen not as a means to prevent conception, but as means to assure that a pregnancy will follow. The drying of dead bodies and of wood is thus thought to prepare for the conception of *noman* in a place and in material.

Noman can be translated as the life-force or energy, which is essential to thought and creativity (*lamonan*) during life. With death and the decomposition of the body, the force is gradually freed, attaining its full strength, which is associated with the heat (*malang*) of fire. The funerary ceremonies following the burial of the body dramatize the dismantling of *noman* by tracing the decomposition of the body. The final ceremony, which culminates in the production of sculptures, consists of four main stages. Linguistically and conceptually, these stages are presented as the "building up of a fire" from ashes to the intense glowing heat or "malangan."

In its liberated stage, the force is hot, polluting and dangerous to life, and has to be recaptured. Its new container in the wooden Malangan sculpture is gradually given form in the enclosure in which *noman* came to be situated.

During every stage of production the carver is paid with money and with food prepared in ways reserved both for this occasion and for the first meal eaten together by husband and wife. In the tripartite scheme of the ritual process, the carver acts as the sacrificer who is stripped of all the temporal aspects of his being during the period of carving. He ceases to garden or to undertake any activity that interrupts the daytime. He does not leave the house in which he is carving, except at night. The further he shapes the wood into an image, the more the rhythm of his waking and sleeping pattern is molded by the stages imposed on the production. The time in which he lives is quite literally transformed into the spatial form of the sculpture.

The carving itself is divided into two phases. The wood is first sculpted in the round until motifs appear in three-dimensional form. The bare frame of motifs is then covered with painted patterns. The patterns completely cover the carved planes like the skin of the body.

The "skin" of the sculpture is thus the visually nonpartible composite of motifs and painted patterns that comes to life with the inserting of the "eye" of Malangan, the art's most distinctive feature. This "eye" is the outer protection of the inner part of a living shell (*turbo petholaurus*). With its "eyes" fitted, the sculpture, now alive, looks back at the person who is viewing the sculpture. The "coming to life" of the sculpture initiates the second stage of the ritual process, in which the captured life-force is dramatically reclaimed.

On the subsequent night, the sculpture is transferred to the graveyard, which is surrounded by a screen. It is set on the grave of the deceased person whose mortuary cycle culminates with the production of the sculpture, and placed in a house that has been built for the occasion of its display. The night (*bot*) is known for the dances (*bot*) performed by hosts and guests in a circle around the slit-drum, which turn into transgressions and violence during the latter part of the night. The progression from dances, simulating nonpartibility through circular movements and the interlocking of dancers, to violence and transgressions enacts the reconquering of *noman* and its transformation into an object of retention through the death of the sculpture that is to take place the following day.

This reconquering, called "the killing" of the Malangan sculpture (*luluk a malangan*), follows instantaneously upon the sculpture's unveiling. It is a highly formalized process in which the hosts and guests form groups, each announcing through a speaker why they have come to participate. One by one, each is called up to throw money on the ground in front of the sculpture. The prestation ['payment'; ed. note] is directed to the sculpture and is fetched by a child, who carries the money to the recipient. The prestations effect the transferences of the image embodied in the sculpture as its "skin." This loss of skin results in the death of the sculpture.

The "dead" sculpture is now carried into the secondary forest to be left to rot. The process of rotting is the final phase of the ritual process, the exit, in which what has been absorbed into the sculpture is released. The decomposition completes the stripping of the image or skin from the medium and transforms the visual representation into memory, which connects those who partook in the sacrifice of the sculpture. The transformation of sculpture into memorized image is an active process that synthesizes other modes of consumption.

Those who share the memory of imagery as a result of such sacrifices call themselves "one skin" and can make claims to land and to residency irrespective of marriage or birth. The mode of address they use in relation to each other is based on affinal kin terminology. With respect to membership in the ritual confederation of "one skin," however, they also conceive of themselves as a nonpartible entity.

The ranking of these ritual confederations is a process that is inseparable from the recall of Malangan imagery. They are like chains that can be fragmented and rejoined and are thus not static groups ranked internally or in relation to each other, but are governed by a process in which any distinction also simultaneously implies connectedness. As distinctions are imposed as patterns of cooperation and competition in exchanges, the confederation expands. This is because both sides come to share the memory of imagery through the sacrifice of a sculpture. When this imagery is recalled for reembodiment in a new sculpture, both are required to cooperate in competition with others who strive to attain rights over the imagery. The language of distinction is thus bound to the transformation of imagery during recall.

Memory production and the development of a regional system

When we recognize that collections document a process of development, rather than a process of decay, assumptions governing the way we approach objects in these collections have to come under revision. In the ethnography of northern New Ireland it soon became apparent that there was no relation between myths and the imagery of sculptures, and that narrative was minimal compared with the abundance of visual imagery. The nontextual frame of Malangan art was initially explained by the breakdown of culture, and after its continuity became undeniable, by the context-bound character of Malangan sculptures (Lewis 1969:22; Brewer 1980).[17] The imagery embodied in sculptures was thought to represent specific groups who cooperated in production and exchange. In a nutshell, so many constellations between groups require so many variations of imagery. Thus a recent analysis by Wilkinson:

> Each Malanggan carving combines different elements in a fixed, as it were copyrighted, form: The pattern consists of this particular collection of units and rarely has an independent mythical or symbolic meaning. Only its owner can have it made for specific Malanggan ceremonies, when it will be displayed with other appropriate patterns to mark one of the important stages of life of a close member of a community" (Wilkinson 1978:227–228).

Every sculpture is thus thought to embody imagery that is copied as it is produced. Variations are not related to the transformation occurring during the recall of imagery from memory, but are thought to mark distinctions between kinship groups. Variations in imagery thus constitute a Malangan "family," according to Wilkinson.

This conception of sculptures as originals raises problems when one shifts the focus of analysis from imagery claimed by a locality to the imagery of the wider region. It quickly becomes apparent that there is no correspondence between kinship-based distinctions and distinctions visible in the form given to sculptures. The nature of the distinctions visible in Malangan sculptures can be illuminated, however, when we consider that sculptures are destroyed after they have served as gifts in mortuary transactions.

The ways in which objects are destroyed show that there is a consistent relation between two different types of medium used in producing sculptures – wood and fiber – and two different ways of dismantling the imagery they embody. Medium and destruction, in turn, correspond to distinct transactional practices and distinctive modes of imagery reproduction.

Sculptures carved in wood are left to rot, while sculptures woven into fiber are burned (Powdermaker 1932:134). Only wooden sculptures reached Western institutions, through a definition of sale as an alternative to leaving them to rot. Rotting sets imagery free in a manner thought to produce "smell" (*musung*). Wooden sculptures and the process of their production and destruction are thus responsible for memory production through their activation of "smell."

Collections are overflowing with wooden Malangan sculptures, yet only two woven sculptures have ever reached the West. The sale of wooden sculptures came to be accepted as an alternative to leaving them to rot partly because the image carved into wood alludes to qualities of pollution and regenerativity that are ascribed to both smell and money;[18] but it is also partly a result of the theme of connectedness that pervades both mode of representation and transaction and that facilitates the integration of both the region and the Western world.[19]

Connectedness is visible in wooden sculptures as part–whole relationships, each image being part of a more encompassing one and ultimately committed to memory with reference to a "template". The allusion to part–whole relationships is absent in sculptures that are woven into fiber. The disconnectedness that is visible in the construction of fiber sculptures as nonpartible wholes is related to the use of fire for their destruction; fire deodorizes, and thus prevents or destroys smell and with it the most important means for recall (Bachelard 1964:103). The image produced in the form of a fiber-sculpture is not recalled from memory and interpreted in terms of its variation upon motifs and their combination, but is understood as re-presentation of a myth of which each version is the original. The imagery of woven sculptures, moreover, is clan-specific and passed on as an undivided and nonfragmentable thing. Such sculptures are produced only for the final mortuary ceremony carried out for deceased women or adolescents and are passed on in such a way as not to leave the place of production.[20]

The stationary and nonpartible character of woven imagery contrasts with the features of movement and assemblage that pervade the imagery of wooden sculptures. The distinction is only apparent, however. This is because the features of stoppage and of nonpartibility represented in woven Malangan sculptures are present as the principles of transformation in the reproduction of imagery carved into wooden sculptures. The images of wooden Malangan sculptures are shattered into fragments and scattered across the region in the course of their repeated reproduction for ceremonial exchange. Each fragment, however, continues to be identified with the path it traces as it moves from the place of the invention of the template (*wune*) to the place where it is reembodied in a sculpture. Knowledge of how such a fragment could be reassembled by retracing its movement through the region is essential to the legitimation of its recall and production.

Each sculpture is thus seen as part of a more encompassing whole that can be further fragmented or reassembled without altering its relation to the whole. This relation between the fragment and the imagery as a whole is also significant for the conception of ritual confederations. They are not based on marriage or birth, but on "membership" (*raso*) in the Malangan complex, which is attained solely on the grounds of sharing the memory of a named image.

Forms of ranking evolved with the efflorescence of gift production, whose integrative capacity governs the expansive and regional character of present-day northern New Ireland; at all levels of complexity, these forms are subject to the conceptions of making and appropriating Malangan sculptures as "gifts to god."

Conclusion

With the help of the particular example of Malangan art I have elaborated on the nature of gifts that are made to be destroyed. Such objects have characteristically representational properties that precipitate their incorporation in ethnographic museums as non-Western art. Object collections of this kind are particularly large, but not as a result of "salvage anthropology" alone. Museums have become the repository of "gift to god" systems, as sale became an alternative measure of removing gifts from circulation.

As gifts, ephemeral objects confound time not through permanence, but through renewal and are thus central to the production of memory in culture and society. They are made as objects of retention and thus display properties that are governed by the assumptions and practices surrounding the repeated recall of the imagery they temporarily embody. The production of gifts, in a system of exchange that features their extraction from circulation through an act of sacrifice, creates a difference in political organization; the transcendence of the technique of gift production by mnemonics allows its imagery to be spread over an expanding region, and to serve as means for the creation and apprehension of new forms of ranking. I have argued that such exchange systems, and the resulting object collections, must be historically situated and analyzed with respect to the dynamic interaction between gift production and changing fields of political and economic influence. As repositories of exchange activities, museum collections contain vital data that can illuminate our understanding of the historical dynamic of societies featuring object destruction. However, in order for these collections to be integrated into research, we have to rethink our conceptions of objects as singular and nonreplaceable things.

Notes

Acknowledgments. A version of this paper was presented to the seminar in the department of anthropology at the University of Virginia, Charlottesville in October 1987. The material is based on two years of field research in northern New Ireland (1982–84) and my dissertation at the London School of Economics, funded by the Volkswagenwerk Research Foundation. I want to thank the faculty and students at the University of Virginia for their illuminating discussion, Gillian Feeley-Harnik for her insightful comments on a later version of the paper and Katherine Verdery for her editorial assistance.

1   This is not meant to be a statement about the history of early collections, which is certainly more complex than can be explained with the conceptions that govern object production in indigenous societies; these conceptions, however, play an important part in the constitution of collections.

2   The example I am utilizing in the analysis appears to be a "special case" as it involves deliberate object destruction through exposing objects and leaving them to rot. It features the temporality of objects and a mode of representation that emphasizes the process of image reproduction. These features also have a bearing, though largely overlooked, on our understanding of objects whose ephemeral character is less pronounced. There is evidence, for example, that the art of the Asmat and the Sepik River region in Papua New Guinea was part of cycles of the production of ceremonial houses that had their own temporal dynamic governed by head-hunting raids, as among the Asmat, or by the seasonal influx of water among the Sepik River cultures (Gerbrands 1967; Hauser-Schäublin 1985); from the Mimika we know that sculptures called *mbitoro* were "brought to the sago marshes and left there to moulder and transmit *kapita* [impersonal life-force] to the sago palms" (Kooijman 1984:9). This paper is not about specific definitions of "ephemeral" versus "permanent," but about the difference created in culture and society by a mode of representation that stresses the reproducibility of images, and its relation to a mode of circulation in which mobile images create new forms of ranking that have the capacity for regional integration.

3   Weiner's article on "inalienable wealth" represents a step toward the analysis of gift objects of the kind discussed in this paper (Weiner 1985). She focuses on objects that are not circulated or that, when circulated, never lose their identity and attachment to those who originally owned them (Weiner 1985:212). These inalienable objects, which are classified as "*immeuble*" according to Mauss's classical scheme, index attitudes, beliefs and practices that revolve around social immortality as they represent "the capital stock of substance belonging to a family" (Weiner 1985:213). The material presented in this paper, however, provides an additional complication that might throw new light on the dichotomy between "alienable" and "inalienable" wealth, because gift objects that are subject to destruction embody imagery that is subject to repeated reproduction; while the gift object is indeed "*immeuble*," the imagery reembodied in a succession of gift objects is transacted and confiscated in a manner Weiner ascribes to things "*meuble*" and "alienable."

4   The term "Malangan" occurs in the literature as "malanggan" or "malagan" depending on the location of research on the island. I am using the Northwest coast pronounciation of the Kara language where I was based during the otherwise regionally focused research (Küchler 1985). See also Louise Lincoln (1987) for recent writings on "image" in northern New Ireland.

5   In an article written during fieldwork, "Malangan of Nombowai," I described sculptures that were found together with mummies in a cave on the edge of an overhanging cliff in the late 1970s (Küchler 1983). I later recognized that it was not the preserving air conditions that led people to place sculptures into the cave, as presumed by museologists and also initially by me; the cave is a landmark for the most important magical performance (the "calling of smell," *wangam a musung*), carried out on the edge of the rift of which the cave is the inland extension. The performance initiates the preparations for a Malangan ceremony and articulates the significance of "smell" and its relation to Malangan art, of which some account is given in this paper. Sculptures can be reused in successive transactions until the transference of rights to the reproduction of imagery, involving indigenous currency and money, has been completed.

6   Weiner's study of the transaction of banana leaves by women in the context of funerals points to the existence of another conception of space-time in the Massim that is complementary, yet opposed, to the inter-island space-time manifest in the circulation of Kula valuables (Weiner 1976). The comparison with the Malangan system is with respect to the inter-island or inter-locality construction of space-time as apprehended visually and conceptually in the objects of gift exchange (cf. Munn 1986).

7   One is reminded of the reflection by a Dakota wise man, reproduced in Lévi-Strauss's work on totemism, according to which things and beings are nothing but materialized forms of creative continuity (Lévi-Strauss 1973:171). I am grateful to Alfred Gell for pointing to this relation between the mode of representation and temporality in Malangan art; each production of imagery creates an imprint in memory that is recalled as part of a "road" connecting people and places which is located, so to speak, "outside" of measured time.

8   Compare Lewis (1969:23); Wilkinson (1978:234); Brewer (1980:89). Others such as Lomas (1973) and Billings (1972) completely ignore the relation between Malangan objects and exchange.

9   The earliest collection was by the missionary George Brown between 1840 and 1870. Later systematic collections concentrate on the period immediately following the advent of German colonial administration between 1884 and 1910. Traders and shipping companies had already brought a number of objects to Germany prior to 1884. The largest and best documented collection of this century was made by Buhler in the 1930s and is today in the ethnographic museum in Basel.

10 This was supported by the sudden cessation of sculptures known as "Uli" produced in central New Ireland until the turn of the century (Gifford 1974). The third culturally distinctive area on the island is the south, which is both linguistically and culturally part of East New Britain (Wagner 1986).

11 In England, the collections are primarily by Romilly (1886) in the Museum of Mankind, London, and by George Brown (1840–1870), scattered today over several museums in England and Japan. In West and East Germany, the main collections are in the museums of Berlin, Bremen, Hamburg, Stuttgart, Dresden and Leibzig (Finsch 1884–1885; Parkinson 1880s–1904; Schlaginhaufen 1906–1910). In America, the largest collections are in the Field Museum in Chicago, the Metropolitan Museum, and the Museum of Natural History in New York (collections primarily from the turn of the century).

12 Compare with material on the art of Australian Aborigines, particularly Morphy (1977, 1985). A detailed analysis of Malangan templates, which would exceed the

present paper, would reveal a scheme of classification that is analogous to the tripartite structure of the process of gift production, which culminates in sacrifice.

13 The fire for baptizing the child (*bungen a lik*) is kindled in the secondary forest called *laten* (literally, the place of the skin).

14 Following Hubert and Mauss (1899), Valeri adds to the scheme of sacrifice an interpretation of sacrificial violence as creating "a strong impression and therefore a memory" (1985:69). Based on the ethnography of Malangan, one could add to the analysis of sacrifice as the production of memory the "death" and destruction of objects of mediation that characteristically display representational properties.

15 The nature of "templates" is not elaborated upon in this essay. Six named templates (to which imagery carved into wood is assigned in memory) are grouped into pairs of two, of which each pair displays in its visual representation the feature of one of the three stages in the process of sacrifice (absorption, containment and ambiguous release/absorption).

16 Cremation used to be a common technique of disposing of the dead; it ceased to be prevalent with mission influence. The transition from cremation to burial had an impact on the length of the mortuary cycle, as each step in the decomposition is marked with a funerary ceremony. The influence on Malangan production is indirect. A longer mortuary cycle corresponds to a more expanded network of debt relationships established through mortuary exchanges. Malangan imagery, concurrently, is known among expanding fields of influence.

17 This relationship between object and context was phrased in more or less empirical terms. See for example Brewer's extreme idealist position: "The relationship between men and the spiritual beings of the world is made concrete and visual in these objects through the form and properties of these objects. . . ." (1980:89).

18 The carver of wooden sculptures is given both money and food with distinctive smell during the shaping of the image into material; the perceived relation between money and smell pervades the ceremonial and exchange system at all levels of complexity and provides the intellectual basis for the interrelation of commodity and gift economy.

19 The relation between mode of representation and mode of transaction is explicated in Küchler (1985 and 1987).

20 Names associated with the imagery of fiber sculptures are place names and are not given to persons as is the case with the imagery embodied in wooden sculptures (cf. Küchler 1987).

References

Bachelard, Gaston (1964) *The Psychoanalysis of Fire*. Alan M. Ross, trans. Boston; Beacon Press.

Bartlett, F. C. (1932) *Remembering*. Cambridge: Cambridge University Press.

Billings, Dorothy (1972) Styles of Culture. Doctoral Dissertation. University of Sydney.

Bourdieu, Pierre (1977) *Outline of a Theory of Practice*. Cambridge: Cambridge University Press.

Brewer, Elizabeth (1980) A Malagan to Cover the Grave. Doctoral Dissertation. University of Queensland.

Campbell, Shirley (1983) Attaining Rank: A Classification of Shell Valuables. In *The Kula*. Jerry Leach and Edmund Leach, eds. pp. 229–249. Cambridge: Cambridge University Press.

Gerbrands, Anthony (1967) *Wow-ipits: Eight Asmat Woodcarvers of New Guinea*. New York: Mouton.

Gifford, D. C. (1974) Iconology of the Uli Figure in Central New Ireland. Doctoral Dissertation. University of California.

Gregory, Chris (1980) Gifts to Men and Gifts to God: Exchange and Capital Accumulation in Contemporary Papua. *Man* (N.S.) 15:626–652.

—— (1982) *Gifts and Commodities*. Cambridge: Cambridge University Press.

Hauser-Schäublin, Brigitte (1985) Not for Collection: Ephemeral Art. In *Authority and Ornament: Art of the Sepik River, Papua New Guinea*. Suzanne Greub, ed. pp. 27–33. Tribal Arts Centre, Basel: Edition Greub.

Hubert, Henri, and Marcel Mauss (1899) Essai sur la Fonction du Sacrifice. *L'Annee Sociologique* 2:29–139. Reprinted in Mauss (1968–69(1):193–307).

Kooijman, Sidney (1984) *Art, Art Objects and Ritual in Mimika Culture*. Leiden: E. J. Brill.

Küchler, Susanne (1983) Malangan of Nombowai. *Oral History*, 11:65–98.

—— (1985) Malangan, Exchange and Regional Integration in Northern New Ireland. Doctoral Dissertation. London School of Economics and Political Science.

—— (1987) Malangan: Art and Memory in a Melanesien Society. *Man* (N.S.) 22: 238–255.

Lévi-Strauss, Claude (1973) *Totemism*. Reissued in Penguin University Books.

Lewis, Philip (1969) *The Social Context of Art in Northern New Ireland*. Fieldiana: Anthropology 58.

Lincoln, Louise (1987) *Assemblage of Spirits: Idea and Image in New Ireland*. New York: George Braziller, in association with The Minneapolis Institute of Arts.

Lomas, Peter (1973) Economic and Political Organization in a Northern New Ireland Village. Doctoral dissertation. Ottawa.

Morphy, Howard (1977) Too Many Meanings: An Analysis of the Artistic Systems of the Yolngu of Northwest Arnhem Land. Doctoral Dissertation. Australian National University.

—— (1985) *Creativity in Yolngu Art*. Paper presented to the Seminar in Anthropology and Art. Oxford University.

Munn, Nancy (1986) *The Fame of Gawa*. Oxford: Oxford University Press.

Powdermaker, Hortense (1932) *Life in Lesu*. London: Williams and Norgate, Ltd.

Valeri, Valerio (1985) *Kingship and Sacrifice. Ritual and Society in Ancient Hawaii*. Chicago: University of Chicago Press.

Wagner, Roy (1986) *Asiwinarong: Ethos, Image, and Social Power among the Usen Barok of New Ireland*. Princeton: Princeton University Press.

Weiner, Annette (1976) *Women of Value, Men of Renown: New Perspectives in Trobriand Exchange*. Austin: University of Texas Press.

—— (1985) Inalienable Wealth. *American Ethnologist* 12(2):210–227.

Wilkinson, G. (1978) Carving a Social Message: The Malanggans of Tabar. In *Art in Society*. Michael Greenhalgh and Vincent Megaw, eds. London: Duckworth.

Wolf, Eric (1982) *Europe and the People without History*. Berkeley: University of California Press.

Chapter 8

Ere the substance fade
Photography and hair jewellery

Geoffrey Batchen

The object

A locket lies here in my hand, coldly at first, and then gradually warming as it absorbs and begins to return my own body heat. Its bronze surfaces are articulated with incised patterns, a combination of star and fleur-de-lis on one side and an abstracted open flower on the other. Designed to be touched, this object touches back, casually grazing the pores of my skin with its textured surfaces. In this mutual stroking of the flesh, object and image come together as one; I behold the thingness of the visual, the tooth of its grain, even as I encounter the visuality of the tactile, the piercing force of its perception. Already, then, a number of my senses have been engaged. For this is an object that has both an inside and an outside, and to be fully experienced it must be handled as well as looked at. A small button on the top of the locket, perhaps a remnant of the watch that it once contained, invites me to press down. When I do, the two halves of the locket spring apart. Opening to an angle of ninety degrees, this mechanism adds an extra geometry to the locket's original circular form and reveals an interior to my gaze for the first time. Suddenly I am made aware that this thing in my hand is in fact a photographic object. On one side of the interior lies a portrait of an elderly man, in the form of a circular tintype behind glass. On the other, also behind glass, is a small clipping of human hair (Figure 8.1).

So what are we to make of such an object? How, in particular, are we to incorporate it into a history of photography? Perhaps the question itself is at fault. Why not instead turn it around and ask another: how have established histories of photography fallen short of this kind of object?[1] For there is surprisingly little published on photographic jewellery as a genre, and this despite the large numbers of these objects that were produced during the nineteenth century.[2] They receive no attention in most survey histories of photography.[3] This last absence is the more easily explained. Since the

Fig. 8.1 Engraved silver locket containing a tintype portrait of a man and human hair *c.* 1855.
Diameter 4 cm. Unknown American maker. (Private collection.)

turn of the twentieth century, photography's published history has largely adopted
the logic of art history and this has neatly excluded most photographs from their own
epic. Organised around a canon of presumed masters and masterworks, with
originality, uniqueness and aesthetic innovation as its principle tropes, photography's
art history has tended to ignore ordinary, commercial photographic practices, of
which photo-jewellery is certainly one. It has also privileged images over their casing
or frames, presenting reproductions of daguerreotypes, to take but one example,
floating miraculously free from the surrounds that always informed their actual
experience in the hand or on the wall.[4] Most importantly, vernacular practices like
photo-jewellery are presumed to have few intellectual or aesthetic qualities beyond
sentimental kitsch, and therefore apparently do not deserve the spotlight of historical
attention or critical analysis.

Given all of this, it is tempting, especially in the context of this volume, to
abandon the discipline of photo-history altogether and adopt in its place the methods
and concerns of material culture, a mode of analysis that explicitly addresses itself to
the social meanings of artefacts. I want to resist this temptation, however, and instead
keep working towards changing photography's history from within (Batchen 2001:
78–9). Otherwise the genre of photographic jewellery will continue to be left out of
photographic histories, finding itself confined to the relative ghettos of social history
or cultural anthropology, or lost in a vast continuum of related, but non-photographic,

representational practices. I want, in contrast, to concentrate on the particularities of my locket's 'photographicness'. For this reason, and for others that should become clear at the conclusion of this chapter, I would prefer to start by regarding this locket in the same way that I might, say, a photograph by Alfred Stieglitz, and then see what happens from there.

We should begin, perhaps, by establishing some sort of genealogy for this locket. Bought on the Internet auction service Ebay.com, it comes into my hand without any information about the identity of either its makers or its subject. All we know is that it is very probably of American manufacture and was made in the later nineteenth century, at some time between about 1860 and the 1890s. A hundred or so years later, it speaks first and foremost of its age, of the undeniable aura of the antique. But then so do all nineteenth-century photographs, to greater or lesser degrees. This one is a tintype portrait unremarkable in pose and features, showing the bust of an elderly man looking directly, almost quizzically, into the camera, his greying hair slightly askew. The collected wisps of fine hair that face him on the other side of the locket have a reddish tint, suggesting that they may have been taken from a younger head — perhaps from this same man several years before his photograph was made, or perhaps from a loved one wanting to stay close to at least this man's image. Already we enter into the seductive realm of speculation. Could it be that this object was put together by a loved one after this man's death, combining a watch locket, a sample of hair taken in the man's younger years, and a photograph made late in life? This would make it a memorial or mourning object rather than a token of ongoing love or friendship. It would also make this locket the intersection of at least five distinct moments (its original manufacture, the taking of a hair sample, the making of a photograph, their later combination in this object and its perception now, here in my hand). Demonstrably collapsing any distinction between being and becoming, my locket demands that we acknowledge that all historical identity is a manifestation of this kind of temporal oscillation.[5]

Photographic lockets

Whatever its intended meaning, this locket now functions as a representative of a genre rather than as a portrait of a known individual or an exceptional masterpiece by a famous photographer. Even the genre itself is unexceptional, for there are frequent references to such photo-lockets in nineteenth-century advertisements and newspaper stories. *The Scientific American* of 1865, for example, reports that a Mr E. N. Foote of New York City had been awarded a patent by the United States Patent Office for a miniature gold locket in the shape of a photographic album, 'with leaves for pictures of friends, so made that each of the golden leaves receives two ferrotypes or other pictures, the number of leaves being varied with the size of the locket'. The reporter mentions seeing an example that held eight portraits, each pair opening out in its leaf like the pages of an album, and with the exterior surfaces 'chased and engraved with elegant designs'. Thanks to this inventor's ingenuity, the writer concludes, an owner 'can have with him always, in this elegant locket, the faces of his dear kindred and friends'.[6]

Lockets are also mentioned in any number of earlier advertisements taken out by photographers to attract new customers. Indeed, from the evidence of such advertisements, it would seem that photographic jewellery was a staple product of the professional portrait photographer of the mid-nineteenth century (Figure 8.2). George Barnard, working in Oswego, New York, informed his fellow citizens in August 1847 that 'he is prepared to take PHOTOGRAPHIC MINIATURES, unsurpassed by any artist in the country . . . and neatly set in Morocco cases, lockets, breast pins, and in a few minutes'. In January 1852, J. H. Fitzgibbon of St Louis, Missouri, encouraged his potential customers to 'secure the shadow ere the substance fade, let nature copy that which nature made'.[7] Having made good use of one of photography's most familiar exhortations, he advises that he can provide 'pictures taken by the most Improved Method, and Colored true to Nature, from the finger ring to the double whole size plate, and put up either in cases or frames, to suit tastes'. Augustus Washington, an African-American daguerreotypist working in Hartford, Connecticut, advised his loyal customers in April 1853 that 'he has also on hand 100 fine GOLD LOCKETS, from six different manufacturers, of every size and variety, suitable for one, two, three or four pictures, which he will sell cheaper than they can be bought at any other establishment'. A Miss M. MacFarlane, of Belfast, Maine, took out a similar advertisement in the *Maine Free Press* in April 1857 to report that her daguerreotype 'miniatures' could be 'neatly inserted in Pins, Lockets, Bracelets, etc.' In September 1854, *Humphrey's Journal* reported that Willard Ellis Geer, 'who is Daguerreotyping on wheels', had written a catchy poem to attract new customers. According to Geer:

> I can put them in Rings, in Keys, or in Lockets;
> Or in nice little Cases to slip into your pockets;
> In a word, I've Cases of all kinds, single and double,
> Lockets too, of all sizes, which saves you all trouble
> Of looking any farther than my Daguerrean Gallery.[8]

The consistent use of the word 'miniature' to describe these early photographic portraits is a reminder that the practice of carrying a small portrait of a loved one predates photography itself by quite a few years. By the late eighteenth century, small portrait paintings of members of the aristocratic class were frequently being incorporated into jewellery and especially into mourning jewellery (a type of ornament that itself goes back to at least the seventeenth century) (see Frank 2000). It was logical that, following the invention of photography in 1839, calotypes, daguerreotypes, ambrotypes, tintypes and albumen prints would also find their way into the pins, rings, pendants, brooches and bracelets that were then so fashionable (Figure 8.2). In a sense, photography allowed the middle classes to adopt a cheaper version of the visual affectations of their betters. There are certainly many examples of daguerreotypes showing their portrait subjects wearing brooches and bracelets that themselves contain photographic portraits. Judging by these and the numerous surviving pieces of photo-jewellery, they came in many shapes and sizes, and varied considerably in cost and fineness of finish.

They also seem to have fulfilled a range of different functions and, indeed, the same piece of jewellery might signify different emotions in different contexts.

Fig. 8.2 Tintype portrait of a young woman in an elliptical metal pendant on a chain, with two samples of human hair, *c.* 1860s. Pendant 3.4 × 2.5 cm. Unknown American maker. (Private collection.)

Often, for example, these objects are clearly organised as declarations of love, or at least of marriage. A single necklace pendant might have portraits of husband and wife on either of its sides, lying back to back, never to be parted. For the object to be experienced in full, it has to be turned from side to side, a form of perpetual caress preordained by its designer. Other examples include photographic lockets containing two facing but separate portraits, such that the man and woman inside initially lie hidden, kissing each other in the dark until liberated into the light of a loved one's gaze. But whatever their exact form or meaning may have been, these are all photographs that turn the body of their owner into an accessory. One displays one's affections in public, wearing them not on the sleeve but as pendants against the chest or hanging off the ears. This is a photography that is literally put in motion: twisting, turning, bouncing, sharing the folds, volumes and movements of the wearer and his or her apparel. No longer seen in isolation, the photograph becomes an extension of the wearer, or more precisely, we become a self-conscious prosthesis to the body of photography.

Although it is tempting automatically to associate these types of object with mourning (as I have already done with my locket), apparently only about 20 per cent of such objects were used for that purpose. But there is no doubt that these are the ones that still tug at the heart. Mourning was a carefully calibrated social ritual during the Victorian period, with fashion, jewellery and photography all playing important roles in the public representation of grief.[9] In fact, the popularity of photographic jewellery as a mourning device is often traced to its adoption by Queen Victoria after her consort Albert's death in 1861 (although she was wearing a daguerreian bracelet featuring his portrait from at least 1848). According to Heinz and Bridget Henisch (1994: 140), 'a memorial ring was designed for the Queen, containing a micro-photograph of the Prince Consort, made in 1861 and attributed to Mayall'. A cabinet card dated 1897 shows her with right arm raised to reveal a portrait of Albert still firmly encircling her wrist, 36 years after his death.[10]

Although there is evidence that adding hair to jewellery was not an exclusively feminine activity, it was certainly one dominated by women. By the mid-nineteenth century, American women in particular were being charged with new social roles as keepers of memory, as mourners and as home-based teachers of religious belief. Even non-Catholic American homes were decorated with religious artefacts of one kind or another, and this pervasive Christian context invests hair lockets like this one with a distinctly sacred aura.[11] The advent of the American Civil War in the mid-1860s added a certain urgency to the practice. Many young men from both sides of the conflict had their photographs taken before heading off for war, perhaps suspecting it might be their last chance. These photos were consulted hopefully in their absence and then, should they die, were incorporated into appropriate ornaments designed specifically for mourning purposes. One striking example comprised a matching set of black and white onyx brooch and earrings, in which an ambrotype of a young man in uniform could be swivelled back and forth, in and out of public view, depending on the context (Kaplan 1998).

The addition of human hair to such objects was already a common practice by the early decades of the nineteenth century.[12] As Thomas Laqueur notes, hair began to enjoy a new prominence as the raw material of memory. 'It became the corporeal auto-icon par excellence, the favoured synecdoche – the real standing for the symbolic – perhaps not eternally incorruptible but long lasting enough, a bit of a person that lives eerily on as a souvenir' (Laqueur 1992: 16–17). Hair, intimate yet easily detached, is of course a convenient and pliable stand-in for the whole body of the missing, memorialized subject. Women in particular were encouraged to use hair in their domestic handicrafts, beginning with horse hair and then, as their skills improved, working with the finer human hair, either bought for the purpose or gathered from friends or even from their own heads. This amateur practice ensured that the hair being used was from an 'authentic' head, there being some fear that professional braiders were not so particular about this. But it also turned the natural hair into a cultural sign, while allowing the braider to involve herself physically with the body of the other as well as with the act of remembrance that braiding entailed.

Custom-made braiding tables were available to facilitate the production of complex patterns, which included pictures of flowers, landscapes and the feathers associated with the late Prince of Wales.[13] The 1856 book *Elegant Arts for Ladies*, for example, devotes a whole chapter to the complex art of 'Weaving or plaiting hair ornaments', including subsections on 'Plaits for rings, lockets, and brooches' and on 'Mourning devices'. The accompanying text underlines the gender-specificity of this practice, while stressing once again hair's memorial function.

> Hair, that most imperishable of all the component parts of our mortal bodies, has always been regarded as a cherished memorial of the absent or lost. Impressed with this idea, it appears to us but natural, that of all the various employments devised for the fingers of our fair country-women, the manufacture of ornaments in hair must be one of the most interesting. Why should we confide to others the precious lock or tress we prize, risking its being lost, and the hair of some other person being substituted for it, when, with a little attention, we may ourselves weave it into the ornament we desire? And the dainty and very tasteful handling hair-work requires, renders it as truly feminine an occupation as the finest crochet or the richest embroidery.[14]

My locket is actually one of the simpler presentations of this material, its lack of visual sophistication suggesting it was put together by a relatively unskilled hand. Some brooches, by contrast, feature a portrait on one side and on the other two artfully organised filigrees of hair behind glass, each teased into exquisite plant-like designs and tied with tiny pearls or precious stones. Samples of hair from two different heads are often woven together in this manner or are simply conjoined in permanent communion with one another, obviously a metaphor of friendship and love or a discreet act of courtship. Thus hair could signify either love or death (or both), and refer simultaneously to past and present. Some oval-shaped brooches were made with a photographic portrait on one side and a small glass viewing-window on the other, so that a sample of the subject's hair could be permanently placed in its own mini-sarcophagus. One elliptical silver brooch, for example, features a tintype portrait of the bust of a young woman on its public side and then behind glass on the other side are two samples of hair woven together, with yet another 'natural' sample laid on top of that. These representative pieces of another's body are thus worn tight against one's own, creating a permanent but entirely private bond cemented by the act of touch. Of course, being behind glass, the hair in this locket offers only an imagined touch of the absent body it signifies. But a pair of bracelets woven from human hair, each with an inset daguerreotype portrait (one of a man and the other of a woman), allow that touch to become real and continuous, resting on the skin of our wrist as a physical, permanent and public reminder of the missing subjects, our relationship to them and their relationship to each other.

Hair was also sometimes plaited into a thick knot of interlinked braids, or, alternatively, woven into a tight grid pattern, so fine that it looks like a piece of cloth. In other instances, human hair was given a functional as well as a symbolic role. In one particularly striking example, the hair was braided into a seven-inch-long ribbon from which hangs a small medallion-shaped tintype. Particularly poignant are those posthumous portraits accompanied by a fragile circle of baby hair and a handwritten text ('Angel on Earth – an Angel in Heaven. Fell asleep with a sweet smile'). In others, a lock of hair is tied up with a simple scrap of silk and placed inside the case next to the photograph, waiting to be encountered (to be touched as well as seen) whenever it is opened.

There is sometimes an intriguing play between the visibility and invisibility of the hair in such objects. One cased tintype shows a soldier sitting in his Union uniform with his hands clenched in his lap. This young man has at some point been given a spectacular headdress of real blond hair, carefully placed around his image under the front glass. This hair cascades down each side of the man's body from a point just above his head, the assembled strands looking gigantic in relation to the reduced scale of the photograph they now frame. Any respect for the integrity of the photograph, and in particular for its reality-effect, has been firmly discounted in favour of a respect for its subject, by the need to memorialise his presence in the owner's life. Conversely, in other examples, memorial locks of hair are placed behind or underneath the image and therefore out of sight (unless the whole object is taken apart). Its existence known only to the owner, this hair remains buried beneath the photograph, part of the total object's signifying morphology but haunting it exclusively in the mind's eye of a single privileged viewer.

Extending indexicality

So what is it doing there? What does added hair, whether visible or not, actually do to the photograph that it accompanies? First and foremost the hair serves a metonymic memorial function, standing in, as we have already noted, for the body of the absent subject. So why isn't the photograph alone enough to fulfil this function? The person pictured has, after all, represented himself or herself through that wondrous intercourse of object, light and chemical reaction that is the photographic process. The body of the subject (be it human, building, landscape or still life) is present as visual trace even when absent as material thing. So why adulterate this already magical process with something as carnal and common as a lock of hair? Perhaps the answer takes us back to where we began, to the reasons why photo-jewellery is worthy of study. Could it be, for example, that the addition of hair to all these otherwise ordinary photographs is a vernacular commentary on tracing itself, on photography's strengths and limitations as a representational apparatus?

This deserves some further consideration. More than any other medium, photography promises an unhindered immediacy of representation. It could even be argued that photography is the manifestation of a desire for a pure opticality, for a visibility without mediation. In a photograph, the thing pictured is automatically transformed into a portable visual sign (mobilising it, but also completing that thing's commodification). But much the same could be said about the photograph itself. For the photograph is certainly nothing if not humble, so ready is it to erase its own material presence in favour of the subject it represents. In most contexts, we are asked to look through the photograph as if it simply isn't there, penetrating its limpid, transparent surface with our eyes and seeing only what lies within. Posing as pure sign, or even as no sign at all, the 'good' photograph offers minimal resistance to this look. Invisible to the eye, it appears to provide a representation generated by the referent itself.

Around the turn of the twentieth century, the American philosopher Charles Sanders Peirce formalised this observation in his taxonomy of fundamental relationships between a sign and its referent. According to Peirce, an iconic sign looks like the object it denotes, whereas an index 'is not the mere resemblance of its Object

. . . but it is the actual modification of it by the Object'. Photographs, Peirce argues, 'are very instructive, because we know that they are in certain respects exactly like the objects they represent . . . But this resemblance is due to the photographs having been produced under such circumstances that they were physically forced to correspond point by point to nature. In that aspect, then, they belong to the second class of signs, those by physical connection' (Peirce 1985: 8, 11). As a footprint is to a foot, so is a photograph to its referent. As Allan Sekula (1983: 218) puts it, photographs are 'physical traces of their objects'. Likewise, Susan Sontag (1977: 154) says that the photograph is 'something directly stencilled off the real', while Rosalind Krauss (1984: 112) describes it as 'a kind of deposit of the real itself'. Indexicality, then, is a major source of photography's privileged status within modern culture. For, unlike other systems of representation, the camera does more than just see the world; it is also touched by it.

Roland Barthes makes much of the physicality of photography's connection to its subject in his 1980 book *Camera Lucida*. 'The photograph is literally an emanation of the referent. From a real body, which was there, proceed radiations which ultimately touch me, who am here . . . a sort of umbilical cord links the body of the photographed thing to my gaze' (Barthes 1980: 80–1). For Barthes, photography's indexical system of representation provides 'a new, somehow experiential order of proof', a 'certificate of presence', of '*what has been*'. According to Barthes, the reality offered by the photograph is not that of truth-to-appearance but that of truth-to-presence, a matter of being (of something's irrefutable place in space/time) rather than resemblance. And, for Barthes, this is an important distinction. 'For resemblance refers to the subject's identity, an absurd, purely legal, even penal affair; likeness gives our identity "as itself", whereas I want a subject – in Mallarmé's terms – "as *into* itself eternity transforms it". Likeness leaves me unsatisfied and somehow skeptical' (Barthes 1980: 102–3). The indexicality of the photograph allows it to transcend mere resemblance and conjure a 'subject', a presence that lingers (the sidelong reference to ghosts and haunting seems no accident). No wonder certain photographs have such a strange effect on him: 'neither image nor reality, a new being, really: a reality one can no longer touch'. These sorts of photographs tantalise Barthes with a nearness made insurmountably distant, 'a mad image, chafed by reality' (Barthes 1980: 115).

Could the addition of a tactile portion of the subject's body to his photograph be an effort to bridge the distance, temporal and otherwise, between viewer and person viewed and between likeness and subject? Contaminating visibility with touch, my locket might then be regarded as an effort to bring the 'mad' photograph back to earth, or at least back to the body of the subject. Truth-to-presence is joined by the actual presence of a portion of the body being signified. In its combination of hair and photograph, my locket has therefore become an indexical sign twice over, two physical traces of the same referent brought face to face, first with each other and then with ourselves.[15]

We could point to many other examples of a doubled indexicality involving photography. Wedding certificates in the nineteenth century often incorporated albumen prints of bride and groom, and sometimes the celebrant as well, together with the signatures of all concerned. This intersection of image and hand is also found in a daguerreotype case containing a handwritten inscription and a lock of hair woven into a circle (both once hidden away behind the image). 'OCala – Florida – July 20th 1859 – "Little things bring back to mind Thoughts of happy bygone times" – Kate – (Dinna Forget).' A portion of Kate's body nestles beneath that same body's photographic imprint, once again bringing touch into the picture and adding a trace of the real (as well as the animation of her presumably Scottish voice) to the simulation of the image (Batchen 1997: 2–11). Barthes suggests throughout *Camera Lucida* that photography allows an imagined exchange of touches between subject, photograph and viewer. In one object's combination of daguerreotype and fabric, this normally invisible exchange is made manifest and thereby repeated for real. It is a daguerreotype portrait of a young girl in a case, taken in about 1850. At some point, a square of cloth from her dress has been added to the inside of the case. We are thus invited literally to touch a piece of the cloth that, we can see from the photograph, once also touched the skin of this long-departed girl (Isenburg 1989: 77). We touch what she touched, turning this square of fabric into a membrane conjoining past and present, the living and the dead. By this creative contrivance, absence and historical distance are temporarily bridged by a moment of shared bodily sensation, turning the remembrance of this girl into an experience at once optical and haptic.

So what are the effects of a doubled indexicality, as opposed to a single one? The photo in my locket is presumably thought to be lacking something that the addition of hair fulfils, but, equally, it would appear that the hair alone is also deemed to be not quite enough – apparently, neither is as effective an act of representation without the other also being present. Like a photograph, the hair sample stands in for the whole body of the absent subject, turning this locket into a modern fetish object; as a mode of representation it 'allow[s] me to believe that what is missing is present all the same, *even though I know* it is not the case' (Durand 1995: 146).[16] A talismanic piece of the body is used to add a sort of sympathetic magic to the photograph, an insurance against separation, whether temporary or permanent. By this means, as we have seen, a secular object is given a potentially sacred aspect. But the hybridity of this object also makes for a stronger portrait experience. By adding a lock of hair to the subject's photograph, the indexical presence of that subject is reiterated and reinforced. The studium of mere resemblance (and the portrait in my locket is of the formulaic kind that offers little more than this) is transformed into the punctum of the subject-as-ghost (a figure simultaneously absent and present, alive and dead). This sorcerer's animation of the missing subject has a temporal component as well. A photograph usually functions as a memory of the past (the moment in which the photograph was taken), while this hair sample stolidly occupies the eternal horizon of the present. The photograph speaks of the catastrophe of time's passing, but the locket as a whole speaks of the possibility of eternal life (a message embodied in its circular form). In short, no matter what its actual size, the combination of photograph and hair turns this locket into a monument to immortality.[17]

All this also enhances the locket's capacity to conjure memory. We usually imagine photographs and memories to be synonymous. The American writer Oliver Wendell Holmes called photography 'the mirror with a memory' as early as 1859 (Newhall 1982: 54), and the Eastman Kodak company has extensively promoted this notion ever since: '[Kodak] enables the fortunate possessor to go back by the light of his own fireside to scenes which would otherwise fade from memory and be lost'

(Frank 2000). And so we have taken our photographs, voraciously and anxiously (Americans take about 550 snapshots per second), as if to fail to do so would be to let our precious memories fade away into the mists of time. The irony in all this is that some of photography's most insightful critics have argued that in fact photography and memory do not mix, that one even precludes the other. Barthes, for example, claimed that 'not only is the Photograph never, in essence, a memory . . . but it actually blocks memory, quickly becomes a counter-memory' (Barthes 1980: 91). Following Proust's lead in *Remembrance of Things Past*, Barthes bases his claim on the presumed capacity of the photograph to replace the immediate, physically embracing experience of involuntary memory (the sort of emotional responses most often induced, before conscious thought, by smells and sounds) with frozen illustrations set in the past; photography replaces the unpredictable thrill of memory with the dull certainties of history.[18]

However, in the examples I have been discussing here, the photograph's capacity to erase memory has been countered by its transformation into an overtly touched and/or touchable object-form. In the process, the subject of each photograph has been similarly transformed, from something merely seen into someone really felt, from just an image set in the past into an exchange you are emotionally (as well as physically) touched by, right now, in the present. The addition of a piece of hair repeats and accentuates this appeal to the mnemonic capacities of touch. Turned into fetish objects devoted to the cult of remembrance, hybrid photographs such as these pieces of jewellery ask us to give up a little something of ourselves if they are to function satisfactorily. They demand the projection on to their constituent stuff of our own bodies, but also of our personal recollections, hopes and fears (about the passing of time, about death, about being remembered only as history and – most terrible of all – about being forgotten altogether).

All this enhances the photograph's capacity to conjure memory, and this at a time when, according to Richard Terdiman, memory itself is in a state of crisis. Of course, memory is always in crisis, always in fearful struggle with its other, with the encroachment of amnesia (Sturken 1997: 7, 17). But Terdiman regards the nineteenth century as a period in which this perpetual memory crisis takes on a more social and systematic character, driven by the often bewildering changes wrought by political revolution and industrial modernity. He argues that Europeans of this period 'experienced the insecurity of their culture's involvement with its past', a type of memory crisis in which 'the very coherence of time and of subjectivity seemed disarticulated' (Terdiman 1993: 3–4). He points to, among other nineteenth-century texts, the commentary in Karl Marx's *Capital* on commodity fetishism, suggesting that, 'because commodities suppress the memory of their own process . . . essentially, "reification" is a memory disturbance: *the enigma of the commodity is a memory disorder*' (Terdiman 1993: 12). Indeed, memory is one of those abstractions increasingly reified in the nineteenth century, turned into lucrative commercial objects of exchange such as keepsakes and souvenirs. One might regard the invention and proliferation of photography as a response to this memory crisis but also as its embodiment and reproduction. The photograph remembers a loved one's appearance, but it is a memory 'hollowed out', disconnected from the social realities of its own production, and also from us, who are doing the remembering.

Might we regard these various examples of photo-jewellery — in which the photograph is touched, worked on, added to, transformed into a personalised, hand-made and often hand-held object and into a multisensory experience — as an attempted resistance or counter to this same memory crisis? They all enact a practice that breaches the virtual walls of the photographic image, forcing us simultaneously to project our mind's eye back and forth, into and out of, the photograph they incorporate. They punctuate the 'chafed reality' of time, for Barthes (1980: 89) the *noeme* or essence of the photographic experience, with the more immediate and tangible realities of physicality. They collapse looking into touching, and history into memory, and, by making their photographs relatively minor, if never incidental, elements of a larger ensemble, they refuse to privilege a pure photography over other types of representational experience.

But the addition of hair to these lockets is not only a modification of the photograph's indexicality and capacity to induce memory. It also constitutes a commentary on photographic representation in general. We have already seen that photography has long been privileged as a direct trace of the real. It is this special form of visuality that allows the photograph itself to pose as invisible, as a 'message without a code' in Barthes's (1977: 17) famous words. But in my locket the real is treated as but one more of these traces, as something not outside the play of signification but very much part of it. The hair sample, for example, is a piece of reality that doesn't just stand in for the symbolic — here, it *is* the symbolic. Equally, this particular photograph is no longer allowed the pretence of invisibility. Turned into a three-dimensional object by its locket frame, that framing, as we have already seen, makes us self-consciously aware of the photograph's thingness by involving our hands as well as our eyes in its perception. Framed in bronze, and then framed again by the embrace of a loved one's hand (and now by my own), the photograph cannot help becoming a sign of itself as well as of its referent. For here it is but one mode of representation among others. We are also made to reflect on the relationship of the image to this referent, a relationship repeated twice over in the confines of this locket. To repeat something is explicitly to declare it as coded, as sign (two knocks on the door signify very differently from just one). This locket thereby takes indexicality to its logical conclusion: 'the thing itself is a sign . . . from the moment there is meaning there are nothing but signs' (Derrida 1976: 48–50). And this declaration could be extended to encompass all the identities incorporated in the locket (hair, photograph, subject, viewer); real and representation are each made continually to signal and (de)generate the other, a physical manifestation of, in Jacques Derrida's words, 'the impossibility for an identity to be closed in on itself, on the inside of its proper interiority, or on its coincidence with itself' (Derrida 1981: 94).

Lockets and photographic history

The same could be said for the identity of the history that would exclude this locket from its purview. It should by now be clear that vernacular photographic practices issue a serious challenge to that history, calling not simply for inclusion in the medium's grand narratives but for the total transformation of the narrative itself.

It should be equally clear that if my locket is indeed to be included in photography's story, an art history centred on origins, great individuals and purity of medium will no longer be adequate. We need to invent a mode of photographic history that matches this object's complexity, and that can articulate its intelligibility both for the past and for our own time. We need also to develop a way of talking about the photograph that can attend to its various physical attributes, to its materiality as a medium of representation. As we have seen, the production of this locket represents certain nineteenth-century social and cultural rituals; a little historical context enhances any reading of it. However, in this particular case we know nothing specific about it, nothing about its subject or owner or their intentions, nothing except what is implied or enacted by the locket's form and design. Refusing to give up its meanings easily, the locket demands I supplement its existence with my own: the locket's meaning amounts to 'an addition: it is what I add to the photograph and *what is nonetheless already there*' (Barthes 1980: 55). My locket thus lends itself to a measure of speculation, to an empathetic, phenomenological style of historical writing that can bridge the temporal and emotional gap between us and it – a century's gap that is, after all, not yet an abyss.

This is a kind of writing already well established in photographic discourse (see Barthes's *Camera Lucida*), but under the guise of a name like Visual Culture it has managed to generate some vigorous opposition in recent times. What is it that makes Rosalind Krauss, Hal Foster, Abigail Solomon-Godeau and other pillars of the postmodern establishment so nervous?[19] Irit Rogoff has described Visual Culture as a shorthand term for 'the critical theorization of visual culture' and argues that its effort to speak *to* as well as *about* particular objects alters 'the very structures by which we organize and inhabit culture . . . It is clearly one of the most interesting aspects of visual culture that the boundary lines between making, theorizing and historicizing have been greatly eroded and no longer exist in exclusive distinction from one another' (Rogoff 1998: 17–18). Foster, for one, sees this as a dangerously 'ethnographic turn', accusing a generic Visual Culture of failing to distinguish subject from object, good art from bad and even art from non-art (Foster 1996: 104). He fears, in other words, the capacity of my locket, and the discourse it generates, to collapse all such binary oppositions into its dynamic supplementary logic.

His argument is not simply against the potential disruptions of deconstruction (although that is part of it) but also attempts a defence of the political function of the avant-garde within mass culture. The artistic avant-garde, so this argument goes, represents a space of resistance to the blandishments of globalised capital. Good historical criticism should privilege this space, thereby offering an alternative model of practice (both artistic and social/political) to that continually propagated by and embodied in the products of a normative capitalist culture. My locket, according to this reading, represents nothing more than Victorian bourgeois sentiment in material form and therefore does not deserve the attention due to, say, a print by Julia Margaret Cameron or Stieglitz. Such an argument of course privileges the sensibilities of the upper middle classes over those of their poorer cousins (both then and now), but it also continues to assume that political agency rests with the object rather than with its reading. It ignores the symbiotic authorial economy described by Rogoff (and before her by Roland Barthes), an economy that in fact pertains to all historical writing and not just the sort that claims the name of Visual Culture (Barthes 1977: 142–8).

But it also turns a blind eye to the contradictions and spaces of critique inherent in all of capitalism's products, including this one. At a time when all things, including memory, are being turned into prescribed commodities, my locket represents a moment of personal resistance to this process. In its unruly turning from life to death and back again, collapsing visuality into touch, and forcing modernity to cohabit with magic, this photographic hair locket conjures an intensely private, unpredictable and even unknowable experience, an experience outside the capacity of capital to control (or, at least, no more in or out of its control than is avant-garde art). For this reason, on top of all the others, I believe my locket deserves our respect and critical attention.

Notes

Thanks go to Bill Jay, Danielle Miller, Monica Garza, Julie Coleman, Catherine Whalen, Anne Ferran, Mary Trasko, Janice Hart and Elizabeth Edwards for all their help with the research and writing of this essay.

1   I have borrowed this reversal from Meaghan Morris's work on women and modernity. She has been cited as saying, 'I prefer to study . . . the everyday, the so-called banal, the supposedly un-or-non-experimental, asking not "why does it fall short of modernism?" but: "how do classical theories of modernism fall short of women's modernity?"' (cited in Burns 1999: 310). For a broad discussion of the place of the vernacular in the history of photography, see Batchen (2001: 199–204).
2   Among the few publications specifically written on this genre of photography are Kappler (1982), West and Abbott (1990) and Spies (1997). For more general histories of jewellery in the modern era, see Cooper and Battershill (1973) and Luthi (2001).
3   Photo-jewellery, for example, is not reproduced in prominent survey histories of photography by Newhall (1982) and Rosenblum (1984). Frizot (1998: 33, 747) reproduces a daguerreotype button and some twentieth-century photo-badges, but discusses neither.
4   In terms of reproductions in photographic histories, the image is consistently privileged over a daguerreotype's casing, not only in the various editions of Beaumont Newhall's *The History of Photography* (1949–82), but also in the much more recent Lowry and Lowry (1998). In contrast, the work of German historian Wolfgang Jaworek (1998) concentrates on the history of the presentation of photographs in frames. Burns (1995) has also emphasised the frame as a means of dating his collection of painted tintype portraits.
5   For a consideration of the historically contingent nature of identity, see Hall (1990).
6   Thanks are due to Bill Jay of Tempe, Arizona, for supplying a copy of this publication.
7   The same phrase, 'secure the shadow ere the substance fade', appears, for example, in the advertisement taken out by Noah North in September 1845 in the *Livingston County Whig* of Geneseo, NY. This advertisement is quoted in Fink (1990: 56). The phrase also appears in an 1843 advertisement published by 'Alvah Ames, Daguerrian Artist', held in the collection of Matthew Isenburg in Connecticut.

8   These examples come from Gary Ewer's invaluable daily Internet DagNews service (http://www.daguerre.org/resource/dagnews/dagnews.html: 1998–2000). See also Palmquist (1980) for an advertisement from a 1902 *Sears Roebuck Catalogue* promising 'an ever present reminder of your relatives or friends, in the form of a photograph on the dial or back cap of your watch . . . done by the Photographic Enamel Process'. He reports that a photographer working in northern California was offering a similar service as early as 1869: 'what could be more appropriate than having the miniature likeness of very dear friends on the dial of one's watch, which would meet the gaze whenever the watch was taken out to tell the time?'

9   For overviews of this tradition, see Morley (1971), Snyder (1971), Meinwald (1990) and Ruby (1995).

10 As the Henisches report, in 1862 Garrard & Company, Goldsmiths to the Crown, supplied Victoria with 'nine gold lockets for photograph Miniatures, with Crown loops and black pearl drops'. Queen Victoria, like Prince Albert, had a keen interest in photography. See Dimond and Taylor (1987).

11 Pointon reports that 'the use of hair in jewellery seems to begin during the Middle Ages and seems to be a peculiarly Christian practice'. She suggests that the practice may stem from a particular reading of the book of Revelations, such that a lock of hair becomes a sign of a possible reunion with the deceased in the afterlife (Pointon 1999a: 198–201, 293). McDannell (1995) mentions gloves, rings and hair art (all pertaining to touch and the hand) as being among those tokens typically exchanged in order to remember the deceased. She also reproduces a mass-produced 1877 certificate designed to memorialise the dead, with this example personalised by the addition (in a vignette space originally intended for a photograph) of a ring of hair tied with a ribbon. Thanks go to Catherine Whalen for directing me to these references.

12 By 1862, advertisements for 'artists in hair' were appearing in such journals as the *Illustrated London News*. In 1855 a full-length, life-size portrait of Queen Victoria, composed only of hair, was exhibited at the Paris Exhibition (O'Day 1982: 36). In England hair jewellery continued to be popular until the 1880s, when, following Queen Victoria's agreement in 1887 to wear some silver jewellery on state occasions, the mourning period for Prince Albert was considered to be at an end and 'hair jewellery was now regarded as being in the worst possible taste'. See Luthi (2001: 29).

13 See O'Day (1982: 36–7) and Trasko (1994). American women were informed by the influential *Godey's Lady Book* of the availability of hair bracelets with clasps made to hold ambrotypes (Kaplan 1998: 9). Particularly instructive is Mark Campbell's *Self-Instructor in the Art of Hair Work: Hair Braiding and Jewelry of Sentiment with a Catalog of Hair Jewelry* (1875 edition). Campbell provides a vast range of possible designs to be made from human hair, including a number that surround a glass-faced locket suitable for photographs. In his Preface, he stresses hair's potent memorial function. 'Persons wishing to preserve, and weave into lasting mementoes, the hair of a deceased father, mother, sister, brother, or child, can also enjoy the inexpressable advantage and satisfaction of *knowing* that the material of their handiwork is the actual hair of the "loved and gone".'

14 *Elegant Arts for Ladies* (1856: 3–4). Interestingly, this book also comes with three pages of advertisements for such things as 'Barnard's Photographic Watercolours' and 'Barnard's Photographic Powder-Colours'.

15 In the context of a memorial locket, hair is an index of the body from which it has been taken because, in Peirce's words, 'it necessarily has some Quality in common with the Object, and it is in respect to these that it refers to the Object'. An index is 'in dynamical (including spatial) connection both with the individual object, on the one hand, and with the senses of memory of the person for whom it serves as a sign, on the other . . . Psychologically, the action of indices depends upon association by contiguity' (Peirce 1985: 8, 13).

16 On this question of fetishism, see Pointon (1999b: 39–57).

17 In *Camera Lucida*, Barthes states: 'Earlier societies managed so that memory, the substitute for life, was eternal and that at least the thing which spoke Death should itself be immortal: this was the Monument. But by making the (mortal) Photograph into the general and somehow natural witness of "what has been", modern society has renounced the Monument' (Barthes 1980: 93).

18 See Barthes (1985: 351–360), Keenan (1998: 60–4) and Edwards (1999). I make a parallel argument to the one in this chapter in Batchen (2003).

19 For instance, Krauss and Foster (1996), Foster (1996), Solomon-Godeau (1998: 33, 39–40). For an overview of this debate, see Moxey (2001: 103–42).

References

Anon. (1856) *Elegant Arts for Ladies*. London: Ward and Lock.

Barthes, R. (1977) *Image–Musk–Text*, trans. S. Heath. New York: Hill and Wang.

Barthes, R. (1980) *Camera Lucida: Reflections on Photography,* trans. R. Howard. New York: Hill and Wang.

Barthes, R. (1985) *The Grain of the Voice: Interviews 1962–1980,* trans. L. Coverdale. Berkeley: University of California Press.

Batchen, G. (1997) *Photography's Objects*. Albuquerque: University of New Mexico Art Museum.

Batchen, G, (2001) *Each Wild Idea: Writing, Photography, History*. Cambridge, MA: The MIT Press.

Batchen, G. (2003) Fearful ghost of former bloom: what photography is. In D. Green and J. Lowry (eds), *Photography / Philosophy / Technology*. Brighton: University of Brighton.

Burns, K. (1999) Urban tourism, 1851–53: sightseeing, representation and 'The Stones of Venice'. Unpublished PhD thesis, University of Melbourne.

Burns, S. (1995) *Forgotten Marriage: The Painted Tintype and the Decorative Frame 1860–1910: A Lost Chapter in American Portraiture*. New York: The Burns Press.

Cooper, D. and Battershill, N. (1973) *Victorian Sentimental Jewellery*. New York: A. S. Barnes & Co.

Derrida, J. (1976) *Of Grammatology*, trans. G. Spivak. Chicago: University of Chicago Press.

Derrida, J. (1981) *Positions*, trans. A. Bass. Chicago: University of Chicago Press.

Dimond, F. and Taylor, R. (1987) *Crown and Camera: The Royal Family and Photography, 1842–1910*. New York: Penguin.

Durand, R. (1995) How to see (photographically). In P. Petro (ed.), *Fugitive Images: From Photography to Video*. Bloomington: Indiana University Press.

Edwards, E. (1999) Photographs as objects of memory. In M. Kwint, C. Breward and J. Aynsley (eds), *Material Memories*. Oxford: Berg.

Fink, D. (1990) Funerary, posthumous, postmortem daguerreotypes. In P. Palmquist (ed.), *The Daguerriean Annual*, 56.

Foster, H. (1996) The archive without museums, *October,* 77: 97–119.

Frank, R. J. (2000) *Love and Loss: American Portrait and Mourning Miniatures.* New Haven, CT: Yale University Press.

Frizot, M. (ed.) (1998) A *New History of Photography.* Cologne: Könneman.

Hall, S. (1990) Cultural identity and diaspora. In J. Rutherford (ed.), *Identity: Community, Culture, Difference.* New York: Lawrence & Wishart.

Henisch H. K. and Henisch, B. A. (1994) *The Photographic Experience 1839–1914: Images and Attitudes.* Philadelphia: Pennsylvania State University Press.

Isenburg, M. (1989) *American Daguerreotypes: From the Matthew R. Isenburg Collection.* New Haven, CT: Yale University Art Gallery.

Jaworek, W. (1998) Wahrnehmungsapparaten und Marketinginstrumente: Präsentationsmittel von Fotografie im 19. Jahrhundert. *Fotogeschichte,* 68/69: 117–30.

Kaplan, D. (1998) Pop photographica in everyday life, 1842–1968, *The Photo Review,* 21(4): 2–14.

Kappler, H. (1982) Fotoschmuck: Fotografie in Dekorativer Fassung, *Fotogeschichte,* 44(12): 11–22.

Keenan, C. (1998) On the relationship between personal photographs and individual memory, *History of Photography,* 22(1): 60–4.

Krauss, R. (1984) *The Originality of the Avant-Garde.* Cambridge, MA: MIT Press.

Krauss, R. and Foster, H. (1996) Introduction, *October,* 77 (Summer).

Laqueur, T. (1992) Clio looks at corporal politics. In *Corporal Politics* (exhibition catalogue). Cambridge, MA: MIT List Visual Arts Center.

Lowry, B. and Lowry, I. B. (1998) *The Silver Canvas: Daguerreotype Masterpieces from the J. Paul Getty Museum.* Los Angeles: The J. Paul Getty Museum.

Luthi, A. L. (2001) *Sentimental Jewellery: Antique Jewels of Love and Sorrow.* Princes Risborough: Shire Publications.

McDannell, C. (1995) *Material Christianity: Religion and Popular Culture in America.* New Haven, CT: Yale University Press.

Meinwald, D. (1990) *Memento Mori: Death in 19th Century Photography.* Riverside, CA: California Museum of Photography.

Morley, J. (1971) *Death, Heaven and the Victorians.* Pittsburgh: University of Pittsburgh Press.

Moxey, K. (2001) *The Practice of Persuasion: Paradox and Power in Art History.* Ithaca, NY: Cornell University Press.

Newhall, B. (1982) *The History of Photography.* New York: Museum of Modern Art.

O'Day, D. (1982) *Victorian Jewellery.* London: Charles Letts Books.

Palmquist, P. (1980) Timely likeness, *History of Photography,* 4(1): 60.

Peirce, C. S. (1985) Logic as semiotic: the theory of signs (c. 1897–1910). In R. Innis (ed.), *Semiotics: An Introductory Anthology.* Bloomington: Indiana University Press.

Pointon, M. (1999a) These fragments I have shored against my ruins. In K. Lippincott (ed.), *The Story of Time.* London: Merrell Holberton and National Maritime Museum.

Pointon, M. (1999b) Materializing mourning: hair, jewellery and the body. In M. Kwint, C. Breward and J. Aynsley (eds), *Material Memories.* Oxford: Berg.

Rogoff, I. (1998) Studying visual culture. In N. Mirzoeff (ed.), *The Visual Culture Reader.* London: Routledge.

Rosenblum, N. (1984) *A World History of Photography.* New York: Abbeville Press.

Ruby, J. (1995) *Secure the Shadow: Death and Photography in America.* Cambridge, MA: MIT Press.

Sekula, A. (1983) Photography between labour and capital. In B. Buchloh and R. Wilkie (eds), *Mining Photographs and Other Pictures 1948–1968.* Halifax: Press of the Nova Scotia College of Art and Design and the University College of Cape Breton Press.

Snyder, D. G. (1971) American family memorial imagery, the photograph, and the search for immortality. Unpublished MFA dissertation, University of New Mexico, Albuquerque.

Solomon-Godeau, A. (1998) Rubrics cubed, *Bookforum* (*Artforum*), Fall, 3: 33, 39–40.

Sontag, S. (1977) *On Photography.* New York: Penguin.

Spies, J. (1997) Collecting 'photographic jewelry': this jewelry is picture perfect!, *Warman's Today's Collector,* July: 36–40.

Sturken, M. (1997) *Tangled Memories: The Vietnam War, The AIDS Epidemic, and the Politics of Remembering.* Berkeley: University of California Press.

Terdiman, R. (1993) *Present Past: Modernity and the Memory Crisis.* Ithaca, NY: Cornell University Press.

Trasko, M. (1994) *Daring Do's: A History of Extraordinary Hair.* Paris/New York: Flammarion.

Wendell Holmes, O. (1859) The stereoscope and the stereograph, *The Atlantic Monthly,* 3 June: 728–48.

West, L. and Abbott, P. (1990) Daguerreian jewelry: popular in its day. *The Daguerreian Annual,* 136–40.

Chapter 9

Preparing and conserving

Samuel J. M. M. Alberti

VERY FEW OBJECTS WOULD SURVIVE long-term retention in the state in which they were found, killed or unearthed. Early in its life in the collection, an artefact or specimen was subject to a series of processes intended to render it stable. However futile, the ultimate aim was to enable it to survive indefinitely.[1] Not only did museum staff spend a significant amount of time preparing specimens as they arrived at the Museum, there was also the continuous cleaning and conserving – ongoing and labour-intensive activities. Several million specimens attracting mould and insects pests, and generally responding to the entropic urge to deteriorate, kept the museum staff on their toes.

The technical challenges of preservation began even before the specimen arrived in the Museum. First, it had to survive the journey, often arduous, from point of collecting to arrival. Transport arrangements varied, but many relied on the post. Insects and plants arrived in envelopes; conchological specimens in crates of 'shell sand', that needed to be painstakingly sifted.[2] The vagaries of the customs process were a frequent challenge for the Museum, such as the crate in 1929 that was held at port for the duty on the preservative spirits.[3] Other specimens were considered too valuable for such routine avenues. One precious insect collection was flown by British Empire Airways from Vienna to Northolt.[4]

Most objects arrived safely at the Museum, there to be subject to a complex set of processes to stabilise and secure them, that is, 'conservation' – the umbrella term that according to the Manchester Museum's Keeper of Conservation encompassed 'both the preservation and enhancement of information embodied in the chemical, physical and biological make-up of the object'.[5] We have already seen how different intellectual approaches clustered around particular kinds of object [see original reading]; so too preparation and conservation methods were highly variable. Some techniques were idiosyncratic to particular staff or institutions, others differed between nations. In the 1890s, fiery debates raged between British and continental entomologists over the appropriate method of pinning Lepidoptera – with flexible European pins or stout, reliable English pins?[6] Part of the challenge of pinning, as with many other techniques, was standardisation. In the herbarium, for example, a great deal depended on the dimensions of the specimen sheets. Donors selected their own sizes to suit their needs, which, to the frustration of curators, did not always match. Of the three major botanical donors first encountered in chapter 2 [see original reading], Charles Bailey based his sheets on those of the British Museum (Natural History), but Cosmo Melvill and Leopold Grindon did not.[7] The gravity in standardising museum techniques exerted by major institutions was significant, but not absolute.

To further illustrate the craft-based contingency of museum practice, I want to turn to the location and personnel of three particular practices developed to care for collections in the Museum's early years: articulation, spirit preservation and cleaning. The taxidermist took the remains of a dead creature and sought to render it as life-like as possible.[8] Given the cost and specialist nature of this skill, some animals were mounted even before they arrived, for example by Rowland Ward's renowned taxidermy company in London – the BM(NH)'s firm of choice.[9] For those specimens that arrived unmounted in Manchester, the Museum at first contracted Harry Brazenor, a taxidermist in nearby Stockport. It was Brazenor who articulated the largest single specimen in the Museum. In February 1896, a sperm whale had beached on the coast of Massachusetts.[10] The fisherman who found the dying beast secured its remains for Henry Ward's Natural Science Establishment in Rochester, New York, a powerful centre for the study and trade of natural history that specialised in supplying museums.[11] The Manchester Museum's keeper, William Evans Hoyle, visited the Establishment while touring North America the following year and, much taken with the skeleton, purchased it for $300. The bones were shipped to Manchester in three cases via the newly opened ship canal. It took Brazenor three weeks, and finally the whale was suspended from the ceiling of the mammal gallery, where it became an iconic specimen, emblematic of the Museum as a whole.

For those vertebrates that arrived untreated, maceration was required – the flesh wasted away to leave only the skeleton. In the Museum's early years, the assistant keeper J. Ray Hardy macerated specimens in a room on the quadrangle, favouring traditional liquid vat techniques.[12] This stood in contrast to 'dry' maceration, used in Dublin and at the BM(NH), in which specimens were buried; later methods used bacteria or insects to eat away the flesh.[13] Other skills demanded of Hardy were equally unpleasant – applying boric acid to bird skins, for example.[14] Reptiles, fish and invertebrates tended to be preserved as 'wet' specimens: a technique developed in the seventeenth century in which organic material was preserved in 'spirit of wine'.[15] This method presented its own peculiar challenges. Wet specimens retained many of the features that mounts did not; but they did suffer some shrinkage and considerable loss of colour.[16] And although the common habit of museum staff purloining the alcohol did not seem to trouble the Manchester Museum, it was nevertheless dangerous and expensive.[17]

Across the collection, from vertebrates to potsherds, objects were picked clean, pieced back together and fixed. But after the labour of preparation, this work was then concealed, 'ironed out'.[18] Perhaps the least visible museum skill – but most fundamental of all – was cleaning. That most mundane of activities, cleaning is not surprisingly almost entirely overlooked in the history of museums. And yet the question of appropriate methods vexed museum professionals of all eras. Cleaning ranged from the careful preparation undertaken by keepers – such as buffing a fossil with a dental engine – to the 'humbler sphere of the charwoman, the pail, the duster, and the broom'.[19] Dust was a particular bugbear of the urban museum. But dust in the case was the problem of the curator or conservator; dust on the floor was not. Rather, the latter was the responsibility of three charwomen the Museum employed. The interface between these two realms was an important boundary, the outer parameter of the museum profession, and those who overstepped the mark in either direction were subject to censure.[20]

On the spectrum of status (and remuneration) of museum workers from charwoman to director, the care of the collections tended to fall to those on the subaltern end of the scale. 'The constant attention which large collections require to protect them from moth and rust and other troubles', proclaimed the Manchester Museum's *Report* in the middle of the twentieth century, 'normally involves a considerable amount of unspectacular work.'[21] This was often in unpleasant circumstances: techniques such as maceration were nasty, smelly tasks.[22] The environment itself was often challenging – the herbarium in particular was an extremely cold place to work. (In the winter of 1978–79, the east corridor was so cold that the specimens themselves began to disintegrate.)[23]

Notes

1   W. Lindsay, 'Time perspectives: what "the future" means to museum professionals in collections-care', *The Conservator*, 29 (2005–6), 51–61.

2   See for example the correspondence cited in S. R. Edwards, 'Spruce in Manchester', in M. R. D. Seaward and S. M. D. FitzGerald (eds), *Richard Spruce, 1817–1893: Botanist and Explorer* (London: Royal Botanic Gardens, 1996), pp. 266–79.

3   Manchester Museum Central Archive (hereafter MMCA) box OMR5, directors' correspondence 1906–33.

4   On the Spaeth Collection, see MMCA box GB5, W. D. Hincks – R. U Sayce, 16 February 1950, and chapter 4 above [see original reading].

5   C. V. Horie, 'Conservation and the specimen', *Newsletter of the Natural History Group of the ICOM Committee for Conservation* (1986), 4–5, p. 4.

6   E. B. Poulton, 'The methods of setting and labelling Lepidoptera for museums', *Report of the Proceedings of the Museums Association*, 8 (1897), 30–6; cf. A. S. Douglas and E. G. Hancock, 'Insect collecting in Africa during the eighteenth century and William Hunter's collection', *Archives of Natural History*, 34 (2007), 293–306.

7   Manchester Museum Herbarium, Accession Register KK, 1906–2006, L. H. Grindon, 'History and description of my herbarium', 1885–86, p. 39; C. Bailey, 'On the contents of a herbarium of British and foreign plants for presentation to the Victoria University, Manchester', *Manchester Memoirs,* 61:5 (1917), 1–13; D. Q. King, 'A checklist of sources of the botanical illustrations in the Leo Grindon Herbarium, The Manchester Museum', *Archives of Natural History,* 34 (2007), 129–39; J. C. Melvill, *A Brief Account of the General Herbarium Formed by James Cosmo Melvill,*

1867–1904: And Presented by him to the Museum in 1904 (Manchester: Sherratt & Hughes, 1904).

8 There is a burgeoning literature on taxidermy, which I review in S. J. M. M. Alberti, 'Constructing nature behind glass', *Museum and Society*, 6 (2008), 73–97.

9 See e.g. MMCA, Manchester Museum Committeee Minutes (hereafter MMCM) vol. 3 (1 June 1908), vol. 4 (20 October 1924); C. Frost, *A History of British Taxidermy* (Lavenham: Lavenham Press, 1987); P. A. Morris, *Rowland Ward: Taxidermist to the World* (Ascot: MPM, 2003); W. T. Stearn, *The Natural History Museum at South Kensington: A History of the British Museum (Natural History) 1753–1980* (London: Heinemann, 1981).

10 Manchester Museum Zoology Archive ZAC/1/146/3, H. A. Ward – W. E. Hoyle, 8 February 1898; ZAC/1/146/4, Ward – Hoyle, 11 January 1898.

11 On Ward's, see M. A. Andrei, 'Nature's Mirror: How the Taxidermists of Ward's Natural Science Establishment Reshaped the American Natural History Museum and Founded the Wildlife Conservation Movement' (PhD dissertation, University of Minnesota, 2006); M. V. Barrow, 'The specimen dealer: entrepreneurial natural history in America's gilded age', *Journal of the History of Biology*, 33 (2000), 493–534; S. G. Kohlstedt, 'Henry A. Ward: the merchant naturalist and American museum development', *Journal of the Society for the Bibliography of Natural History*, 9 (1980), 647–61; R. H. Ward, *Henry A. Ward: Museum Builder to America* (Rochester, NY: Rochester Historical Society, 1948).

12 MMCM vol. 1 (1 October 1890), (24 March 1893).

13 A. C. Western, Interview with Kay Prag, 2006, abstract in MMCA; R. F. Scharff, 'On a dry system of macerating bones', *Museums Journal*, 10 (1911), 196–8.

14 See e.g. MMCM vol. 1 (28 October 1892); H. H. Higgins, 'Life history groups. Suggestions on the desirability of exhibiting in museum drawers of unmounted skins of birds', *Report of the Proceedings of the Museums Association*, 2 (1891), 49–56; R. Newstead, 'The use of boric acid as a preservative for birds' skins, &c.', *Report of the Proceedings of the Museums Association*, 4 (1893), 104–6; cf. S. L. Olson 'Correspondence bearing on the history of ornithologist M. A. Carriker Jr. and the use of arsenic in preparation of museum specimens', *Archives of Natural History*, 34 (2007), 346–51.

15 R. Down, '"Old" preservative methods', in C. V. Horie (ed.), *Conservation of Natural History Specimens: Spirit Collections* (Manchester: University of Manchester, 1989), pp. 33–8; J. J. Edwards and M. J. Edwards, *Medical Museum Technology* (London: Oxford University Press, 1959).

16 MMCA, *Manchester Museum Report* (hereafter *MMR*) (1890–94); P. Rainbow and R. J. Lincoln, *Specimens: The Spirit of Zoology* (London: Natural History Museum, 2003).

17 Cf. M. G. Rhode and J. Connor, 'Curating America's Army Medical Museum', in A. Levin (ed.), *Defining Memory: Local Museums and the Construction of History in America's Changing Communities* (Lanham, MD: AltaMira, 2007), pp. 177–96.

18 *MMR* (1950–51). Only later did archaeologists value the associated matter on finds: see M. Corfield, 'The reshaping of archaeological metal objects: some ethical considerations', *Antiquity*, 62 (1988), 261–5; E. Pye, *Caring for the Past: Issues in Conservation for Archaeology and Museums* (London: James and James, 2001); United Kingdom Institute for Conservation of Historic and Artistic Works, *Guidance for Conservation Practice* (London: Tate Gallery, 1983). On the 'silencing' of museum practice see Alberti, 'Constructing nature behind glass'; S. Macdonald (ed.), *The*

Politics of Display: Museums, Science, Culture (London: Routledge, 1998); S. L. Star, 'Craft vs. commodity, mess vs. transcendence: how the right tool became the wrong one in the case of taxidermy and natural history', in A. E. Clarke and J. H. Fujimura (eds), *The Right Tools for the Job: At Work in Twentieth-Century Life Sciences* (Princeton: Princeton University Press, 1992), pp. 257–86.

19 C. Nördlinger, 'The cleaning of museums', *Report of the Proceedings of the Museums Association*, 9 (1898), 108–11, p. 108; *MMR* (1896–97); R. A. Bather, 'How may museums best retard the advance of science?', *Report of the Proceedings of the Museums Association* (1896), 92–105.

20 On professional boundary work, see T. F. Gieryn, 'Boundary work and the demarcation of science from non-science: strains and interests in professional interests of scientists', *American Sociological Review,* 48 (1983), 781–95; Gieryn, *Cultural Boundaries of Science: Credibility on the Line* (Chicago: University of Chicago Press, 1999).

21 *MMR* (1947–48), p. 4.

22 Western, Interview with Kay Prag; Kohler, *All Creatures*; Scharff, 'On a dry system'.

23 *MMR* (1978–79).

PART II

Experiencing objects

Introduction to Part II

Sandra H. Dudley

H AVING EXPLORED DIFFERENT FORMS AND QUALITIES of objects, the book now moves on to examine ways in which objects and their material characteristics are perceived, interpreted and experienced by human subjects. It addresses the senses, the historically and culturally constituted nature of sensory perception, and the notion of embodied experience. Readings include perspectives influenced by a range of methodologies and theoretical paradigms, including conservation science, neuroscience, phenomenology, psychology and science technology studies.

The short reading by David Morgan sets up this part of the book. It overviews the wider and by now conventional paradigm of studying material culture – that objects are exchanged and in the process acquire a range of shifting values and meanings, all of which can tell us much about the social, historical, economic disciplinary and/or political contexts of the objects – before ending with the emphatic observation that objects are not simply 'projectiles bearing [human] intentions', and that 'meaning is not only abstract and discursive, but embodied, felt, interactive'. In other words, Morgan argues that objects and their meanings are material not only in their form (as the readings in Part I of this book made clear), but also in how they are experienced.

Ernst van de Wetering's article, written for conservators, follows on neatly from the first reading to demonstrate very clearly the material nature of our everyday encounters with, and thus knowledge of, objects. He reflects thoughtfully on the impact of surface qualities on our experience of objects, bringing our attention both to those surface qualities *per se* and to how ubiquitous our awareness of them and of their meanings and values actually is. Material expertise is not just the preserve of specialists, but something we all acquire as part of social experience.

The next reading is the first of three exploring – in very different ways – how the senses might 'work'. Semir Zeki, a leading neuroscientist who has coined the field of 'neuroaesthetics', allows us a glimpse into a neurological perspective on the visual perception of objects – specifically of art objects – and perception of the material world by artists themselves. Part of his wider attempt to develop a biologically founded theory of art, in this article he aims to bring together neuroscience with Plato and other philosophers, and the views of artists such as Michelangelo, Mondrian, Cézanne, Matisse and others, in order to unpick the physical, active process of vision from a neurobiological perspective. He seeks to tie the function of the visual brain to the function of art – both, he argues, are 'a search for constancies with the aim of obtaining knowledge about the world' – and he suggests that artists too are essentially neurologists, studying the brain.

Olga Belova also focuses on seeking to understand the visual sense in particular, but from a very different viewpoint. Taking a phenomenological approach and coming out of organisational studies, her paper considers the sense of sight as, contemporary critiques of ocularcentrism notwithstanding, fundamental but nonetheless embodied and non-detachable from the other senses. She demonstrates that rather than the senses operating within a hierarchy,[1] all are part of an interlinked, lived experience of the world. This is an important perspective worth reflecting upon in the context of other settings, including the museum.

Liz James's chapter continues this focus on how the senses operate, and like Olga Belova she takes a view in which all the senses potentially interact, each informing and triggering others. Her engaging piece, focusing on Byzantine art, looks at a mosaic of the Virgin and Child in the Hagia Sophia in Istanbul not as a piece of art or visual culture but 'as an installation set into and reacting with its physical location, and . . . designed to appeal to all the senses'. As a result, she is able to understand far more about how the mosaic worked for, and was experienced by, ninth-century worshippers in Byzantium. A similar approach could illuminate other sorts of objects, in museums and elsewhere.

Anna Gibbs's article is the first of three readings that take us into the realm of the feelings, and the relationships between objects, sensation and emotional response. Gibbs explores distinctions between various notions of 'emotion' and 'affect', arguing first that affect should be understood as fundamentally embodied and inseparable from the materiality of the body and sensation of the material world, and second that there is no such thing as 'pure cognition . . . uncontaminated by sensate experience, including affective experience'. She argues too that cultural perspectives on human perception and response should be informed by and work with, those of the cognitive and biological sciences. She suggests that such an approach has real value for her own field of media studies – and it clearly has considerable potential too for material culture studies and museum studies.

Peter de Bolla's chapter continues the focus on the affective and emotive aspects of the experience of objects. He explores what precipitates and constitutes 'the state of wonder', specifically in the context of contemplating art. He discusses the 'aesthetic experience' in this art context, and reflects on his own powerful responses to Marc Quinn's *Self*, a frozen sculpture of the artist's head made from 4.5 litres of the artist's own blood. While de Bolla's reflections on aesthetic experience and wonder are focused around responses to art objects, it is worthwhile reflecting too upon such issues in non-art contexts: as Rosenstein made clear in his article in Part I, aesthetic experience does not necessarily involve only those things we are happy to call 'art'; and powerful responses such as those de Bolla calls 'wonder' (or even those we might call 'disgust') do not occur only on encountering 'art' objects.

The following reading is a short reflection on the embodied, sensory and material manifestations of the exile experienced by an anthropologist working in a refugee camp (ironically already a place of exile, of course, for those living therein). It links the physicality of aspects of the refugee camp environment, and bodily experience of it, with emotional response in the short and long term. Worthy of reflection, too, is how far the kind of displaced experience described here can be metaphorically applied to the process of observing others' objects in museum and heritage settings. Cultural objects in museums, like refugees, are displaced; and those from other cultures who come to observe them are, like anthropologists, usually outside their familiar environment. What makes the time in the camp most understandable and memorable is full engagement with the refugees and the physicality of the camp on sensory and emotional levels, not simply cognitive examination. How far, one might ponder, could such engagement happen in museums and other contexts, thus enabling greater connections?

At the end of this part of the book, Thomas Hardy's poem leads us to meditate upon still wider, sensory and historical imaginings that can be triggered by engagements with evocative objects.

Note

1   Cf. Foucault's argument in favour of a historical development of a hierarchy of the senses in which, with the rise of modernity and in particular of the discipline of natural history, sight has become dominant over smell and touch in European perspectives (Foucault 1970). This Foucauldian perspective has been influential, but it has also been criticised by some more recent scholars as placing too heavy an emphasis on the dominance of sight from the seventeenth century onwards and thus diminishing the actual role of other senses, particularly taste and smell, in shaping Western modernity and notions of individualism and class (e.g. see Howes and Lalonde 1991, Smith 2007).

References

Foucault, M. (1970) *The Order of Things*, London: Tavistock.
Howes, D. and M. Lalonde (1991) 'The history of sensibilities: of the standard of taste in mid-eighteenth century England and the circulation of smells in post-revolutionary France', *Dialectical Anthropology* 16: 125–35.
Smith, M. M. (2007) *Sensory History*, Oxford: Berg.

Chapter 10

The materiality of cultural construction

David Morgan

WHAT DO I MEAN BY MATERIAL CULTURE? If culture is the full range of thoughts, feelings, objects, words, and practices that human beings use to construct and maintain the life-worlds in which they exist, material culture is any aspect of that world-making activity that happens in material form. That means things, but it also includes the feelings, values, fears, and obsessions that inform one's understanding and use of things. But that's not all. As I understand it, the study of material culture gives special attention to the scrutiny of practices, that is, what people do with things. As a field of inquiry, material culture assumes that meaning does not inhere in things, but is activated by them. Meaning is a complex process of interaction in which people, objects, environments, histories, words, and ideas take part. To be sure, some objects seem to function only as denotations of codes. Like traffic signs: once you know the code, the signifier is devoid of interest. The sign tells you to stop or go, nothing more. But most things aren't so ancillary to meaning-making. They enter into it much more integrally, messily. Most objects acquire their significance through engagement with people and an object user's interaction with other people and objects.

This means at least two very important things for the study of material culture. First, it foregrounds the study of exchange and its complicated and varied forms since the value of an object will draw powerfully from its social career, that is, its circulation among people. As an object moves from one person to the next, from one social setting or one culture to the next, it acquires different values and associations, negotiating differences and carrying with it veneers of significance that will tell us much about what objects do. Second, rather than understanding objects as projectiles bearing the intentions of their makers, it is more productive to study the response to objects as they are displayed, exchanged, destroyed, and circulated in order to determine what they mean to people, that is to say, how they build and maintain life-worlds. Meaning is not only abstract and discursive, but embodied, felt, interactive, and cumulative. This means that the cultural construction of reality is not a wispy evocation of words about objects, but a concrete process that invites us to take a careful look at objects.

Chapter 11

The surface of objects and museum style

Ernst van de Wetering

THERE ARE NEGATIVE UNDERTONES IN DESCRIBING someone as superficial. A person is more highly valued if his views and feelings are perceived to have depth. We also tend to mistrust our attitudes toward the surfaces of objects; we would rather wait and see whether the surface of an object really corresponds in quality to that which lies beneath. Emphasis on the surface provokes thoughts about appearances being deceptive, about glitter rather than gold.

You may thus imagine that my ears perked up when, in her significant paper at the last seminar in Veszprém, Hanna Jedrzejewska concluded that "the most important and the most representative part of an object is its surface."[1]

Museum objects are – unfortunately – only there to be *seen*. Thousands of people earn their living preventing untold thousands of others from touching the objects. But what, other than the surface, can be seen of an object? Moreover, it is the surface that bears the finishing touches and the finest workmanship of the original artist or craftsman. It is, however, also the surface that is most exposed to environmental influences and rarely resembles its original appearance. And that is the crux of a very complex problem. The term "patina dilemma" has already been used in this connection. In attempting to resolve this dilemma, it is most important to consider the peculiarities of our perception.

The moment one consciously concentrates on surface phenomena, one is overwhelmed – at least I was – by the unbelievable diversity in the appearance of the objects all around us. That sensing these surface appearances intensively should cause a near-psychedelic experience without recourse to drugs indicates that we consciously experience relatively few of these impressions in our daily lives. Instead, we generally use them without identifying and assessing an object; we then know whether we are likely to bump into it, whether we will dirty our hands if we touch it, how heavy it might be if we were to try to lift it, et cetera.

Objects are often identified by other means in which the appearance of the surface plays no part. When, as a seventeen-year-old, I went to France for the first time and, after traveling all night, found myself walking through the streets of a typical hilly southern French town, a solitary ball suddenly rolled round the corner in the gutter. Wanting to be helpful by returning the ball to its unseen owner, I kicked it – and then limped for the rest of the day: the ball was made of iron. The fact that it was rolling down the street and that it was round (I had never heard of the game of *boules*) sufficed to prevent me from noticing any of its other properties, such as the appearance of the surface or even the clattering noise it must have made. The only material I could even begin to consider that ball to have been made of was rubber.

The realization that we are able to form an idea of the surface characteristics of an object by indirect means also explains why we easily accept working with countless photographs of the objects that occupy us professionally in museums. It hardly troubles us that the subtleties of the appearance of the surface are lost or falsified in these reproductions. In looking at the photographs we imagine the surface on the basis of our visual memory bank.

In this one kind of "seeing" the image is thus based to a great extent on memories and on the expectations based on these memories. The appearance of the object before us is conveyed to our minds by a quick glance – in daily life also by means of the other senses: hearing, smell, touch. Our readiness to see what we expect to see causes us to overlook a lot. It is for this reason that the museum visitor overlooks damage of all sorts as well as very crude restorations; this could be taken to imply that we need not expend too much effort on restorations.

On the other hand, this same, average museum visitor perceives surfaces very sensitively – not only in the course of intensive examination, but also in daily life while casually glancing at things in passing. We often pass verdicts on our fellow human beings based on the tiniest stains, on minute blemishes, on specks of dust. Entire industries are built on the inclination people have to repair the smallest deficiencies in surfaces of the most varied types: in clothing, furniture, cars, tableware, the human skin, et cetera. Here our perception is apparently very sophisticated – even at the briefest glance.

Oddly enough, it is precisely the small areas of surface damage perceived at speed – either consciously or much more often subconsciously – that do not really disturb us (unless, of course, they affect our own property); on the contrary, we use these surface deficiencies to identify and assess the objects around us. Our sensitivity to these small signposts is great. We are all profoundly knowledgeable about the signs of aging on the outer skins of things. My knowledge of the ways in which a paint layer on a wooden ground forms blisters and *craquelure*, how it separates from the ground, was essentially acquired in childhood, as I sat next to the green-painted coal bunker in my parents' garden, absentmindedly breaking off flakes of paint and squashing blisters that collapsed with a cracking sound. A refined understanding of the nature and appearance of iron corrosion was developed by observing the rusty nail on which the coal shovel hung. The familiar wooden door handles in my grandparents' house are the basis for lovingly acquired impressions of the ways and means by which wood wears and becomes shinier in some spots than in others through constant handling. We could surely all spend hours telling one another about the development of the enormous range of knowledge of the surfaces of things that each of us possesses.

A knowledge of what we now somewhat abstractly call "natural aging" is acquired early in life. We use this knowledge daily in order to find our way around objects. Although we may not be aware of it, it is specifically the signs of natural aging and of wear that often provide us with significant information about the material of which an object is made. These signs also provide instant information about the meaning of an object and about the ways and means in which it is used; they even let us know the extent to which it is valued — or neglected. The early Flemish painters already incorporated small signs of damage in the painted objects in their panel paintings to enable the observer to identify the materials of which these objects were made. An example is the detailed portrayal of the chipped stone on the niches in Gerard David's *Annunciation*. The painters in Rembrandt's circle were able to represent the relationship between the persons depicted in their paintings and the objects around them, such as books and furniture, by emphasizing signs of the objects' use in their depictions.

Both the signs of aging and the signs of wear may be disturbed severely in the course of restoration; even if they are consciously respected by the restorers, an alien effect may result. The surface acquires a look that does not occur "in nature": one has the feeling that something has happened to the object although one does not usually get as far as asking oneself consciously just *what* is odd about it. Yet the piece has acquired the characteristics of a museum object. It becomes an intermediate object between a carefully preserved object of daily use — such as a well-polished shoe, its brittle leather smeared with shoe cream, a process we take for granted as a sign of diligence and cleanliness — and an object that has aged at its own pace, and carries an air of having been left untouched for a long time. By its untouched condition it spans, amazingly, the gap between us and the distant past, and unexpectedly gives us the feeling the Dutch historian Huizinga called *de historische sensatie*: the propulsion into a direct experience of the past.

Many carefully conserved objects have had surface treatments that have either interfered with the evidence of the materials of which they are made or have blocked direct access to their past; the objects have thus become, through such treatment, stylized objects of our own time.

A frequently occurring example of this kind of alienating condition is the nearly invisible protective layer that is applied to many objects. As we accept this in the case of the above mentioned shoe, so we also accept the pleasing domestic layer of wax on the polished surface of furniture, the obligatory varnish layer on a painting. With many other sorts of objects, however — archaeological objects, tools, utensils, et cetera, but above all with objects that to some extent convey the sense of decay as a process — such a layer can have a very disturbing effect. This layer often reveals minor surface damage or defects in the outer layer of engravings as well as in pits of corrosion on metal objects. At those points where the surface recedes or advances to a different level, these layers tend to create small catchlights that alert the observer to the fact that the object is covered with a thin layer that is meant to be invisible. One begins to get the unpleasant feeling that a momentary state in the movement through time has been indiscretely fixed.

Another example of the alienating effect of interference with the skins of objects is the partial interruption in the continuity of the signs of aging. We have a pronounced sense of the logic of a given form of damage; for example, we have a clear expectation of the way in which a crack will develop in stone, in wood, in terracotta or in porcelain. If such a crack is partly closed in the course of restoration because the surface of the object demands continuity at that point – for example, in connection with the retouching of a painted motif – our expectations of the behavior of this material are confused. It seems as though the entire object has been transformed from its familiar state of brittleness into a viscous mass.

Yet another example is the type of retouching in which the color on the surface is continued by the restorer into the depression of a damaged area of an object that is not apparently massive. This sort of interference profoundly affects the appearance of the object, because it is no longer possible to have confidence in the integrity of the surface layer as an authentic whole.

If only one single aspect of the aging of the surface is obliterated during restoration, while others remain, the results can be most disturbing. The connections between the signs of aging are dissolved, so that the object is partly displaced in time, resulting in a common form of museum stylization.

Although they are perceived only subconsciously, the examples of alienating conservation and restoration treatments described here may cause a slight feeling of revulsion, which can disturb or even eliminate any sympathy with the object.

Patina has long been highly esteemed in the broadest sense and considered to be a part of the identity of the object. In this sense the prevailing significance of patina is as a symbol, as a sign that something is old, worthy of respect, and genuine; and as with all symbols, a general indication suffices to give the idea. As a result, an industry of patina kitsch has developed whereby these symbolic values are "glued" onto objects in the cheapest way possible. The tin rusk box with printed-on *craquelure* and gradual darkening toward the edges commonly appears on many Dutch breakfast tables. It radiates coziness and seems to have been around since granny's day. But make no mistake: this patina kitsch is to be found in antique shops, and if we are not careful, it will be promoted in museum showcases as well. It is the result of searching for a balance between stability and cleanliness on the one hand, and on the other hand, the emanation of a worthy venerability. The increasingly sophisticated facilities, ingenious showcases and theatrical lighting in museums are leading to the taming and stylization of the often somewhat unintentionally savage air that clings to many objects, hinting at past calamities. Many restoration and conservation treatments have, often unintentionally, a subtle cosmetic effect that leaves the objects imperceptibly well groomed, so that they comply with museum style.

One might ask another question about museum style: How much influence does incessant confrontation with reproductions have on our aesthetic expectations and demands? One might, for instance, ask to what extent our concept of a beautiful surface is influenced by modern color reproductions. Could there be a parallel with a phenomenon known to have affected the early American symphony orchestras? Somewhat tinny tones were discernible in their sound, tones typical of those heard in recordings of the renowned European orchestras of the time: these records represented the ideal sound to contemporary American musicians.[2] It might be thought to follow that the splendid reproductions available today have such an influence. Every shade of each color is saturated, thanks to the glossy paper and the properties of the printer's ink: many, not always necessary, surface treatments in the restoration studio result in similarly saturated colors, and this gives rise to a singular perception of the authentically historical. On the other hand a diffuse refraction of light, which results in a somewhat dusty appearance, is very rarely seen with objects in museum exhibition cases. However, it occurs commonly on the surfaces of old objects in "the natural state" and contributes greatly to the experience of authenticity.

In describing the effect of interventions on the character of the surface – many more examples of which could, of course, be given – the object thus treated was several times compared to a similar object as it occurs in "the natural state." It should be clear what is meant by "the natural state" in this context: those conditions in which objects are left to age, change, and wear out in their own way. Also meant by "the natural state" is the immense picture book of the manifestations of aging that we build up in our visual memories from childhood on; one might almost say a pattern book into which the surface appearance of many restored or conserved objects does not really fit. And that leads to the alienating effect that occurs more often than one is aware of consciously. It goes without saying that the "naturalism" here being defended has nothing to do with nostalgia. It also is certainly not "capitalist culture-fetishism" as an academic critic has described my efforts. It concerns the ability to recognize the object undistorted, to perceive it unobstructed.

When objects are in need of conservation, it admittedly sometimes seems inevitable that the character of the surface is changed by treatment. The argument may then be that the change was technically unavoidable, that the alteration occurred inadvertently. What makes the work of the restorer so interesting, however, is that he does not limit himself to the technically *possible*; on the contrary, he regards the technically *impossible* as a personal challenge. It was precisely the ethical and aesthetic demands of restoration that caused many traditional solutions to conservation problems to be considered unsatisfactory and made the need for quasi-impossible new solutions unavoidable.

Minimalism in conservation and restoration can be defended in various ways. The most significant argument is surely the need to preserve the many-layered documentary evidence that every historic object bears. No one can foretell what sort of questions will be asked of the object in connection with future attempts at interpretation; in examining (art) historical objects one all too often discovers that essential traces have been made unintelligible or destroyed during treatment because their meaning went unrecognized. The argument against minimalism is that the object ought to be presentable and stable in its present function and should therefore be thoroughly restored. The discussion above is intended to bring some shades of distinction to this objection.

Notes

1. HANNA JEDRZEJEWSKA, "Basic Problems in the Conservation of Stone," *Problems of the Completion of Art Objects: Second International Seminar for Restorers, Veszprém, Hungary, 15–27 July 1978*, ed. Adam Szemere (Budapest: Institute of Conservation and Methodology of Museums, with the support of UNESCO, 1979), 36.
2. V. ZUCKERKANDL, *Sound and Symbol*, Bollingen series 44 (New York: Pantheon Books, 1956); G. C. Kop, *Mens en Muziek: Inleiding tot de paedagogische muziekpsychologie* (Amsterdam: J. Muusses, 1958), 155–56.

Chapter 12

Art and the brain

Semir Zeki

"les causeries sur l'art sont presque inutiles"[1]

Paul Cézanne

"More often than not, [people] expect a painting to speak to them in terms other than visual, preferably in words, whereas when a painting or a sculpture needs to be supplemented and explained by words it means either that it has not fulfilled its function or that the public is deprived of vision."[2]

Naum Gabo

I

Much has been written about art but not in relation to the visual brain, through which all art, whether in conception or in execution or in appreciation, is expressed. A great deal, though perhaps not as much, has been written about the visual brain but little in relation to one of its major products, art. It is therefore hardly surprising that the connection between the functions of art and the functions of the visual brain has not been made. The reason for this omission lies in a conception of vision and the visual process that was largely dictated by simple but powerful facts, derived from anatomy and pathology. These facts spoke in favour of one conclusion, to which neurologists were ineluctably driven, and that conclusion inhibited them, as well as art historians and critics, from asking the single most important question about vision that one can ask: Why do we see at all? It is the answer to that question that immediately reveals a parallel between the functions of art and the functions of the brain, indeed ineluctably drives us to another conclusion, that the overall function of art is an extension of the function of the brain. In that definition lie the germs of a theory of art that has solid biological foundations and which unites the views of modern neurobiologists with those of Plato, Michelangelo, Mondrian, Cézanne, Matisse and many other artists.

The concept of the functions of the visual brain inherited by the modern neurobiologist was based on facts derived between 1860 and 1970. Chief among these was the demonstration by the Swedish neuro-pathologist Salomon Henschen and his successors in Japan and England that the retina of the eye is not diffusely connected to the whole brain or even to half the brain, but only to a well-defined and circumscribed part of the cerebral cortex, first called the visuo-sensory cortex and later the primary visual cortex, area V1, which therefore constituted ". . . the only entering place of the visual radiation into the organ of psyche".[3] This capital discovery led to a prolonged battle between its proponents and its opponents, who thought of it as "*une localisation à outrance*";[4] they had conceived of the visual input to the brain as being much more extensive and to include large parts of the cerebral cortex that were known to have other functions, a notion more in keeping with the doctrine of the French physiologist Flourens. The predecessor of the American psychologist Karl Lashley, Flourens had imagined that each and every part of the cortex is involved in every one of its activities. It was not until early this [20th] century that the issue of a single visual area located in an anatomically and histologically defined part of the cortex was settled in favour of the localisationists.[5] There was much else to promote the idea of V1 as the "sole" visual centre. It had a mature appearance at birth, as if ready to "receive" the visual "impressions formed on the retina",[6] whereas the cortex surrounding it matured at different stages after birth, as if the maturation depended upon the acquisition of experience; this made of the latter higher cognitive centres, the *Cogitatzionzentren*, whose function was to interpret the visual image received by V1, or so neurologists imagined. As well, lesions in V1 lead to blindness, the position and extent of which is in direct proportion to the position and size of the lesion; by contrast, lesions in the surrounding cortex resulted in vague visual syndromes, referred to first as mind blindness (*Seelenblindheit*) and then as agnosia, following the term introduced by Freud. Together, these facts conferred the sovereign capacity of "seeing" on V1, leading neurologists to conceive of it as the "cortical retina", the cerebral organ which receives the visual images "impressed" upon the retina, as on a photographic plate – an analogy commonly made. Seeing was therefore a passive process while understanding what was seen was an active one, a notion that divided seeing from understanding and assigned a separate cortical seat to each.

This concept left little room for the fundamental question of why we see. Instead, seeing was accepted as a given. Asked the question today, few would suppose that it is to enable us to appreciate works of art; most would give answers that are specific, though related in general to survival of the species. The most general of these answers would include all the specific ones and define the function of seeing *as the acquisition of knowledge about the world*.[7] There are of course other ways of obtaining that knowledge; one can do so through the sense of touch or smell or audition. Vision happens to be the most efficient way of obtaining it and there are some kinds of knowledge, such as the colour of a surface or the expression on a face, that can only be obtained through vision.

It takes but a moment's thought to realise that obtaining that knowledge is no easy matter. The brain is only interested in obtaining knowledge about those permanent, essential or characteristic properties of objects and surfaces that allows it to categorise them. But the information reaching the brain from these surfaces and objects is in continual flux. A face may be categorised as a sad one, thus giving the brain knowledge about a person, in spite of the continual changes in individual features or in viewing angle or indeed in the identity of the face viewed; or the destination of an object may have to be decided by its direction of motion, regardless of its speed or distance. An object may have to be categorised according to colour, as when judging the state of ripeness of an edible fruit. But the wavelength composition of the light reflected from an object is never constant; instead it changes continually, depending upon the time of day, without entailing a substantial shift in its colour. The ability of the brain to assign a constant colour to a surface or a constant form to an object is generally referred to as colour or object constancy. But perceptual constancy is a much wider phenomenon. It applies as well, for example, to faces that are recognisable when viewed from different angles and regardless of the expression worn. There is also what I shall call situational constancy, when the brain is able to categorise an event or a situation as a festive or a sad one, and so on, regardless of the particular event. There is even a narrative constancy when, for example, the brain is able to identify a scene as the Descent from the Cross, regardless of variations in detail or the style of the painting. The brain, in each case, extracts from the continually changing information reaching it only that which is necessary for it to identify the characteristic properties of what it views; it has to extract constant features in order to be able to be able to obtain knowledge about them and to categorise them. Vision, in brief, is an active process depending as much upon the operations of the brain as upon the external, physical, environment; the brain must discount much of the information reaching it, select from that information only that which is necessary for it to be able to obtain knowledge about the visual world and compare the selected information with its stored record of all that it has seen. A modern neurobiologist should approve heartily of Matisse's statement[8] that "Voire, c'est déja une operation créatrice, qui exige un effort".

How the brain achieves this remarkable feat remains a puzzle, indeed the question has only been seriously addressed in the last thirty years, which have witnessed a prolific output of work on the visual brain. Among the chief discoveries is that it is composed of many different visual areas that surround V1.[9] Each group of areas is specialised to process a particular attribute of the visual environment by virtue of the specialised signals that each receives from V1.[10] Cells specialised for a given attribute such as motion or colour are grouped together in anatomically identifiable compartments within V1, different compartments connecting with different visual areas outside V1,[11] thus conferring their specialisations on the relevant areas. V1, in brief, acts much like a post office, distributing different signals to different destinations; it is but the first, though essential, stage in an elaborate machinery designed to extract the essential information from the visual world. What we now call the visual brain is therefore V1 plus the specialised visual areas with which it connects, directly and indirectly. We therefore speak of parallel systems devoted to processing simultaneously different attributes of the visual world, a system comprising the specialised cells in

V1 plus the specialised areas to which these cells project. Vision, in brief is modular. The reasons for evolving a strategy to process in parallel the different attributes of the visual world have been debated but it seems plausible to suppose that they are rooted in the need to discount different kinds of information when acquiring knowledge about different attributes.[12] With colour, it is the precise wavelength composition of the light reflected from a surface that has to be discounted whereas with size it is the precise viewing distance and with form the viewing angle.

Recent evidence has shown that the processing systems are also perceptual systems in that activity in each can result in a percept without reference to the other systems; each processing-perceptual system terminates its perceptual task and reaches its perceptual end-point at a slightly different time from the others, thus leading to a perceptual asynchrony in vision – colour is seen before form which is seen before motion, the advantage of colour over motion being of the order of 60–100 ms.[13] Thus visual perception is also modular. In summary, the visual brain is characterised by a set of parallel processing-perceptual systems and a temporal hierarchy in visual perception.[14]

These findings lead me to propose that there is also a modularity, a functional specialisation, in visual aesthetics. When area V4, the colour centre, is damaged the consequence is an inability to see the world in colour.[15] But other attributes of the visual scene are perceived normally. When area V5, the motion centre, is damaged, the consequence is an inability to see objects when in motion but other attributes are seen normally. Damage to a region close to V4 leads to a syndrome characterised by an inability to see familiar faces. There are other specific syndromes, for example the inability to recognise certain categories of objects and neurology is continually uncovering new syndromes of selective visual loss. I do not mean of course to imply that the aesthetics of colour are due solely to the activity in V4 or the aesthetics of kinetic art are due solely to activity in V5 but only that the perception of colour and of motion is not possible without the presence and healthy functioning of these areas. It is little good asking a patient with a V4 lesion to appreciate the complexities of fauvist art or a patient with a V5 lesion to view the works of Tinguely. These are aesthetic experiences that such patients are not capable of.

II

The definition of the function of the visual brain – a search for constancies with the aim obtaining knowledge about the world – that I have given above, is applicable with equal vigour to the function of art. I shall thus define the general function of art as a search for *the constant, lasting, essential and enduring features of objects, surfaces, faces, situations, and so on, which allows us to acquire knowledge* not only about the particular object, or face, or condition represented on the canvas but to generalise from that to many other objects and thus acquire knowledge about a wide category of objects or faces. In this process, the artist, too, must be selective and invest his work with attributes that are essential, and discard much that is superfluous. It follows that one of the functions of art is an extension of the major function of the visual brain. Indeed philosophers and artists often spoke about art in terms that are extremely similar to the language that a modern neurobiologist of vision would use, except that he would substitute the word brain for the word artist. It is striking, for example, to compare Herman von Helmholtz's statement about "discounting the illuminant" in which a coloured surface is viewed (in order to assign a constant colour to a surface) with the statement of Albert Gleizes and Jean Metzinger in their book on *Cubism*.[16] Discussing Gustave Courbet, they wrote that, "Unaware of the fact that in order to display a true relation we must be ready *to sacrifice a thousand apparent truths*, he accepted, without the slightest intellectual control, all that his retina presented to him. He did not suspect that the visible world can become the real world only by the operation of the intellect" (my emphasis). I interpret "intellect" to mean the brain or, better still, the cerebral cortex. In order to represent the real world, the brain (or the artist) must discount ("sacrifice") a great deal of the information reaching it (or him), information which is not essential to its (or his) aim of representing the true character of objects.

It is for this reason that I hold the somewhat unusual view that artists are neurologists, studying the brain with techniques that are unique to them and reaching interesting but unspecified conclusions about the organisation of the brain. Or, rather, that they are exploiting the characteristics of the parallel processing-perceptual systems of the brain to create their works, sometimes even restricting themselves largely or wholly to one system, as in kinetic art. These conclusions are on canvas and are communicated and understood through the visual medium, without the necessity of using words. This may surprise them since most of them, naturally enough, know nothing about the brain and a good many still hold the common but erroneous belief that one sees with the eye rather than with the cerebral cortex. Their language, as well as the language of those who write about art, betrays this view. But however erroneous their views about the seeing organ or the role of the visual brain may be, it is sufficient to glance at their writings to realise the extent to which they have defined the function of art in a way that a modern neurobiologist would not only understand but feel very sympathetic to. Thus, Henri Matisse once said that, "Underlying this succession of moments which constitutes the superficial existence of things and beings, and which is continually modifying and transforming them, one can search for a truer, more essential character, which the artist will seize *so that he may give to reality a more lasting interpretation*"[17] (my emphasis). Essentially, this is what the brain does continually − seizing from the continually changing information reaching it the more essential one, distilling from the successive views the essential character of objects and situations. Similar statements abound, and it is sufficient to give just one more example. Jacques Riviere, the art critic, wrote:[18] "The true purpose of painting *is to represent objects as they really are*, that is to say differently from the way we see them. It tends always to give us their sensible *essence*, their presence, this is why the image it forms does not resemble their *appearance* . . ." (my emphasis), because the appearance changes from moment to moment. A neurologist could hardly have bettered on that statement in describing the functions of the visual brain. He might say that the function of the brain is to represent objects as they really are, that is to say differently from the way we see them from moment to moment if we were to take into account solely the effect that they produce on the retina.

To summarise, therefore, both the brain and one of its products, art, have a task which, in the words of artists themselves, is to depict objects as they are. And both face a problem, which is how to distil from the ever changing information in the visual world only that which is important to represent the permanent, essential characteristics of objects. Indeed this was almost the basis of Kant's philosophy of aesthetics – to represent perfection; but perfection implies immutability, and hence arises the problem of depicting perfection in an ever changing world. I shall therefore define the function of art as being a search for constancies, which is also one of the most fundamental functions of the brain. The function of art is therefore an extension of the function of the brain – the seeking of knowledge in an ever changing world.

Notes

1 Mack, G. *La Vie de Paul Cézanne*, quoted by C. Gray (1953) in *Cubist Aesthetic Theories*, The Johns Hopkins Press, Baltimore.
2 Gabo, N. (1959). *Of Divers Arts*, The A.W. Mellon Lectures in the Fine Arts, National Gallery of Art, Washington, Pantheon Books, Bollingen Foundation, New York.
3 Flechsig, P. (1901). Gehirnphysiologie und Willenstheorien, Fifth International Psychology Congress, pp 73–89. [Translated by G. von Bonin (1960), in *Some Papers on the Cerebral Cortex*, C.C. Thomas, Springfield.]
4 Vialet, M. (1894). Considérations sur le centre visuel cortical à propos de deux nouveaux cas d'hémianopsie suivis d'autopsie, *Archs. Ophtalmol. (Paris)* 14, 422–426.
5 Monbrun, A. (1939). Les affections des voies optiques rétrochiasmatiques et de l'écorce visuelle, in *Traité d'Ophtalmologie*, Vol. 6, Baillart et al. (Eds), Masson, Paris.
6 These are the terms of neurologists, not mine; they were current until the last two decades.
7 Zeki, S. (1993). *A Vision of the Brain*, Blackwell, Oxford.
8 Matisse, Henri, *Ecrits et propos sur l'art*, Hermann, Paris, 1972, pp 365.
9 Zeki, S.M. (1978). Functional specialization in the visual cortex of the rhesus monkey, *Nature, Lond.*, 274, 423–428.
10 Zeki, S.M. (1978). *loc. cit.*
11 Livingstone, M.S. and Hubel, D.H. (1984). Anatomy and physiology of a color system in the primate visual cortex. *J Neurosci*, 4: 309–356.
Livingstone, M.S. and Hubel, D.H. (1987). Connections between layer 4B of area 17 and the thick cytochrome oxidase stripes of area 18 in the squirrel monkey. *J Neurosci*, 7: 3371–3377.
Shipp, S. and Zeki, S. (1985). Segregation of pathways leading from area V2 to areas V4 and V5 of macaque monkey visual cortex. *Nature*, 315: 322–325.
12 Zeki, S. (1993), *loc. cit.*
13 Moutoussis, K. and Zeki, S. (1997). A direct demonstration of perceptual asynchrony in vision, *Proc. R. Soc. Lond. B.*, 264, 393–399.

14 Zeki, S. (1998). Parallel processing, asynchronous perception and a distributed system of consciousness in vision, *The Neuroscientist* (In Press).

15 Zeki, S. (1990). A century of cerebral achromatopsia, *Brain*, 113, 1721–1777.

16 Gleizes, A. and Metzinger, J. (1913). *Cubism*, Fisher Unwin, London

17 Matisse, Henri, Notes d'un peintre, *La Grande Revue*, LII, 24, pp 731–745. Reproduced in Flam, J.D. (1978), *Matisse on Art*, Phaidon, Oxford.

18 Riviere, J. (1912). Present tendencies in painting, *Revue d'Europe et d'Amérique*, Paris, March 1912, pp. 384, 406. Reproduced in *Art in Theory*, (1992). C. Harrison and P. Wood (eds), Blackwell, Oxford.

Chapter 13

The event of seeing

A phenomenological perspective on visual sense-making

Olga Belova

We never look just at one thing;
we are always looking at the *relation* between things and ourselves.
Berger (1972), Ways of Seeing, p. 9.

Introduction

The domination of vision in our knowing and thinking about the world, or ocularcentrism, has long been a topic of many critical discussions (e.g. Levin, 1993; Jonas, 1966; Brook, 2002). One of the most comprehensive analyses of these debates has been presented in Jay's *Downcast Eyes* (1993), which examined the rise and fall of sight in French thought which has been as vehement in putting the Cartesian vision-centred rationality on a pedestal as in taking it down. Within organisation studies, the objectivist and disembodied understandings of reality that resulted from ocularcentric perspectives have also been attacked on many occasions (e.g. Dale, 1997, 2001; Lennie, 2000; Kavanagh, 2004). These arguments played an important part in revealing the role of the eye in producing knowledge, scientific methods of inquiry and creating a society of surveillance and order. Dale (1997: 95) argues that the scientist's eye dissects in order to perform an 'invasive investigation, fragmentation and re-organization' of the object of study, and that this anatomising urge pervaded almost all areas of knowledge, both as a metaphor and a form of representation. Thus, the critique of 'culture of dissection' presents vision as an incising, objectifying, and ordering activity aimed to seize and appropriate the other.

To provide alternatives to vision-centred perspectives, research was undertaken to explore other senses such as hearing (Pihlajamaki, 1990; Carpenter and McLuhan, 1966), touch (Candlin, 2003; Frank, 1966), smell (Baxter and Ritchie, 2004; Bone and Ellen, 1999) and their role in organising experience of a workplace. One can hardly deny, however, that whilst being sites of olfactory, tactile, kinaesthetic and auditory experiences, organisational artefacts continue to have a strong appeal to our visual senses: inside them, we are surrounded by a vast array of visual artefacts (e.g. documents, uniforms, interiors, architecture) which are designed to make management philosophy visual, 'available to senses' (Berg and Kreiner, 1992: 41); outside organisations, the visual often remains the main way of reaching out to the public by conveying organisations' identity through logos, TV advertisements, visual displays, billboards, glossy brochures and packaging that lure us into the utopian world of fantasy and pleasure. The very word 'image', meaning both 'a visual representation' and 'a reputation', transmits the sense of visibility of organisations on all levels. The visual, Kavanagh claims, is so deeply entrenched in language and thinking that we would need 'to remain either silent or unintelligible without it' (2004: 459).[1] So if our concern with the visual is to continue, how can it usefully go beyond the much-attacked Cartesian legacy?

The phenomenology of the French philosopher Merleau-Ponty (1964, 1968, 1993a, 1993b) provides a useful starting point from which we can re-visit the ontological and epistemological status of the practice of looking. While being deeply suspicious of the Cartesian dualistic philosophy of sight, Merleau-Ponty was still fascinated by vision as a mode of our embodied involvement with the surrounding world, characterised not by a superficial surveying of distant objects but by a fundamentally reversible relation between the seer and the seen, the visible and the invisible, and an intertwining of all sensory perceptions which open onto the world in its pre-reflective rawness (Merleau-Ponty, 1968; 1993b). In his understanding, it is the body, not the eye or the mind, that looks. Merleau-Ponty shifts our focus from *the structure of the visual sign* (Barthes, 1977; Williamson, 1978; Goldman, 1992) to *the event and meaning of visual experience* as our everyday engagement with the surrounding world.

The purpose of this paper is to continue our concern with the visual from a phenomenological perspective, and to elaborate on Merleau-Ponty's ideas using illustrative examples from a larger research project. In the framework of this project focus group participants were asked to comment on images that appeared on cover pages of the University of Essex advertising materials. One may ask why images of a rather 'Cartesian' institution, which a university today is, were chosen. An answer to this is twofold: on the one hand, it is exactly for this reason that it is interesting to see what reaction advertising images of a University provoked; on the other hand, it is not a certain interpretation of images that is at the focus of this paper, but various ways in which people engage with visual materials. In this sense, these could be images of any other organisation, or, indeed, works of art. Since the aim of this paper is to make a theoretical contribution to phenomenological understanding of the practice of seeing, I do not propose to *explain* participants' experiences (from Latin *explanare* 'to flatten') but try to *explicate* (from Latin *explicare* 'to unfold') those aspects of the visual encounter that have been *sensed by* Merleau-Ponty and *overlooked* by the modernist accounts.

The paper starts with a short discussion of the Cartesian understanding of sight to outline the principles that Merleau-Ponty sought to overcome, such as an objectified and static nature of the gaze, its separation both from the body that it inhabits and the seen object, and the superiority of mind over sight and sight over other senses. It concludes with a brief note on ways in which an instrumental understanding of sight influenced subsequent visual investigations, such as semiotic studies of imagery. The second section gives a sense of the situation in which comments on imagery were received from focus group participants. In the last three sections I explore some of these comments in the light of Merleau-Ponty's phenomenology with a particular emphasis on three themes: embodied and pre-reflective nature of visual perception, intertwining of all senses in a visual encounter, and seeing as a lived experience. This focus on embodied aspects of vision aims to complement existing explorations into the practice of seeing.

Descartes and the disembodied eye

Descartes was perhaps the first to lay foundations for the modern inquiry into the visual as a primary source of human experience and knowledge (Descartes, 1637–1701/1954). For him, sight was an objective and accurate way of discovering the external world of which images served as tangible and recordable evidence (evidence from Latin *videre* 'to see', 'observe', 'understand'), leading him to believe that only what one could see with one's eyes is true. Knowing through seeing was 'knowing through staring' (Jay, 1993), that is via an immobile, fixed gaze which examined objects from a distance. As Descartes observed, one seeks true knowledge by 'fixing their eyes on a single point, [to] acquire through practice the ability to make perfect distinctions between things, however minute and delicate' (Descartes, 1637–1701/1985: 33). This allowed the mind to concentrate and make sense of visual perceptions in an unbiased rational manner: 'the objects that I thought I saw with my eyes, I really comprehended only by my mental power of judgement' (Descartes, 1637–1701/1954: 74). As Jay points out, Descartes himself, in his philosophical quest, sought to be 'a spectator rather than an actor' (Jay, 1993: 81). This passive intellectual engagement with the object of study complemented by a physical detachment from it gave rationale to a clear-cut distinction between the body and the outside world, the seer and the seen.

By arguing that conscious acts have no affinity with corporeal acts (Descartes, 1637–1701/1954: 132), Descartes helped legitimise the separation of the mind, as a source of intellectual powers, from the body, as a source of senses, desire and animality. This separation, as well as the idea of sight being an opening of the mind rather than the body, led to establish, at least in the materialist tradition, observation as an objective, neutral activity, characterised as a detachment rather than an engagement with the object of scrutiny. Mind (= sight) was thought to be able to perceive primary measurable qualities of an object, e.g. shape, quantity, and magnitude, while body (= senses of touch, smell, etc.) could appreciate only its secondary qualities such as odour, texture, and taste. The latter could not be quantified and therefore almost polluted visual perceptions of the primary qualities (Descartes, 1637–1701/1954: 194–196, 199). Against the later British 'empiricist' tradition, Descartes argued that the body with its corporeal acts could not be trusted in knowing the world; it was the mind, which grasped the true essence of things (ibid.: 131–132).

This conception of sight as an extension of the powers of the mind left an indelible mark on most human sciences, and can be traced in the semiotic/structuralist (e.g. Barley, 1983; Schapiro, 1996) and content analysis methods of analysing an image (e.g. Millum, 1975; Lutz and Collins, 1993). These studies were usually undertaken by an analyst who provided an interpretation of the image by skilfully unmasking and interpreting social codes used by advertisers to manipulate the public into desiring their products. The titles of such inquiries often speak for themselves: in *Mythologies* Barthes sets the rules for unveiling the myths created by advertisers (1972), while in *Decoding Advertisements* Williamson further refines structuralist analysis by deciphering complex games that advertisers play with their audiences (1978; see also Goldman, 1992). The analysis of visual materials was undertaken in an explicatory manner whereby images took on meaning under the objectifying eye and mind of the researcher, and where the point of visual interaction was reduced to identifying, explaining and appropriating the essence of the object. As Burgin wittily notes, these methods represent a hunt for *the* meaning undertaken in the belief that 'meanings are to be found in the world much in the same way that rabbits are found on downs, and that all that is required is the talent to spot them and the skill to shoot them' (Burgin, 1982: 40). Such is, for example, Millum's endeavour in his study of advertisements in women's magazines where he asks: How is one to decide the connotations, to interpret symbols or metaphors (Millum, 1975: 37)? It seems that what he is really asking is: How do we decide what the meaning of the message is? Who determines it? The task for Millum is to find a quasi-scientific and tested procedure, an almost magic formula that would give no excuse for indulging in a personal and subjective account based on examples chosen for reasons of individual whim (ibid.).

But what if we were to break from this search for a recipe that holds the key to *the* meaning of signs? What if we asked ordinary people with no particular training in visual skills to share their ways of making sense of the visual? Studies involving viewers making sense of imagery are possible (see for example Warren, 2002) but extremely rare, as is research into imagery from phenomenological perspectives (King, 2003). In this paper I illustrate the idiosyncrasies of visual encounters on the basis that vision might be better explored as a fundamental way of being and making sense, and as an embodied exploration of the present circumstance which always implies the next move. This perspective allows us to distinguish between 'the thought of seeing' or purified vision, severed from its body and senses, and 'active vision', that which happens in the midst of things, 'squeezed into a body – its own body', and 'of which we can have no idea except in the exercise of it' (Merleau-Ponty, 1993b: 136). From this perspective, vision does not cut across mind and physical sensations but unites them in the event of embodied being.

Source of illustrative materials

In the rest of the paper a selection of comments obtained during a focus group discussion will be taken up for reflection. These comments were gathered during a larger research project in which participants were offered a set of images that appeared on the covers of the University of Essex prospectuses and were invited to comment on them. At the preparation stage various sets of images were tried out and those that stimulated the most responses were kept for the main study. In the limited space of this paper only two of these images will be discussed to pursue certain themes. I am conscious that a selective approach to images and comments might attract criticisms of 'engineering' a certain interpretation. My point, however, is not to be objective but to present one of the countless ways in which these, and perhaps any other, images can be experienced. What interests me most is not so much the meaning that respondents draw from the materials, but the ways in which they engage with them.

It must be noted that discussions generated a wide variety of responses and involved participants beyond a simple interpretation of meaning. For example, one of the respondents, a professional printer, was fascinated by the expensive satin paper and pondered on the cost and waste involved in its production. Perhaps not surprisingly, he was particularly receptive to the physical qualities of photographs, to their feel and touch. Another respondent, a keen photographer, was particularly attentive to the photographic quality of the images, discussing the sharpness of the focus, lighting, and depth of field. They had different opinions towards the institution represented in the images: some were sceptical of Universities' educational rather than commercial interest, while others enthusiastically believed in opportunities for learning, achievement and growth that Universities provide. Wider issues concerning recycling, racism, and attitudes of young people today were raised. As well as rationalising the content, value, and meaning of images respondents engaged with their aesthetic qualities, and reacted to images' appeal to their physical as well as cognitive self. In this sense, participants responded to the imagery with their whole life-worlds and meaning systems. My intention, however, is not to analyse participants' phenomenological worlds, although this would undoubtedly be an interesting direction to pursue, and not to engage with their 'talk' only from the textual point of view. Such speech-based approach, as noted by Letiche (2004), would make an analysis of sense-making 'flat' and 'one-dimensional'. Instead, the aim is to render explicit those aspects of visual encounters that are often taken for granted in formal analyses, to conceptualise vision as a lived event, always embodied and interactional, where sense-making happens in a variety of ways. With this in mind, comments taken up for reflection will serve as starting points in the theoretical discussion and will be drawn upon as illustrative examples rather than empirical data which 'proves' a theory.

Making sense with the body: the phenomenal and pre-reflective nature of visual engagement

Comments offered whilst viewing [the cover page of the University of Essex 1998 Graduate Prospectus] allow us to probe into the embodied aspects of visual experience. One of the respondents noted:

I like that one [clock image]. It's good because it is a warm picture and you instantly think: oh, this looks interesting because something is happening and you wanna look inside it. That's what it says to me.

Before attempting an interpretation of its meaning, the viewer engages with the image on a bodily level: it evokes sensual feelings and invites him to physically cross the space and reach for it. The bodily rootedness of being-in-the-world and its deep pre-reflective involvement with the surroundings is an essential feature of Merleau-Ponty's phenomenology (1964; 1968; 1993a; 1993b). He argues that more than anything we are carnal beings who move around, smell, touch and hear, so that every visual contact with the world becomes a *lived-out*, not a *thought-out* experience of it. This makes us embodied 'agent[s]-at-grips-with-things' (Taylor, 1989: 7) who make sense of the world by acting in and on it. Perception becomes conditioned by one's stance in space, his/her movement towards or away from the object, specific tactile and other sensory perceptions of it. It is in these momentary and perhaps seemingly insignificant dealings with things around that we recreate the shape, the feel, the colour and the spatial orientation of the visual object each for ourselves so that the visual interaction of beings and things, like in the above instance, becomes a 'uniquely "shaped" circumstance which, although invisible, is *felt* by all who are involved as participants' (Shotter, 2002).

This interconnection of body and things indicates that visual engagement with the world occurs on the border between body and its surroundings, at its margins, described by Merleau-Ponty as *flesh* (1968). *Flesh* is not a substance in-between the body and the world but is to be understood 'functionally, as *texture, articulation, framework, joints*, as an *element* in which we live and move . . . An *intertwining* forms between things, others and myself, a *chiasmus* or a *chiasma* . . . [where] [w]hat is one's own and what is not constantly more or less overlap but never entirely coincide with each other' (Waldenfels, 1998: 288–289). Being made of the same stuff, body and the world are part of *flesh*.

> The thickness of flesh between the seer and the thing is constitutive for the thing of its visibility as for the seer of his corporeity; it is not an obstacle between them, it is their means of communication (Merleau-Ponty, 1968: 135).

Flesh is sharing a continuous bond, a fabric of experience in which body and thing interconnect in the event of *living-in-the-world*. By creating a relationship of connection rather than opposition between the body and the world, *flesh* substantiates Merleau-Ponty's thesis of the indivisibility of seer and seen. They are no longer ontological opposites, as Descartes would have it, but are included in the same 'horizon', the same dimension, because 'he who sees is of it (flesh) and is in it' (Merleau-Ponty, 1968: 100). This leads Merleau-Ponty to 'reject the age-old assumptions that put the body in the world and the seer in the body, or, conversely, the world and the body in the seer as in a box' and wonder: 'Where are we to put the limit between the body and the world, since the world is flesh?' (ibid. 138). This question takes issue with the Cartesian perspective of sight as a unidirectional activity in terms of power (subject intellectually appropriating the object by assigning it a meaning) and action (subject passively gazing at objects at a distance). As Evans and Lawler argue, 'consciousness is always consciousness of something' (2000: 3) so any attempt to separate the object from the subject and vice versa is a crucial distortion of their relationship. They continue:

> to sever objects from their relationship to subjects, to consider them as fully
> determinate entities, is to ignore that they are present to us as reflecting our
> hold on them (their 'immanence') as well as their inexhaustibility in relation
> to our perception and thoughts about them (their 'transcendence') (ibid.).

In this process the object and subject gain a clearer sense of the direction of their dialogue as well as establish a basis for the next stage of perceptual engagement that will enable them to move forward in their exchange, making the body-subject 'a continuous movement of acquisition and transcendence' (ibid.). Evans and Lawler further suggest that 'like a dialogue, perception leads the subject to draw together the sense diffused throughout the object while, simultaneously, the object solicits and unifies the intentions of the subject' (2000: 4). Importantly, 'this dialogue provides a direction for the becoming of both subjects and objects and yet retains the degree of indeterminacy or ambiguity required for the creative contributions of subjects and for the surprises that the world harbors' (ibid.).

This calls us to further pursue Merleau-Ponty's collapsing of the subject–object dichotomy. Rather than dispassionately contemplating an image, the respondent continues his active engagement with it:

> It's a warm thing attracting you to open the book up. It says: look, open me,
> have a look inside me.

The looked-at-object, as this comment points out, addresses the viewer on a kinaesthetic level, almost calling for taking it, for physically engaging with it. This is what Merleau-Ponty talks about in terms of reversible relations between subject and object: since the seen and the seer are part of the *flesh*, the object has the same power over the looking subject as s/he has over it (the looked-at object). The roles between the seer and the seen become reversed: from the subject controlling the image spatially to the image directing the gaze and the physical actions of the beholder. Merleau-Ponty describes a similar experience of an object taking on the active role of a felt presence that occurred to Paul Klee:

> In a forest, I have felt many times that it was not I who looked at the forest.
> Some days I felt that the trees were looking at me, were speaking to me . . .
> I was here, listening . . . I think that the painter must be penetrated by the
> universe and not want to penetrate it . . . (1993b: 129)

In reaching towards the object and going back, the seer becomes aware of his own humbleness in front of the object at which he is looking. He is not approaching the object with the intent of appropriating it, as Descartes would have it, but simply opens himself up to the object and sensitises himself to what the object has to express. This relation can be described as chiasmic (Merleau-Ponty, 1968) in that one holds and lets oneself be held at the same time, allows dispossession without considering it as a loss or defeat. As Mallin argues, our age, following the celebration of order, logic, and causality, is characterised by possession where we

> . . . hold to ourselves by holding back unyieldingly and keeping secure whatever we already possess; while at the same time extending our grasp (*saisir*) aggressively in order to possess the other by taking back whatever we can to ourselves as if each of us was the only legitimate subject (Mallin, 1989: 223).

Chiasm, instead, lets the other exist because it is through the other that one's own being is determined. It requires that the links between them, while bending onto each other, remain separate 'without collapsing, being absorbed or broken in the process' (Mallin, 1989: 221). They cannot produce an organic whole without being internally connected but also without merging their independence, as in intertwining of fibres in linen, strata in stone or threads in a rope.

Remarkably, an artist, on the one hand, and someone with no training in aesthetics, on the other, both seem to describe their visual experiences in ways which suggest that visual encounter is a fundamentally reciprocal event. In his bodily involvement with the image the respondent gives up the ambition to imperiously pierce the object as if to discover its essence. It is no longer only him that endows the object with meaning, it is also the object that guides his perceptions. The image invites grasping and feeling it, subtly conditioning the kind of interaction and meaning it will have for its viewer. It is no longer clear who guides whom in a visual experience:

> The look . . . envelops, palpates, espouses the visible things. As though it were in relation of pre-established harmony with them, as though it knew before knowing them, it moves in its own way with its abrupt and imperious style, and yet the views taken are not desultory – I do not look at a chaos, but at things – so that finally one cannot say if it is the look or if it is the things that command (Merleau-Ponty, 1968: 133).

Intertwining of senses in perception

It is not by accident that the last quote describes the look as 'enveloping, palpating, espousing the visible things'. The intertwining of vision and touch comes through in some comments on the 'clock' image:

> It's warm colour, yeah, the terracotta colour. Plaster, is that plaster, isn't it?

As one knows from their own experiences, colours may 'feel' 'warm' or 'cold', irritating or soothing, as if the gaze could touch them or the colours could reach to the viewer. The very expression 'terracotta' colour, based on the analogy with the colour of baked clay, suggests the warmth and a coarse feel of it. Looking at an image seems to go beyond a purely optical disembodied contact and has other senses filling it with texture. As Danto put it, they form a "'densely felt fabric" of perceptual experience, in which the various modalities are always present, even if we lack a good relational term to express the way they are in mutual presence without being metaphorical' (1991: 202), which perhaps explains why one can see taste or wetness, or smell a shape. This impregnation of quality with texture transpires in the respondent's perception of the image in terms of its material and texture ('is that plaster?'). Merleau-Ponty suggests that sight and touch belong to the same order of perception (making little difference between 'tactile palpation' and 'palpation with the look') and that they function in similar ways:

> We must habituate ourselves to think that every visible is cut out in the tangible, every tactile being in some manner promised to visibility, and that there is encroachment, infringement, not only between the touched and the touching, but also between the tangible and the visible, which is encrusted in it, as, conversely, the tangible itself is not a nothingness of visibility, is not without visual existence. Since the same body sees and touches, visible and tangible belong to the same world (1968: 134).

By way of analogy, Merleau-Ponty refers to Cézanne's paintings which, he argues, depict existence itself.

Cézanne's canvasses present what seems to be a distorted perspective, a mass of colours, a space that vibrates instead of being stable. This is because he strived to depict things as they appear to us in the world, in their wholeness, without being separated by the five senses. Cézanne endeavoured to preserve this raw state of nature in his work, to replicate through his paintings 'this indivisible whole' in order to give it 'the imperious unity, the presence, the insurpassable plenitude which is for us the definition of the real' (ibid.). In his various paintings of Mont Sainte-Victoire (1902–1906), Cézanne suggests depth through colour rather than perspective, making it appear as it would be experienced by the senses. For this reason, many of his paintings need to be looked at from a distance to allow separate touches to form the image. Merleau-Ponty said of Cézanne's works: 'We *see* the depth, the smoothness, the softness, the hardness of objects; Cézanne even claimed that we see their odour' (Merleau-Ponty, 1993a: 65). So intense was Cézanne's perception of the connections and tensions between objects that he tried to recreate a life of objects in which they would be linked in the same way as humans exchange glances and words. In his private correspondence, for example, Cézanne said of fruits that: '[they] come to you in all their odours, tell you about the fields that they left, about the rain that nourished them, about the dawns that they searchingly watched . . .' (Benedetti: 1995, 31, my translation[2]). For Cézanne, objects formed part of the essence of life and complex but harmonious relations between its elements, which was what he tried to express in his art.

It is not my point to claim that images of an organisation have the same capacity to recreate the invisible and holistic essence of being as much as paintings of great artists do. Rather, I would like to suggest that regardless of the nature of images they are not made sense of only intellectually. We seem to experience the visual with our whole embodied being, with all senses that come together to form a presence to things, without separating the rational from the perceptual and the visual from other sensations. Distinctions between senses blend into an organic whole that immerses us in an overall experience. It was Cézanne's belief that we have learned to distinguish between, say, sight and touch only as a result of the development of science:

> Cézanne did not think he had to choose between feeling and thought, as if he were deciding between chaos and order. He did not want to separate the stable things which we see and the shifting way in which they appear; he wanted to depict matter as it takes on form, the birth of order through spontaneous organisation. He makes a basic distinction not between 'the senses' and 'the understanding' but rather between the spontaneous organisation of the things we perceive and the human organisation of ideas and sciences (Merleau-Ponty, 1993a: 63–64).

Here Merleau-Ponty, as well as participants' comments, clarifies what we tend to take for granted: that various senses, in this case touch and vision, can hardly be separated in a lived-out experience of being, that both merge in our immediate response to our surroundings, and only part ways in the rationalising of perceptions.

The kinaesthetic ability of the body to move and change perspectives also becomes an integral part of a visual encounter. As one of the respondents commented:

> It's a warm thing attracting you to open the book up. It says: look, open me, have a look inside me [takes the booklet in his hands and starts browsing through it].

He is responding to the image by changing his spatial position, by taking it in his hands. His seeing is not rigidly positioned in one point of space but shifts its location, expressed by Merleau-Ponty in saying: 'The world is around me, not in front of me' (1993b: 138). He and the image are no longer ontological opposites but are brought closer so that vision and movement become part of the same sense-making process:

> . . . body [which] is an intertwining of vision and movement . . . I have only to see something to know how to reach it and deal with it, even if I do not know how this happens in the nervous system. My moving body makes a difference in the visible world, being a part of it; that is why I can steer it through the visible . . . This extraordinary overlapping, which we never give enough thought to, forbids us to conceive of vision as an operation of thought that would set up before the mind a picture or a representation of the world, a world of immanence and of ideality. Immersed in the visible by his body, itself visible, the see-er does not appropriate what he sees; he merely approaches it by looking, he opens onto the world.
>
> (1993b: 124)

The fact that vision is closely interrelated with movement refutes the immobile gaze with which the Cartesian observer surveys the world. We never stare, argues Merleau-Ponty, our eyes run over the surface we look at, accumulating the different viewpoints and examining its different parts. We do not see an object as a whole at once and then formulate its meaning but swiftly examine its parts gathering together the multiple perspectives to form a whole. Any movement performed by the body has implications for what comes within its visual field and its physical reach and consequently for its experiential existence: 'every experience of the visible has always been given to me within the context of the movements of the look' (Merleau-Ponty, 1968: 134).

The interrelation of vision and motility shows another aspect of reversibility as a principle of existence whereby all objects intertwine in a process of reciprocation and movement, and where we find ourselves in the centre of the world by looking at it from our absolute position, and at the same time at its periphery by locating all other objects around us and by changing our own location. The body moves in order to interrogate the things and beings around it, 'its motility is a response to the questions the world raises' (Dillon, 1997: 146). Thus the kinaesthetic ability expands the receptive, responsive character of body's involvement with the world and its search to understand others.

It is worth emphasising that phenomenological visual experience cannot be described as perceptions only, as this term is often associated with the 'five peepholes' through which the body is linked to its environment. This is surely not what Merleau-Ponty meant by entitling his work *Primacy of Perception*. Gendlin (1992: 345) makes this clear by affirming the primacy of body rather than perception. He says:

> What the word 'perception' says cannot usually include how the living body *consists of* interactions with the world. 'Perception' is usually something that appears before or to a body. But the body is an interaction also in that it breathes, not only in that it senses the cold of the air. It feeds; it does not only see and smell food. It grows and sweats. It walks; it does not only perceive the hard resistance of the ground. And it walks not just as a displacement between two points in empty space, rather to go somewhere – to answer 'the call of the things', as Merleau-Ponty said. The body senses the whole situation, and it urges, it implicitly shapes our next action. It senses itself living-in its whole context – the situation.

Gendlin cannot emphasise enough that we do not act on the basis of separate sensations coming from five sources but out of the whole bodily sense of the situation, which is inseparable from the awareness of who, what and where we are. The bodily presence is not pre-linguistic and pre-thought, but is with us at every moment. Through it, we are always already engaged with our surroundings which are not "'there" before us as a picture is there, but it is there *for* us as a set of "invitations" and "resistances", as a set of openings and barriers to our actions – all given in relation to our present "position" within "it" (Shotter, 2005: 118).

An account of a lived experience

As is suggested above we respond to what is in our visual horizon with our whole bodies, so that an act of seeing becomes an event of *lived experience* rather than an immobile and detached survey that is often taken as the primary way of making sense of the seen. Seeing as a lived experience and as an instrumental scrutiny can be contrasted through some other comments offered in the discussion. In what follows one of the respondents explains how he makes sense of images *in general*, without talking about any particular picture:

> When I look at the picture I look at it for a variety of reasons. I look at it as a picture. The first thing I do when I see anything is I look upon it as a picture whether it's photographically pleasing to the eye, I look at the technical aspects of the photograph. And once I've got that in my mind I look at it as to what use it's got on the cover. So I get a judgement in my own mind. I think we all do this maybe without realising it as to whether we like the picture. And then we look at the suitability of the picture in relation to what's inside the book.

From the first sight it seems that the emotional matters little in his perception of images. Being knowledgeable about photography, he pays attention to the technical, 'photographically pleasing' aspects of the image, to its functionality and suitability in relation to the context of its appearance. His account is linear, explanatory, logical and almost mechanistic in the way he goes through particular stages of his visual understanding. This bears considerable similarity to Descartes' rules for the direction of the mind (1954) where he says that: we fix our gaze upon them to scrutinise the minute details; we study only those objects that 'our intellectual powers appear competent to know certainly and indubitably' (Rule II); we need to find 'truth about things' (Rule IV); we organise pertinent points in an 'adequate and orderly enumeration' (Rule VII); we break the phenomena down into its elementary parts, and go over them in a sequence so that we do not miss any part but grasp them all in a logical and rational manner (Rule IX, XIII). It is important to remind ourselves at this point that the viewer was trying to formulate how he approaches *any* visual image and describes his *general* view of the understanding process.

The same respondent then proceeds to give a detailed description of Figure 13.3 [see original reading], which was his favourite of the lot offered for discussion.

> I chose this one because to me it had most impact. I think it's very important to have things against a plain background. 'Cause a lot of these are very fussy and your eyes are not focused on a lot of things. I mean the ducks and the elephant [which appear on covers of other brochures], they are silly, the University is not about this . . . From this [cloth], I draw a lot from it. What it is, and this is very artistic, a lot more artistic than any of these [other images], simply because what they've done, this is a much deeper picture than the rest of them. Because what they've done, they haven't done

very . . ., nothing is even about that, everything is slightly disjointed which is how it is in life, and they've got different colours which is how it is in life. And they've got it in a plain black background, a lot more impact than it would be against a white background. And I don't think there is any ethnic minority reasoning behind the black background, it's not important. But what they've done is that they've got each piece of cloth is not wonderfully trimmed, it's a bit like people, a bit like the world we live in, it's not perfect, so what they are saying is that because you've got a bigger gap there than here that means more to me than all of the rest of these [other images] put together . . . You see because what it's doing and, I am not sure whether you see it, these two bits that I've pointed out before. I am not really sure whether they were designed into that, that they are translucent that you can see through them, I'm not sure. The red and the yellow, I'm not sure whether it was intentional or just how it ended up. There's no particular colour that stands out, there's nothing to stand out on that cover.

This account lets the event of the viewer's engagement with the image, as it appeared to him there and then, come through wonderfully. He is no longer too much concerned with the photographic aspects of the picture, its function as a cover of a University publication, or any sequence of intellectual operations that rationalise its impact. He personally and very passionately engages with the image: to him, a little element of the picture, 'a bigger gap there than here', tells a story of life in a beautiful and artistic way. It tells him that the world is made of many diverse episodes, people and experiences, none of which exists on their own. They all intertwine and depend on each other to form a mosaic in which one does not live in isolation but takes on meaning in relation to others. The mosaic's parts are not in order; they are somewhat irregular and disorganised, and their shape is of all sorts, like a motley crew of life experiences. Pieces of the cloth are translucent and he can see one stripe through another, which is exactly how he understands this picture: all its parts being interlinked and each of them indirectly but significantly affecting the experience of the whole image. He does not so much look *at* an image but sees *according* to it. As Merleau-Ponty suggests in one of his examples, we see tiles of a swimming pool not *despite* the water that inhabits it but *according* to it, mediated by the water movement, reflections, its 'syrupy and shimmering' power (1993b: 142). For the viewer here, meaning does not arise from isolated perceptions, but from the stream of relations, associations and experiences which are variegated and yet intimately interconnected.

These two accounts of a visual encounter capture different ways in which the event of seeing can be understood. It can be conceptualised as an attempt to seize the impalpable, to generalise the unique, to impose rules and limits on a spontaneous and vivid dimension of 'lived experience', and to provide an *explanation* of it. While our engagement with the visual certainly does the above, I suggest that it is not the only or the principal way in which we respond to what we see. Seeing as *living-in-the-world* has an endless potential to be a personal, emotional and deeply embodied *relation* to the world. Meanings unfold temporally during viewers' engagement with the presence of the image and embodied others, and emerge not as 'individual achievement[s]' but as 'joint action[s]' that takes place in the 'interactive moment' (Shotter and Katz, 1996) of perception that cannot be defined only in linguistic, physiological, or individualistic terms. It forms an inalienable part of people's being-in-the-world and lived-out circumstances of their perceptions, making the meaning of each text, be it visual or verbal 'individual, unique, and unrepeatable, and herein lies its entire significance' (Bakhtin, 1986: 140).

Concluding remarks

What I hope to have achieved in this probing into the phenomenological aspects of seeing is not to arrive at a 'better' and more 'accurate' account of visual sense-making but to re-frame our discussion of vision in order to reveal other aspects of it. In a visual encounter, we position ourselves in relation to what comes into our visual horizon, evaluate it aesthetically, engage with it in a bodily and practical manner, in other words, understand it in an 'actively responsive' way. Shotter describes such engagement as 'relational-responsive understanding' (2002) whereby one enters into a dialogue with the surroundings, explores them for possible meanings and lets them be a guide in this search rather than *a priori* imposing or discovering some fixed meaning in them. It also means that objects that we perceive with our senses have living embodied dimensions and, having an equal power of meaning-making, form a reversible relation with us. If visual perception is conceptualised as a reversible or 'dialogically-structured' activity (Shotter, 2002) qualitatively new forms of understanding may result. It might be then described as:

- *Spontaneous*, because it is immediate and not pre-meditated. Visual perception precedes reflection and rationalisation, and therefore grasps the actual present world in its wholeness and primordiality.
- '*Bodily*, in that it is not hidden inside individual people's heads' (Shotter, 2002, when describing any 'dialogically structured activity') but involves *sharing* an embodied material space, where the body is both the seer and the seen, senses intertwine to form a rich, deep, but also impure and concrete vision, and where visual perceptions cannot be distilled from other senses.
- *Reversible* in that it is deeply rooted in the 'activities of the others and otherness in its surroundings' (ibid.). The object is not a passive 'something' that takes on meaning under the gaze of the subject but becomes an active part of the meaning-making process by returning the gaze and guiding the beholder in their look. Thus, the meaning of the visual experience originates in the object of seeing (the looked at) as much as in the subject (I who look).
- *Temporal and processual* because it becomes an event, an experience that lasts in time (Silverman, 1987: 68–69). Meanings unfold temporally and emerge not as 'individual achievement[s]' but as 'joint action[s]' that takes place in the 'interactive moment'. Sight can be of a momentary nature, but it can also 'intertwine past, present, and future into a meaningful whole' (Kavanagh, 2004: 454).

Thus, vision cannot be limited to the dimensions which Descartes and his critics pointed out ('fixating', 'atemporal', 'objectifying', 'appropriating', 'controlling', etc.) and which determined much of the modern epistemology. By being interested in the impure, sensorial and concrete vision Merleau-Ponty establishes the *primacy of perception and body*, which, being reversible, open onto the world. Merleau-Ponty brings together the various planes on which embodied being takes place: in the moment of perceiving 'here and now', in the inter-involvement of self and other as bodies that share the common ground of *flesh*, and a profound sociality of interaction where understanding hinges on the *frontier* of an intermingling of subjects, consciousnesses, and corporalities. This makes vision a view *in* the world, rather than *on* it.

One can only speculate whether producers of University images ever expected their 'target groups' to engage with images in ways described above. Most probably not. But this confirms that one can hardly underestimate the complex nature of our engagement with the visual, and while every effort can be made to aim and produce a certain effect and calculate its impact, these efforts can only be successful to a certain extent (which perhaps gives hope in the age of limitless proliferation of imagery and advertising). Just as brand images get jammed in ways most unpredicted by global advertisement makers, the event of visual sense-making is much more complex than those following the Cartesian tradition might suggest. This is not to claim an absolute relativity of meaning. As Evans and Lawler note, 'each body-subject is a different perspective on the *same* world and hence one that holds out the promise of social and political unity without nullifying diversity' (2000: 8). So it seems that while a particular visual horizon can make different sense to those inhabiting it, those different perspectives form a 'total part', at one singular and universal, which becomes 'the expression *of every possible being*' (Merleau-Ponty, 1968: 218). If this paper managed to convey a sense of some of these possibilities, its goal has been achieved.

Acknowledgement

I would like to thank Dr Ian King from Essex Management Centre at the University of Essex and Dr Jonathan Vickery from the Centre for Cultural Policy studies at Warwick University for their very helpful comments on the earlier draft of this paper. I am also grateful to anonymous reviewers for their valuable suggestions. Any remaining deficiencies, however, are my sole responsibility.

Notes

1. Examples of how the English language is permeated with visual metaphors are available in Jay (1993: 1); Tyler (1984).
2. "Ils [les fruits] viennent à vous dans toutes leurs odeurs, vous parlent des champs qu'ils ont quittés, de la pluie qui les a nourris, des aurores qu'ils épiaient".

References

Bakhtin, M.M. (1986) *Speech Genres and Other Late Essays*, Vern W. McGee (trans.), Caryl Emerson and Michael Holquist (Eds) (Austin: University of Texas Press).

Barley, S.R. (1983) Semiotics and the study of occupational and organisational cultures, *Administrative Science Quarterly*, **28**, pp. 393–413.

Barthes, R. (1972) *Mythologies* (London: J. Cape).

Barthes, R. (1977) *Image – Music – Text* (London: Fontana Press).

Baxter, L.F. and Ritchie, J.M. (2004) The sensation of smell in researching a bakery: from the yummy to the abject. Paper presented at 22nd conference, Standing Conference on Organizational Symbolism, July 2004, Halifax, Canada.

Benedetti, M.T. (1995) *Paul Cézanne: sa vie, son œvre* (Paris: Gründ).

Berg, P.O. and Kreiner, K. (1992) Corporate architecture: turning physical settings into symbolic resources, in P. Gagliardi (Ed.) *Symbols and Artefacts: Views of Corporate Landscape* (New York: Aldine de Gruyter).

Berger, J. (1972) *Ways of Seeing* (based on the BBC television series with John Berger [and others]) (London: British Broadcasting Corporation).

Bone, P.F. and Ellen, P.S. (1999) Scents in the marketplace: explaining a fraction of olfaction, *Journal of Retailing*, **75**(2), pp. 243–262.

Brook, I. (2002) Experiencing interiors: ocularcentrism and Merleau-Ponty's redeeming of the role of vision, *Journal of the British Society for Phenomenology*, **33**(1), pp. 68–77.

Burgin, V. (Ed.) (1982) *Thinking Photography* (London: Macmillan).

Candlin, F. (2003) Blindness, art and exclusion in museums and galleries, *International Journal of Art and Design Education*, **22**(1), pp. 100–110.

Carpenter, E.S. and McLuhan, M. (1966) Acoustic space, in E.S. Carpenter and M. McLuhan (Eds) *Explorations in Communication* (Boston: Beacon Press).

Dale, K. (1997) Identity in a culture of dissection: body, self and knowledge, in K. Hetherington and R. Munro (Eds) *Ideas of Difference: Social Spaces and the Labour of Division* (Oxford: Blackwell), pp. 94–113.

Dale, K. (2001) *Anatomising Embodiment and Organisation Theory* (Basingstoke: Palgrave).

Danto, A. (1991) Description and the phenomenology of perception, in N. Bryson, M.A. Holly and K. Moxey (Eds) *Visual Theory: Painting and Interpretation* (Cambridge: Polity), pp. 201–216.

Descartes, R. (1637–1701/1954) *Philosophical Writings*, E. Anscombe and P.T. Geach (trans.) (Edinburgh: Nelson).

Descartes, R. (1637–1701/1985) *The Philosophical Writings of Descartes*, J. Cottingham, R. Stoothoff and D. Murdoch (trans.) (Cambridge: Cambridge University Press), volume 1.

Dillon, M.C. (1997) *Merleau-Ponty's Ontology* (Evanston, IL.: Northwestern University Press).

Evans, F. and Lawler, L. (2000) The value of flesh: Merleau-Ponty's philosophy and the modernism/postmodernism debate', in F. Evans and L. Lawler (Eds) *Chiasms: Merleau-Ponty's Notion of Flesh* (Albany, NY: State University of New York Press), pp. 1–22.

Frank, L.K. (1966) Tactile communication, in E.S. Carpenter and M. McLuhan (Eds) *Explorations in Communication* (Boston: Beacon Press).

Gendlin, E. (1992) The primacy of the body, not the primacy of perception, *Man and World*, **25**(3/4), pp. 341–353.

Goldman, R. (1992) *Reading Ads Socially* (London: Routledge).

Jay, M.(1993) *Downcast Eyes: The Denigration of Vision in Twentieth-Century French Thought* (Berkeley: University of California Press).

Jonas, H. (1966) The nobility of sight: a study into the phenomenology of senses, in H. Jonas (Ed.) *The Phenomenon of Life:Towards a Philosophical Biology* (NewYork: Harper and Row), 135–156.

Kavanagh, D. (2004) Ocularcentrism and its others: a framework for metatheorctical analysis, *Organization Studies*, **25**(3), pp. 445–464.

King, I. (2003) Laissé rêver une ligne: an exploration of the sinuosity of the line, working paper.

Lennie, I. (2000) Embodying management, in J. Hassard, R. Holliday and H. Willmott (Eds) *Body and Organization* (London: Sage), pp. 130–146.

Letiche, H. (2004) 'Talk' and 'Hermès', *Culture and Organization*, **10**(2), pp. 143–161.

Levin, D.M. (1993) *Modernity and the Hegemony of Vision* (Berkeley: University of California Press).

Lutz, C.A. and Collins, J.L. (1993) *Reading National Geographic* (Chicago: University of Chicago Press).

Mallin, S.B. (1989) Chiasm, line and art, in H. Pictcrsma (Ed.) *Merleau-Ponty: Critical Essays* (Washington, D.C.: Center for Advanced Research in Phenomenology), pp. 219–250.

Merleau-Ponty, M. (1964) *The Primacy of Perception* (Evanston: Northwestern University Press).

Merleau-Ponty, M. (1968) *The Visible and the Invisible* (Evanston: Northwestern University Press).

Merleau-Ponty, M. (1993a) Cézanne's doubt, in G.A. Johnson (Ed.) *The Merleau-Ponty Aesthetics Reader: Philosophy and Painting* (Evanston, IL: Northwestern University Press), pp. 59–75.

Merleau-Ponty, M. (1993b) Eye and mind, in G.A. Johnson (Ed.) *The Merleau-Ponty Aesthetics Reader: Philosophy and Painting* (Evanston, IL: Northwestern University Press), 121–149.

Millum, T. (1975) *Images of Woman: Advertising in Women's Magazines* (London: Chatto and Windus).

Pihlajamaki, K. (1990) The organisational sensory system, in B.A. Turner (Ed.) *Organisational Symbolism* (Berlin: de Gruyter), pp. 237–253.

Schapiro, M. (1996) *Words, Script, and Pictures: Semiotics of Visual Language* (New York: G. Braziller).

Shotter, J. (2002) *'Real Presences'* – The Creative Power of Dialogically-Structured, Living Expression. Available online at: http://pubpages.unh.edu/~jds/KCCoutline.htm (accessed 14 December 2003).

Shotter, J. (2005) 'Inside the moment of managing': Wittgenstein and the everyday dynamics of our expressive-responsive activities', *Organization Studies*, **26**(1), pp. 113–135.

Shotter, J. and Katz, A.M. (1996) *Articulating a Practice from Within the Practice Itself: Establishing Formative Dialogues by the Use of a 'Social Poetics'*. Available online at http://pubpages.unh.edu/~jds/Beinum1.htm (accessed 13 December 2003).

Silverman, H.J. (1987) *Inscriptions: Between Phenomenology and Structuralism* (New Cork: Routledge & Kegan Paul).

Taylor, S. (1989) Embodied agency, in H. Pietersma (Ed.) *Merleau-Ponty: Critical Essays* (Washington, D.C.: Center for Advanced Research in Phenomenology), pp. 1–21.

Tyler, S.A. (1984) The vision quest in the West, or what the mind's eye sees, *Journal of Anthropological Research*, **40**(1), pp. 23–39.

Waldenfels, B. (1998) Merleau-Ponty, in S. Critchley and W.R. Schroedcr (Eds) *A Companion to Continental Philosophy* (Maiden, MA: Blackwell), pp. 281–292.

Warren, S. (2002) Show me how it feels to work here: using photography to research organizational aesthetics. *Ephemera: Critical Dialogues on Organization*, 2(3), pp. 224–245. Available online at http://www.ephemeraweb.org (accessed 15 December 2003).

Williamson, J. (1978) *Decoding Advertisements: Ideology and Meaning in Advertising* (London: M. Boyars).

Chapter 14

Senses and sensibility in Byzantium

Liz James

THE MOSAIC OF THE VIRGIN AND CHILD in the apse of the church of Hagia Sophia in Istanbul, dedicated on 29 March 867, is positioned 30 m above the floor of the church (figure 14.1). The figure of the Virgin is more than 4 m tall, and that of the Child just less than 2 m.[1] The artist is unknown and the only names associated with the mosaic are those of the two emperors in whose reign it was put up and the patriarch Photios, who celebrated its unveiling with a homily.[2] The mosaic was the first monumental work of figural art to be installed in the most public church in the capital of the Byzantine empire after the end of the period known as Iconoclasm.[3] It is an image that has been approached in a variety of ways. It has been discussed in terms of its formal qualities of style and iconography; in terms of how it fits into the art-historical schema of the decorative programme of the Byzantine church; in terms of its social, cultural, theological and political history; and, most recently, in terms of its visuality.[4]

These are all methodologies practised within art history and they all share one underlying theme. They discuss the mosaic as a work of art, that is, as a conscious creation, something set apart and different, noted for certain formal qualities, and located within an historical and cultural context. Treating the mosaic as a work of art overlooks, partly through its focus on the purely visual, how this object functioned when it was not a 'work of art', a piece of 'high culture' in today's terms.[5] As such, the objects of Byzantine art have often been considered in isolation. An icon or a mosaic may be compared in iconographic, stylistic and functional terms to other icons or mosaics or art objects, but they are rarely considered in their wider physical settings. Even when the decorative schemata of churches are considered, they are perceived as just that: church ornamentation, where scenes are seen together as part of a common iconographical plan, conforming – or not – to certain rules and conditions. There is a widely accepted convention that medieval art is 'for' decoration, narration or

Fig. 14.1 The Virgin and Child mosaic, apse, Hagia Sophia, Istanbul. Dedicated 867. The traditional view. Photograph by Liz James.

education, and it was in this context that Otto Demus developed a concept of three hierarchized levels of church decoration: saints at the lower level; the life of Christ in the middle; and the Virgin, angels and Christ in heaven at the top. Demus's plan has continued to dominate ideas about the decorative programmes of Byzantine churches.[6] It is rare for scholars to relate the images in a church to each other in any other way and for the physical nature of the building as a whole to be considered.[7] Thus, within studies of the apse mosaic at Hagia Sophia, the Virgin has remained essentially detached, suspended alone in space, speaking only to her surroundings in terms of the three levels of church decoration or of Photios's homily on the image's inauguration. She is usually illustrated alone, in colour or in black and white, as she is here (figure 14.1).

The methodologies covered by the terms 'art history' and 'visual culture' alike privilege the visual nature of the things discussed, considering them in purely visual terms. This paper will side-step the squabble between art history and visual culture, which seems to be one essentially of terminology, and will take into account what happens when art, or the visual, is considered in its interactions with the other senses, and the ways in which art history might wish to exceed the visual. Rather than treat the apse mosaic as simply a work of art or a piece of visual culture, explicable only through its formal visual qualities, I will consider it as part of an installation set into and reacting with its physical location, and as an installation designed to appeal to all the senses. What was the purpose of the 'installation' and how did it move beyond the visual in order to manipulate the full range of the senses to disrupt the everyday world of ninth-century Byzantium?

In thinking about how Byzantine art functioned in ways beyond the purely visual, contemporary installations offer an odd but effective parallel. Contemporary installation art can be defined as constructions or assemblages conceived for specific interiors, or self-contained and unrelated to the gallery space. Either way, their interaction is with the space in which they are located, matching it or dislocating it.[8] They often physically dominate the entire space in which they take place. In addition, installations are rarely only visual. They bring together disparate objects and sensations, appealing not only to sight but to hearing, smell and even touch. They invite the viewer to enter the work of art, demanding the viewer's active engagement on a variety of levels, upsetting the modernist conception of the self-sufficiency of the art object in favour of a sense of the art object's dependence on contingent, external factors such as audience participation.[9] The spectator's share matters – and the spectator is asked to be more than a spectator. In Mona Hatoum's *Current Disturbance* (1996), for example, the fizz and crackle of the electric wires formed an intrinsic part of the installation; in Helen Chadwick's *Cacao* (1994), the spectator was overwhelmed with the smell of molten raw chocolate. Where one might argue that pure visuality and visual culture undermine the emotions in the reception of art, installations, by badgering all the senses, invite and even expect the emotional. Installation art offers an awareness of the significance of material objects located in space, potentially unsettling that space and gaining their effect not simply by what they offer in visual terms but also in their interaction with the viewer's senses and the viewer's experience.

These are all issues relevant to the study of the Byzantine church. A Byzantine church is a space that dominates the congregation; it is a space that appeals to all the senses; and it is a space that places the body and the body's relation to the spiritual at the centre of its display. In the ways in which religious services and their ritual actions were constructed, the viewer, or member of the congregation, was not able to remain a passive, isolated spectator but was compelled to engage with what was going on, with the church itself and with other worshippers. In the Byzantine church, the total sensory programme disturbs the world in an unexpected fashion, for it seeks to reveal God to man. The art historian is confronted with a paradox within Byzantine art, that of the use of the material and sensual to achieve the spiritual, a placing of the body at the centre of religious experience, whilst attempting to transcend the body through the use of the senses. It is a paradox embedded within the visual that the visual alone cannot convey.

As Jonathan Rée has suggested, sight does not stand alone, for people relate to the world through a single sense organ, the body, in which all the senses are united.[10]

Sight is only one means of apprehending the world and only one dimension in which images may operate. It is the traditions of Western philosophical thinking about the senses, based on Plato and Aristotle, that have placed sight and then hearing as the most significant and spiritual of the senses, relating them to the higher functions of the mind, and which have relegated smell, touch and taste to the lower functions of the body, considering them base and corporeal.[11] As a result, smell, touch and taste are the senses least considered in an historical context, yet all three are senses that make a difference in relating to the visual.

Inside a Byzantine church, inside Hagia Sophia, around the image of the Virgin and Child, things smelt and people smelt.[12] Apart from damp and bodies, burning candles and oil lamps provided their own aromas. Incense and perfumes, burnt in censers and in oil lamps, formed an intrinsic part of any church service; even very small churches had their own incense burners. Incense was an appropriate gift to offer at the shrines of saints. When praying for a child, the mother-to-be of St Symeon Stylites the Younger filled a censer with incense so that the whole church was filled with its strong perfume.[13] The early Christian theologian Clement of Alexandria stated that some fragrances were good for the health. However, smell, considered as one of the baser senses, could also be problematic. Clement was neither the first nor the last to raise the spectre of the effeminate charm and unmanly softness of perfume, and John Chrysostom, who believed in subduing the passions through controlling the senses, also denounced smell as dangerous.[14]

Smells did not simply offer physical sensations. Clement also suggested that perfumes could have an allegorical meaning, one that conveyed the fragrance of Christ's divine nature, and many authors described pleasant scents as creating an impression of the sweet aroma of Paradise. God could make his presence known through smell. The eighth-century patriarch Germanos, who, in his work on the divine liturgy, sought to show how 'the church is an earthly heaven in which the super-celestial God dwells and walks about', said that 'the censer denotes sweet joy' and that 'the sweet-smelling smoke reveals the fragrance of the Holy Spirit.'[15] Sight was of no real use in apprehending the Holy Spirit, the invisible member of the Trinity, so its presence in Byzantine images was signalled by symbols: a dove, a ray of light, even real light itself; its presence in worship was indicated by the sweet smell of incense.[16] A recurring imagery of prayers as the incense of the faithful also underlines the significance of smell within religious worship.

The odour of sanctity, the divine scent that infused right-living Christians, was not so much a feature of Byzantine writings as it was in the medieval West. Nevertheless, there are still cases of the righteous smelling good as a sign of their virtue. St Polycarp was said to have given off a 'fragrant odour as of the fumes of frankincense' when he was burnt at the stake.[17] Some saints had it both ways. St Symeon Stylites the Elder, whose smell was such that no one could bear to share a cell with him and who described himself as a 'stinking dog' (a claim that seems both literal and metaphorical), nonetheless expired in an odour of sweetness. His corpse emitted a 'scented perfume which, from its sweet smell, made one's heart merry'.[18] Where saints might stink to emphasize their rejection of sensual earthly luxuries (like baths) and their transcending of worldly values in pursuit of the divine, others might smell bad as a sign of the depravity of their lives. Several villains of

Christianity, including King Herod, died in the stench of corruption, their bodies eaten by worms. The eighth-century Byzantine emperor Constantine V was accused by his enemies of having defecated in the baptism font as a baby, 'a terrible and evil-smelling sign' that foretold the evils of his reign.[19] Smells thus carried a spiritual dimension and could reveal inner truths that were otherwise hidden: the good saint, the evil emperor.

What role taste played for the Byzantines within the church building is difficult now to detect; compared to the other four senses, references to sensations of taste are infrequent. Part of the issue may lie in the links made in Late Antiquity and afterwards between taste and gluttony, one of the major sins. The fourth-century church father Gregory of Nyssa, for example, described taste as the 'mother of all vice'.[20] Nevertheless, within Byzantine writings, there is a recurrent motif of sweet speech and of words tasting as sweet as honey. Although there is some discussion of the taste of the Eucharist in Byzantium, there does not appear to be the same emphasis as there was in the later medieval West.[21] In these discussions, however, the taste of the Eucharist is seen as offering an access to deeper spiritual truths.[22]

Touch, however, was a key element in the experience of any Byzantine worshipper. Sensations of touch are immediately apparent on entering a Byzantine church today as the cool air inside strikes the body. Touch was also an active sense as worshippers engaged on a physical level with objects within a church. Worshippers kissed doors, columns, relics and, above all, icons. They made gestures with the whole body: bowing, kneeling, prostrating themselves. Touch enabled the congregation to show love and respect for the holy.[23] Icons were 'cult objects', to be handled and venerated.[24] Such practices continue within Orthodoxy. At the exhibition, *Treasures of Mount Athos*, in Thessaloniki in 1997, several of the most venerated icons in Orthodoxy were publicly exhibited for the first time.[25] Many visitors to the exhibition were observed crossing themselves in front of the icons, praying in front of them and even kissing the glass of the exhibition cases. The objects were not regarded as 'works of art' displayed to be admired at a distance for their formal qualities; they were powerful vehicles of the holy.

Touch was a crucial means of assuring oneself of the reality of spiritual truths. The New Testament is full of stories of people touching Christ, culminating in that of doubting Thomas, who needed to put his hand into Christ's wounds to be assured that Christ had risen. The eighth-century Byzantine theologian and Iconophile Theodore the Studite noted how the godhead in the incarnate Christ was comprehended through both sight and touch. A range of Byzantine saints performed their miracles through touch. St Artemios, the patron saint of genital injuries, would appear in visions to the afflicted and heal them through painfully squeezing their diseased testicles or cutting his way through flesh and muscle.[26] John Chrysostom held his icon of St Paul whilst reading aloud Paul's epistles, as if contact with the saint served as the medium through which the believer and God could interact. St Daniel the Stylite was physically defrosted by his followers. Relics were kissed, touched and even gnawed away by the faithful.[27] One of the most significant of all holy images, the Mandylion of Edessa, was formed not through painting but through touch. It was an *acheiropoietas* image, an image not made by human hands, but one that had been created when Christ washed his face and, in drying it on a cloth, left the imprint of his features on it. As the cloth touched other objects, so the image replicated itself still further.[28] Touch, like smell and even taste, could be employed to cross the boundaries between the holy and the human. It was a sense that the Byzantine worshipper expected to deploy.

Within the church, besides the rustles of the congregation, there was the singing and hypnotic chanting of the liturgy, responses and counter-responses from the congregation, the reading and preaching of the word of God.[29] It has been suggested that parts of homilies were designed almost like miniature playlets, with dialogues and dramatizations in which the preacher took different parts, playing off one voice against another.[30] Inside a building like Hagia Sophia, or, indeed, any other church, it is possible to guess at the acoustics of the building. Domes, semi-domes and vaults probably provided different echoes which could have been employed during religious services.[31] Hearing is not simply about understanding words that made sense but also taking in words as musical sounds. In a culture that valued rhetoric, the sound of the speech must have mattered as well as the significance of the words.

Seeing the images in a church appears to have afforded an intensely pleasurable experience in which, beyond the iconography of a scene, the colour and the light effects were regularly emphasized.[32] Often Byzantine churches are thought of as dark and gloomy, yet many were full of light. Church architecture reveals a use of external light that alters as the time of day or year changes, and can be potentially different for each service. The very space itself is altered.[33] Churches were decorated with light-reflective materials: mosaics and wall-paintings, gleaming marble, metalwork, textiles and icons; and lit by flickering candles and oil lamps. Mosaics above all, made of thousands upon thousands of glass tesserae, all acting as little mirrors, formed one vast reflective surface which glinted and sparkled as light played across it. Offsetting the tesserae of a mosaic changed the spatial relations around the mosaic and encouraged a sense of movement. It could also change the appearance of an image. In the apse of Hagia Sophia, the Virgin's robe alters in colour as the light moves around it. That the Byzantines themselves valued and enjoyed their art for these qualities of dazzle and polychromacity is clear in surviving written sources from the fourth century to the fourteenth. Time and again, writings about being in church reveal a sensuous pleasure in light and in the dizzying interplay of reflections of light. 'The roof is compacted of gilded tesserae from which a stream of golden rays pours abundantly and strikes men's eyes with irresistible force. It is as if one were gazing at the midday sun in spring when it gilds each mountain top' is how one sixth-century author described Hagia Sophia.[34]

As with the other senses, so too with sight there was a dimension beyond the physical. Correct sight allowed one to see with spiritual vision. St Theodore of Sykeon, unlike those around him, was able to see that the silver of the vessel bought for communion was in reality blackened and tarnished, thanks to the metal having previously been used as a prostitute's chamber pot.[35] Saints, the Virgin and even Christ might be seen through visions.[36] Light itself carried a spiritual dimension. The eyes were regarded as the lamps of the body; churches were said to shine with radiant spiritual light; dead saints not only smelt good but also glowed with light; light was often a precursor of divinity and of miracles. This is reiterated in verbal imagery. At the Transfiguration, Christ was revealed as 'an earthly body shining forth divine radiance, a mortal body the source of the glory of the Godhead'.[37] Thus the actual visible play of light within a church carried meaning on a spiritual level.

The senses did not act in isolation. They interacted in creating a sensory effect. Hearing and taste, for example, might be linked. Theodore of Sykeon tasted sweetness in hearing the Scriptures.[38] Sight was understood not as a disembodied sense but as a tactile one: vision was believed to work through intromission or extra-mission, but both involved contact between the eye and the thing seen. Once sight is conceived of as tangible, then one's view of the world changes.[39] One touches the world, grasps it, carries it back to the mind. Touching an icon becomes a form of seeing and vice versa. Sight and hearing were frequently conjoined: 'Just as words speak to the ear, so the image speaks to the sight; it brings us understanding.'[40] The effect of combining the experiences of all the senses could be overwhelming. Photios wrote that entering the church of the Virgin of the Pharos was

> as if one had entered heaven itself . . . and was illuminated by the beauty in all forms shining around like so many stars, so is one utterly amazed. Thenceforth it seems that everything is in ecstatic motion and the church itself is circling around. For the spectator, through his whirling about in all directions and being constantly astir, which he is forced to experience by the variegated spectacle on all sides, imagines that his personal condition is transferred to the object.[41]

It is apparent that pleasurable sensory experiences related to all five senses were allowed and even encouraged within a Byzantine religious context and that experiencing the church was portrayed as a sensory, corporeal experience, underlining the bodily dimension to seeing.[42]

The eighth- to ninth-century period known as Iconoclasm in Byzantine history marks a point when the East Christian world was affected by a dispute over the role and function of images in religious worship. This clash was perhaps the most wide-ranging and disruptive quarrel ever about pictures, lasting for over a century and affecting the entire Byzantine Empire. The results of its final resolution in 843 are still present in Orthodoxy today, in the presence and use of images in religious devotion. This dispute about the place of images in religious worship came down, in many ways, to a debate over the primacy of sight or hearing in apprehending the divine: whether seeing the image or hearing the Bible was the better or more valid route to God. The major Iconophile theologian John of Damascus, writing in the eighth century, was clear about this: 'We use all our senses to produce worthy images of [God] and we sanctify the noblest of the senses which is sight.'[43] Hearing was more dubious. The late eighth-century Iconophile patriarch Nikephoros summed it up when he said that 'Often what the mind has not grasped while listening to speech, sight seizes without risk of error, and has interpreted more clearly.'[44] Speech could lie and be deceitful; chatter could be vain and foolish; vision, it seems, was less easy to deceive. Although the Seventh Ecumenical Council of 787, which affirmed the Iconophile triumph, appeared to equate the two when it declared that 'that which the narrative declares in writing is the same as that which the icon (or image) does', in reality, it was sight that came out on top.[45] Patriarch Nikephoros summed up this victory: '[words] enter hearing, for first the sounds of the things spoken encounter those listening, then, second, the listener achieves understanding of the given facts through analogy' but '[painting] directly and immediately leads the minds of the viewers to the facts themselves, as if they were present already, and from the first sight and encounter, a clear and perfect knowledge of these is gained.'[46] Words mattered but understanding through sound came second and through analogy; with vision, the facts were clearly visible and needed no mediation. Nevertheless, both sight and hearing interacted in the overall comprehension of the image; the visual did not act alone.

This composite picture of the senses serves to locate the apse mosaic of the Virgin and Child at Hagia Sophia as a part of a wider sensory experience, one involving all five senses. The mosaic is set in a church, above the altar, and is thereby a focal point of religious services (figure 14.2). The church itself is a vast space, with a great central nave crowned by an immense dome, the largest dome in Christendom until St Peter's.

Fig. 14.2 Hagia Sophia, Istanbul, interior looking east towards the apse and the mosaic of the Virgin and Child. Photograph by Liz James.

It is a space that is sensory. Sounds echo and reverberate, are caught and lost in the maze of domes and semi-domes, vaults and high walls; light flickers and changes; it is cool; it smells. The mosaic of the Virgin and Child is installed within a vast surround of gold mosaic that, in the Byzantine period, seems to have stretched unbroken, apart from a handful of figural scenes, throughout the church at the level of the springing of the galleries. It is accompanied on either side by two archangels, each almost 5 m tall, evoking the heavenly court.[47] The building was used for religious services, for processions involving emperor, court and patriarch, services celebrating all the great Christian and imperial festivals, full of lights, candles, incense, gold and silver ware, jewelled and embroidered textiles and icons. Although the mosaic of the Virgin and Child appears unchanging, it is not. Its appearance changes as the light changes in the church – daily and throughout the year. Beyond the visual aspect, the significance and impact of the image on its audience also altered with the perceptions and memories of that audience.[48] The senses provided access to a double reality, one both physical and spiritual. The mosaic did not exist only to be looked at; rather, the interplay of the five senses around the object opened its audience to a fuller perception of its meaning and purpose.

Photios's homily on the inauguration of the apse mosaic embodies this concept of its installation. This homily was delivered in Hagia Sophia from a pulpit close to the mosaic. It celebrates the triumph of the Iconophiles over the Iconoclasts and the restoration of both Orthodoxy and imagery in Hagia Sophia.[49] Its purpose was to engage its audience with the image of the Virgin and to convey to them the theological truths that this image revealed. To achieve this, Photios needed to persuade his audience to see the image not with physical vision but with spiritual, or even conceptual, vision.[50] His homily drew his audience to look at the apse mosaic not in terms of what they could see but in terms of what their sight might lead them to apprehend. The image in itself was not mysterious. Any Byzantine viewer who could see it would have immediately identified it as the Virgin and Child. What it meant, however, was a different matter. Photios did not describe the mosaic. Instead, he told his audience that what was there in the apse was:

> A virgin mother carrying in her pure arms, for the common salvation of our kind, the common Creator reclining as an infant – that great and ineffable mystery . . . A virgin mother with both a virgin's and a mother's gaze, dividing in indivisible form her temperament between both capacities yet belittling neither by its incompleteness. With such exactitude has the art of painting, which is a reflection of inspiration from above, set up a lifelike imitation. For she fondly turns her eyes upon her begotten child in the affection of her heart . . . You might think her not incapable of speaking . . . To such an extent have the lips been made flesh by the colours that they appear merely to be pressed together and stilled as in the mysteries, yet their silence is not at all inert neither is the fairness of her form derivatory but rather it is the real archetype.[51]

Photios talks of the Virgin mother carrying her child, but from the perspective not of aesthetics but of salvation. He reports the lifelikeness of the image, that 'you might think her not incapable of speaking'; thus viewers might expect both to see her and to hear her. Her lips have been made flesh; the fairness of her form is not derivatory but the real original. It is as if she were alive. Such a view has caused consternation among art historians for, to eyes accustomed to classical and Renaissance 'lifelikeness', there is little alive about this mosaic.[52] This misses Photios's point. For him, 'lifelikeness' is not an aesthetic judgement; it is a conceptual necessity. As the first monumental figural representation placed in the most important church in Byzantium after the end of Iconoclasm, the mosaic needed to reflect the triumph of the Iconophiles.[53] Installed as she is in Hagia Sophia at this point in Byzantine history, and at this moment in the Byzantines' definition of the nature of images, the Virgin must appear lifelike. Photios's speech echoes Nikephoros and John of Damascus about the crucial role of religious images in revealing religious truths, the fundamental paradox of Byzantine religious art that man could depict God truthfully and accurately through base materials. For an image to be a true image, it had to resemble the archetype, or model; it had to be lifelike. That the Virgin existed here in Hagia Sophia in this lifelike form with the Christ Child on her lap was proof positive of the Incarnation of Christ and hence of the truth of the Christian message.[54] To enable his audience to see this, Photios had to make it possible for them to use their earthly senses to see further than the visual surface of the mosaic. He had to explain to them the facts (the reality of the Incarnation and the existence of the image) through analogy (the image and the lifelikeness of the image), so that they could 'look at things with the eyes of sense and understand them with the eyes of the spirit'.[55] Important, though, was the concept that it was the eyes of the body that led to the eyes of the spirit. In the context of the homily, Photios's audience was invited to use its senses to go beyond the sensual. The overall environment of the church facilitated this engagement.

Each of the five senses had a role to play in achieving this transformation of the material 'installation' of the church into heaven upon earth. It was the evocation called up by all the senses that broke the world apart in a way that looking alone could not. In part, this was achieved through a conditioned awareness of the bridge that the senses provided between the physical and the spiritual: everyone 'knew' that the smell of incense indicated holiness, that touching an icon was touching a saint, that the image of Christ meant that Christ was there.[56] This is an area where cultural memories, which can work in the context of all five senses, were triggered.[57] Art as a part of the whole sensory continuum allowed the believer to pass beyond the physical realm to the spiritual: the role of the human senses was to reveal spiritual truths that might otherwise be hidden.

In this context of the senses, there was another paradox: the use of the material and sensual to achieve the spiritual, a placing of the body at the centre of religious experience, whilst attempting to transcend the body through the use of the senses. This seems to contradict Western philosophical thinking about the body's subservience to the spirit. Instead, the senses breached the boundaries of both 'culture' and materiality. One of the fundamental issues in the Iconoclastic dispute was whether base materials could convey divinity: was the work of art as a material object able to portray the holy and non-material? For the Iconoclasts, this was impossible but after the triumph of the Iconophiles, who believed that the material could convey the divine, material objects that now would be defined as 'art' – mosaics, for example – became 'not art' so that they could function as gateways to the divine. That the image of the Virgin is life-like', can 'speak', is the 'real archetype', actually moves her one step further away from the material world. That the image might be real would make the Virgin flesh and blood and divine, all at once, like the child she holds, and this is the crux of the paradox of Byzantine art.[58] For the Byzantine believer, the existence of the mosaic of the Virgin disturbed the religious space by promising to make the divine real.

In this way, the appeal to and the response of the senses formed a crucial part of the Byzantines' engagement with their images.[59] By using all the senses, the worshipper – who was viewer, listener, smeller, toucher, taster, all at once – was transported into a visionary world beyond objects, to the point where the onto-logical differences between the artist's imitations and their objects was erased: there was no boundary between the object and the living body, between the physical realm and the spiritual. To put this another way, we might follow Edward Casey, who, drawing on Merleau-Ponty, suggests that to be in a place is to know, to be aware of one's consciousness and sensuous presence in the world. For Casey, place is a fusion of self, space and time, which might be one means of articulating the Byzantine worshipper's ideal state.[60] In 988 the envoys of Vladimir of Kiev reported on the Hagia Sophia experience. As angels seemed to descend from the mosaics to join in the celebration of the liturgy, 'we knew not whether we were in heaven or on earth. For on earth there is no such splendour or such beauty and we are at a loss how to describe it. We only know that God dwells there among men.'[61] If, as Rée proposes, art exists to challenge and disturb our shared engagement with reality, then Byzantine art intended to do this as spectacularly as possible for its audience. It was the senses that allowed the worshipper to make contact with God, crossing the gap between the sensible and the in-sensible. John of Damascus explained it thus: 'If we sometimes understand forms by using our minds, but other times from what we see, then it is through these two ways that we are brought to understanding. It is the same with the other senses; after we have smelled or tasted or touched, we combine our experience with reason and thus come to knowledge.'[62] Art's installation in the sensory and spatial allows the viewer to cross between this world and the next. Visuality was only one part of this experience, visual culture only a part of the story, and the mosaic only partly to be categorized as something called 'art' and thus belonging to art's history. To the Byzantine viewer, the incorporeal God himself could be known through all the senses. As John of Damascus wrote, 'When we speak of the holy and eternal Trinity, we use the images of the sun, light, and burning rays [sight]; or a running fountain or an overflowing river [sound]; or the mind, speech and spirit within us [hearing]; or a rose tree, a flower and a sweet fragrance [smell].'[63]

Notes

My thanks to Michelle O'Malley, the editors of *Art History*, and to seminar audiences at the University of Sussex and at the Lawrence Seminar in Cambridge for their contributions and insights. Where English translations of original written sources exist, I have cited these; otherwise, references are to the Greek texts. *PG* = J.P. Migne, ed., *Patrologia Cursus Completus. Series Graeca*, Paris, 1857–66.

1   For the dimensions and a description of the mosaic, see Cyril Mango and Ernest J.W. Hawkins, 'The apse mosaics of St Sophia at Istanbul, Report on work carried out in 1964', *Dumbarton Oaks Papers*, 19, 1965, 115–51 and pls 1–56.
2   The emperors are Michael III and Basil I. The Greek text of Photios's homily, *Homily 17*, on the mosaic is published in Basil Laourda, ed., *Photios, Homilies*, Thessaloniki, 1959 and trans. Cyril Mango in Cyril Mango, *The Homilies of Photios, Patriarch of Constantinople: Translation and Commentary*, Harvard, 1958, 286–96.
3   There is a vast literature on Byzantine Iconoclasm. Alexander Kazhdan et al., eds, *The Oxford Dictionary of Byzantium*, Oxford, 1991, 'Iconoclasm' gives a brief and easily accessible potted history and useful references; see also Leslie Brubaker and John Haldon, *Byzantium in the Iconoclast Era (c.680–850)*, Aldershot, 2001; John Haldon, *Byzantium in the Seventh Century*, Cambridge, 1990, esp. 405–424; A.A.M. Bryer and Judith Herrin, eds, *Iconoclasm*, Birmingham, 1977; Peter Brown, 'A Dark Age crisis: aspects of the Iconoclastic controversy', *English Historical Review*, 88 (1973), 1–34.
4   From an extensive bibliography on the mosaic, Mango and Hawkins, 'The apse mosaics', describes it fully in terms of style and iconography, and dates it; Robin Cormack, 'Interpreting the mosaics of St Sophia at Istanbul', *Art History*, 4:1, March 1981, 131–49, esp. 135–8, and Robin Cormack, *Writing in Gold*, London, 1985, chap. 4, set it within its social, religious and political contexts; Robert S. Nelson, 'To say and to see: ekphrasis and vision in Byzantium', in Robert S. Nelson, ed., *Visuality before and beyond the Renaissance*, Cambridge, 2000, 143–68, discusses visuality in the context of the mosaic.
5   On the problem of 'giving objects back to the Middle Ages', see Robert S. Nelson, 'The discourse of icons, then and now', *Art History*, 12:2, June 1989, 144–57.
6   Otto Demus, *Byzantine Mosaic Decoration*, Oxford, 1948.
7   An important exception to this is Thomas F. Mathews, 'The sequel to Nicaea II in Byzantine church decoration', *Perkins Journal*, 41, 1988, 11–21. For a wider approach to icons, see Robin Cormack, *Painting the Soul. Icons, Death Masks and Shrouds*, London, 1997.
8   Robert Storr, *Dislocations*, MOMA, New York, 1992. Deborah Cherry, 'Contemporary Art and the Senses', inaugural lecture, University of Sussex, 2002.
9   Discussed by Andrew Benjamin, 'Matter and meaning: on installations', in *Installation Art, Art and Design*, London, 1993, 31–3.
10 Jonathan Rée, 'The aesthetic theory of the arts', in Peter Osborne, ed., *From an Aesthetic Point of View. Philosophy, Art and the Senses*, London, 2000, 57–70, esp. 64.
11 For Plato and Aristotle on the senses a good introduction is Richard Sorabji, 'Aristotle on demarcating the five senses', in Richard Sorabji et al., eds, *Articles on Aristotle*, vol. 4, Psychology and Ethics, London, 1997, 134–65. As yet, relatively little work has been done on how the Byzantine conception of the senses related to classical philosophy, and how closely the Byzantines might have followed Aristotle and Plato.
12 For smell in Byzantium, see Béatrice Caseau, 'Christian bodies: the senses and early Byzantine Christianity', in Liz James, ed., *Desire and Denial in Byzantium*, Aldershot, 1999, 101–110; Susan Ashbrook Harvey, 'St Ephrem and the scent of salvation', *Journal of Theological Studies* 49, 1998, 109–128. A more general study is Constance

Classen, David Howes, Anthony Synnott, *Aroma. A Cultural History of Smell*, London, 1994.

13 Paul van den Ven, ed. and trans., *La vie ancienne de Symeon Stylites le jeune*, 2 vols, Brussels, 1962–70. A whole variety of written sources mention the use of perfumes in these contexts: see Caseau, 'Christian bodies'.

14 Clement of Alexandria, *Paedogogus*, trans. S. W. Wood, *The Instructor*, New York, 1953; John Chrysostom, *On Vainglory and the Education of Children*, trans. in M. L. W. Laistner, *Christianity and Pagan Culture in the Later Roman Empire*, Cornell, 1967.

15 Germanos, *On the Divine Liturgy*, 1,2; 30. Parallel Greek and English texts in John Meyendorff, *St Germanus of Constantinople, On the Divine Liturgy*, New York, 1984.

16 For the Holy Spirit as light, see, for example, the ninth-century *Life* of Ioannikios by the monk Peter, chap. 35, trans. in Alice-Mary Talbot, ed., *Byzantine Defenders of Images. Eight Saints' Lives in English Translation*, Washington, DC, 1998, 315.

17 Eusebius, History *of the Church*, chaps 15 and trans. 40, G. A. Williamson, *Eusebius. The History of the Church*, London, 1965, reprinted many times.

18 Antonius, *Life of Symeon Stylites*, chaps 8 and 29 (English trans. Robert Doran, *The Lives of Symeon Stylites*, Kalamazoo, 1982).

19 Theophanes, *Chronographia*, Anno Mundi 6211; trans. Cyril Mango and Roger Scott, *The Chronicle of Theophanes Confessor. Byzantine and Near Eastern History AD 284–813*, Oxford, 1997.

20 Gregory of Nyssa, *De Virginitate*, chap. 21, *PG* 46, col. 401C.

21 See Caroline Walker Bynum, *Holy Feast and Holy East. The Religious Significance of Food to Medieval Women*, Berkeley, 1987.

22 Georgias Frank, '"Taste and see"; the Eucharist and the eyes of faith in the fourth century', *Church History*, 70:4, December 2001, 619–43.

23 For something of why and when people did this, see Mathews, 'The sequel to Nicaea II'; also Nelson, 'Discourse of icons', 154–5 on kissing manuscripts. More generally on touch, see Georgia Frank, *The Memory of the Eyes*, Berkeley, 2000.

24 This is the distinction made by Hans Belting, *Likeness and Presence. A History of Images before the Era of Art*, Chicago, 1994.

25 Athanasios A. Karakatsanis, ed., *Treasures of Mount Athos*, exhib. cat., Thessaloniki, 1997.

26 In the miracles of St Artemios, touch and smell played a big part. Several of the stories describe how the afflicted person in their sleep or in a vision felt the saint squeezing their testicles and smelt an intolerable odour of blood and pus, after which they were healed. See Virgil S. Crisafulli and John W. Nesbitt, eds, *The Miracles of St Artemios*, Leiden, 1997, for example Miracles 13, 29, 35.

27 Significantly, the story of Chrysostom and the icon of St Paul is told by the great defender of icons, John of Damascus, *On the Divine Images* 1, Commentary, trans. David Anderson, *St John of Damascus on the Divine Images*, New York, 1980, 46; see also the comments in Nelson, 'Discourse of icons', 148–9. Daniel the Stylite, *Life of Daniel the Stylite*, chap. 43, trans. Elizabeth Dawes and Norman H. Baynes, *Three Byzantine Saints*, Oxford, 1948. Egeria describes pilgrims taking bites out of the True Cross in the fourth century, *Itinerarium Egeriae*, 37.3, trans. John Wilkinson, *Egeria's Travels to the Holy Land*, Jerusalem and Warminster, 1981.

28 For the Mandylion, see Averil Cameron, 'The history of the image of Edessa: the telling of a story', in Cyril Mango and Omeljan Pritsak, eds, *Okeanos, Studies presented to Ihor Ševčenko*, Cambridge, Mass., 1984, 80–94; and Herbert Kessler and Gerhard Wolf, eds, *The Holy Face and the Paradox of Representation*, Milan, 1998.

29 Egon Wellesz, *A History of Byzantine Music and Hymnography*, Oxford, 1961.

30 See the remarks in Pauline Allen, Cornelis Datema, *Leontius, Presbyter of Constantinople. Fourteen Homilies*, Brisbane, 1991, 14–16.

31 A contemporary parallel is offered by the choir of York Minster which has a two-second echo. I am grateful to Dorothy Scruton for this information.

32 See Liz James, *Light and Colour in Byzantine Art*, Oxford, 1996; Rico Franses, 'When all that is gold does not glitter: on the strange history of looking at Byzantine art', in Antony Eastmond and Liz James, eds, *Icon and Word. The Power of Images in Byzantium*, Ashgate, 2003, 13–24.

33 Andrjez Piotrowski, 'Architecture and the Iconoclast Controversy', in B.A. Hanawalt and M. Kobialka, eds, *Medieval Practices of Space*, Minnesota, 2000, 101–121 looks at this in the context of light in Hosios Loukas; Nadine Schibille, 'Light and the Architecture of Hagia Sophia', unpublished PhD thesis, University of Sussex, 2004, explores the changing nature of light in Hagia Sophia. Also, in a different temporal context, Michael Baxandall, *The Limewood Sculptors of Renaissance Germany*, New Haven and London, 1980, 172ff. and 189ff. (my thanks to Nigel Llewellyn for this reference).

34 Paul the Silentary, *Ekphrasis*, Paul Friedländer, ed., *Johannes von Gaza und Paulus Silentarius*, Leipzig, 1912, lines 668–72. These lines are translated in Cyril Mango, *The Art of the Byzantine Empire*, Toronto, 1972, 86.

35 *Life* of Theodore of Sykeon, chap. 42, trans. Dawes and Baynes, *Three Byzantine Saints*.

36 Visions appear in almost every saint's life, almost certainly in all those cited in this article. To cite just one example, see Crysafuli and Nesbitt, *St Artemios*, chaps 15, 16, 18.

37 John of Damascus, *Homily on the Transfiguration*, 2, 35, *PG* 94, 1003C. On this theme, see Andrew Louth, *St John Damascene*, Oxford, 2002, 324–43.

38 *Life* of Theodore, chap. 13. How far this is a literal or a metaphorical synaesthesia is unclear. Christoph Catrein, *Vertauschte Sinne. Untersuchungen zur Synästhesie in der römischen Dichtung*, Munich and Leipzig, 2003, is almost the only place where synaesthesia has been considered in the context of classical studies.

39 On theories of vision and how they affected the Byzantines' perception of the world, see Nelson, 'To say and to see'. For these aspects in the medieval West, see Suzanne Biernoff, *Sight and Embodiment in the Middle Ages: Ocular Desires*, Palgrave, 2002.

40 John of Damascus, *On the Divine Images 1*, 17; *De Fide Orthodoxa*, 2, 18, *PG* 94, 933D–936A; a further conjoining of the two is apparent in Nikephoros, *Refutatio et Eversio*, fol. 273v, quoted in Paul J. Alexander, *Patriarch Nicephoros of Constantinople*, Oxford, 1958, 211 and n. 3, and in the Sixth Session of the Seventh Ecumenical Council, 220E–221A, trans. in Daniel J. Sahas, *Icon and Logos. Sources in Eighth-Century Iconoclasm*, Toronto, 1986, 61.

41 Photios, *Homily 10*, 5, trans. from Mango, *Homilies of Photius*, 186.

42 Patricia Cox Miller has begun to explore how the aesthetically wrought media in which God was worshipped aroused the affective responses of their participants: i.e., shrines filled with mosaics, jewelled reliquaries, candlelit vigils, sermons, incense; sight; touch; hearing; smell; even taste. The sensory experience could unite the single bodies of worshippers into the corporeal body worshipping. Patricia Cox Miller, '"The little blue flower is red": relics and the poetizing of the body', *Journal of Early Christian Studies*, 8, 2000, 213–36.

43 John of Damascus, *On the Divine Images 1*, 17.

44 Nikephoros, *Antirrheticus*, 3, 3, *PG* 100, 380D–381A.

45 Sixth Session of the Seventh Ecumenical Council, 232C, Sahas, *Icon and Logos*, 69.

46 Nikephoros, *Antirrheticus*, 3, 3, *PG* 100, 381C–384B, and *Apologeticus*, 61, *PG* 100, 749–52.

47 On angels and the junctures between the heavenly and earthly courts, see Henry Maguire, 'The heavenly court' in Henry Maguire, ed., *Byzantine Court Culture from 829 to 1204*, Washington, DC, 1997, 247–58. In the same publication, see George Majeska, 'The emperor in his church: imperial ritual in the church of St Sophia', 1–12, for details of imperial ceremonies within the building.

48 What to Photios was new and revolutionary did not get a mention in a twelfth-century description of the church: Cyril Mango and John Parker, 'A twelfth-century description of St Sophia', *Dumbarton Oaks Papers*, 4, 1960, 233–45; and barely warrants a reference in the accounts of Russian pilgrims in the fourteenth and fifteenth centuries: George Majeska, *Russian Travellers to Constantinople in the Fourteenth and Fifteenth Centuries*, Washington, DC, 1984.

49 See the introduction by Mango, *Homilies of Photios*, 279–86, esp. 282–3.

50 For Byzantine rhetoric in this context, see Leslie Brubaker, 'Perception and conception: art, theory and culture in ninth-century Byzantium', *Word and Image*, 5, 1989, 19–32; Liz James and Ruth Webb, '"To understand ultimate things and enter secret places": ekphrasis and art in Byzantium', *Art History*, 14:1, March 1991, 3–17. For a definition of *ekphrasis*, see Ruth Webb, 'Ekphrasis ancient and modern: the invention of a genre', *Word & Image*, 15, 1999, 11–15. For a view that it was 'mere' rhetoric, see Beat Brenk, 'Discussion', in Eve Borsook, Fiorella Gioffredi Superbi and Giovanni Pagliarulo, eds, *Medieval Mosaics. Light, Color, Materials*, Milan, 2000, 180.

51 Photios, *Homily*, 17, 2; translation from Mango, *Homilies of Photios*, 290.

52 There has been a genuine debate about whether or not the apse mosaic in Hagia Sophia was the apse mosaic described by Photios because his account of it was seemingly so inaccurate: he claimed the Virgin is standing and she is clearly seated; he said she looks lifelike and to eyes accustomed to seeing in ways conditioned by classical and Renaissance art, she is clearly not. Thus Nikolas Oikonomides, 'Some remarks on the apse mosaic of St Sophia', *Dumbarton Oaks Papers*, 39, 1985, 111–12. The archaeology of the mosaic refutes this argument: see Mango and Hawkins, 'The apse mosaics of St Sophia', 142–8.

53 From a vast bibliography, two good introductory papers to Iconoclasm and the theory of images, are G.B. Ladner, The concept of the image in the Greek Fathers and the Byzantine Iconoclast controversy', *Dumbarton Oaks Papers*, 7, 1953, 1–34; and Leslie Barnard, 'The theology of images', in Bryer and Herrin, eds, *Iconoclasm*, 7–14.

54 For Byzantine faith, see Mary Cunningham, *Faith in the Byzantine World*, Oxford, 2002. For rhetorical strategies for turning listeners into spectators and enabling them to see with spiritual eyes, see Ruth Webb, 'Imagination and the arousal of the emotions in Greco-Roman rhetoric', in S.M. Braund and C. Gill, eds, *The Passions in Roman Thought and Literature*, Cambridge, 1997, 112–27, and James and Webb, 'Ekphrasis and art'.

55 The phrase is that of Nikolaos Mesarites, 'Description of the Church of the Holy Apostles in Constantinople', chap. 12 (text, trans. and commentary by Glanville Downey, *Transactions of the American Philosophical Society N.S.*, 47:6, 1957, 855–924.); see also James and Webb, 'Ekphrasis and art'. On these ideas in an early Christian context, see Frank, 'Eucharist and eyes of faith', who discusses the fourth-century

debate between the physical and spiritual senses that resulted in both having a part to play.

56   'Conditioned' is a gesture towards Foucault and geographies of struggle and resistance. Certainly, Christianity was the dominant ideology in the Byzantine empire and it can be read as a tool through which the masses were kept under control (Walter Benjamin's portrayal of religion as ritual rather than belief). Nevertheless, it was also an ideology that the rulers believed in and a crucial difference between it and twentieth-century ideologies is that Christianity offered eternal life to its devotees, so rulers and ruled had an investment to get it right as well – if anything, the ultimate oppressor was God.

57   There is a considerable body of work on geographies of sense and place, dating back to trends in humanistic geography in the 1970s. See, for example, Yi-Fu Tuan, *Topophilia*, New York, 1974; John Eyles, *Senses of Place*, Warrington, 1985; and the reworking of the concept by Doreen Massey, 'Power-geometry and a progressive sense of place', in Jon Bird et al., eds, *Mapping the Futures: Local Cultures, Global Change*, London, 1992, 59–69. For archaeologies of the senses, see Yannis Hamilakis et al., eds, *Thinking through the Body*, London, 2001. I am grateful to Yannis Hamilakis for sending me a copy of his paper 'Material culture, the senses and sensory memory', read at the Lawrence Seminar, University of Cambridge, May 2003. For memory in the classical and Late Antique worlds, see Susan E. Alcock, *Archaeologies of the Greek Past*, Cambridge, 2002; Frank, *Memory of the Eyes*.

58   For this concept, see James and Webb, 'Ekphrasis and art', 11–13; Ruth Webb, 'The aesthetics of sacred space: narrative, metaphor and motion in *ekphrasis* of church buildings', *Dumbarton Oaks Papers*, 53, 1999, 69; and Nelson, 'Discourse of icons', on the links between the image and the beholder.

59   Here, Hal Foster's remarks about a contemporary shift from a vertical to a horizontal conception of art are interesting. Foster suggested that in a vertical conception of art, the artist investigates the disciplinary depths of a given genre or medium, whereas, in a horizontal conception, art activity is conceived of as a terrain on which different areas of discourse are brought together. This is precisely what the mosaic appears to have done. 'The artist as ethnographer', in Hal Foster, *The Return of the Real*, Cambridge, Mass., 1996, esp. 199–202.

60   Edward S. Casey, 'How to get from space to place in a fairly short stretch of time', in Steven Feld and Keith H. Basso, eds, *Senses of Place*, New Mexico, 1996, 13–52. Another issue here is the church as both place of exile and as home within the context of Christian belief.

61   Described in the *Russian Primary Chronicle*, Samuel H. Cross and Olgerd Sherbowitz-Wetzor, *The Russian Primary Chronicle: Laurentian Text*, Cambridge, Mass., 1953, 110–11.

62   John of Damascus, *On the Divine Images*, 3, 24.

63   John of Damascus, *On the Divine Images*, 1, 11, and again at *On the Divine Images*, 3, 21.

Chapter 15

Disaffected

Anna Gibbs

ACROSS THE DISCIPLINES, FROM MUSIC THERAPY in medicine to Martha Nussbaum's (2001) study of the emotions as a form of ethical intelligence, interest in 'the emotions' is at a new high. In Cultural Studies, 'affect' seems to be emerging as a key term in the wake of expressed feminist desires to think 'through the body'. But what is meant by the 'emotions' in other disciplines and by 'affect' in Cultural Studies is somewhat variable, and there exist different usages (consonant with different theoretical positions and having quite different theoretical and political implications) for the term 'affect' itself. It has been thought on the one hand – and most famously – as that which is lost or missing: Jameson's phrase the 'waning of affect' refers to the loss of cultural authority (including the authority of authorship) rather than simply to emotion or feeling, or to affect as it has been thought by various biologies (Jameson, 1991, p. 10). The site of either mourning or occasionally its obverse, celebration, this loss represents instead a kind of disaffection which manifests either in alienation and indifference, or anomie and nostalgia. On the other hand, and arguably more radically, affect in Cultural Studies has been taken up (especially by Brian Massumi) in the Deleuzian/Spinozist sense of capacity or force (Massumi, 1993), in keeping with the need to which Foucault long ago pointed, to think beyond the horizon of anthropomorphism: for Deleuze, affects are precisely what offer opportunities for becomings through which bodies may be remade.

What these uses of the term 'affect' share, however, is a certain distance from affect in its biological sense. This paper instead sets out to start to rethink the role of innate or categorical affect in human communication and, more specifically, to point to some ways in which such a rethinking might make possible a new approach to media studies.[1] Such a project, which implies of necessity a re-engagement with certain clinical and scientific disciplines (especially biology, neurobiology and neuropsychology as well as with certain psychotherapies), seems unhappily at odds with a Cultural Studies generally more given to textualizing, representational modes of thinking communication — and this in spite of the important role cybernetics played in the development of a semiotics of communication by writers such as Anthony Wilden, even as he was constructing a critique of scientific discourse as 'propaganda' (Wilden, 1972, p. 413). In fact, as Eve Kosofsky Sedgwick and Adam Frank (1995) argue in their introduction of the affect theory of American psychologist Silvan Tomkins (1962–1992) to the field of Cultural Studies, the biological per se (with its erstwhile connotations of political fixity, for example of gender) has long been exiled from the Humanities as a whole by the anti-essentialist project of denaturalization that sought to reveal the operations of social and cultural construction which everywhere turned nature into second nature. Sedgwick and Frank, diagnosing in advance the reasons for the lack of uptake of Tomkins' work in Cultural Studies, argue that it poses a major challenge to the fundamental premises of the various poststructuralisms (feminist, psychoanalytic, philosophical and new historical, for example) which comprise contemporary critical theory (Sedgwick and Frank, 1995, p. 1). However, while Elizabeth A. Wilson unhesitatingly takes up the challenge of this analysis and the methodological example set by Sedgwick and Frank in the introduction to her *Neural Geographies: Feminism and the Microstructure of Cognition* (1998), little other feminist work since has sought to address the implications of their critique of the founding exclusions of contemporary theory.

Here I wish simply to point — as Wilson has also done (Wilson, 1996) — to the apparent perversity of the wholesale rejection of the biological in the face of the recent (especially feminist) concern with the body in Cultural Studies. In the event, it seems that the body has been conceived in this field largely as a body of words, the sum of discourses about it. Perhaps this is not altogether surprising when one considers the prevalence of textual models (and the role of English Departments) in the development of Cultural Studies generally. Moreover the long dominance, especially in mainstream psychology, of cognitivism and behaviourism, and the concomitant empiricism and even scientism of so much work in this field, as well as the dominance of linguistic models in places, such as psychoanalytic thought, that might have provided a challenge to this, has meant that there has been little inducement for feminist Cultural Studies to reconsider either questions of nature and human nature or the question of whether 'essentialism' was too simple a concept in the first place, especially given the complexity of relations between nature and culture as they are now thought, at least, in some disciplines outside the Humanities.

As the work of writers like Oyama (1995) and Varela *et al.* (1993) points out, it is now not so much a question of trying to work out what is nature and what second nature, but rather to see that the question of nature versus nurture is an artificial one, once we recognize that the human organism and its environments are 'mutually unfolded and enfolded structures' (Varela *et al.*, 1993, p. 199). The biological body, then, may mark a constraining, but not determining, limit on the nature of the human. Biologist Humberto Maturana (sometime collaborator of Varela) has argued that it is 'the configuration of [what he calls] "emotioning" that we live as Homo sapiens [which] specifies our human identity' rather than our cognitive capacity, rationality or technology (Maturana, 1997). To understand this may, as he argues, enable us to approach questions of human communication, technology and the media in quite new ways.

Maturana does not use the term affect, but recent work in the fields of neurology, infant research, and attachment studies and clinical psychotherapy have all converged on it. Of germinal importance here is the evolutionary perspective of Darwin in *The Expression of Emotion in Man and Animals* (Darwin, 1998). It is on the basis of Darwin's work that the major affect theorist of our time, American psychologist Silvan Tomkins (1962–1992), identifies nine discrete human affects, each with its own neurological profile and distinct pattern of physiological response. Recent clinical research has affirmed that affective experience, especially the capacity to use differentiated affects as feedback to the self, plays the major role in the organization of self-experience, in creating intersubjective relatedness and a shareable inner universe. In fact, infant researcher Daniel Stern (1985) has framed affect as the 'supramodal currency' which translates between all other modalities of infant perception and cognition: intensities, shapes, temporal patterns, 'vitality affects', and hedonic tones. This process of translation is what initially enables experience to be ordered into familiar patterns, including the formation of 'affective scripts' designed to manage punishing negative affect and maximize rewarding positive affect (Tomkins, 1962). The resulting emergent constellations of experience operate outside of awareness but form an experiential matrix which is the source of ongoing affective responses to and constructions of the world. In translating, in other words, affect *organizes*, both intra- and inter-corporeally, and is crucial to social responsiveness.

The attachment system, which means that children will stay close to their parents who can provide physical protection, which was identified by Bowlby (1969, 1973) in the 1960s and 1970s,[2] may in fact have been hijacked for the purposes of affect regulation, as Peter Fonagy (2001) suggests, since mutual regulation on the part of parent and child is crucial to the child's survival (in as much as it solicits and sustains parental responsiveness) and to the development of a relatively stable self structure and of the social responsiveness facilitated by this. It is now recognized within neuropsychology that the process of mutual affective regulation, while it relies on innate human capacities, also actively shapes the brain itself, inaugurating a complex feedback process between body and environment – a process Maturana and Varela (1992, pp. 75–80) would term 'structural coupling' – part of the process of 'unfolding and enfolding'.

For Tomkins, affects are the primary human motivational system, amplifying the drives and lending them urgency, since the drives on their own are relatively weak motivators. Moreover, unlike the drives, affects are '*general* motivating responses capable of powering *any* type of response, cognitive, perceptual or motor' (Tomkins, n.d.). Each of the nine discrete innate affects[3] has its own specific gradient of neural firing and therefore a precise and chartable relation to other affects (e.g. enjoyment–joy as the reduction of interest–excitement, shame as the attenuation of enjoyment or interest). This is distinct from other theories which see affect as undifferentiated except by social elaboration (e.g. the James–Lange theory) and which are therefore unable to account in precise ways for the particular 'affective economy' of the individual. Here I think that to date, leaving aside the work of Brian Massumi (1993) and more recently the work of Elspeth Probyn (2000), the Humanities as a whole have also been handicapped by a refusal to consider affect as anything more than culturally constructed 'feelings' and 'emotions' substantially divorced from the materiality of the body. By contrast, Tomkins' work provides a detailed account of the inherence of affect in the body, of its evolutionary importance as a motivational system, and of different modes of socialization of the innate affects as well as an account of the results of particular forms of socialization on a wide variety of areas of social and cultural life as well as on individual affective economies.

Of particular potential importance to Cultural Studies is his account of affect contagion. Because affects (with the exception of surprise–startle) are innate activators of themselves (fear makes the hair stand on end which produces more fear via physiological feedback), and because affects are communicated rapidly through facial expression, affect is also contagious between people, and in fact this characteristic of contagion

> is critical for the social responsiveness of any organism. It is only when the joy of the other activates joy in the self, fear of the other activates fear within, anger of the other activates anger within, excitement of the other activates one's own excitement that we may speak of an animal as a social animal. It is now known that the distress cries of animals taped and reproduced over a loud speaker are capable of evacuating from a small town all animals of that species. In such a case it is a matter of indifference *who* is emitting a distress cry so long as it is heard (Tomkins, 1962, pp. 296–297).

It may even be that social contagion precedes self-contagion: that

> the phenomenon of contagion within the organism is an indirect consequence of the similarity of one's own responses to social activators. Since it is known that the smile of the face of another is a specific activator of the smile of the one who sees it, the awareness of the smile in the self may release another smile either on the basis of the similarity of the smile in the visual and the smile in the proprioceptive modality, or on a learned basis, since one's own smile was often preceded by the smile of another (Tomkins, 1962, p. 297).

More broadly, affect contagion falls within the domain of 'sympathetic communication'. Sympathetic modes of communication involve form-sharing, especially sharing of movement and affect, and they not only persist alongside linguistic modes, but inhabit and actively shape them. These are not rudimentary, infantile, or so-called 'primitive' modes of communication: rather, they are the essential prerequisites for, and accompaniments of, verbal communication. Trevarthen, following Bateson (1975), terms them 'proto-language' (Trevarthen, 1990). This is to say that they are not noise in the system: they are (part and parcel of) the system. Indeed, sympathetic or mimetic knowledge may be the earliest form of knowledge of both self and other, as recent infant research seems to indicate.

It is in this broad context, then, that we might begin to think about the means by which biological capacities for affective response, mimetic communication and cross-modalization are co-opted in and by the cultural world and to formulate a new view of the relationship between media and audiences. Here we might seek to say what a theory of the discrete innate affects can actually contribute to our understanding of feedback (amplification, magnification and contagion) processes between human bodies and various communicational media, including text. Central to such a project would be Virginia Nightingale's conception of the media as non-anthropomorphic cyborgs which function by co-opting aspects of the human in a series of 'transitory appropriations':

> These electronic chimeras borrow human qualities by enticing humans into their flowing. They cathect human bodies to provide them with energy; they amass human bodies to command power. Without human service these cyborgs cease to exist; they evaporate almost without trace (Nightingale, 1999, p. 228).

I would want to argue – as I have elsewhere in relation to a particular instance (Gibbs, 2001) – that what is co-opted by the media is primarily affect, and that the media function as amplifiers and modulators of affect which is transmitted by the human face and voice, and also by music and other forms of sound, and also by the image. Moreover, the media inaugurate and orchestrate affective sequences (for example, startle–terror–distress–anger, in the recent 'Attack on America' and the subsequent 'War on Terror'). While for neurophysiological reasons certain affects may be more likely to have a sequential relation to some affects rather than others (anger is more likely to follow shame than joy), affects are also socialized in ways particular to historical period, cultural and social setting, as well as to unique family organizations which mean that individuals will develop characteristic affect profiles. Such profiles refer to the range of affects available to any one person, and to the band of intensity within which such affects are characteristically experienced (for example: whether one knows one is angry, or whether this knowledge is too dangerous to be admitted to awareness; whether anger is only ever able to be experienced as irritation, or whether it escalates rapidly and uncontrollably to overwhelming rage). Affect sequences are thus the characteristic ways in which one responds to particular affects with other affects – for one individual it might be shameful to be angry, while for another it might be exciting.

Tomkins uses the term 'magnification' to refer to the process by which an affect is given salience across an increasing range of contexts. Importantly, he informs us, 'magnification refers *equally* to the individual and social construction of [any given affect]. It is therefore a process which must be understood in terms of both socialization and individualization' (Tomkins, 1990, p. 511). Moreover, 'the socialization of affect is not independent of either the ideology of the larger society or the events of international relations'. But nor, he says, 'are these interrelationships . . . simple, readily demonstrable, or unchanging' (Tomkins, 1990, p. 511).

In this optic, it seems to me, media and bodies appear as vectors, and affect itself as the primary communicational medium for the circulation of ideas, attitudes and prescriptions for action among them. Here I would want to draw on work in the field of somatics to begin to elaborate the linkages, often automatic and outside awareness, between affects, attitudes, ideas and action. The work of Feldenkrais (1949), among many others (including practitioners of yoga), points to the ways in which physical and affective processes are inextricably intertwined such that a physical posture may call up an affect, and vice versa. This body of work also suggests that affective states experienced in particular contexts call up the unconscious beliefs and characterological dispositions or attitudes familiar to them. After all, as Feldenkrais realized early on, and psychoanalysis and infant research both reiterate, we learn 'to speak, to walk, to adjust [ourselves] to [our] parents, and to other members of [our] society all at once' (Feldenkrais, 1949, p. 99). It is in this context that we develop what in the clinical field has been called 'emotional memory' (Orange, 1995, p. 105). Emotional memory differs from representational memory in that it is not subject to conscious recall. It manifests in dreams, moods, in various forms of somatization, and in habitual actions and reactions (Orange, 1995, p. 105). In fact it comprises the majority of all memory, forming the relatively stable pattern of ideo-affective schemata that constitutes the self. In Tomkins' terms, this represents an informational compression necessary because consciousness is 'a limited channel' (Tomkins, 1992, p. 287).

Such compression compacts affective, sensory and so-called cognitive forms of knowledge, and this prompts a rethinking of just what is meant by cognition at all. Tomkins insists on the complexity of what he calls 'the cognitive system', given the importance in it of sensory and motor modes of knowledge which not only 'operate outside consciousness and permit consciousness to restrict itself to other objects of knowledge', but which – in the case of sensory knowledge – give rise to a plethora of different kinds of knowledge, beyond the different senses: drive, affect and muscle sensations, as well as the proprioceptive sense (Tomkins, 1992, p. 16). In elaborating on the different kinds of knowing produced by these various functions, Tomkins makes clear that they (the forms) are all integral to the cognitive system which would include all of the above and he suggests that cognition has been at once too narrowly defined and too easily imagined as an independent 'high command mechanism' which would assess and arbitrate other ways of knowing. Instead, he argues against the existence of a separate cognitive mechanism at all, and for 'a more democratic system with no special mechanism completely in charge or, if in charge, able to endure as a stable mechanism' (Tomkins, 1992, p. 17). What results from this picture is a 'distributed authority' that makes cognition 'as elusive to define as the "power" in a democratic form of government or the "meaning" in a sentence' (Tomkins, 1992, p. 17).

(Perhaps this is easier to grasp if we remember that the octopus, which has no cortex, has instead a sensory intelligence in each of its arms that enables it to learn how to unscrew a jar to retrieve food in less than thirty seconds, a task which would take a monkey thirty days. As this example perhaps also suggests, the implications of such a reframing of cognition would be to put paid to any idea of an evolutionary hierarchy that places Man at the top of the tree.)

At the limit, then, Tomkins makes clear that there can be no 'pure cognition', no cognition uncontaminated by the richness of sensate experience, including affective experience. His work produces an extraordinarily rich phenomenology via a seemingly endless stream of examples of different combinations of scene (the basic unit of affective salience), script (strategy for affect management), and socialization. Over and over again he shows how, from a few simple parameters, something immensely complex is generated and simultaneously maintained and transformed. In this respect, Tomkins' modelling of affective scenarios approaches a practical working out of a dynamic systems theory of affective transmission.

Central to the idea of system is feedback. What this implies is that the nature of the relation between people and media is one of complex imbrication between individuals, texts and institutions, such that the electronic media (for example) are no longer necessarily the point of origin or cause of 'effects', but simply a vector in a larger process which we might term, following Massumi, 'effects and their interweavings': in other words, 'syndromes' (Massumi, 1993, p. 31). Syndromes may not be predictable nor fully analysable, as Massumi suggests; however, they are open to local interventions. Here, perhaps, there is an explicit political role to be played by a hitherto disaffected Cultural Studies which has, in recent years, seemed increasingly unable to intervene in any domain except itself.

Notes

1   This work forms part of the project of the Affect-Image-Media Research Group of the University of Western Sydney, and I would like to thank Maria Angel and Virginia Nightingale, members of the group, for a number of very helpful discussions of what is presented here.
2   This concept was rejected by feminism in the 1970s for the anti-feminist arguments it might have sustained at a time when women were seeking the right to full-time paid employment in the face of prevalent feeling that their place was in the home, occupied with childcare, and by classical psychoanalysis for its concerns with a world beyond 'psychic reality'.
3   The nine affects are Interest–Excitement, Enjoyment–Joy, Surprise–Startle, Distress–Anguish, Shame–Humiliation, Contempt–Disgust, Anger–Rage, Fear–Terror, and Dissmell.

References

Bateson, M. C. (1975) Mother–infant exchanges: the epigenesis of conversational interaction, in D. Aaronson and R. W. Reiber (eds), *Developmental Psycholinguistics and Communication Disorders* (Annals of the New York Academy of Sciences), vol. 263. New York: New York Academy of Science, pp. 101–113.

Bowlby, John (1969) *Attachment and Loss*. Vol. 1: *Attachment*. London: Hogarth Press and the Institute of Psycho-Analysis.

Bowlby, John (1973) *Attachment and Loss*. Vol. 2: *Separation: Anxiety and Anger*. London: Hogarth Press and the Institute for Psycho-Analysis.

Darwin, Charles (1998) *The Expression of Emotion in Man and Animals*. London: HarperCollins.

Feldenkrais, Moshe (1949) *Body and Mature Behaviour: a Study of Anxiety, Sex, Gravitation and Learning*. Madison, CT: International Universities Press.

Fonagy, Peter (2001) Training Workshop in the Coding of Reflective Function from Attachment Narratives at the NSW Institute of Psychiatry, July.

Gibbs, Anna (2001) Contagious feelings: Pauline Hanson and the epidemiology of affect, *The Australian Humanities Review*, http://www.australianhumanitiesreview.org/AHR/archive/Issue-September-2001/gibbs.html

Jameson, Fredric (1991) *Postmodernism, Or, The Cultural Logic of Late Capitalism*. London and New York: Verso.

Massumi, Brian (1993) Everywhere you want to be: introduction to fear, in Brian Massumi (ed.), *The Politics of Everyday Fear*. Minneapolis and London: University of Minnesota Press.

Maturana, Humberto (1997) Metadesign, http://www.inteco.cl/articulos/metadesign.htm

Maturana, Humberto and Francisco Varela (1992) *The Tree of Knowledge: the Biological Roots of Human Understanding*, Boston and London: Shambala.

Nightingale, Virginia (1999) Are media cyborgs? in Angel Gordo-Lopez and Ian Parker (eds), *Cyberpsychology*. London: Macmillan.

Nussbaum, Martha (2001) *Upheavals of Thought: the Intelligence of the Emotions*. London: Cambridge University Press.

Orange, Donna (1995) *Emotional Understanding: Studies in Psychoanalytic Epistemology*. New York: Guilford Press.

Oyama, Susan (1995) *The Ontogeny of Information*. Cambridge: Cambridge University Press.

Probyn, Elspeth (2000) *Carnal Appetites: Food, Sex, Identities*. New York and London: Routledge.

Sedgwick, Eve Kosofsky and Adam Frank (1995) Shame in the cybernetic fold: reading Silvan Tomkins, in Eve Kosofsky Sedgewick and Adam Frank (eds), *Shame and its Sisters: a Silvan Tomkins Reader*, Durham, NC and London: Duke University Press.

Stern, Daniel (1985) *The Interpersonal World of the Infant*. New York: Basic Books.

Tomkins, Silvan S. (1962–1992) *Affect, Imagery, Consciousness*, 4 vols. New York: Springer.

Tomkins, Silvan S. (n.d.) Letter to Heidi Sigal. The Silvan Tomkins Papers, M694, History of Psychology Archives, University of Akron, Ohio.

Trevarthen, Colwyn (1990) Signs before speech, in Thomas A. Sebeok and Jean Umiker-Sebeok (eds), *The Semiotic Web*. Berlin: de Gruyter, pp. 689–755.

Varela, F., E. Thompson and E. Rosch (1993) *The Embodied Mind: Cognitive Science and Human Experience*. Cambridge, MA: MIT Press.

Wilden, Anthony (1972) *System and Structure Essays in Communication and Exchange*. London: Tavistock Publishing.

Wilson, Elizabeth A. (1996) Projects for a scientific psychology: Freud, Derrida and connectionist theories of cognition, *Differences: A Journal of Feminist Cultural Studies* 8 (3), pp. 21–52.

Wilson, Elizabeth A. (1998) *Neural Geographies: Feminism and the Microstructure of Cognition*. New York and London: Routledge.

Chapter 16

The state of wonder

Peter de Bolla

THE STATE OF WONDER IS MORE hospitable than awe, which has the capacity to trouble or disturb us, and it is less engrossing than rapture, which seems to swallow up all sense of self. Wonder has a residue of comfort or safety, a bolt-hole for when things get too far away from the possibility of understanding. It is distinct from surprise, which may nevertheless often accompany a sense of wonder, act as a prompt or prelude to it. The big difference here is that I can remain *in* wonder, be in it, whereas the structural formation of surprise requires that the feeling die away almost as soon as it comes upon me. Wonder has an identifiable architecture; it comprises a variety of rooms we inhabit, moving from fascination and curiosity through admiration toward, at the lowest levels below ground, as it were, stupor or stupefaction. That is when wonder runs out, when all the energy of the spell-binding has been exhausted.

Surprise is a frequent component of my affective responses to art, but if my experience of the work stays with this response I quickly lose interest: surprise often fails to be converted into something more compelling, like wonder. This is why artworks that shock, whether or not their authors consciously set out to provoke such a reaction, provide us with weak *aesthetic* experiences: we are brought up short, confronted with something new and for which we are unprepared, but sooner or later (and very often simply sooner) we find it very easy to accommodate the new and to render the force of the shock unremarkable. Furthermore, by and large the more shocking something is initially the faster and more facile the accommodation becomes. Wordsworth had a good phrase for that which takes a little longer; he called it the "shock of mild surprise," and the milder the surprise, generally speaking, the more enduring the shock. Artworks that court this sensation are generally less compelling or interesting to me than those that may begin by surprising me but end up leading me into something else, say, amazement. Much contemporary visual art has the capacity to shock in spades: many of the works in the Saatchi Collection displayed at the 1998 Royal Academy *Sensation* show would provide good examples – the sculptures produced by the Chapman brothers that distort the human body and displace the sexual organs come to mind – of how surprise quickly runs out of steam, loses its appeal, fades into the familiarity of being shocked. The interest of this show was severely diminished for me by the frequency of this structure of response in the face of many of the works displayed.

Adam Smith noted that surprise may lead to wonder if we find ourselves unable to reconcile the new with the familiar, but once again the milder the surprise the greater the propensity for difficulty in reconciliation. Wonder is an aesthetic state, it engrosses the mind only to lead it to a kind of distraction. Being in breathless wonder is a form of inattention. When I find myself in wonder I try to remain there, poised in this state, deliberately holding off the onset of expectation or the moment of release. I feel absorbed but unable to touch the source of that absorption, keenly aware, in a heightened state of perception yet at the same time lacking focus. It is almost as if my self lacks consistency, or precision. Being in wonder is a kind of contemplation without object, a suspension in attentive inattention; I am at the same time both completely absorbed and distracted. Such dumbfounderment may cause a sense of inadequacy in the face of the object that prompted the wonder, as if I am forced to recognize the limits of my perceptual powers. But this feeling is also often replaced by an intensification of self-presence. The state of wonder, then, may be both compelling and disabling at the same time: it leaves me wanting more but also slightly relieved when the moment has passed. I am certain that our fascination with great works of art derives from this push-me-pull-me state of knowing. We both want or seek out the mysterious powers of *aesthetic* contemplation and at the same time feel slightly apprehensive about what might be revealed in the moment of wonder. Or, to put it another way, we are certain that with time and effort (or sometimes just plain luck) we will be able to penetrate to the core of our cherished works of art but know that they are cherished to the extent that they will never, completely, give up what it is they know.

What makes *aesthetic* experience distinct from other forms of experience is its absolute divorce from the ordinary or everyday. Yet, in a strange way, the inattentiveness of the habitual is a correlate of affective experience; wonder is, as I have said, a kind of distraction. It also feels as if it comes, as it were, before knowledge, since, as Socrates remarked, the primary motivation of wonder is the recognition of ignorance. Wonder requires us to acknowledge what we do not know or may never know, to acknowledge the limits of knowledge. It is, then, a different species of knowledge, a way of knowing that does not lead to certainties or truths about the world or the way things are. It is a state of mind, of being with the world and oneself that, like being in love, colors all that we know we know. And that can, on occasion, certainly appear to be like thaumatology: the science or knowing, of wonders and miracles.

In conclusion a sculpture that was also shown in the *Sensation* show: Marc Quinn's *Self*. As noted, no other work moves me more than this compellingly beautiful cast made from the artist's own blood. I feel both the chill sense of an intellectualization in my response – this work is "about" mortality, making art in the age of AIDS, the futility of art's wager against time – and a more visceral, elemental sensation of being in the presence of beauty. Sometimes it feels as if tears, perhaps tears of blood, might be the only appropriate response to its cold majesty. As formally perfect as any sculpture, indeed as any work of art in any medium, it persists in time only on account of its electromechanical lifeline, the refrigeration unit that keeps the blood in a solid state. Even this technology is unable to prevent the head from "weathering," which, like the patina on a classical bronze sculpture, merely adds to the poignancy of the object.

But it is not the semantic content of the work that finally contains or produces the wonder of this art; it is its knowing fragility. I do not mean to point to the literal fragility of the object even though certain aspects of its materiality intrigue me, cue my curiosity. I want to touch the object, feel its temperature, smell the blood. I certainly feel a physical register to my response – almost as if the somatic responds in its own terms, on its own account. Hence at one moment I am keenly aware of the absence of skin and bone – as if the head in front of me has been flayed – while at another the pose of the artist seems to take on a set of resonances that idealize sculpture or casting the head as a form. In these moments I want to place *Self* in a history of sculpted and cast forms: I call to mind the craggy ruggedness of Giacometti's heads or the simple purity of shape and form I find in Gaudier Breszka's hieratic head, or Henry Moore's morphing of the human body into dazzling contour. When this happens the frozen blood seems to transmute into different material forms, into bronze or stone. And then I find myself wondering about the pose struck by the artist, if indeed it should properly be called a pose. Is this the cold but finally arid triumph of art, the ultimately unsuccessful wager against time: Shelley's "sneer of cold command"? Or is it resignation, equanimity in the face of that defeat, in the knowledge that at the end of time all one can do is accept, as gracefully as is humanly possible, the fact of solitude?

It sometimes feels as if this is the pose of prayer, and when this occurs a corresponding sense arises in me: the calm inward agitation associated with the activity of praying. But then again the pose seems lifeless, without the sustaining life-blood of percipience. It remains inert, frozen in front of me, both blind and dumb, a reminder of the dark interior secret of knowing otherwise, a stark outpost of the resistance to propositional knowledge: a monument to art's wonder.

But at the end of this itinerary I find dignity: facing up to the transient nature of being human. This work, in a profound way, teaches me the value of dignity, the slow but finally telling realization of the acceptance of solitude. And behind or alongside all this I sense fragility: this might be called the cognitive component of my *aesthetic* response. This helps me to understand why I am moved so powerfully by this sculpture: its state of fragility chimes so clearly with the vulnerability, the evanescence of art's wonder, the sense I have of knowing this for myself as only I can, yet feeling the pressure toward the habitation of a shared knowing. Here I feel familiar, on nodding terms at least, with the wonder that results from the acceptance of solitude, and I know this as deeply in the presence of *Self* as any other place art has led me.

Chapter 17

Sensory exile in the field

Sandra H. Dudley

A S AN ANTHROPOLOGIST IN THE FIELD, I too experienced a form of displacement, albeit a voluntary one. Intriguingly, sensory and sensual components of such an exile are still surprisingly little addressed (a notable and excellent exception being Stoller 1989). Yet when one begins to recall experiences in the field, it is often if not always a *sense* of it — tastes, sounds, bodily sensations, smells, and of course sights — that comes to mind first. And if we pause to reflect upon that often fleeting sensory recall before moving swiftly on — as we usually do — to cogitate, analyse and write, the specifics of what is recollected are somehow *felt* again, albeit this time within the imagination rather than literally within the feet or the mouth or other appropriate part of the body. As I have written this book, for example, inevitably I have thought a great deal about my own experience in the field — and if I pause to notice it, before I even begin self-consciously to reflect upon and theorise my field data, all my memories of refugee camp life are wrapped up in how it felt, for me, to be there.

It is of course crucial that my or any other researcher's own sensory matrices do not unconsciously structure those with which the subject community is imputed — just because, say, sound is of particular significance in an anthropologist's memories of his or her time in the field, it does not necessarily follow that it is of the same level of importance in how members of the community order and interpret their world. Interestingly, however, as I later outline it is for the Karenni, for me the sensual domain of eating is especially significant in my field recollections. Discussing his own experiences, Stoller has much to say about food, for example telling a tale about his own sensual disgust, provoked in the field by a deliberately badly cooked sauce (1989).

The sense of taste is, as Stoller demonstrates, important and complex in its own right, rich with cultural meanings. But eating is so much more of a multi-layered sensorial experience than one involving taste alone. My own field memories of food and its associations are at once immediate, powerful, frequently still strongly physical in manifestation and sometimes poignant. I still clearly recall – and actually, greedily, still salivate at – both the tastes and smells of fish paste and ground soya bean cakes cooked with chilli. These favourite food items of mine during my time in the camps, have lingered long in my sensorial memory vaults. But so too have the connected sensations of touch, bodily movement, and internal responses to the food: when I break down my memories of mealtimes in the camps, be they situated in my or another's house, I realise that as well as visual pictures in my mind of what the cooking and dining areas looked like, and in addition to recollections of tastes and smells, the other, still integral components of those memories involve the physical feelings of walking barefooted over the springy, uneven bamboo planks of the suspended floor to the low table, of sitting – sometimes slightly uncomfortably after a few minutes had passed – on the floor to eat, of feeling the pleasant breeze blowing gently through the house wall onto my face as I perspired from the heat of both the day and the chilli, of the wetness and different textures of the rice and sauces on my fingers and thumb as I tried to learn to eat with my hand, and of the warmth in my throat and stomach as the spicy food went down. All this has stayed in my memory and can be rekindled – and re*felt* – almost as if it were being directly experienced all over again. This would clearly be so even had I worked with a non-displaced group of people.

In research with refugees, however, there is a double exilic layer, with the subject community's displacement deepening the anthropologist's own exile in the field. Indeed, while sensory experience in the refugee camps was generally not so 'other' for the Karenni refugees as it was for me, we had some commonality in undergoing a kind of sensual exile from the familiar past. My situation was clearly incomparable with theirs – I had not experienced the horrors they had, and I could leave at any time – but none of us was really 'at home', including in the culinary terms that turned out to be of mutual importance.

But did my conceptualisation of exile have anything more in common with theirs? Or does such a comparison risk oversimplifying, even trivialising the refugee experience? The physical and conceptual journeying and the transcending of national, cultural and metaphorical boundaries that characterise anthropological fieldwork are well understood (see Gupta and Ferguson 1997). The anthropologist's 'strong trope of movement, of migrancy' (Wilding 2007: 334) arguably also has additional implications for anthropological interpretations of forced displacement; indeed, Wilding develops this theme in the related context of transnationalism (2007). She argues that the traditional ethnographic approach 'privilege[s] a certain worldview' and has had 'a problematic effect on the understandings that are developed about the lives of the people being researched' because the individual anthropologist's emphasis tends to reflect the researcher's own concerns and circumstances rather than necessarily those of the research subjects (2007: 332–3). Part of the problem, she suggests, is that the ethnographer is unable to escape the traditional conception of fieldwork in which 'the field' is a fixed, singular place, and thus they 'continue to seek to *place* their research' (ibid.: 336) while contradictorily and simultaneously focusing not on the places *per se* but on the migration of an idea, commodity or relationship (ibid.: 337). The researcher, in other words, according to Wilding remains unable ultimately to see the world in a way other than one still informed by their, rather than their informants', basic premises – and here, this means seeing culture as still emplaced, even when it is displaced and mobile, as it is for refugees and transnational migrants.

Yet this assessment of the researcher as unable to attain the right viewpoint upon displacement because of his or her own background in a rooted, emplaced world, is, I suggest, too simple – and ultimately, it risks failing to hear the voice of the displaced subject even more than the approach it critiques. Like Malkki's attempt to demolish the pertinence to refugees of the global framework of nation-states (1995), it ignores the extent to which the displaced themselves may still conceive of themselves within the terms of the framework being dismissed by the analyst. Refugees may be displaced, but they may nonetheless work hard to maintain conceptual, metaphorical and physical relationships with place, with the result that their experience is exilic but still somehow emplaced. That far at least, my own experience in the field is indeed analogous with the Karenni refugee experience.

Importantly too, the physical feelings of bodily sensations were for me as much as for the Karenni essentially inseparable from the other kind of 'feeling', which we commonly gloss as emotion and affective response. Indeed, when we remember a physical sensation we tend also to recall emotions associated with the same situation or action. In turn, these emotions are closely linked to values we attribute to them – in a broad sense, to an aesthetics of experience (cf. Coote 1992). This is true for my personal memories of field experiences; it is equally true of the experiences of refugees. Focusing and reflecting back upon the physical and emotional experiences, and aesthetics, of the subjects of research – upon their pains, pleasures and rationalisations thereof – enables 'a fuller view of *what is at stake* for people in everyday life' (Lutz and White 1986: 431; emphasis original). These interlinkages between the physical world, refugees' bodily senses, emotion, memory and aesthetics, underpin and run throughout this book [see original reading].

References

Coote, J., (1992) '"Marvels of everyday vision": the anthropology of aesthetics and cattle-keeping Nilotes', in J. Coote and A. Shelton (eds) *Anthropology, Art and Aesthetics*, Oxford: Clarendon, pp. 245–73.

Gupta, A. and J. Ferguson (eds) (1997) *Anthropological Locations: boundaries and grounds of a field science*, Berkeley (CA): University of California Press.

Lutz, C. and G. M. White (1986) 'The anthropology of emotions', *Annual Reviews in Anthropology*, 15: 405–36.

Malkki, L. H. (1995) *Purity and Exile: violence, memory, and national cosmology among Hutu refugees in Tanzania*, Chicago: University of Chicago Press.

Stoller, P. (1989) *The Taste of Ethnographic Things: the senses in anthropological perspective*, Philadelphia (PA): University of Pennsylvania Press.

Wilding, R. (2007) 'Transnational ethnographies and anthropological imaginings of migrancy', *Journal of Ethnic and Migration Studies*, 33 (2): 331–48.

Chapter 18

In the British Museum

Thomas Hardy

'What do you see in that time-touched stone,
    When nothing is there
But ashen blankness, although you give it
    A rigid stare?

'You look not quite as if you saw,
    But as if you heard,
Parting your lips, and treading softly
    As mouse or bird.

'It is only the base of a pillar, they'll tell you,
    That came to us
From a far old hill men used to name
    Areopagus.'

—'I know no art, and I only view
    A stone from a wall.
But I am thinking that stone has echoed
    The voice of Paul,

'Paul as he stood and preached beside it
    Facing the crowd,
A small gaunt figure with wasted features,
    Calling out loud

'Words that in all their intimate accents
    Pattered upon

That marble front, and were wide reflected,
 And then were gone.

'I'm a labouring man, and know but little,
 Or nothing at all;
But I can't help thinking that stone once echoed
 The voice of Paul.'

Contexts of experiencing objects

Introduction to Part III

Sandra H. Dudley

THE PREVIOUS PART OF THE BOOK looked at ways in which objects and their material characteristics are perceived, interpreted and experienced by human subjects, looking particularly at the senses, embodied experience and the emotions. This section continues the examination of sensory and emotional experience, but now with a special focus on the particular influence of where and when the experience occurs. A range of contexts of experience are explored, ranging from a historic house and the museum, through cross-cultural settings, to a decaying homestead and an outdoor heritage site. Questions are raised about the impact on experience of the restriction of some of the body's senses (as happens in most museum environments), the power and aura that objects can appear to have because of the emotional responses we may have to them, the relative importance of different sensory and other components of our experience, issues in trying to interpret and empathise with other people's experience, and the matter of authenticity.

The readings begin with Kim Christensen's discussion of the delicate – and variable – balance between ideas and things in interpretation in American historic house museums. She primarily discusses a museum-in-process, the Matilda Joslyn Gage House, but also reviews practices in relation to object use in a number of other historic house museums. Demonstrating the disadvantages of both an uncritical focus on objects and an attempt to leave objects behind and concentrate on ideas, she argues instead for allowing visitors to experience – and thereby come to understand – objects and associated meanings through engaging with their historically contemporary uses.

Lending a sense of continuity with the de Bolla chapter in the last part of the book, the second paper comprises Julie Marcus's discussion of the experience of wonder. In Marcus's case, the exploration concentrates on wonder in relation to the visual, to loss, to desire and to the poetic possibilities of the experience of objects – all specifically in a museum setting. Marcus thereby seeks to develop a poetics, and ultimately what she calls an 'erotics', of that museum experience. It is a reading which enables extensive reflection on the potential affective power of the museum object and gallery space.

A historical perspective and a sensory focus underpin the third chapter. Jan Geisbusch examines sight and touch in relation to religious relics, and the role of these sensory apprehensions on the development of Western notions of the sacred. In so doing, Geisbusch explores experience in the contexts of both museum and the Catholic reliquary, subtly considering the not only complementary but also competing linkages of the senses in human experience of the material world. Comparing the museum setting and sacred space, Geisbuch concludes that in both contexts touch, though often proscribed, is sometimes essential if the 'magic' of certain objects is truly to be 'met and experienced'.

In the following text, Jeremy Coote's exploration of the experience of objects in a traditional West African cultural context brings the focus to cross-cultural settings. He looks at engagement with objects, principally cattle and other objects connected with them in some way, particularly in relation to visual experience and the attribution of aesthetic value. In the process, he discusses the cross-cultural possibilities of the notion of aesthetics – can such a notion be applied cross-culturally at all? Others certainly also argue that it can, where aesthetics is defined in the broad, useful way in which Coote applies it here (see also, for example, Morphy 1992).

Celmara Pocock's paper follows on the last reading's consideration of the context-dependent attribution of aesthetic value to material objects, here exploring changes over time in the predominant forms of sensory experience of, and consequent aesthetic valuing of, the Great Barrier Reef. The article is helpful in exploring the multi-sensory and sensual components of aesthetics, the importance and subjectivity of aesthetic value, and the significance of place as the context of experience. It also examines such questions in relation to heritage preservation and interpretation – and the role of aesthetic value as a criterion in assessing heritage places. Pocock argues that current heritage management practice has not engaged with the literature on aesthetics and thus has a rigid and narrow view of sensory experience which mistakenly confines it to a certain class or culture and misses a whole spectrum of non-visual aesthetic appreciation. As a result, as she shows, there has unfortunately been a change in the landscape and a loss of value.

A new approach to conservation and interpretation is also called for in the next reading, although from a different perspective. Here, Caitlin DeSilvey's article explores material change and deterioration, reflecting on the experience of objects in the context of abandonment and decay. Based on the author's work on a deserted homestead in Montana, the chapter problematises conventional museum and heritage paradigms that emphasise the 'stasis and preservation' of the object. DeSilvey calls for an alternative approach she terms 'entropic heritage', focusing on material process and revealing the ultimate transience of physical things and 'the complexity of our entangled material memories'.

DeSilvey's article demands an honesty of approach in following the true life cycle of objects and materials. Truth of interpretation and authenticity in the object is also the concern of the next text in this third part of the book: Victoria Rovine's chapter on African textiles. This reading allows a focused problematising of the notion of 'authenticity', here entirely in relation to the material quality of texture and the ways in which it is experienced, as the textiles move through different global markets. It thus encourages reflection on the issue of shifting contexts, in relation to the very physicality of the objects.

In the last reading, Christina Kreps reflects on cultural context and differing notions of museum-mindedness, in particularly discussing her experience of preparations for an exhibition at Museum Balanga in Central Kalimantan, Indonesia. Her text raises fascinating and important questions about culturally constituted ideas about, responses to and experiences of objects – questions that have a bearing not only on issues of conservation and interpretation, but also on the very notion of for what and for whom museums, and museum objects, exist.

Reference

Morphy, H. 1992. 'Aesthetics in a cross-cultural perspective: some reflections on Native American basketry', *Journal of the Anthropological Society of Oxford* 23 (1): 1–16.

Chapter 19

Ideas versus things
The balancing act of interpreting historic house museums

Kim Christensen

Introduction

Historical house museums have a rich history within the United States, dating to mid-nineteenth-century efforts to save two sites associated with George Washington. In 1850, Hasbrouck House, Washington's Revolutionary War military headquarters in New York became the first historic residence preserved by state efforts and opened to the public. Likewise, Ann Pamela Cunningham's efforts to preserve Washington's Mount Vernon plantation as a public shrine to his memory, which began in 1853, were the first of their kind (Butler 2002). Both of these founding historic house museums were created with particular purposes in mind – to hearken back to the nation's founding and inspire patriotism during the tumultuous period leading up to the American Civil War (West 1999, Stahlgren and Stottman 2007). Since these early efforts to preserve houses associated with significant historical figures, historic house museums have become a commonplace feature of the American museum landscape. The use of these house museums has continued to be implicitly linked to concerns of the present, although these concerns themselves have necessarily shifted through time.

Over the past several decades, beliefs regarding the proper purpose of historic house museums have shifted toward a more explicit embrace of linking past issues with present-day concerns. As part of a larger emphasis on creating 'useable pasts' by public historians and museum professionals, historic house museums have come under criticism for their static, object-centred, apolitical, and idealised presentations of the past. This concern mirrors that within the historical archaeology profession, where calls for making explicit links between the past and present and using archaeological research for emancipatory or civic engagement purposes have become increasingly common (Shackel and Chambers 2004, Little 2007, McGuire 2008).

In this article, I reflect on my archaeological research undertaken at a fledgling historic house museum, the Matilda Joslyn Gage House in Fayetteville, New York, in terms of the tenuous balancing act between 'ideas' and 'things' necessitated by the desire to avoid replicating the features for which historic house museums have been critiqued. In particular, I will comment on how historic house museums have traditionally depicted the past, with special regard to issues of domesticity and women's lives. I compare and contrast the Gage House's proposed interpretive plan with other politically-minded house museums, and argue how material culture can be effectively used in bridging past and present for museum visitors without falling into the trap of a nostalgic, apolitical domesticity. Specifically, I demonstrate how mundane material culture – such as ceramic tea wares – can simultaneously be used to interpret family life, gendered Victorian practices, and radical political action.

The Matilda Joslyn Gage Foundation

The Matilda Joslyn Gage Foundation (hereafter the Foundation or the Gage Foundation) is a non-profit educational organisation created in 2000 dedicated 'not only to educating current and future generations about the lifelong work of this major women's rights thinker, author and activist, but also its power to drive contemporary social change' (Matilda Joslyn Gage Foundation, Inc. 2009). A large component of this effort is the Foundation's restoration of the Gage property to its 1880s appearance which began during the summer of 2009. My archaeological research on the property, undertaken between 2005 and 2008, was conducted prior to these restoration efforts in order to determine the presence and state of cultural deposits on the property for historic preservation purposes and to recover information on the household's daily practices. In the process, I excavated portions of a sheet midden extending from the kitchen door to the area immediately behind the house. The material culture assemblage recovered from these excavations provides a rich picture of the Gage household's material surroundings, as well as those of the occupants before and after the Gages.

While my archaeological research was conducted collaboratively with the input of the Gage Foundation, I found myself somewhat puzzled with regard to how I could advocate incorporating the material found archaeologically when it spoke primarily to the domestic context of the site – which was in contrast to the stated intention of the Gage Foundation to focus on Gage's ideas. As an archaeologist, my focus is on things – the stuff of everyday life, and what objects can tell us about past practices and beliefs. The Gage Foundation's emphasis – in contrast, has been on the concepts – the interpretive themes – to be showcased in the new museum. This emphasis on ideas rather than things stems largely from an aversion to replicating the typical historical house museum – the 'fussy, dusty' house interior full of period-correct furnishings that has little connection to concerns of the present day. Instead, the Gage Foundation seeks to create a historic house museum which, while utilising the domestic space of the Gage family, portrays the radical history of Matilda Joslyn Gage by emphasising the four major areas of social reform she was involved in – women's rights, abolition and the Underground Railroad, Native American sovereignty, and the separation of church and state – and by making links to the current manifestations of these concerns. This will be accomplished by utilising different rooms of the house for exhibits focused on one of these themes; for instance, the rear parlour of the house will be the Women's Rights Room, whereas the dining room will be the Religious Freedom Room. While Gage's household life – including the presence of her husband, Henry Gage, and their four children Thomas Clarkson, Helen Leslie, Julia Louise, and Maud – will be interpreted in the house's front parlour as the Family Parlour and Oz Room, it by no means predominates within the museum.

Before moving on to discuss the specific nature of historic house museum depictions of the home, let me set the stage for the Gage House by relating why the family was, and is, significant.

History of the Gages

The Gage family, including Matilda and Henry and their three children – Helen Leslie, Thomas Clarkson, and Julia Louise – moved to Fayetteville, New York, from the nearby village of Manlius in 1854 and purchased the house in 1858 after renting it for several years. Their youngest daughter, Maud, was born here in 1861.

Henry owned a dry goods store located in the central business section of Fayetteville a few blocks from the house. We have some, but not much, historical evidence of Henry's political reform involvement. As an abolitionist, he was involved in the local Republican party, and we know that he proudly displayed the 1862 Emancipation Proclamation in his store window, decorated with patriotic bunting. Previously, he had draped the store display in mourning for the day of John Brown's execution in 1859. The house itself was almost certainly used by the family to house enslaved fugitives escaping northward on the Underground Railroad, and this would have required the cooperation of both Henry and Matilda (Wagner 2004).

In contrast, we know much more about Matilda Gage's activities, and her story predominates. Besides her involvement in the abolition movement, Matilda was a tireless activist for woman suffrage, women's rights, the separation of church and state, and Native American sovereignty throughout her life. Gage made her debut in the woman suffrage arena at the third national woman's rights convention held in Syracuse, New York, in 1852, and in 1869 was a founding member of the National Woman Suffrage Association (NWSA) with Elizabeth Cady Stanton and Susan B. Anthony (Wagner 1998).

Gage remained involved in the NWSA until 1890, acting as Chair of the Executive Committee for many years, in addition to holding the offices of president, vice president, and treasurer at various times. She also founded the New York state chapter of the NWSA and held the office of president for its first nine years of existence. Over the course of these 20 years of suffrage activity, Gage remained a sought-after speaker and very prolific writer, and was considered one of the 'Suffrage Triumvirate' along with Stanton and Anthony (Boland 2006).

She split from the national suffrage organisation in 1890, when the NWSA merged with the more conservative American Woman Suffrage Association, which included members of the Women's Christian Temperance Union. Gage viewed the merger as a betrayal by Anthony as it was based solely on the shared desire for suffrage, but elided the vastly different reasons *why* women wanted the vote and the different ends to which they wanted to use it. Gage called the threat of religious fundamentalism and the merging of church and state 'the danger of the hour' and devoted the last years of her life to the Freethought movement.[1] Upon her death in 1898, her children – who had all moved west to the Dakota territories by this time – sold the house (Wagner 1998, Boland 2006).

While much of Gage's work was distributed on the state and national level, the place of her Fayetteville home was of crucial importance. Like most of the other female reformers of her time, she essentially worked from home – including acting as editor of *The National Citizen and Ballot Box*, the official newspaper of the NWSA. It was also here that she wrote her many articles and books and collaborated on the three-volume *History of Woman Suffrage* with Stanton and Anthony in the 1870s and 1880s. She hosted many abolition, suffrage, and freethought activists in the house over the years, whether for a short visit or an extended stay to work collaboratively on projects. In the case of the Gage House, then, the traditional rhetoric of 'the domestic sphere' does not hold, as the domestic arena was a primary space of explicitly political work and general hell-raising (Boland 2006).

In turning the Gage House into a historic house museum today, it is obvious that merely creating a showcase for Victorian home life would not be appropriate as it would not do justice to the lives of the Gage family. The Gage Foundation is quite aware of this fact, and is committed to creating a 'museum of ideas' rather than one focused on decorative arts and objects. This is in keeping with Matilda Gage's own wishes; she very much resisted media attempts to identify her based primarily on her home life and status as a wife and mother. In an 1890 letter to Lillie Devereaux Blake, then the President of the NWSA, Gage wrote: 'This sketch is not enough in line of a biography to require my age, number of children, etc. I always look upon the latter as an impudent question to us woman suffragists, and was not at all pleased when Susan B. wrote us all up that way once' (Gage 1890).

The Foundation's decision to have themed interpretation rooms in the restored house makes sense, then, given Gage's own desire to be known for her work. As the plan currently stands, the front parlour of the house will be the only one restored to its nineteenth-century appearance, and it will be the Family Parlour & Oz Room. This is partly because this is the only room of the house of which we have a period photograph. It is also where Gage's youngest daughter Maud married L. Frank Baum, the author of *The Wonderful Wizard of Oz*, in 1882. The rest of the rooms will be restored with period-appropriate wall and floor coverings – some based on physical evidence recovered during the exploratory period of the restoration – while the space itself will be filled with exhibits pertaining to each room's interpretive theme. My interest has been in figuring out where the archaeological research can come to play in this setup. In order to find a place for the archaeology, we must first understand what the Gage Foundation is reacting to in its efforts to create a new kind of house museum.

Historic house museums, depictions of domesticity, and material culture

As mentioned earlier, American historic house museums were first created in the mid-nineteenth century and focused on the homes of the nation's Founding Fathers. Public historian Patricia West has noted that these early efforts by women to rescue the homes of famous American figures played off of the nineteenth-century emphasis on women's domesticity, as well as the belief that the home and its physical space and furnishings were a crucially important part of imparting morals to those who dwelled within. Thus, the Mount Vernon Ladies' Association was one part of a movement which emphasised 'the political and social benefits of public exposure to the lives of American forefathers' (West 1999, p. 160).

These early efforts to preserve, restore, and study the homes of American forefathers circumscribed the types of households presented by historic homes as primarily white, male, and elite; in their interpretation, focus was centred on the male head of household and objects on display were seen as the end point of interpretation (Donnelly 2002), presenting static scenes of domestic furnishings. In this formulation of the historic house museum, the experiences of different household members – including women, children, servants, or enslaved labourers – were typically overlooked.

At the same time, an internal contradiction was at play. While the historical significance of the male head of a household was typically the reason for establishing a house museum in the first place, the domestic realm was historically – and in many instances is to this day – attributed to the domain of women.

Thus, the image of the past presented at house museums centred on the domestic surroundings of a significant family, while the interpretive significance was 'the business or political acumen of the "great man" after whom the museum is named' (West 1994, p. 456). This dichotomy is a legacy of the ideology of 'separate spheres' dating to the nineteenth century, which specified that man's place was in the public sphere and woman's in the domestic (Kerber 1988). This ideology emerged with the separation of economic production from the domestic arena which took place among emerging middle-class American households during the first half of the nineteenth century. Attendant with this separation was a shift in gender roles; women became the moral heads of the household and were responsible for ensuring the social and moral status of their household through intensive child-rearing and the proper consumption of material goods (Laslett and Brenner 1989, Wall 1994). The 'cult of true womanhood' emerged during this period which idealised women's place within the home by celebrating their innate cardinal virtues: purity, piety, submissiveness, and domesticity (Welter 1966).

While these ideals were widely circulated throughout nineteenth-century society through etiquette books, household manuals, magazines, and sermons, they were still precisely that – ideals. Neither the 'separate spheres' nor the 'cult of true womanhood' were inclusive ideologies, as they proposed lifestyles which only the upper and emerging middle classes could afford; likewise, they were racially and ethnically exclusive (Wilkie 2003). Women's placement as managers of the household brought with it an elaboration of domestic tasks, which required the employment of domestic servants, who were typically themselves young female immigrants. Thus,

> For every nineteenth-century middle-class family that protected its wife and child within the family circle, there was an Irish or a German girl scrubbing floors in that middle-class home, a Welsh boy mining coal to keep the home-baked goodies warm, a black girl doing the family laundry, a black mother and child picking cotton to be made into clothes for the family, and a Jewish or Italian daughter in a sweatshop making 'ladies'' dresses or artificial flowers for the family to purchase.
>
> (Coontz 2000, pp. 11–12)

Moreover, even among those families who had the means to adhere to these precepts, many did not subscribe to these ideologies.

Nonetheless, the explosion of material culture options for the home during the nineteenth century has long been a subject of fascination for contemporary scholars (e.g. Grover 1987, Grier 1988, Ames 1992, Foy and Schlereth 1992, Williams 1996). Most of this literature highlights several recurring themes which link material culture to prevailing ideological attitudes – belief in the home environment to shape personal character, and class-based anxiety over propriety, presentation of the self, and etiquette. As Williams (1996, p. 52) has stated, 'A woman was charged with the responsibility of creating a household environment that would nurture taste, civility, and Christian ideals in her husband and children, thereby influencing them to be moral and productive members of society'.

In material terms, these concerns were expressed in a variety of ways. Use of gothic-styled architecture and ceramics, as well as natural motifs (or actual plants) can be seen as expressions of the 'cult of home religion', whereby the home was cast as a Christian sanctuary from the corrupt public sphere (Beecher and Stowe 1869, Spencer-Wood 1996). The elaboration of meals and an increased specialisation in dining and serving wares was related to the role of middle-class women in maintaining the family's standing within the social structure, as well as acting as a guiding moral spirit of the family (Williams 1987).

As a result of this fascination with the dominant socially-endowed meanings of Victorian material culture, I argue that historic house museums of this period can easily fall into the trap of presenting a rather fixed and uncomplicated image of past household life. As West (1994, p. 456) notes, 'American house museums, tidy and tastefully furnished, are arrestingly formulaic: on tour one often feels a peculiar *déjà vu*, perhaps as the silver tea service or the portrait of the colonel is pointed out'. This is what can occur, I contend, when the notion of the domestic as the sole domain of women is taken for granted, when all interesting political, social, and economic action is seen as located outside of the home, and the hegemonic meanings attached to domestic material culture are taken as universal fact rather than prescribed ideals to be investigated within particular contexts. This is the historical house museum that the Gage Foundation vehemently resists being, why it seeks to emphasise ideas over things.

Ideas vs. things at the Stanton and Alcott house museums

It is instructive to look at other historic house museums that interpret the lives of high-profile women and the very different approaches taken in their interpretations. The Elizabeth Cady Stanton house in Seneca Falls, New York, and the Orchard House of Louisa May Alcott in Concord, Massachusetts, show the difficulty of balancing things with ideas and illustrate how different museums opt for emphasising one over the other. The Elizabeth Cady Stanton house in Seneca Falls is a National Historic Landmark and part of the Women's Rights National Historical Park operated by the National Park Service. The historical park commemorates the first known women's rights convention, held in July 1848 at Seneca Falls' Wesleyan Chapel, where Stanton's *Declaration of Sentiments* (modelled on the *Declaration of Independence*) first put forth women's demand to vote.

The Stanton house, a Greek Revival farmhouse dating to the 1840s, was occupied by the family between 1847 and 1862. Stanton herself referred to the house as 'the centre of the rebellion'. The house is open by tour for most of the year and comprises the main site of interpretation at the park in addition to the visitors' centre and the Wesleyan Chapel.

The Stanton house interpretation is of interest because it largely eschews objects. Besides a desk and chair Stanton owned when living in Tenafly, New Jersey (years after leaving Seneca Falls), a piano and a loveseat, the house is largely empty. Restoration work has re-created the wall treatments in place when the Stantons occupied the house, but the house itself is largely a shell interpreted by Park Ranger-led tours which focus on her life and thought (Melosh 1989, Rose 1997, NPS 2009). The National Park Service's choice to not fully furnish the Stanton house with period pieces is notable, as it has allowed the focus of the tours to be on Stanton's work rather than her domestic surroundings; here, ideas trump things.

At the other end of the spectrum falls Orchard House in Concord, Massachusetts, home to the Alcott family between 1858 and 1877 and where Louisa May Alcott penned *Little Women* in 1868. Established as a house museum by the Concord Woman's Club in 1912, Orchard House in its early twentieth-century configuration emphasised largely non-existent linkages between the Alcott family's life and the idealised domestic world of *Little Women* (West 1994).[2] Instead of recognising Louisa May Alcott's involvement in the woman's suffrage movement and her status as an unmarried and working woman, the fully period-furnished Orchard House was used to present an image of 'traditional domesticity' seen as endangered by increasing immigration and the spectre of woman's suffrage. In so doing, Orchard House was reinvented 'as a curious hybrid of a progressive-era, neo-colonial, single-family suburban home and an idealised nineteenth-century cottage' in which domestic life was interpreted to the visiting public at the expense of discussions of the people who actually lived there (West 1994, p. 465). In this case, objects – many of which were actually owned and used by the Alcotts – were used to impart a very particular image of nineteenth-century domestic life and gender roles that overlooked the actual, iconoclastic ideas put into practice by their users.

The examples provided by the Stanton and Alcott houses show the rather extreme contrasts in interpretive strategies possible in terms of emphasising ideas or things. In order to create a model for the Gage House that incorporates both, I turn to the example of the Lower East Side Tenement Museum.

A model for balancing things and ideas: the Lower East Side Tenement Museum

The Lower East Side Tenement Museum in Manhattan was founded in 1988 with the purpose of telling the stories of America's nineteenth- and twentieth-century working-class immigrants. The tenement at 97 Orchard Street was built in 1863, containing 20 small apartments among its five floors, and was home to over 7000 immigrants before its closure in 1935 (Abram 2002).

Today, the museum consists of six apartments restored to reflect the stories of particular immigrant families that lived in the building between the 1860s and 1930s (Abram 2007). Various tours are available which highlight the experiences of German-Jewish, Irish, and Italian-Catholic immigrant families in New York through their restored apartments.

The tours are immersive, richly textured, and evocative. The tour I have personally taken, entitled 'The Moores: An Irish Family in America', combined music, historical documents and artefacts, and a tour of Bridget and Joseph Moores' ca. 1869 apartment to learn the family's story and discuss broader issues related to nineteenth-century Irish immigration, anti-Irish sentiment, religion, public health issues, and tenement reform. The apartment setup, which showed how the apartment parlour would look for the funeral wake of the Moores' five-month-old Agnes, who died of marasmus (malnutrition) most likely due to contaminated milk, provided an evocative link to broader concerns of public health and pure food.

The Lower East Side Tenement Museum is also notable for its practice of explicitly linking the stories of its nineteenth- and early twentieth-century immigrant families with current concerns related to immigration. Connections between past and present immigration are made throughout the apartment tours, but until recently a landmark programme called 'Kitchen Conversations' was also held after select tours, with an average of 80% of visitors opting to participate (Russell-Ciardi 2008).[3] Over juice and cookies, visitors discussed links between the stories of New York's immigrant ancestors – whom many visitors identify with due to their own family history – and continuing debates related to immigration today, including whether everyone should be required to learn and speak English, whether immigrants should receive help and support on arrival, and what it means to be an American. These conversations tended to highlight the false distinctions made between the hard-working 'good immigrants' of the past and the 'lazy, dependent, and disloyal' immigrants of today (Abram 2007, p. 63). These dialogues, then, allowed visitors from different backgrounds to 'react to what they were hearing, share their own knowledge, and exchange ideas about the ways in which the new information they were learning did and did not resonate with their previous understanding of the issues' (Russell-Ciardi 2008, p. 47).

In addition, the museum has taken steps to ensure its place as a community institution, rather than simply a history museum. As part of its mission to engage with issues of contemporary immigration, the museum has hosted a programme since

2002 called 'Shared Journeys' for recent immigrants in Adult English for Speakers of Other Languages (ESOL) classes. The programme is comprised of six workshops in which participants tour one of the restored tenement apartments and learn about the parallels between the issues facing that particular immigrant family and their own contemporary struggles. Each workshop tackles a single issue, including challenges on arriving in the United States, housing laws, sweatshops and labour laws, obtaining government assistance, health and medical care, and sharing immigration stories. These workshops share the goal of teaching participants the vocabulary needed to advocate for themselves and make them aware of laws and available resources (Russell-Ciardi 2008).

Finally, the museum also utilises space within the 97 Orchard Street building to host art shows and performances by recent immigrants. This has allowed artists and performers to showcase their personal experiences and present multiple contemporary perspectives on immigration; in the meantime, this has forced the museum to share ownership of the immigration narratives being shown at the museum and directly engage with different stakeholders (Russell-Ciardi 2008).

The Lower East Side Tenement Museum thus utilises the sense of an active history as embodied by the restored living spaces of these immigrant families to make explicit linkages to contemporary issues we still struggle with. This model, I argue, is an effective one at balancing ideas and things, and shows that material culture and nuanced family histories can indeed be an ideal venue for bridging the microscale with macroscale ideas relating to both the past and present. Moreover, the museum's involvement with contemporary immigration issues ensures its placement as a community centre and resource which separates it from many other history museums depicting past living contexts.

Prospects for linking ideas and things at the Matilda Joslyn Gage House

The examples given by the Stanton and Alcott houses detailed earlier illustrate the complexity of balancing interpretive priorities in historic house museums. Likewise, the Lower East Side Tenement Museum provides a commendable model for balancing broad concepts and household material culture within the context of a historic site that is unequivocally engaged in current politics and issues. Based on their example, I propose that one means by which the Matilda Joslyn Gage House can include domestic material culture in the final museum planning that serves to reinforce, rather than distract from, their central focus on Gage's ideas and actions, could be through the display, interpretation, and use of tea wares.

Studies of the place of tea in Victorian culture have emphasised its feminisation by the second half of the nineteenth century, as men working outside of the home were no longer able to return home for meals during the day (Wall 1994). These gatherings were an important means of socialising for women, and could either be held for close friends and female family members, or more competitively focus on maintaining the family's social status (Williams 1987, Wall 1991). Diana Wall's (1991, 1994, 1999, 2000) studies of archaeologically-recovered tea wares from nineteenth-century New

York City have focused on how the use of gothic-style ceramics, in particular, indicated that women embraced the gender ideology of the cult of domesticity and/or the cult of home religion. Conversely, households which did not use these ceramics have been interpreted as not participating in this ideology (i.e. Wall 1999). More elaborately decorated porcelain tea wares have been interpreted, on the other hand, as signalling the status of the household when used in entertaining other women for tea (Wall 2000).

In the archaeological excavations at the Gage House, we uncovered more or less what one would expect to find at a middle-class Victorian household, including what were considered crucial accoutrements for a proper, moral home by prescriptive literature of the period: Gothic ironstone china, a porcelain tea service, and various house wares exhibiting floral or other natural design elements (Beecher 1841, Beecher and Stowe 1869). Moreover, these are the material indicators that we as archaeologists have tended to use as evidence for a past household's acceptance of and participation in the cult of domesticity (Wall 1991, 1994, 1999, 2000, Rotman 2001, 2005).

The image of Matilda Joslyn Gage as a moral keeper of the home, exhibiting purity, piety, submissiveness, and domesticity suggested by the material culture of the household, however, contrasts markedly with what we know about her historically. As she actively struggled to expand women's role in the world and reform social and political relations throughout her lifetime, I argue that the material culture associated with her household simply *cannot* be taken as reflecting the prescriptive gender ideologies of the period. Rather, it seems much more likely that she was utilising the trappings of domesticity for her own ends; that is, working from 'within the system'. This then leads to the question of how this complexity can be interpreted to future visitors to the museum.

The key, I argue, is consideration of practice: How were these ceramics actually used within the Gage household?[4] What part did they play in Matilda Gage's reform efforts? What meanings could these have held for the Gage family and their guests? In the absence of a discussion of actual everyday practices, prescriptive ideals regarding what things *should* have been like stand in instead – in this case, Victorian domestic womanhood – and simply reify whatever we already think we know about the past.

In this regard, these tea wares, as well as other artefacts, can be highlighted as emblematic of different social relations and practices which took place in the home, rather than simply being bric-a-brac in the parlour. Instead of reinforcing images of Victorian ladies, pinkies raised, having afternoon tea in the formal parlour, we can envision Gage working over tea with Stanton and Anthony to plan their protest at the 1876 Philadelphia Centennial convention, or writing *The History of Woman Suffrage*. Given that we know that the Gages entertained reformers such as Lillie Devereux Blake, Gerrit Smith, Belva Lockwood, Lucretia Mott, William Lloyd Garrison, and Wendell Phillips, in addition to Stanton and Anthony, I can see both the taking of communal meals and ladies' afternoon teas as enacting challenges to prevailing ideologies (Matilda Joslyn Gage Foundation, Inc. 2006).

What is interesting is that these historical practices actually fit quite well with the contemporary practices of the Gage Foundation staff and volunteers, who are by and large fuelled by gallons of Earl Grey tea. Teas are used as the basis for day-to-day work at the Foundation, as well as discussion groups and fundraisers – such as an 'afternoon tea' fundraiser with Gloria Steinem held in the summer of 2009. There are also plans to initiate conversations with museum visitors in a programme similar to the Tenement Museum's 'Kitchen Conversations', which would take place in the rear parlour – the 'Women's Rights' room – over tea.

Thus, by interpreting these tea wares as simultaneously engaged in family gatherings, reform actions, and community-making, the Gage Foundation has the potential to augment their interpretation of Gage's work rather than distract from it or eschew discussion of household life altogether.

Concluding thoughts

Decisions regarding how to create interpretive narratives at historic house museums are complicated, even more so when a museum seeks to break with the established way of doing things. In the push to create a politically-informed, community-enhancing institution, it is tempting to jettison traditional conceptions of household interpretation, as has the Stanton house. However, as the model of the Lower East Side Tenement Museum suggests, it is more than possible to utilise household material culture to deal with contentious and difficult historical subjects, link microscale histories with larger concepts, and prompt museum visitor engagement with contemporary social issues.

In much the same way, the restoration and interpretive plan of the Matilda Joslyn Gage House seeks to make links between the past and the present – between nineteenth-century slavery and human trafficking today; the fight for woman suffrage and the continued fight for gender equality; and the continuing issue of the proper relationship between religion and the state. By utilising the domestic space of the Gage House to interpret Gage's radical works, the Foundation can powerfully turn traditional, supposedly apolitical notions of what a nineteenth-century home was on their head.

Likewise, using the Gage's ceramic tea wares to illustrate their varying uses and meanings then leads us to foreground the fact that material culture is not a mere reflection of meaning, but that past peoples quite actively endowed mass-produced material culture with a wide array of symbolic meanings through their daily practices (de Certeau 1984, Beaudry et al. 1991, Spencer-Wood 1996, Little 1997). While the particular context of the Gage House provides a well-documented instance of the alternate meanings imbued to material culture through practice, it should not be considered an exceptional case. Rather, by approaching the interpretation of material culture from the perspective of practice, we should remember that all past peoples imbued their material culture with meanings through their use, and thus all sites have the potential for exploring the non-hegemonic meanings attributed to material culture.

By emphasising how the Gages used their tea wares within the context of their reform efforts, and continuing to use teas as a venue for discussions and community-making within the Foundation and the museum, these icons of Victorian feminine domesticity can be shown as the complex resources for creating meaning that they were. In so doing, the Gage House has the potential to be a noteworthy and iconoclastic historic house museum that emphasises ideas over things, while not overlooking the significance that they embodied for those who used them to create their world.

Notes

1   Gage's magnum opus, *Woman, church and state*, was published in 1893 and exhaustively detailed her case against organised religion in creating and maintaining the subordination of women. While some readers embraced the book, it was also the subject of heated opposition and attracted the attention of Anthony Comstock, enforcer of obscenity laws. Publication of the book served to further estrange Gage's relations with the NWSA.

2   As West (1994) discusses how Orchard House was presented to the public during the first half of the twentieth century, please note that this is not a negative comment on their current interpretive strategies. For information on the site currently, see their website at http://www.louisamayalcott.org.

3   As of my visit to the Tenement Museum on 15 September 2009, the Kitchen Conversations programme was no longer available, replaced by a 'Super Tour' which combined a walking tour of the neighbourhood with one of the standard tours of the tenement building. More information on the museum's tours and programmes can be accessed at their website: http://www.tenement.org.

4   Practice theory approaches, derived from the work of Bourdieu (1977), Giddens (1979), and de Certeau (1984); have been fruitfully applied in archaeological contexts from various places and time periods. Just a few examples include Silliman (2001) and Lightfoot *et al.*'s (1998) use of practice theory in colonial California, and Gillespie (2000) and Hendon's (2004) use of it in Mesoamerica. Still other archaeologists, for example Clark and Wilkie (2006) and Joyce (2000), have further incorporated Judith Butler's (1990, 2004) concept of performativity into considerations of practice and the construction of personhood.

References

Abram, R.J., 2002. Harnessing the power of history. *In*: R. Sandell, ed. *Museums, society, inequality*. New York: Routledge, 125–141.

Abram, R.J., 2007. Kitchen conversations: democracy in action at the Lower East Side Tenement Museum. *The Public Historian*, 29 (1), 59–76.

Ames, K.L., 1992. *Death in the dining room and other tales of Victorian culture*. Philadelphia: Temple University Press.

Beaudry, M.C., Cook, L. and Mrozowski, S., 1991. Artifacts and active voices: material culture as social discourse. *In*: R.H. McGuire and R. Paynter, eds. *The archaeology of inequality*. Oxford: Blackwell, 150–191.

Beecher, C., 1841, reprinted 1977. *A treatise on domestic economy*. New York: Schocken Books.

Beecher, C. and Stowe, H.B., 1869, reprinted 2008. *The American woman's home: principles of domestic science*. Bedford: Applewood Books.

Boland, S., 2006. Partners in suffrage: Matilda Joslyn Gage and Susan B. Anthony, 1869–1882. Paper presented at the Susan B. Anthony and the Struggle for Equal Rights Women's History Conference, University of Rochester, NY. 30 March–1 April 2006.

Bourdieu, P., 1977. *Outline of a theory of practice*. Cambridge: Cambridge University Press.

Butler, J., 1990. *Gender trouble: feminism and the subversion of identity*. New York: Routledge.

Butler, J., 2004. *Undoing gender*. New York: Routledge.

Butler, P.H., 2002. Past, present, and future: the place of the House Museum in the museum community. *In*: J.F. Donnelly, ed. *Interpreting historic house museums*. Walnut Creek, CA: AltaMira Press, 18–42.

Clark, B.J. and Wilkie, L.A., 2006. The prism of self: gender and personhood. *In*: S.M. Nelson, ed. *The handbook of gender in archaeology*. Walnut Creek, CA: AltaMira Press, 333–364.

Coontz, S., 2000. *The way we never were: American families and the nostalgia trap*. New York: Basic Books.

De Certeau, M., 1984. *The practice of everyday life*. Berkeley: University of California Press.

Donnelly, J.F., 2002. Introduction. *In*: J.F. Donnelly, ed. *Interpreting historic house museums*. Walnut Creek, CA: AltaMira Press, 1–17.

Foy, J.H. and Schlereth, T.J., eds., 1992. *American home life, 1880–1930: a social history of spaces and services*. Knoxville: University of Tennessee Press.

Gage, M.J., 1890. Letter to L.D. Blake, dated 11 May. Matilda Joslyn Gage Foundation, Inc. archival collection.

Gage, M.J., 1893. *Woman, church and state*. Chicago: Charles H. Kerr & Company.

Giddens, A., 1979. *Central problems in social theory: action, structure and contradiction in social analysis*. Berkeley: University of California Press.

Gillespie, S., 2000. Personhood, agency and mortuary ritual: a case study from the ancient Maya. *Journal of Anthropological Archaeology*, 20, 73–112.

Grier, K.C., 1988. *Culture and comfort: parlor making and middle-class identity, 1850–1930*. Washington, DC: Smithsonian Institution Press.

Grover, K., ed., 1987. *Dining in America: 1850–1900*. Amherst: The University of Massachusetts Press.

Hendon, J.A., 2004. Living and working at home: the social archaeology of household production and social relations. *In*: L. Meskell and R. Preucel, eds. *A companion to social archaeology*. Malden, MA: Blackwell, 272–286.

Joyce, R.A., 2000. Girling the girl and boying the boy: the production of adulthood in ancient Mesoamerica. *World Archaeology*, 31 (3), 473–483.

Kerber, L.K., 1988. Separate spheres, female worlds, woman's place: the rhetoric of women's history. *The Journal of American History*, 75 (1), 9–39.

Laslett, B., and Brenner, J., 1989. Gender and social reproduction: historical perspectives. *Annual Review of Sociology*, 15, 381–404.

Lightfoot, K., Martinez, A. and Schiff, A., 1998. Daily practice and material culture in pluralistic social settings: an archaeological study of culture change and persistence from Fort Ross, California. *American Antiquity*, 63 (2), 199–222.

Little, B.J., 1997. Expressing ideology without a voice, or obfuscation and the enlightenment. *International Journal of Historical Archaeology*, 1 (3), 225–241.

Little, B.J., 2007. Archaeology and civic engagement. *In*: B.J. Little and P.A. Shackel, eds. *Archaeology as a tool of civic engagement*. Lanham, MD: AltaMira Press, 1–22.

Matilda Joslyn Gage Foundation, Inc., 2006. Visitors summary; draft research for Historic Structures Report. On file at the Matilda Joslyn Gage Foundation, Inc.

Matilda Joslyn Gage Foundation, Inc., 2009. *The Gage home* [online]. Available from: http://www.matildajoslyngage.org/ [Accessed 28 September 2009].

McGuire, R., 2008. *Archaeology as political action*. Berkeley: University of California Press.

Melosh, B., 1989. Speaking of women: museums' representations of women's history. *In*: W. Leon and R. Rosenzweig, eds. *History museums in the United States: a critical assessment*. Urbana: University of Illinois Press, 183–214.

National Park Service (NPS), 2009. *Women's Rights National Historical Park* [online]. Available from: http://www.nps.gov/wori/index.htm [Accessed 28 September 2009].

Rose, V., 1997. Preserving women's rights history. *CRM: The Journal of Heritage Stewardship*, 20 (3), 25–28.

Rotman, D.L., 2001. *Beyond the cult of domesticity: exploring the material and spatial expressions of multiple gender ideologies in Deerfield, Massachusetts, ca. 1750–1911*. Thesis (PhD). University of Massachusetts Amherst.

Rotman, D.L., 2005. Newlyweds, young families, and spinsters: a consideration of developmental cycle in historical archaeologies of gender. *International Journal of Historical Archaeology*, 9 (1), 1–36.

Russell-Ciardi, M., 2008. The museum as a democracy-building institution: reflections on the shared journeys program at the Lower East Side Tenement Museum. *The Public Historian*, 30 (1), 39–52.

Shackel, P.A. and Chambers, E.J., eds. 2004. *Places in mind: public archaeology as applied anthropology*. New York: Routledge.

Silliman, S., 2001. Agency, practical politics, and the archaeology of culture contact. *Journal of Social Archaeology*, 1 (2), 190–209.

Spencer-Wood, S., 1996. Feminist historical archaeology and the transformation of American culture by domestic reform movements, 1840–1925. *In*: L.A. DeCunzo and B. Herman, eds. *Historical archaeology and the study of American culture*. Knoxville: University of Tennessee Press, 397–437.

Stahlgren, L.C., and Stottman, M.J., 2007. Voices from the past: changing the culture of historic house museums with archaeology. *In*: B.J. Little and P.A. Shackel, eds. *Archaeology as a Tool of Civic Engagement*. Lanham, MD: AltaMira Press, 131–150.

Wagner, S.R., 1998. *Matilda Joslyn Gage: she who holds the sky*. Aberdeen SD: Sky Carrier Press.

Wagner, S.R., 2004. Heritage NY Underground Railroad Heritage Trail designation nomination. On file at the Matilda Joslyn Gage Foundation, Inc.

Wall, D.D., 1991. Sacred dinners and secular teas: constructing domesticity in mid-19thcentury New York. *Historical Archaeology*, 25 (4), 69–81.

Wall, D.D., 1994. *The Archaeology of gender: separating the spheres in urban America*. New York: Plenum Press.

Wall, D.D., 1999. Examining gender, class, and ethnicity in nineteenth-century New York. *Historical Archaeology*, 33 (1), 102–117.

Wall, D.D., 2000. Family meals and evening parties: constructing domesticity in nineteenth-century middle-class New York. *In*: J. Delle, S. Mrozowski, and R. Paynter, eds. *Lines that divide: historical archaeologies of race, class, and gender*. Knoxville: University of Tennessee Press, 109–141.

Welter, B., 1966. The cult of true womanhood: 1820–1860. *American Quarterly*, 18 (2), 151–174.

West, P., 1994. Gender politics and the 'invention of tradition': the museumization of Louisa May Alcott's Orchard House. *Gender and History*, 6 (3), 456–467.

West, P., 1999. *Domesticating history: the political origins of America's house museums.* Washington, DC: Smithsonian Institution Press.

Wilkie, L.A., 2003. *The archaeology of mothering: an African-American midwife's tale.* New York: Routledge.

Williams, S., 1987. Introduction. *In*: K. Grover, ed. *Dining in America: 1850–1900.* Amherst: University of Massachusetts Press, 3–23.

Williams, S., 1996. *Savory suppers and fashionable feasts: dining in Victorian America.* Knoxville: The University of Tennessee Press.

Chapter 20

Towards an erotics of the museum[1]

Julie Marcus

WITHIN THE LITERATURE EXPLORING THE NATURE of the museum, one can discern two broad strands of thought regarding its origins. One of them sees in the modern museum a clear departure from the pre-Enlightenment model of a cabinet of curiosities; while the other draws attention to continuities between those older cabinets of curiosities and their wondrous collections, and the great collections and collection houses of the nineteenth century. The genealogies proposed through both strands of that literature mask a set of concerns with what the museum is, and does, today. Is the museum a teaching institution aligned with the universities, or, is it more appropriate to see the museum as a form of theatre, which can best be approached through analyses of performance and spectatorship? Yet the question of the museum is a broader one.

Successful museum displays and exhibitions conjure into existence particular visions of the nature of the world. In doing so, they provide at least some of the spectators, as well as museum curators, with those moments of illumination which could be thought of as resembling the Heideggerian 'flash' of insight that offers a glimpse of a truth. That truth is not, of course, necessarily 'true'. But in those flashes of understanding which bring into light an unseen order which bears upon the worlds of daily life, there lies a moment which both offers truth *and* a way towards the truth, a moment of new knowledge. It is this moment, always visual in the museum, where offer and promise, the power of looking, and the approach of 'truth' are collapsed within a poiesis which is so seductive, and so pleasurable.

This moment of pleasure and wonder is the sense of the marvellous that traditional genealogists of the museum associate with the pre-modern museum, with the cabinets of seventeenth-century curiosities now so well-documented and critiqued. Yet the ordered display of natural and cultural objects found in the great modern museums of the nineteenth and twentieth centuries presented marvels no less wondrous for being ranged in modern taxonomies of one kind or another. While ordered differently, that new order produced and represented new relations, new knowledges and new possibilities to a broader audience, but the distinction between the old and new museum orders is not as fixed as some have imagined. It is incorrect to think of the old cabinets of curios and wonders as either necessarily heterogeneous or as existing only in the past. Neither is it correct to think of those well-ordered Linnaean taxonomies exemplified through natural history displays as being either homogeneous or entirely absent from the collections of the past. In particular, the visual conventions of the older forms have carried on into the new in very interesting ways. In the museum both forms of displays worked within the recognisable and specific visual conventions found in painting and it is this that I shall explore shortly.

But where *does* the wonder of the museum come from? Perhaps Brecht was wrong in saying that 'Facts can very seldom be caught without their clothes on . . . they are hardly seductive' (Crew, Spencer and Sims 1991: 159). Objects in museums might well be thought of as facts without their clothes on. And this capacity for revelation is why collections and museums are so seductive. The museum's object is often thought of as revealing the naked truth, as making visible some essential detail of the truth that would be hard to grasp through words alone. Among the propositions explored in this chapter are those that within the museum, truth and desire are inextricably bound up within each other: that the pleasures of the museum are essential to it; 'facts' collected in it in the form of its collections and presented through visual display are immensely seductive, and that both the pleasure and seduction of the museum constitute an erotics which arises from two sources. First, that erotics arises from the electric flash of a comprehended truth that comes with the moment of enlightenment, a flash which is procreative and charged with desire; and second and equally significantly, that erotics emerges from the relations and deployment of power itself, power's relation to the creation of truths and to the ordering of the collections which museums contain. The question here is one of how a particular aesthetic and visual order is established to represent either the museum's heterogeneity or the museum's epistemologies of homogeneity, its claims to rationality, order and completion. It is in this context that questions concerning the essential nature of the museum, visual pleasure and the pleasures of looking must be set.

Donato's work on the origins of the museum and its fundamental and compromising epistemological contradictions is well known. It forms the basis of a number of commentaries, including Douglas Crimp's (1983: 43–56) which focuses on the art museum, its discipline of art history, and photography. Through these essays, Flaubert's work *Bouvard and Pécuchet* has again become familiar to a broader English-speaking readership. Flaubert's tale of the attempts of two retired copy clerks to grapple with representations of the world in the early part of the nineteenth century, their eventual construction of a museum and the gathering and writing of the fragments of the world they seek both to understand and to write into a 'Book', can be read as constituting a critique of representation and of the ordering of knowledge. Donato's reading of Flaubert's novel and its characters points to the ways in which the erasure of difference and time ensure the essential heterogeneity of the project of the nineteenth-century museum. The 'Book' that Bouvard and Pécuchet wished to write would contain all knowledge and is never written, but their lives were filled with the collecting of material for it. What they could not, or would not, do, was discriminate or understand the differences between representations and reality, between information and content, between homogeneity and heterogeneity. Theirs was a world of difference erased, value-free and thus inevitably incomprehensible.

I should like to have read Flaubert's unwritten second volume of *Bouvard and Pécuchet*, which was to be the 'Book' that his two asexual bachelor characters wanted to write, the book which was made entirely of a collage of quotations (Donato 1979: 213–38). The new Museum of Sydney uses what might be called the Bouvard-and-Pécuchet principle in presenting its displays and labels, in its collages of quotations, its erasure of distinctions and the absence of evaluation. With those erasures and absences go both desire and the erotics of enlightenment which have always been essential to the success of the museum, so that it is particularly appropriate that Flaubert's two old bachelor boys have no sexuality. And with them goes the possibility of comprehension and evaluation. In their absence, there will remain only the values of heterogeneity, of no-value; but because there cannot be a cultural domain outside or without power, the relations of power which create the absence of value turn back upon themselves, to make the question of the nature of the Museum of Sydney perverse.

The Museum of Sydney

In 1995, a new museum opened in Sydney. Set on the site of Australia's first Government House, the museum was a troubled project from its inception. The Aboriginal owners of the Sydney region wanted a museum which reflected their history; the descendants of the colonial families wanted a museum reflecting 'settlement' rather than 'invasion'. Amid considerable public controversy, a form of 'reconciliation' emerged which saw the commissioning of a major public art work from both an Aboriginal and non-Aboriginal artist for the courtyard of the museum and the introduction of Aboriginal displays in the museum's gallery space. This troubled project offers insights into the ways in which aesthetics and certain postmodernist philosophies produce a poetics which, in the final analysis, blots out desire and slips easily into a non-confrontational and reactionary nihilism.

At the Museum of Sydney, the heterogeneity which curators place at the heart of the museum and at the heart of knowledge itself is carefully displayed through an enormous display case containing hundreds of beautifully hung fragments of domestic pottery and rural machinery. The truth of that heterogeneity is used to reveal the artifice of knowledge, the absent space of truth, and to devastate narratives of space and time. What is not displayed is the guiding hand which determines what knowledge shall be revealed, the hand of power. The display of fragments focusing on Sydney's foundation and its colonial culture therefore constitutes a lie – the lie that because truth is ever fragmentary, evaluation and narrative are impossible, because the truth can never be known let alone reconstituted from a vast distance, that there are no regimes of truth. And the really big lie that follows from these is that you-the-spectator do not need to know what curators and designers know about you. This is the museum as theatre, the author hidden, with the actors speaking about theatricality and their relations to it – the audience left in the dark.

The display of fragments of colonial Sydney which cannot be reconstituted by the viewer, the use of unrecognisable objects from an undated past and unknown location, the ordering of objects according to an aesthetic convention which breaks any links between them, the highlighting of the fragment and the conceal-ment of the whole, and the removal of written text from display is an effective way of breaking up narratives of time and place relating to colonialism and colonisation. The massed presentation of beautifully placed archaeological fragments is also an effective way of creating a truly Flaubertian unreadable visual text. At the Museum of Sydney, this display is supported by panels of text which consist entirely of quotations.

Such an approach is an effective way of evading the moment of colonisation and of presenting the claim that truth can never be properly known, that the story of what happened when Sydney was founded will vary so much according to who is speaking, that its only truth will lie in the gathering together and presentation of its multiple fragments – make what you will of them. In this way, knowledge and the power to constitute it are each denied to those who most need to have it – those who have come to see and learn something of the past other than what they already know, and those whose pasts and knowledge of them have been denied them. This is to say that Aboriginal people, lesbians and gays, women and other marginalised sectors cannot recognise themselves or their experience and cannot discover it within the fragmented colonial narratives presented through collage, pastiche and irony. Representations of heterogeneity hold no promise because they need to be reconstituted into a homogeneity which, in the absence of opportunity, can only be that which already exists.

Bricolage and pastiche, disruptions of time and place, and hyper-aestheticisation – all of which offer radical political interventions – in this case, seem to work to open up racialised readings of past, present and future that are very difficult to subvert. When these techniques are applied to the objects of Aboriginal culture, the impact is even more worrying. Because of the racialisation of Australian culture, the bitter contests over land ownership and human rights for Aboriginal Australians, all museum displays referring to Aboriginal culture are necessarily difficult and contentious.[2] In the Museum of Sydney, it seems to me that the radical refusal to evaluate is underpinned by conservatising notions of balance and equality which, in other contexts, curators might wish to disavow. In referring to the aesthetics of high art, the use of objects to create a field without value and a text which is intelligible only to a small elite familiar with the interests and concerns of high art, the display refuses to engage with the bulk of its audience.

The Museum of Sydney therefore offers a view in which European settlement in the Sydney region is dealt with through disruption and fragmentation to the extent that most visitors cannot read the text being presented and, if they can, they see that the bric à brac of colonial life has no truth-value and museums less; and furthermore, that Aboriginal history and culture is dealt with through Aboriginal objects illuminated and displayed in ways which leave Aboriginal people where they have always been, on the margins and outside history.

Fiona Foley's sculptures, carried out partly in conjunction with Janet Laurence, illustrate this point. The courtyard or forecourt to the building contains the Fiona Foley sculptures. These magnificent poles combine references to either Aboriginal history, colonisation and Aboriginal life and culture in the present – some are of wood, some of burnished rusted metal, and each bears a reference either to colonisation or Aboriginal culture. Foley and Laurence have combined the shells of middens with concrete in one of the anti-historical panels embedded in the pole. In another there are swathes of the hair that had to be removed from Aboriginal heads before Aboriginal people could be admitted into the more hygienic colonial presence. A number of the poles contain sound, Aboriginal voices speaking, reciting remnant words of Aboriginal languages, names of colonists. You wander in and around 'From the edge of the trees' in a small powerfully evoked sensory landscape that is lodged against the noise of the street and the urban backdrop to it. At least you would, if you stopped or even glanced that way. Most visitors to the museum walk straight past. The poles are tall; they are set in a small space to one side of the approach to the entrance, and most adults simply do not register their presence. Children, however, with their sharper ears and their complete lack of interest in the mechanics of getting family from car to museum to ticket office and with their propensity to simply run away from their minders, hurry into 'the forest' and catch the muted voices. They pause and listen, hug the wood and touch the metal, try to remove the shells, climb up the footholds until called to come inside to go to the museum.

Had the museum been serious about recognising Aboriginal culture – Aboriginal claims to be first in the history of Sydney, Aboriginal claims to own the land – then Foley's forest of poles could have been placed across the front of the museum so that visitors had to pass through them to get in the doors. Instead, the poles stand marginalised, as ever, leaving the heavy paving of the empty forecourt as a Nuremburg style approach to a temple of doom. The museum's concept brief places the space for the sculpture as intersecting with the entrance foyer of the museum. In the course of development, this intersection shifted further from the foyer until even this slight recognition of who owned the land was lost.

The initial concept brief for the public art work states that the museum required a work which would allow visitors to approach the entrance to the museum along the 'edge of the trees', along a line conceptualised as being on the edge of contact. The phrase used to title the public art work being commissioned, 'Edge of the trees', is taken from an essay of Rhys Jones: '. . . the "discoverers" struggling through the surf were met on the beaches by other people looking at them from *the edge of the trees*. Thus the same landscape perceived by the newcomers as alien . . . was to the indigenous people their home, a familiar place, the inspiration of dreams'.[3] There is no Aboriginal voice in the theme of this project of 'reconciliation'; the description naturalises Aboriginal bodies, again, and the concept of 'contact' enshrined within a fragment of text, presents a benign and slippery language which camouflages its facts in the process of presenting them.

Visitors were to approach the museum along the edge of the trees, but the open plaza design ensures that only a random minority of visitors will follow the trajectory of the concept. Were visitors to approach the museum along the 'edge of the trees', there is nothing to make them remark upon them. The labelling is inconspicuously placed so that it is immediately behind the backs of those entering. Those few who leave the museum along the 'edge of the trees' need to be very observant to spot the reasonably large metallic sheet which blends so well with the granite in which it is embedded.

The problem is this. I love museums and have always done so. Especially the old-fashioned ones. But when I visited the new Museum of Sydney I found myself in a quandary. First, this very new museum that had been built on a very large budget, had access to state of the art technology, and had hired very distinguished staff and advisers appeared, at least at first sight, to have paid little attention to Aboriginal claims to be represented within it. And a second puzzle arose from the displays within the museum which seemed, again at first sight, to veer from bricolage to pastiche, and from muddle back to traditional and very familiar narratives of colonialism. Had the big budget, high technology, intellectualised museum turned out to be a cabinet of curiosities, a hall of colonial fragments referring, after all, only to itself? It was all so good looking: it had Fiona Foley's wonderfully imaginative sculptured poles at the front of the museum and which seemed to lay out an Aboriginal land claim; it had Aboriginal voices and faces on video inside; it had used sound as well as sight in order to grab the visitor's attention, and at several points the visitor seemed to be invited to question the concept of the museum itself. What was wrong with a museum which aspired to get so many things 'right'? Why did I feel it did not actually work? Could the problem be located in its aesthetics, pedagogy, architecture, technology, epistemology, history, cultural politics or government? An analysis of the visual strategies of the museum helps to indicate where an answer might lie.

Visual strategies

To appreciate some of the elements of the visual strategies involved and their relation to desire, it is important to recall that those older, fustier museum collections and displays which laid out the order of a natural history of the world were intricately involved in what Foucault referred to as the triumph of the visual (Jay 1988: 187). The visualising of knowledge and the play of visual politics with power and its manifestations in objects is therefore one of the critical aspects of the success or failure of museum displays. Aesthetic conventions informing museum displays can be linked into those informing other areas of artistic production.

The paintings made by the Dutch in the seventeenth century, the century of curios and cabinets, provide a useful starting point for exploring the visual order of the museum. Those well-known landscapes, domestic scenes, still lifes and lively portraits with their shimmering detail and odd perspective can 'best be understood as being an art of *describing* as distinguished from the *narrative* art of Italy' (Alpers 1983: xx). The question of narrative is important because of the ways in which the destruction of the master narratives of Western histories is placed at the heart of so many radical attempts to work outside their discursive constraints. The distinction between narrative and descriptive painting proposed by Svetlana Alpers is helpful, I believe, in providing ways of considering narrative within the museum and can offer insights into the visual tradition of museum displays.

If the visuality of the narrative space of the museum is a *descriptive* visuality, the principles of which were well understood and enunciated in the descriptive picturemaking of the Dutch from the seventeenth to the late nineteenth centuries, then the conventions of narrative picturing will mislead. Alpers distinguishes the descriptive tradition by pointing to the absence of a specific viewing position, a play with great contrasts of scale, the absence of a prior frame so that the world within the work is either cut off by the edges of the picture or extends beyond its bounds, a sense of the picture as surface (rather than as a window) on which words and objects can be replicated or inscribed, an insistence upon the craft of representation so as to recraft surfaces and finally, little stylistic development. Such pictures are not telling the tale of history; they are non-narrative and static. They stand in contrast to the principles of Italian painting during the Renaissance where the picture shows a strong narrative content and aesthetic, and picturing involves the representation of a few large objects which are modelled by light and shadow rather than by surface detail, where the image is framed and where the viewer is strongly positioned as a result of particular conventions of perspective which place both the viewer's and the artist's eye very specifically.

While the Italian form has been the norm for Western iconography and art history, with the Dutch seen as a secondary tradition, it is the descriptive picturing of the Dutch which seems to be particularly relevant to the natural history and history museum (Alpers 1983: xxv and 44). Were this so, then it would follow that Crimp's claim that art history was the discipline and discourse of the museum could be accepted as appropriate for understanding the visuality of both the art museum and the natural history/history museum (Crimp 1983). This is because the Renaissance notions of perspective underpinning what Martin Jay refers to as the 'visual régime of the modern' are worked out in traditional histories of art in conjunction with Cartesian ideas of subjective rationality (Crimp 1983). The perspectives he is referring to are those developed in Italy rather than the conventions of the Dutch painters, but it is the link between perspective and subjectivity which is important, for the exclusion of subjectivity puts into place the hierarchy which makes Dutch painting secondary to the modernism of narrative forms and museum displays 'objective'.

Some of these factors can be seen at work in the museum's *diorama*, for example, a very specialised and technical form of picturing that might be compared with the great panoramic paintings of the Dutch in the seventeenth century.[4] Its deceptive perspective, its large foregrounded figures, often large birds or mammals, and tiny background figures; the absence of a frame, a meticulous concern with surfaces and detail, and of course the parallel interests in text, mapping and mirroring are commonly found in the Dutch panorama. Similarly, the flat display cases of insects, stones and artefacts of old-fashioned museums could again be seen as descriptive picturing. While the objects are in cases, the display itself is generally unframed, the objects are rendered so that surface detail and richness is clear and highlighted, with no modelling by shadow and light, and no positioning of the viewer. The surface qualities are the qualities which mattered as they were the bases of the taxonomic series into which each object fitted. The use of traditional *descriptive* picturing in the Museum of Sydney displays of fragments uses a nostalgia without recognising the quite different narrative form that is being both recalled and destroyed.

Alpers (1983: xxi) points out that because the Dutch paintings were not made within the narrative tradition of the south, because they did not narrate a text, they were considered meaningless. Their meaninglessness also derived from the static nature of some of the pictures. In their stillness they play with space rather than with time, and this too, fits well with the tradition of museum aesthetics, the visuality of the display case, the diorama or the whale skeleton set on a platform, unframed and three dimensional.

Let me summarise my argument so far. It is that the characterisation of Dutch art of the seventeenth century as 'descriptive' (in the sense of their rejecting the framing of the picture, the focus on surfaces, the absence of a constrained viewing point, and their preference for a static image) points to an alternative tradition of representation which can be traced through to the present in museum displays. This tradition offers a way of understanding the aesthetics of museum displays of natural and historical objects in display cases as well as a way of understanding the displays found in art museums. It draws ethnographic, historical and natural history museum displays into the realm of art history and its traditional concerns, and it offers some insights into current debates about aesthetics in history museums.[5] While the descriptive tradition has been seen as generally unconcerned with desire and erotics, this is not necessarily the case.

Discussions now taking place around the erotics of art, particularly in rereadings of the Baroque and the conventions of perspective, are particularly relevant to understanding the erotics of the visual strategies of the museum.[6] Martin Jay (1988: 8), for example, points to the role of Renaissance perspective and its relation to the single eye as ushering in a new 'de-eroticising of the visual order'. 'The moment of erotic projection in vision – what St Augustine had anxiously condemned as "ocular desire" – was, Jay says, 'lost as the bodies of the painter and viewer were forgotten in the name of an allegedly disincarnated, absolute eye' (Jay 1988: 8). While the developing rationalism of what we construe as the dominant tradition provides the basis for a range of theories of the disembodied eye, the gaze and hegemonic visuality, I suspect that the eroticising moment was never lost from art in quite such an absolute way. Rather, the rationalisation of the body was never convincing, particularly in the nude, so that the shift was to a dishonest voyeurism which is absent from the perspective of Dutch descriptive paintings but very much a characteristic of Western constructions of difference, sexuality and modernity. In other words, eroticism and desire were not lost as rationalism advanced, but displaced (as in the Baroque) and reconfigured into a disembodied form. It is the secrecy and its power, the pleasure of the hidden eye that sees intimacy through the window of the picture; it is the power of looking that is thenceforth eroticised, rather than desire itself.[7]

This brief reference to the conventions of the Baroque, then, concerns the distinction I want to make between the erotics of vision, visualising, picturing and art on the one hand, and the erotics of the creation of knowledge itself with its sexualising of relations of power and bodies, and their interplay in the institutional space of the museum on the other. I now return to the museum itself, to consider how best to think about it.

Death, desire and redemption

The museum is often theorised as a space of death or ruination. Douglas Crimp (1983: 43–5), for example, cites Adorno's etymological equivalence of 'museum' and 'mausoleum' and Adorno's view that 'Museums are the family sepulchres of works of art'; he also cites Hilton Kramer's claim that art museums have 'death-dealing capacities'. And Baudrillard (1994: 13) proposes that the completion of the collection would be the death of the collector, a fact of which I wish I had been aware when I was in charge of the National Museum of Australia's social history collections. In a different way, Alpers suggests that the transformation of the object effected by its introduction into the museum, what she calls 'the museum effect' and its way of seeing, might also be construed as the death of the object in order that the object might live, but this is the museum as a space of redemption, a space peculiarly suited to an era of commodity fetishisation (Alpers 1991: 25–7). Are museums so deathly, and if so, why then are museums so seductive, at least to some? Is it the stillness of death, the fascination with the absolutely unknowable, that made the museum such a wonderful place to visit? Should we follow Alpers, and see it as a redemptive space, or at least a space of reification? Should we note that Freud's death drive is tinged with eroticism and pursue an analysis that sought out analogies between classifying, death and erotics? Or is it, as some have suggested, the relief that comes from being able to see the world frozen, as in a single still from a moving film? Or perhaps the satisfaction of the eye? Or the ultimate satisfaction of order itself?

Foucault, Heidegger, in-sight

Foucault (1980: 98) claims that from the sixteenth century, sex and the revelation of truth came to be linked together so that the apparatus of sexuality was articulated onto power. In thinking about the implications of Foucault's proposal as it relates to the museum and the academic knowledges it eventually represented, it is particularly important to reflect upon that section of his work in which he relates the pleasure that comes from exercising a power which questions, watches, spies out and brings to light that which it seeks to show is truly there (Foucault 1978: 45). It is the visuality, the invasive quality of the disembodied gaze, and the power of sight to bring truth into light that is significant in his understanding of power. And it is the sexualisation of the order of knowledge that set in with the Enlightenment, that provided the power and pleasure of an increasingly normalised heterosexual gender order.[8]

Foucault's shift away from phenomenological modes of thinking make the realigning of Foucault and Heidegger an adventurous task. In discussing Heidegger's phenomenology of Being, I note his opposition to the particular kinds of seeing that are concerned with the discourses of objectivity and rationality which inform so much of Western knowledge. However, it is precisely the procreative moment of coming into illumination that brings forth knowledge and understanding that is theorised in Heidegger that creates the space in which Foucault's analysis of the centrality of sexuality and the eye can be placed to produce an understanding of desire and the erotics of knowledge.

In this configuration, Foucault's analytics brings to Heidegger's phenomenology the dimension of power; it brings Being back to bodies and subjectivity. This is because, in Foucault's view, the individual is conceptualised as the product of a relation of power and truth exercised over and through bodies. That is to say that truth is produced through power onto bodies, and power cannot be exercised except through the production of truth.

There are other ways of approaching erotics, of course, particularly in the visual arts. Pemiola (1989: 237), for example, sees eroticism in the 'figurative arts' as 'a relationship between clothing and nudity' and as conditional upon movement or transit between one state or another. But what I am configuring here is the eroticising of knowledge itself, and more specifically, the eroticisation of the moment of illumination at which knowledge, understanding or truth comes into light and into sight.

In making a distinction between the erotics of knowledge, of coming to know, and the sexualising of an order of knowledge, I am pointing to what I see as a relation of power which informs an ontology and an aligned epistemology that can be seen as being deployed within the practices of daily life. This is one reason for sexual difference becoming so central to philosophy and metaphysics at the present time, for the Western sexual order which claims to be, as I have said, essentially heterosexual.[9] When Foucault discusses the productive capacities of power, and points to the ways in which it induces pleasure, forms knowledge and produces discourse, he brings us to a position where we can consider the production of knowledge as pleasurable in itself (Foucault 1980: 63).[10]

In order to consider the proposition that the enlightenment offered by the museum is eroticised, I leave aside the museum for a moment in order to examine the pleasures of knowledge and knowing. I begin with a cautious reading of the metaphysics of Martin Heidegger. While it might be objected that Heidegger's phenomenology contains a strong attack on the ocularcentrism of Western philosophy and science, I think that his concern with illumination and the generation of in-sight can be carried into the discussion of the ontology and epistemology of the museum and its forms of representation.[11] In his discussion of technology and its mode of knowing and being, he proposes that a knowing is always a *poiesis*, a bringing forth. That 'bringing forth' (and here I use Heidegger's own terminology) occurs when something which is concealed comes into what he labels as unconcealment (Heidegger 1977: 47). As Heidegger develops his understanding of the nature of technological knowledge, the most important proposal from my point of view is that the revealing and the unconcealing of knowledge is always simultaneously an excluding and a concealing. The control of this moment must be of immense importance and is the moment of power and genesis.

In the essay called 'The turning', Heidegger sets out the view that within the danger surrounding knowledge of the true, lies also what he calls the saving power. What is required is for the 'turning' of the danger so that it can be made to reveal Being. This 'turning' is experienced, he suggests, as a lighting up, a sudden flash which is the glance. This is the moment and circumstance of in-sight. But the origin of the flash in the unlighted is concealed so that again, there is a bringing into light that is simultaneously part of a darkening or concealing (Heidegger 1977: 47).

The simultaneous disclosing into light and casting into darkness that in-sight and new knowledge imply, offer a way of approaching the relations of power that inhere in knowledge itself and the ways in which the creation of a truth is always shadowed by its necessary exclusions. In the creation of natural and historical taxonomies, for example, the bringing into light of the similarities on which their order is to be based will never be exhaustive, can never register the totality, and will simultaneously exclude similarities in order to create the differences upon which taxonomic categories are based. This order is present and recoverable from cabinets of curiosities as well as from nineteenth-century museum displays. The appreciation of this hidden order, its bringing into light, is an aspect not only of the museum's displays and their aesthetic, but also of the spectator or viewer's experience of them.

In the moment of illumination that exposes the order that was hidden, lies the promise and seduction of the taxonomies on display. The taxonomies and keys to the order of nature and human nature offer not only a truth but the totalising possibility of closure. In other words, they offer the possibility that the persistent and overwhelming diversity of the world can be ordered in total, that limitless systems can be bounded and limited. It is this aspect of the museum that causes them to be seen sometimes as absolute heterogeneity and sometimes as totally homogenising. And it is both the homogeneity and its narratives which constitute the big lie. Yet in a sense, that moment of illumination which brings into view the taxonomic order of the world does not lie. For it appears to bring into view the principles of that order, whether they be true or false. It is the claim of those orders and the claim that vision (their seeing) guarantees their truth which is false, not their conjuring into view. In order to leave behind something less than the seventeenth-century cabinet of curiosities from whence we came, the *very* modern Museum of Sydney, of course, does away with taxonomies altogether. Techniques of pastiche, collage and irony present an informed and aestheticised political statement about the nature of the museum itself but nothing about the nature of the world or its histories – that so much difficult theoretical work should take the Museum so far!

Conclusion

The museum's *poiesis*, however, is explicitly pictorial. The unframed nature of the museum exhibit or display and the unpositioned viewer are critical elements in creating the conditions for this bringing forth, this unconcealing of order. The flash of in-sight that comes with the objectifying gaze of the spectator is therefore specifically visual. This moment of seeing and knowing, a moment of bringing into light is a moment of power. As a moment of subjection and control, within Western knowledges it is always sexualised, gendered, eroticised.

The proposition explored in this chapter is that the pleasures of the museum are essential to it, that the 'facts' collected in it and presented through visual display are immensely seductive, and that both the pleasure and seduction of the museum constitute an erotics in which race and sexuality are never absent. In the Museum of Sydney, the pleasure of the order of knowledge has been restricted to a point where it becomes accessible to a tiny minority who believe that a nihilistic emptiness is somehow miraculously emptied of power, race and sexuality, to leave a purified aesthetic which is thought to be subversive.

These are the failings that leave the Museum of Sydney in something of a cultural, political and aesthetic mess, failings which are illustrated particularly clearly in the visual choices being made in the display of Sydney's foundational colonial moments. The visitor follows a carefully defined trajectory, entering not along the edge of the trees, at a moment of contact no matter how evasive that might be, but rather across the plaza of governance, moving from a glimpse of the original foundations of Government House, to a further glimpse of foundations displayed at the street level entrance, and then on to a first floor gallery that utilises postmodern theory in ways which replicate the colonial narrative they seek to subvert. The Museum of Sydney collapses into a traditional tale of urban foundations, an essentially European dream of reconciliation based on the continuing marginalisation of Aboriginal people, their rights and their concerns.

Notes

1   I should like to thank the convenors of the theme year in the Graduate Research Centre for Culture and Communication at the University of Sussex for the opportunity to join them and for the stimulus to begin to prepare an essay on a topic that had been endlessly deferred. I am particularly grateful for the assistance of Catherine Rogers, who made the images for [the original version of] this essay, in drawing relevant literature to my attention and for the opportunity to discuss aspects of art and art theory with her, and to Andrea Malone for bearing with me while it happened.

2   Most Australian museums have Aboriginal advisers to assist with displays and exhibitions relating to Aboriginal culture. Institutional politics and personal relationships make for some very difficult decisions, out of which emerge self-justifying defences against critique. The Museum of Sydney utilised Aboriginal advice for this display.

3   This passage is taken from Rhys Jones (1985) 'Ordering the landscape' in Ian and Tamsin Donaldson (eds) *Seeing the First Australians*, Sydney. It is engraved close to the Laurence and Foley sculptures. Given the author's ambiguous relationship to some of the most critical aspects of Aboriginal views of their own history and the ownership of cultural property, the use of his phrasing in this context is not particularly appropriate.

4   Panoramic picturing has an interesting history with photographers taking up some of the earlier problems it poses. It is widely used in ethnographic and scientific texts. For a recent commentary, see Peter Emmett's (1996) exhibition catalogue. Compare Ann Reynolds (1995).

5   Martin Jay (1993: 52–3) also refers to this point: '. . . it [perspective] functioned in a similar way for the new scientific order. In both cases [painting and science] space was robbed of its substantive meaningfulness to become an ordered, uniform system of abstract linear coordinates. As such, it was less the stage for a narrative to be developed over time than the eternal container of objective processes. It was not

until the time of Darwin that narrative regained a significant place in the self-understanding of science'.

6 Compare Stafford (1991).

7 Kenneth Clark's (1956) attempt to define the nude illustrates the point: 'In the greatest age of painting the nude inspired the greatest works.' (*ibid.*: 1) 'We do not wish to imitate [the body]; we wish to perfect it. (*ibid.*: 4) 'No nude, however abstract, should fail to rouse in the spectator some vestige of erotic feeling, even although it be the faintest shadow – and if it does not do so, it is bad art and false morals.' (*ibid.*: 6)

In Sir Kenneth's work we see at work the nexus between power, sexuality and gender which is partly traced out by Foucault in his account of the history of heterosexuality, perversion and power from the Enlightenment to the present. Secrecy is critical to Foucault's analysis and it is precisely this which forms the viewing eye as a voyeuristic one.

8 How else to explain Queen Victoria's apocryphal puzzlement over what on earth lesbians could actually do, and how, too, to account not only for the complete ignorance of students and the media over how women could possibly have sex with each other without a dildo, let alone find it stunningly erotic.

9 Compare Monique Wittig (1992), Luce Irigaray (1984 and 1985), Elizabeth Grosz (1994).

10 'A discursive formation must be grasped in the form of a system of regular dispersion of statements', Foucault (1980: 63).

11 See also Martin Jay (1993: 273–5).

References

Alpers, Svetlana (1983) *The Art of Describing. Dutch Art in the Seventeenth Century*, Harmondsworth: Penguin.

Alpers, Svetlana (1991) 'The museum as a way of seeing', in I. Karp and S. D. Levine (eds) *Exhibiting Cultures. The Poetics and Politics of Museum Display*, Washington DC: Smithsonian Institution Press.

Baudrillard, Jean (1994) 'The system of collecting', in J. Elsner and R. Cardinal (eds) *The Cultures of Collecting*, Melbourne: Melbourne University Press.

Clark, Kenneth (1956) *The Nude*, Harmondsworth: Penguin Books.

Crew, Spencer R. and Sims, James E. (1991) 'Locating authenticity: fragments of a Dialogue', in I. Karp and S. D. Lavine (eds) *Exhibiting Cultures. The Poetics and Politics of Museum Display*, Washington, DC: Smithsonian Institution Press.

Crimp, Douglas (1983) 'On the museum's ruins', in Hal Foster (ed.) *The Anti-Aesthetic. Essays on Postmodern Culture*, Seattle, WA: Bay Press.

Donato, E. (1979) 'The museum's furnace: notes toward a contextual reading of "Bouvard and Pécuchet"', in J. V. Harari (ed.) *Textual Strategies. Perspectives in Post-Structuralist Criticism*, Ithaca: Cornell University Press.

Emmett, Peter (ed.) (1996) *Sydney Vistas. Panoramic Views 1788–1995*, Sydney: Museum of Sydney.

Foucault, Michel (1978 [1976]) *The History of Sexuality. Volume 1: An Introduction*, Harmondsworth: Penguin.

Foucault, Michel (1980) *Power / Knowledge. Selected Interviews and Other Writings 1972–1977*, edited by Colin Gordon, New York: Pantheon Books.

Grosz, Elizabeth (1994) *Volatile Bodies. Toward a Corporeal Feminism*, Sydney: Allen & Unwin.

Heidegger, Martin (1977 [1954]) *The Question Concerning Technology and Other Essays*, New York: Harper Colophon Books.

Irigaray, Luce (1984) *Ethique de la différance sexuelle*, Paris: Minuit.

Irigaray, Luce (1985) *This Sex Which is not One*, Ithaca NY: Cornell University Press.

Jay, Martin (1988) 'Scopic régimes of modernity', in Hal Foster (ed.) *Vision and Visuality*, Seattle, WA: Bay Press.

Jay, Martin (1993) *Downcast Eyes. The Denigration of Vision in Twentieth Century French Thought*, Berkeley and Los Angeles: University of California Press.

Pemiola, Mario (1989) 'Between clothing and nudity', in Michel Feher (ed.) *Fragments for a History of the Human Body*, part 2, New York: Zone Books.

Reynolds, Ann (1995) 'Visual stories', in Lynne Cooke and Peter Wollen (eds) *Visual Display. Culture Beyond Appearances*, Seattle, WA: Bay Press.

Stafford, Barbara Maria (1991) *Body Criticism. Imaging the Unseen in Enlightenment Art and Medicine*, Cambridge, MA: MIT Press.

Wittig, Monique (1992) *The Straight Mind and Other Essays*, Hemel Hempstead: Harvester Wheatsheaf.

Chapter 21

For your eyes only?
The magic touch of relics

Jan Geisbusch

Introduction

'It hit the spectator like a bullet, it happened to him, thus acquiring a tactile quality.'
Walter Benjamin is alluding to the way Dadaist art had exploded the solemnity and
intellectual detachment that formerly characterised the reception of artworks
(1937/1999, 231). Whatever the merits of this particular appraisal, we are interested
here in the connection Benjamin establishes between impact and tactility. It is this
kind of sensuous 'drive-by shooting' that I explore here, though its ammunition is
sacred objects rather than art (notwithstanding some overlap between the two
categories, as discussed in this chapter). Our central concern is what might be termed
'modalities of perception' and their experiential and social implications with regard
to the sacred.

Seeing and touching – as well as hearing, tasting, and smelling, though these are
not our focus – represent complementing, but more often competing, modes of
sensory experience. This chapter argues that they are implicated in broader issues
over the development of a Western subject, its agency within the world, and, more
specific to the topic, how it has conceptualised the sacred.

Relics

First of all, we need to clarify what is meant by 'relics'. The *Oxford Dictionary of the
Christian Church* provides a workable definition: 'In Christian usage the word is applied
to the material remains of a saint after his death and to sacred objects which have been
in contact with his body' (Livingstone 1996, 433). Historically, such relics, especially
the major ones, present themselves to us boxed into reliquaries, permanently installed

in tombs and shrines. Typically, scholarly literature addressing the subject understands relics primarily as fixed, localised objects. Even analyses such as Geary's *Furta Sacra* (1978) and 'Sacred commodities' (1990), which show medieval relics in motion through gift giving, theft, or trade, assume that this state is only temporary, a movement between two points of immovability.

The natural condition of relics, it is implied, is that of motionlessness as the centre of sacred space. Their occasional movement is something of a liminal state, erasing, or at any rate threatening, the relic's ascribed cosmological position and authority; this authority has to be reconfirmed once the relic is installed in a new location – through miracles or heavenly signs, and through the incorporation into the new physical and institutional setting (the shrine and the religious community).

Yet there are also relics, and a vast multitude of them, the purpose of which is not to stay put but to circulate. These are the sort of relics that are available from religious congregations, religious goods shops, and even eBay, the Internet auction house. The Carmelite Sisters of Lisieux, for example, distributed an estimated 17 million (!) relics of their co-sister, St Theresa of the Child Jesus (1873–1897), between 1897 and 1925 (Erret 2003, 12). Even today, religious congregations often use the distribution of relics to promote the cause of a candidate for sainthood or foster the devotion to a saint already canonized. Orders may give away actual particles of the body, typically bone fragments placed in a *theca*, a small metal locket secured by a wax seal; or they issue prayer cards or medals of inexpensive material carrying particles of cloth that was either used by saints during their lifetime or touched to a body relic. Relics such as these can be manufactured cheaply on a large scale and, in the case of contact relics, ad infinitum. They are the kind of relic that is destined to serve private devotions, or at any rate often enough ends up in private hands.

The magic touch

What role does touch play in these devotional practices? The mittens of Padre Pio serve as an illustration. Born Francesco Forgione in 1887, Padre Pio was a priest and Capuchin friar living in Southern Italy. In 1918 he received the stigmata, the wounds of Christ, and soon his reputation as a mystic and miracle worker began to spread. This brought him into conflict with the Church hierarchy, which accused him of various sorts of misdeeds, from financial fraud to sexual abuse of female parishioners. With his name eventually cleared, he became the centre of a popular cult[1] during his lifetime. While working for the spiritual salvation of his flock, Padre Pio also managed to turn around the economic fortunes of San Giovanni Rotondo, the rural backwater where he lived, by founding a large hospital. After his death in 1968, this 'hospital industry' was further complemented by a 'pilgrimage industry', which today draws pilgrims in numbers comparable to Lourdes or Fatima. In 2002 Padre Pio was canonized, in one of the most high-profile cases of recent times (see McKevitt 1991).

Relics of Padre Pio, especially cards and medals (sometimes of dubious origin) are widely and easily available from his order, religious goods shops, or eBay. Not so easy to obtain – in fact highly limited in their availability – are more substantial relics, such as his mittens (which he used to cover the stigmata in his hands), although quite a few of them are extant. At least one such pair of mittens is in the UK, in the possession of MD, a devotee who uses the mittens in her pastoral work. Being partly of Italian stock, MD had known of Padre Pio since her childhood, though he became a significant presence in her life only after the sudden death of her husband, which left her in deep and lasting distress. It was during a special Padre Pio Mass, held at a church in her vicinity, that something like a healing process dramatically set in. It was at this point that the 'magic touch' made itself felt. In her words:

> At the close of the Mass, the priest placed a mitten of Padre Pio on the head of each individual. This was the first time for me. As soon as the mitten was placed on my head, I can only describe the feeling as a bolt of lightning going through me. I felt as though I was stuck to the floor and could not move away. I also felt I was standing there for a long time, although this could not have been possible. I made my way to the back of the church, turned to my friend [who had brought her there], and instantly burst into tears. I asked her if she felt anything. She replied 'Wow, did I feel that.' It was a very emotional night.
>
> (pers. comm. 2004)

MD then became a regular worshipper at this Mass and eventually was given a mitten of Padre Pio as a gift:

> She placed the mitten in my hand and then her hand on top. I felt the plastic covering the mitten very cold, yet the mitten was burning hot. I cannot explain that. She prayed to Padre Pio to make his presence known to me and show me I was not alone.
>
> (pers. comm. 2004)

MD then became increasingly involved with the friars of San Giovanni Rotondo, working as a translator for them and distributing information material on Padre Pio. The mittens continue to play an important part in her local pastoral activities:

> Mainly, people ask us to visit friends/relatives who are sick. . . . Many feel the comfort of holding the mitten. As far as I know, other mittens used (which have been 'entrusted' and are eventually returned to the Friary) are encased in plastic. My mitten was gifted to me, and so I have chosen not to cover it. I have never believed that Padre Pio would put his hand inside a plastic bag before he would allow people to touch him. . . . Also, my mitten had some crusts/scabs from Padre Pio's hand inside it, and I know it comforts people to see these.
>
> (pers. comm. 2004)

There were also occurrences when the mittens made themselves felt in a different way, emitting a scent of violets – a phenomenon known as 'odour of sanctity' and a well-worn hagiographic topos also reported by other sources on Padre Pio. It is not necessary here to determine the veracity of this phenomenon or explain its occurrence; what is interesting is the appeal to senses other than visual perception, which is perhaps the sense most commonly associated with relics in particular, and with Roman Catholicism more generally.

What, then, are we to make of these practices? For an answer, or at least for some suggestions, we turn to the notion of magic. While the work of Frazer has lost much of its significance in anthropology, his writings on magic (notwithstanding the theoretical problems relating to the term) are still useful. The notion of 'contagious magic' can especially help to focus attention on the very materiality of the object, making it clear that the connection between the relic, the saint, and the saint's power is not metaphorical. The relic is remarkable (and potent) because it has been in actual physical contact with, or is indeed derived from, the very substance of the saint.

Though the theology behind them is subtler and more complex, often downplaying the material aspect, relics are typically perceived not just as reminders but remainders, not *like* but *of* the saint. While doctrinally not quite correct, the relic thus frequently evokes an image of being inhabited, animated, by the saint, imbued with something like a 'real presence' (Dinzelbacher 1990). As MD put it to me: 'I understand what you say about praying only [when asked about the relation to praying of internal faith as opposed to external objects], but I think it helps the sick to feel "closer" to the Saint from whom they ask intercession' (pers. comm. 2004).

Visual piety: when seeing is believing

We need to remember that relics are not only experienced through touch but also, and perhaps more so, through sight. *Schaufrömmigkeit* (visual piety) is a core element of Catholic devotion with a most venerable tradition, reaching back at least to the mid-to-late twelfth century, when reliquaries first became transparent through the use of crystal windows that allowed a view of the relic inside. As Diedrichs points out, this was a development with far-reaching art historical and devotional consequences: 'The medium of veneration turns into its object; the believer becomes spectator. . . . Face to face with the new kind of reliquary the observer confronts, as subject, the object of his contemplation' (2001, 9; translation my own). Diedrichs regards this development as the starting point of a growing externalisation of devotion and an increase in superstitious practices, a case of popular piety subverting the spiritual and intellectual principles of the Church's teachings.

We might ask whether the rise of visual piety as characterised by Diedrichs did not rather prefigure the first dawn of our uneasy, incomplete modernity. What we witness is the slow rise of an 'era of art' after an 'era before art' (Belting 1994) that would no longer recognise objects serving as conduits of the sacred, but only objects of (supposedly) disinterested contemplation. Heidegger speaks of the 'world as picture', distinguishing the modern age, where 'man' is no longer 'the one who is looked upon by that which is', but instead 'that which is . . . come[s] into being . . . through the fact that man first looks upon it' (quoted in Pinney 2002a, 360).

Apart from Heidegger, a substantial body of scholarship (e.g. Merleau-Ponty 2002 [1962]; Foucault 1975; Jay 1988) critically connects the emergence of the modern Western subject with the rise of sight as the privileged mode of perception, thus engendering a relation of detachment from the world. Disembodied and disinterested, the world is positioned as the passive subject of man's dissecting eye. Of course, as Pinney notes, there are still aspects of Western visual culture that are predicated on an engaged beholder (citing pornography and the iconography of sport, to which I add advertising). They constitute not so much an aesthetics – a system of scholarly, disengaged reflection – but what Pinney terms *corpothetics*, the 'sensory embrace of images, the bodily engagement that most people (except Kantians and modernists) have with artworks' (2001, 158).

Arguably, Catholicism too has always been responsive to corpothetic practices. At the same time as we see the rise of visual piety, there is ample evidence that the sacred retained its material quality: we may think of the (alleged) comb of St Hildegard (1098–1179), now kept at the Bayerisches Nationalmuseum, which was used by the Benedictine nuns of Eibingen (Hesse, Germany) to cure their headaches (van Os 2001, 157ff); or of the German altar piece, *The Blood Miracle of the Franciscan Martyrs of Morocco* (ca. 1460; Germanisches Nationalmuseum Nürnberg) that shows the faithful crouching around the saints' shrine, rubbing off its power with pieces of cloth (a type of contact relic known as *brandea* since antiquity). Similar evidence can be found on a Dutch altar piece (ca. 1500; Museum Catharijnenconvent, Utrecht) depicting the shrine of St Kunera, from the railings of which hang strips of cloth to be wrapped around injured limbs by devotees seeking a cure. Even today, liturgy, the images of saints, the architectonic splendour of churches, incense, music, and, of course, relics can be seen as constituting a network in which the believer, instead of being an aloof observer, willingly gets caught up with all senses.

Exactly how comfortable are institutions like the Church hierarchy (or the museum, as we shall discuss later) with the 'performative dimension of the artefact' (Pinney 2001, 157)? Do they not rather assert 'those European subject/object distinctions which have insisted on the triumph of discourse over figure as part of its strategy to degrade the agency of objects' (Pinney 2002b, 139f)? Already in the 1960s Mary Douglas argued that, due to an overly intellectual training, large parts of the Catholic hierarchy are debilitated in that they 'cannot conceive of the deity as located in any one thing or place' (2003 [1970], 52).

I would argue that there is a strong inclination within the Catholic Church to disentangle the religious self from the 'sticky touch' of objects, to marginalise certain devotional forms (tellingly subsumed under the heading 'popular piety') and, animated by the same dynamics, to displace certain objects from the shrine to the museum. During fieldwork I often noticed how aesthetics rather than corpothetics resonate with the sensibilities of many of today's clergy. They prefer to 'read' the relic, to understand it in a symbolic fashion as a sign of exemplary virtue, of hope, of salvation, of historic continuity, or of institutional memory. It is rarely (and only if carefully hedged by theological subtleties) a repository of a tangible and powerful presence.

Making the sacred tangible

In contrast to the ideology of the eye, touch recognises that subjects are not really detachable from the world. It is the only sensual perception that works as a mutual, two-way process – while touching I am being touched, while being touched I touch the other – allowing the experience of the world as contingent and interconnected, questioning the sharp divide between object and subject. It is eminently human and potent, as is shown in the case of Padre Pio's mittens: the close and prolonged contact with the unprotected relic, its plastic cover removed, creates a deeper intimacy between saint and devotee than could sight alone.

I would argue that touch remains central to certain religious practices like, for example, the cult of relics. For what are relics if not touch made permanent? The whole concept of the relic is based on the idea of transfer through physical proximity. Once the sacred has entered the world, has taken residence in the bone and flesh of a holy person, it spreads through contact, through contagion. Certainly, devotees may and do converse with the sacred through vision, yet often enough it is the tactile, corporeal encounter that prompts visual piety as, for example, with the shroud of Turin, or the *sudarium* (Veronica's veil upon which Christ left an impression of his face), or the blood-stained bandages from Padre Pio's hands, which were shown to me at the Capuchin headquarters in Rome. These are remarkable (or holy, if you are a believer) not because they depict or signify something but because they have been in actual contact with something (or rather, someone).

'*Dreikönigenzettel* (literally, Three-Kings slips) are just printed pieces of paper or fabric and their linguistic/pictorial representations may stimulate piety and devotion. Yet their capacity to protect from 'dangers while travelling, falling sickness, headaches, sudden death, poison and witchcraft' derives from the fact that they have been touched to the 'heads and relics of the Magi at Cologne'" (Beer & Rehm 2004, 1; translation my own). *Thecas* usually have little loops so they can be worn as a pendant or attached to a rosary, which of course encourages their handling.

Visual contemplation thus easily blurs with other forms of perception: a *theca* may be fondled during prayer; holy pictures given away at pilgrimage sites are proof that the devotee has undertaken not just a spiritual but a geographical journey, experiencing all the attendant physical sensations and discomforts of such an undertaking; little devotional prints (*Schluckbilder*, literally, swallow pictures) could be ingested for purposes of healing and protection, a practice that draws an intriguing connection to medical drugs, whose distribution and dispensation, like that of relics, can also be fraught by disputes between experts and lay users.

Touch reminds us how much the sacred is predicated on the material and the corporeal, how much it is a corpothetics rather than an aesthetics (or a theology) – a matter of engagement, interest, desire, captivation, manipulation rather than dispassionate contemplation, study, or belief. Sight *can* do this too, as demonstrated in detail by Pinney (2001, 2002a, 2004) and Morgan (1998, 2005). But in the West at least sight is also deeply implicated in the radical subject/object divide of our supposed modernity that privileges the dissociating vision of contemplation over the associating vision that permeates popular cultures. As Miller (2005, 1) reminds us, '[t]here is an underlying principle to be found in most of the religions that dominate recorded history. Wisdom has been accredited to those who claim that materiality represents the merely apparent, behind which lies that which is real. . . . Nevertheless, paradoxically, material culture has been of considerable consequences as the means of expressing this conviction.' No wonder, then, that hands-on experiences are often frowned upon or seen with concern as prone to slippage into heterodoxy and superstition. It is the unease felt at the return of the repressed.

The recalcitrant sensuous cannot but assume a haunting and troublesome aspect to a disembodied gaze that has imagined itself to be rid of the world and its things and is therefore now unable to recognise what confronts it. The fetish – often disparagingly invoked by clerical informants as the pitfall of the naïve believer – is thus indeed a figure of misapprehension, but less a misapprehension of the fetishist (so-called) than of its enlightened critic. Magic, superstition, fetishism – those traps into which relic practices are apparently so liable to fall – thus come to be seen as disparities of perception and at the same time as disparities of social interests: elite interests that are (can afford to be) conceptual, intellectual, cosmological, one step removed from everyday necessities – ocularcentric; and 'popular' interests that are (cannot escape being) down-to-earth, pragmatic, and banal, but pressing nonetheless – tangible in more than one sense. As Bourdieu put it: 'Each dominated practice or testimony of belief is condemned to appear as a profanation to the extent that it represents, through its mere existence and even without profane intent, an objective contestation of the monopoly to administer the sacred, that is to say of the legitimacy of the owners of this monopoly' (Bourdieu 2000, 66; translation my own). Differences in sensory experience thus have their specific material and institutional locations; in fact, they could be said to be expressive as well as constitutive of these locations.

Magic behind glass

Like the Church hierarchy, the museum is another site where touch is relegated to the margins. In the UK, and possibly in most countries outside the Catholic Mediterranean, relics are today usually encountered in museums rather than in their natural habitat – they have become museological artefacts. More precisely, what one encounters (and what is privileged) is inevitably the *reliquary*, the container, with little or no mention of whether it still contains any relics and what their nature may be. Given the precious and intricate design of many medieval and early modern pieces this is understandable, and yet it is somewhat perverse. It is like preferring the gift box to the gift. Furthermore, what tends to be collected and preserved are the outstanding pieces of craftsmanship, those of high material and aesthetic value, as, for example, the Eltenberg Reliquary at the Victoria and Albert Museum or the Holy Thorn Reliquary of Duke Jean de Berri at the British Museum.[2]

Often overlooked are the myriad devotional objects of humble appearance and little value – the ones we consider here – the medals and prayer cards, the *thecas* and paper sachets containing a bit of holy dust that belong to the ill-defined domains of private devotion and popular religion. While there can be no doubt that museums have saved many sacred objects, they have done so *in their fashion*, preserving their physical existence, yet bleaching them of energy and meaning. It is the museological gaze that Foucault saw as emblematic of Western modernity, imprisoning the object within discourse, 'abstracted in a space beyond touch' (Pinney 2002b, 140).

The question is: Can our museums be more than just dutiful but impassive guardians content to salvage the raw material for monographs on twelfth-century enamel techniques or seventeenth-century goldsmithing? Indeed, curators themselves are aware that something may be amiss. The catalogue of a French exhibition opens with the statement that 'more and more have reliquaries become an object of the museological type. . . . One admires the art work, the technique; one studies the messages revealed through iconography; but the sacred has today nearly vanished' (Musée d'Art Sacré du Gard 2000, 5; translation my own). But has it? Or is the museum simply ill-equipped for its presentation? In a poem on the ethnographic collection of the Pitt Rivers Museum in Oxford, James Fenton brings out the fascination that objects can hold, even within this classical space of Enlightenment rationality. Tellingly, though, it is a childhood experience he recalls, not yet organised by the quest for meaning and its control, but open to an 'affective intensity' (Pinney 2002b, 132), that is to say, to fascination, enchantment, and desire. The poem mixes the exotic – witches' hair, earth from a grave, tigers – with the danger of encountering the unknown and getting lost in it; yet, with the danger also comes the allure of imagination, of creating one's own magical world (Fenton 1983, 83).

Looking at the questions of whether and how relics could be featured within the museum or heritage sector, three main issues confront us: presentation, conservation, and propriety.

If the sacred has vanished, part of the reason is that the typical museum setting is not especially conducive to its aura. As the bourgeois temple of elite culture, the museum's cult is a secular one (Duncan 1995). To let devotional objects shine will therefore, at least in part, be a matter of presentation. While educational requirements must be taken into account, so should sensuous qualities. The presentation of devotional objects should allow the visitor not only to learn but also to experience. Curators, exhibition designers, and architects may want to address this question. While there is a long tradition of visual piety, there is a crucial difference between the vision of worshippers, who are immersed in a numinous presence, and the vision of the curator, who strongly influences how the visitor is going to look at an object.

Hands-on experience: enabling a culture of touch

Visual presentations, of course, have the advantage of causing the least wear and tear and are therefore the preferred solution from a conservator's point of view. Yet, to look at a relic is only half the story. That it is possible to create a more physical experience is illustrated by the example of Louis Peters. A lawyer from Cologne, Germany, he owned until recently one of *the* major relic collections not in ecclesiastical hands,[3] one containing around five hundred pieces, ranging from tiny *thecas* to sizeable shrines, dating mostly from the eighteenth and nineteenth centuries. The collection was shown in a number of exhibitions around Germany and Austria during the 1980s and 1990s.

The 1989 show at the renowned Schnütgen Museum for medieval art in Cologne marked something of a watershed because it generated renewed interest in relics and popular piety among curators and scholars alike. Peters himself has always attached great importance to the haptic dimension of his pieces and he has been scathing of 'overprotective' curators. He deplores the decline of our 'culture of touch', due to the 'fixation of our art historians and conservators who would much prefer to let their objects rot in deserted rooms, protected from light and breath. And yet our relic and shrine culture is utterly a cult of touch, badly in need of rejuvenation' (Peters 1994, 104; translation my own).

During the exhibition of 1989 many objects were therefore freely accessible, and in guided tours Peters would pass around *thecas* to be handled by visitors. Obviously, we would not want to find the Eltenberg Reliquary passed around a class of sixth formers; but the sacred objects that concern us here – the *thecas*, holy cards, relic medals – are usually neither rare nor valuable. Within certain limits, it is therefore possible to allow greater proximity between visitors and objects. Of course, objects will be worn out in this process. But perhaps we can contemplate the possibility that using up an object in this way is not the museum's loss so much as the visitors' profit.

If this is an unusual concept for curators and art historians, it is not necessarily so for anthropologists. Susanne Küchler (1988) points out, in an article on *malanggan*, how time can be confounded and memory produced through destruction rather than preservation. Wooden sculptures created for funereal ceremonies by the natives of New Ireland, Papua New Guinea, *malanggan* are intentionally left to rot as part of the ritual process, transforming the sculpture into a memorised image. I would argue that relics can activate a similar process. As they carry a strong message of *vanitas*, the remains of the saints, ingeniously, speak not only of life everlasting but also of the fact that all things must come to perish. They present death as the mirror in which to reflect on ourselves.

Conservation does not need to be an intractable problem. We could look instead at propriety: how appropriate is the presentation of sacred objects in a museum context and what difference does it make if we allow or even encourage their touching by visitors? Recalling incidents like the condemnation by Christian groups of the BBC's broadcasting of *Jerry Springer: The Opera*, or the cancellation of a production of *Idomeneo* in Berlin over fears of possible violent actions by Muslim extremists, it is clear that religion and its representation within the culture industries has become a touchy issue.

In a related, though less threatening way, many museums have been under pressure from indigenous groups to sort out their holdings of sacred objects and human remains, through removal from display, repatriation, or by allowing native worshippers access to them on museum premises. The British Museum's *A'a*, for example, the wooden sculpture of a deity from Rurutu, Polynesia, is still being visited by Rurutuans to pay homage through song, performance, and offerings. Another good example even closer to this subject matter is the 1999 exhibition 'La mort n'en saura rien – Head Relics from Europe and Oceania' at the Musée National des Arts d'Afrique et d'Océanie (MNAAO) in Paris. A colloquium of curators, scholars, and government officials discussed the questions of whether these artefacts could be exhibited at all (and, if so, how). Since these head relics, the skulls of ancestors, are regarded as highly potent, curators first obtained the agreement of elders, who released them for display after having ritually removed the skulls' indwelling 'souls' (to be reinstalled upon their return). In the particular case of Christian relics, the relevant interest groups to consult might include the local ordinary, the Vatican Congregation for the Causes of the Saints (which has technical authority over relics), the religious community to which the saint belonged, or the place of worship from which the relic originally came, if it can be identified.

Conclusion

I have presented an analysis of religious practice centred around two modalities of perception: vision and touch. Visual piety has a long and vital tradition, and vision possibly constitutes the dominant mode of perception in our society, being nearly coterminous with the project of modernity and the emergence of a particular modern subjectivity. But touch remains a central part of religious practice, a transmitter of equally powerful and possibly more intimate experiences of the sacred.

Relics play an important part in this experience, notwithstanding a theology that tends to aestheticise their function, that is to say, to read them in an abstract symbolic fashion, thus distancing them from all-too-physical experiences. Yet the intimacy of the religious touch is often beset with unease: Does its sensual, affective quality imply an inherent power? Can it be contained within the religious field or is it destined to be marginalised as magic, fetishism, and superstition from an institutional point of view? Unlikely candidates, perhaps, for such an assessment, yet in their very characterisation of certain practices as magic, fetishism, or superstition, both theology and the Church hierarchy appear strongly committed to the project of modernity. In this contest over orthopraxis (could one say, ortho-perception?) the respective significance of vision and touch is revealed as a function of social position.

The corporeal nature of the relic poses certain problems to the Catholic Church. The relic offers a direct route to the sacred, bypassing institutional mediation, and thus necessitating institutional control and ideological safeguarding. One such measure of control was the medieval directive that the remains of the saints must be kept in reliquaries (Fourth Lateran Council, 1215). On the whole, it would seem to me that visual piety is a safer alternative to channel religious desires than tangible experience.

Next to the Catholic hierarchy, I have described the museum as the other locus of modernist ocularcentrism. No longer the *Wunderkammer* of the sixteenth and seventeenth centuries, the museum has nonetheless often become the repository of the miraculous – or, more exactly, the once-miraculous. For practical as well as ideological reasons (if a neat separation can be made), touch is usually discouraged by the museum. Thus the magic of touch may be just as much the (supposed) antithesis of science as it is of religion. Yet, I argue, there are objects – relics among them – that need to be met and experienced in a different way, a way that allows fascination and fetishism to flourish alongside science, learning, and education. The sacred, after all, is not for your eyes only.

Notes

1   'Cult' is the technical term used by the Catholic Church; it implies systematic and continuous veneration based on a reputation of holiness. It does not have the derogatory connotations of the colloquial English usage.

2   The Eltenberg Reliquary must be one of the museum's most precious treasures:
     a large reliquary of bronze and copper gilt in the shape of a domed basilica,
     decorated with enamel, ivory, and figures of prophets and apostles (Rhenish, ca.
     1180). The Holy Thorn Reliquary is a rather theatrical construction of gold and
     enamel, depicting the Last Judgement, and lavishly adorned with rubies and pearls
     (French, ca. 1410).
3   The collection has since been acquired by the French government, which apparently
     plans to present it in a specifically dedicated museum.

References

Beer, M., Rehm, U. 2004. Die Macht der kleinen Bilder. Zur Sammlung Kleiner
     Andachtsbilder im Museum Schnütgen. In Manuela Beer and Ulrich Rehm (eds.),
     Das Kleine Andachtsbild: Graphik vom 16. bis zum 20. Jahrhundert. Hildesheim: Georg
     Olms Verlag, 1–5.
Belting, H. 1994. *Likeness and Presence: A History of the Image before the Era of Art*. Chicago:
     Chicago University Press.
Benjamin, W. 1999 [1937]. The work of art in the age of mechanical reproduction. In
     Hannah Arendt (ed.), *Illuminations*. London: Pimlico, 211–35.
Bourdieu, P. 2000. *Das religiöse Feld: Texte zur Ökonomie des Heilsgeschehens*. Konstanz:
     Universitätsverlag Konstanz.
Diedrichs, C. 2001. *Vom Glauben zum Sehen: Die Sichtbarkeit der Reliquie. Ein Beitrag zur
     Geschichte des Sehens*. Berlin: Weissensee-Verlag.
Dinzelbacher, P. 1990. Die 'Realpräsenz' der Heiligen in ihren Reliquiaren und Gräbern
     nach mittelalterlichen Quellen. In Peter Dinzelbacher and Dieter R. Bauer (eds.),
     Heiligenverehrung in Geschichte und Gegenwart. Ostfildern: Schwabenverlag, 115–74.
Douglas, M. 2003 [1970]. *Natural Symbols*. London: Routledge.
Duncan, C. 1995. *Civilizing Rituals: Inside Public Art Museums*. London and New York:
     Routledge.
Erret, G. 2003. *Die heutige Bedeutung und Anziehungskraft des Reliquienkultes*. Retrieved 26
     April 2004 from [http://www.pfarrer.at/reliquienbuchenhuell.pdf].
Fenton, J. 1983. *The Memory of War and Children in Exile: Poems 1968–1983*. Harmondsworth:
     Penguin.
Foucault, M. 1975/1995. *Discipline and Punish: The Birth of the Prison*. New York: Vintage.
Geary, P. 1990. Sacred commodities: the circulation of medieval relics. In Arjun Appadurai
     (ed.), *The Social Life of Things*. Cambridge: Cambridge University Press, 169–91.
—— 1978. *Furta Sacra: Thefts of Relics in the Central Middle Ages*. Princeton: Princeton
     University Press.
Jay, M. 1988. The scopic regimes of modernity. In S. Lash and J. Friedman (eds.), *Modernity
     and Identity*. Seattle: Dia Press, 178–95.
Küchler, S. 1988. Malangan: Objects, sacrifice, and the production of memory. *American
     Ethnologist* 15(4): 625–37.
Livingstone, E. (ed.). 1996. *The Concise Oxford Dictionary of the Christian Church*. Oxford:
     Oxford University Press.
McKevitt, C. 1991. San Giovanni Rotondo and the shrine of Padre Pio. In J. Eade and
     M.J. Sallnow (eds.), *Contesting the Sacred: The Anthropology of Christian Pilgrimage*.
     London, New York: Routledge, 77–97.

Merleau-Ponty, M. 2002 [1962]. *Phenomenology of Perception*. London: Routledge.

Miller, D. 2005. Materiality: an introduction. In D. Miller (ed.), *Materiality*. Durham and London: Duke University Press, 1–50.

Morgan, D. 2005. *The Sacred Gaze: Religious Visual Culture in Theory and Practice*. Berkeley: University of California Press.

—— 1998. *Visual Piety: A History and Theory of Popular Religious Images*. Berkeley: University of California Press.

Musée d'Art Sacré du Gard. 2000. *Reliquaires* (exhibition catalogue). Nîmes: author.

Os, H van. 2001. *Der Weg zum Himmel: Reliquienverehrung im Mittelalter*. Regensburg: Schnell & Steiner.

Peters, L. 1994. Reliquien und ihr Publikum. In Diözesanmuseum Paderborn (ed.), *Heilige und Heiltum: Eine rheinische Privatsammlung und die Reliquienverehrung der Barockzeit in Westfalen* (exhibition catalogue). Paderborn: Diözesanmuseum Paderborn, 103–105.

Pinney, C. 2004. *'Photos of the Gods': The Printed Image and Political Struggle in India*. London: Reaktion.

—— 2002a. The Indian work of art in the age of mechanical reproduction or, what happens when peasants 'get hold' of images. In F.D. Ginsburg, L. Abu-Lughod and B. Larkin (eds.), *Media Worlds: Anthropology on New Terrain*. Berkeley: University of California Press, 355–69.

—— 2002b. Creole Europe: The reflection of a reflection. *Journal of New Zealand Literature* 20:125–61.

—— 2001. Piercing the skin of the idol. In C. Pinney and N. Thomas (eds.), *Beyond Aesthetics: Art and the Technology of Enchantment*. Oxford and New York: Berg, 157–79.

Chapter 22

'Marvels of everyday vision'
The anthropology of aesthetics and the cattle-keeping Nilotes

Jeremy Coote

The current idea that we look lazily into the world only as far as our practical needs demand it while the artist removes this veil of habits scarcely does justice to the marvels of everyday vision.

(E. H. Gombrich, *Art and Illusion*)

Introduction

This essay is written out of a conviction that progress in the anthropological study of visual aesthetics has been hampered by an undue concentration on art and art objects. The cattle-keeping Nilotes of the Southern Sudan make no art objects and have no traditions of visual art, yet it would be absurd to claim that they have no visual aesthetic. In such a case as this, the analyst is forced to attend to areas of life to which everyday concepts of art do not apply, to attend, indeed, to 'the marvels of everyday vision' (Gombrich, 1977: 275) which we all, not just the artists and art critics amongst us, experience and delight in. It is my contention that such wide-ranging analyses will produce more satisfactory accounts of the aesthetics of different societies – even of those with art traditions and art objects. With this in mind, then, I present the cattle-keeping Nilotes of the Southern Sudan as a sort of test-case for the anthropology of aesthetics.

The anthropology of aesthetics

While it is generally recognized that aesthetics concerns more than art and that art is about more than aesthetics, anthropologists, along with philosophers and aestheticians in general, have tended to work on the assumption, made nicely explicit in the 'Aesthetics' entry in the *New Encyclopaedia Britannica* (Pepper, 1974: 150), that 'it is the explanation that can be given for deeply prized works of art that stabilizes an aesthetic theory'. In their accounts of the aesthetics of other cultures, anthropologists have concentrated on materials that fit Western notions of 'works of art', at times compounding the problem by making the focus of their studies those objects which are 'deeply prized' by the Western anthropologist, rather than those most valued by the people themselves. Moreover, what has passed for the anthropology of aesthetics has often been little more than talk about such 'art'; for many years, anthropologists' or art critics' talk, more recently, indigenous talk as systematized by the anthropologist.

While one doubts that works of art are ever deeply prized for their aesthetic qualities alone, it is probably true that in Western societies, and in others with highly developed art traditions, aesthetic notions are most perfectly manifested in works of art, and are given their most refined expression in that type of discourse known as the philosophy of art. But the aesthetic notions so manifested and refined are those of members of the art world, not necessarily those of the general population. For most of us – or, perhaps more accurately, all of us most of the time – our aesthetic notions have more to do with home decorating, gardening, sport, advertising, and other areas of so-called 'popular' culture. The presence of art having become almost a defining feature of Western notions of the civilized, anthropologists have been loath to say of any other society that it has no art. There is, it is true, probably no society that has no art-form at all, but there are certainly societies with no visual art traditions. A Western preoccupation with the visual has led both to the undervaluation of the poetic, choreological, and other arts, and to the widening of the definition of visual art so as to embrace all those objects or activities which have 'artistic' or 'aesthetic' qualities. So, for example, body decoration has been reclassified as art in recent years. While I have no fundamental objection to 'art' being defined in such broad terms, I find it more satisfactory to talk rather of the aesthetic aspect of a society's activities and products.

All human activity has an aesthetic aspect. We are always, though at varying levels of awareness, concerned with the aesthetic qualities of our aural, haptic, kinetic, and visual sensations. If art were to be defined so broadly as to encompass any human activity or product with an aesthetic aspect, then none could be denied the status of art. This seems to me unwarranted; the possible insight seemingly captured by such an argument is adequately caught by saying that all human activity has an aesthetic aspect.

I am encouraged in arguing for such a view by a trend that seems to characterize some recent anthropological and philosophical literature, a trend towards recognizing that aesthetics may be usefully defined independently of art. The anthropologist Jacques Maquet, for example, has argued repeatedly (e.g. 1979: 45; 1986: 33) that art and aesthetics are best treated as independent. Among philosophers, Nick Zangwill (1986: 261) has argued that 'one could do aesthetics without mentioning works of art! Sometimes I think it would be safer to do so.' And T. J. Diffey (1986: 6) has remarked how it is not just philosophers of art who require a notion of aesthetics; philosophers of religion require one too, and 'a notion of it as that which has no especial connection with art, but which, rather, is closer to perception'. Diffey regards 'aesthetic experience' as an as yet 'inadequately understood expression', as a term 'that extends thought, stretches the mind and leads us into new and uncharted territory' (ibid. 11). The task of philosophy, as he sees it, is to clarify and explicate what ordinary language has already 'inchoately discovered'. It is my view that rather than waiting for the clarifications and explications of philosophy, the anthropology of aesthetics should follow such ordinary language usage, disconnect itself from art, and get closer to perception.

I hope that what is meant by this admittedly vague contention will become clearer through the course of this essay. It might be thought too easy to have recourse to 'everyday usage', for probably any definition at all can be supported by judicious selection from the flux of everyday language. I am able, however, to adduce here non-specialist usages of 'aesthetic' and its cognates by three of the authors whose writings on the peoples of the Southern Sudan are drawn on in this essay. These authors do not discuss aesthetics as such, but make passing references which I find significant. Evans-Pritchard (1940a: 22) refers to 'those aesthetic qualities which please him [a Nuer] in an ox'. Elsewhere, Jean Buxton (1973: 7) tells us that 'marking and patterning are very highly estimated in the Mandari visual aesthetic', and John Burton (1981: 76) refers to a particular cattle-colour configuration as being 'the most aesthetically pleasing for the Atuot'. In none of these cases does the author explain what he or she means by the term. They can all be taken to be using the term in an everyday sense which they expect their readers to understand. I take them to mean by an 'aesthetic' something like 'the set of valued formal qualities of objects' or 'valued formal qualities of perception'.

The anthropology of aesthetics as I see it, then, consists in the comparative study of valued perceptual experience in different societies. While our common human physiology no doubt results in our having universal, generalized responses to certain stimuli, perception is an active and cognitive process in which cultural factors play a dominant role. Perceptions are cultural phenomena. Forge touched on this some twenty years ago when he wrote (1970: 282) concerning the visual art of the Abelam of New Guinea:

> What do the Abelam see? Quite obviously there can be no absolute answer to this question: it is impossible literally to see through the eyes of another man, let alone perceive with his brain. Yet if we are to consider the place of art in any society . . . we must beware of assuming that they see what we see and vice versa.

I should argue that, more than just being wary of making assumptions, we must in fact make the attempt to understand how they see. The study of a society's visual aesthetic, for example, should be devoted to the identification of the particular qualities of form – shape, colour, sheen, pattern, proportion, and so on – recognized within that society, as evidenced in language, poetry, dance, body decoration, material culture, sculpture, painting, etc. A society's visual aesthetic is, in its widest sense, the way in which people in that society see. Adapting from Michael Baxandall's studies of Western art traditions (1972: 29 ff.; 1980: 143 ff.) the phrase 'the period eye', anthropologists might usefully employ the notion of 'the cultural eye'. It is a society's way of seeing, its repertoire of visual skills, which I take to be its visual aesthetic, and it is with this that I believe the anthropological study of visual aesthetics should be concerned. Such an anthropology of aesthetics will be a necessary complement to any anthropology of art, for it surely must be essential to any anthropological consideration of art, however conceived, that an attempt is made to see the art as its original makers and viewers see it.

The study of aesthetics as it is taken here is to be distinguished from both art criticism and the philosophy of art. These disciplines are concerned with aesthetics, but not exclusively so. The evaluations of art criticism involve considerations of form, but also of content and meaning. The philosophy of art tends towards analysing the relations between art and such matters as the True and the Good, matters which are beyond the formal qualities of works of art. It is perhaps worth emphasizing that practices similar to those of Western art criticism and philosophy are to be found in other cultures. These practices are worthy of study in their own right. According to the terminology adopted in this essay, however, they are not the aesthetics of a society, but its art criticism or its philosophy.

The cattle-keeping Nilotes

The cattle-keeping Nilotes need little introduction here. This essay focuses on the Nuer, Dinka, Atuot, and Mandari of the Southern Sudan, concerning each of whom there is a substantial and easily accessible literature, while making passing reference to the closely related Anuak of the Southern Sudan and the more distantly related Pokot and Maasai of East Africa. The Nuer and Dinka in particular are well known to all students of anthropology.[1] What does perhaps require some explanation is their being taken together as 'the cattle-keeping Nilotes'. The million or so people who are referred to by the names 'Nuer', 'Dinka', 'Atuot', and 'Mandari' do not compose a homogeneous society – but then, neither do any of the four 'peoples' themselves. There are, for example, variations in the ecological situation, economic life, degree of political centralization, and particularities of religious belief and practice both within and between these peoples.

However, they also share many social and cultural features, not least of which is the importance of cattle in their lives.[2] Cattle are not just a food source, but a central factor in all aspects of their social and cultural activities, being used to mediate social relationships through the institutions of bridewealth and bloodwealth, as well as to mediate man's relationship with God through their role as sacrificial victims. Moreover, the Nuer, Dinka, Atuot, and Mandari share a common history,[3] live in geographical proximity, and have extensive interrelations across the 'borders' that might be supposed to exist between them.

The picture of Nilotic visual aesthetics painted here is an analyst's abstraction. It is founded on the current state of anthropological knowledge concerning the group of peoples which provide the ethnographic focus, peoples who are related linguistically, historically, geographically, and culturally. Further research may reveal significant differences between and amongst the aesthetics of these four peoples. It might, however, also reveal significant similarities between these four peoples and other

Nilotic-speaking peoples. The analysis presented here is ahistorical. This is for the sake of convenience only. A full understanding of an aesthetic system must include the historical dimension. I hope to be able to deal with aesthetic change among the Nilotes elsewhere.

Nilotic aesthetics

Little attention has been paid by scholars to aesthetics amongst the Nilotic-speaking peoples of Southern Sudan and East Africa.[4] In his thesis on Western Nilotic material culture, Alan Blackman (1956: 262–73) devotes a chapter to 'Aesthetics', but only to discuss representational art – or, more accurately, the lack of it. Ocholla-Ayayo's discussion (1980: 10–12) of 'Aesthetics of Material Culture Elements', in his account of Western Nilotic Luo culture, is a purely theoretical account of the abstract notion of beauty and its relation to value, appearance, use, and society, drawing on thinkers such as Santayana, without entering into a discussion of the particularities of Luo aesthetics as such. Harold Schneider's short but often quoted article on 'The Interpretation of Pakot Visual Art' (1956) is the best-known contribution to the study of Nilotic aesthetics, and is worth commenting on at some length.

Schneider defines his terms rather differently from how they are defined here. He defines 'art' as 'man-made beauty', but recognizes that what the Pokot themselves find beautiful should not be assumed by the analyst but has to be discovered. To do this, he analyses the meaning and use of the Pokot term *pachigh*, which his interpreter variously translated as 'beautiful', 'pretty', 'pleasant to look at', and 'unusual'. *Pachigh* is distinguished from *karam*, which means 'good', and which Schneider glosses as 'utilitarian'. The Pokot apply the term *pachigh* to non-utilitarian, aesthetically pleasing objects of the natural world or of non-Pokot manufacture, as well as to the non-utilitarian embellishments of Pokot utilitarian objects. Cattle, for example, are utilitarian (*karam*), but the colours of the hides are *pachigh* (ibid. 104). People are also *karam*, though a woman 'may have aspects of beauty such as firm round breasts, a light, chocolate-coloured skin, and white even teeth' (ibid. 104); and a fully decorated man may be referred to as beautiful but 'it is clear that they mean only the aesthetic embellishments' (ibid. 105).

Through his analysis of the term *pachigh*, Schneider is able to identify what it is that the Pokot find aesthetically pleasing, but he tells us little about *why* these particular objects and embellishments are considered *pachigh*. In recognizing that what is of interest is not a category of objects – art – but a category of thought – aesthetics – Schneider makes an important contribution – being 'forced' to, perhaps, by the very lack of Pokot art – but he tells us little about what characterizes this category of thought, merely listing those objects to which it is applied. While he refers in passing to contrast, which is discussed below – and to novelty, which I hope to discuss elsewhere – the discussion of aesthetic qualities, the very stuff of aesthetics, is not developed. It is on the aesthetic qualities which Nilotes appreciate, rather than on the category of objects in which these qualities are observed, that this essay concentrates.

For Nilotic-speaking cattle-keepers, cattle are the most highly valued possessions. This analysis of Nilotic aesthetics is, therefore, centred on cattle. The importance of

Fig. 22.1 Dinka ox of the *marial* configuration; Bekjiu, near Pacong, Agar Dinka. Photograph by Jeremy Coote, February 1981.

cattle for the Nilotes is well known, and I do not propose to summarize the literature here. I wish to concentrate on the perceptual qualities of cattle as they are appreciated by their owners. These concern the colour configuration and sheen of the hide, the shape of the horns, and the bigness and fatness of the body including particularly the hump (see Fig. 22.1). These are discussed first, and then their ramifications into other areas of Nilotic life are traced.

Of primary importance for this discussion are the cattle-colour terminologies which are so characteristic of the cattle-keeping peoples of East Africa.[5] Nilotic languages in general have many terms to describe the colour configurations of cattle. Even people who no longer keep cattle or depend upon them materially may maintain cattle-colour terminologies. The Anuak, for example, who, according to Evans-Pritchard (1940*b*: 20), can only have been a pastoral people 'a very long time ago', still based their metaphorical praise-names upon cattle-colour configurations when Lienhardt studied them in the 1950s (Lienhardt 1961: 13 n.). Cattle-colour terms rarely refer to pure colours or shades of colours, but rather to configurations of colours or, in a loose sense of the term, patterns.

For the Western Dinka, Nebel (1948: 51) recorded twenty-seven terms, while for the Ngok Dinka, Evans-Pritchard (1934) recorded thirty. For the Nuer, Evans-Pritchard (1940*a*: 41–4) showed that there are 'several hundred colour permutations' based on ten principal colour terms multiplied by at least twenty-seven combination terms. In his 1934 article on Ngok Dinka terms, he promised that he would publish a full account of Nuer terms, a promise repeated in *The Nuer* (1940*a*: 44). The fact that the promised lengthy analysis, of what he noted in 1940 was a 'neglected' subject (ibid. 41 n.), has never appeared suggests how difficult such an analysis would be. Indeed, the application of the abstract terminology to real animals is not always straightforward for Nilotes themselves. According to Deng (1973: 96), 'the colour-patterns are so intricate among the Dinka that frequent litigation centres on their determination'. And Ryle has described (1982: 92) – in interesting terms, given the subject of this essay – how

> When discussing the colour pattern of an animal – as they do for hours – the Dinka sound more like art critics than stockbreeders. For instance, when does *mathiang* – dark brown – become *malual* – reddish brown? If the animal has brown patches, are they large enough to make it *mading* or are they the smaller mottling that identifies *malek*?

Such discussions are a matter of both appreciation and classification, perhaps more akin to the discussions of antique-dealers or wine connoisseurs than to those of art critics.

It is not necessary to analyse these terminologies at length here. It is sufficient to identify briefly the principles underlying the perceived configurations. For Mandari, the colours red, white, and black have much symbolic importance (Buxton, 1973). With cattle, however, they are not so interested in pure colours; what is important is that an ox should be piebald or variegated. When a piebald is born, its owner is delighted and the beast is set aside as a display ox (ibid. 6). Similarly, Ryle has described (1982: 93–6) the 'hopeful expectation' that attends the birth of a new calf amongst the Agar Dinka. He relates how in one instance Mayen, the cow's owner, 'was ecstatic, beaming with pleasure and singing snatches of song, because the calf was a much desired *mariai*'. It is the destiny of such well-marked male calves to become 'song', or 'display' oxen, being castrated when they are eight or nine months old. Animals with the most highly valued configurations are thus excluded from breeding. Ryle was told that one cannot anyway predict the occurrence of such colour patterns, 'and therefore there is no point in trying to breed for them' (ibid. 93; cf. Howell *et al.*, 1988: 282). For the Western Dinka Lienhardt (1961: 15) records how, when a male calf of a highly valued configuration is born, 'it is said that . . . the friends of its owner may tear off his beads and scatter them, for his happiness is such that he must show indifference to these more trivial forms of display'. If the dam that has produced the well-marked calf is a good milch cow, Dinka may find it hard to choose whether to keep the calf for stud purposes, knowing that it is likely to produce further good milch cows, or castrate it for display. They may hope that the dam will produce another, not so well-marked, male calf later, and castrate the one it has already produced. Mandari also choose their stud bulls from the progeny of good milch cows. All other things being equal, they will choose well-coloured ones; but, significantly, not the piebald or variegated but the plain black or red calves, trusting that these will produce offspring which are well-marked (Buxton, 1973: 6).

In fact, most cattle are not well-marked. Buxton noted that the majority of Mandari cattle are a nondescript white (ibid.), and my own experience would support this. Amongst the Agar Dinka to the west, the situation is much the same; greyish, off-white cattle are preponderant, as aerial photographs have demonstrated.[6]

Fig. 22.2 Dinka man with decorated song-ox. Photograph by Survival Anglia, 1975.

That they are relatively rare helps to explain why well-marked beasts are valued to such an extent that the Agar Dinka, for example, 'will trade two or three oxen of unexceptional colourings for one particularly desirable beast, if the owner is willing to part with it' (Ryle, 1982: 92). It follows that it is the cattle of less aesthetic interest, as well as those beyond breeding, which are marketed by those Nilotes, such as some Atuot, who have entered the incipient Southern Sudanese cattle trade (Burton, 1978: 401).

The sheen of the hides is also appreciated and valued. Though sheen is not a factor in cattle-colour terminologies, its appreciation can be amply illustrated by the amount of time and effort expended in the grooming of cattle, and by frequent reference to it in poetry and song. An Atuot song, for example, includes the words: 'the back of my ox is as white as the grazing in the new grass' – the image, as Burton explains (1982: 274), being 'of morning dew glittering in the sunlight'. A song by Stephen Ciec Lam, a Nuer, refers to 'my sister's big ox/ whose glossy hide shines against the compound' (Svoboda, 1985: 32). Another by Daniel Cuor Lul Wur, also a Nuer, refers to an ox whose hide 'is like the sun itself: he is the ox of moonlight' (ibid. 19). And yet another by Rec Puk relates how 'Jiok's hide is as bright as moonlight,/ bright as the sun's tongue./ My Jiok shines like gold,/ like a man's ivory bracelet' (ibid. 11). In this last example, specific comparison is made between the white-on-black cattle-hide and the whiteness of the ivory bracelet shining against the black Nuer skin.

The training of ox-horns is practised by cattle-keeping peoples all over the world. Nilotes cut the horns of young display oxen so that they grow into shapes which their owners find particularly pleasing. They are cut with a spear at an oblique angle, and the horns grow back against the cut.[7] To describe such horn shapes the Nuer have six common terms, as well as 'several fancy names' (Evans-Pritchard, 1940*a*: 45). In combination with the cattle-colour configuration terms, these considerably increase the number of possible permutations to specify individual beasts – logically, to well over a thousand. As can be seen in Fig. 22.2, the horns may also be adorned with buffalo-tail hair tassels to accentuate the effect. When Burton (1982: 279) was carrying out his field-work among the Atuot, such tassels were exchanged at the rate of one tassel for six cow-calves. Cutting also thickens the horns, and large and heavy horns are especially characteristic of display oxen among the Mandari (Buxton, 1973: 7).

Appreciation of horns is expressed in song. A Dinka song, for example, tells of an 'ox with diverging horns, / The horns are reaching the ground; / The horns are overflowing like a boiling pot' (Deng, 1972: 84). The range of imagery is vast: Cummins (1904: 162) quotes a Dinka song in which an ox's horns are said to be 'like the masts of ships' – presumably referring to the masts of sailing ships which once plied the Nile and its tributaries. Horns are also sometimes decorated with ash, when oxen are exchanged in bridewealth, for example, the effect being to make them stand out more against the dull background of sky and landscape.[8]

In his discussion of the Nuer attitude to their cattle, Evans-Pritchard (1940*a*: 22) referred to 'those aesthetic qualities which please him [a Nuer] in an ox, especially fatness, colour and shape of horns'. And, according to him (ibid. 27), it is fatness which is most important, for 'colour and shape of horns are significant, but the essential qualities are bigness and fatness, it being considered especially important that the haunch bones should not be apparent'. He goes on (ibid.): 'Nuer admire a large hump which wobbles when the animal walks, and to exaggerate this character they often manipulate the hump shortly after birth.' This admiration of humps is shared by the Dinka and Atuot. A Dinka song (Deng, 1972: 81) has the lines: 'My ox is showing his narrow-waisted hump. / The hump is twisting like a goitered neck, / Staggering like a man who has gorged himself with liquor; / When he walks, the hump goes on twisting / Like a man traveling on a camel.' Another Dinka song, quoted by Cummins (1904: 162), refers to an ox whose hump is 'so high that it towers above the high grass'.

The qualities of bigness and fatness are also referred to in songs. An Atuot song recorded by Burton (1982: 272) refers to the ox which is the subject of the song as 'the mahogany tree', thereby likening the size of the ox to the tree. Another Atuot song (Burton, 1981: 107) tells of an ox which is said to be 'so large like an elephant'. A Dinka song recorded by Cummins (1904: 162) tells of an ox which is 'so big that men can sit and rest in his shadow'. It should be stressed that bigness and fatness are not appreciated because they will lead to a better price at market, or to a larger meal on the death or sacrifice of the animal: cattle are primarily a feast for the eyes, and only secondarily a feast for the stomach.

Before going on to trace some of the ramifications of these elements of Nilotic 'bovine' aesthetics into the Nilotes' appreciation of, and action in, the world, it is worth making the attempt to understand why the particular perceptual qualities identified are so appreciated.

The appreciation of a large hump and of bigness and fatness are presumably at least partly explicable as indicators of healthy and well-fed beasts. And the same can presumably be said for the appreciation of sheen – it indicates a sleek and healthy hide; though it should be noted that sheen is perceptually exciting in and of itself, so its appreciation can be understood as a particular manifestation of the universal appreciation of brightness.

The appeal of horn shapes is not difficult to understand in the field. One quickly learns to appreciate the variety of trained and untrained shapes in a forest of horns in the cattle camp. Both the symmetrical and the asymmetrical curving shapes of Nilotic cattle horns have great visual appeal, especially when they are seen moving through space as the cattle move their heads, and when the arcs the horns make in the air are exaggerated by the swinging movements of the tassels. Fagg (e.g. 1973) has drawn attention to the frequent use of exponential curves in African art: the Nilotic appreciation of the curving shapes of cattle horns can be seen as yet another instance of this theme in African aesthetics.

As with horns, the appeal of particular cattle-colour configurations cannot be explained by reference to the healthiness or well-being of well-marked beasts. The majority of such beasts, though, are likely to have larger body proportions than other beasts, as the majority of well-marked beasts are castrated, and neutering encourages body growth. They also spend no energy in sexual activity and much less than uncastrated cattle in fighting; so their body growth is further encouraged and they remain physically unblemished. In general, more care is lavished on them by their owners, and one can expect this to have a beneficial effect on their health and well-being. Well-marked beasts are thus also likely to be big and fat, and vice versa. It would, however, be a strange argument which explained the appeal of well-marked beasts by the fact that they are healthier, when their being healthier depends upon their being well-marked.

As aestheticians stabilize their theories by explaining why highly prized works of art are so valued, the explanation for the Nilotes' appreciation of well-marked cattle might be sought in what they value most highly. For the peoples who are the focus of this essay, it is bold pied markings. For the Western Dinka at least, it is in particular the black-and-white configurations *majok* and *mariai* (Lienhardt, 1961: 15). The former is most simply described as a black animal with a white chest, the latter as a black animal with a white flash on its flank. Black-and-white configurations provide strong contrasts. Buxton offered an explanation of the appeal of such contrasts, noting (1973: 7) that 'marking and patterning are very highly estimated in the Mandari visual aesthetic; and the strong contrast markings of black on white, red on white, or a combination of all three, stand out so strikingly in a landscape devoid of strong colour that the importance given to it can be readily understood'. Such an explanation can only be partial at best, but when one remembers that the vast majority of cattle are a nondescript white, the appeal of strongly contrasting black-and-white or red-and-white markings can be appreciated more readily.

The visual stimulation offered by both black and red markings amongst a herd of greyish cattle is not to be doubted. It might be expected, then, that it should be the pure black or red beasts which are most highly valued. This is not the case, for while the appreciation of well-marked beasts should be understood in the context of a dull and pale landscape and herds preponderantly off-white in colour, it is the contrast of black and white or red and white in the single beast which provides the greatest aesthetic satisfaction. The individual beast, then, provides the locus for stimulating visual experience.

Aesthetics in the wider world

Having introduced some elements of Nilotic aesthetics, it is possible to trace their ramifications in the Nilotes' appreciation of, and action in, the world in which they live.

The cattle-colour terms are associated with a wide range of phenomena apart from cattle. At its most simple, this involves the recognition of connections between, for example, the ox *makuac* – that is, an ox of the *kuac* configuration – and the leopard, *kuac*. In their poetic imagery, however, the Nilotes go beyond these relatively straightforward linguistic connections to more complex associations. Evans-Pritchard recorded (1940*a*: 45) some 'fanciful elaborations of nomenclature' among the Nuer where, for example, 'a black ox may be called *rual mim*, charcoal-burning or *won car*, dark clouds'. And amongst the Western Dinka, according to Lienhardt (1961: 13), a man with a black display ox may be known not only as *macar* 'black ox', but also as, for example, *Him atiep*, "the shade of a tree"; or *kor acom*, "seeks for snails", after the black ibis which seeks for snails'.

It is not just that Nilotes make metaphorical connections between cattle-colour configurations and other phenomena; it is not just poetic play. In a real sense they see the world through a sort of grid or matrix of cattle-colours:

> The Dinkas' very perception of colour, light, and shade in the world around them is . . . inextricably connected with their recognition of colour-configurations in their cattle. If their cattle-colour vocabulary were taken away, they would have scarcely any way of describing visual experience in terms of colour, light, and darkness.
>
> (Lienhardt, 1961: 12–13)

This is not, of course, to say that they could not perceive the black ibis or the shade of a tree if it were not for the existence of black oxen, but it is to say that their visual experience and appreciation of the ibis and the shade is inseparable from their appreciation of the *macar* colour configuration in cattle.

Those cattle-colour terms, such as *makuac*, which are clearly related linguistically to natural phenomena, are no doubt derived from the term for the phenomenon and not vice versa. Presumably the Dinka called the leopard *kuac* before they called the spotted ox *makuac*. However, the *kuac* configuration in cattle is not called after the leopard because of some significance of the leopard as such, but because it is like the pattern to be found on *kuac*. Children will learn the names of cattle-markings, and apply them to natural and cultural phenomena, before they ever see the source of the name of the markings. A Dinka child will know what *kuac* means as a marking pattern, and will be applying it to cattle and to spotted cloth, for example, well before he or she ever — if ever — sees a leopard. The visual experience of young Dinka is focused on cattle and their markings, and the cattle-colour terminology is learned through listening to daily discussions about cattle. As Lienhardt (ibid. 12) writes, 'a Dinka may thus recognize the configuration in nature by reference to what he first knows of it in the cattle on which his attention, from childhood, is concentrated'. This fact is of greater significance than the possible historical origins of the terms.[9] That the Nilotes' visual perception of their natural and cultural world is thus shaped by their interest in, and experience of, the colour configurations of their cattle is amply attested, both by their complex cattle-colour terminologies and by the rich poetic and metaphorical elaborations of these terminologies by which associations are made between the most diverse visual experiences and cattle-colours. These associations are not by any means always obvious; part of the pleasure of composing and staging songs is in making creative connections which one's audience has to work at to comprehend.

That these associations are not made only in poetic contexts, however, is shown by Lienhardt's remark (1961: 19) that Dinka 'frequently pointed out to me those things in nature which had the *marial* colour-configuration upon which my own metaphorical ox-name was based'. One might expect a man to become particularly attuned to the colour-configuration of his own name or song ox, but, as Lienhardt's anecdote makes clear, this attuning is not exclusive; Dinka recognize and appreciate a wide range of colour-configurations. Agar Dinka friends called me Makur, explicitly referring to the dark rings around my eyes like the black patches round the eyes of the ox *makur*. Other Agar to whom I was introduced immediately grasped why I had been so called.

It is not just in their perception of their world, and their poetic expressions concerning it, that we can trace these elements of the Nilotic aesthetic. They can also be traced in the ways in which Nilotes act in the world. For example, they decorate their bodies with ash, the decoration being always (as far as I know) non-representational, but very commonly geometric.[10] Buxton tells us (1973: 401) that among the Mandari 'young people decorate their faces with white ash to imitate the facial markings of oxen and cows'. This is what one might expect to be the case for the Nilotes in general, though I know of no other report of such decoration as conscious imitation. The appearance of ash-covered bodies is, in any case, not unlike the colour of the majority of poorly marked, greyish cattle. Even if it is the case that when they decorate themselves with ash they are not consciously imitating the markings of cattle, it is surely not too much to assume that the appreciation of the markings of cattle and of the ash-covered bodies are similar, and that the former affects the latter.

More clearly, perhaps, the black-and-white animal skins, like that of the colobus monkey, which are part of 'traditional' Nilotic dress, can be seen as reflecting the contrasts appreciated in cattle-hides.[11] In recent years it has been possible for Nilotes to buy plastic accoutrements with which to adorn themselves; the man pictured with his ox in Fig. 22.2 is wearing a striking black-and-white plastic leopard-skin belt.

The contrasts that Nilotes appreciate in their cattle, and in the world around them, they also achieve in their decorative work. Mandari incise patterns on pots and gourds and blacken them with the heated point of a knife or spear, and contrasts are also made by rubbing white clay or ash into black or red surfaces. Black-and-white contrasts can also be seen in the frequent use of ivory bracelets in body decoration: as noted above, the whiteness of the ivory gleams against the wearer's black skin. Necklaces and bracelets made of indigenous materials such as wood and shell are also characterized by black-and-white contrasts.[12] It seems that contrast continues to be an important aspect of the aesthetics of beadwork, even with the immense range of hues now available in imported plastic beads.[13]

The forked branches erected in cattle camps, like the Agar Dinka example in Fig. 22.3, are decorated by the removal of alternate sections of bark to produce a banded, hooped, or straked effect.[14] In the 1980s, Mandari had access to acrylic paints, and took to painting the tall poles they erect in cattle camps. Instead of stripping alternate sections of bark to produce the desired effect, the whole bark was stripped off and alternate sections painted black and white, or, as in one example I saw, bright red and brilliant yellow.

The asymmetrical branching shape effected by horn-training can be seen in the tree branches erected as shrines amongst the Dinka, Mandari, and Atuot.[15] Although, as can be seen in Fig. 22.4, they also have a practical purpose, in that their shape makes them suitable to lean spears against and hang things from (Lienhardt, 1961: 257–60), it seems unlikely that shapes so reminiscent of the trained horns of oxen are accidentally so. One is encouraged to think that the resemblance is deliberate by the fact that the place marked by such forked-branch shrines is known amongst the Dinka as 'the head of the cattle-hearth' (ibid. 258); and Cummins (1904: 158) recounts a Dinka myth of origin in which it is said that where God lives there is a tree 'that is leafless with only two branches, one to the right and the other to the left like the horns of a bull'. For the Atuot, at least, 'the imagery of the spreading branches is consciously associated with the horns of a cow sacrificed on the occasion when the power was brought into the homestead' (Burton, 1979: 105 n.).

Whatever the case with forked-branch shrines, there can be no doubt that in other areas of life the representation of horns is conscious. Both symmetrical and asymmetrical shapes are imitated and represented. Some Nilotic scarification patterns can be seen as being based on cattle-horns; perhaps even the forehead marks of some Dinka and Mandari might be seen in this way.[16] Amongst Agar Dinka, at least, it is not unusual to see cattle-horn-shaped scarification on various parts of the body.[17]

After initiation, Nuer youths endure much pain and discomfort to imitate the horns of their oxen. They render useless their left arms by fixing a set of bracelets to them. This temporary deformation holds down their left arms as the left horns of oxen are trained downwards (Evans-Pritchard, 1956: 256–7).[18]

Lienhardt describes various ways in which Dinka imitate cattle in stylized action, remarking (1961: 16) that 'a characteristic sight in Western Dinkaland is that of a young man with his arms curved above his head, posturing either at a dance or for his own enjoyment when he is alone with his little herd'. Such posturing has been illustrated frequently and can be seen here in Fig. 22.5 where, as they dance at a sacrifice, Agar Dinka women raise their arms above their heads in imitation of the horns of cows.[19] This curving of the arms in imitation of cattle is, for the Dinka, 'one of the forms of "handsomeness" (dheng [or dheeng]), a bodily attitude which the Dinka consider graceful' (ibid. 16); it is 'a gesture of pride and triumph' (ibid. 269).

Fig. 22.3 Forked-branch post in an Agar Dinka cattle-camp. Photograph by Jeremy Coote, February 1981.

Fig. 22.4 Forked-branch shrine in an Apak Atuot homestead, near Aluakluak. Photograph by Jeremy Coote, February 1981.

Fig. 22.5 Agar Dinka dancing at a sacrifice, near Pacong. Photograph by Jeremy Coote, February 1981.

Evans-Pritchard (1940*a*: 38; cf. 1956: 251) colourfully describes how

when a Nuer mentions an ox his habitual moroseness leaves him and he speaks with enthusiasm, throwing up his arms to show you how its horns are trained. 'I have a fine ox,' he says, 'a brindled ox with a large white splash on its back and with one horn trained over its muzzle' – and up go his hands, one above his head and the other bent at the elbow across his face.

In one type of Atuot dance, 'men leap high into the air with their arms outstretched, imitating the girth and pattern of the horns of their personality oxen' (Burton, 1982: 268). Even when ox songs are sung in a sitting position a Dinka 'holds his hands up as the horns and moves his head and body in imitation of the ox' (Deng, 1972: 83).

Horn shapes are also found in Nilotic ornament. MacDermot (1972: pl. opp. p. 49) illustrates Thiwat, a Nuer man, wearing two leopard teeth fastened to a piece of leather around his neck, the resultant shape being very reminiscent of horns. Fisher (1984: 42) illustrates a Nuer wooden necklace with a central forked pendant 'shaped to resemble cows' horns'. She also illustrates (ibid. 54, 57) ivory pendants 'shaped like cows' horns' suspended from bead necklaces. And Ray Huffman (1931: fig. 3.6, opp. p. 17) illustrates a 'two-pronged wristlet' – in fact a ring – in which the shape formed by the prongs is again reminiscent of the horns of an ox.

It is not just horns which are imitated. In dance, it can be the whole animal, or groups of animals. In the same Atuot dance as that referred to above, young women imitate cows. Burton (1982: 268) describes it as follows:

a line of six or eight young women forms directly in front of the drummers. Here they perform a movement which attempts to imitate the slow gallop cows make as they saunter across a pasture. A girdle of colored beads reaching well above their heads sways back and forth, suggesting the manner in which the hump of a cow shifts back and forth when running.[20]

Deng (1972: 78–80) discusses a number of dances in which men and women act out the roles of bull, ox, and cow. And Lienhardt (1961: 17) describes a Dinka dance which is based upon 'the running of oxen with cows in the herd'. In considering fully the aesthetics of such dances, we should have to take into account more than just the purely visual; the major element is presumably the kinetic experience of the dancers themselves, though there are oral, and aural, elements too (ibid.). The visual appearance of cattle – the horns, the hump, and the general posture – are imitated as part of a more complete imitation the analysis of which is beyond the scope of this essay.

Nilotes have no developed tradition of figure sculpture or painting. There are, however, examples of modelling and drawing in which the aesthetic elements identified above are manifested. Through an examination of such models and drawings, we can deepen our understanding of the ideal forms in terms of which actual cattle are assessed and appreciated.

The making of clay, mud, or baked-earth models of cattle is a common occupation of Nilotic children. Generally speaking, the models are made by children for children's play, as is illustrated by the Dinka boy featured in a Survival Anglia film (1983) and in Fig. 22.6 here.[21] Amongst the Nuer, children play games with their oxen, 'taking them to pasture and putting them into byres, marrying with them and so on' (Evans-Pritchard, 1937: 238; cf. 1940a: 38), and Deng (1972: 60) tells of Dinka children making cattle camps using either shells or clay figures as cattle.[22] Such mud oxen may have their horns decorated with tassels in imitation of the real-life song oxen, as has the one at furthest left in the group illustrated in Fig. 22.7. They may also be coloured with ash or charred wood (Huffman, 1931: 65; Blackman, 1956: 273) in imitation of the markings of real animals.

In the examples illustrated in Fig. 22.7,[23] it is evident that what are emphasized and exaggerated are the hump, the horns, and the general fatness of the body: the head, legs, and hooves are of much less importance. A most satisfying example of such exaggeration, in which these features have been abstracted to produce a form which at first sight it takes a little imagination to see as a whole beast, are a group of five mud cows collected by Jean Brown among the Pokot in the 1970s and illustrated in Fig. 22.8. While not from a people within the particular focus of this essay, they are so striking that they are well worth illustrating here. In these examples, the aesthetically central aspects of the physical form of cattle – the fatness of the body, the hump, and the horns – have been brought together to produce a form which, though it bears little resemblance to the form of the animals themselves, is in itself aesthetically pleasing. That such models are made by children for children's play, or, as in the Pokot case, by mothers for their children, does not lessen their interest for an understanding of Nilotic aesthetics. They can be taken as an indication of what is aesthetically pleasing for the older brothers of these children, that is, for themselves when they grow up.[24]

Two-dimensional representations of cattle as illustrated in Fig. 22.9 are found on external hut walls amongst the Agar Dinka. Although there are reports of such mural drawings amongst the Nuer (e.g. Evans-Pritchard, 1937: 238; Jackson, 1923: 123–4), there are no published illustrations to provide comparative examples. They may be compared, however, with the figures of cattle incised on gourds by the Anuak as illustrated in Fig. 22.10. Here the cattle have triangular humps, and the colour configurations on their rectangular bodies are geometrically stylized.[25] They are more reminiscent of flag designs than the configurations actually found on cattle. If clay modelling reflects the Nilotic appreciation of the physical qualities of bigness and fatness, then the geometricized representations of cattle on gourds and walls can be seen to reflect the importance of colour configurations. That the bodies are rectangular and the configurations geometricized suggests that the cattle-colour classification represents a set of ideals which can be abstractly stated – or represented – even though real cattle only ever approximate to them.

Aesthetics and society

So far I have discussed some of the qualities of perceptual experience recognized and appreciated by Nilotes. Little reference has been made to 'art', 'beauty', or 'the good', which are so often taken to be defining terms of the aesthetic. Nor has reference been made to those traditional concerns of anthropology, such as social organization and social structure, to which analysts have attempted to link aesthetics. The discussion of elements of visual appreciation in a given culture is an end in itself, contributing to an understanding of what it is to be a member of that culture. Nevertheless, I shall try to address, albeit briefly, some of the wider concerns often discussed in what has been taken elsewhere to be the anthropology of aesthetics. My concern is to bring out what I take to be the implications for the anthropology of aesthetics of the material presented above.

As for 'art', I have referred to body decoration, mural drawing, and clay modelling, all of which might well have been discussed under a heading of 'art'. I indicated my response to such an approach in the introduction to this essay. Such activities as body decoration and clay modelling have an aesthetic aspect, as all human activity does, and it is the aesthetic aspect of these activities which has been of concern in this essay. No good purpose would be served for the anthropology of aesthetics, as I understand it, in separating such activities as 'art', or in restricting any discussion of aesthetics to them.

As for 'beauty', it is hoped that the terminology adopted in this essay avoids the problems that beset attempts to use such vague terms in accounts of other cultures. An understanding of the aesthetic qualities which we have identified is, of course, relevant for any understanding of Nilotic ideas approximating Western notions of beauty. For example, Lienhardt (1963: 87) quotes a Dinka song in which the singer compares his own 'dazzling array' – glossed by Lienhardt as 'shining beauty' – with that of the ugliness of 'a big coward' to whom a girl in whom the singer is interested has been promised by her father: 'This dazzling array is a poor man's truculence, ee/ [That her father] gives her to that big ugly coward to play with, ee/ This dazzling array

Fig. 22.6 Dinka boy modelling a mud cow. Photograph by Survival Anglia, 1975.

Fig. 22.7 Nuer mud toy cattle, collected by E. E. Evans-Pritchard in the 1930s (all but one, far right, labelled 'Anuak', though they are almost certainly all Nuer); maximum height 14.0 cm; Pitt Rivers Museum, Oxford (d.d. Evans-Pritchard 1936).

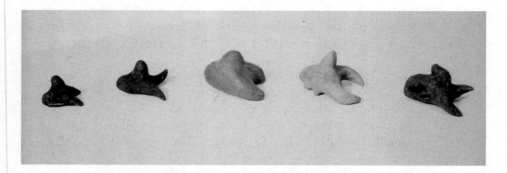

Fig. 22.8 Pokot mud toy cattle, collected by Jean Brown in the 1970s; largest 11.0 × 9.5 cm; Pitt Rivers Museum, Oxford (1978.20.194–8).

Fig. 22.9 Agar Dinka hut-wall drawings of a young man with two tasselled oxen (*majok*, left; *makuac*, right); near Pacong, Agar Dinka. Photograph by Jeremy Coote, February 1981. The human figure is approximately 23 cm high.

Fig. 22.10 Anuak gourd bowl, incised with figures and decorative designs; collected by E. E. Evans-Pritchard in the Southern Sudan in the 1930s; 20.0 cm high, 36.0 cm max. diameter; Pitt Rivers Museum, Oxford (1936.10.79).

is just truculence'. The words for 'dazzling array' and 'ugly' are, in fact, the cattle-colour terms *marial* and *malou*. As noted above, *marial* is one of the most highly valued black-and-white configurations signifying a black ox with a white splash on its flank. *Malou* is a grey ox, the implication in this context being dullness – *lou* is the Dinka name for a large bustard, probably the visually uninteresting kori bustard (*Ardeotis kori*) (Nebel, 1979: 52, 56). That *rial* combined with *nyin*, 'eye', is the Dinka term for 'to dazzle' gives some indication of the Dinka conceptualization of the visual stimulation of the *rial* black-and-white configuration (ibid. 76). In some contexts, 'pied' and 'beautiful' might be virtually interchangeable: Deng (1972: 63) quotes a song in which some young girls are said to wear 'pied and beautiful beads'.

But what is aesthetically pleasing and what is beautiful are not necessarily the same thing. A better appreciation of Nilotic ideas concerning beauty can be achieved through a discussion of indigenous concepts, such as the Dinka notion *dheeng*, mentioned in passing above. In a discussion of the virtues and dignity of a 'gentleman', Deng (1972: 14) glosses the term as follows:

> *dheeng* . . . is a word of multiple meanings – all positive. As a noun, it means nobility, beauty, handsomeness, elegance, charm, grace, gentleness, hospitality, generosity, good manners, discretion, and kindness. The adjective form of all these is *adheng*. Except in prayer or on certain religious occasions, singing and dancing are *dheeng*. Personal decoration, initiation ceremonies, celebration of marriages, the display of 'personality oxen', indeed any demonstration of an esthetic value, is considered *dheeng*. The social background of a man, his physical appearance, the way he walks, talks, eats, or dresses, and the way he behaves towards his fellowmen are all factors in determining his *dheeng*.

In the context of this essay it is the perceptual qualities contributing to *dheeng* which are of significance, and some of these, as they relate particularly to cattle, have been identified. But it is clear from Deng's discussion that for the Dinka there is more to 'beauty' than meets the eye.

It is also in the notion of *dheeng* that aesthetics and morality are linked. What is morally good is expected to display valued aesthetic qualities, and what displays valued aesthetic qualities is expected to be morally good. It is recognized, however, that this is far from always being the case. A Dinka man is *adheng* if he has social status, whether ascribed or achieved, if he is virtuous in his relations with others, or if he is physically attractive. Ideally, these three aspects should go together, but Dinka recognize that they do not always do so.

Some of the recent literature in the anthropology of aesthetics attempts to relate aesthetics to social organization or social structure. As presented here, Nilotic aesthetics seems rather to be a contingent product of these cattle-keepers' experience of the world which they inhabit, and to have little to do with any social facts. In his account of the aesthetics of the Fang of Gabon, Fernandez (1971: 373) claims to identify basic principles of opposition and vitality at work in Fang society and culture: 'in both aesthetics and the social structure the aim of the Fang is not to resolve opposition and create identity but to preserve a balanced opposition'. This is achieved in the social structure, he argues, through complementary filiation, and in their ancestor statues through skilful aesthetic composition. Should it not be possible to make such a profound summation concerning the material presented in this essay?

To some extent, one's answer to such a question depends upon one's intellectual temper. No doubt many would find it intellectually satisfying to relate the high value of piedness to the segmentation of Nilotic political structure and to the divided world of Nilotic cosmology. The combination of black and white, or red and white, in the pied ox, the argument might run, is valued because it fits with the principles of the social organization and religious thought. It is probably the case that an intellectually diverting picture of the anthropological material concerning Nilotic aesthetics could be constructed along such lines. But what would it mean? That social structure and cosmology are products of aesthetic principles, or that aesthetic principles, and cosmology, are products of social structure, or that they are all products of underlying principles? For anyone wishing, despite these ontological puzzles, to make links of this sort, there are some suggestive facts in the ethnography to which one might point. They do not, however, stand up to closer inspection.

There is, most famously, the Nuer leopard-skin priest, amongst whose duties it is to resolve conflicts between disputing factions, and to act as an intermediary between man and God. Is it not, therefore, most suitable that he is the *leopard-skin* priest? The leopard-skin is pied, and combines within itself the opposites of black and white. However, the priest is not usually known by this title by the Nuer themselves. The more usual title can be translated as 'earth (or soil) priest'; as Evans-Pritchard (1956: 291) points out, 'the leopard-skin title is taken only from his badge [of office] whereas the earth title is derived from a symbolic association with the earth of deeper significance'. He is, therefore, not in fact a leopard-skin priest, but a priest of the soil who wears a leopard-skin as a badge of office. There is no hint that the Nuer regard a pied skin as suitable, *qua* its piedness, for a priest who is in an intermediate position and whose duty it is to resolve disputes. There is no reason to suppose any more profound reasons for the wearing of the leopard-skin than the symbolic associations of the leopard itself, which are beside the point here, and that it is a visually attractive and bold material symbol.

While Nilotes do not, in general, picture God to themselves,[26] Lienhardt relates (1961: 46) how some Western Dinka conceive of Nhialic, God, or Divinity, as being pied:

> Some people claim to have had visions of Divinity. Two youths, at different times, told me that their mothers had once seen Divinity . . . In one vision Divinity was seen as an old man, with a red and blue pied body and a white head. In the other he appeared as a huge old man, with a blue-green body (the colour of the sky) and again a white head. Other Dinka who have heard of such visions seem usually to be agreed that in them the body of Divinity is strikingly pied, but with a white head, a mark of age and venerability.

The blue-green body, it is worth noting at the outset, is not pied blue and green, but a single blue-green colour – the colour of the sky, *nhialic*, in which Divinity is conceived as living. The red-and-blue pied configuration is not found in cattle, but represents one of the strongest perceptual contrasts. It is an extreme form of piedness. Among the Atuot, similarly, one of the powerful spirits of the sky, the power of rain, is 'usually referred to by its ox-name *awumkwei*', and according to Burton (1981: 76), 'this color pattern is the most aesthetically pleasing for the Atuot; it signifies a boldly marked black and white animal, with a fully white head and red nose'.

That Nhialic and Awumkwei should be thought of as pied is not surprising, given how much the Dinka and Atuot value such configurations. The high aesthetic value of pied configurations, whether in cattle or elsewhere, is sufficient reason for Divinity to be though of as pied, when Divinity is thought of as displaying any perceptual qualities at all.

Lienhardt (1961: 46) goes on to explain that 'white oxen or oxen boldly marked with white are especially appropriate for sacrifice to Divinity'. Significantly, it is not the piebald which is especially suitable, but the white ox – or, in the case of the piebald, one that is marked with white. Similarly for the Mandari, Buxton's careful and sophisticated analysis of their colour symbolism (1973: esp. 385–94) makes it clear that, despite the high aesthetic valuation of variegated beasts, they have no symbolic importance and no especial place in sacrifice over and above their being cattle like any other. The appropriateness of different colour configurations for sacrifice to different divinities – or Divinity – amongst the Dinka, however, is exemplified in a number of cases in Lienhardt's study. In particular, the black-and-white configurations in cattle are especially suitable for sacrifice to the free-divinity Deng, which is particularly associated with celestial phenomena such as rain, thunder, and lightning. It is, however, not the piedness as such which makes beasts of black-and-white configurations suitable for sacrifice to Deng, but rather the imaginative connections between the quality perceived in the black-and-white ox and the quality of the lowering skies: 'the black-and-white configurations in cattle . . . impress themselves upon the minds of the Dinka as does the lightning in dark, overcast skies which signifies the activities of Deng' (Lienhardt, 1961: 162). The symbolic action is thus inexplicable without an understanding of the workings of the Dinka imagination, and our appreciation of the workings of the Dinka imagination involves, I should argue, an appreciation of Dinka aesthetics.

Conclusion

Cattle provide the primary aesthetic locus of Nilotic society. This is a given of their pastoral life-style and the well-documented centrality of cattle in their lives. The particularities of the Nilotic aesthetic relate to their deep appreciation of the physical qualities of their cattle and their ideals of bovine form. Their appreciation of cattle-colour configurations can be understood in the context of the environment in which the cattle are perceived, and as a particular instance of the universal appeal of contrast, manifested here in the appreciation of black-and-white and red-and-white beasts in herds of mostly off-white, greyish cattle. Elements which have their origins in this 'bovine' aesthetic can be traced through the ways in which Nilotes perceive, appreciate, enjoy, describe, and act in their world.

The underlying assumptions of this essay are that, all other things being equal, people act in the world to maximize their aesthetic satisfaction, and that an awareness of this aspect of human activity may help us to understand what we might otherwise seek to explain with reference to social structure, cosmology, symbolism, etc. I do not imagine that I have established beyond doubt the worth of these assumptions here, but I hope that I have provided at least an insight into how the Nilotes of the Southern Sudan take pleasure in the lives they lead, as well as into some of the marvels of their everyday vision.

Notes

This essay is based primarily on literary research, although, thanks to the British Institute in Eastern Africa and the Social Science Research Council, I was able to visit Agar Dinka and Apak Atuot country in 1981 and Mandariland in 1982. I am grateful to Survival Anglia and the Pitt Rivers Museum, Oxford, for permission to reproduce photographs. For comments on earlier drafts of this essay I am grateful to Gerd Baumann, Nigel Fancourt, Wendy James, Godfrey Lienhardt, John Mack, Andrew Mawson, Howard Morphy, Michael O'Hanlon, John Penney, and Simon Simonse.

1 For the Nuer, see Evans-Pritchard (1940a); for the Dinka, Lienhardt (1961); for the Atuot, Burton (1987); and for the Mandari, Buxton (1973).
2 See, for the Nuer, Evans-Pritchard (1940a: 16–50); for the Dinka, Lienhardt (1961: 10–27); and for the Mandari, Buxton (1973: 5–11).
3 This includes the war currently being waged in the Southern Sudan, in which Nuer, Dinka, Atuot, and Mandari have been involved as combatants, victims, and refugees.
4 In his comprehensive overview of the literature on 'African Aesthetics', Van Damme (1987) mentions only one work on a Nilotic people, Schneider (1956) on the Pokot. Klumpp (1987) includes a brief discussion of Maasai aesthetics. There are a number of works which discuss body decoration, material culture, and so on amongst Nilotic peoples; this literature contains material relevant to the study of aesthetics, but rarely discusses aesthetics specifically.
5 See e.g. Turton (1980) on the Mursi.
6 For illustrations, see e.g. Ryle (1982: 17, 26–7, 34–5, 139); Howell et al. (1988: 287, 288, pls. 21, 22); and Fig. 22.1 here, in which the 'background' of off-white cattle is an accidental feature of the photograph. The veterinary officer Grunnet (1962: 7) claimed that 60% of Dinka cattle, were 'greyish white or dirty white'.
7 On Nuer practice, see Evans-Pritchard (1940a: 37–8; 1956: pl. xiii, opp. 256); for the Dinka, see Lienhardt (1961: 17), and the illustrations in Ryle (1982: 65, 94–5), and in Howell et al. (1988: 205, pl. 18); for the Atuot, see Burton (1981: fig. A, opp. 36); and for the Mandari, see Buxton (1973: 7, pl. 1, opp. 6).
8 For an illustration, see Ryle (1982: 39).
9 The fact that similar patterns are highly valued by geographically contiguous peoples who do not keep cattle – such as the Uduk (James, 1988: 28–9) – suggests that these elements may have been part of Nilotic aesthetics even before the Nilotes became cattle-keepers. This is, however, irrelevant to an understanding of the appreciation of

such patterns by Nilotic cattle-keepers today, which is founded in their daily experience of their cattle.

10 For illustrations, see e.g. Ryle (1982: 62–5).

11 See e.g. the photograph of a Dinka wearing a colobus monkey skin and other finery in Howell *et al.* (1988: 205, pl. 18).

12 For illustrations, see e.g. Fisher (1984: 42).

13 Schneider (1956: 105) noted the importance of contrast in Pokot beadwork, and Klumpp (1987) has discussed the importance of both contrast and complementarity in contemporary Maasai beadwork. I hope to discuss Nilotic beadwork at length elsewhere.

14 See also e.g. the post illustrated in Buxton (1973: pl. 2, opp. 78).

15 For the Dinka, see Lienhardt (1961: pl. vi, opp. 176); for the Mandari, see Buxton (1973: 54, fig. 1; pl. 7, opp. 371; and app. ii at 419); for an Anuak example, see Evans-Pritchard (1940b: pl. ivb, opp. 40).

16 For illustrations, see, for the Dinka, Fisher (1984: 48, 50, 52); for the Mandari, Caputo (1982: 366).

17 For illustrations, see Ryle (1982: 7, 18, 70–1).

18 For an illustration, see Evans-Pritchard (1956: pl. xii, opp. 234).

19 For other illustrations, see, for the Dinka, Deng (1972: 18); Ryle (1982: 15, 58–9); Lienhardt (1961: pl. 1, opp. 16); and the various sequences including dances interspersed throughout the film *Dinka* (Survival Anglia, 1983), especially the sacrifice sequence.

20 For illustrations of such girdles, or corsets, see Fisher (1984: 50, 51); Howell *et al.* (1988: 205, pl. 18).

21 Lienhardt (1961: 264), however, found mud models of bulls hanging in a shrine he visited.

22 Lienhardt (1963: 82) also refers to children playing at cattle-herding with snail-shells. I do not know what form these shells have, but I should not be surprised if they resembled in some ways the schematized cattle forms represented in the abstracted Pokot examples in Fig. 22.8.

23 These examples are in the Pitt Rivers Museum, Oxford, and were collected by Evans-Pritchard. All but one are inscribed as having been collected among the Anuak, but it is almost certainly the case that they were all collected among the Nuer.

24 In his discussion of Dinka arts, Caravita (1968: 366) suggests that painting and sculpture remain undeveloped and marginalized because they are the work of people, that is, women and children, who are marginalized within Dinka society.

25 Huffman (1931: 69) remarks that the figures drawn by Nuer children and those incised on gourds by Nuer women always have rectangular bodies.

26 Evans-Pritchard (1956: 123) says that 'Nuer do not claim to see God', while, according to Buxton (1973: 19), Mandari say 'Creator has not been known or seen', and among the Atuot, according to Burton (1981: 138), '"God the Father" is never said or imagined to exist in any physical form'.

References

Baxandall, Michael (1972). *Painting and Experience in Fifteenth-Century Italy: A Primer in the Social History of Pictorial Style*. Oxford: Oxford Univ. Press.

—— (1980). *The Limewood Sculptors of Renaissance Germany*. New Haven, Conn.: Yale Univ. Press.

Blackman, A. A. (1956). 'The Material Culture of the Nilotic Tribes of East Africa'. B.Litt. thesis, Univ. of Oxford.

Burton, John W. (1978). 'Ghost Marriage and the Cattle Trade among the Atuot of the Southern Sudan', *Africa*, 48/4: 398–405.

—— (1979). 'Atuot Totemism', *Journal of Religion in Africa*, 10/2: 95–107.

—— (1981). *God's Ants: A Study of Atuot Religion*. Studia Instituti Anthropos 37. St Augustin, Germany: Anthropos Institute.

—— (1982). 'Figurative Language and the Definition of Experience: The Role of Ox-Songs in Atuot Social Theory', *Anthropological Linguistics*, 24/3: 263–79.

—— (1987). *A Nilotic World: The Atuot-Speaking Peoples of the Southern Sudan* (with a foreword by Francis Mading Deng). Contributions to the Study of Anthropology, No. 1. New York: Greenwood Press.

Buxton, Jean (1973). *Religion and Healing in Mandari*. Oxford: Clarendon Press.

Caputo, Robert (1982). 'Sudan: Arab-African Giant', *National Geographic*, 161/3: 346–79.

Caravita, G. (1968) 'L'arte dei Dinka', *Africa* (Rome), 23/3: 350–69.

Cummins, S. L. (1904). 'Sub-Tribes of the Bahr-el-Ghazal Dinkas', *Journal of the Royal Anthropological Institute*, 34: 149–66.

Deng, Francis Mading (1972). *The Dinka of the Sudan*. New York: Holt, Rinehart & Winston.

—— (1973). *The Dinka and their Songs*. Oxford Library of African Literature. Oxford: Clarendon Press.

Diffey, T. J. (1986). 'The Idea of Aesthetic Experience', in Michael H. Mitias (ed.), *Possibility of the Aesthetic Experience*. Martinus Nijhoff Philosophy Library 14. Dordrecht: Nijhoff, 3–12.

Evans-Pritchard, E. E. (1934). 'Imagery in Ngok Dinka Cattle-Names', *Bulletin of the School of Oriental and African Studies*, 7/3: 623–8.

—— (1937). 'Economic Life of the Nuer: Cattle', *Sudan Notes and Records*, 20/2: 209–45.

—— (1940a). *The Nuer: A Description of the Modes of Livelihood and Political Institutions of a Nilotic People*. Oxford: Clarendon Press.

—— (1940b). *The Political System of the Anuak of the Anglo-Egyptian Sudan*. London School of Economics Monographs on Social Anthropology, No. 4. London: Lund, Humphries.

—— (1956). *Nuer Religion*. Oxford: Clarendon Press.

Fagg, William (1973). 'In Search of Meaning in African Art', in Anthony Forge (ed.), *Primitive Art and Society*. London: Oxford Univ. Press, 151–68.

Fernandez, James W. (1971). 'Principles of Opposition and Vitality in Fang Aesthetics', in Carol F. Jopling (ed.), *Art and Aesthetics in Primitive Societies: A Critical Anthology*. New York: Dutton, 356–73 (first published 1966).

Fisher, Angela (1984). *Africa Adorned*. London: Collins.

Forge, Anthony (1970). 'Learning to See in New Guinea', in Philip Mayer (ed.), *Socialization: The Approach from Social Anthropology*. ASA Monographs, No. 8. London: Tavistock, 269–91.

Gombrich, E. H. (1977). *Art and Illusion: A Study in the Psychology of Pictorial Representation*, 5th edn. Oxford: Phaidon (first published 1960).

Grunnet, N. T. (1962). 'An Ethnographic–Ecological Survey of the Relationship between the Dinka and their Cattle', *Folk* (Copenhagen), 4: 5–20.

Howell, Paul *et al.* (1988). *The Jonglei Canal: Impact and Opportunity.* Cambridge: Cambridge Univ. Press.

Huffman, Ray (1931). *Nuer Customs and Folklore* (with an introduction by D. Westermann). London: Oxford Univ. Press.

Jackson, H. C. (1923). 'The Nuer of the Upper Nile Province', *Sudan Notes and Records*, 6/1: 59–107; 6/2: 123–89.

James, Wendy (1988). *The Listening Ebony: Moral Knowledge, Religion, and Power among the Uduk of Sudan.* Oxford: Clarendon Press.

Klumpp, Donna Rey (1987). 'Maasai Art and Society: Age and Sex, Time and Space, Cash and Cattle'. Ph.D. thesis, Columbia Univ., New York.

Lienhardt, Godfrey (1961). *Divinity and Experience: The Religion of the Dinka.* Oxford: Clarendon Press.

—— (1963). 'Dinka Representations of the Relations between the Sexes', in I. Schapera (ed.), *Studies in Kinship and Marriage: Dedicated to Brenda Z. Seligman on her 80th Birthday.* Royal Anthropological Institute Occasional Paper No. 16. London: Royal Anthropological Institute, 79–92.

MacDermot, Brian Hugh (1972). *Cult of the Sacred Spear: The Story of the Nuer Tribe in Ethiopia.* London: Hale.

Maquet, Jacques (1979). *Introduction to Aesthetic Anthropology*, 2nd edn. Other Realities 1. Malibu, Calif.: Undena Publications (first published 1971).

—— (1986). *The Aesthetic Experience: An Anthropologist Looks at the Visual Arts.* New Haven, Conn.: Yale Univ. Press.

Nebel, Arthur (1948). *Dinka Grammar (Rek-Malual Dialect) with Texts and Vocabulary.* English text rev. by C. W. Beer. Museum Combonianum 2. Verona: Missioni Africane.

—— (1979). *Dinka–English, English-Dinka Dictionary: Thong Muonyjang Jam Jang Kek Jieng, Dinka Language Jang and Jieng Dialects.* Museum Combonianum 36. Bologna: Editrice Missionaria Italiana (first published 1954).

Ocholla-Ayayo, A. B. C. (1980). *The Luo Culture: A Reconstruction of the Material Culture Patterns of a Traditional African Society.* Studien zur Kulturkunde 54. Wiesbaden: Steiner.

Pepper, Stephen (1974). 'Aesthetics', in *New Encyclopaedia Britannica: Macropaedia*, i. Chicago: Beaton, 149–63.

Ryle, John (1982). *Warriors of the White Nile: The Dinka.* Amsterdam: Time-Life.

Schneider, Harold K. (1956). 'The Interpretation of Pakot Visual Art', *Man*, 56: art. 108, 103–6.

Survival Anglia (1983). *Dinka.* The Vanishing Tribes of Africa 3. Film. Norwich: Survival Anglia.

Svoboda, Terese (trans.) (1985). *Cleaned the Crocodile's Teeth: Nuer Song.* Greenfield Center, NY: Greenfield Review Press.

Turton, David (1980). 'There's No Such Beast: Cattle and Colour Naming among the Mursi', *Man*, n.s., 15/2: 320–38.

Van Damme, Wilfried (1987). *A Comparative Analysis Concerning Beauty and Ugliness in Sub-Saharan Africa.* Africana Gandensia 4. Ghent: Rijksuniversiteit.

Zangwill, Nick (1986). 'Aesthetics and Art', *British Journal of Aesthetics*, 26/3: 257–69.

Chapter 23

Sense matters
Aesthetic values of the Great Barrier Reef

Celmara Pocock

Heritage assessments and aesthetics

The earliest legislation and administration governing the identification and protection of cultural heritage places was developed within Old World countries, and
exported to the New World in colonial contexts. The way in which heritage places are
identified and assessed around the world continues to share many features of this
colonial legacy, in spite of the diversity of cultural and social contexts in which they
operate.[1] Many of the conservation frameworks developed under these regimes
include a series of criteria by which the significance of heritage places can be assessed.
Although there have been some shifts in how criteria are interpreted and defined, the
underlying premises on which they are based have remained unchanged. This is clearly
illustrated by criteria used to assess aesthetics of heritage places.

Many heritage-management systems make provision for the aesthetics of natural-
and cultural-heritage places to be considered in deciding significance and conservation
measures. Like the heritage-conservation regimes, the philosophy and judgement of
aesthetics emerged within the Old World, and is most commonly associated with the
visual arts of Europe. However, the study of aesthetics is controversial and complex.
There is a broad and elaborate literature on aesthetics in the areas of philosophy,
psychology, music, art history, architecture and an increasing number of studies
relating to the aesthetics of the environment and the everyday.[2] A significant portion
of the debate stems back to Kant's *Critique of judgement* in 1790, and the arguments
are, to some extent, exhausted.[3] However, they are in no way conclusive and the
concept is constantly challenged and expanded, contracted and reinstated.

In contrast, the issue of aesthetics is barely debated within heritage management,
even though decisions about aesthetic value continue to be made on a daily basis by
practitioners. It is not the intention of this paper to review or summarise the extensive

body of literature on the subject or to provide an overview of philosophical or psychological cognition of aesthetics. Rather, its purpose is to demonstrate that the failure of heritage-management practice to engage with theoretical discourse has produced inadequate assessment methods and processes. Through the consideration of a case study, the paper illustrates how professional use of aesthetics, as a criterion to assess heritage significance, is simplistic and subject to misrepresentation. The example of the Great Barrier Reef is used to demonstrate how a lack of engagement with philosophies and theories can result in naïve assessments and the loss of value.

Great Barrier Reef Heritage Listing

The Great Barrier Reef, off the northeast coast of Australia, is regarded by many as one of the wonders of the world. It is a place deemed to have superlative natural attributes and is included in the World Heritage List. The Reef is also recognised by the Commonwealth Government of Australia through its inclusion in the Register of the National Estate. World Heritage and National Estate processes share characteristics with other heritage-listing regimes in the world, including their capacity to assess aesthetic qualities in making decisions about significance. The aesthetics of the Reef are considered to be an important contributor to the current heritage status of the Reef under both the Australian and the World Heritage systems.

World Heritage Listing

The Great Barrier Reef has been included on the World Heritage List since 1981. It is listed, among other things, for its aesthetic qualities. At the time of listing, the criterion used to assess aesthetic values stated that World Heritage places should 'contain unique, rare and superlative natural phenomena, formations and features and areas of exceptional natural beauty'. The Reef was hence recognised for its natural beauty, including its 'unparalleled aerial vista' and an 'abundance and diversity of shape, size and colour of marine fauna and flora in the coral reefs'.[4]

The criteria for assessing places for World Heritage listing have since changed. A report by Lucas et al., to expand and clarify the basis on which the Reef can be included on the World Heritage List, found that natural heritage attributes contributing to natural beauty and aesthetics 'were the poorest documented and least known set of attributes'.[5] This is a problem that continues to plague the assessment of aesthetic values, and to some extent is a result of the criteria themselves. The World Heritage Convention[6] articulates separate criteria for natural and cultural values, and both are defined to include aesthetic perspectives. The way in which aesthetics are incorporated into each definition is quite different. In the case of cultural heritage, defined under Article 1, aesthetics are mentioned in relation to sites, but in relation to buildings and monuments it is art that defines aesthetic judgement. Sites are judged to be of outstanding universal value 'from the historical, aesthetic, ethnological or anthropological point of view', but monuments and buildings must have outstanding universal value 'from the point of view of history, *art* or science' (my emphasis).

In contrast, natural heritage is defined in a way that is more generally inclusive of scientific and aesthetic values and is expressed as the 'outstanding universal value from the aesthetic or scientific point of view' and 'from the point of view of science, conservation or natural beauty'. Underlying this division between cultural and natural aesthetic criteria are some strongly held associations between fine art and beauty in a cultural context, and the presupposed aesthetic qualities of the natural world.

The operational guidelines of the World Heritage Convention go further in showing these two distinct approaches to assessing aesthetic value. The cultural assessment is clearly focused on the arts, citing monumental arts and architecture. The word 'aesthetic' is absent altogether. On the other hand, the natural assessment retains its inclusiveness and requires that sites 'contain superlative natural phenomena or areas of exceptional natural beauty and aesthetic importance'.[7] The first indicates that cultural assessment is about established concepts of Western art; the second that natural aesthetics are presumed to be independent of cultural influence. Both clearly indicate that UNESCO regards aesthetic values as existing without a cultural context and that they are assessable objectively. This can be attributed to the emphasis given to monuments in early legislative regimes,[8] and reflects the lag between cultural heritage practice and academic debate.

Lucas et al. consider the inclusion of the phrase 'aesthetic importance' in the World Heritage criteria since 1996 as an important avenue through which to consider 'the range of values which the community places on the Great Barrier Reef World Heritage Area'.[9] However, in the World Heritage operational guidelines this phrase is included only in the context of natural heritage values. The interpretation given to it by Lucas et al. highlights the nexus between cultural and natural heritage values[10] by recognising that communities may in fact attribute these values. Within the current World Heritage framework, however, there is no scope to allow for the intersection of cultural and natural values. The criteria lead directly to the problems that the Lucas et al. report warns against, in particular that aesthetic qualities are reduced 'solely to visual amenity', and that there is a lack of consistency in methods used to document and assess aesthetic value.[11]

The problems of assessment and documentation of aesthetics highlighted by Lucas et al. result from a failure to regard aesthetics in a social context. Under some legislative and management regimes in Australia, heritage places may be assessed and listed for their social values. These are very broadly understood to be the values attributed to places by communities and are much like the values Lucas et al. have seen as arising out of aesthetic value. In some instances, social value is defined to include aesthetics, and in others social and aesthetic values are assessed through separate criteria.

Australian Heritage Commission Listing

The Australian Heritage Commission is an Australian Commonwealth Government statutory authority responsible for natural and cultural heritage places of significance. It was established to identify, assess and list heritage places in the Register of the National Estate. As a national body, it has been a leader in developing guidelines, policies and practices for the assessment and management of heritage places. The Commission uses the same principal criteria to assess both natural and cultural heritage places for inclusion in the Register of the National Estate, and defines separate criteria for social and aesthetic values. However, the Commission criterion used to assess aesthetics has some social context, and is less general than the World Heritage criterion. Criterion E under the Australian Heritage Commission Act 1975 provides for a place to be included in the Register of the National Estate for 'its importance in exhibiting particular aesthetic characteristics valued by a community or cultural group'. This goes some way to recognising that aesthetic appreciation is determined by cultural groups themselves, and thus partly addresses research that demonstrates the interconnectedness of class, culture, education levels and aesthetic judgement.[12] While a diversity of aesthetic appreciation may be recognised through factors like class, gender, ethnicity and Aboriginality, the phases of human lifecycles can have an equally important impact on aesthetic appreciation and values. The Australian Heritage Commission criterion for aesthetic value has the capacity to consider and include the aesthetic values of cultural groups within society brought about not only by historical change but also by the transformation of individuals throughout their lives.

As an explanation of the formal criterion, aesthetic value is defined broadly by the Australian Heritage Commission to include:

> aspects of sensory perception (sight, touch, sound, taste, smell) for which criteria can be stated. These criteria may include consideration of form, scale, colour, texture and material of the fabric or landscape, the smells and sounds associated with the place and its use.[13]

The definitions provided by the Australian Heritage Commission are inclusive of cultural difference and a range of sensory experiences that may contribute to a sense of place. However, the recognition of these experiences does not translate into practice in the assessment of heritage places. In the case of the Great Barrier Reef, the Australian Heritage Commission's statement of significance includes only visual aesthetics in recognising that '[t]he reef is an area of exceptional natural beauty with some of the most spectacular scenery on earth'.[14]

Aesthetic assessment has remained the primary domain of non-Indigenous, historic built heritage and scenic landscapes. Only the most cursory attention is given to aesthetics in other contexts. For example, it can be argued that aesthetic qualities may manifest themselves as very different concepts within Aboriginal society,[15] but Aboriginal paintings and engravings are often superficially judged to be of aesthetic importance by non-Aboriginal experts. The focus on built heritage may partly be attributed to the appropriation of this aspect of heritage by conservation architects,[16] and the strong association of aesthetics with Western art and particular social strata. Similarly, appreciation of landscapes is linked strongly with Western landscape painting.[17]

The focus on the physical aspects of heritage places poses problems for heritage management in Australia and elsewhere in the world,[18] and the assessment and management of aesthetic value is similarly restricted by this bias. Because aesthetic values are assessed separately from social values, heritage practitioners tend to regard aesthetics as a set of attributes that can be observed impartially by an expert, at a distance and in isolation from other communities who may attribute values to the place. Although seeing can be a tactile experience,[19] the physical and emotional distance required by the objectivity of heritage assessments restricts the consideration of aesthetics to visual characteristics that are less 'grossly sensuous'[20] than other aesthetic experiences.

The assessment of aesthetic values, as with other characteristics of heritage places, is therefore reduced to fabric and material evidence significant to a restricted number of individuals. This objectifying process displaces the consideration of emotional and sensory experience and knowledge that underpins other people's attachment to place.[21] The result is that aesthetic judgement remains the realm of aesthetes for whom visual pleasure is pre-established and does not meet the broader objective of aesthetic criteria as defined by the heritage profession. Aesthetic value is also used as a generic criterion, to support arguments about 'natural' landscape values or as support to arguments about scientific significance. In this context, aesthetic value is sometimes (sub)consciously used by scientists as a way of expressing attachment that is not reflected in standard identification of natural attributes.

So in spite of the inclusive definitions of aesthetic value, which go some way to recognising that aesthetics are culturally constructed and that smell, taste, touch, and sound can all be strongly evocative of place, the predominant interpretation of aesthetics is a visual one, constituted by a particular social construction.

The implications of this bias are that experiences of place go unrecognised and unassessed. According to established processes of Article 6 of the Burra Charter, management of a heritage place 'must be based on an understanding of its cultural significance'.[22] In other words, the values must be assessed before they can be managed. This principle is generally regarded as standard, if not best, practice in Australian heritage conservation. In the case of aesthetics, it is apparent that only a very narrow range of values is considered. Many additional aesthetic values, both from different cultural and social perspectives, and those resulting from different sensory experiences, are ignored. The aesthetic experiences of people of differing abilities are also marginalised.

In this paper, the preliminary results of research into changes in social values associated with the Great Barrier Reef are used to show how aesthetic appreciation of the Reef has changed over time. It also explores how the failure to recognise non-visual aesthetics has resulted in the loss of significant values.

Aesthetic experiences of the Great Barrier Reef

Representations of the Great Barrier Reef enter people's lives through advertisements, documentary films, television, advertising, posters, books, magazines and postcards. This material is overwhelmingly colourful, and images abound of blue seas, green islands, white beaches and kaleidoscopic underwater life. These vivid visual images are readily accepted as representing an important aesthetic experience of the Great

Barrier Reef. As discussed above, these scenic visual aesthetics are recognised as contributing to the heritage values of the Reef.

There are, however, a number of different aesthetic and sensory experiences associated with the Great Barrier Reef that hold significance. In her book *Reefscape*, Rosaleen Love[23] explores a variety of spiritual and sensory experiences of the Reef, both beneath and above the surface of the sea, and in that intermediate zone between the two worlds. A particularly memorable description by Love is of the unmistakable smell of a coral cay. Her description may be conspicuous because it seems unconventional among the more common experiences portrayed in Reef advertising. It seems unlikely that the 'distinctive fertiliser smell of the true coral cay'[24] would be used in contemporary promotion of the Great Barrier Reef.

The accounts of several people who spent a number of months camping on small islands during Reef excursions in the 1920s and 1930s disclose distinctive elements of the environment. Their encounters with the region are more holistic – evocative of smell and tastes of food, water and air; skin sensations of heat, moisture, insects, and sand; and of sounds of birds, insects and trees.

At the beginning of the last century, one of the Great Barrier Reef's most renowned long-term residents, E. J. Banfield, gave a lengthy account of the different smells of Dunk Island in its various seasons and moods. For him the smells of the island were a distinctive part of the experience of this place:

> It has long been a fancy of mine that the island has a distinctive odour, soft and pliant, rich and vigorous. Other mixtures of forest and jungle may smell as strong, but none has the rare blend which I recognize and gloat over whensoever, after infrequent absences for a day or two, I return to accept of it in grateful sniffs.[25]

A contemporary Reef experience is regarded as incomplete without a venture into the underwater world. For many people the associated aesthetics are quite thrilling and unique. This is sometimes the first and only time they will dare to immerse themselves in the ocean. They float, taste salt and hear underwater sounds as completely new experiences. However, even these sensations are frequently reduced to the two-dimensional visual reproductions found in the mass of popular colour images of the Reef.

In early 20th-century Reef tourism, underwater experiences were not only impracticable but also undesirable.[26] It was a long time before large groups of people snorkelled and dived on coral reefs. Although the 1930s were an important period of expansion of Reef tourism,[27] personal immersion in an underwater world was not an important aspect of Reef experiences. Instead, the Reef was peeked at through a waterscope or glass-bottomed boat. The experience was more voyeuristic than participatory.

The brilliant colours for which the Reef is known are now taken as synonymous with Reef images. However, in the historic past people would have had no notion of the colours of the Reef except through direct experience. Photographs of the Reef and its islands were in black and white, and the colours of the underwater world difficult to communicate. In writing of the living corals in the 1930s, Mel Ward says that the 'colours are elusive and frequently indefinable'.[28] Similarly, in her reminiscence of a Reef holiday, Hilda Marks says, 'No words can describe what we saw.'[29] Early colour reproductions in the form of hand-tinted photographs and postcards are pale and subtle in comparison with the photographic images of today. Even in the 1960s it was difficult to re-create the colours of the underwater world, and coral displays were a poor substitute. Coral samples quickly died out of water and subsequently lost their colour. Bleached white specimens were hand-painted to re-create the colours visible underwater. In writing to the Commonwealth Government in support of her own skill in re-creating the colours of living corals, coral artist Shirley Keong stressed that:

> [O]verseas displays of coral should not be of the 'icing sugar' colourings, that have been sent in past years, (to me it has been the worst form of false advertising in relation to one of the worlds [sic] Greatest Wonders). Shirley Keong, 20 December 1965[30]

Only those who had visited and viewed the Reef beneath the sea would have realised and remembered the colours. Brilliant colour was therefore regarded more clearly as only one aspect of a broader visual aesthetic experience, and the textures and diversity of coral shapes were prominent. Without the emphasis on underwater ventures, activities on the Reef more readily included a range of land-based aesthetic experiences. Forms of trees and silhouetted shapes of people, mountains, islands and boats were important visual images. But beyond this, people's experiences of sounds, smells and tastes were also given greater emphasis.

Sighing she-oaks

One example of non-visual aesthetics that stands out in the historic texts is the sound of *Casuarina equisetifolia*, also known as casuarinas or she-oaks, on islands of the Great Barrier Reef. Elsewhere I have presented an argument about the transformation of Reef landscapes from Australian bush to generic ideal.[31] Prior to the transformation of environments around island resorts, many native species of trees and bushes were present in areas frequented by visitors. Casuarinas are only one such species. However, the prominence of these trees is notable in that they were identified primarily through a non-visual aesthetic experience.

Casuarinas are a colonising tree of coral cays, and fringe the beaches of Great Barrier Reef islands. Although they are found and are valued elsewhere in the world, she-oaks are distinctively Australian and bring with them a characteristic audible aesthetic. In the experiences of early Reef visitors, casuarinas were not regarded as particularly beautiful to look at, but they were frequently recalled for their sound. In writing of Dunk Island, Banfield describes these trees as 'ever-sighing beech oaks'.[32]

The sound of the she-oaks on the Reef islands is one that is deeply impressive, and is an important aesthetic experience of early Reef visitors. Mel Ward, a naturalist who spent many months living on Reef islands, writes of being '[l]ulled by the music of the sea and the sighing trees' on Lindeman Island.[33] The trees are part of an experience of being on the Reef. In a newspaper article, Mel Ward recalls she-oaks as 'haunted trees'.[34] The spiritual quality he ascribed to the trees is also prominent in his other writing:

> The . . . casuarinas at first appeared drab and even bedraggled in the daylight
> – their forlorn foliage hanging in shreds but at night they seemed to become
> imbude [sic] with some mystical spirit at first scarcely definable but as the
> inevitable nights followed each other, this nameless presence claimed the
> imagination.[35]

The presence of casuarinas is visually testified in numerous newspaper and personal photographs in the early part of the 20th century. In terms of visual qualities, the casuarinas are not given particular attention, but their abundance on Reef sands assures them a place at the edges and in the background of many photographs of the period.

In contrast, contemporary promotion rarely includes casuarinas as part of Great Barrier Reef depictions. Casuarinas are still found in significant numbers on the islands and along the coastline of the Great Barrier Reef. However, in hundreds of Reef-related tourism brochures gathered at the 2001 Townsville Travel Show, only two include glimpses of these trees. In one photograph, small casuarina saplings peek out of the sand, and in the other the casuarina is mostly obscured by a superimposed image. The vegetative framing of photographs has given way overwhelmingly to the palm.[36]

And yet for Captain Tom McLean, a long-time tourism operator in the Whitsundays from the mid-1940s to the 1980s, casuarinas were an important part of a Reef experience:

> From afar [the Reef islands] are outlines of green apparently suspended
> above the sea. On closer approach they resolve into wooden humps indented
> with bays from which shine curving crescents of white sand, often with the
> touch of a few coconut palms that most people expect on a tropical island.
> The palms are not an essential part of the enchantment for many a beach is
> shaded by the pine-like casuarinas known as she-oaks in Australia. These have
> their own magic in the soft sigh the wind makes through them, a sound
> infinitely more subtle than the rustle of palm fronds.[37]

This contrasts strongly with the permit provisions for tourist operators in the late 1980s, who were prohibited from allowing their patrons to sit in the shade of the sole remaining casuarina on Lizard Island.[38] The heavy planting of palms around tourist areas has removed casuarinas from the environments that people visit. Although present on many beaches of the Reef, they have disappeared from the dominant discourse that frames Reef experiences.

Discussion

For Reef visitors in the early 20th century, casuarinas imparted a real sense of place and are entwined with their knowledge of the region. Unlike many elements of contemporary Reef experiences, she-oaks were valued through sound rather than for their visual attributes. Although casuarinas persist on Reef islands and cays today, they are no longer a central conception of the Reefscape for visitors.

The Great Barrier Reef is renowned for its brightly coloured visual aesthetics, and in this context casuarinas may not be particularly conspicuous. However, the sound of these trees was an integral and evocative element in early Reef experiences. Sound is at least as important as visual quality in the experience and appreciation of place,[39] but in the case of the Reef these values have been diminished. This can be attributed, in part, to the way in which aesthetics are assessed and managed. Without the recognition of the value of the sound in aesthetic experiences of place, palms have displaced casuarinas[40] and the continuity of visitor experiences has been broken. It is possible that if a full range of aesthetic values were identified, casuarinas may have been more carefully managed and maintained within and around the resorts of the Great Barrier Reef that are inundated with exotic palms today. This may have maintained the value of the she-oak as an important aspect of visiting the Reef.

While the Reef is managed and conserved primarily for natural attributes, the failure to identify social aesthetic values has led to the loss of some natural attributes. The contemporary management regime, with its focus on scientific values, highlights the conservation needs of vegetation such as *Pisonia* trees that are recognised as being at risk.[41] The casuarina is not regarded as endangered or under threat and is therefore overlooked in the management regime. Although the trees are abundant generally, they have lost their place in the environmental and social contexts in which they were valued. In some instances this has in fact led to a loss of natural attributes, as seen in the case of Lizard Island.

The data suggest not only that aesthetic values have been lost, but also they are historically constituted through both social and technological factors. Visual appreciation is strongly tied with tourists' experiences of places,[42] and the 'taking of photographs seems almost obligatory to those who travel about'.[43] Photography is a predominant force in contemporary capitalist societies[44] and provides a literal framing mechanism of contemporary Reef experience.

The Great Barrier Reef and its highly regarded aesthetics are closely linked with the role of the camera and the purposes to which it has been put. Photographs provide a means by which people can acquire knowledge and experience.[45] The development of new types of technology made new forms of knowledge available and shaped people's aesthetic experiences of the Reef. In the early 20th century, photographs were black and white still images taken from above the water surface. Technological development of underwater cameras, colour film emulsions, motion film and macroscopic lenses gave people access to new experiences and aesthetics and impacted directly on how people perceived the Reef. Before colour photography was available, people had to experience the colours of the Reef themselves or not at all. Improvements in photographic technology, particularly the advent and improvement of colour film and underwater cameras, have focused aesthetic appreciation of the Reef to particular visual qualities. This has come at the expense of other sensory experiences that contribute to a sense of place.

The realisation that the way in which aesthetics are valued changes over time raises some interesting questions for cultural heritage managers. Heritage vision statements and definitions inevitably consider the value of places in an intergenerational context.[46] The aim of heritage management is to conserve and maintain heritage in respect of the past, and for appreciation and use in both the present and the future. The implication of historic change is that aesthetics, as a criterion to assess significance, require constant reassessment and re-evaluation. The values are constantly changing and subject to the influence of technology, society and management. It is therefore worth considering, in a contemporary heritage context, how these values might best be assessed so as to allow aesthetic values of the past, present and future to be included in a management regime.

Conclusions

People construct places through sensual experience that is mediated by technology and structured by society. There is a body of literature dealing with space and place in which the first is thought to exist without reference to people, the latter constructed through human knowledge. Similar arguments have been made in relation to environment and landscape.[47] However, in considering non-visual aesthetics, heritage professionals seek to identify sensations that are evocative of place, rather than recognising that these sensations may in fact constitute the place. While technology and society effect temporal changes in aesthetic appreciation, the way in which heritage practitioners assess these values has remained static. This is particularly problematic in heritage contexts that are multicultural and conflicting.

Some regimes have attempted to broaden definitions and adjust criteria to account for the greater diversity of situations in which they operate. For instance, the strong emphasis given to monuments in very early legislation has been balanced by broader definitions that include other types of sites and landscapes.[48] However, the colonial history of heritage legislation, and the association of aesthetics with a Western tradition of fine art and architecture has left a strong bias in the types of places listed for their aesthetic qualities. There is a further bias towards the visual aspect of aesthetics that stems from the dominance of the visual in Western philosophy, and the objective scientific paradigm in which cultural heritage management operates.

The contentious issue is that, within heritage practice, assessment continues to reinforce Western notions of natural and cultural aesthetics, and its bias towards the visual. Heritage practitioners' assessments of significance are undertaken uncritically, based on cultural prejudice and assumption. While aesthetics are regarded as an important element in significance assessment, the individuals making these judgements operate in isolation from the debates on aesthetics.[49] Aesthetics are assumed to be understood and unambiguous by heritage practitioners, whereas the theoretical literature on the subject suggests this is anything but the case. The criterion is therefore poorly understood and used by most practitioners, particularly in newer contexts of landscape and social assessment.

In many parts of the world, there is an increasing recognition of the nexus between cultural and natural heritage values. In response to this, the criteria for World Heritage listing are currently under review. It would also be timely to disentangle aesthetics criteria from their colonial origin, and to reconsider the elements that contribute to aesthetic values in a range of heritage contexts. This may require the use of different terminology to clarify the role of sensuousness in the experience of place. It may only be once the term is understood within particular heritage conservation regimes that it will be possible systematically to assess and conserve these elements of heritage places.

Acknowledgements

This research is made possible through the support of the Cooperative Research Centre for the Great Barrier Reef World Heritage Area. I would like to thank Drs David Collett, Shelley Greer, David Roe and Marion Stell for commenting on earlier versions of this paper.

Notes

1.   H. Cleere, 'World cultural resource management: problems and perspectives', in H. Cleere (ed.) *Approaches to the archaeological heritage: a comparative study of world cultural resource management systems*, New Directions in Archaeology, Cambridge and New York: Cambridge University Press, 1984; Henry Cleere, 'Introduction: the rationale of archaeological heritage management', in Henry Cleere (ed.) *Archaeological heritage management in the modern world*, One World Archaeology, London: Unwin Hyman, 1989; F.P. McManamon & A. Hatton, 'Introduction: considering cultural resource management in modern society', in F.P. McManamon & A. Hatton (eds) *Cultural resource management in contemporary society: perspectives on managing and presenting the past*, One World Archaeology, London and New York: Routledge, 2000.
2.   See, for example, D. Inglis & J. Hughson, 'The beautiful game and the proto-aesthetics of the everyday', *Cultural Values*, Vol. 4, No. 3, 2000; H. Grace, 'Introduction: aesthesia and the economy of the senses', in H. Grace Kingswood (ed.) *Aesthesia and the economy of the senses*, Sydney: Faculty of Visual and Performing Arts, University of Western Sydney, Nepean, 1996; A. Berleant, 'Toward a phenomenological aesthetics of environment', in D. Ihde & H.J. Silverman (eds) *Descriptions*, Selected Studies in Phenomenology and Existential Philosophy, Albany: State University of New York Press, 1985; A. Berleant, *The aesthetics of environment*, Philadelphia: Temple University Press, 1992; S.C. Bourassa, *The aesthetics of landscape*, London and New York: Belhaven Press, 1991; P. Bourdieu, *Distinction: a social critique of the judgement of taste*, London: Routledge & Kegan Paul, 1984; T. Eagleton, *The ideology of the aesthetic*, Oxford and Cambridge, MA: Blackwell, 1990; R. Lamb, 'Advancing arguments for the conservation of valued landscapes', Barton, ACT: Australian Heritage Commission, 1994; R. Burton Litton, Jr, 'Visual assessment of natural landscapes', in B. Sadler & A. Carlson (eds) *Environmental aesthetics: essays in interpretation*, Victoria, BC: University of Victoria, 1982; R.B. Riley, 'The visible, the visual, and the vicarious: questions about vision, landscape and experience', in P. Groth & T.W. Bressi (eds) *Understanding ordinary landscapes*, New Haven and London: Yale University Press, 1997; J.D. Porteous, *Environmental aesthetics: ideas, politics and planning*, New York: Routledge, 1996.

3. Grace, op. cit.
4. Environment Australia, 'Great Barrier Reef World Heritage values', available from http://www.environment.gov.au/heritage/places/world/great-barrier-reef/values.html, accessed 25 April 2001.
5. P.H.C. Lucas, T. Webb, P.S. Valentine & H. Marsh, *The outstanding universal value of the Great Barrier Reef World Heritage Area*, Townsville: Great Barrier Reef Marine Park Authority, 1997.
6. UNESCO, 'Convention Concerning the Protection of the World Cultural and Natural Heritage', available from http://whc.unesco.org/en/conventiontext, accessed 25 April 2001.
7. UNESCO, 'Operational Guidelines for the Implementation of the World Heritage Convention', available from http://whc.unesco.org/en/guidelines, accessed 25 April 2001.
8. H. Cleere, 'The World Heritage Convention in the Third World', in McManamon & Hatton, op. cit.
9. Lucas et al., op. cit., pp. 52–53.
10. D. Lowenthal, 'Environment as heritage', in K. Flint & H. Morphy (eds) *Culture, landscape and the environment; the Linacre lectures 1997*, Oxford: Oxford University Press, 2000.
11. Lucas et al., op. cit., p. 39.
12. I. Hunter, 'Aesthetics and the arts of life', in Grace op. cit. (note 2); Bourdieu, op. cit.; Eagleton, op. cit.; W.D. Lipe, 'Value and meaning in cultural resources', in Cleere, 1984, op. cit.; J.F. Weiner et al., '1993 debate: aesthetics is a cross-cultural category', in T. Ingold (ed.) *Key debates in anthropology*, New York: Routledge, 1996; J. Coote & A. Shelton, *Anthropology, art, and aesthetics*, Oxford: Clarendon Press, 1992.
13. Australian Heritage Commission, 'Glossary of heritage terms', available from http://www.environment.gov.au/soe/2001/publications/theme-reports/heritage/glossary.html, accessed 25 April 2001.
14. Australian Heritage Commission, 'Register of the National Estate', available from http://www.environment.gov.au/heritage/places/rne/index.html, accessed 21 January 2002.
15. See, for example, L. Taylor, *The aesthetics of a Kunwinjku site*, Barton, ACT: Australian Heritage Commission, 1994; H. Morphy, 'From dull to brilliant: the aesthetics of spiritual power among the Yolngu', in Coote & Shelton, op. cit. (note 12).
16. D. Byrne, H. Brayshaw & T. Ireland, *Social significance: a discussion paper*, Sydney: Research Unit, Cultural Heritage Division, NSW National Parks and Wildlife Service, 2001.
17. Bourassa, op. cit. (note 2).
18. Byrne, Brayshaw & Ireland, op. cit. (note 16); Cleere, 'Introduction: the rationale of archaeological heritage management'; Lipe, op. cit.
19. Berleant, 1985, op. cit. (note 1); M. Taussig, *Mimesis and alterity: a particular history of the senses*, New York and London: Routledge, 1993.
20. Eagleton, op. cit., p. 3.
21. See, for example, J. Carles, F. Bernáldez & J. de Lucio, 'Audio-visual interactions and soundscape preferences', *Landscape Research*, Vol. 17, No. 2, 1992; S. Feld, 'Waterfalls of song: an acoustemology of place resounding in Bosavi, Papua New Guinea', in S. Feld & K.H. Basso (eds) *Senses of place*, Santa Fe: School of American Research Press, 1996.

22. Australia ICOMOS, 'Burra Charter', available from http://australia.icomos.org, accessed 1 May 2001.

23. R. Love, *Reefscape: reflections on the Great Barrier Reef*, St Leonards: Allen & Unwin, 2000.

24. Ibid., p. 20.

25. E. Banfield, *The confessions of a beachcomber*, Sydney: Angus & Robertson, 1908, p. 14.

26. P. Harvey & G. Borschmann, 'Interview with Perry Harvey, Great Barrier Reef tourist operator', Canberra: National Library of Australia, 1994.

27. T. Barr, *No swank here? The development of the Whitsundays as a tourist destination to the early 1970s*, Department of History and Politics in conjunction with Department of Tourism (ed.) Studies in North Queensland History, Townsville: James Cook University, 1990.

28. C. Melbourne (Mel) Ward, 'Papers of Mel (Charles Melbourne) Ward Lindeman Island', Australian Museum AMS 358 Box 4, Item 60, Sydney: n.d.

29. H.V. Marks, *A Christmas holiday on the Great Barrier Reef, 1932–1933*, Sydney: Harris & Sons, 1933, p. 14.

30. Prime Minister's Department, 'Expo 67 – Great Barrier Reef Exhibit', National Archives of Australia (National Office): A463/50; 1965/4559, Canberra: 1965–1966.

31. C. Pocock, 'Australian landscape to tropical fantasy: Great Barrier Reef' (in preparation).

32. Banfield, op. cit. (note 25), p. 9.

33. Charles Melbourne (Mel) Ward, op. cit., Box 3, Notebook 31, Sydney: 1939.

34. Mel Ward, 'The grinding trees', *The Sunday Sun and Guardian*, 10 February 1935.

35. Ward, op. cit.

36. Pocock, op. cit.

37. G.T. McLean, *Captain Tom*, Mackay: Boolarong Publications, 1986, p. 2.

38. Personal communication with staff at the Great Barrier Reef Marine Park Authority, Townsville.

39. Carles, Bernáldez & de Lucio, op. cit. (note 21); Feld, op. cit. (note 21).

40. Pocock, op. cit.

41. D.R. Wachenfeld, J.K. Oliver & J.I. Morrissey, *State of the Great Barrier Reef World Heritage Area 1998*, Townsville: Great Barrier Reef Marine Park Authority, 1998, p. 29.

42. J. Urry, *The tourist gaze: leisure and travel in contemporary societies*, London: Sage, 1990.

43. S. Sontag, *On photography*, New York: Farrar, Straus and Giroux, 1973, p. 162.

44. Ibid.

45. Ibid., pp. 155–156.

46. Cleere, op. cit. (note 1), p. 126; Lipe, op. cit., p. 10.

47. B. Cunliffe, 'Landscapes with people', in K. Flint & H. Morphy (eds) *Culture, landscape and the environment; the Linacre lectures 1997*, Oxford: Oxford University Press, 2000.

48. H. Cleere, 'Cultural landscapes as world heritage', *Conservation and Management of Archaeological Sites*, Vol. 1, No. 1, 1995; Cleere, 'The World Heritage Convention in the Third World'; Lipe, op. cit.

49. Many heritage practitioners have disciplinary backgrounds in archaeology, which similarly uses aesthetics without theoretical context. See C. Gosden, 'Making sense: archaeology and aesthetics', *World Archaeology*, Vol. 33, No. 2, 2001.

Chapter 24

Observed decay
Telling stories with mutable things

Caitlin DeSilvey

> If you are squeamish
> do not poke among the beach rubble
>
> Sappho (Barnard, 1958)

Introduction

The ideas in this article germinated at a derelict homestead in Montana where I spent several years poking about in a scrambled deposit of domestic and agricultural rubble. My excavations performed an ad hoc archaeology of the recent past in a place not yet old enough to be interesting to (most) archaeologists (though see Buchli and Lucas, 2001) and too marginal and dilapidated to be interesting to historic preservationists. The farm, settled with a homestead claim in 1889, lay a few miles north of the city of Missoula, tucked into a swale in the bare foothills of the Rocky Mountains. For most of the 20th century, the Randolph family ran a market garden and subsistence operation on the site, but by the 1990s these days of productivity were long past. The youngest son in the family died in 1995, leaving behind a complex of ramshackle sheds and dwellings crammed with the debris of decades (Figure 24.1). I came along in 1997 and began to work with the site's residual material culture, first as a volunteer curator and later as a research student working towards a doctoral degree in cultural geography.

As I worked in the homestead's derelict structures, I often came upon deposits of ambiguous matter – aptly described by Georges Bataille as the 'unstable, fetid and lukewarm substances where life ferments ignobly' (1993: 81). Maggots seethed in tin washtubs full of papery corn-husks. Nests of bald baby mice writhed in bushel baskets. Technicolor moulds consumed magazines and documents. Repulsive odours escaped miscellaneous matter. Against the shed's back wall, under a long bench behind a heap of baling twine and feed sacks, sat a dingy wooden box, roughly two feet wide by four feet long. I pulled off a covering piece of corrugated tin to disclose a greyish mass of fibre, bits of woody material, seeds and plum pits filling the chest up to the rim. But then I noticed a leather book cover, and another. A stack of battered volumes nestled in among the litter. Leaning closer, I saw that scraps of torn paper made up part of the box's grey matter. I picked out a few legible pieces: 'shadowed', 'show', 'here', 'start', 'Christ'. The words mingled with mouse droppings, cottony fluff, and leaf spines (and the odd mouse skeleton). Tiny gnaw marks showed along the spines of the books, half-moons of stolen print. I opened one mottled text, *Bulwer's Work*, to a chapter on 'The Last Days of Pompeii' and read a purple passage about the inhabitants of that ill-fated town.

An *Encyclopaedia of Practical Information* occupied pride of place in the top centre of the box. The chunky reference text (copyright 1888) seemed to be intact, save for a small borehole in the upper right corner of the first page I turned to. I carefully lifted the brittle sheets to page 209, and a table on the 'Speed of Railroad Locomotion'. Page 308 detailed cures for foot rot in sheep; page 427 offered a legal template for a 'deed with warranty'; and page 608 informed me that 'Ecuador lies on the equator in South America, and is a republic'. The borehole tracked my progress through the inches of brittle paper. At page 791, a table recording the population of world cities (Osaka, Japan, 530,885, Ooroomtsee, Turkestan, 150,000) I had to stop, lest I crack the book's stiff spine. Below, the pages disappeared into the litter of seeds and scraps, the single hole still tunnelling down into the unknown.

Faced with a decision about what to do with this curious mess, I baulked. The curator in me said I should just pull the remaining books out of the box, brush off the worst of the offending matter, and display them to the public as a damaged but interesting record of obsolete knowledge. Another instinct told me to leave the mice to their own devices and write off the contents of the box as lost to rodent infestation. I could understand the mess as the residue of a system of human memory storage, or I could see an impressive display of animal adaptation to available resources. It was difficult to hold both of these interpretations in my head at once, though. I had stumbled on a rearrangement of matter that mixed up the categories I used to understand the world. It presented itself as a problem to be solved with action – putting things in their place. But what I found myself wanting to do most, after I recovered from my initial surprise, was to take what was there and think about how it got there. I wanted to follow the invisible bookworm into the encyclopaedia.

Object as process

In the box-nest, I had come up against a moment of ambiguous perception in which my interest was torn between two apparently contradictory interpretive options. To borrow a turn of phrase from environmental archaeology, I found myself with a decision to make about whether I was looking at an *artefact* – a relic of human manipulation of the material world – or an *ecofact* – a relic of other-than-human engagements with matter, climate, weather, and biology (Jones, 2005: 85). Cultural matter had taken on an explicitly ecological function. To see what was happening required a kind of double vision, attuned to uncertain resonances and ambivalent taxonomies. 'Thinking about natural history and human history is like looking at one of those trick drawings', writes Rebecca Solnit, 'a wineglass that becomes a pair of kissing profiles. It's hard to see them both at the same time' (Solnit, 1999: 91).

If you're only attuned to see the wineglass – the evidence of explicitly human activity – then the onset of decay and entropic intervention may look only like destruction, an erasure of memory and history. Paying attention to one aspect of the object's existence deflects attention from another. But I want to argue in this article that if we can hold the wineglass and the kiss in mind concurrently, decay reveals itself not (only) as erasure but as a process that can be generative of a different kind of knowledge. The book-box-nest required an interpretive frame that would let its contents maintain simultaneous identities as books *and* as stores of raw material for rodent homemaking. Michael Taussig touches on a similar theme in an essay on the peculiar character of bogs and swamps. He muses on the ways boggy, rotting places expose 'the suspension between life and death', flitting 'between a miraculous preservation and an always there of immanent decay' (Taussig, 2003: 15–16). Taussig acknowledges how difficult it can be to encounter amalgamated deposits of cultural and biological memory in these places: 'What you have to do is hold contrary states in mind and allow the miasma to exude', he writes (2003: 16).

Taussig's advice seems promising, but how exactly do we go about letting the miasma exude? This is not a particularly easy thing to do, especially when curatorial work assumes a certain responsibility for stabilizing things in frames of reference that make them accessible to those who come along afterwards. I soon came to realize, however, that the drive towards stabilizing the thing was part of the problem.

In the past few decades, theoretical approaches that stabilize the identity of a thing in its fixed form have given way to more complex notions of identity as a mutable and living process (Appadurai, 1986; Buchli, 2002; Thomas, 1991). As Rudi Colloredo-Mansfeld recently observed in a special issue of this journal [see original reading], however, there remains in museum and material culture studies a pervasive identification between the social significance of an artefact and its physical permanence (2004: 246). Colloredo-Mansfeld and other authors show how routines of daily life depend, often, on the material transformation of physical objects: people use things up, expose them to the elements, consume and combine (2004: 250). Objects generate social effects not just in their preservation and persistence, but in their destruction and disposal (Hansen, 2003; Hetherington, 2004; Lucas, 2002; Van der Hoorn, 2003). These processes facilitate the circulation of material and the maintenance of social codes; the death of the object allows for the continued animation of other processes.

This is also true of objects transformed or disfigured by ecological processes of disintegration and regeneration. These things have social lives, but they have biological and chemical lives as well, which may only become perceptible when the things begin to drop out of social circulation (Edensor, 2005a: 100). The disarticulation of the object may lead to the articulation of other histories, and other geographies. An approach that understands the artefact as a process, rather than a stable entity with a durable physical form, is perhaps able to address some of the more ambiguous aspects of material presence (and disappearance). The book-box-nest is neither *artefact* nor *ecofact*, but both – a dynamic entity that is entangled in both cultural and natural processes, part of an 'admixture of waste and life, of decadence and vitality' (Neville and Villeneuve, 2002: 2). Of course, in order to think this way it's necessary to defer the urge to 'save' the artefact. Interpretation requires letting the process run, and watching what happens in the going. Though this might seem wilfully destructive to those who locate the memorial potency of the object in its unchanging physical form, I want to suggest that a different kind of remembrance becomes possible in this kind of work.

In a broader sense, I want to engage with the question: 'What are the consequences of seeing certain orderings and not others?' (Harrison et al., 2004: 16). What difference does it make to refuse to discard objects that are mired in advanced states of decay? What kinds of alternative orderings become accessible when interpretation tries to scrutinize things on their way to becoming something else? Others have drawn political, economic, and aesthetic insights from engagements with degraded and fragmented things (Benjamin, 1999; Edensor, 2005a; Hawkins and Muecke, 2003). Although these themes weave through the fringes of the analysis I put forth here, the article is not directly concerned with this body of work. I turn, instead, to a discussion of how the homestead's mutable artefacts inhabit the 'blurred terrain where nature and culture are not so easily (as if they ever were) distinguished and dichotomised' (Harrison et al., 2004: 9). It is here, where what we call 'human' unravels into what we call 'other', that the ambiguous perceptions seem to lie most thickly, and promise most fully.

Matrix of memory

Edward Casey has written, 'everything belongs to some matrix of memory, even if it is a matrix which is remote from human concerns and interests' (2000: 311). In my dictionary, the ninth (and final) definition for the word 'memory' reads, 'the ability of a material to return to a former state after a constraint has been removed' (*Collins English Dictionary*, 1991 edition). The matter that makes up the homestead's structures and features exhibits just this kind of tracking backward, as well as a dynamic evolution into other states. Human labour introduced temporary arrangements – clear window glass, milled lumber, tempered fence wire. But these arrangements are unstable. Century-old glass develops cloudy irregularities in its gradual recrystallization. Faded scraps of newspaper mingle with the husks of fallen leaves. Lichen grows on a standing building, a symbiotic association of fungus and algae breaking down milled clapboards to make them available for recycling into new saplings. A lump of soft coal, pulled from the nearby mine 70 years ago, recalls the organic matter of a 25 million year-old forest. The homestead, like the abandoned Welsh farms described by Michael Shanks and Mike Pearson, is a place where 'the very processes of the archaeological are apparent: mouldering, rotting, disintegrating, decomposing, putrefying, falling to pieces' (Pearson and Shanks, 2001: 158). The formation processes that mould the archaeological record are here just getting under way.

It is exactly these processes of mouldering and disintegration that most conservation practices work to forestall. In conventional terms, in order for the object to function as a bearer of cultural memory it must be held in perpetuity in a state of protected stasis. Acts of counting, sorting, stacking, storing and inventory convert things from the category of 'stuff' to the status of museum object, and, as a curator at one Montana heritage site commented to me, 'if it's museum property it needs to be taken care of and preserved forever – that's kind of the responsibility of it being in that category'. Conservation technologies slow or halt physical decay, while interpretive strategies present the objects as elements of a static, unchanging past. Ephemeral things, decontextualized and catalogued, acquire a 'socially produced durability' in carefully monitored environments (Buchli, 2002: 15). Objects are kept in climate-controlled, rodent-proofed storage areas. Special paint protects artefacts from damaging ultraviolet rays; chest freezers decontaminate cushions and clothing of any lingering moulds and microbes. 'Arrested decay' – the maintenance policy applied to buildings to uphold their structural integrity yet preserve their ruined appearance – also works at the scale of individual objects. Most places designed to preserve 'the past' take great pains to ensure that the physical and biological processes that underlie that past have been neutralized (DeLyser, 1999). The memory encapsulated in these buildings and cushions is a resolutely human history, and any loss of physical integrity is seen as a loss of memorial efficacy – an incremental forgetting. But the state of affairs is, of course, more complicated than it appears to be. Strategies to arrest decay always destroy some cultural traces, even as they preserve others. And decay itself may clear a path for certain kinds of remembrance despite its (because of its?) destructive energies.

A thicket of box elder trees crowds the fenceline at the bottom of the homestead's decadent orchard. Given their girth and height, the trees appear to have seeded within the last half-century. Long before then, the area along the fence accumulated an assortment of farm implements and stockpiled materials: a spike-toothed harrow, a stack of boxcar siding, a grain binder. Unneeded objects came to rest in the widening shade of the weedy trees, and no one paid them much attention. Eventually, the trees began to draw the snarl of iron and steel into their generous vegetal embrace. The edge of a studded wheel fused into grey bark; a branch thickened and lifted over the binder's mass, carrying with it, and gradually consuming, a loose length of chain; roots twined around steel tines. The binder – designed to cut, gather, and fasten sheaves of grain – became bound in place. Pale lichens encrusted the driving chains that wound round the body of the machine. One of the binder's moulded iron handles now protrudes from a slim trunk as if to invite an adjustment of the systems of multiplying cell and running sap. The hybrid tree-machine works away at a perennial chore, binding iron and cellulose, mineral and vegetable. The binder is too broken down and biodegraded for recuperation in a conventional heritage strategy. If you start to think about the decay of the binder in another way, however, it is possible to see the ongoing intervention of the trees and the soil as productive of other resources for recalling the past in this place. An example from far afield might help explain what I mean by this.

Susanne Küchler's work in Papua New Guinea has documented the construction of *malanggan*, monuments to the dead. Mourners construct these assemblages of wood or woven vines and decorate the surface with carvings of animals, birds, shells, and human figures. The perishable monument is placed over a human grave as a marker. After a certain amount of time has passed (when the human soul is understood to have escaped the body), the *malanggan* are taken from the graves and set in a location (often near the sea) where they are left to rot. Once the *malanggan* have decomposed, the remains are gathered to fertilize gardens. Küchler describes how this vital memorial tradition turns 'the finality of death to a process of eternal return' (Küchler, 1999: 57). The mode of remembrance practised in the *malanggan* ritual, Küchler argues, does not require a physical object for its operation, but draws instead on the absence of this physical presence, the 'mental resource created from the object's disappearance' (Küchler, 1999: 62).

In her work, Küchler emphasizes the 'anti-materialism' of this memorial practice. What strikes me, however, is not the rejection of materiality *per se*, but the embrace of the mutable character of material presence, the transformative powers of decay and revitalization. Küchler (drawing on Walter Benjamin) asserts that 'ephemeral commemorative artefacts' might 'instigate a process of remembering directed not to any particular vision of past or future, but which repeats itself many times over in point-like, momentary . . . awakening of the past in the present' (Küchler, 1999: 63). Cultural remembering proceeds not through reflection on a static memorial remnant, but on the process that slowly pulls the remnant into other ecologies and expressions of value – accommodating simultaneous resonances of death and rebirth, loss and renewal.

I wonder if it is possible to approach the grain binder as a *malanggan* of the American West, which, too, releases its meaning in decay. An artefact of technological innovation sinks into the dark loam under the box elder trees and recalls its origins in veins of ore under the dark earth. The ruined machine sparks reflections on once robust economies, the changing markets and agricultural consolidations that precipitated the transformation of the western landscape (and the gradual obsolescence of diversified farms like the homestead). Raw material returns to the earth or is seized into the lignin and cellulose of a tree – the tree itself an import from another part of the continent, brought to the West to domesticate unfamiliar places. Now, the weedy trees signal the inexorable 'rewilding' of places that are left to their own ecological devices (Cronon, 2003; Feldman, 2004). These suggestive interpretive resources would not be available if the binder were sawed from the tree, repaired and polished, and set alongside other mechanical agricultural dinosaurs (such an action is probably impossible, at any rate, and would lead to the destruction of both the tree and the implement). The binder suggests a mode of remembrance that is erratic and ephemeral – twined around the past and reaching imperceptibly into what has yet to come. In a sense, the trees participate in the production of cultural memory as 'an activity occurring in the present, in which the past is continually modified and redescribed even as it continues to shape the future' (Bal et al., 1999: vii). Memory, in this sense, is based on chance and imagination as much as evidence and explanation; the forgetting brought on by decay allows for a different form of recollection. Such recollection fosters an acknowledgement of agencies usually excluded from the work of interpretation.

Other editing

The farm's root cellar – a cavernous space with crumbling earth walls and a pervasive scent of sour rot – contained several maps in its dim corners and crates, each one spectacularly degraded in its own way. One excavation turned up a US Forest Service map of the Beaverhead and Deer Lodge forest management districts, just west of Missoula. When I unrolled it, I discovered an ornate fringe along the bottom edge where an insect had consumed the map's gridded territory (Figure 24.2). The insects had intervened to assert the materiality of the map, and in doing so they offered their own oblique commentary on human intervention in regional ecologies. The forests in the physical territory depicted by the disfigured paper map suffered from decades of poor management and fire suppression, which made them vulnerable to the depredations of other organisms. Over the last few decades, an infestation of destructive bark beetles has killed many of the trees represented by the map's green patches. The destruction on the root cellar's map can be read as a metonym for the destruction of the surrounding forest. The *dis*articulation of a cultural artefact leads to the articulation of other histories about invertebrate biographies and appetites. In this speculative allegorical example, 'objects have to fall into desuetude at one level in order to come more fully into their own at another' (Gross, 2002: 36).

Other documents showed equally impressive evidence of insect and rodent editing. In their degraded condition, these documents carried an unusual charge. I came up against an absence in the record, but an absence that seemed to carve out a window in the wall that usually keeps cultural analysis separate from the investigation of ecological processes. It required some imagination to work past the initial awareness of missing information, but once this had been overcome I could see the emerging shape of an engagement with the past that draws part of its force from absence and incompletion (Küchler, 1999: 59). Christopher Woodward (2002), in his observation

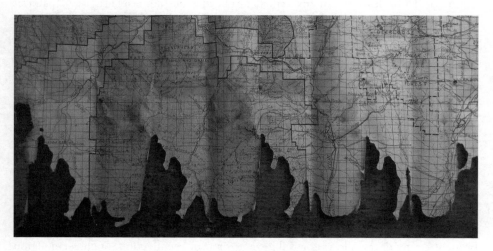

Fig. 24.2 The forest map with insect-eaten fringe. Photograph by Caitlin DeSilvey.

of the creative resources that people generate when confronted with ruins and remnants, identifies a sympathetic association between structural incompletion and imaginative invention. Degraded artefacts can contribute to alternative interpretive possibilities even as they remain caught up in dynamic processes of decay and disarticulation. The autonomous exercise of human intention gives way to a more dispersed sharing of the practices of material editing and curation.

Miles Ogborn, in a recent essay on the ecology of archives, comments on how archives and their contents, which arise out of a patently cultural desire to preserve the human past, are also amalgams of animal skin and wood pulp, chemical compounds and organic substances (2004). The elements that make up the archive are open to breaches and interventions – from heat, light, moisture, mould, insects, rodents. Ogborn writes, 'The storehouses of memory, the central cortices of social formations of print and the written world, are ecologies where the materials of remembrance are living, dying, and being devoured' (Ogborn, 2004: 240). The 'nature of cultural memory' becomes apparent in the gradual consumption of evidence and images.

I found one of my favourite examples of these cultural ecologies at work in a battered copy of *National Geographic* magazine, which had been stored with others of its kind in a set of cranberry crate shelves in the farmhouse kitchen. In the 40-year interval between human habitation of the dwelling and my intervention hungry moulds and rodents consumed the glossy pages. This particular copy peeled apart reluctantly, to reveal a patchy scene brushed with delicate pink. The mould had eaten away an image of a mountain town to expose a few bars of music, an area of green, shards of unintelligible text. There was a curious loveliness to the transformed scene – mountains and music and mould in a montage of indeterminate effect. The cultural spore of mass printed matter was caught up in the fungal ecologies of decay, its authority an impartial documentation of a world 'out there' undermined by the microscopic imperatives of a world 'in here'. These were the kinds of knowledges produced as other-than-human influences peeled back layers of natural and social history sedimented in the homestead's fragmentary materials.

Co-habitation

There was another register in which the homestead's entangled artefacts worked to remember the past in place in unfamiliar ways. The shacks and sheds at the site were full of collections of miscellaneous material: sacks stuffed with feathers and leaves, bushel baskets of wool and fibre, neat stacks of twigs, jars of seed and sand. It was not always clear to me how these gatherings of materials were assembled. The tidy collections troubled the distinction I tried to draw between animal and human labour. The homestead's tack shed contained a few tin cans packed with fruit stones – rough pits from the wild plums that grow in the gully and the hard seeds of the orchard pie cherries. Each of the stones was neatly scraped down to the woody centre, and marked with a tidy chewed hole through which an animal had extracted the edible core. In the farmhouse pantry, I found dozens of jars of saved garden seeds that were linked into a similar collecting impulse. The root cellar's dusty shelves held cloudy jars of cherries, rhubarb, and tomatoes. In a crate below the shelves I found a 1937 postmarked envelope full of flower seeds, and a twist of catalogue paper around a handful of white snail shells. Nearby a pillowcase hung from a nail, the bottom eaten through to let out a slow leak of feathers.

An odd affinity seemed to hang over these animal accumulations; intertwined memories of seasonal harvest and hoarding seeped out of the jars and tins and bins. As I worked along these lines, the human activity that went into constructing the homestead began to look like just another layer of habitation. I developed an appreciation for how other organisms draw in the raw material of their world and animate it through their modifications – and an altered perspective on the material practices of human dwelling (Hinchliffe, 2003; Ingold, 2000; Lorimer, in press). If the boundary of the organism is 'a process that continually redefines what is considered living and non-living' (Harrison et al., 2004: 34), this place presented a curious record of several different species of extended organisms. The memory in these accretions of matter spoke to decades of co-habitation, of entangled lives and habits. People inhabit places with books and tools and clothes; mice inhabit places with pits and leaves and bones, and the matter people leave behind.

The finest grain of the (elusive) boundary between animal and human habitation lay in the dust. As one of my first curatorial acts at the homestead, I sorted the contents of the long-abandoned kitchen junk drawers. After I had pulled out the household objects and set them aside, a layer of minuscule detritus lay on the wooden bottom slats. I identified bits of mouse droppings, rubber shreds, wood splinters, paper, lint, wire, insect wings, plant stems, seeds, human hairs. An even finer grain of residue underlay these legible fragments, a slightly greasy amalgam of human skin, tiny fibres, crumbled deposits of mineral and animal origin. I remember feeling dizzy while I examined these leavings, sharply aware that I had reached the base level of materiality, the place where human artefacts blended imperceptibly into mass of worldly matter (Edensor, 2005a: 122). As Phil Dunham points out, encounters with dust raise questions about 'what (if anything) is consistent or whole about our bodies, and where (and indeed whether) a line can meaningfully be drawn between the human and nonhuman worlds' (Dunham, 2004: 100). These encounters, though disagreeable, also served as a powerful reminder of my own entangling with these borderline materials and their active ecologies.

My early decision to let the dust and the detritus into my interpretive frame was not without its risks. As I began to allow myself to yield to these messy remains (McAllister, 2001), I realized that in order to meet them (so to speak) on their own terms, I had to accept that the outcome of the situations I found myself in was not entirely in my hands. '[E]xpelling and discarding is more than biological necessity – it is fundamental to the ordering of the self', comment Gay Hawkins and Stephen Muecke (2003: xii). In choosing not to discard materials that would, in other circumstances, have been quickly consigned to the rubbish bin, I also opened myself up to influences that unsettled my sense of curatorial authority and allowed the material to 'act back' on me in unexpected ways (Buchli and Lucas, 2001: 5). With the dissolution of standards of value and significance, the sheer excess of eligible material mocked my attempts at recovery and rationalization. Sometimes I found myself pushing back against the chaos to assert some kind of (usually ineffectual) order. But I also experimented a bit with strategies that took the forces of decay on as allies, rather than adversaries.

Collaboration: synchronic handiwork

One day I came across an over-stuffed bushel basket in the homestead's harness shed. I pulled out the top layer of stained clothes to disclose a stew of paper, fabric, and animal leavings. I tipped the whole thing on the grass, where I could see scraps of printed matter mixed in with a mass of pits and seeds, woolly fibre and feathers, long johns and holey socks, a 1928 licence plate and a few delicate mouse spines. I had come across similarly scrambled deposits countless times in my excavations, and I usually gave in to the impulse to discard or burn all but the most discrete items (only the licence plate, in this case). This time, however, something about the mess drew me in, and I began to pick out the shards of text from the other litter.

Later, I took some liberties and drafted a poem from the fragments:

the camera	cardboard box
may	on the wall
record	behind a picture
odd	parts will
invented	have a
museums	numerous
placed at	synchronic
glare horizon	handiwork
your service	that of
makes	invention in
value	minimum
almost anywhere	delight

I like to think that the mice and I share authorship for this work – with some credit due as well to the authors of the articles in the shredded magazines (which I have tentatively identified as an amalgam of *Popular Mechanics* and Seventh Day Adventist religious tracts). I suppose I should also mention Tristan Tzara, whose dadaist poem instructions run like so: Take a newspaper / Take some scissors / Choose from this paper an article of the length you want to make your poem / Cut out the article / Next carefully cut out each of the words that makes up this article and put them all in a bag / Shake gently / Next take out each cutting one after the other / Copy conscientiously in the order in which they left the bag / The poem will resemble you (Tzara, 1992: 39). The poem, perhaps, says more about my intervention in the homestead's sedimented histories than it does about the content of those histories. But I include it here to suggest the terrain that might be explored by an interpretive practice willing to engage in serious play with artefacts that might otherwise be overlooked entirely.

This experimental engagement with some of Douglas's dangerous things allows other 'sensible forms' to work alongside the curator in the generation of research materials (Whatmore, 2003). In this instance, an act of 'synchronic handiwork' takes up the raw material of the past and works it into a missive that speaks both to that past and to the lived present. The method celebrates the artefact's status as 'a temporary arrangement of matter, always on its way to being something else. At Hyde Park Barracks, near Sydney, Australia, rats collected the ephemera of daily life in their nests between the floorboards. When restorationists and curators discovered these hoards they decided to create a display to celebrate the findings. 'Rats are honoured at this site as the minions of history,' writes Barbara Kirshenblatt-Gimblett (1998: 168). I occasionally attempted a similar strategy at the homestead, opening up my curatorial activities to the intervention of other organisms. Such strategies may generate 'interpretive ambiguities' (Cronon, 2003: 42), but they also open up different ways of ordering the world, working past an entirely negative reading of material dislocation and dissociation.

In conclusion

The interpretive approaches I sketch out in this article – observed decay, ephemeral commemoration, collaborative curation – are presented in a speculative spirit. I am more interested to spark reflection than I am to propose new orthodoxies. I recognize that the kind of material dissolution and disappearance I advocate here would be difficult to implement in most recognized historic sites. If the homestead were to perform as a truly ephemeral monument, for example, the processes I have been describing would be allowed to consume it altogether. This kind of interpretive work is more likely to occur with materials that lie at the fringes of conservation practice, or with things held in a state of limbo before more formal arrangements around preservation and public access take hold. It is possible, however, to imagine how established museums and heritage sites might begin to introduce a focus on material process (and a whiff of miasma) into a mode of interpretation that tends to come down heavily on the side of stasis and preservation. The potential for 'entropic heritage' practice remains, for the most part, untapped (DeSilvey, 2005a).

Even a subtle shift in interpretive focus would require some attempt to hold those contrary states in mind – to accept that the artefact is not a discrete entity but a material form bound into continual cycles of articulation and disarticulation. When I was able to pull it off, this kind of approach allowed me to see things that otherwise would have been invisible to me simply because I lacked discursive frames to fit them in. Interpretation, in this sense, constituted otherwise unconstituted matter (Buchli and Lucas, 2001). I was able to read the messages on a wall of tattered newspaper scattered with box-elder seed, the occluded histories in a rodent nest. Such work stakes out an expanded field for the telling of local histories, allowing for the inclusion of inhabitants usually entered in the margins, or consigned to their own separate texts. Instead of asking the artefact to speak to a singular (human) past, such a method works with an ecology of memory – things decay and disappear, reform and regenerate, shift back and forth between different states, and always teeter on the edge of intelligibility. Remembrance comes into its own as a balancing act, an 'art of transience' (Hawkins, 2001) which salvages meaning from waste things and reveals the complexity of our entangled material memories.

Note

1. The state university's lead archivist took one look at the clutter and reached for a black plastic sack. The curator from the local historical museum refused to even

touch the homestead's documents and artefacts for fear of spreading their moulds to her collection. The degraded condition of the materials mediated against their inclusion in public collections and archives – my decision to carry on the work of excavation and curation despite this official rejection is part of a story I do not have room to tell here (DeSilvey, 2005b).

References

Appadurai, Arjun, ed. (1986) *The Social Life of Things: Commodities in Cultural Perspective.* Cambridge: Cambridge University Press.

Bal, Mieke, Crewe, Jonathan and Spitzer, Leo, eds (1999) *Acts of Memory: Cultural Recall in the Present.* Hanover, NH: University Press of New England.

Barnard, Mary (1958) *Sappho: A New Translation.* Berkeley: University of California Press.

Bataille, George (1993) 'Volume II: The History of Eroticism', in *The Accursed Share: An Essay on General Economy*, pp. 21–191. New York: Zone Books.

Benjamin, Walter (1999) *The Arcades Project* (trans. H. Eiland and K. McLaughlin). Cambridge, MA and London: Belknap Press.

Buchli, Victor, ed. (2002) *The Material Culture Reader.* Oxford: Berg.

Buchli, Victor and Lucas, Gavin (2001) *Archaeologies of the Contemporary Past.* London: Routledge.

Casey, Edward S. (2000) *Remembering: A Phenomenological Study.* Bloomington: Indiana University Press.

Colloredo-Mansfeld, Rudi (2004) 'Matter Unbound', *Journal of Material Culture* 8(3): 245–54.

Cronon, William (2003) 'The Riddle of the Apostle Islands', *Orion*, May/June: 36–42.

DeLyser, Dydia (1999) 'Authenticity on the Ground: Engaging the Past in a California Ghost Town', *Annals of the Association of American Geographers* 89: 602–32.

DeSilvey, Caitlin (2005a) 'Rot in Peace', *Slate Magazine* 5 December. URL (accessed July 2006): http://www.slate.com/id/2129660/

DeSilvey, Caitlin (2005b) 'Salvage Rites: Making Memory on a Montana Homestead', unpublished PhD thesis, Open University.

Douglas, Mary (1966) *Purity and Danger.* London: Routledge.

Dunham, Phil (2004) 'Dust', in Stephan Harrison, Steve Pile and Nigel Thrift (eds) *Patterned Ground: Entanglements of Nature and Culture*, pp. 98–100. London: Reaktion.

Edensor, Tim (2005a) *Industrial Ruins: Aesthetics, Materiality, and Memory.* Oxford: Berg.

Edensor, Tim (2005b) 'Waste Matter: The Debris of Industrial Ruins and the Disordering of the Material World', *Journal of Material Culture* 10(3): 311–32.

Feldman, James Wyatt (2004) 'Rewilding the Islands: Nature, History and Wilderness at Apostle Islands National Lakeshore', unpublished PhD thesis, University of Wisconsin.

Gross, David (2002) 'Objects from the Past', in Brian Neville and Johanne Villeneuve (eds) *Waste-site Stories: The Recycling of Memory*, pp. 29–37. Albany: State University of New York Press.

Hansen, Karen Tranberg (2003) 'Fashioning Zambian Moments', *Journal of Material Culture* 8(3): 301–9.

Harrison, Stephan, Pile, Steve and Thrift, Nigel (2004) 'The Curious, the Exalted, the Occult, the Passion', in Stephan Harrison, Steve Pile and Nigel Thrift (eds) *Patterned Ground: Entanglements of Nature and Culture*, pp. 15–25. London: Reaktion.

Hawkins, Gay (2001) 'Plastic Bags: Living with Rubbish', *International Journal of Cultural Studies* 4(1): 5–23.

Hawkins, Gay and Muecke, Stephen, eds (2003) *Culture and Waste: The Creation and Destruction of Value*. Lanham, MD: Rowman and Littlefield.

Hetherington, Kevin (2004) 'Secondhandedness: Consumption, Disposal, and Absent Presence', *Society and Space* 22(1): 157–73.

Hinchliffe, Steve (2003) '"Inhabiting" – Landscapes and Natures', in Kay Anderson, Mona Domosh, Steve Pile and Nigel Thrift (eds) *Handbook of Cultural Geography*, pp. 207–25. London: Sage.

Ingold, Tim (2000) *The Perception of the Environment: Essays in Livelihood, Dwelling and Skill*. London: Routledge.

Jones, Martin (2005) 'Environmental Archaeology', in Colin Renfrew and Paul Bahn (eds) *Archaeology: The Key Concepts*, pp. 85–9. London: Routledge.

Kirshenblatt-Gimblett, Barbara (1998) *Destination Culture: Tourism, Museums and Heritage*. Berkeley and Los Angeles: University of California Press.

Küchler, Susanne (1999) 'The Place of Memory', in Adrian Forty and Susanne Küchler (eds) *The Art of Forgetting*, pp. 53–72. Oxford: Berg.

Lorimer, Hayden (in press) 'Herding Memories of Humans and Animals', *Society and Space*.

Lucas, Gavin (2002) 'Disposability and Dispossession in the Twentieth Century', *Journal of Material Culture* 7(1): 5–22.

McAllister, Kirsten Emiko (2001) 'Captivating Debris: Unearthing a World War Two Internment Camp', *Cultural Values* 5(1): 97–114.

Neville, Brian and Villeneuve, Johanne, eds (2002) *Waste-site Stories: The Recycling of Memory*. Albany: State University of New York Press.

Ogborn, Miles (2004) 'Archives', in Stephan Harrison, Steve Pile and Nigel Thrift (eds) *Patterned Ground: Entanglements of Nature and Culture*, pp. 240–2. London: Reaktion.

Pearson, Mike and Shanks, Michael (2001) *Theatre / Archaeology*. London: Routledge.

Sloterdijk, Peter (1987) *Critique of Cynical Reason*. Minneapolis: University of Minnesota Press.

Solnit, Rebecca (1999) *Savage Dreams: A Journey into the Landscape Wars of the American West*. Berkeley: University of California Press.

Taussig, Michael (2003) 'Miasma', in Gay Hawkins and Stephen Muecke (eds) *Culture and Waste: The Creation and Destruction of Value*, pp. 9–23. Lanham, MD: Rowman and Littlefield.

Thomas, Nicholas (1991) *Entangled Objects: Exchange, Material Culture, and Colonialism in the Pacific*. Cambridge, MA: Harvard University Press.

Tzara, Tristan (1992) *Seven Dada Manifestos and Lampisteries*. London, Paris, New York: Calder Publications.

Van der Hoorn, Melanie (2003) 'Exorcizing Remains: Architectural Fragments as Intermediaries between History and Individual Experience', *Journal of Material Culture* 8(2): 189–213.

Whatmore, Sarah (2003) 'Generating Materials', in Michael Pryke, Gillian Rose and Sarah Whatmore (eds) *Using Social Theory*, pp. 89–104. London: Sage.

Woodward, Christopher (2002) *In Ruins*. London: Vintage.

Chapter 25

Handmade textiles
Global markets and authenticity

Victoria L. Rovine

Styles went ethnic everywhere this summer, from Saks Fifth Avenue to the 99-cent store.

N. Bernstein, The New York Times

A recent article in *The New York Times* focusing on a merchant in Astoria, Queens, described the fad for Indian tunic blouses with sequined embroidery. The article offered a vivid illustration of the phenomena that characterize many contemporary fashion markets: (1) the globalization of clothing styles and fashion manufacture; (2) the changing identities associated with garments, textiles, and styles of dress; (3) the revival and re-creation of forms associated with "tradition"; and (4) the adaptation of new production techniques to suit changing markets. This essay focuses on one element that remains constant in the midst of fashion's global markets and shifting terrains: the role of texture, both literal and conceptual, in the production of "authentic" styles of clothing.

The markers of authenticity in dress, the features that signify distinctive cultural characteristics and practices, are often preserved or imitated as garments move between markets. By exploring one of these markers, texture, I seek to elucidate the construction of authenticity in the realm of dress. How does texture communicate authenticity, and what information does it encode? What does this information reveal about the expectations that are attached to garments in various markets, both Western and non-Western? After introducing the issues through the case of Indian blouses sold in the United States, I will turn to African garments, which vividly illustrate the shifting markets and meanings of garments associated with "authentic" cultures. I will also detour into classic Western haute couture, a market in which authenticity has distinct connotations, many of which are also connected to texture. These worlds come together through discussion of contemporary African haute couture design, in which textiles associated with "authentic" cultures are employed, drawing on the histories out of which these associations emerge to create entirely new forms.

This investigation addresses the literal as well as the figurative meanings of texture, both of which are at play in the production of authenticity. The literal meaning of texture in the realm of fabrics and clothing is determined by factors including the type of fibers, the manner in which they are spun or otherwise prepared for the loom, and the nature of the weave. These variables produce a quality that can be perceived through the skin. The figurative texture of a fabric, the *feeling* it evokes, is also closely related to the techniques and circumstances of its manufacture, but it is the stories that reverberate from a textile's manufacture that lend it authenticity in this second sense, as I will describe. In order to address these multiple incarnations of texture, this exploration of the production and the perception of authenticity combines technical analysis with discussions of the emotional impact of clothing and textiles. Understanding texture requires a range of methodologies, from the "hard data" of manufacturing techniques to the ineffable realm of "feelings."

"Authentic" fashions and global markets

The Indian- or Pakistani-style shirts featured in the *New York Times* article are part of an international system whereby a garment's association with local "tradition" propels it onto global markets. The change in markets often relocates the manufacture of garments to completely new contexts where new populations are drawn into the production, in this case, to China and to a small factory in Brooklyn which is "staffed primarily by Latin American immigrants" (Bernstein 2005: 21). The identities that are attached to particular clothing styles, "Indian," "African," or any other cultural or regional designation, may have little to do with their actual provenance, for the idea of "Indian-ness" or "African-ness" is preserved through key features. In this case the fabrics and adornments create their recognizably "Indian" style when reproduced and readjusted, as are the production techniques such as "shortcuts like ready-made rolls of sequins instead of the kind sewn on one-by-one" (ibid.). Yet the value of handmade production is preserved, if only through the efforts made to imitate it: "And though Chinese factories now have the technology to mimic handwork, [one wholesaler] said he sometimes turned back to India for real handwork" (ibid.). The garments may also be produced for several distinct markets, from inexpensive outlets aimed at local South Asian immigrants to $3,000 designer versions sold at Saks.

The meanings of these tunics shift in global markets, their reception among new consumers affects their significance for their original audience. Thus, the South Asian immigrant owner of the boutique in Astoria noted a change in her own attitude: "I felt embarrassed with these clothes . . . Now I feel proud, because everybody's wearing them" (ibid.). Such cycles of authenticity and fashion complicate the classifications of clothing. As Joanne Eicher and Barbara Sumberg noted, ethnic dress can be defined in opposition to fashion: "Often known as traditional, ethnic dress brings to mind images of coiffure, garments, and jewelry that stereotypically never change . . . In other words . . . the terms 'traditional' and 'ethnic' imply non-fashionable dress . . ." (1995:

300–301). Yet, garments shift between categories, sometimes propelled by their aura of authenticity.

Texture, manufacture, and authenticity

Although customarily separated, the realms of high fashion and of non-Western dress often intersect and overlap, as the Indian tunics illustrate. Exploration of the role of texture as a marker of authenticity reveals a striking consistency between the markets for high-fashion and for non-Western attire. In both markets, texture serves as a barometer of the expectations attached to authenticity. In the realm of dress and adornment, our eyes may tell us if something is beautiful, but we rely on our hands to tell us if fabrics are "genuine," if a garment is "authentic." Touch is the sense most deeply used in questions of authenticity.

Texture provides information about production, a key factor in the evaluation of authenticity. Handmade manufacture is key to the creation of authenticity in the worlds of both Western haute couture and "ethnic" attire associated with non-Western cultures, though for very different reasons. Handmade manufacture is, in fact, the key defining feature of haute couture fashion. Official designation by the French fashion syndicate requires that a design house employ at least twenty people, with the presumption that all their work will be by hand. This handwork produces a sense of exclusivity through high price. In a feature on the fashion industry *The Economist* pointed out a designer dress can require "700 hours of painstaking labour" and cost more than $100,000 ("Fashion's Favorite" 2004: 5).

In a discussion of the development of the fashion system in the early decades of the twentieth century, Ellen Leopold notes haute couture long has had a special role as a bastion of handwork, with garments "presented as one-off style 'creations' that enhanced the originality and individuality of the consumer in a world of increasingly mass-produced goods" and further that "the imagery of advertising sought to play down if not conceal entirely the contribution of machinery to the production of clothing" (1992: 109). Handmade manufacture has become an ideal as much as it is an actual method. In the 1950s, Angela Partington observes, Christian Dior "pioneered the system through which manufacturers and retailers could sell an 'Original-Christian-Dior-Copy'" (1992:151). In the high-fashion economy, thus, the hand of the designer has been abstracted, signified by a name on a label that continues to represent their identity. The originality of the handmade is translated into the conceptual realm, a move echoed in African textiles and fashion.

Production by hand has powerful implications in the market for non-Western garments and textiles as well as in high fashion, for it carries associations with authenticity, tradition, and local cultures. In his discussion of the success of Oriental carpets in Western markets, where they are associated with "authenticity," Spooner notes: "[T]he fact of their being hand-made became a significant characteristic, and as the craft was gradually drawn into the world economy the survival of traditional relations of production became an additional factor [in their success on the international art market] – the rug was an exotic product made in its own exotic production process for its own exotic purpose" (1986: 222). Ronald Waterbury describes a similar focus on the handmade as a central element of the globalization of the market for Oaxacan embroidery, noting that for many consumers "a handcrafted object evokes the aura of human tradition, the sweat and skill of its individual maker, and – since craftsmanship avoids the repetitive precision of a stamping machine – uniqueness and originality" (1989: 245).

As these examples demonstrate, the value of handmade manufacture lies in its evocation of lives and stories, offering consumers a means by which to partake physically in those narratives. The power of the handmade to evoke such stories crosses cultural boundaries. Just as the detailed stitches of a high-fashion garment may allude to the so-called "little hands" of the seamstresses in Dior's atelier, so too may carpets call to mind the Central Asian nomads to whom they are often attributed, or as a Mexican blouse evokes Oaxacan villagers.

African textiles/African authenticity

Turning to Africa, a strip-woven, indigo-dyed wrapper embodies the physical presence of weavers and dyers in a Malian village. Adam Levin, a dealer, art promoter, and author of the recent book *The Art of African Shopping*, encapsulates this animation of the handmade: "Like all handmade textiles, this cloth 'lives'" (2005: 98). The cloth in question, an indigo-dyed cotton wrapper, epitomizes the texture, both literal and symbolic, that results from handmade manufacture (Figure 25.1). Levin purchased the cloth quite close to its point of production and he evoked the hands (in this case, the arms) of the maker in his description of the fabric: "I bought my favorite

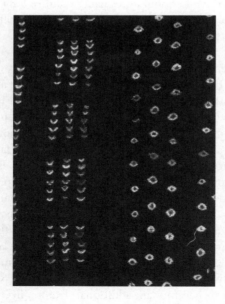

Fig. 25.1 Indigo-dyed cloth, strip-woven cotton, Dogon region, Mali, late twentieth century. Private collection.

piece of cloth on the cliffs of the Dogon in Mali, from a woman whose brown arms gleamed a deep, iridescent blue in the Sahel sunshine" (ibid.). The cloth and its maker are, thus, intimately linked, to the point of being the same color. The life out of which this cloth emerges is, by implication, the life of this Dogon woman, working in her rural village.

While the texture and color of specific handmade textiles and garments might evoke the circumstances of their production, this elision of African culture and handmade production has in some instances been broadly generalized and applied to African artistic production as a whole. Thus, in a popular publication on the adaptability of African textiles and other art forms to American home décor, Sharne Algotsson and Denys Davis declare: "African art . . . evokes a time when fabric dyes were derived from plants, earth, and minerals; when cloth was produced from the pounding of tree bark; and when wooden objects were carved with rudimentary tools" (1996: 10). African-ness itself thus evokes the technology of the handmade.

Feel, a broad, ineffable term that encompasses texture, is also implicated in the determination of authenticity. It is the "feeling" of garments that allows consumers to insert themselves into the stories the clothing evokes. Such was the case for one male, African American consumer of a *bogolan* (mudcloth) suit who described the impact of the ensemble on his own sense of identity as he tried it on: "So what if the shop didn't have a mirror? I didn't need one to tell me how wearing the African clothing made me feel. The weight and regal cut of the cloth made me feel, well, reconnected" (Marriott 1997: section 9, 1). Or, as cited in the exhibition catalog, *Wrapped In Pride*, on the changing roles of Ghanaian *kente* cloth in global markets, one American wearer of the cloth explicitly connected her feelings with its handmade manufacture: "Having been there and actually watched the weaving . . . gives me a special feeling, and I think I do feel a little different" (K. Smith-Phillips in Quick 1998: 262). The texture and weight of the garment evokes feelings in the wearer; feelings produced at the intersection of texture and authenticity.

Mass production of the handmade

The connection between texture and authenticity is reflected in the mass production of cloth and garments that retain the stylistic signifiers of the handmade. *Kente* cloth is but one prominent example of factory-produced textile reproductions wherein the strips of woven patterns mechanically printed in a variety of media are marketed as "authentic." *Bogolan*, the Malian textile, offers another example (Rovine 2001). In its original form, this cloth is woven on narrow strip looms using locally spun cotton. It is then dyed using a labor-intensive process that involves applying a mineral pigment to the areas around the geometric patterns, darkening the background so that the motifs remain white.

As *bogolan* has been adapted to new, international markets, the elements that mark it as handmade have been carefully preserved or reproduced. The application of dyes has been accelerated by the reversal of the positive/negative space, so that cloth can be quickly adorned by painting simple linear patterns. Even stencils have been adapted to *bogolan* production, so that patterns can be even more efficiently applied.

Yet, such streamlining of technologies has only minimally impacted the texture of *bogolan*, which is, along with its geometric patterns, crucial to its authenticity. The vast majority of the cloth made for sale in both domestic tourist markets and in international markets as "ethnic" textiles and clothing is made of the same strip-woven fabric that has long given *bogolan* its distinctive texture.

In a revealing twist on the many adaptations of this textile in diverse markets, American designer Daryl K. recently took a strikingly different approach to the use of *bogolan* by literally inverting the cloth in order to emphasize its handmade production (Horyn and Armstrong 2002: 81). Daryl K. created pants made of *bogolan* that appear to focus entirely on its handmade texture, to the exclusion of the patterns that usually define the cloth. The designer turned *bogolan* inside out, revealing the strips and the saturated browns and yellows that bleed through the seams along with a shadowy echo of the linear patterns. This reversal of the cloth's orientation (the side that has been adorned is now invisible) dramatically accents the strips, and the stitches that hold them together are the most important elements for the designer.

In a fascinating exception to this preservation of *bogolan*'s strip-woven texture, the textile's distinctive patterns have been adapted to factory-printed textiles, severing the patterns from the textured support of the strip-woven cloth. Yet, the handmade cloth is still referenced even in the mass-produced fabric. Patterns are surrounded by an "aura" of the handmade in the form of an encircling ring of "smudged" edges, reproducing the imperfection of the hand-painted cloth. In one prominent example of this phenomenon, leading Malian fashion designer, Chris Seydou, designed a *bogolan*-inspired textile produced by a Malian factory in 1991 (Rovine 2001: 116) (Figure 25.2). The pattern incorporated subtle variations in color

Fig. 25.2 Bogolan or mudcloth, strip-woven cotton, Bamako, Mali, late twentieth century. Private collection.

saturation and soft edges around the linear patterns. Thus, Seydou hints at manual production, a crucial element of *bogolan*'s popularity both at home and abroad, even as he initiates industrial production of the cloth to meet new demands and find new markets.

Other fabrics, too, have been translated from literal to symbolic references to the handmade. Along with the woven patterns of *kente* and the carefully painted motifs of *bogolan*, the vast array of effects that result from tie-dye and other resist dyeing techniques from many West African textile traditions have been painstakingly replicated in the medium of screen printing and other technologies of mass production. The factory-printed versions of resist-dyed fabrics also reproduce key markers of the handmade, such as fuzzy edges and uneven seams. Thus, through visual cues, these textiles allude to the handmade production crucial in the perception of authenticity. In a dramatic example, a Senegalese factory print, purchased in the early 1990s, imitates the explosion of rippling color that is the result of tie and dye techniques used with multiple plunges into dye vats of diverse colors (Figure 25.3).

A particularly rich discussion of the visual re-creation of texture is provided by Leslie Rabine, who describes the work of designers in the SOTIBA textile factory in Dakar, Senegal. These designers employ a variety of techniques in their efforts to reproduce the visual cues of handmade wax resist (batik). Their work is part of a long history of global markets and technical innovations that began with Indonesian batiks and continued with European reproductions of batiks intended solely for African markets. Thus, these designers partake in a multilayered production and reproduction of authenticity, as Rabine describes: "Sotiba fabric began not simply as a copy of Indonesian batik, but as the French copy of the English imitation wax" (2002: 139).

Fig. 25.3 Factory-printed reproduction of resist-dyed cotton fabric, SOTIBA textile company, Senegal, late twentieth century. Private collection.

Rabine describes the efforts of designers to ensure that the markers of handmade manufacture are reproduced in the factory cloth, including elements such as "Le misfit," which "imitates the leaky border between motif and background that results from the wax-resist dyeing technique" (ibid.: 145). The final step in the printing process is the application of "Le crack," a design element that imitates the cracking effect of wax-covered cloth that has been crumpled as it is submerged into the dye vat. The complexity of effectively reproducing what was an accidental, even an undesirable, by-product of the handmade batik required intense effort on the part of the designer: "It took him a whole month and many frustrating tries to produce a realistic representation of dye bleeding through a wax crack" (ibid.: 146). Of a cloth that had been carefully designed to incorporate "certain irregularities," "the designer said, 'You feel the African in it'."Thus, the cloth's authentic African-ness is located in the deliberate imperfections that mark manufacture by hand.

Adding yet another layer to this nexus of the handmade and the mass-produced, Rabine notes that, in fact, factory production need not eliminate the human element. In an ironic twist, "almost all the work, from beginning the design to mounting it on the print cylinders, *is* done by hand – with the help of huge rolls of cellophane tape, themselves symbolic of the workers' efforts to keep the old factory equipment patched together" (ibid.: 147). Thus, the SOTIBA workers who use elaborate machinery to imitate closely the appearance of the handmade must manipulate those machines by hand.Yet this element of hand manufacture does not lend the cloth the texture of authenticity so desirable on the market. The manipulation by hand of outdated or broken machinery is not compatible with the notion of handmade as authentic. That is, not all work by hand carries connotations of authenticity.

Isishweshwe and the scent of authenticity

Along with the use of carefully designed patterns to communicate the tactile attributes of authenticity visually, in at least one case *smell* features in the sensory reproduction of the handmade. The iconic South African textile *isishweshwe* (or *shweshwe*) has a rich local history dating back more than a century (Leeb du Toit 2005). The cloth, also known as "German Print," and characterized by its small, neatly ordered geometric patterns, was originally made using indigo dye and, in the late nineteenth century, a synthetic form of indigo developed in Germany (Figure 25.4). In South Africa, its status as imported (arriving with German settlers in the nineteenth century) and, until recently, its foreign manufacture, has precluded its inclusion in conventional conceptions of "authentic" South African attire.

Since the late 1990s, however, *isishweshwe* has become a symbol of national identity and, as such, the market for *isishweshwe* and *shweshwe* imitations has grown. Only one manufacturer, Da Gama Textiles, still produces the cloth using the nineteenth-century process associated with "authentic" *isishweshwe*: copper rollers etched with patterns that are used to apply an acid solution to blue-dyed cotton percale, bleaching out white patterns. Several experienced textile consumers in South Africa told me they can smell the difference between the Da Gama technique and other printing technologies. The sound and texture of the cloth offer other clues

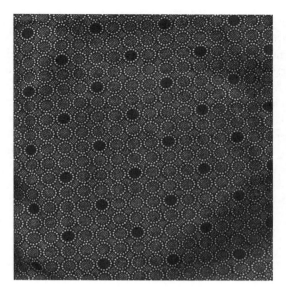

Fig. 25.4 Shweshwe fabric, South Africa, 2001. Private collection.

to its authenticity – the name *isishweshwe* itself is said to be a reference to the sound the stiff-textured cloth makes when its folds rub together. At least one *isishweshwe* imitator was trying to reproduce the cloth's authentic smell! Thus, authentic production, whether by hand or by machine, can be communicated – and imitated – through several senses.

Isishweshwe brings us back to the realm of fashion trends in which handmade manufacture is a key feature. Numerous South African designers have made use of *isishweshwe*, and many have been inspired to use it because of its "authenticity." In the words of one young design student, "shweshwe is the celebration of a cultural heritage that embraces the new" (Counihan 2005: 63). Or, as Adam Levin describes it, the cloth has been transformed from the attire of matrons who have little access to fashion trends into the garb of choice for trendsetters: "*Shwe-shwe* fabric – once the domain of overweight aunties – is now a favorite of young black and white women" (Levin 2005: 173). In South African fashion, the texture of the past is thus melded with the cutting-edge styles of the present.

Coming full circle?

In Western fashion markets, the association between handmade manufacture and authenticity is embodied by the handwork of haute couture. Parisian fashion designer Jean Paul Gaultier frequently borrows from African and other non-Western dress practices, but without concern for their cultural authenticity. In his winter 2004 collection, he presented an entire African line with a richly beaded dress as the crowning ensemble. The dress is authentically haute couture in its complex handwork, creating multiple layers of texture and color. But it is culturally inauthentic; that is, elements from everywhere have been cut and pasted into Gaultier's personal aesthetic vision without acknowledging their cultures of origin. A spread in *The New York Times* magazine in March, 2005, offered another view of these distinct versions of authenticity (Hirshberg and Barnes 2005). Pairs of bags, one by a named designer, one identified only by the non-Western culture from which it originated, emphasized the apparent synchronicity between these two distant realms, creating a contrast that seems aimed at lending the Western designs a veneer of authenticity. One of those bags, of a type used by Yoruba diviners in Nigeria, appeared in both realms, stripped of its authenticity in one culture to be literally stitched into another. The desire to produce and reproduce authenticity drives these transpositions of form and translations of meaning. Texture plays a crucial role in negotiations over authenticity in the realm of dress, providing a sensitive barometer of shifting local identities and changing perceptions of other cultures.

References

Algotsson, S. and Davis, D. (1996), *The Spirit of African Design*, New York: Clarkson Potter Publishers.

Bernstein, N. (2005), "In Craze for Tunic Blouses, It's See and Be Seen in Sequins," *The New York Times* (September 11): 21.

Counihan, H. (2005), "Shweshwe: The Long History of the Latest Trend," *Urban Fabrics* (July): 63–4.

Eicher, J. B. and Sumberg, B. (1995), "World Fashion, Ethnic, and National Dress," in J. B. Eicher (ed.), *Dress and Ethnicity: Change Across Space and Time*, Oxford: Berg, pp. 295–306.

"Fashion's Favorite." (2004), *The Economist* (March 6–12) 370 (8,365): 4–5.

Hirshberg, L. and Barnes, R. (2005), "The Things They Carried," *The New York Times Magazine* (March 20): 72–9.

Horyn, C. and Armstrong, D. (2002), "She Wears the Pants: Daryl K. is back in charge" and "Oh, K!" *The New York Times Magazine* (September 22): 77–83.

Leeb du Toit, J. (2005), "Sourcing Amajamani/Isiswhweshwe and Its Indigenization in South Africa," Unpublished paper.

Leopold, E. (1992), "The Manufacture of the Fashion System," in J. Ash and E. Wilson (eds), *Chic Thrills: A Fashion Reader*, Berkeley: University of California Press, pp. 101–17.

Levin, A. (2005), *The Art of African Shopping*, Cape Town: Struik Publishers.

Marriott, M. (1997), "Meaning in a Suit from Mali," *The New York Times* (October 26) section 9: 1, 5.

Partington, A. (1992), "Popular Fashion and Working-Class Affluence," in J. Ash and E. Wilson (eds), *Chic Thrills: A Fashion Reader*, Berkeley: University of California Press, pp. 145–61.

Quick, B. (1998), "Pride and Dignity," in D. Ross (ed.), *Wrapped in Pride: Ghanaian Kente and African-American Identity*, Los Angeles: Fowler Museum of Cultural History, pp. 203–65.

Rabine, L. W. (2002), *The Global Circulation of African Fashion*, New York: Berg.

Rovine, V. L. (2001), *Bogolan: Shaping Culture through Cloth in Contemporary Mali*, Washington, DC: Smithsonian Institution Press.

Spooner, B. (1986), "Weavers and Dealers: The Authenticity of an Oriental Carpet," in A. Appadurai (ed.), *The Social Life of Things: Commodities in Cultural Perspective*, New York: Cambridge University Press, pp. 195–235.

Waterbury, R. (1989), "Embroidery for Tourists: A Contemporary Putting-Out System in Oaxaca, Mexico," in A. B. Weiner and J. Schneider (eds), *Cloth and Human Experience*, Washington, DC: Smithsonian Institution, pp. 243–71.

Chapter 26

Museum Balanga as a site of cultural hybridization

Christina F. Kreps

THE PROVINCIAL MUSEUM OF CENTRAL KALIMANTAN, Museum Balanga, is located in the provincial capital of Palangka Raya. The town, with a population of approximately 100,000, is a "frontier" community carved out of the once thick forests of Central Kalimantan.[1] It is the commercial and government center of the province, situated some 80 miles (or 130 kilometers) from the Java Sea. The primary means of accessing Palangka Raya is by boat or airplane since few roads exist in the province that are navigable year round. In the eyes of some, Palangka Raya's remote location makes it an unlikely place to find a museum. As one Australian visitor wrote in Museum Balanga's comment book: "I hardly expected to find a museum in Palangka Raya or in all of Borneo, for that matter." This visitor's comment reflected not only the prevalent image of Borneo as a wild and "uncivilized" land, but also popular attitudes regarding the context in which one expects to find a museum.

Museum Balanga was first established as a regional museum (*museum daerah*) in 1973. According to a former director of Museum Balanga, the idea to create a museum in Palangka Raya originally came from an Australian dignitary who visited the town back in the early 1970s. Several leading community members who were concerned about the preservation of Central Kalimantan's cultural heritage decided to follow through with the idea. As stated in one of the museum's publications:

> For a long time the people of Central Kalimantan longed for a museum which would give a picture of the various aspects of life of the people of Central Kalimantan and its natural environment. This desire led to the establishment of a museum in Palangka Raya.
>
> (Mihing 1989:3)

In 1989, Museum Balanga was officially designated a provincial museum (*museum negeri*), which placed it under the purview of the Directorate of Museums and the central government. In an interview with the Director of Museum Balanga in 1991, I was told that before the museum was incorporated into the national museum system it was not a "real" museum. By this he meant that previously the museum was not being managed in line with the state bureaucracy and according to professional museum standards as dictated by the Directorate of Museums.

Museum Balanga functions to collect, preserve, document, study, display, and disseminate information on the cultural and natural history of the province. The museum is primarily devoted to the collection and representation of Dayak culture, although the province is ethnically diverse and home to immigrants from other Indonesian islands. The name "Dayak" is a generic term that refers to the non-Malay, non-Chinese indigenous inhabitants of Indonesian Borneo. A number of different Dayak groups exist in Central Kalimantan who possess their own names, languages, and cultural traditions. Despite this diversity, even among the Dayaks, Museum Balanga mostly concentrates on Ngaju-Dayak culture. This is partly due to the fact that the Ngaju are the most numerous Dayak group in the province. In 1994, it was estimated that there were between 500,000 to 800,000 Ngaju-speakers in a province with a total population of some 1.5 million (Schiller 1997:14). The Ngaju are also the most politically and economically powerful Dayak group in Central Kalimantan.

Historically, Dayaks have lived in villages along the banks of Kalimantan's many rivers. Their livelihood has rested on the cultivation of rice in addition to hunting, fishing, and gathering forest products for trade such as rattan, resins, rubber, and aromatic woods. Most Dayaks today are also engaged in some form of wage labor, working in timber camps, mining operations, or as civil servants.

In keeping with the Directorate of Museum's assertion that Indonesians are "not yet" museum-minded, Museum Balanga appeared to be a foreign idea in the eyes of the local community. Outside of visiting government officials and dignitaries, school groups, and occasional tourists, few people visited the museum on a regular basis. Many local people surveyed did not know the museum existed despite its formidable presence on the edge of town. (Museum Balanga consists of nine buildings enclosed in a 3-hectare complex. The word "museum" is also inscribed in large letters on the façade of its main building.) For some, it was just a place to "keep old things," while for others it was just another cluster of government buildings whose real purposes and functions were unknown.

The museum idea was also alien to many of the individuals who worked in Museum Balanga. Museum workers were civil servants who, for the most part, had had no formal museological training before coming to work at the museum. The majority of Museum Balanga workers were also Dayaks, who retained, to varying degrees, ties to their traditional culture. They received their training on the job and under the guidance of the Directorate of Museums.[2] Consequently, the Directorate was charged with instilling a sense of museum-mindedness not just in the public, but also in the people working in provincial museums.

Bearing on the museum staff's lack of museum-mindedness, I was interested in how museological tasks were performed in Museum Balanga in comparison with work in European and American museums. Museum Balanga resembles western

Fig. 26.1 The Provincial Museum of Central Kalimantan, Museum Balanga. Photograph by Christina Kreps, 1991.

ethnographic museums in its functions and exhibition style. However, the ways in which museum work was actually carried out often reflected local values, beliefs, and perceptions on the uses and treatment of objects, which at times, appeared to conflict with those of professional, western museum culture.

Western museum culture operates with a particular set of standards, practices, and value systems regarding the collection, care, interpretation, and representation of objects. Within this museum culture objects are made museum pieces or "special" by meeting criteria established by anthropologists, art historians, scientists, curators, and collectors. Standard criteria for evaluating an object's value may be its provenience, or where and when it was made; its formal aesthetic properties; its rarity, uniqueness, or authenticity; its monetary value as determined by an art or antique market; and its scientific value as evidence of natural or cultural phenomena (Clavir 2002, Clifford 1988, Kirshenblatt-Gimblett 1991).

Most of the objects in Museum Balanga's collection are classified as "ethnographic," representing various aspects of Dayak culture. According to the Directorate of Museums' classification system, an ethnographic object is anything made by local people and still in use. For the most part, objects are displayed using an exhibition style similar to western ethnographic museums' whereby objects are grouped thematically and shown in a reconstructed cultural context. For example, one exhibition leads visitors through the stages of life by showing objects used in rituals related to birth, courting, marriage, and death. This "life-cycle" exhibit is a standard feature of nearly all provincial museums in Indonesia and was originally designed and installed by Directorate staff from Jakarta. A life-size diorama features a house on the river complete with canoes, hunting and fishing gear such as traps, weirs, blowpipes, spears, and nets. Other displays include implements used in traditional gold mining and agriculture as well as tools and materials used in the production of basketry and bark cloth. Also on display are ritual paraphernalia and objects associated with Kaharingan ceremonies. Kaharingan is the traditional religion of the Ngaju and other Dayaks of Central Kalimantan. What actually constitutes Dayak culture is a matter of debate, but to many, Kaharingan is the basis of Ngaju-Dayak culture and provides the inspiration for much of its unique cultural expressions (Schiller 1997).

Many of the objects on display in the museum are examples of things still being used in everyday life, and found in people's homes, in the market, or in villages.

Not surprisingly then, objects such as baskets, fishing and hunting gear, and tools were seen as ordinary by the staff and local people. This quotidian perception of objects was reflected in the way staff members handled objects and managed the collection, which, from the perspective of a professional curator, might be considered careless or improper. The perceived ordinariness of the objects was also the reason why many local people did not visit the museum. They saw no point in visiting a place to view objects they had in their homes and used on an almost daily basis.

Conventionally, in western museums, once an object enters the museum it takes on a new life and usually does not leave the museum except for purposes deemed acceptable by the curators. Museum workers are obliged to safeguard objects so their museum value is preserved. Rarely are objects used for the same purposes they were originally made. However, in Museum Balanga, objects were often borrowed by local people for use in ceremonies, performances, and for community events such as festivals, official ceremonies, and festivities related to the observance of national holidays. The following incident is a case in point.

One day I arrived at the Museum in time to see the staff preparing a float for a parade commemorating Indonesian Independence Day, August 17, 1945. Staff members were busily carting objects out of the museum to create a display on the back of a truck. The display was designed to represent a traditional Dayak mortuary ceremony known as a *tiwah*. Large brass gongs had been arranged on the bed of the truck along with 5-foot-tall wooden figures known as *sapundu*. An antique ceremonial cloth was being nailed onto the side of the truck while two other workers were giving the only masks in the museum's collection a new coat of paint.

Observing these actions, I was confronted with the dilemma of whether or not to intervene in the staff's activities. As a person trained in "proper" and "professional" museum practices, I felt compelled to inform the workers about the potentially damaging effects of their actions on the objects. When I expressed my concerns to one staff member, who was wrestling a *sapundu* onto the truck, he turned to me with a perplexed look and said: "Oh, it doesn't matter. There are lots of them in the villages." Obviously, this approach to the objects challenged my own sense of museum-mindedness and the idea that the carvings, masks, and other objects were "special" by virtue of the fact they were in the museum. It also underscored the differences between my views of and relationship to the objects and those of the staff. To this man, as well as to many other members of the museum staff, they were objects still

Fig. 26.2 Float created for Indonesian Independence Day parade by Museum Balanga staff. The banner on the side of the truck reads: "The Museum and the Preservation of Regional Cultural Arts. Supporting the Development of the People." The float features structures and objects used in a Ngaju-Dayak *tiwah* ceremony. Photograph by Christina Kreps, 1991.

embedded in Dayak living culture. But to me, they were "ethnographic specimens" whose value rested on their status as examples of Dayak "material culture."

In western ethnographic museums, objects are made "ethnographic" by the act of detaching them from their original cultural context and recontextualizing them into western scientific frames of reference. As Kirshenblatt-Gimblett has observed: "Ethnographic artifacts are objects of ethnography . . . Objects become ethnographic by virtue of being defined, segmented, detached, and carried away by ethnographers. Such objects are ethnographic . . . by virtue of the manner in which they have been detached" (1991:387).

As previously noted, most of the objects in Museum Balanga's collection were classified as ethnographic, and the museum's approach to exhibiting objects was modeled after western-style ethnographic museums. Nevertheless, at the time of my research, none of the museum workers were trained in anthropology or ethnographic methods.[3] They were using a classification system for objects and exhibition styles formulated by the Directorate of Museums. Consequently, the practice of conceptually detaching objects from their larger sociocultural contexts and perceiving them in an abstract manner was incongruous to the way in which many of the staff members viewed the objects. This incongruity became clear to me while observing the preparation of an exhibit on traditional carving of Central Kalimantan.

The title of the exhibition was *The Art of Traditional Carving of Central Kalimantan*, and was held at Museum Balanga from February 29 to March 3, 1992. The exhibition displayed a total of twenty-seven pieces, which were arranged to highlight the objects' aesthetic or formal qualities as well as their functions. The objects included weapons, musical instruments, and carvings originally used in Kaharingan ceremonies and rituals.

A few days before the exhibit was to open, staff members responsible for making object labels and interpretative texts told me they were having trouble preparing the texts. I thought their problem stemmed from difficulties in finding information about the objects. In an effort to help them, I drew their attention to several publications on Dayak woodcarving. However, the workers were reluctant to use these materials because they said the objects illustrated in the books were not the same objects in the museum's collection. Initially, I thought this response reflected the staff's lack of training in formal research methods. But later I learned their reluctance had more to do with the nature of the objects and who had the right to interpret them.

The exhibition included various types of *hampatung* and *karuhei*, which are carved wooden figures created by ritual specialists, or *basir*, for use in religious rituals or ceremonies. Each object is considered a unique creation, endowed with meanings and powers known only to the *basir* who created it. Knowledge about an object and how to use it is sacred, non-public, and only acquired through lengthy apprenticeship (Schiller 1986, Sellato 1989, Taylor and Aragon 1991). It is also highly personal and based on individual interpretations of Kaharingan. In describing the work of one ritual specialist, Basir Muka, Schiller writes:

> Like other ritual specialists Muka possesses a highly personalistic under-standing of his religion based upon his own experience, and the conclusions he has formed about the relationship between man and the supernatural. Basir Muka has produced a permanent record of his religious beliefs in a sculpture that is both sacred artifact and an attempt to preserve Kahayan mythology.
>
> (1986:232)[4]

Therefore, "without the detailed information from the individual who created them, it is impossible to interpret completely the ritual objects . . . or to understand the use of Dayak magical paraphernalia" (Taylor and Aragon 1991:49).

Because objects were made for specific purposes and endowed with singular meanings, museum workers were cautious about usurping the *basir*'s authority and writing generalized statements on exhibit labels about the objects. This attitude stands in contrast to how ethnographic objects are viewed and used in western museum culture where a single artifact is made to represent an abstract totality, such as Dayak woodcarving, art, or culture. As Clifford has pointed out, museum collections and displays "create the illusion of adequate representation of the world by first cutting objects out of specific contexts and making them 'stand for' abstract wholes" (1988:220). Museums deny objects their singularity as "exhibition classifications . . .

shift the grounds of singularity from the objects to a category within a particular taxonomy" (Kirshenblatt-Gimblett 1991:392).

The modern museum is typically considered a public entity. Museum collections are theoretically owned by or held in the public trust, and are to be made accessible to the public. Information about collections is, in principle, available for public consumption. "Museums are . . . apparatuses for public rather than private consumption . . . The public museum was established as a means of sharing what had been private and exposing what had been concealed" (Hooper-Greenhill 1989:68). But in traditional Dayak society, particular kinds of objects, such as *karuhei*, and knowledge about them have not been considered part of the public domain. In fact, knowledge and rights to the ownership and interpretation of some objects, because of their sacred nature, have been the sole preserve of *basir* or other select members of the society.

Out of respect for traditional customs and beliefs associated with certain objects and rights related to the authority of ritual specialists, Museum Balanga workers looked to *basir* for guidance on how to interpret and present objects used in Kaharingan rituals. They also called upon *basir* to assist them in the production of exhibits related to Kaharingan. For instance, on one occasion the museum hired three *basir* to help renovate an exhibit on the *tiwah* ceremony. The *basir* were engaged to advise the staff

Fig. 26.3 Basir, or ritual specialists, conducting rites at a *tiwah*. The site features *sapundu* (effigy poles), a *sangkaraya* (bamboo structure covered with cloth and festooned with flags), and a *pasah pali* (platform that holds ritual offerings). Photograph by Christina Kreps, 1991.

Fig. 26.4 Re-creation of *tiwah* site in Museum Balanga, complete with *sapundu*, *sangkaraya*, and *pasah pali*. Photograph by Christina Kreps, 1991.

on how to make the exhibit more authentic or closer to the image of a real *tiwah*. But the *basir* did more than merely advise. They selected objects for display, constructed models of ceremonial structures, and arranged them in their appropriate positions. All the work was carried out in accordance with Kaharingan prescriptions. After the renovation was completed, the *basir* performed a cleansing ritual to cast out any lingering bad spirits and to summon good spirits to bestow their blessings on the museum, staff, and visitors.

Collaboration with *basir* is one example of how Museum Balanga was a site of cultural hybridization where local approaches to the interpretation and representation of cultural materials were being mixed with those of a wider, international museum culture. However, to some administrators, these collaborative efforts were unprofessional, too closely tied to religion, and not in keeping with the idea of a museum as a modern, secular institution based on scientific principles and professionalism. As a result, such practices were being discouraged in Museum Balanga.

Notes

1   The island of Borneo is divided among the states of Malaysia, Brunei, and Indonesia. Indonesian Borneo, known collectively as Kalimantan, is comprised of the provinces of East, West, South, and Central Kalimantan.

2 Between 1991 and 1992, several Museum Balanga workers participated in the previously mentioned Dutch-sponsored museum training workshops. One worker was selected for participation in the Indonesian Museum Training Program, and in 1994, studied museology at the Burke Memorial Museum at the University of Washington in Seattle for six months.

3 When I visited Museum Balanga in 2000 I met a new staff member who was trained in anthropology. While conducting research at the museum in 1991 and 1992, the Director of the museum told me that the Directorate of Museums was trying to place an anthropologist in the museum. Thus, the Directorate was finally successful in meeting this objective.

4 One of Basir Muka's *hampatung karuhei* is in the collection of Museum Balanga. This piece is featured in Sellato's book, *Hornbill and Dragon* (1989: 226).

References

Clavir, M. (2002) *Preserving What is Valued: Museums, Conservation, and First Nations*, Vancouver: University of British Columbia Press.

Clifford, J. (1988) *The Predicament of Culture: Twentieth Century Literature, Ethnography, and Art*, Cambridge: Harvard University Press.

Hooper-Greenhill, E. (1989) "The Museum in the Disciplinary Society" in S. Pearce (ed.) *Museum Studies in Material Culture*, London: Leicester University Press, pp. 41–72.

Kirshenblatt-Gimblett, B. (1991) "Objects of Ethnography" in I. Karp and S. Lavine (eds) *Exhibiting Cultures. The Poetics and Politics of Museum Display*, Washington, DC: Smithsonian Institution Press, pp. 386–443.

Mihing, T. (1989) *Sekelumit Koleksi Museum Negeri Kalimantan Tengah*, Palangka Raya: Departemen Pendidikan dan Kebudayaan Kantor Wilayah Propinsi Kalimantan Tengah.

Schiller, A. (1986) "A Ngaju Ritual Specialist and the Rationalization of Hindu-Kaharingan," *Sarawak Museum Journal*, 36 (new series):231–242.

—— (1997) *Small Sacrifices: Religious Change and Cultural Identity among the Ngaju of Indonesia*, New York and Oxford: Oxford University Press.

Sellato, B. (1989) *Hornbill and Dragon*, Jakarta: Elf Aquitaine Indonesie.

Taylor, P. and L. Aragon (1991) *Beyond the Java Sea*, Washington and New York: National Museum of Natural History and Harry N. Abrams.

PART IV

Object/person distinctions

Introduction to Part IV

Sandra H. Dudley

S O FAR, THE BOOK HAS CONSIDERED objects, our contingent and embodied experience of them, and some of the effects of the contexts of that experience. It now moves on to explore aspects of the particular relationships between persons and things. In fact, as the readings will demonstrate, while things' and persons' identities and meanings could be said to be always dependent on other things or persons, there are a number of different ways in which their linkages can be conceptualised, described, utilised and theorised. Indeed, perspectives on the relationships and distinctions between people and things differ not only with academic perspective, but also across cultures and periods. Views vary markedly, for example, on whether or not objects can be said to have agency — that is, whether they can be said actively to cause or have effects in some way. As some of the texts illustrate, even amongst those who do consider that objects can be said to have agency, quite what agency means and how it is thought to manifest, may be articulated in a number of different ways.

In the first reading, Anita Herle reflects on the agency and power of objects now in museum collections to connect persons and happenings that are geographically, culturally and temporally distant from one another. Her discussion of the dialogical co-production of an exhibition in Cambridge to mark the centenary of the 1898 Torres Strait anthropological expedition, demonstrates the dynamic lives that objects may continue to have long after they have been accessioned into museum collections. Such entanglement and agency are both qualities of active things far from the 'dead' objects museum artefacts are so often thought to be. They both revolve around narrative, culture and meaning — and all are inseparable too from the objects' particular material forms, decorative features and qualities.

As Herle's analysis moves between objects' form and subjective meanings, demonstrating the blurred line between them, so too, in different ways, does Gabriel Moshenska's exploration of the heritage potential of applying historical archaeology and oral history techniques to understand and interpret German sites damaged by Allied aerial bombing in the Second World War. Examining the cross-cutting themes of ruins, fragments, wounding and depth, and probing the differences between 'bottom-up and top-down views of the world', Moshenska investigates different forms of narrative and varied approaches to the material remains themselves, and the tensions and similarities between them. Ultimately, the objects – the ruins – and the subjects here, ebb and flow into one another depending upon the perspective one takes.

The third reading is then the first of five which reflect directly on the relationships between people and things. Focusing on the relationships between an object and its meanings, Simon Knell makes the case that ultimately objects only do and mean things because people make them do so, and argues strongly that the material object is mute and has no agency of its own. Drawing on art, science and a number of specific examples, he connects and contrasts the material object with its conceptual twin, the intangible object we construct and negotiate in our minds. For Knell, our interpretations of and responses to objects come from us and are informed by our experiences; the material qualities of the object alone are of little significance in how we come to *know* about an object, and whether or not we understand it as authentic. As the author points out, this perspective raises interesting questions and possibilities for museums.

A very different perspective is then introduced with the next reading, an extract from Alfred Gell's now classic *Art and Agency*. In it, Gell briefly outlines his theory on the possession of agency by objects as well as by persons. He includes a section addressing the common objection that to have agency (i.e. to cause things to happen) you need to *intend* things to happen, and things – it is commonly objected – cannot have intentions. He avoids this objection by incorporating into his discussion both *primary* and *secondary* agents, as well as *patients* on whom the agents have effect. He then outlines the basic application of his theory to art objects, in his anthropological theory of art. In the following paper, another leading anthropological theorist, Howard Morphy, outlines some key objections to Gell's imputation of agency to objects. He carefully sets out too why he disagrees with Gell's rejection of the significance of the aesthetic and semantic aspects of art to an effective anthropological theory. Importantly, and as both Gell and Morphy point out, their arguments can be extended to other kinds of things as well as to art objects alone.

Theoretical conceptualisations of the relationships between persons and things comprise the preoccupation of Lambros Malafouris's paper, too, though his focus is not on agency but on the dividing line, physical and conceptual, between subject and object. Elaborating upon the Blind Man's Stick hypothesis found in older literature, Malafouris asks where man and stick – and, by extension, prehistoric man and stone tool – each begin and end, and what that in turn implies for our understanding of early hominid cognitive development. There are some echoes with Gell's claim in the earlier chapter that a soldier's weapons are *part* of him – though Gell takes this in an ultimately different and more elaborate theoretical direction than does Malafouris.

Lastly, Tim Ingold examines the creation of objects, asking if we might not think of it rather as a sort of growth. His discussion of the autopoietic processes through which form emerges from the engagements over time between maker and materials and 'the temporal rhythms of life are gradually built into the structural properties of things', ends this part of the book's focus on object–person relationships and differences in a dynamic and productive way, emphasising their mutual and ongoing entwinement. It also, because of its focus on material form and its production, returns us to many of the concerns of the beginning of the volume too – thus helpfully reminding us that the categories into which this book's papers have been divided are ultimately as artificial in their boundary lines as are the worlds of people and things.

Chapter 27

Objects, agency and museums

Continuing dialogues between the Torres Strait and Cambridge

Anita Herle

I feel like I've met the people, the artists who created these magnificent artefacts.

(Alick Tipoti 2000)[1]

This exhibition includes artefacts which are in themselves visual expressions of belief, culture and traditions of profound social and spiritual values. The Haddon collection enables the modern Torres Strait Islander to re-discover and re-interpret the truth about himself in the light of the wisdom and strength of his ancestors throughout the ages. And enables him to revive, recreate and extend his culture in ways beneficial to our future generations to come.

(Bishop Passi 2001)[2]

Objects in museum collections have the potential of connecting people and events over time and space. Against the familiar criticism that museum objects have been ripped from their cultural context only to languish in mausoleums, objects may have entangled and transitive lives both before and after they enter a museum's collection. Nor does the museum context necessarily alienate material from the knowledge and interests of people in source communities. Through its role in preserving and documenting important cultural materials, the museum may provide opportunities for cross-cultural dialogue and innovative collaborations.

In the late twentieth century, much research on material culture has drawn attention to the biographies or social lives of objects as a means of illuminating complex social interactions and systems of value, meaning and exchange.[3] The underlying notion is that objects do not necessarily have fixed meanings but that meanings are attributed by the social contexts through which the objects pass. Yet, is the intrinsic or original meaning of particular objects so weak that it is lost by successive interpretive frameworks? What about the agency of the objects themselves?

The production and reception of *Torres Strait Islanders: An Exhibition to Mark the Centenary of the 1898 Cambridge Anthropological Expedition to the Torres Strait*[4] provides an opportunity to reflect on the role of the museum and the meanings associated with specific objects. I am particularly interested in the resonance that certain objects collected in the late nineteenth century by Alfred Haddon, the leader of the Expedition, have for Islanders and researchers today. Throughout my discussion the museum emerges as a particular kind of 'contact zone' (Clifford 1997: 188–219), a space charged by the agency of the objects emerging through the intersecting interests of producers and collectors, Islanders and curators. To clarify, my concept of the word agency here is not classificatory, it is relational and context dependent (Gell 1998). Whereas Gell uses abduction to analyse the agency of objects in a wide variety of historical and cross-cultural settings, here the process of re-interpreting material collected by Haddon enables both the observation of and participation in dynamic relationships between people and things. Turtle-shell masks, feather head-dresses, models, photographs and texts make important intercultural links between past and present, and between Cambridge and the Islands.

The visual and textual material collected by the 1898 Expedition, and often generated by the encounter between the Islanders and the Expedition members, embodies successive layers of meaning. It contains ethnographic information about the people of the Torres Strait at the end of the nineteenth century. Some items are associated with named individuals and have specific biographies. Haddon recorded who made them, how they were used, and the circumstances of their collection. A close analysis of the production and collection of Islander material reveals the entangled and multilateral relationships between the Islanders, Expedition members, missionaries, colonial officials and academic communities. On another level the objects reveal trends in Western intellectual history. In Cambridge and elsewhere Torres Strait collections were placed within changing systems of classification and used for the dissemination of anthropological knowledge to specialist and popular audiences. More recently the collections have provided the opportunity to re-open a dialogue between Cambridge and the Torres Strait.

Over the last few decades, Islander interest in the Expedition's work has heightened. As noted by David Moore (1984: 7) in the preface to his comprehensive book, *The Torres Strait Collections of A.C. Haddon*, '[t]he catalogue will be of particular interest to the Torres Strait Islanders themselves, since they are now attempting a reconstruction of their own culture in order to clarify and consolidate their identity as a people.' The social and political implications of the Expedition's research has been reinforced by recent political events, notably the 1992 'Mabo Case', where information contained in the Expedition's *Reports* became crucial documents in contemporary struggles for Islander self-determination.[5] Images of Torres Strait objects and the designs they carry have become symbols of a strong resurgent Islander identity and sources of inspiration for contemporary artists. Some retain a powerful spiritual presence, directly connected to personal and family stories.[6]

The Expedition

The 1898 Cambridge Anthropological Expedition is a significant part of several distinct yet intersecting histories. In British academic and intellectual history the Expedition is noted for its comprehensive research agenda and its influence on the professionalisation of social anthropology in Cambridge and beyond.[7] Haddon, a natural scientist and ethnologist, had first been to the Torres Strait ten years earlier to study marine biology, but the focus of his attention soon shifted to the Islanders among whom he lived and worked. Concerned that Islander customs were fast disappearing as a result of the influence of colonialists, missionaries and the marine industry, Haddon determined to organise an anthropological expedition to return to the Torres Strait to collect ethnographic data 'before it was too late'. Within a paradigm of salvage ethnography, Haddon designed the Expedition as a multi-disciplinary project encompassing anthropology in its broadest sense.

The seven members of the Expedition included scholars in the fields of psychology, physiology, medicine, linguistics and natural sciences. Haddon recorded local customs, studied decorative art, oversaw the collection of artefacts and took anthropomorphic measurements. William Rivers, in charge of experimental psychology, investigated vision, and once in the field, developed a method of recording local genealogies. William McDougall studied tactile sensation while Charles Myers, a skilful musician, concentrated on hearing and music. The Expedition's linguist, Sidney Ray, compiled word lists, constructed grammars and assisted with translations. Charles Seligman researched native medicine and local pathology and also compiled comparative ethnographic data in Cape York and coastal Papua. Anthony Wilkin worked as the official photographer under Haddon's direction and investigated house construction and land tenure.

Driven by his concern for comprehensive and accurate recording, the work of the Expedition and their Islander assistants generated an enormous corpus of information: the six official volumes of the *Reports of the Cambridge Anthropological Expedition to Torres Straits* (1902–35) (hereafter *Reports*), numerous scholarly and popular publications, a collection of approximately 1,500 artefacts, over 400 photographs, several short sequences of moving film, sound recordings and extensive associated archival material. The majority of this material is now housed at the University of Cambridge, the main sponsor of the Expedition. The range of objects includes elaborate masks, ritual objects, body ornaments, musical instruments, clothing, baskets, household items, tools, weapons, commissioned models and samples of raw materials. Significant Torres Strait collections are held in numerous museums throughout Europe, Australia and the United States, but overall the material at Cambridge is acknowledged as the most comprehensive and well documented.[8]

The results of the Expedition have remained an important resource for subsequent researchers in the region as well as for Islander knowledge about the past. In contrast to the practices of many early ethnographers, Haddon took great care to acknowledge the sources of the Expedition's data. Islanders and other informants were referenced and often quoted verbatim, many of the people in the photographs were identified, and the names of an object's maker or previous owner were sometimes recorded. The attribution of knowledge to named individuals is of particular significance to people from Mer and Mabuiag, the islands where Expedition members spent the most time and home to the descendants of many of Haddon's assistants and friends. Haddon appears to have been unaware of the full implications of recording the names of the Islanders who provided the Expedition with information. Islander notions of ownership are directly related to kinship and include rights over land, sea resources and objects as well as knowledge of stories, songs, dances, etc. (Philp 1998a, 1998b). For contemporary Islanders, the *Reports* are also a record of the people who had the knowledge and authority to speak about particular things. An awareness of the source of information is a means by which some Islanders attempt to verify or challenge some of the details presented in the *Reports*. Access to particular types of knowledge is traced through kinship and used to ascertain whether an informant was in a position to have both the 'deep' knowledge and the right to tell a particular story.

Despite some inaccuracies, the details in the *Reports* and associated archival material allude to complex relationships that developed between researchers and local informants. The Expedition's work was greatly assisted by people such as Pasi, Jimmy Rice, Jimmy Day, Debi Wali, Gisu, Ulai, Enoch, and Wano on Mer and Nomoa, Gizu, Waria, Peter and Tom on Mabuiag and Maino on Tudu. These and other Islanders were actively involved in the work of the Expedition: demonstrating 'traditional' practices, sharing cultural stories, re-enacting rituals, participating in physiological and psychological tests, trading artefacts, producing commissioned objects and so forth.

Some Islanders were aware of the intended destination for the material collected by the Expedition. Although their knowledge of museums was limited, the exhibition of objects owned by named individuals was seen by some as an opportunity to display cultural status. Maino of Tudu was one of the first Islanders with whom Haddon established a lasting relationship, meeting with him several times in 1888, 1898 and finally in 1914. At their first meeting Maino organised a dance for him and later traded objects which had belonged to his famous father Kebisu.[9] Haddon recorded the transaction in his diary:

> I did not ask for them as I felt he valued them highly – he offered them to me and then I asked him what he wanted and I paid his price (a small oval looking glass, 2 pocket knives, a blue bead necklace, 2 clay pipes and 11 sticks of tobacco) . . . he wanted me to have them and he also wanted them to be exhibited in a big museum in England where plenty people could see his father's things.
>
> (Haddon 1888–9: 66)

It is worth noting that other objects owned by Kebisu are still owned and valued by his direct descendants.[10] Although local people appeared keen to trade some objects, they were reluctant to part with others and refused to give up items such as the sacred drum Wasikor, which remains on Mer today. Haddon was persistent in his efforts to record and collect as much as possible, often cajoling people to make models or replicas of sacred material that no longer existed or that was inappropriate to remove. He self-consciously recorded his intentions to trade fairly, but the negotiations reveal the political asymmetry and the discrepancies between different value systems.

On Mer Haddon persuaded Gisu to trade a *doiom*, a stone charm used in rainmaking, and refused to return it when Gisu regretted the transaction the following day, 'the collecting instinct was stronger than pure sentiment, and I had to inform him that it was then too late' (Haddon 1901: 26).

In due course some Islanders became aware of the results of the Expedition's research and saw themselves and their work represented in print. Haddon sent copies of his publications back to the Torres Strait for comment, where they generated much interest and discussion.[11] Some Islanders soon recognised the potential of written texts and both Pasi of Mer and Waria of Mabuiag sent manuscripts to Haddon. Written in the Mabuiag language, Waria's 300-page account begins, 'I am Ned Waria. I wrote this book so that men coming afterwards might know' and his introduction finishes with the genealogies of the people with dugong and crocodile totems who lived at Panai village (*Reports*, Vol. III: 192). These and other stories were partially translated by Ray in the *Reports*. An awareness of the process of transforming oral stories into written text highlights the agency of specific Islanders in the production of anthropological knowledge.

The Exhibition as process

Nearly a hundred years after the Expedition, preparations for a centenary exhibition provided an opportunity to reflect on the Expedition and its legacies and to reactivate links between Cambridge and the Torres Strait. A brief account of the process of creating the exhibition will illuminate both its content and varied reception. As the curator responsible for the collections, I recognised that an adequate account of the complexity of this particular encounter and its multiple and diffuse legacies would necessarily have to include the insights of contemporary Islanders. To this end, I went to the Torres Strait in 1996 to discuss plans for the exhibition with members of the indigenous government, the Torres Strait Regional Authority (TSRA) established in 1994, and other political and cultural leaders both in the Strait and on the Australian mainland. From 1995–6 Jude Philp, then a research student in the Department of Social Anthropology at Cambridge, conducted fieldwork in the Torres Strait. Her insights and alliances were crucial to the preparations for the exhibition. In Australia I also made contact with Mary Bani, a Torres Strait Islander working at the National Museum of Australia, and invited her to come to Cambridge to research the collections (Bani and Herle 1998).[12] With the assistance of Philp and Bani, a short exhibition brief was prepared which was sent to over 60 people, mainly Islanders in the Strait and on the mainland and other specialists including anthropologists and curators. Although direct written responses were limited, the importance of the consultative process cannot be over-emphasised, both in terms of sharing information and generating support. Overall, the dialogue ultimately influenced both the content of the exhibition as well as various responses to it.

The overall aim of the exhibition was to review the Expedition and its legacies critically while presenting the strength and richness of *Ailan Kastom* (Island Custom), past and present.[13] The approach sought a nuanced understanding of historically and culturally specific encounters. A central concern in the preparations for the exhibition was the extent to which a presentation of contact history can be balanced, inclusive and consensual. Yet notions of inclusion and consensus may not be appropriate in relation to Islanders' understanding of authority and ownership, where knowledge is owned and selectively transmitted to descendants. Throughout the exhibition different types of knowledge were highlighted in order to illustrate some of the historical and cross-cultural complexities involved in the relationship between the Expedition members, Islanders, missionaries and colonial officers. The juxtaposition of narratives was intended to multiply the shifting and overlapping contexts of the objects on display. The Expedition *Reports* and associated archival material provided historical insights into the views of different individuals and groups while more recent 'voices' were drawn from contemporary field notes, publications, informal discussions and correspondence. Numerous comments, opinions and stories from named individuals were thus directly incorporated into the storyline of the exhibition, providing a forum for the transmission of anthropological and indigenous perspectives both past and present. The approach of interweaving historic and contemporary voices was also intended to highlight the dynamic strength and vitality of *Ailan Kastom*.

Throughout the exhibition preparations Philp and I were conscious of Islanders' notions of privacy and avoided topics that would be likely to cause offence. While reference was made to esoteric knowledge, we did not attempt to explain it. Some material, such as objects associated with sorcery or death, was rejected for display as these items may retain an inherent dangerous potency. Explicit permission was sought for the inclusion of some sacred material; in particular, the section on Malo-Bomai required careful consideration and negotiation. The name of Bomai continues to be a sacred name for the Meriam people. Bomai has such power that commonly even his name is not spoken, instead, people refer to this *agad* (god) as Malo. In 1898 Haddon commissioned Wano and Enoch to create two cardboard models of the sacred Malo-Bomai masks, originally made of turtle-shell and worn at the climax of a secret initiation ceremony.[14] The production of the masks provoked a strong emotive response in many of the senior men and eventually the Expedition members were privileged to witness parts of the performances relating to the Malo ceremonies. Detailed information about Malo-Bomai was recorded in the *Reports*, a re-enactment of the ceremony was photographed and filmed, related objects were purchased for the museum, and the stories and the associated songs were recorded on wax cylinders.

Given the centrality of Malo-Bomai to the Meriam and the complex interactions involved in the production of the masks and re-enactment of the ceremonies, we were keen to include this material in the exhibition. However, our concerns regarding cultural sensitivity and ownership of knowledge included not only the question of the public display of the masks but the stories associated with them. The movements of Malo (that is, Bomai) created the social structure of Mer, its laws, tenancy and instruction. Each of the eight tribes of Mer had quite specific duties and privileges associated with Malo which were restricted to initiates and passed on only to their descendants. As such, the story of Malo's arrival on Mer has very real socio-political implications for Meriam today. Over time, with the assistance of Ron Day, the Chairman of Mer, and Meriam elders, the display text was discussed, modified and eventually approved. Although the changes to the text appear to be relatively small, concerning the sequence of Malo's movements and details of his encounters, the narrative alludes to a deeper knowledge regarding initiation and ownership which was not disclosed.

The exhibition intentionally and somewhat inevitably contained a number of tensions and ambiguities. Objects and information collected in 1898 with the intention of recording Torres Strait culture 'before it was too late', were displayed 100 years later to reinforce the ongoing vitality of *Ailan Kastom*. Even in Haddon's own writings there was a noticeable contrast between his laments for a dying culture and the lively vignettes of Islander life recorded in the journals, letters and more popular publications.[15] The contrast between the motivating goals of the Expedition members and the personal relationships that were developed in the field were highlighted in adjacent sections in the exhibition entitled 'Recording, Measurement and Collecting' and 'Fieldwork and Friendship'. The colonial infrastructure facilitated the movements of the Expedition members and nourished the desire to record, measure and collect data about distant peoples and places. But once in the Islands, the Expedition's fieldworkers had to improvise and Islander responses often challenged Eurocentric assumptions about cultural and racial differences.

In addition to nearly 300 Islander objects, the exhibition included the material culture of the Expedition: callipers, a microscope, a colour wheel, Lovibond's tintometer, cameras, a recording phonograph and a magic lantern projector. The technology used by the Expedition members along with its associated knowledge and skills played an important role in mediating between the Expedition members and the Islanders, often with unexpected results. For example, photography was initially a means of surveillance and scientific analysis, but photographs soon became objects of exchange, anthropometric photography shifted into portraiture, family photographs were made at Islander's request, and Haddon's magic lantern shows were popular local entertainment (Edwards 1998). The exhibition attempted to contextualise the anthropological practices that were developed during this period, not glorify the work of the Expedition members. It was crucial to acknowledge the active role of Islanders in the Expedition's research, as confirmed by both the historical records and Islander memory. However, a lingering curatorial concern was whether the assertion of indigenous agency in the production of anthropological knowledge inadvertently downplayed the devastating effects of colonisation and the Expedition's role in removing important cultural artefacts. As one reviewer commented,

> A cross-cultural exhibition that fails to display tensions, instead of coherence, exceptions as well as rules, and at least several stories rather than one is probably not doing justice to whatever, art, culture or history it is supposed to be representing.
>
> (Thomas 2000: 73)

Responses

Over the last few years, the Museum has welcomed over 30 Islander visitors. Awareness of the exhibition was heightened through occasional updates in the *Torres*

Strait News and radio broadcasts on Radio Torres Strait (Torres Strait Islander Media Association, *Voice Blo Ilanman*). Some individuals used the exhibition as an incentive to visit the UK. Other visits were more lengthy and formal. For example, an official delegation represented the TSRA at the opening of the exhibition on 1 July 1998. In attendance were Ron Day, Chairman of Mer, and Terrence Whap, Chairman of Mabuiag, both direct descendants of Haddon's close assistants and representatives of the two Islands where the Expedition members conducted most of their research. Shortly after the exhibition opened, John Abednego, then Chairman of the TSRA, came to Cambridge specifically to see it. The flag of the Torres Strait, presented to the museum when I first discussed the exhibition with the Regional Authority in 1996, hung over the final section of the exhibition that outlined the efforts of the TSRA and other Islander community groups.[16] In 1999 a delegation of five elders (David Passi, Goby Noah, Florence Kennedy, Ephraim Bani, Frances Tapim), and Leilani Bin-Juda, a representative of the National Museum of Australia, spent approximately two weeks in Cambridge. They came specifically to see the exhibition, to conduct their own research in the reserve collections and archives of the museum, and to recommend possible loan objects for the opening of the new National Museum in Australia in 2001 (Figure 27.1). Finally, artist Alick Tipoti, well known for his detailed and vibrant lino-cut prints, came to 'close' the exhibition in December 2000. Islanders have continued to be attracted to the Museum and there have been several visits in 2001–2, including a visitation by five members of the Mualgau Minarral Art Collective based on Moa Island.

Fig. 27.1 Torres Strait Islander delegation recording information about material in the Haddon collections at MAA, (l–r) Frances Tapim, Florence Kennedy, Ephraim Bani, David Passi. 1999. Photograph by Anita Herle.

Interactions with and between various Islanders and staff within the Museum have been extremely productive. The storyline of the exhibition and the varied objects on display roused strong and mixed emotive responses, animating conversations about the past and its relevance to the present. Some of the objects remain connected to particular families and islands, highlighting the ongoing relationship between people and things as well as the distinction between members of various communities. They are often linked to stories that both convey and selectively encode important cultural knowledge. Other objects are re-appropriated as symbols of a resurgent Islander identity and are used as a source of inspiration for contemporary Islander artists.

Day, Whap and others were keen to see the exhibition and the material in the reserve collections but they also expected a detailed explanation of why and how the exhibition was arranged. Initially Islanders tended to be overwhelmed by the richness of the collections and the amount of material on display. Some of the objects sparked excited conversations, others less familiar provoked sadness – a reminder of the devastating impact of colonisation, the loss of knowledge, and the things that no longer exist on the Islands. Where possible the labels noted an object's maker or previous owner. The care with which we attempted to associate people and things, attributed quotes and identified individuals in the photographs had a powerful effect on Islander visitors. These were not simply 'multiple voices' but named ancestors – we heard stories about them and were reminded of their living descendants.

The importance of family connections was and continues to be central to people's interest in and understanding of the collections in Cambridge. People are identified through their relationships with others – as someone's child, sibling, cousin, auntie, uncle, wife, husband and so forth. The emphasis on family was particularly apparent when looking at the historic photographs in the exhibition and the archives.

Family relationships also animate specific objects, which in turn stimulate further discussions about how and to whom people are related. In the collection there is a group of six rather roughly carved and painted male figures, *ad giz*, each representing a Meriam ancestor figure associated with a particular district and lineage. It is uncertain whether these types of figures were ever made and used locally, the examples in Cambridge were specifically made for Haddon via Jack Bruce (the schoolteacher on Mer), their production encouraged by Haddon's investigations into the existence of ancestor cults. In Cambridge, the Meriam representatives, Passi, Noah and Tapim, were keen on seeing the *ad giz* models and the unpacking of these figures prompted a long and detailed discussion conducted both in English and Meriam Mir. The men looked closely at the carved figures as they recited genealogies, comparing details with each other and with Rivers' genealogical tables in *The Reports* (Vol. 6).[17] People frequently referred to the *Reports* while looking at the objects in the reserve collections. The volumes and their contents were treated with great respect and nearly everyone asked if it would be possible to get them reprinted.

Objects with totem marks were also of great interest. Totems such as crocodiles, turtles or hammerhead sharks were incised on personal items such as the characteristic hourglass shaped drums, *warup* or bamboo tobacco pipes. Viewing these objects often prompted long discussions about characteristics of various totems and some Islanders used it as an opportunity to reveal their own totems. The style and execution of totem designs were of particular interest to artists, as discussed below.

Some of the objects in Cambridge continue to be directly linked to stories and legends that illustrate characteristics distinctive to each Island and define the relationship between individuals, communities and the physical world. While much of the 'deep' knowledge contained within stories is restricted and only selectively revealed,[18] their overall importance as a means of transmitting knowledge is highly valued (Lawrie 1970). When Ephraim Bani, a noted cultural leader from Mabuiag, first came to the museum in 1995, he saw an elaborate composite turtle-shell mask on display in the main anthropology gallery. The mask, a human face with outstretched hands surmounted on top of a crocodile head, was made by Gizu of Nagir and collected in 1888. Significantly, the story of this mask was never recorded by Haddon. Upon seeing this mask, Bani spontaneously and with great emotion told the story of Uberi Kuberi, a man who was eaten by a crocodile kept as a pet by his daughter. His initial encounter and reaction to the mask were recorded on film.[19] In the exhibition, the sequence of Bani telling the story of Uberi Kuberi was positioned beside the object, a strong reminder of the link between contemporary Islander knowledge and the objects collected by the Expedition.

Stories are related to particular families and places, yet some stories link people and islands. A 'complete' story may be made up of numerous versions, each 'owned' by a different family. A group of dance staffs, which were collected by Haddon at Mer, an Eastern Island, refer to legendary figures believed to have originated from Mabuiag or Western Island stories.[20] Upon seeing these staffs, Bani (from Mabuiag) discussed the imagery with Passi, Noah and Tapim (all from Mer). These flattish wooden staffs, originally carried during dance ceremonies, are distinguished by a carved anthropomorphic head that protrudes above a sinuous painted line. The more elaborate staffs are further decorated with tufts of cassowary feathers with small white feather highlights. Bani explained that the imagery on the staffs alludes to *muri*, small spirits who employ waterspouts as spears for catching turtle and dugong and he told a story about them. Exceptionally, here it was appropriate for someone from the Western Islands to speak about a Meriam object. Generally, Islander visitors to the museum would only talk about objects that are either general to the Torres Strait or specifically associated with their own island community. The distinction between the Eastern and the Western islands is particularly marked, linguistically and ethnographically. When looking at photographs and objects in store, the delegation of elders divided themselves into groups based on family and community affiliations.[21]

For many contemporary Torres Strait artists, historic objects, particularly those collected by Haddon, are an important source of inspiration. Many have closely studied images of these objects reproduced in the *Reports* and Moore's (1984) *Torres Strait Collections of A.C. Haddon*. A more recent source that draws substantially from the collections made by Haddon is Lindsay Wilson's (1988) *Thathilgaw, Emeret Lu: A Handbook of Traditional Torres Strait Islands Material Culture*.[22] Wilson was a skilled artist and illustrator and his book contains detailed line drawings with clear and informative captions. Artists tend to prefer this format, which highlights the clarity of detail and facilitates a better understanding of the construction techniques.

Expressing his excitement at seeing the actual objects at the Cambridge Museum, artist Alick Tipoti said 'these are the designs that inspired me as an artist to produce my lino-cuts. These are the *exact* designs I've looked at in books so many times and thought, *wow*, my forefathers did that!' (pers. com. December 2000). When Tipoti left Horn Island to study art at the TAFE in Cairns,[23] he chose to focus on lino-cut printing, a skill that he further developed when awarded a place at the National Art School in Canberra. Although using different materials and techniques than his ancestors, Tipoti relates the process of print-making to carving and compares the cutting of intricate designs into the lino with the low relief carving found on 'traditional' objects such as bamboo pipes and drums. The patterns and totem marks carried by nineteenth-century objects are elaborated and form imaginative and complex designs, which fill the background and give a dynamic quality to the overall composition. But it is often difficult to discriminate between the apparent subject matter of the prints and the background. In Tipoti's more recent work, significant totemic images may be hidden in the background; they become visible only when the viewer is informed of their existence. As with other ways of encoding knowledge, such as stories expressed orally and through dance, 'deeper' meanings may be concealed and only made visible when deemed appropriate.

Tipoti and other artists such as Dennis Nona and Joseph Dorante also directly incorporate representations of historic materials, including objects and models collected by Haddon, into their work. Masks, drums, sardine scoops, coconut water containers and pearlshell ornaments, as well as characteristic creatures such as dugong, turtle, hammerhead shark and crocodile, are used as symbols of an enduring *Ailan Kastom*. Figures referencing a general heroic past or depicting the legendary exploits of fierce warriors, such as Kwoim, are common subjects.

The first Islander artist to study the Haddon collections directly was Victor McGrath, a noted carver and engraver of marine materials such as pearlshell, turtle-shell and ivory. In 1991 he conducted research at Cambridge and several other British museums in order to analyse the design and construction methods of selected objects. Describing his experience he wrote, 'I have vivid recollections of handling those rare and beautiful treasures, utmost respect for their [often] nameless and faceless creators and privilege in having had an experience denied to so many people back home' (McGrath 1998: 104). McGrath's comments raise the issue of Islander access to historic collections and he notes the difficulty of reproducing 'traditional' objects without frequent reference to 'the outstanding quality of workmanship in the old artefacts' (ibid.). The potential of objects to embody and convey distinctive cultural knowledge is highlighted by a report on the arts environment in the Torres Strait conducted by Mosby on behalf of the Torres Shire Council.[24]

Despite the limitations on the production of 'traditional' art in the Torres Strait, feathered head-dresses (*dharis*), dance objects, personal ornaments and domestic items such as mats and baskets are still being made. Dance is a central feature of *Ailan Kastom* and the movements, costumes and music are the principal forum for artistic creativity. Islanders are great connoisseurs of performances. Dance paraphernalia from Haddon's 1898 collections include hand-held ornaments and story-boards, many of which relate to a detailed knowledge of the movement of the stars, the currents of the sea and the changing seasons. These objects collected a hundred years ago are the precursors of the articulated dance machines, elaborate and distinctive objects held or worn during performances.[25] Ken Thaiday Senior's hammerhead shark masks, Patrick Thaiday and Ken Thaiday Junior's hand-held dance machines are outstanding examples of contemporary creations which intensify the dramatic nature of the choreography while advancing a multi-layered narrative sequence.

Islander artists, often based or trained on the mainland, are producing a wealth of material ranging from the lino-cuts mentioned above to the installations of Ellen José. For many of these artists, historic objects are seen to have the potential of providing a direct link to the past as well as being a source of inspiration for the future. An impressive range of contemporary material set against a smaller number of nineteenth-century pieces was recently brought together for the first major exhibition of Torres Strait art in Australia. Organised by two Islander curators, Tom Mosby and Brian Robinson, *Ilan Pasin (this is our way) Torres Strait Art*, opened at the Cairns Regional Gallery in November 1998 and travelled to numerous venues in Australia before closing in Canberra in February 2001. The ongoing dialogue with Cambridge is apparent – a *dhari* collected by Haddon is featured on the cover of the lavishly produced catalogue[26] and the then chairman of the Torres Strait, John Abednego, acknowledged the co-operation between Cambridge Museum and the Torres Strait in the preface.

Conclusion

Torres Strait Islanders: an exhibition to mark the centenary of the 1898 Anthropological Expedition attempted to emphasise the multiple and shifting contexts of the objects on display. The material collected by Haddon has been entangled in distinct but overlapping narratives for over a century. The objects embody information about Islanders in the late nineteenth century, but they were also agents in the relationships which developed between specific Islanders and the members of the Expedition. Once considered remnants of a 'traditional' past that had all but disappeared, specific objects have remained embedded in Islander knowledge and today are symbolic of a strong resurgent Islander identity.

The museum itself has become a fieldsite – a place for cross-cultural encounter and creative dialogue. A more inclusive and multi-perspectivist approach to material in museum collections is crucial in illuminating the multiple meanings of specific objects as well as the complex processes involved in their production, collection and interpretation. Working with members of source communities provides an opportunity for developing productive relationships and collecting contemporary material for future generations. Yet, one must also acknowledge practical limitations and political constraints. It would be impossible for Cambridge museum staff to work closely at any given time with people from the many Pacific (and other) communities represented by our collections. In this example, our approach was facilitated by numerous factors including: the historical and cultural specificity of the encounter between Expedition members and Islanders, the richness of the collections, the detailed information that was produced and recorded, the generous assistance of numerous Islanders, Philp's doctoral fieldwork, and sabbatical leave for the curator.

The renewed dialogue between Cambridge and the Torres Strait continues. The centenary of the 1898 Anthropological Expedition was just one more stage in the life histories of the objects made and used by Islanders and collected by Haddon. In collaboration with the National Museum of Australia and a Torres Strait Islander reference group, a special exhibition on loan from Cambridge, *Past Time: Torres Strait Islander Material from the Haddon Collection, 1888–1905*, is currently on display at the National Museum in Canberra (2001–2) and will then travel to the Cairns Regional Gallery (2002). Further meanings will be illuminated when these objects are made more accessible to Islanders and a broader Australian audience.

Acknowledgements

My main thanks go to the many Islanders who generously shared their time and knowledge with me, in particular Ephraim Bani, Mary Bani, Leilani Bin-Juda, Ron Day, Florence Kennedy, Victor McGrath, Goby Noah, David Passi, Frances Tapim, Alick Tipoti and Terrence Whap. I am also grateful to Jude Philp, who has been an invaluable collaborator. Support for background research and the production of the exhibition was provided by the British Academy, the Crowther-Beynon Fund and Smuts Memorial Fund (University of Cambridge). Support for Islanders to conduct research in Cambridge was provided by the National Museum of Australia, the Australian Arts Council, Winston Churchill Memorial Trust Fellowship grant, Crowther-Beynon Fund (University of Cambridge) and the Torres Strait Regional Authority.

Notes

This paper is a slightly abbreviated and revised version of an article by the same name in A. Herle, N. Stanley, K. Stevenson, R. Welsch (eds) (2002) *Pacific Art: Persistence, Change and Meaning*. Hindmarsh: Crawford House Press (pp. 231–49).

1 Personal communication with Alick Tipoti, a Torres Strait Islander artist from Badu and Horn Island, Cambridge University Museum of Archaeology and Anthropology, December 2000.

2 Elder Bishop Passi from Mer commenting on the exhibition of material from the Haddon collection at the National Museum of Australia (Philp 2001: viii). Passi is the grandson of one of Haddon's main assistants and he came as part of a delegation to Cambridge in 1999 to help select Torres Strait material for the exhibition in Australia.

3 Numerous writers have looked at the social life of things following on from Appadurai (1986).

4 *Torres Strait Islanders: An Exhibition to Mark the Centenary of the 1898 Cambridge Anthropological Expedition to the Torres Strait* was at the University of Cambridge Museum of Archaeology and Anthropology from 1 July 1998 to 2 December 2000.

5 The Murray Island Land Case, commonly known as the 'Mabo Case' after one of the plaintiffs, overturned 200 years of *terra nullius* and marked the first time that the

Australian Government recognised the prior ownership of land by an indigenous group. Information from the *Reports*, in particular Rivers' genealogies, provided crucial evidence.

6　My interest here in an object's agency is somewhat over-determined in that Islanders often refer to the animate power of particular things. For example, inappropriate contact with certain objects is potentially dangerous.

7　The significance of the Expedition's work has been discussed in disciplinary histories (Herle and Rouse 1998; Kuklick 1991; Stocking 1983, 1995; Urry 1993). The Expedition is primarily credited for its methodological innovations: the integration of field research with scholarly interpretation, Rivers' development of the 'genealogical method', and the use of film and photography.

8　See Cooper (1989) for an overview of the locations of Islander collections. The majority of the Torres Strait material collected by Haddon in 1888 is housed in the British Museum (Moore 1984).

9　Maino's father was described as 'Kabagi' in Haddon's unpublished journal (1888–9: xx).

10　Kebisu's great grandson, Mr Arther Kebisu, retains one of his clubs, gaba-gaba (Mosby and Robinson 1998: 33).

11　Cf. Letter from Bruce to Haddon, 26 December 1902, Haddon Papers Envelope 1004. Letter from Ned Waria to Haddon 21 July 1904, Haddon Papers, Envelope 3012.

12　Mary Bani came to Cambridge for three months and used the museum as a base to compile information about Torres Strait collections in Cambridge, in numerous museums throughout the UK, and in Dublin and Berlin.

13　*Kastom* is defined as 'the body of customs, traditions, observances and beliefs of some or all of the Torres Strait Islanders living in the Torres Strait area, and includes any such customs, traditions, observances and beliefs relating to particular persons, areas, objects or relationships' (Aboriginal and Torres Strait Islander Commission Act 1989).

14　Haddon states that the original masks had been burnt, presumably by zealous missionaries (Haddon 1898–99: 204). Local oral tradition asserts that Malo had been burnt but that Bomai was buried at the village of Las on Mer. For a more detailed discussion on the creation of the masks and the re-enactment of the Malo-Bomai ceremony, see Herle (1998: 77–105).

15　Despite Haddon's emphasis recording and preserving past practices, Philp (1998b) has convincingly argued that the *Reports* tell us more about what was happening in the present. See also Beckett (1998).

16　Abednego presented the museum with a framed photograph of the 20 recently elected representatives of the TSRA, and this was incorporated into the final section of the exhibition.

17　These men are well aware of the political significance of Rivers' genealogies; David Passi was one of the plaintiffs in the Murray Island land case.

18　Haddon's concern that the young men no longer know the old ways and hence his emphasis on salvage ethnography may have been exaggerated by his lack of awareness of how significant cultural knowledge was transmitted. Younger people often declined, as they continue to do today, to speak about things that are the domain of specific elders or inappropriate to reveal to outsiders. The suppression of 'traditional' beliefs and practices by missionaries and colonial officials would have reinforced Islanders' reluctance to speak about certain issues.

19 Ephraim Bani first came to the museum with Francis Calvert as the protagonist in her film *Cracks in the Mask*. The film focused on Ephraim's reactions to various museum collections in the UK and Europe, and thus Ephraim's activities in the museum were recorded.

20 Meriam legends and cults were noted for their tendency to borrow elements from elsewhere and re-interpret them (Beckett 1998: 40).

21 There are two main language groups in the Torres Strait: Meriam Mir, the language of the people of the Eastern islands and Kala Lagaw Ya, the language of the Western, Northern and Central islands (the latter with mutually intelligible regional dialects). *The Reports* (Vol. 5) *Sociology, Magic and Religion of the Western Islanders* (1904) and *The Reports* (Vol. 6) *Sociology, Magic and Religion of the Eastern Islanders* (1908) were based on research primarily conducted on Mabuiag and Mer respectively.

22 Published by the Department of Education in Queensland to coincide with the Australian bicentenary and the centenary of Haddon's first expedition to the Torres Strait.

23 A Visual Arts Course began in 1984 the Faculty of Aboriginal and Torres Strait Islander Studies at the TAFE in Cairns. A unique style of Torres Strait Islander art has developed within the Printmaking Department under the direction of Anna Eglitis. Islander printmakers have included Annie Gela, Dennis Nona, Brian Robinson and Alick Tipoti (Eglitis 1998: 135–41).

24 There is a growing interest, supported by the TSRA, in establishing a cultural centre with appropriate facilities to care for historic as well as contemporary material.

25 In the exhibition a large section on dance includes video sequences showing a variety of dances from the 1993 Cultural Festival on Thursday Island, which are intended to animate the objects on display and incorporate contemporary manifestations of a distinct cultural form.

26 There are several levels of symbolism at work here: the *dhari* has become the symbol of the unity of the Torres Strait, but this particular *dhari* has also become the symbol of the Haddon collection, appearing on the cover of the comprehensive illustrated catalogue, *The Torres Strait Collections of A.C. Haddon* (Moore 1984). Its placement on the cover reinforces the continuity between past and present and acknowledges the links between the Torres Strait and Cambridge. On another level it may be interpreted as either an act of re-appropriation or a demonstration that some objects in museum collections may never be fully alienated from their original cultural owners.

References

Appadurai, A. (ed.) (1986) *The Social Life of Things: commodities in cultural perspective*, Cambridge: Cambridge University Press.

Bani, M. and Herle, A. (1998) 'Collaborative projects on Torres Strait collections', *Journal of Museum Ethnography*, 10: 115–20.

Beckett, J. (1998) 'Haddon attends a funeral: fieldwork in Torres Strait, 1888, 1898', in A. Herle and S. Rouse (eds), *Cambridge and the Torres Strait: centenary essays on the 1898 anthropological expedition*, Cambridge: Cambridge University Press.

Clifford, J. (1997) 'Museums as contact zones', in J. Clifford, *Routes: travel and translation in the late twentieth century*, Cambridge, Mass.: Harvard University Press.

Cooper, C. (1989) *Aboriginal and Torres Strait Islander Collections in Overseas Museums*, Canberra: Aboriginal Studies Press.

Edwards, E. (1998) 'Performing science: still photography and the Torres Strait Expedition', in A. Herle and S. Rouse (eds), *Cambridge and the Torres Strait: centenary essays on the 1898 anthropological expedition*, Cambridge: Cambridge University Press.

Eglitis, A. (1998) 'A new art from the Torres Strait', in T. Mosby and B. Robinson (eds), *Ilan Pasin (this is our way) Torres Strait art*, Cairns: Cairns Regional Gallery.

Gell, A. (1998) *Art and Agency: an anthropological theory*, Oxford: Clarendon Press.

Haddon, A. C. (1901) *Head-Hunters: black, white and brown*, London: Methuen.

Herle, A. (1998) 'The life-histories of objects: collections of the Cambridge Anthropological Expedition to the Torres Strait', in A. Herle and S. Rouse (eds), *Cambridge and the Torres Strait: centenary essays on the 1898 anthropological expedition*, Cambridge: Cambridge University Press.

Herle, A. and Rouse, S. (eds) (1998) *Cambridge and the Torres Strait: centenary essays on the 1898 anthropological expedition*, Cambridge: Cambridge University Press.

Kuklick, H. (1991) *The Savage Within: the social history of British social anthropology 1885–1945*, Cambridge: Cambridge University Press.

Lawrie, M. (1970) *Myths and Legends of the Torres Strait*, Brisbane: Queensland University Press.

McGrath, V. (1998) 'Contemporary Torres Strait Arts', in T. Mosby and B. Robinson (eds), *Ilan Pasin (this is our way) Torres Strait Art*, Cairns: Cairns Regional Gallery.

Moore, D. (1984) *The Torres Strait Collections of A. C. Haddon: a descriptive catalogue*, London: British Museum Press.

Mosby, T. and Robinson, B. (eds) (1998) *Ilan Pasin (this is our way) Torres Strait Art*, Cairns: Cairns Regional Gallery.

Philp, J. (1998a) 'Owning artefacts and owning knowledge: Torres Straits Island material culture', *Cambridge Anthropology*, 20 (1–2): 7–15.

—— (1998b) 'Resonance: Torres Strait Islander material culture and history', unpublished PhD thesis, University of Cambridge.

—— (2001) *Past Time: Torres Strait Islander Material from the Haddon Collection, 1888–1905: a National Museum of Australia exhibition from the University of Cambridge*, Canberra: National Museum of Australia.

Stocking, G. W., Jr. (ed.) (1983) *Observers Observed: essays on ethnographic fieldwork*, Madison: University of Wisconsin Press.

—— (1995) *After Tylor: British social anthropology, 1888–1951*, Madison: University of Wisconsin Press.

Thomas, N. (2000) 'Islands of history: reflections on two exhibitions of Torres Strait Islander culture', *ART Asia Pacific* 28: 70–7.

Urry, J. (1993) *Before Social Anthropology: essays on the history of British anthropology*, Chur: Harwood Academic Publishers.

Wilson, L. (1988) *Thathilgaw, Emeret Lu: a handbook of traditional Torres Strait Islands material culture*, Brisbane: Queensland Department of Education.

Chapter 28

Resonant materiality and violent remembering

Archaeology, memory and bombing

Gabriel Moshenska

RUIN AND FRAGMENTATION HAVE BEEN AMONGST the most powerful and pervasive cultural themes in Western society from at least the Romantic period onwards, serving as allegories, analogies and metaphors for a wide range of social, cultural and natural processes.[1] In this paper I use ruins and fragments as organising concepts to explore the connections between my principal research interests: archaeology, memory, and bombing; specifically the commemorative potential of an archaeology of bombsites.

The aerial bombardment of civilian populations is one of the most powerful, iconic and despicable innovations of the recent past. Bombing has played a central role in shaping the nature of warfare for almost a century, from the first bombs dropped by Italian aircraft on Libya in 1911 to the annihilation of Hamburg and Tokyo and the 'smart bombs' of modern high-tech warfare.[2] My interest in bombing is primarily an archaeological one, studying bombsites, air-raid shelters, and crashed aircraft, as well as the more portable material culture or ephemera of civilian life in wartime. The historical archaeology of these sites and materials leads inevitably to encounters with first-hand memories of the war on the Home Front.

Aside from its revolutionary influence in the conduct of warfare, bombing has also had an extraordinary impact on modern culture; the horror of death from the air and the gothic desolation of bombsites have influenced artists and writers including Picasso, Henry Moore and Virginia Woolf. The devastation of aerial bombing featured in science fiction and dystopian visions of the future from as early as 1670. In the 1930s the impersonal destructive potential of the aircraft became a powerful symbol of the dehumanisation of technology in the works of Lewis Mumford, Rex Warner and others.[3]

Further reading in and around my three fields of research has left me entangled in a web of symbolism and wordplay that links archaeology, memory and bombing in rich and often unexpected ways. The roots of these metaphorical strands lie in the ambiguities and opaque language of memory theory, the powerful trope of archaeology both as practice and material record, and the struggle to comprehend and describe the devastation of bombed cities. The risks of over-interpretation of apparently trivial figures of speech have been highlighted by Holtorf, but as a technique for demarcating a field of interest and potential value I will argue it can at least have a limited use.[4] Moreover, it is worth exploring the possibility that analogies and metaphors might have a discursive as well as a descriptive role. This paper is an attempt to explore the points of correspondence, opposition and friction between my three fields, highlighting themes, particularly ruin and fragmentation, that might lead to a clearer understanding of the strengths and potential outcomes of an archaeology of bombing. In examining these themes I have asked the question: in what ways might an archaeology of bombing become an archaeology of the *memory* of bombing?

Archaeology/memory – into the depths

> People believe that a deep underlying 'essence', an unchanging reality from the past, exists underneath the sedimented layers of history. But as they dig, the past becomes a ghostlike presence.[5]

The use of archaeological metaphors for memory and other functions of the mind is a familiar one, most notably in the works of Freud and Walter Benjamin. The latter outlined his somewhat belaboured analogy in his very short essay 'Excavation and Memory'. Benjamin argues that memory

> is the medium of that which is experienced, just as the earth is the medium in which ancient cities lie buried. He who seeks to approach his own buried past must conduct himself like a man digging. Above all, he must not be afraid to return again and again to the same matter: to scatter it as one scatters earth, to turn it over as one turns over soil.[6]

There are two key elements here: the memory/earth analogy, passive and natural, and the 'emblematic description of the rememberer as archaeologist', active and purposeful. Wallace traces Benjamin's model further, attempting to link the reshaping of memory by the subconscious to taphonomic processes in the archaeological record.[7] However, compared to Benjamin's image of the excavator Wallace's passive, naturalistic analogy has more in common with Freud's archaeologies of the mind.

Freud's repeated use of archaeological analogies in his writings is striking. Kuspit has suggested that this was partly a cynical pitch aimed at the public, associating the unpopular practice of psychoanalysis with the highly popular one of archaeology.[8] Ruins are an image that Freud exploits in several cases, most notably his comparison of the subconscious to catacombs in a ruined city. However, this comparison is not so successful: the processes of entropy at work in physical structures are the antithesis of Freud's notion of burial, in which objects and memories survive, concealed but complete:

> Freud's example of the city of Rome highlights the limits of archaeological analogy for the mind, for the city has crumbled and decayed over time whereas painful memories do not . . . 'only in such rare circumstances as those of Pompeii', Freud wrote, could the direct analogy be made between the 'psychical object' and the 'archaeological object'.[9]

Clearly human agency in the forms of preservation and restoration affects the uses of ruins as sites of memory. Ruined buildings and cities are a powerful source of imagery and metaphor in themselves, as the sections on bombing will demonstrate. But we need not dig for ruins; they confront us. In the Dora case Freud compared himself to a 'conscientious archaeologist', giving his cautious but informed interpretation of the fragments of memories. The idea of fragmentation or atomisation of memory, both individual and collective, is an important link between my diverse fields of interest: 'The fragmentary nature of the archaeological find becomes a metaphor for the real content of memory.'[10] Similarly, the metaphor of burial used by Benjamin is better served by Freud:

> Like the archaeologist, the analyst also relies upon the fact that his patient has actively repressed or buried particular memories so that they have been preserved and can be later studied . . . All of the essentials are preserved, even things that seem completely forgotten are present somehow and somewhere, and have merely been buried and made inaccessible to the subject.[11]

But for Freud burial is not an inevitable effect of nature, and here as elsewhere the analogy begins to break down. The concept of 'resistance', a crucial aspect of Freud's theories, represents an active unwillingness to remember, and operates through the distortion or evasion of memories. Resistance must be actively maintained over time, and Freud compares this to the building up of layers of stratigraphy above archaeological remains.

What are the key themes in the metaphors and analogies of memory and archaeology? The performativity of the archaeological process and the physicality of its findings provide dynamic and material terms for abstract and invisible processes of memory, a 'roadmap of melancholy and mourning'.[12] In the works of W. G. Sebald, Remmler identifies 'an archaeology of remembering that relies heavily on spatial metaphors and the experience of place [in which] texts enact cultural memory through the metaphorical excavation of sites of destruction, disaster, and atrocity'.[13] Implicit in this uncanny imagery of destruction, disturbance and penetration is the idea of remembering as a dangerous and potentially damaging process. All of these elements must be taken into account: the popular perception of connections between archaeology and memory, digging and remembering appear to have become a popular mythology; perhaps they always have been. The archaeological process can be a process of remembering, and potentially of forgetting.

Archaeology/bombing – vertical aggression

Archaeology and war have an enduring and ambiguous relationship – both create in the very act of destroying.[14]

In comparison to memory, bombing is not normally linked with archaeology but I believe that there are equally interesting points of connection and contrast. Again the most important themes in this relationship are ruins and fragmentation, and I will outline some of the particular complexities of these themes in this comparison. In this context the Allied bombing of Pompeii in 1943 acquires a darkly humorous element, raining destruction down on the hitherto un-ruined ruins of Freud's model of memory.[15]

The comparison of the ruins of a bombed city with archaeological remains is an obvious one, based on physical appearance but with deeper connotations of epic struggle, fallen empires and dead civilisations. The need to familiarise or contextualise the trauma of devastation is another powerful source for this analogy. The author W. G. Sebald examined the phenomenon of bombing in great depth in his extraordinary work *On the Natural History of Destruction*, in which he considers the human face of the bombing war in Germany, the physical destruction, and what he perceived to be the inadequate cultural response. Archaeological imagery is a central theme in Sebald's analysis of bombing and of memory, as recognised by Remmler:

> Sebald's writing employs archival and archaeological methodologies for remembering atrocity and other forms of destruction by human hand that is bound to an allegorical poetics of remembrance, even as it demands a turn towards a visceral and material engagement with sites and objects of memory.[16]

To Sebald, 'The empty facades of Hamburg look like triumphal arches, Roman ruins, or stage sets for some fantastic opera'. But what about the future trajectory of these ruins, these 'bits of buildings, cornices of churches, shattered pediments'? Sebald suggests that if, as was briefly considered by the allies, post-war Germany had been reduced to a purely agrarian economy, the ruins of the cities might soon have been covered by grass and woodland, leaving only lumps and bumps in the rolling landscape.[17] This never came to pass: the rubble was cleared and the cities were rebuilt over the ruins. In an extraordinary image of this process, taken from Peter de Mendelssohn's *Die Kathedrale*, Sebald describes the protagonist

> putting to sea in one of the great barges used to clear the ruins; as the rubble sinks into the depths, he sees the whole city down on the sea bed, complete and undamaged, another Atlantis. 'All that was destroyed above is intact down here, and everything that is left standing up above, in particular the cathedral, is not present down here'.[18]

This raises another curious analogy in bombing and archaeology: the contrasting views from above and below, 'the up–down division [which] is one of the central metaphors we live by'.[19] The archaeologist's view of a bombsite, on a human scale that highlights fragmented remains of domestic life, contrasts with the bombardier's view: '"I didn't see much of the city at all as I recall", says a British airman who participated in the raids over Dresden'.[20] This difference in perspective has important connections with memory work, although it should be noted that both the archaeologist and the bombardier destroy that which is the focus of their efforts.

The process of reconstruction in bombed cities is also a process of forgetting. Sebald laments this eliding of memory, even as he raises the idea that bombsites might become the archaeology of the future. In the present the burial of bombed ruins, their transformation into archaeological sites, is the antithesis of the grand, almost classical remains on the surface:

> The rebuilt cities leave few traces of their previous destruction, even as practiced archaeologists would have a heyday in uncovering the many-layered remnants, the bones and the artifacts, forgotten or bulldozed into the ground. It is the remnants in plain sight that interest Sebald's narrators, just as archaeological metaphors inscribe the work of memory.[21]

The fragmented remains of bombed homes and cities will inevitably be salvaged – for materials by the forces of reconstruction, for meaning by the poets and artists stalking the rubble, and for patterns and order by the archaeologists: 'The project of salvage means the cataloguing of specificity'.[22] In contrast to the chaos and violence of bombing, the archaeologists uniquely bring order to the bombsites: even as the bombing of London revealed some of its greatest archaeological treasures, the archaeologists' work preceded and heralded the work of reconstruction. Rose Macauley described the process: 'Excavators had begun their tentative work, uncovering foundations, seeking the Middle Ages, the Dark Ages, Londinium, Rome . . . a civilised intelligence was at work among the ruins'.[23]

But for some the impact of archaeology on ruins is a negative one, applying 'civilised' order where none ought to be, removing the innate aesthetic qualities of the ruins, their romance. Woodward regards the archaeologists' work on spectacular ruins, in restoration and conservation, as a battle against the forces of nature. In doing so he raises the important issue of perspective: today's ruins, symbols of violence, dispossession and death, will be the delightfully melancholy and evocative beauty spots to inspire future generations of poets and artists, 'the butchered families and their burnt homes . . . mulched into a soil of delirious fertility'. After all, he argues, in the early modern period 'the ruins of the eight hundred medieval abbeys which had been seized, plundered and sold by Henry VIII . . . seemed as raw, bare and painfully explicable as bomb sites are to the modern age'.[24] An archaeology of remembering must acknowledge the necessity of forgetting.

Bombing/memory – trauma, wounding and resistance

> New ruins are for a time stark and bare, vegetationless and creatureless; blackened and torn, they smell of fire and mortality.[25]

Within the broad and diverse field of memory studies, memories of violent conflict feature prominently: 'Work on the memory of war has lain at the heart of the broader memory project'.[26] Bombing is by far the most common manifestation or experience of war for the civilian populations of twentieth-century Europe. Historian Horst Boog argues that 'Whenever Germans think of the Second World War, they mostly think of the bombing war, because it affected them directly and left an enduring impression on their minds'.[27]

Here again the crucial metaphor is the up/down, above/below dichotomy, which connects bombing and memory twice over; both in the physical relationship of the bombers above and the people below, and in the disparities between history-from-above and history-from-below. Compared to Portelli's airman who 'didn't see much' of Dresden, 'those who, like rats, await their fate in the hole of the air-raid shelter, see nothing of the majesty of war – if there is such a thing. Anguished waiting is their lot'.[28]

The idea of bombing as an irresistible force lasted far longer than the reality; nevertheless Stanley Baldwin's warning that 'the bomber will always get through' struck a chord with many.[29] The idea of bombers as inhuman, even godlike in their power is a common theme in memories of war: 'There is a fatalistic perception of the war as destiny, of the bombs as a "bolt" from above, unleashed by an invisible hand'.[30] However, Jörg Friedrich's claim that 'the Allies could feel like the gods, who hurl lightning bolts at the vileness of the enemy' belies the appalling losses suffered by the Allied air-forces.[31] The air-crew's view was somewhat different: Richard Hillary compared fighter pilots like himself to duellists, but suggested that bomber crews were merely satisfying a childish urge to smash things.[32]

This contrast of gods and humans in bombing emerges from the same powerful above/below metaphor. Portelli makes a powerful argument that this metaphor transcends the immediate experience of bombing, drawing in themes of science, rationality and history:

> The top down, outside, emic view from above possesses a *superior* (literally, higher) *power* to perceive the global context, the general picture. The bird's eye or bomber's radar view of the world sees farther, and retains the wholesome detachment, the capacity for abstraction, the rational ability to concentrate on the *objective* and the relevant (the target) and dismiss the irrelevant . . . On the other hand, the lower, (literally, *inferior*) point of view is narrowly focused, irretrievably bound to the detail, to the concrete – shall we say, down-to-earth, grassroots – immediacy of material experience, and is inevitably twisted into and limited by the personal, emotional identification and involvement.[33]

Memory-based work is best placed to provide a link between these two histories of bombing: the official history-from-above of bombing surveys, hectares burnt, dead numbered in thousands, and the history-from-below of the 'I was there' experience.

Another curious feature of bombing and memory is the use of terminology of wounding and injury as a metaphor for bombing and destruction; the city or its population as a human body or 'body politic' is itself a common enough analogy. The physicality and visibility of these wounds presupposes a process of healing in which they will disappear; presumably as the visible symbols of traumatic memory vanish the memories fade too. In contrast, bombsites and destroyed cities that are deliberately left as ruins are often used as memorials, as symbols of a refusal to forget. Examples of this include bombed churches in London and Portsmouth, and the town of Oradour-sur-Glane in France.[34] In societies where ruins are so readily accepted as symbols of traumatic memory, archaeological work will inevitably be regarded as reopening old wounds. As Holtorf observes, the archaeologist who explores beneath the ground is an ambivalent figure: 'revealing secret truths undoes the status quo and causes change'.[35] In some cases reconstruction rather than redevelopment of bombed sites has been used to promote amnesia and forgiveness; the most famous recent example being the Frauenkirche in Dresden rebuilt with funds partly donated from Britain and America.[36]

Bombed buildings are clearly a potent physical metaphor for memory. The themes of ruin and ruins are powerful ones; ruins preserved, hidden, or rebuilt are never without meaning and intent as wounds to be flaunted, healed or left to become scars. Equally, the process of bombing provides an analogy for its own histories from above and below. The memory of the people on the ground is a history-from-below; the narratives of war written by the victors take a top-down view in every sense. The power of this metaphor forcefully outlined by Portelli cannot be underestimated, as it includes a call to action: the memories of the bombarded people must become part of the historical discourse.

An archaeology of the memory of bombing?

I have argued that the archaeological process is closely linked to memory and remembering; that the relationship between archaeology and bombing is one of tension and contradiction; and that an archaeology of bombing will be a difficult and painful process. But can it be a productive one? As I asked at the start: what might an archaeology of bombing tell us about the memory of bombing? Moeller has argued for a history of bombing that puts memory at its core: 'a history of the bombing war . . . in which all the dead have names and faces, might get us closer to the multiple meanings of the war'.[37] To return to Portelli's argument, a history of bombing must include these names, faces and memories if it is to become anything other than a top-down, bombardier's-eye view of events. For Portelli the mechanism for bridging official history and personal experience is oral history:

> Oral history, in essence, is an attempt to reconnect the local, native point of view from below and the global, scientific point of view from above: to contextualise the local, and to enable the global to recognise it. Oral history, then, brings history from above and history from below into the same text – as it were, to the negotiating table – creating an equal dialogue between the historians' awareness of broad spatial and temporal patterns, and the local narrator's closely focused personal narrative.[38]

This impassioned plea is rooted in the awareness that an inability to view bombing from the viewpoint of the bombarded makes its future use easier; Portelli cites examples drawn from the NATO bombing of Yugoslavia as well as Allied and German bombings of Italy during the Second World War. He concludes that 'our capacity to see the whole world depends on seeing single, small details like that . . . if only we could see them'.[39] Which brings us back to the archaeology.

As Mellor has noted, the violence of bombing has the power to render metaphors into brutal truisms. What can this discussion of archaeology, memory and bombing contribute to the study of real conflicts and the real lives they transform and destroy? I believe the answer lies in the fragments of everyday life destroyed by bombing, the fragmented memory of bombing, and the capacity of archaeological work to salvage and interpret both of these. The power of objects and places from the past to evoke memory in the present has been described as resonance: 'Resonance is understood as the power to be heard, to be seen, to be felt, and to be responded to through the existence of a physical marker or an evocation of place'.[40] This highlights the rhetorical power of material things and their use in literary symbolism: Mellor describes how Eliot's *The Waste Land*

> stacks up broken and resonantly jumbled material stuff. In this Eliot seems to have typified how swathes of first-wave modernism had a yearning for locating in the urban landscape violently disordered debris – and then for attempting the extraction of meaning from it.[41]

The power of an archaeological incursion into memory work is the ability to make its very literal intervention into this resonant debris a spectacular and performative one.

Bombsite archaeology in practice

A bombsite is a ruin amidst fragments. While a ruined building can stand as a memorial, the clearing of fragmented remains from the structure is a finite process of commemoration. This distinction is clearest if we compare the preservation of bombsites as heritage sites, with the excavation of bombsites as sites of lived memory. Schofield estimates that 'in England some 20–30 buildings damaged in the Blitz, and otherwise during the Second World War, now stand as ruins . . . amounting on average to less than one bomb site per major targeted city'.[42] In his analysis Schofield notes the rarity of these structures, and their unique role in commemorating the civilian casualties of war on a local scale, as arguments for their preservation and continued protection.

In contrast to their stated importance, excavations of bombsites as bombsites rather than as sites for development are extremely rare: it is worth considering a short case study. The Museum of London's Shoreditch Park community archaeology project in Hackney, East London in 2005 aimed to recover the remains of bombed houses and their contents; the importance of community involvement and memory work were recognised by the organisers from the very beginning. The excavation focused on a row of four terraced houses from an area that was heavily bombed both during the Blitz and during the later V weapon campaigns. The foundations of the houses were revealed, as well as the remains of concrete garden paths and outside toilets. A quantity of domestic material culture dating from the Victorian period to the 1940s was also discovered, including sewing equipment and children's toys. In the three weeks of the dig more than 4000 local people visited the site, including hundreds who helped out with the excavation itself. In addition, more than 20 people who had lived on or near the site during the war took part in an oral history project based around the excavation and using the artefacts recovered from it. Towards the end of the project a multi-faith service of remembrance was held at the site in memory of those killed in the Blitz. For the few weeks before the site was back-filled and the area restored, the bombsite served as a focus for commemoration in different ways and on a number of levels: individuals, families, local communities and faith communities. By design and by circumstance the dig became a site of memory.[43]

From the relatively comfortable and often triumphalist memory of the Second World War in Britain it is worth examining the very different memory of conflict in Germany, and the potential cultural and mnemonic impacts of an archaeology of bombing. In the last few years the memory of the bombing of German towns has been taken up by historians, journalists and writers across the political spectrum. Foreign visitors have noted a popular willingness and eagerness to discuss the bombing, encouraged in part by parallel discourses in Britain and elsewhere around the ethics of the bombing campaign.[44] The prophet of German memory of bombing was W. G. Sebald: too young to remember the war, Sebald grew up in a country laid to waste by bombs, where the physical evidence of bombing was constantly visible, and yet the events themselves were passed over in silence:

> the sense of unparalleled national humiliation felt by millions in the last years of the war had never really found verbal expression, and those directly affected by the experience neither shared it with each other nor passed it on to the next generation.[45]

This pattern of unspoken trauma together with an absence of shared narratives of the past has been characterised as atomised memory or 'fragmented memories'. Sebald (who notably ignores the works of Günter Grass) highlighted in particular the failure of German writers to produce works that reflected the wartime and immediate postwar experiences of Germans: he regarded this absence of a literature of bombing as a 'scandalous deficiency'. He was equally scathing of the self-imposed silence of German historians on the subject of bombing, although he singled out for praise the military historian Jörg Friedrich's early work on the Allied bombing strategies, noting that 'his remarks have not aroused anything like the interest they deserve'.[46]

Between Sebald's untimely death in 2001 and the present, the public discourses of bombing and memory in Germany have changed beyond recognition. Indeed, the response to his book on bombing, published in German in 1999, is regarded as one of the triggers. Moeller observed that 'In remarkable ways, for the last five years, Germans have been fighting the war all over again'. Together with Sebald's book and Grass' *Crabwalk*, the spark that ignited this extraordinary national discussion was the serialisation and publication of Jörg Friedrich's *Der Brand: Deutschland im Bombenkrieg*

1940–1945.[47] Moeller argues that Friedrich's achievement is his description of 'the face of mass death':

> Suffering that is cordoned off in accounts that detail the 'balance of destruction' in cubic meters of rubble and totals of lives lost, houses destroyed, and people displaced, or even the photographs of moon landscapes of bombed out cities, can only begin to convey a sense of the consequences for those who lived their lives between bomb shelters and bombed-out residential areas and for whom sirens, blackouts, uncertainty, death and fear became part of a daily routine.[48]

In this respect, Friedrich's writings answer Portelli's call for a history-from-below of bombing, focused on the physical and emotional experiences of those on the ground. But Friedrich's work does not draw extensively on memory; rather, he trumpets its absence, and his history-from-below remains a curiously impersonal one. Schulze notes that even 60 years on 'victims of the Allied air raids on German towns still feel the need to have their voices heard'.[49]

Urban rescue archaeology in German cities frequently encounters the remains of the bombing war: rubble, ruins and occasionally unexploded bombs. The possibility of creating a public or community archaeology of bombsites in these circumstances is challenging, but if the pattern observed in the British example above can be replicated even in part the effects could be remarkable, and the archaeology of bombing could become an element in the wider debates. In these circumstances an archaeology of the memory of bombing could be of value as an arena for debate and discussion on several levels including the academic, political and local.

Conclusion

Archaeologists do not dig grand narratives; we will never unearth the strategy of area bombing or the moral debates that surrounded it then and now. The most useful thing we can offer is the immediacy of small views of everyday life annihilated by bombing; the debris of individuals, their homes and their possessions. Most importantly these fragments and ruins are located in modern towns and cities in the present: more than any 'then and now' photographs, this brutal juxtaposition detaches the suffering and death from dominant narratives of memory and locates it firmly in the local, detailed and specific, as Portelli demands. An archaeology of bombsites contributes to those smaller scale, local narratives of war in which the dead have names and faces. I have no doubt that the archaeology of bombsites will remain troubling and deeply controversial, both in its practice and in its findings.

Many of the themes, tropes and metaphors that I have examined in the course of this study have shown themselves to be representative of the real processes of memory around bombsites, sites of bombing and their archaeologies. These powerful and essential themes include digging as remembering, the bonds between ruins and fragments of landscapes and memories, and the resisting memories and archaeologies from below versus histories from above. I have suggested an arena in which they could most fruitfully be explored; it remains to be seen whether they can make a substantial contribution. If nothing else, the pitiful shards of shattered domesticity should be an abject and resonant presence in the modern world; their excavation a challenging and discordant practice.

Notes

1   Thomas, 'Assembling History', 177–178.
2   Fletcher, 'The Hammering of Society', 308; Lindqvist, *A History of Bombing*.
3   Beer, 'The Island and the Aeroplane'; Mellor, 'Words from the Bombsites'; Saint-Amour, 'Air War Prophecy and Interwar Modernism'; Warner, *The Aerodrome: A Love Story*.
4   Holtorf, *From Stonehenge to Las Vegas*.
5   Till, *The New Berlin*, 10.
6   Benjamin, 'Excavation and Memory', 576.
7   Wallace, *Digging the Dirt*, 15.
8   Kuspit, 'A Mighty Metaphor', 133.
9   Ibid., 137; Wallace, *Digging the Dirt*, 95.
10 Remmler, 'On the Natural History of Destruction', 45.
11 Wallace, *Digging the Dirt*, 94–95.
12 Prager, 'Air War and Allegory', 37.
13 Remmler, 'On the Natural History of Destruction', 60.
14 Saunders, 'Excavating Memories', 101.
15 Descoeudres, *Pompeii Revisited*.
16 Remmler, 'On the Natural History of Destruction', 59
17 Sebald, *On the Natural History of Destruction*, 41–43; Mellor, 'Words from the Bombsites'.
18 Sebald, *On the Natural History of Destruction*, 56.
19 Holtorf, *From Stonehenge to Las Vegas*, 16.
20 Portelli, 'So Much Depends on a Red Bus', 30.
21 Remmler, 'On the Natural History of Destruction', 52.
22 Mellor, 'Words from the Bombsites', 89–90.
23 Ibid., 86.
24 Woodward, *In Ruins*, 81, 97.
25 Macauley, *Pleasure of Ruins*, 453.
26 Finney, 'On Memory, Identity and War', 5.
27 In Moeller, 'On the History of Man-made Destruction', 128.
28 Lindqvist, *A History of Bombing*, 172.
29 Grayling, *Among the Dead Cities*, 148.
30 Portelli, 'So Much Depends on a Red Bus', 36.
31 In Moeller, 'On the History of Man-made Destruction', 124.
32 Hillary, *The Last Enemy*.
33 Portelli, 'So Much Depends on a Red Bus', 30.
34 Baker, 'Archaeology, Habermas and the Pathologies of Modernity'; Schofield, 'Monuments and Memories of War'; Stone, 'A Memory in Ruins?'; Uzzell, 'The Hot Interpretation of War and Conflict'.
35 Holtorf, *From Stonehenge to Las Vegas*, 50.

36 James, 'Undoing Trauma'.
37 Moeller, 'On the History of Man-made Destruction', 125.
38 Portelli, 'So Much Depends on a Red Bus', 30.
39 Ibid., 41.
40 Greenblatt quoted in Remmler, 'On the Natural History of Destruction', 43.
41 Mellor, 'Words from the Bombsites', 77.
42 Schofield, 'Monuments and Memories of War', 151.
43 Blair et al, 'The Archaeology of the Blitz'; Moshenska, 'Oral History in Historical Archaeology'.
44 Confino, 'Telling about Germany'; Grayling, *Among the Dead Cities.*
45 Sebald, *On the Natural History of Destruction*, viii.
46 Ibid., 70; Schulze, 'Review Article: Memory in German History', 637.
47 Nolan, 'Germans as Victims During the Second World War', 10.
48 Moeller, 'On the History of Man-made Destruction', 109.
49 Schulze, 'Review Article: Memory in German History', 647.

References

Baker, F. 'Archaeology, Habermas and the Pathologies of Modernity'. In *Writing the Past in the Present*, edited by F. Baker and J. Thomas, 54–62. Lampeter: St David's University College, 1990.

Beer, G. 'The Island and the Aeroplane: The Case of Virginia Woolf'. In *Nation and Narration*, edited by H. K. Bhabha, 265–290. London: Routledge, 1990.

Benjamin, W. 'Excavation and Memory'. In *Walter Benjamin: Selected Writings Vol. 2*, edited by M. W. Jennings, 576. Cambridge, MA: Harvard University Press, 1999.

Blair, I., F. Simpson and G. Moshenska. 'The Archaeology of the Blitz'. *Current Archaeology* 201 (2006): 486–492.

Confino, A. 'Telling about Germany: Narratives of Memory and Culture'. *Journal of Modern History* 76 (2004): 389–416.

Descoeudres, J.-P. *Pompeii Revisited: The Life and Death of a Roman Town.* Sydney: Meditarch, 1994.

Finney, P. 'On Memory, Identity and War'. *Rethinking History* 6 (2002): 1–13.

Fletcher, R. 'The Hammering of Society: Non-correspondence and Modernity'. In *Matériel Culture. The Archaeology of Twentieth Century Conflict,* edited by J. Schofield, W. G. Johnson and C. M. Beck, 303–311. London: Routledge, 2002.

Friedrich, J. *Der Brand: Deutschland in Bombenkrieg 1940–1945.* Munich: Propyläen Verlag, 2002.

Grass, G. *Crabwalk.* London: Faber, 2004.

Grayling, A. C. *Among the Dead Cities: Was the Allied Bombing of Civilians in WWII a Necessity or a Crime?* London: Bloomsbury, 2006.

Hillary, R. *The Last Enemy.* London: Pimlico, 1997.

Holtorf, C. *From Stonehenge to Las Vegas: Archaeology as Popular Culture.* London: AltaMira, 2005.

James, J. 'Undoing Trauma: Reconstructing the Church of Our Lady in Dresden'. *Ethos* 34 (2006): 244–272.

Kuspit, D. 'A Mighty Metaphor: The Analogy of Archaeology and Psychoanalysis'. In *Sigmund Freud and Art: His Personal Collection of Antiquities*, edited by L. Gamwell and R. Wells, 133–152. London: Thames & Hudson, 1989.

Lindqvist, S. *A History of Bombing*. London: Granta, 2002.

Macauley, R. *Pleasure of Ruins*. New York: Barnes & Noble, 1953.

Mellor, L. G. 'Words from the Bombsites: Debris, Modernism and Literary Salvage'. *Critical Quarterly* 46 (2004): 77–90.

Moeller, R. G. 'On the History of Man-made Destruction: Loss, Death, Memory and Germany in the Bombing War'. *History Workshop Journal* 61 (2006): 103–134.

Moshenska, G. 'Oral History in Historical Archaeology: Excavating Sites of Memory'. *Oral History* 35 (2007): 91–97.

Nolan, M. 'Germans as Victims during the Second World War: Air Wars, Memory Wars'. *Central European History* 38 (2005): 7–40.

Portelli, A. 'So Much Depends on a Red Bus, or, Innocent Victims of the Liberating Gun'. *Oral History* 34 (2006): 29–43.

Prager, B. 'Air War and Allegory'. In *Bombs Away! Representing the Air War Over Europe and Japan*, edited by W. Wilms and W. Rasch, 25–43. Amsterdam: Rodopi, 2006.

Remmler, K. 'On the Natural History of Destruction and Cultural Memory: W. G. Sebald'. *German Politics and Society* 23 (2005): 42–64.

Saint-Amour, P. K. 'Air War Prophecy and Interwar Modernism'. *Comparative Literature Studies* 42 (2005): 130–161.

Saunders, N. J. 'Excavating Memories: Archaeology and the Great War, 1914–2001'. *Antiquity* 76 (2002): 101–108.

Schofield, J. 'Monuments and Memories of War: Motivations for Preserving Military Sites in England'. In *Matériel Culture: The Archaeology of Twentieth Century Conflict*, edited by J. Schofield, W. G. Johnson and C. M. Beck, 143–158. London: Routledge, 2002.

Schulze, R. 'Review Article: Memory in German History: Fragmented Noises or Meaningful Voices of the Past?', *Journal of Contemporary History* 39 (2004): 637–648.

Sebald, W. G. *On the Natural History of Destruction*. London: Penguin, 2003.

Stone, M. 'A Memory in Ruins?' *Public Archaeology* 3 (2004): 131–144.

Thomas, S. 'Assembling History: Fragments and Ruins'. *European Romantic Review* 14 (2003): 177–186.

Till, K. *The New Berlin: Memory, Politics, Place*. Minneapolis, MN: Minnesota University Press, 2005.

Uzzell, D. 'The Hot Interpretation of War and Conflict'. In *Heritage Interpretation Volume 1: the Natural and Built Environment*, edited by D. Uzzell, 33–47. London: Belhaven, 1989.

Wallace, J. *Digging the Dirt: the Archaeological Imagination*. London: Duckworth, 2004.

Warner, R. *The Aerodrome: A Love Story*. London: Harvill, 1996.

Woodward, C. *In Ruins*. London: Vintage, 2001.

Chapter 29

The intangibility of things

Simon J. Knell

IN HIS CLASSIC STUDY OF ILLUSION IN ART, art historian Ernst Gombrich (1977: 176, 190–1) observed in practitioners of his discipline, a 'readiness to start projecting, to thrust out the tentacles of phantom colours and phantom images which always flicker around our perceptions.' He continued, 'what we call "reading" an image may perhaps be better described as testing it for its potentialities, trying out what fits.' In other words, while art historians believed the object was communicating to them they were really talking to it, infusing it with their thoughts and desires; the flow of communication was quite the reverse of their perception of it. If Gombrich understood that 'the artist of the Western tradition came to rely upon the power of indefinite forms', he knew too that the reception of works of art also played upon these ambiguities, permitting artist and art historian alike to find creative potential in the same uncertainties.

Of course, we cannot deny the material specificity of the art object; it is a thing of definite form and composition. Even a constructivist engages with an object of surfaces and textures, weight and temperature, and other properties, and never with a 'blank slate'. The arguments developed in this essay, however, privilege the interpretive process. They suggest that such things as the bold ribbing on a shell do not 'speak' to the viewer but are perceived. Indeed, speech itself does not, of course, reach the listener's mind without this act of perception and interpretation. So, if we take this page as an object bearing clear marks which seem to speak, we understand that they do so only because we have learned their meaning. Indeed, those who invented writing, those who designed type, those who write and those who read bear a cultural connection which permits this page-object to work. However, not all objects exist within such connected cultural systems – all must first be admitted into these worlds, including Nature's shell. We detect and value such things as its ribs, and perhaps even value them when they are barely perceptible, and can hardly be said to whisper let alone speak. This selective valuing of one feature over another is a choice that has been made and then adopted. Were this page to arrive from some alien culture we might decide that it is not the black marks that matter but the white patterns that surround them. Of course, it is hard for us to imagine this, but it is entirely possible and no less possible than choosing to value the black characters.

So the boundaries between an object's material form and our presumptions and interpretations of it are unclear. 'Culture', an inextricable part of 'material culture studies', is fundamental to our working with objects. For example, those materially vague but firmly intentional hints and indications of the form of cloth in Velázquez's later works seem hardly up to the task of describing their subject matter. Materially they are blobs and streaks of pigment. But step back five paces and these indefinite forms take on the appearance of the thing they were meant to represent. However, they do so because Velázquez's masterful use of paint chimes with our experiences of cloth. He had simply wrapped up an idea in these blobs and streaks which we were then able to unwrap because of our shared experiences of the things he was representing. The material aspect of the object here is however in this pattern of marks, the cloth that forms in our minds is of our own making. Had we no prior experience of cloth, the blobs and streaks may have helped little in explaining what cloth might be like.

The material aspect of the object also forms an important baseline for judgments of authenticity, though even here opinion can take possession of these material components. In older art objects *attribution* plays a central role in giving these objects significance and mapping out the geography of art history. In art, interpretation is all; the material object cannot become an *art* object without additional interpretation. Art is, so we are told, a judgment or a 'meaning' attached to the material thing by those who make and particularly by those who receive. Many social theorists, however, have argued that reception alone confers an object with this status. But this is not how the art object seems to those who engage with it. For them it is born an art object and it *is* an art object; art and object are inseparable. Indeed, it is possible to argue that art is a functional aspect of the object; art and object are inextricably entwined at birth in the same way that a bowl is made a bowl and does not become one simply through use. The art in the object is an intention, not a measure of elevation. This does not mean that we all share identical ideas about the artistic merits of an art object or that just because a maker conceives of her object as art that an audience will do the same.

The artwork, and all those individuals and institutions engaged in the production and reception of a work of art, might be understood ethnologically as forming a cultural grouping built around systems of belief which are produced and permeated by traditions and performances (Appadurai 1986), which reify, consolidate and shape mutual values and understandings of the objects in their possession. I shall refrain from calling this the 'art world' (Danto 1964; Dickie 1974; Becker 1982; Bourdieu 1993) as that makes it too special. What I am talking about is little different from those cultural groupings formed around racing pigeons and racing cars, collecting fossils or making glass beads. By suggesting a similarity, I do so in terms of an ethnologically understood cultural group with its objects, beliefs, roles and performances; I am not suggesting that the performances are identical in each of these groups. Our aim, as museologists, cultural historians or ethnologists, must be to stand on the outside of such performances and look in.

So what of the art object in its peculiar cultural world? Here things get a little more complicated, for this art aspect – a meaning bound to the material object through functional intent – is mutable. It is an intangible held in constant negotiation by those who experience the object. The material aspect of the art object is, by contrast, progressively reduced and diminished (relatively speaking) as the mythology of the object's artistic significance grows. Indeed, as many of the most famous works of art are consumed in reproductions and the printed word, and held in negotiation in our thoughts and conversations, the materiality of the art object may contribute little to its place in this cultural world. But is this not true of all objects? '[W]hen we look at how people experience and negotiate authenticity through objects, it is the networks of relationships between people, places and things that appear to be central, not the things in themselves' (Jones 2010: 181).

Now this entanglement between the tangible object in our collections and its intangible counterpart in our recollections is interesting for its complex psychological effect. When we stand before the material object, its intangible qualities seem a part of it; we cannot isolate them. In a similar way, the material reality of the object seems implicitly present whenever we think about or discuss the object even though our conversations only ever invoke its intangible and mutable form. In both cases we perceive only one object. The illusion, then, is this: that this one object is actually two, one tangible and real but not always present, the other intangible, the product of experience and negotiation, which seems to us to be the real object but is not. The intangible object exists in our world but is made in our thoughts; it is ever present and inescapable. The material object also exists in our world but it never really exists in our thoughts.

This notion of an unavoidable detachment between the thing, and our understanding of it, is many centuries old. A central debate in Western philosophy, Descartes expressed his concerns as long ago as 1641 (Descartes 1975). Our present constructivist reading, which privileges the experience of reality over its actuality, owes much to Berger and Luckmann's (1967) phenomenology. They argued, as did Gombrich implicitly, that 'Consciousness is always intentional; it always intends or is directed *towards* objects' (Berger and Luckmann 1967: 34, my emphasis). Morrissey reflected on Husserl's comprehensive and radical account of this phenomenological outlook: 'the objects that surround us function less "as they are" than "as they mean", and objects only mean for someone . . . To see implies seeing meaningfully' (Tauber 1997: 399). Bertrand Russell observed, 'It is not correct to say that I am believing the actual event; what I am believing is something now in my mind . . . since the event is not occurring but the believing is . . . What is believed . . . is not the actual fact that makes the belief true, but a present event related to the fact. This present event, which is what is believed, I shall call the "content" of belief' (Aquila 1977: 96). Finally, Schulz (1963: 3): 'Even the thing perceived in everyday life is more than a simple sense presentation. It is a thought object, a construct of a highly complicated nature.'

This should suggest to us that museum objects are things that 'seem to be' rather than 'are'. But to think this is to undermine the very justification for museums. These institutions came into being with an Enlightenment view, that emerged with the consolidation of the natural sciences, which suggested that by detecting, collecting and preserving material reality society could escape the clutches of myth and speculation, and all the ill consequences that arise from it. For example, Peter the Great promoted the pickling of deformed still-born babies, on public display even today at the Kunstkammer in St Petersburg, in order to quash a mythology of monsters that fostered irrational science and social relations. Perhaps surprisingly, even early historians of art, such as Giovanni Morrelli (1816–1891) and Bernard Berenson (1865–1959), adopted a natural science model to establish a framework for the study and connoisseurship of art objects. They did so not by blind adoption but through sophisticated adaptation. And while many disciplines have since found more liberal frameworks for their studies, in their museum manifestations at least, all remain true to principles which foreground the fundamental reality and authenticity of the object. It is through this lens that museum professionals see their objects, rarely considering the boundaries to the realities they believe they curate. They see only the material object which seems to speak to them and never an intangible thing constructed in their thoughts. This, Husserl (1913) observed, is the 'natural attitude'. They, their institutional and disciplinary world, and the objects within it, are locked in an unquestioned, and seemingly natural, relationship (Knell 2007). Arguments for greater cultural democracy, such as Bourdieu's (1984) convincing demonstration that museum objects are political (suffused with meanings and manipulated by an elite) rather than neutral (material) things, did nothing to displace this. Objects were, for him, real. We might argue, however, that this political aspect exists as a component in an intangible object deployed in social relations; it never existed in the real object.

The material object, from which our conceptual or intangible object is negotiated into existence, remains simply that: material and mute but implicitly, we must believe, bearing authentic witness to its origins and original context. We can take the intangible, immaterial or conceptual object wherever we like and deploy it in our imaginings and communications in a wide variety of ways. The silent, material, object – the real museum object – however, remains in a drawer or case. Situated in the tame environment of a collection formed to serve the particular needs of an intellectual discipline, the material object nevertheless sits apart from the field which seeks to understand it, always belonging to a reality beyond. Being real, it is to be used to question and doubt the knowledge produced, invested in, and represented by, its intangible twin; the material object is there to be the subject of new investigations as new knowledge, fashions, desires and technologies permit. Of this tangible–intangible pairing, it alone holds the potential to reveal the ultimate truth but this truth must always be negotiated and represented using its intangible form.

By adopting this approach I am denying the material object independent agency of any kind (unlike Callon's (1986) famous oysters, for example, for which see also Collins and Yearley 1992). Our thinking about an object, our surprise at first meeting it, even our involuntary bodily reactions to it, emanate from us and reflect our prior cultural experiences.

I would argue that this twin existence of things allows the development of that natural attitude, of which Husserl so disapproved, to operate without impeding processes of cognition. It alone permits the performances necessary to make sense of, and utilise, the real world using rational tools. It does so by ensuring that inaccuracies and mistaken beliefs, established during the negotiation of the intangible object, remain separated from reality by an invisible and impenetrable barrier; the factuality of material objects is never dependent upon the vagaries of belief or knowledge. History shows that the *reality* of objects has never been affected by thought; they have proven immune to designer gods and successive creations, untouched by the Flood and all variants of theory. These thought fashions manifested themselves only in the intangible object. This intangible, conceptual, immaterial, evidential object *appeals* to the truth of the material object; but its connection to its material twin is detached and fluid – it lives in another world. The object in our thoughts may seem material, definite and fixed but it is in fact intangible, contingent and transient.

But, again, this is not how things seem. Scientists, for example, work on the basis that the real thing is entirely within reach. How else might a scientist know that she has seen a greenfinch? That truth, however, which might arrive in her thoughts with great assurance, does so at the end of a rather convoluted journey spanning centuries. It might be explained: bird seen down barrel of gun; bird shot; bird skinned and preserved, drawn, described, compared, named, classified, published; other birds shot etc.; bird featured in an identification guide; book sold; book read; bird seen; intangible greenfinch held in constant negotiation; intangible greenfinch appears immutable; intangible greenfinch seems tangible. Through this grand performance the intangible thing I have in my mind seems indistinguishable from the material thing I saw. Science theorists might evoke paradigms, falsification episodes, correspondence theory, and so on, to explain this, but most scientists work with a more innate sense of science practice. This, in the natural sciences, includes the belief that there can only be one truth which must correspond with nature. This is a moral and ethical obligation central to the sciences but not shared so fundamentally by other disciplines. This obligation is embedded within a culture which implicitly believes in the possibilities of discovery, the accessibility of reality, the necessity of disinterestedness, the distancing terminology of theories, hypotheses, paradigms and models, the superiority of measurement and exact science, the need for open and testable data, and so on. This is instilled into scientists, to echo Bourdieu's arguments concerning taste and class, during their 'upbringing' and education. This thinking is fundamental to science but it must be understood that it is so only in relation to science's own particular performances. This permits scientists to live in a world which can negotiate absolute truth with no sense that a 'natural science attitude', to use Husserl again, is in any sense naive or unwarranted.

The art object is different. It exists in a field which understands that reality is just one dimension to knowledge; subjective understandings are admissible. This permits art history to be something of a theological discipline, critically questioning its beliefs, whilst also setting up idols and gods. In the museum, a curatorial priesthood might be understood to disseminate this gospel which we, the masses, lap up. How else can we explain the performances that daily greet Velázquez's *La Meninas* (1656) at the Prado Museum in Madrid? Every day, a crowd assembles before this painting and remains there. Its constituent actors may come and go but nevertheless a crowd remains. At nearby Reina Sofia, a similar spectacle can be observed in front of Picasso's *Guernica* (1937). Here the air is alive with the chatter as a public discusses the form, meaning and significance of this work, and in so doing makes it a part of their lives.

But what in these museums is making these objects perform in this way? On their own, and without any contextual information (historical or art historical), I doubt that these objects would provoke these performances. At the Kunsthistorisches Museum in Vienna, Raphael's famed *Madonna of the Meadow* (1506), perhaps rather surprisingly, attracts no such fuss. My point is simply that we have, on the one hand, the material object, detached from the everyday and presented in the museum, and on the other we have an intangible object formed through experience. The material object, if left to its own devices, might have little or no impact upon us as we need to learn how to appreciate objects. But what we learn, of course, is how to make our own intangible objects from real things. It is not the real *Guernica* that is causing all the hubbub, but a nebulous immaterial version forming in minds and in the exchanges between individuals, and between individuals and the object. In neighbouring galleries art (paintings, sketches, posters and photographs) performs as historical context supported by labelling which assures the visitor that this painting is the great antifascist symbol uniting the people of Spain. Picasso understood the functional purpose of his artwork at the moment it was made. He was the first among many who constructed the intangible *Guernica* that would forever accompany it.

The modern guidebook to the Prado tells us that this museum is 'considered by many to be the greatest public collection of paintings in the world' (Museo Nacional del Prado 2009: 5). To believe this, I would argue, one would need to have never visited the Hermitage, the Louvre, the Kunsthistorisches Museum, the National Gallery in London, the Museum of Fine Arts in Budapest or a number of other leading European galleries. One would also need to believe that the Prado is, like these other museums, rather more the international survey museum than is actually the case. If we chose to see it in its very Spanish colours then we might also compare it with the great national collections of paintings such as the wonderful Russian Museum in St Petersburg or the magnificent Hungarian National Gallery in Budapest. To elevate the Prado, we would also have to accept that the tastes and patronage of a seventeenth-century monarchy remain central to the idea of great art. But I tease a little here, the Prado is most certainly amongst the greatest of art museums. Its greatest attribute, however, is that it sees itself primarily as the keeper of 'the Spanish tradition' (Museo Nacional del Prado 2009: 23). It is its Spanish collections, nurtured over four centuries, that make it exceptional, together with its direct relationship to the active production of art in Spain over that period. The museum actively promotes the Spanish School, but in doing so also promotes its own significance: 'It is not by chance that the Prado's inauguration coincided with the international discovery of the "Spanish School" in general, and of the most emblematic of its painters, Velázquez, in particular. Indeed, the characteristics regarded as typical of the "Spanish School" can largely be said to be those associated with the most outstanding paintings by these artists at the Prado' (ibid.). Vast numbers of paintings by Velázquez, Goya, El Greco, Ribera and Murillo, and a lesser number by Zurbarán, are here turned into great pillars upon which the notion of an artistic tradition has been built. So effective is the museum's performance, one could believe that these paintings spring from a people, from a territory, from the national culture, from the very soil of the country. Viewed from within this carefully constructed cultural world, visitors learn to believe and seek to locate those characteristics said to be typical which connect the prodigiously talented royal painter, Velázquez, to the Caravaggist, Ribera, and the idealised beauty of Murillo, and these in turn to the more extraordinary work of Goya and El Greco. Stood in room 12, looking at *La Meninas*, am I simply seeing the material object? Thrusting 'out the tentacles of phantom colours and phantom images', my thoughts affected by curators and historians who insert the lenses of Titian, Italian travel, the formality of court portraiture, and late nineteenth-century French Impressionism before my eyes, am I not making my own intangible *La Meninas*? And in doing so are not these lenses as important as the material object to this act of making?

It might appear, then, from the examples of the greenfinch and Spanish art that the negotiations of intangible objects taking place in the arts and sciences are fundamentally different, but this is not really the case. The arts and humanities also possess in some measure science's desire for rationalism, dispassionate objectivity and truth. And, as I shall explain, scientists cannot live in a wholly rational and objective world; they too admit subjective experiences. Different disciplinary worlds – or cultural worlds – do not distinguish themselves at a fundamental level, it is rather that each values and privileges particular performances. Indeed, it is possible, through detailed study, to reveal these performances and show how these shape the object in the mind. What is particularly interesting about these performances is that they are structured not by disciplinary rigour but by social experience.

To explore this, I will, as a final example, discuss a group of materially insignificant, ambiguous, and yet evocative, objects. In doing so I am going to be a little circumspect about the nature of these things. If I state overtly what they are, you will be inclined to presume to know the arcane world to which they seem to belong. You might then be tempted to stop reading, believing that these objects are concerns only of that particular field. This all-pervasive act of pigeonholing things into their supposedly natural intellectual homes must, however, be resisted. Paintings and fossils don't belong to artists and palaeontologists, they both belong also to – and to no lesser extent – artists, children, collectors, television viewers, advertising agents, military historians, knick-knack sellers, and so on. The approach we are using here does not arise from within the disciplinary worlds we are exploring. Our goal must be not to think as participants do *within* the field but to stand on the outside of the field and see it and its participants as engaged in forms of negotiation and attached to particular objects without them ever reflecting on the cultural strangeness of it all. We should aspire to see this strangeness. And although I shall be discussing a world formed around a curious group of objects, my aim is not to focus on the objects but on the manner of the negotiations taking place.

The objects I chose for this study are small; vanishingly small. So small, in fact, that you could fit several on the head of a dress-making pin. The world collection, totalling millions of these things, could be made to fit into a few shoe boxes, if poured like so many grains of sand. But put these Lilliputian things under a microscope and they show themselves to possess extraordinarily exotic form. They are translucent and jewel-like. Some might even say they are beautiful. Were they considerably bigger then we might convince ourselves that they are like animal teeth though in many respects they are not like teeth at all. Their other special quality is that they are puzzlingly old. As material things, they seemed to me, to echo Thomas Mann's (1927) eloquent description of atoms, 'so small, such a tiny, early, transitional mass, a coagulation of the unsubstantial, of the not-yet-substantial and yet substance-like, of energy, that it was scarcely possible yet – or, if it had been, was now no longer possible – to think of it as material, but rather as mean and border-line between material and immaterial.'

What are these things? Well, the truth of the matter is that all who have looked – and this has included the great and good – have never quite managed to agree on the answer to that question. They have been attributed to almost every group of animals you might imagine (and others you have never heard of) and at least three times they have been considered the remains of plants! Over the 160 years they have been known they have become, rather ironically, the great unknown. The degree to which they were unknown spawned a myth and even a rather jolly song. Nevertheless objective and rational people still managed to make use of them – quite remarkable use of them. This, then, was my object but it was not its strangeness that concerned me but the strangeness of the world that surrounded it – a world consisting of a global population of 300 or so workers who made this thing central to their being. How did this group live with such an ambiguous thing and yet make it function for them?

So I set out not to study the thing but those who had thought about it. I positioned myself outside their arcane and expert world – for these objects were possessed by an enclosed community – never seeking to be drawn into their way of looking or to believe that I could know these things as they did. Instead I took the view that each actor possessed his or her own contingent knowledge (Weber 1968). It did not matter that each thought differently about the object or that each possessed, within his or her 'knowledge', a complex mix of truths, errors and orthodoxies. At that moment, for each individual, all these things composed 'the truth' and this truth shaped the intangible object at the centre of their studies. I was not concerned with what the objects were, only with what these people believed them to be (Latour 1987). I could not, as Evans-Pritchard (1937) did, begin by believing that 'Witches, as the Azande conceive them, clearly cannot exist'; in my study, belief alone brought intangible things into existence. By this means I could separate the reality of the material thing from the objects that existed only in the minds of those who worked with them.

It soon became apparent that my actors made no attempt to differentiate their disciplinary knowledge – knowledge belonging to that arcane field focused on these objects – from other knowledge and experiences arising from lunchtime conversations, casual reading, babies, pets and so on (Strawson 1979; Geertz 1983; Rapport 1993; also Wenger et al. 2002 and Fish 1990). What each person thought about these objects, then, arose from direct study of them, but seen through the lens of heterogeneous experience. Iterative exposure to the object and to these other lens-forming experiences gave their understanding of the object a high degree of reliability; it also exposed unknowns and uncertainties which could then be corralled and contained. Rather interestingly, the exterior sources which affected each individual's looking and believing – which shaped the intangible objects in their heads – were never revealed in the papers written about the objects. But, then, how could they – exterior experience is boundless and uncontained and constantly in negotiation. The performances recorded in the scientific papers they wrote referred only to the work they had undertaken on the objects themselves, though the manner of that work was sometimes motivated by things off stage. If they referred to external influences, it would only be to papers published by others. As in a play it seemed that part of the performance remained in the rehearsal room; no public ever saw it.

Now despite what seems at first sight a rather formalised approach to knowledge production, participants were well aware of the vagaries of interpretation. One worker argued that the field possessed 4000 specifically defined types of these objects, 500 examples where different kinds had been found together, and partial remains of five animals possessing these objects; 'All the rest is really speculation or, if you will, interpretation', he said. Another worker also recognised this speculative aspect, stating that when one has one object one also has one type. When one has two slightly different objects, then one must believe one has two types. When one has 100 objects all differing slightly in some way, then one might feel brave enough to believe that one has just one somewhat variable type. His point was that even in the sciences knowledge of the thing – the object – results from connoisseurship which in turn relates directly to the simple matter of how many of these things are known. The intangible object being formed in this way, which is held differently in each mind, but which is also acquiring shared understandings through conversation, is locked in negotiation, and subject to waves of phantom thoughts which envelop it and make it.

As someone on the periphery of this particular field noted, 'The road to good scholarship is paved with imagined patterns'. The intangible object might be regarded as a pattern which sits in the mind and which seems to possess a poetic and cognitive logic; a constellation of thoughts, 'readings' and projections. These patterns are constrained by what seem to be the material possibilities of the thing. In the 1950s one observer, a respected authority from another field, seemed to demonstrate conclusively that these tooth-like objects were not teeth after all. This silenced a generation. A language based on the teeth, which had been used to describe these things, was abandoned. Hardly anyone dared consider what form of life had possessed them. This phase ended when the field itself adopted a more liberal intellectual outlook and developed an aspiration for grand theory and creative thinking in the 1970s. This permitted workers to use reason to manifest functional roles for the objects. Intangible objects now developed rapidly but because they included a higher level of creative opinion new tensions grew between them as conflicting interpretations were given room to develop.

This was not the first time that incompatible objects were produced. In the 1930s, differing interpretive communities developed in Chicago, Washington, Missouri and Göttingen. Local negotiations, in an era when long-distance communication was rather more onerous, produced localised beliefs, and localised forms of the intangible object. By this means geography shaped the object, and would continue to do so as centres later developed in Iowa and Marburg, then Ohio, and lastly in the English midlands. Each possessed a particular outlook and saw the object differently. In this field of knowledge, then, sub-communities disrupted that sense of universality often claimed as a scientific necessity.

Key to this localisation was the training of PhD students. These new workers, on entering this field, were allocated to physical and intellectual territories by their supervisors. This positioned them uniquely in the field and ensured they were to complete their projects without risk of personal rivalry or interference. It meant that each individual had an in-depth knowledge of a particular space and the objects that occupied it. Thus while the field as a whole relied upon the ability to test the data of other workers, it also structured itself so that no two workers would possess precisely the same material. The social necessities of working relationships had made this necessary (Merton 1976). There was, then, in this division of labour, a peculiar balance between the agonistic and communal which was determined and achieved through control over part of the global resource of these tiny things. If the intangible object was held in constant negotiation then the performance of these negotiations was in part preconfigured in social relations.

However, on occasion individuals found themselves in possession of key objects – powerful objects capable of producing major advances in the field – which also permitted them to have influence far beyond anything these objects themselves could offer. These empowered individuals mobilised their own intangible objects to great political effect, attracting new monies, expanding their research teams, and acquiring control of popular media. Lesser objects, in the hands of particularly innovative thinkers, also became powerful, forming new readings which affected whole communities of workers, shaping their thoughts and their conceptions of the object. But in most cases these shifts in thinking were ephemeral. Occasionally, a fashionable idea would later find rejection but more often ideas simply slipped into the backwaters without a fight. The intangible object mutated through acts of letting go.

Repeatedly workers started out along a particular path that seemed to offer a solution to contemporary unknowns about the thing, but before the destination of that research trajectory was reached – before the once-imagined definitive result had been delivered – those on the path were drawn into new things. This happened because at the moment when particular questions were asked and the map of progress was drawn up, the features on that map were composed of things already within view. But, as these workers voyaged forwards, they soon hit seas disrupted by new ideas. They looked again at their map, and saw that the features marked upon it were not those imagined at the moment of departure. They needed a new ship and new map, and a new direction in which to voyage. It was not simply that the expenditure of effort in this field had entered a phase of diminishing returns but rather that changes around that field of research had diminished its value. In this way, once fashionable ideas drifted out of sight, joined by those ideas rejected by new knowledge, or which were never promoted or defended, or which had only persisted while their proponents remained alive. In this scientific world, the thought object – the intangible object – was never on a simple and progressive trajectory. It was never simply an objective and rational thing, but rather a palimpsest recording experiences that the individual still considered legitimate.

I have discussed elsewhere, and in a rather less abstract way, the manner in which these enigmatic objects journeyed through scientific minds (Knell in press). My aim here has simply been to demonstrate that while we partition knowledge into disciplines in museums, and define those disciplines in terms of ethical expectations and learned performances, there is another side to these human–object relationships which can be explored culturally or, as Swedish workers might describe it, ethnologically. By invoking the notion of an intangible object, we can extract ourselves from the norms of disciplinary engagement, and view the object as produced and existing within particular cultural worlds. Few museums have attempted to do this.

At the Historiska Museet in Stockholm, however, one gallery which uses the metaphor of the airport departure lounge, deconstructs the social and intellectual presumptions of archaeological knowledge. It permits the archaeological past to be understood as contingent upon present-day perceptions and performances. The past and the objects that seem to speak of it are all things held in contemporary negotiation. Other displays in this museum also reveal a sophisticated museological deployment of objects quite unlike those found in other historical museums. Similarly, across the city at the Nordiska Museet, Swedish ethnologists reveal with striking effect the power of this form of museological interrogation. An ethnological museum dealing with the Nordic present and past, curators here expose the anthropological strangeness of society, its objects and performances. The contrast between this and a British class-based social history tradition in museums could not be more profound. In Sweden, the curators privileged a commonality of human experience across time in order to evoke this sense of strangeness. In doing so they had swept aside that historical distancing which also tended to distance the subject from the viewer as something academic, arcane and rather irrelevant, approachable only through empathy, sympathy and reminiscence. By contrast, at the Nordiska Museet, life and culture seemed to be something worth celebrating, even if the beautifully designed displays themselves never took this stance. The museum simply asked visitors to look at everyday objects afresh, to see them as part of rather than remote from their culture and consider the peculiarity of the human condition. This is possible, I feel, because the intangible object does not remain hidden – it is not sold to visitors as existing within the material thing on display – but revealed as something to be wondered at.

References

Appadurai, A. (ed.) (1986) *The Social Life of Things: Commodities in Cultural Perspective*, Cambridge: Cambridge University Press.

Aquila, R. E. (1977) *Intentionality: A Study of Mental Acts*, University Park: Pennsylvania.

Becker, H. S. (1982) *Art Worlds*, Berkeley: University of California.

Berger, P. L. and Luckmann, T. (1967) *The Social Construction of Reality*, London: Allen Lane, Penguin Press.

Bourdieu, P. (1984) *Distinction: A Social Critique of the Judgement of Taste*, Cambridge, Mass.: Harvard University Press.

Bourdieu, P. (1993) *The Field of Cultural Production*, London: Polity Press.

Callon, M. (1986) 'Some elements of a sociology of translation: domestication of the scallops and the fishermen of St. Brieuc Bay', in J. Law (ed.) *Power, Action and Belief*, London: Routledge and Kegan Paul, 196–233.

Collins, H. M. and Yearley, S. (1992) 'Epistemological chicken', in A. Pickering (ed.) *Science as Practice and Culture*, Chicago: University of Chicago Press, 301–26.

Danto, A. (1964) 'The Artworld', *J. Philosophy*, 61: 571–84.

Descartes, R. (1975) *The Philosophical Works of Descartes*, vol. 1, Cambridge: Cambridge University Press.

Dickie, G. (1974) *Art and the Aesthetic: An Institutional Analysis*, Ithaca, N.Y.: Cornell University Press.

Evans-Pritchard, E. E. (1937) *Witchcraft, Oracles and Magic among the Azande*, Oxford: Clarendon Press.

Fish, S. E. (1990) *Is There a Text in This Class? The Authority of Interpretive Communities*, Cambridge, Mass.: Harvard University Press.

Geertz, C. (1983) *Local Knowledge*, New York: Basic Books.

Gombrich, E. H. (1977) *Art and Illusion*, Oxford: Phaidon, fifth edition.

Husserl, E. (1913 [2010]) *Ideas: An Introduction to Pure Phenomenology*, London: Taylor and Francis.

Jones, S. (2010) 'Negotiating authentic objects and authentic selves', *J. Material Culture*, 15: 181–203.

Knell, S. J. (2007) 'Museums, reality and the material world', *Museums in the Material World*, London: Routledge.

Knell, S. J. (in press) *The Great Fossil Enigma*, Bloomington: Indiana University Press.

Latour, B. (1987) *Science in Action*, Cambridge, Mass.: Harvard University Press.

Mann, T. (1927) *The Magic Mountain*, New York: A. A. Knopf.

Merton, R. K. (1976) *Sociological Ambivalence and Other Essays*, New York: Free Press.

Museo Nacional del Prado (2009) *Prado Guide*, Madrid: Prado Museum.

Rapport, N. J. (1993) *Diverse World Views in an English Village*, Edinburgh: Edinburgh University Press.

Schulz, A. (1963) *Collected Papers I: The Problems of Social Reality*, The Hague: Martinus Nijhoff.

Strawson, P. F. (1979) 'Perception and its objects', in G. McDonald (ed.) *Perception and Identity*, London: Macmillan, 41–60.

Tauber, A. I. (ed.) (1997) *Science and the Quest for Reality*, Basingstoke: Macmillan Press.

Weber, M. (1968) *Economy and Society*, New York: Bedminster Press.

Wenger, E., McDermott, R. and Snyder, W. M. (2002) *Cultivating Communities of Practice*, Cambridge, Mass.: Harvard Business School Press.

Chapter 30

'Things' as social agents

Alfred Gell

T HE IMMEDIATE 'OTHER' IN A SOCIAL relationship does not have to be another 'human being'. My whole argument depends on this not being the case. Social agency can be exercised relative to 'things' and social agency can be exercised by 'things' (and also animals). The concept of social agency has to be formulated in this very permissive manner for empirical as well as theoretical reasons. It just happens to be patently the case that persons form what are evidently social relations with 'things'. Consider a little girl with her doll. She loves her doll. Her doll is her best friend (she says). Would she toss her doll overboard from a lifeboat in order to save her bossy elder brother from drowning? No way. This may seem a trivial example, and the kinds of relations small girls form with their dolls are far from being 'typical' of human social behaviour. But it is not a trivial example at all; in fact it is an archetypal instance of the subject-matter of the anthropology of art. We only think it is not because it is an affront to our dignity to make comparisons between small girls showering affection on their dolls and us, mature souls, admiring Michelangelo's *David*. But what is *David* if it is not a big doll for grown-ups? This is not really a matter of devaluing *David* so much as revaluing little girls' dolls, which are truly remarkable objects, all things considered. They are certainly social beings – 'members of the family', for a time at any rate.

From dolls to idols is but a short step, and from idols to sculptures by Michelangelo another, hardly longer. But I do not wish to confine the notion of 'social relations between persons and things' to instances of this order, in which the 'thing' is a representation of a human being, as a doll is. The concept required here is much broader. The ways in which social agency can be invested in things, or can emanate from things, are exceedingly diverse (see Miller 1987 for a theoretical analysis of 'objectification').

Take, for instance, the relationship between human beings and cars. A car, just as a possession and a means of transport is not intrinsically a locus of agency, either the owner's agency or its own. But it is in fact very difficult for a car owner not to regard a car as a body-part, a prosthesis, something invested with his (or her) own social agency *vis-à-vis* other social agents. Just as a salesman confronts a potential client with his body (his good teeth and well-brushed hair, bodily indexes of business competence) so he confronts the buyer with his car (a Mondeo, late registration, black) another, detachable, part of his body available for inspection and approval. Conversely, an injury suffered by the car is a personal blow, an outrage, even though the damage can be made good and the insurance company will pay. Not only is the car a locus of the owner's agency, and a conduit through which the agency of others (bad drivers, vandals) may affect him – it is also the locus of an 'autonomous' agency of its own.

The car does not just reflect the owner's personhood, it has personhood as a car. For example, I possess a Toyota which I esteem rather than abjectly love, but since Toyotas are 'sensible' and rather dispassionate cars, my Toyota does not mind (it is, after all, Japanese – cars have distinct ethnicities). In my family, this Toyota has a personal name, Toyolly, or 'Olly' for short. My Toyota is reliable and considerate; it only breaks down in relatively minor ways at times when it 'knows' that no great inconvenience will result. If, God forbid, my Toyota were to break down in the middle of the night, far from home, I should consider this an act of gross treachery for which I would hold the car personally and morally culpable, not myself or the garage mechanics who service it. Rationally, I know that such sentiments are somewhat bizarre, but I also know that 99 per cent of car owners attribute personality to their cars in much the same way that I do, and that such imaginings contribute to a satisfactory *modus vivendi* in a world of mechanical devices. In effect, this is a form of 'religious belief' (vehicular animism) which I accept because it is part of 'car culture' – an important element in the *de facto* culture of twentieth-century Britain. Because this is a form of 'animism' which I actually and habitually practise, there is every reason to make mention of it as a template for imagining forms of animism that I do not happen to share, such as the worship of idols.

So, 'things' such as dolls and cars can appear as 'agents' in particular social situations; and so – we may argue – can 'works of art'. While some form of hedged agreement to these propositions would, perhaps, be widely conceded in the current climate of conceptual relativism and pragmatism, it would be facile in the extreme not to observe that unwelcome contradictions arrive in their wake.

Paradox elimination

An agent is defined as one who has the capacity to initiate causal events in his/her vicinity, which cannot be ascribed to the current state of the physical cosmos, but only to a special category of mental states; that is, intentions. It is contradictory to assert that 'things' such as dolls and cars can behave as 'agents' in contexts of human social interactions, since 'things' cannot, by definition have intentions, and moreover, such causal events as occur in their vicinity are 'happenings' (produced by physical causes) not 'actions' referable to the agency exercised by the thing. The little girl may, possibly, imagine that her doll is another agent, but we are obliged to regard this as an erroneous idea. We can preoccupy ourselves with detecting the cognitive and emotional factors which engender such erroneous ideas – but this is very different from proposing a theory, as I seem to be bent on doing, which accepts such palpable errors in agency-attribution as basic postulates. This appears a dangerous course indeed. A 'sociology of action' premised on the intentional nature of agency, undermines itself fatally by introducing the possibility that 'things' could be agents, because the whole interpretative enterprise is founded on the strict separation between 'agency' – exercised by sentient, encultured, human beings – and the kind of physical causation which explains the behaviour of mere things. However, this paradox can be mitigated, initially, in the light of the following considerations.

Whatever happens, human agency is exercised within the material world. Were the kinds of material cause and effect with which we are familiar not in place, intentional action, action initiated in a social context and with social objectives in view, would be impossible. We can accept that the causal chains which are initiated by intentional agents come into being as states of mind, and that they are orientated towards the states of mind of social 'others' (i.e. 'patients': see below) – but unless there is some kind of physical mediation, which always does exploit the manifold causal properties of the ambient physical world (the environment, the human body, etc.), agent and patient will not interact. Therefore, 'things' with their thing-ly causal properties are as essential to the exercise of agency as states of mind. In fact, it is only because the *causal milieu* in the vicinity of an agent assumes a certain configuration, from which an intention may be abducted, that we recognize the presence of another agent. We recognize agency, *ex post facto*, in the anomalous configuration of the causal milieu – but we cannot detect it in advance, that is, we cannot tell that someone is an agent before they *act as an agent*, before they disturb the causal milieu in such a way as can only be attributed to their agency. Because the attribution of agency rests on the detection of the effects of agency in the causal milieu, rather than an unmediated intuition, it is not paradoxical to understand agency as a factor of the ambience as a whole, a global characteristic of the world of people and things in which we live, rather than as an attribute of the human psyche, exclusively. The little girl's doll is not a self-sufficient agent like an (idealized) human being, even the girl herself does not think so. But the doll is an emanation or manifestation of agency (actually, primarily the child's own), a mirror, vehicle, or channel of agency, and hence a source of such potent experiences of the 'co-presence' of an agent as to make no difference.

I am prepared to make a distinction between 'primary' agents, that is, intentional beings who are categorically distinguished from 'mere' things or artefacts, and 'secondary' agents, which are artefacts, dolls, cars, works of art, etc. through which primary agents distribute their agency in the causal milieu, and thus render their agency effective. But to call artefactual agents 'secondary' is not to concede that they are not agents at all, or agents only 'in a manner of speaking'. Take, for instance, the anti-personnel mines which have caused so many deaths and mutilations in Cambodia in recent years. Pol Pot's soldiers, who laid these mines, were, clearly, the agents responsible for these crimes against innocent people. The mines themselves were just 'instruments' or 'tools' of destruction, not 'agents of destruction' in the sense we mean when pinning moral responsibility on Pol Pot's men, who could have acted differently, while the mines *could not help* exploding once trodden on. It seems senseless to attribute 'agency' to a mere lethal mechanical device, rather than its culpable user.

But not so fast. A soldier is not just a man, but a man with a gun, or in this case with a box of mines to sow. The soldier's weapons are *parts* of him which make him what he is. We cannot speak of Pol Pot's soldiers without referring, in the same breath, to their weaponry, and the social context and military tactics which the possession of such weaponry implies. Pol Pot's men were capable of being the kind of (very malign) agents that they were only because of the artefacts they had at their disposal, which, so to speak, turned them from mere men into devils with extraordinary powers. Their kind of agency would be unthinkable except in conjunction with the spatio-temporally expanded capacity for violence which the possession of mines makes possible. Pol Pot's soldiers possessed (like all of us) what I shall later discuss as 'distributed personhood'. As agents, they were not just where their bodies were, but in many different places (and times) simultaneously. Those mines were components of their identities as human persons, just as much as their fingerprints or the litanies of hate and fear which inspired their actions.

If we think of an anti-personnel mine, not as a 'tool' made use of by a (conceptually independent) 'user', but, more realistically, as a component of a particular type of social identity and agency, then we can more readily see why a mine can be seen as an 'agent' – that is, but for this artefact, this agent (the soldier + mine) could not exist. In speaking of artefacts as 'secondary agents' I am referring to the fact that the origination and manifestation of agency takes place in a milieu which consists (in large part) of artefacts, and that agents, thus, 'are' and do not merely 'use' the artefacts which connect them to social others. Anti-personnel mines are not (primary) agents who initiate happenings through acts of will for which they are morally responsible, granted, but they are objective embodiments of the *power or capacity to will their use*, and hence moral entities in themselves. I describe artefacts as 'social agents' not because I wish to promulgate a form of material-culture mysticism, but only in view of the fact that objectification in artefact-form is how social agency manifests and realizes itself, via the proliferation of fragments of 'primary' intentional agents in their 'secondary' artefactual forms.

Agents and patients

Many more examples of social agency being attributed to 'things' will be provided as the discussion proceeds, but there is another issue which needs to be dealt with in this connection. There is a special feature of the concept of agency that I am advancing to which I must draw particular attention. 'Agency' is usually discussed in relation to the permanent dispositional characteristics of particular entities: 'here is X, is it an agent or not?' And the answer is – 'that depends on whether X has intentions, a mind, awareness, consciousness, etc.' The issue of 'agency' is thus raised in a classificatory context, classifying all the entities in the world into those that 'count' as agents, and those that do not. Most philosophers believe that only human beings are *pukka* agents, while a few more would add some of the mammals, such as chimpanzees, and some would also include computers with appropriately 'intelligent' software. It is important to emphasize that I am not raising the question of 'agency' in anything like this 'classificatory' sense. The concept of agency I employ is relational and context-dependent, not classificatory and context free. Thus, to revert to the 'car' example; though I would spontaneously attribute 'agency' to my car if it broke down in the middle of the night, far from home, with me in it, I do not think that my car has goals and intentions, as a vehicular agent, that are independent of the use that I and my family make of my car, with which it can co-operate or not. My car is a (potential) agent with respect to me as a 'patient', not in respect to itself, as a car. It is an agent only in so far as I am a patient, and it is a 'patient' (the counterpart of an agent) only is so far as I am an agent with respect to it.

The concept of agency I employ here is exclusively relational: for any agent, there is a patient, and conversely, for any patient, there is an agent. This considerably reduces the ontological havoc apparently caused by attributing agency freely to non-living things, such as cars. Cars are not human beings, but they act as agents, and suffer as patients 'in the (causal) vicinity' of human beings, such as their owners, vandals, and so on. Thus I am not really indulging in paradox or mysticism in describing, as I shall, a picture painted by an artist as a 'patient' with respect to his agency as an artist, or the victim of a cruel caricature as a 'patient' with respect to the image (agent) which traduces him. Philosophers may rest content with the notion that, in such locutions, the only *pukka* agents are the human ones, and that cars and caricatures (secondary agents) could never be *pukka* agents. I, on the other hand, am concerned not with the philosophical definition of agency *sub specie aeternitatis*. I am concerned with agent/patient relationships in the fleeting contexts and predicaments of social life, during which we certainly do, transactionally speaking, attribute agency to cars, images, buildings, and many other non-living, non-human, things.

In what follows, we will be concerned with 'social agents' who may be persons, things, animals, divinities, in fact, anything at all. All that is stipulated is that with respect to *any given transaction* between 'agents' one agent is exercising 'agency' while the other is (momentarily) a 'patient'. This follows from the essentially relational, transitive, and causal implications of our notion of 'agency'. To be an 'agent' one must act with respect to the 'patient'; the patient is the object which is causally affected by the agent's action. For the purposes of the theory being developed here, it will be assumed that in any given transaction in which agency is manifested, there is a 'patient' who or which is *another 'potential' agent*, capable of acting as an agent or being a locus of agency. This 'agent' is momentarily in the 'patient' position. Thus, in the 'car' example just considered, if my car breaks down in the middle of the night, I am in the 'patient' position and the car is the 'agent'. If I should respond to this emergency by shouting at, or maybe even punching or kicking my unfortunate vehicle, then I am the agent and the car is the patient, and so on. The various possibilities and combinations of agency/patiency will be described in detail later on [see original reading].

It is important to understand, though, that 'patients' in agent/patient interactions are not entirely passive; they may resist. The concept of agency implies the overcoming of resistance, difficulty, inertia, etc. Art objects are characteristically 'difficult'. They are difficult to make, difficult to 'think', difficult to transact. They fascinate, compel, and entrap as well as delight the spectator. Their peculiarity, intransigence, and oddness is a key factor in their efficacy as social instruments. Moreover, in the vicinity of art objects, struggles for control are played out in which 'patients' intervene in the enchainment of intention, instrument, and result, as 'passive agents', that is, intermediaries between ultimate agents and ultimate patients. Agent/patient relations form nested hierarchies whose characteristics will be described in due course [see original reading]. The concept of the 'patient' is not, therefore a simple one, in that being a 'patient' may be a form of (derivative) agency.

The artist

However, we still have not specified the situation sufficiently to circumscribe the scope of an 'anthropological theory of art'. Agency can be ascribed to 'things' without this giving rise to anything particularly recalling the production and circulation of 'art'. For this to be the case it seems necessary to specify the identity of the participants in social relations in the vicinity of the 'index' rather more precisely.

The kinds of 'index' with which the anthropological theory of art has to deal are usually (but not always) artefacts. These artefacts have the capacity to index their 'origins' in an act of *manufacture*. Any artefact, by virtue of being a manufactured thing, motivates an abduction which specifies the identity of the agent who made or originated it. Manufactured objects are 'caused' by their makers, just as smoke is caused by fire; hence manufactured objects are indexes of their makers. The index, as manufactured object, is in the 'patient' position in a social relationship with its maker, who is an agent, and without whose agency it would not exist. Since art-making is the kind of making with which we are primarily concerned, it might be most convenient to call the one to whom the authorship of the index (as a physical thing) is attributed, 'the artist'. Wherever it is appropriate, I shall do so, but it is important to note that the anthropology of art cannot be exclusively concerned with objects whose existence is attributed to the agency of 'artists', especially 'human' artists. Many objects which are in fact art objects manufactured by (human) artists, are not believed to have originated in that way; they are thought to be of divine origin or to have mysteriously made themselves. The origins of art objects can be forgotten or concealed, blocking off the abduction leading from the existence of the material index to the agency of an artist.

The recipient

Art objects lead very transactional lives; being 'made by an artist' is only the first of these. Often an art object indexes, primarily, not the moment and agent of its manufacture, but some subsequent, purely transactional, 'origin'. This applies, for instance, to ceremonial valuables in Melanesia (such as Kula shells) whose actual makers (who are not in the Kula system) are forgotten – Kula shells 'originate' with whoever possessed them as a *kitoum*, that is, as unencumbered ceremonial property (Leach and Leach 1983).

Similarly, in the Victoria and Albert Museum, one may see the beautiful carved onyx cup of the Mogul emperor, Shah Jehan. This cup is Shah Jehan's *kitoum* for all that it is now British government property. But there is a difference, in that in Shah Jehan's cup, we see, first and foremost, the power of the Mogul emperor to command the services of craftsmen possessing more skill and inventiveness than any to be found nowadays. Shah Jehan's agency is not as a maker, but as a 'patron' of art, and his cup indexes his glory in this respect, which contemporary potentates can only emulate in feeble, vulgar, ways.

Thus a second abduction of agency which an index in the form of an artefact normally motivates is the abduction of its 'destination', its intended reception. Artists do not (usually) make art objects for no reason, they make them in order that they should be seen by a public, and/or acquired by a patron. Just as any art object indexes its origins in the activity of an artist, it also indexes its reception by a public, the public it was primarily made 'for'. A Ferrari sports car, parked in the street, indexes the class-fraction of 'millionaire playboys' for whom such cars are made. It also indexes the general public who can only admire such vehicles and envy their owners. A work of contemporary art indexes the contemporary art public, who constitute the intended recipients of such work. If the work is to be seen in the Saachi gallery, it indexes this famous collector and his patronage of contemporary art. And so on. In the course of their careers, art objects can have many receptions. While I am able to feel that I belong (as a gallery-goer and occasional reader of *Art Now* and similar periodicals) to the 'intended' public for contemporary art, I know perfectly well that the Egyptian art in the British Museum was never intended for my eyes. This art permits the vicarious abduction of its original, or intended reception, as a component of its current, non-intended reception.

The public, or 'recipients' of a work of art (index) are, according to the anthropological theory of art, in a social relationship with the index, either as 'patients' (in that the index causally affects them in some way) or as 'agents' in that, but for them, this index would not have come into existence (they have caused it). The relation between the index and its reception will be analysed in greater detail in due course [see original reading]. For the present it is sufficient to stipulate that an index has always to be seen in relation to some specific reception and that this reception may be active or passive, and is likely to be diverse.

The prototype

To complete the specification of the network of social relationships in the vicinity of art objects, we need only one more concept, one which need not always apply, but which very commonly does. Most of the literature about 'art' is actually about representation. That representation is the most complicated philosophical and conceptual problem stemming from the production and circulation of works of art there is no doubt. Of course, by no means all 'art' actually is representational, even in the barest sense, and often it is the case that the 'representational content' of art is trivial, even if the art is representational (e.g. the bottles and guitars in Cubist still lifes, or the botanically arbitrary flowers and leaves in textile patterns). I do not propose to discuss the problem of representation as a philosophical problem in any detail. I should, however, state that I espouse the anti-Goodmanian view which has been gaining ground recently (Schier 1986). I do not believe that iconic representation is based on symbolic 'convention' (comparable to the 'conventions' which dictate that 'dog' means 'canine animal' in English). Goodman, in a well-known philosophical treatise (1976), asserts that any given icon, given the appropriate conventions for reception, could function as a 'representation' of any arbitrarily selected depicted object or 'referent'. The analogy between this proposition and Saussure's well-known postulate of the 'arbitrary nature of the sign' does not need to be underlined. I reject this implausible claim as an overgeneralization of linguistic semiotics. On the contrary, and in accordance with the traditional view, I believe that iconic representation is based on the actual resemblance in form between depictions and the entities they depict or are believed to depict. A picture of an existing thing resembles that thing in enough respects to be recognized as a depiction or model of it. A depiction of an imaginary thing (a god, for instance) resembles the picture that believers in that god have in their minds as to the god's appearance, which they have derived from other images of the same god, which this image resembles. The fact that 'the picture that people have in their minds' of the god's appearance is actually derived from their memories of images which purport to represent this appearance does not matter. What matters to me is only that people believe that the causal arrow is orientated in the other way; they believe that the god, as agent, 'caused' the image (index), as patient, to assume a particular appearance.

It is true that some 'representations' are very schematic, but only very few visual features of the entity being depicted need to be present in order to motivate abductions from the index as to the appearance (in a much more completely specified form) of the entity depicted. 'Recognition' on the basis of very under-specified cues is a well-explored part of the process of visual perception. Under-specified is not the same as 'not specified at all', or 'purely conventional'.

References

Goodman, N. (1976) *Languages of Art*, Indianapolis: Hackett.

Leach, J. and Leach, E. (eds) (1983) *The Kula: New Perspectives on Massim Exchange*, Cambridge: Cambridge University Press.

Miller, D. (1987) *Material Culture and Mass Consumption*, Oxford: Basil Blackwell.

Schier, F. (1986) *Deeper into Pictures*, Cambridge: Cambridge University Press.

Chapter 31

Art as a mode of action
Some problems with Gell's Art and Agency

Howard Morphy

REVIEWS OF ALFRED GELL'S *Art and Agency* have been sharply divided between those who see the book as making a major theoretical contribution to the anthropology of art (e.g. Hoskins, 2006), indeed in some cases making art for the first time a relevant subject for anthropology, and those who see it as a thought-provoking but significantly flawed work characterized by significant exclusions and internal contradictions in the argument (see Winter, 2007). Interestingly, the latter camp includes mainly anthropologists who have devoted much of their time to the study of art, and the former largely those who have not. Many of the more critical have qualified their comments by noting that if Gell had lived he might have modified his argument (e.g. Layton, 2003: 457). Those who have heaped praise have had no need for such qualifications.

As one of the anthropologists of art at whom Gell drew his critical bow, perhaps it is not surprising that I belong in the more critical camp. While the book makes a very rich read and is replete with interesting case studies, insightful asides and raises innumerable topics for research, as a whole it is very problematic.[1] The problems with the book lie not so much in the details as in more general features of the argument, and these are symptoms of some underlying problems in recent developments in anthropological theory. Two problems that I might highlight, and that are central to Gell's book, are a difficulty in coming to terms with complexity and an over-narrow definition of the central focus of anthropology. Bisecting these issues is a major gap between the theoretical positioning of the book and the methods of analysis that Gell employs (see Arnaut, 2001: 206).

Although the book is titled *Art and Agency* the argument overall is one that obscures the role of human agency in artistic production and fails to provide a theoretical basis for understanding how art can be a mode of action – a means of intervening in the world. This is partly because the concept of agency – 'actions' caused by prior intentions (Gell, 1998: 17) – is applied both to humans and to the objects that they produce and interact with (e.g. 1998: 153). While the extension of agency to inanimate objects is a central topic for anthropological analysis, as a theory of what kinds of things objects are, it poses certain problems. On the whole objects do not change themselves. While it is possible to imagine agentive objects existing in cyberspace and in the realm of robotics and artificial intelligence, these are not the objects that Gell is referring to. What human beings think an object is capable of doing needs to be separated from that which it is actually known that objects can do. My own intuition is that Gell's agentive object, however seductive the idea may at first seem, is a case of an analogy gone too far, and that he might have modified his treatment of it in subsequent rewritings of the book. Hints of that occur in the distinction he draws between primary and secondary agents, secondary agents being ones that are known to be incapable of intentional action.[2] The latter however would seem to be a contradiction in terms.

Gell's analysis also confuses the phenomenological with the analytical. Certain people may indeed ascribe agency to inanimate objects that are believed to be capable of intentional actions. They may indeed not make any distinction on the basis of intention between the hand of God and the hand of man. While for many purposes it may be sufficient for the anthropologist only to know that the object concerned is believed to have agency, just as it is to know that a particular magical act is believed to be effective, the question must be explored ethnographically. There is no reason why every anthropologist should be interested in religious experience, but if an anthropologist is interested in the phenomenology of religious experience, then how people come to believe in the magical properties or spiritual power, or affect of a particular object becomes a central question. Indeed Gell recognizes this briefly when writing about Hindu idol worship 'the animacy and imputed subjectivity of the idol is not attained except by surmounting the stark difference between an inert image and a living being. How does this happen?' (1998: 118).

I see the 'how' question as one of the most important questions in the anthropology of art and Gell does not really attempt to answer it.[3] In the case of the Hindu god he fixes on a single argument. The attention of the viewer is focused on the eye of the god, the god looks at the viewer just as the worshipper looks at the god. The viewer imagines he is being looked at as he sees himself reflected in the gaze of the god. This reciprocal process provides the image with agency (Gell, 1998: 120). I will not provide a detailed critique of this analysis but will list the kind of problems I see with it. While it may be a reasonable hypothesis to interrogate one aspect of the process of viewing an idol, Gell makes no attempt to garner the evidence that would prove the hypothesis. Without ethnography it has the status of the 'if I were a Nuer' explanation.[4] Secondly, it brackets off or takes for granted all that is outside the immediate context of viewing, the belief system of the viewer, Hindu iconology, socialization into viewing and so on. It also brackets off – almost provides shutters to – all other aspects of the form of the object and the context of viewing. At later stages of the book Gell does provide a theoretical perspective that would bring these elements in, but he does so in ways that do not connect with the original hypothesis about the reciprocal viewing that endows the object with agency. For example, the set of Hindu deities and their representations could be treated as a distributed object in the way that Marquesan images are: a domain of images that reflects both structural features of the society and is an analogue for the mind of the individual. While I find both of these formulations highly problematic, they do deal with the wider historic contexts and with details of form. However, at this early stage of his argument Gell is setting up a theoretical framework that excludes most of these contextual features that could be labelled cultural or structural.

Gell provides a deliberately, almost provocatively, narrow definition of what an anthropological theory is about, stating that the 'subject matter is "social relationships" – relationships between participants in social systems of various kinds' (1998: 4). 'Culture', he writes, 'has no existence independently of its manifestation in social interactions' (1998: 4). Adopting this position enables him to place semantic and aesthetic analysis, for the most part, outside the province of anthropological theory, making such analyses irrelevant to understanding the agentive dimension of objects. He defends this position partly by creating a series of straw men: aesthetics is equated with beauty,[5] contemplation is seen to be a requirement for an aesthetic response, aesthetics is separate from function,[6] semantic and symbolic analyses of art involve treating the objects as texts and so on. However, it is precisely through these particular dimensions of objects that artworks become indices of agency and indeed create the particular form of agency concerned. However, while dismissing aesthetics and semantics as part of his general theory, what most people might refer to as the aesthetic and semantic dimension of objects are central to his analyses.

Gell (1998: 7) eschews definition of art objects by arguing that the definition must be determined by the theoretical framework he adopts to analyse it. However, having dismissed the need to develop a substantive definition of art, Gell states that objects which people normally identify as art objects will illustrate the book. By coincidence, his pre-theoretical category coincides with his post-theoretical category. It may be that Gell could have centred his argument on a quite different set of objects, ones that do not coincide with the objects conventionally categorized as artworks. Certainly many of his theoretical arguments apply equally well to other bodies of material culture objects but that is not surprising since few would argue that the attributes of art objects are exclusive to those objects placed in that category.

The fact that Gell chooses to select objects that others define as art objects may not be entirely arbitrary, but indeed may be explicable in part even in terms of his own theory. While not denying art objects, Gell states that they are mediating objects in human action, or later on, in a somewhat differently phrased statement, he says: 'the anthropology of art . . . deals with those situations in which there is an index of agency, which is normally some kind of an artefact' (Gell, 1998: 66). While not a defining characteristic of art objects, I think that Gell is right to emphasize their role in mediation. To use a convenient 'Gellism' I would argue that art objects tend to be those objects where mediation is thematic. Mediation is always a component of material culture objects but the mediating role is fundamental to art objects. They mediate between domains of existence, they mediate between artist and audience, and they mediate between an object that they are an index of and the person interacting with that object.

Gell is interested in precisely those aspects of an object that have previously been referred to by many as its symbolic significance. Thus Gell is interested in a Ferrari not as a mode of transport but as an index of male status and in Abelam yams not as food but as an index of male power. While most would agree that much symbolic analysis is simplistic and often deflects analysis away from the way the object contributes to rather than represents aspects of socio-cultural processes, my point is that Gell's analysis is often based on similar interpretations and presuppositions. It would not be unfair to argue that in parts of his thesis Gell argues for a reflectional theory of social meaning. Gell's art objects are often simply social parrots.[7] On the whole Gell fails to demonstrate how art objects can be part of the process of creating power, status, role differentiation; why they can be powerful gifts; how they can create a sense of the presence of God, be understood or experienced as sources of spiritual power, or invoke the idea of a supra-human mind. Where he does provide valuable analytic insights, it is often because he strays outside the limitations of his own theoretical framework to analyse the objects in terms of specific aspects of their form.

By implying a direct relationship between the object as index and the agent that it is connected to Gell has engaged in a sleight of hand that both creates problems for him and is the means whereby he can exclude from his analysis what others have seen as central topics of an anthropology of art. Gell (1998: 14–15) argues that indexes are kinds of sign from which meaning is abducted. He refers briefly to the theoretical literature on abduction citing Boyer (1994: 147) citing Holland that 'Abduction is "induction in the service of explanation, in which a new empirical rule is created to render predictable what would otherwise be mysterious"' (Gell, 1998: 14). However he then brings the discussion back closer to the interpretation of a Peircian index by the example he uses. He argues that there is a direct relationship between a person smiling and the emotion of happiness (just as there is a relationship between smoke and fire). He then argues that a picture of a person smiling is going to be subject to the same interpretative process as an actual person smiling: 'the appearance of person smiling [in a picture] triggers . . . an inference that (unless they are pretending) this person is friendly . . . We have access, in short, to another person's mind' (1998: 13).

While Gell cites as his initial example of an indexical sign the classic Peircean example of smoke from a fire, most of the examples he goes on to discuss are highly complex representations that do not derive their form in the same way that natural signs are connected to their maker – it is the human beings who perceive, respond to and conceptualize the objects and who make the connections. Understanding those responses – how the objects are understood in the way they are and how that relates to the ways in which they are used in context and in turn how that contributes to ongoing socio-cultural processes – are all central components of an anthropology of material culture and art. The analysis must include, in the broadest sense, the meaning that the object has in cultural context, where meaning is more than a simplistic reading of the signs on the object, something that Gell's parody reduces it to. Gell, however, is almost explicit in stating that part of his motivation for using the concept of abducted meaning is so that he does not have to explore these issues: 'there seems to be something irreducibly semiotic about art . . . I am anxious to avoid the slightest imputation that (visual) art is "language like" and that the relevant forms of semiosis are language-like' (1998: 14).[8]

There is no fully developed theory of representation in *Art and Agency* and indeed in his general theoretical framing theories of representation do not have a central place. One might argue that representations are replaced by indexical signs or abductions of agency. However, the absence of a theory of representation or semiosis is problematic precisely because abduction of agency in the form of indexical signs requires a theory of signs in order to show the senses in which they are indexical (see Layton, 2003). The failure to provide a clear theory of meaning results in Gell's index sliding across the entire spectrum of the Peircean set of signs of which Gell's index is explicitly taken to be a member (see Arnaut, 2001 for a relevant discussion). Constable's *Salisbury Cathedral* is seen as a spin off from the Cathedral itself, in the same way that exuviae are detached fragments of a victim's distributed personhood. The absence of theoretical discussion of representational process makes much of Gell's analysis appear to be naively realist: the form of the apple is a secondary agent in its own representation, Rigaud's portrait of Louis XIV shows Louis XIV as he wishes to look, Churchill does not like Donald Sutherland's portrait of him because it looks too much like him: 'the problem for Churchill was that he was unable to come to terms with his own ugliness' (1998: 37). What is the basis for attributing ugliness to Churchill? How do we know that Sutherland was motivated by a strict criterion of realism? What are the particular conventions of Sutherland's portraiture and how do his portraits differ from those of other artists? Does cultural background and knowledge of art affect a person's interpretation and response to a portrait? The conventions of representation in the case of Louis XIV that make him look as he wants to look provide vital information for historical and anthropological analysis.

Gell in his analysis depends on assumptions about what objects represent and communicate but he fails to engage with how they do this. The presence and absence of aesthetic factors in his work prove equally problematic. Gell does indeed devote a great deal of attention to analysing properties of objects that other people would define as aesthetic. He avoids addressing the issue of cross-cultural aesthetics by adopting a particularly narrow definition of aesthetics that rhetorically collapses it into western ideas of beauty.

He writes that the question of 'indigenous aesthetics is essentially geared to refining and expanding aesthetic sensitivities of the Western art public by providing a cultural context in which non-Western art objects can be assimilated to the categories of Western art appreciation' (1998: 3). Yet of course, as Gell acknowledges elsewhere, the anthropological critique of primitivism in western art has been directed towards precisely the opposite effect – to remove non-western art from being interpreted according to the aesthetics of modernism (see e.g. Errington, 1998; Price, 1989). Indeed that does have as a consequence a transformation of western categories of art appreciation.

Ironically, Gell's own aesthetic commentary at times appears uninfluenced by such discourse and he produces almost archetypal modernist descriptions of non-western art. Writing of Iatmul lime containers he comments 'examining this gourd container, we are able to see that it is decorated with beautiful patterns, formed from motifs that do not obviously resemble real world objects . . . a free exercise in the deployment of curves, ovals, and spirals and circles in symmetrical or repetitive arrangements' (Gell, 1998: 74). The description is a-ethnographic, and presumes a universal viewer who responds to and interprets the object in the same way as Gell. Gell is also happy to make confident value judgements about particular artworks: '*A'a* from the Austral Islands is arguably the finest piece of Polynesian sculpture' (1998: 137).

In excluding indigenous aesthetics from the province of anthropology Gell draws an analogy with the anthropology of law as to why ethical principles such as conceptions of right and wrong are outside the province of the discipline.[9] He argues that the anthropology of law is not the study of people's ideas of right and wrong – but of disputes and their resolution, echoing a functionalist agenda.

Gell creates a straw man by, on the one hand, asserting that 'aesthetic' properties cannot be abstracted anthropologically from the social processes surrounding the deployment of candidate art objects in specific social settings and, on the other, by collapsing aesthetics and beauty. Thus Gell is able to ridicule aesthetic interpretations of the form of New Guinea shields by asserting that rather than being contemplative objects of beauty, the designs inspire terror in the minds of enemies (see O'Hanlon, 1995 for a relevant analysis). Later he evocatively refers to the designs on Asmat shields 'seeming to have been composed in a mood of terror' (Gell, 1998: 31), looking into them is like looking into the eye of a tiger.

People writing about aesthetics today seldom restrict its realm to beauty, which itself is a complex concept and not necessarily opposed to sensations of terror.[10] Moreover, it is quite insufficient to simply assert that the shields are effective because they inspire terror. Such statements need to be demonstrated ethnographically and require the same methods that would be used to analyse objects that create a sense of serenity. The terror in Asmat designs is a projection of Gell's own interpretative perspective and does not necessarily reflect Asmat views. Ironically, Gell is the universalist here who has no need to turn to the agency of the Asmat to support his interpretations.

However, the rhetoric against aesthetics is not strictly followed in his analysis and in several sections of the book he explores the form of artworks to determine 'why social agents in particular settings, produce the responses they do to particular works of art' (1998: 4). The two areas he explores in most detail are the creation of illusions of movement and relationships among sets of objects and/or the component parts of objects that are consonant with the idea that the object or object sets have attributes of mind.

He argues that the unstable and dynamic nature of certain patterns creates the illusion of movement 'whereby the dynamic aspect of the act of perception is subjectively experienced as a dynamic property of the object being perceived' (1998: 78). The theoretical construction of his argument does not require that artworks actually show properties of living things. However, because agency plays such a large role in his theory it is not surprising that Gell pays a great deal of attention to ways in which objects can be seen or thought to have agency. In these analyses he is not examining the objects merely as indexes from which meaning is abducted but as complex entities that can be analysed from a multiplicity of different perspectives, all of which contribute to understanding how in the particular case, objects can be thought to have agency. Thus in spite of his denials, his analysis centres on what are generally considered to be aesthetic and semantic attributes of objects.

Gell focuses on the dynamic component of works of art in two other areas. One is the vocabulary associated with the technology of enchantment and the associated concept of entrapment (see also Gell, 1996). Both of these are productive concepts echoing the conventional language of art appreciation. However Gell's conception of enchantment is a very unexpected one, for although it builds on the wonder a person gets from viewing a particular artwork, whether it is a Vermeer or a Kula prow board, the wonder takes for granted the effect and is transformed into a sense of awe and inadequacy in the face of such overwhelming technical accomplishment – 'the spectator's inability to mentally rehearse the origination of the index from the viewpoint of the originator, the artist' (Gell, 1998: 71).

In analysing style, Gell develops a slightly different angle on this argument, but one that shows another way in which objects can be seen to be active agents. Analysing the form of decorative objects, he points out that designs create part–whole relationships. As well as having the potential to create dynamic illusions, they are inherent containers of complexity that often elude easy interpretation. By this Gell means not that their meaning is difficult to interpret, but that it is hard to see how the parts fit together, in particular, how they are constructed. He chooses as an example 'an intricate oriental carpet' and asks who 'can say that they have entirely come to grips with its pattern; yet how often the eye rests on it and singles out now this relationship, this symmetry, now that' (1998: 80). While a core example, somehow this 'reflective viewing' is not seen by Gell as part of the aesthetic experience; decoding its complexity is what gives the pattern power, not how it looks. This seems to be a problematic and very subjective perspective. An emphasis on how something is constructed, how the parts relate to the whole, may be what engages Gell most with the artefact concerned but its visual effect is at least as relevant to other people's viewing of it. Certainly the issue of complexity of a design is a relevant one to address, but there seems no a priori reason to privilege it. Moreover, each case of complexity requires analysis and ethnographic contextualization. Gell seems to assume that his own subjective interpretation of a design is both universal and culturally relevant, but he provides no evidence. His discussion of the Kolam design from south India provides a good example: 'we want to see the figure as one continuous line, but we know it is four separate threads' (1998: 86). I have yet to find anyone else who wants to interpret the figure as continuous line.

While at the level of theory Gell excludes semantic and aesthetic factors from his analysis, he does not exclude the analysis of form altogether. I have mentioned earlier that the final section of the book centres on detailed formal analyses of sets of objects. He begins with an almost classic analysis of formal variations within the body of Marquesan art based on published illustrations of objects. He then develops two related theories that link the results of his stylistic analysis to the form of Marquesan society and then to artworks as a manifestation of the extended mind of the artist, or collective agency of the group. In both these cases he leaps from the level of the individual to an abstract collective domain that takes on characteristics of a living organism. Gell provides an immensely detailed analysis of formal variations in Marquesan art, deliberately excluding meaning from his analysis (1998: 159). He argues that style exists at a level of relative autonomy in which its structural core or axes of coherence are produced purely by the relations between the objects.

Ultimately, in the Marquesan case, this can be reduced to the principle of the least difference. Gell then connects this principle of the least difference to the fact that a similar principle lies at the core of Marquesan society: the core of Marquesan society according to Gell is a 'prevailing preoccupation with differentiation in the context of dissolution' (1998: 219).[11] He earlier states that artworks 'come in families, lineages, tribes, whole populations, just like people. They have relations with one another as well as with the people who create them as individual objects. They marry, so to speak, and beget offspring, which bear the stamp of their antecedents' (Gell 1998: 153).

I have no doubt that there may be a connection between structural features of art styles and aspects of social organization.[12] I also believe in the relative autonomy of form and the importance of formal analysis as part of anthropological method. I do not find Gell's analysis of style convincing, however, precisely because he makes no attempt to place the art in the context of its production and use. In the end, Marquesan art is reduced to being a structural analogue for Marquesan society rather than shown to be integral to the processes of its reproduction and transformation over time – in contrast to his insightful analyses of Polynesian tattooing (Gell, 1993). In *Art and Agency* there is no attempt to connect the different strands of his argument together to connect to the context of production and use.

* * * * *

In the discussion so far I have argued that Gell uses a problematic concept of agency that confuses different levels of analysis (Winter, 2007). By focusing at the level of social action with objects as agents, Gell's theory excludes consideration of those factors that make it possible for members of the society to use objects as agents of their individual action and indeed, in some circumstances to conceive of certain objects as having agency in themselves.[13] Meaning pre-exists action and indeed is one of the things that makes agency possible; the meaning of social action is not circumscribed solely by the relationships that it entails, even though those relationships are going to be part of its meaning, broadly defined. Meaning also includes the content of those relationships and the purposes for which people come together in action.

People who use works of art, interact with works of art, respond to works of art, do so with some background of knowledge and experience which may include detailed knowledge of the artwork itself and of innumerable previous interactions involving it, or similar objects. Likewise, people respond to the physical properties of an artwork, to the complexity of its composition, partly in the context of the moment but also in the light of a history of viewing artworks and other things. Their viewings are influenced by how those experiences are interpreted in relation to their cultural background, their religious beliefs, their social status or gender and so on.

Early on in his book Gell writes 'I view art as a system of action' (1998: 6), a view with which I totally concur; however to this he adds a codicil 'intended to change the world rather than encode symbolic propositions about it'. While I too would reject the idea that art is primarily concerned with encoding symbolic propositions about the world, I do think that in many cases the semantic component of art can be integral to its being a mode of acting in the world, which may be directed towards change or any other objective that motivates the person who uses it. In the second section of this critique I will illustrate the perspective I adopt on art as a way of acting in the world by summarizing the way that Yolngu art is used in one of its contexts – paintings on the chest of a boy at his circumcision ceremony – showing the complex interaction between semantic and aesthetic factors but also emphasizing the need to place a particular art performance in the wider context of Yolngu society as a whole, taking into account the multiple contexts of viewing and the different positions of the viewers. I will also problematize the idea of the archive of images as a distributed mind separated from the agency of the individuals who produce the paintings. The system of Yolngu art is undoubtedly supra-individual but the anthropologist must focus on the production of art in context and have as his or her subject the archive of images that are produced by the minds and imaginations of the interacting individuals, as part of the body of knowledge they have about the world and the means and prescriptions they have for acting in it.

In many societies and for many people, artworks, or objects that can be defined as such from particular perspectives, are an integral part of the processes that socialize people into ways of seeing things, that inculcate beliefs, create meanings and understandings about the world. Artworks are produced and producing. Works of art differ radically in the way that they are involved in these processes and the ways in which they are used or encountered. In many cases encoded meaning may be quite irrelevant to the process, in other cases central. It depends on the art and on the expectations that the viewer brings to it (see Morphy, 2007, chapter 6 for a comparative analysis of Yolngu and Abelam art). But in cases where encoded meaning is relevant it is unlikely to be communicated in a single viewing by the object being 'read'. Iconographic meaning is not read on the spot and acted upon like a sentence in ordinary language. Indeed even in cases where objects are dense with iconographic meaning, that meaning may be quite irrelevant to the impact of the object in the particular context.

Yolngu body paintings are dense with iconographic and sociological meanings, yet in some contexts and to some participants the iconographic meaning may be largely irrelevant. The paintings are completed in semi-restricted spaces. Few people, apart from the artists, may look directly at the painting until it is completed, when it is exposed for a short while to inspection and, certainly today, to the admiring gaze. Even then it is likely that most viewers will treat it as ceremonial regalia, dressing up for a special occasion, rather than wearing an item to be decoded. (Yet of course the context is one of the things that adds to its meaning and contributes to the power it subsequently has.) In the Yolngu case many viewers will know little about the meaning of the particular artwork: people are not supposed to show too much knowledge of the meanings of a distant clan's art, and women and young people in general defer to others. The main impact of the design may be through its aesthetic effect – the shimmering brilliance of the design which is relatively autonomous of its semantic meaning but which is interpreted as an index of ancestral power (Morphy, 1992).

Any particular painting may be produced only on rare occasions and then only glimpsed for a few minutes, and any instance of a painting is only going to be seen by a small segment of the society. However the significance of the work and its role in cultural process cannot be understood or seen to exist only in the particular contexts of its viewing. The painting exists as a much more widely connected and durable object than the instances of its production allow. Far from being disconnected from life it is linked everywhere to people and places. It exists in the mental archive that is Yolngu art and in the imaginations of the artists who can produce it on the occasions when it is required. The semantic dimension of the object is vital as far as Yolngu conceptions of the transmission of religious knowledge are concerned, indeed Yolngu today refer to paintings as their texts. The ability to produce paintings is a sign of a person of knowledge, and the ability to produce intricate designs is seen as a form of supreme technical skill, which in the Yolngu case is attributed to the creative genius of the ancestral beings – and in this respect is an exemplification of Gell's technology of enchantment (Gell, 1992). The meanings encoded in the form of the paintings are referred to in many other contexts through the singing of clan songs and by observing features of the landscape, in the personal names that refer to the ancestral places that are represented in the paintings and so on.

Gell ridicules semantic interpretations of ritual art by assuming that the elements are to be 'read' on the spot, and his own theoretical framework often simply makes the iconography redundant. This comes out clearly in Gell's highly reductionist analysis of the viewing of Indian idols. He argues that the impact of viewing 'imagistic devotion' is accomplished entirely 'looking into the eyes of god, union comes from eye contact, not the study of all the other details that the image may show' (1998: 118). Indeed in Gell's analysis these details remain unanalysed. However, it is wrong to imagine that the cultural significance of design forms can be understood by relating them to a single context of viewing. The significance of the detailed composition of images requires that it be connected to the producer of the work, to the process of learning about it, to the chants and stories and places that relate to it, to the work as it is performed, not simply as it is 'looked at'. Iconographic analysis cannot be reduced to, or seen to be coincident with, particular contexts of action, or agentive events, but is broadly relevant to understanding how the object is believed to have power and its contribution to a wider system of meanings linked to social process.

Yolngu *miny'tji* (ancestral designs) are generally produced for specific contexts – as a body painting, on a hollow log coffin, or as a sand sculpture and so on. As physical objects they are of short duration, seldom lasting more that a few days. Many paintings today exist in more permanent forms in museums and art galleries in Australia and around the world, and as illustrations in books. On the whole, however, as far as Yolngu are concerned, paintings remain as part of a virtual archive – a vast resource of paintings from different places that exist for the most part in people's minds and are produced on occasions as instances of ancestral action in the context of ceremony, and in some cases for sale to outsiders. The production of Yolngu art in a ceremonial context is a creative act which influences the way in which the painting is going to be seen and interpreted on that occasion and it also contributes to its significance in the virtual archive of Yolngu art and consequently to the production of artworks on subsequent occasions. The decisions made are part of a process that is productive and potentially innovative on each occasion that an image is produced. The painting chosen can affect anything from the journey of the soul of the dead person, to the relationships between clans and the spiritual identity of a boy being circumcised. In the case of circumcision the painting used may be a 'gift' from a mother's mother's clan (*märi*) or a sister clan (*yapa*) cementing a relationship that may in the long term influence patterns of marriage and succession to land (for a detailed discussion see Morphy, 1991).

As with any human action, there are more or less habitual components, some of which are conventionalized and routine and normally produced with little reflection. There are aspects of the painting process that are just like riding a bicycle! If we take the example of the painting on an initiate's chest at circumcision we can illustrate the types of choices that are made. The painting will be selected from a category of paintings that represent major places associated with particular ancestral beings. The paintings are characterized by intricate and complex designs finished off with fine crosshatched lines painted with a brush of human hair (Figure 31.1). The paintings are among the most important possessions of a clan. The painting will occur on the day of the boy's circumcision and will take some four hours to complete during which time the boy must lie completely still. The painting has to be completed in the late afternoon since the circumcision itself must take place a little before sunset.

These factors are shared, are common to every circumcision ceremony and leave limited room for choice. However the particular sequence of events and forms can

Fig. 31.1 The final stages of completion of one of the paintings. The painting represents the journey of two ancestral women, the Djan'kawu sisters, who created waterholes in the countries of Dhuwa moiety clans and gave birth to members of the clans. In this case the painting belongs to the Djapu clan. One meaning of the background pattern is the clouds that build up in the wet season – the reflections of the sun and the penetration of its rays creating patterns in the sky and on land and sea. Photograph by Howard Morphy.

reasonably be thought to have evolved over the *long durée* and the nature of the painting contributes greatly to the effectiveness of the occasion and the power of the ritual, which in turn adds to the significance of paintings as objects. The boy lying for hours in a trance-like state remembers the occasion for the rest of his life; the painting provides the focal point for the afternoon's rituals, creating a set-aside space around which people sing and dance. The aesthetic effect of the painting is considerable, and together with the feather armbands and dilly bags creates the boys in the image of ancestral beings. The whole performance is stage-managed by the ritual leaders to create a great event and people ensure that the most accomplished artists play a major role in producing the body painting.

So far we have been considering attributes that belong to body paintings as a class; meaning has not entered the analysis. Yet each painting produced on a boy's chest at a circumcision ceremony is likely to differ from every other in details of its form. The choice of paintings is made on the basis of kinship and alliance. A painting will be chosen that belongs to a clan of the boy's own moiety, either his own clan or one that he is closely related to by descent. If the painting comes from another clan it is seen as a gift and the recognition of relationship. The painting on the child's chest is an important statement of his social position and of the ways he is connected to sources of spiritual power. The fact that paintings effectively encode the relationship between social group, ancestral beings and place is an important part of their significance, and their use in a circumcision ceremony makes a strong statement about group identity and personal and intergroup relationships – an excellent example in Gell's terms of art as a mediating object. If all the paintings were identical they would not have this same discriminating function. The paintings are thought to have the power to define group identity but it is human agency that creates this potential. The fact that a painting is used in a circumcision ceremony creates a close bond between that painting and the person that may be reflected in the person's name; it also becomes part of the archive of memory associated with the paintings, that links the potential designs with a wide range of significances ranging from the personal to the institutionalized. A painting is a named and known place with certain characteristics but it is also a named and known person.

Yolngu art is a dynamic social process that involves continual innovation through the process of production – each time an instance of the virtual archive is realized there is potential for change. That change may involve changing the relationships between groups by authorizing the transfer of a design from one group to another, or it may involve radical changes in design form or context. In recent years new design contexts have included petitions to Parliament, the Yirrkala church panels,[14] designs on clan motor vehicles, and dressing people in ceremonial regalia for investitures or graduation ceremonies (see Morphy, 2007). Changes in design form have involved the transfer of designs to new materials such as screen printed cloth and batik, the use of wood glue as a fixative for earth pigments and a continuous process of subtle changes in design form over time. These changes have occurred through interaction with outside and often invading cultures but are also clearly continuations of endogenous processes. There has been a general shift of crosshatched designs from relatively closed to relatively open contexts. There has been an elaboration of the figurative component of some paintings and certain design effects have been emphasized relative to others. These changes both maintain and transform the value and forms of the artworks produced – they engage the artworks in ever-wider networks of interaction, and affect the design form by creating wider contexts of use, response and influence (see Morphy, 1991 for a detailed analysis). The changes that occur are not restricted to any one context but move back and forward across contexts creating a dialogical relationship between Yolngu society and the encompassing world. Innovations that occur first in art made for sale in a Sydney gallery may the following year be painted on the chest of a boy at circumcision. All this occurs in the case of a society, a community of artists, who tend to deny that any innovations have occurred and to assert the continuity of an unchanging tradition.

In relation to meaning Gell's 'theory' oversimplifies and privileges social action, it makes objects exist for the moment and fails to take into account the knowledge and presuppositions that people bring to bear when acting in relation to objects. People act in relation to objects as a part of a history of relating to objects, a history that is supra-individual yet reproduced through individual action. The knowledge, meanings, interpretations, and experiences that people bring to bear on objects cannot be reduced to individual agency nor can they be thought to be contained in the sets of objects that have been produced over a given historical period of time.[15] In his analysis of Marquesan material culture objects Gell, ironically, slips from the context of action and interaction almost directly to the set of material culture objects themselves. And yet that set of Marquesan designs is only partial, both in the sense that it is what has remained from history, but also in a more fundamental and theoretically salient sense, it represents only those objects that have been produced. A finished artwork is a stage in a process of action in which most paintings are never produced, most objects are never finished – the actual Yolngu paintings that are produced are instances of what could potentially have been produced. Every painting produced in a circumcision ceremony is a representative of the many paintings that were not produced on that occasion but are still part of the archive of possible paintings. I applaud Gell's formal analysis of Marquesan designs but it is vital that such analyses place the designs in the context of their production and use in social contexts and in relation to their distributions in time and space.

To reduce paintings to sets of concrete objects that can then be imagined to breed, also elides the spaces between the objects. It obscures the many possible relationships between them that can be seen, the interpretations that vary according to the viewer and the context of time of viewing, and perspectives that can entirely disrupt any presumed historical sequence. The sets of objects that have been produced are not in any sense directly equivalent to the processes that produced them, though they do provide vital information as to what those processes were. In order to use them as evidence they need to be reconnected to the actual process of their manufacture, use and interpretations in action. They will exist, not as a separated off set of recorded forms, but as a partial and contextual set of images contained in whatever model of cultural memory or the cultural imagination that we would like to construct. The analyst's job is to position himself or herself at the moment of action when the archive of emergent designs produces one of its instances, to take into account the history of the object as it comes to the actor in context, not as it resides in a museum or archive, and show how that body of knowledge and experience is used to produce the object in context, how it influences the perception of objects, how it moulds the interaction of objects. Objects do not breed as Gell seems to suggest (1998: 153), they are created for use in particular contexts, and in order to understand how a new object is created, one needs to focus on individual agency in the context of systems of knowledge and in relation to historical and contextual factors.[16]

*   *   *   *   *

To an extent the problem with Gell's analysis reflects a key problem with social theory in general and British anthropology in particular: the difficulty of modelling the supra-individual prerequisites of action — knowledge, perceptions and conceptions, understanding, technology, beliefs and ideology — that are an essential component of any social situation. The issue has been formulated as the relationship between structure and/or culture and/or society and agency. The level of reality which was for long occupied in American anthropology by culture and in British anthropology by social structure, which contains at different times concepts such as values, knowledge systems, beliefs and ideational systems, has proved highly problematic in recent years. This is partly because of the slippage between culture as process and cultures as bounded groups. The latter while never a part of culture as a theoretical concept is always imposed on theories of culture in the form of a simplistic critique. And it is partly because the domain that we are dealing with is so abstract and unbounded in any absolute sense. It depends on imminent structures, and contains things at very different levels of reality and consciousness — language, knowledge, beliefs and values for example. The problem of trying to avoid the inevitability of the supra-individual is that theorists substitute for it agency in material culture objects, affordances to the environment or embodiment in humans, or invent processes like 'structuration' and 'habitus' and hope that no one notices that the abstract structures and albeit 'fuzzy' boundaries that they imply remain largely unexamined. As a consequence much recent social theory has been both reductive and individualistic on the one hand and scientistic on the other; society is reduced to the relationships in which individuals engage in the context of power relations that constrain them, that are magically transformed into the cognitive basis for action. We need an anthropology that is not reductive, that is not afraid of complexity and multi-determination, that is analytical and capable of making sense of vast bodies of diverse data, and that develops explanatory frameworks that are sensitive to context and which locate events and actions historically. Such a programme inevitably means an alliance with other disciplines and concerted efforts to see synergistic relations between the concepts of anthropology and those of other disciplines including those of linguistics, art history and cognitive science.

Gell attempts to limit the scope of anthropology and define too narrowly the nature of anthropological theory — emphasizing the short *durée*, focusing on social relations, with its echoes of Radcliffe-Brown, and excluding aesthetics and semiotics. In pushing agency beyond the limits of its meaning he is in danger of creating another of those fuzzy concepts that, while directing the attention of anthropologists to an important dimension of the phenomena under consideration – in this case recognizing art as a means of acting in the world[17] – reaches a conclusion by avoiding the analysis that is necessary to demonstrate the argument. By attributing agency to the objects themselves Gell deflects the focus of the anthropology of art away from the many ways in which art contributes to social action and the production of identity.[18] Yet ironically the book is full of rich insights and suggestive analyses of particular cases that show how much art as a source of data can contribute to anthropology if it is given the centrality that his engagement with the subject demonstrates rather than the marginal place he has constructed for it in his theoretical encapsulation.

Acknowledgements

This article has a long history. I first drafted it in response to reading the page proofs of Alfred Gell's book for a conference published as Thomas and Pinney (2001). I revised it for the ASA decennial conference in Manchester and then rewrote it adding the ethnographic exemplification for a seminar at the Australian National University in 2005. My argument has been sharpened by the participants in those seminars, but I owe my greatest debt to Karen Westmacott and Frances Morphy for their critical engagement with the argument.

Notes

1   There have been a number of critical review articles of *Art and Agency*. Excellent and generous reviews have been undertaken by Karel Arnaut (2001) and Bob Layton (2003) and a somewhat less generous one by Ross Bowden (2004).
2   The core of his argument can be approached from his discussion of children's dolls (1998: 17). He argues that dolls are social beings because people show agency in relation to them. He recognizes that objects such as cars cannot really have agency since they cannot produce intentional actions, but then slips into an argument that, in effect, makes them prosthetic components of human action. We cannot abduct agency (in Gell's terms) unless we see people in action. People act using things, therefore objects and customs are part of the same whole, therefore objects appear to have agency. The logic of this however could as easily be modified to: we cannot see the objects in action unless we see people using them; hence objects have no agency themselves but only with respect to the ways in which they are used by people.
3   As I will argue later in the article, part of Gell's problem with semantic analysis is because he assumes that semiotic analyses must involve treating objects as texts to be read. On the whole anthropologists have seldom treated art objects as texts and how something means is every bit as important as what something means (see Guss, 1989: 91; Morphy, 1991: 142–5). Indeed in many respects, while not acknowledging it, Gell's analysis is concerned with gaining insights into the how and what of meaning through placing the objects concerned within the wider framework

of society as a whole (see Arnaut, 2001). However because he denies this is what he is doing he fails to locate these processes in the context of the production of the objects by agentive subjects, while simultaneously endowing the objects themselves with agency.

4   I agree with Layton (2003: 457) when he writes 'Gell's argument [is] weakened by his use of the Victorian strategies of either imagining oneself in the position of a member of another culture ([Gell, 1998:] 125), or drawing a parallel between the behaviour of western children and adults in other cultures ([1998:] 129, 134).'

5   Gell's arguments against analysing art from the perspective of cross-cultural aesthetics were first developed in his inspirational article on the technology of enchantment (Gell, 1992) that was in turn inspired by his reading of Shirley Campbell's 1984 doctoral thesis on the art of the Kula (see Campbell, 2002). His argument involves the application of the concept of methodological atheism in the study of religion to the study of art. Methodological atheism is the principle that 'whatever the analyst's own religious convictions, or lack of them, theistic and mystical beliefs are subjected to sociological scrutiny on the assumption that they are not literally true – religion becomes the emergent property of the relations between various elements of the social system' (Gell, 1992: 41). By analogy with this, methodological philistinism is 'an attitude of resolute indifference towards the aesthetic value of works of art' ([Gell] 1998: 42). There is however a distinction that needs to be made between the anthropologist's own aesthetic response to the object and the aesthetic value it has in the context of the producing society. The matter is more a question of suspending aesthetic judgement rather than adopting a position of philistinism.

6   Gell's position on aesthetics is full of ambiguities. Thus in criticizing the art historian Freedburg he writes that 'In India . . . idolatry flourishes as a form of religiosity, and nobody in their right minds would try to drive a wedge between the beautiful form and religious function of venerated idols' (Gell, 1998: 97). Certainly no anthropologist should separate the aesthetic dimension from the functional, hence the point he is making is no argument against anthropologists paying attention to the aesthetic dimension of artworks. Indeed, to neglect them would be equally absurd since it would be to neglect a dimension of the object that is vital to understand its effect. However Gell continues in the same paragraph to hint at an evolutionary argument, which, as a consequence of his own reflections, positions the aesthetic as logically subsequent to the religious dimension of the work. 'Since it is impossible to separate the religious from the holy the anthropologist of art inevitably contributes to the anthropology of religion, because the religious is – in some contexts, though not all – prior to the artistic' (Gell, 1998: 97). This conclusion may be a consequence of Gell assuming for the moment 'the Western post-Enlightenment point of view that [separates] the beautiful and the holy' (1998). Because aesthetic experience is often a component of religious performance it is no argument for assuming that the religious is prior to the aesthetic.

7   The analysis is often deliberately reflectional. What the Hindu idol sees is the devotee looking back (Gell, 1998: 118ff.), 'the doll's thoughts are a reflex of the child's thoughts' (1998: 129). While the reflectional component of the viewing of objects and performances is an important one to pursue, Gell's analysis is somewhat formulaic and he fails to provide the evidence for his interpretations.

8 This position stems from a particularly narrow conception that Gell has of both meaning and language, which is restricted to what he refers to as natural language:

> I entirely reject the idea that anything except language itself has 'meaning' in the intended sense. Language is a unique institution (with a biological basis). Using language we can talk about objects and attribute meanings to them in the sense of finding something to say about them, but visual art objects are not part of a language for this reason, nor do they constitute an alternative language.
>
> (Gell, 1998: 6)

9 Gell acknowledges aesthetics may be necessary to understand the affective response to objects and actions in particular contexts and writes that 'in so far as there can be an anthropological theory of aesthetics, such a theory would explain why social agents in particular settings, produce the responses they do to particular works of art' (1998: 4). This perspective is indeed quite compatible with that argued for by Coote and Morphy in Ingold (1996). Indeed I would argue that Gell implicitly follows that method in his analysis of the illusion of movement created in art objects.

10 Indeed at one point Gell appears to acknowledge this 'Melanesian aesthetics is about efficacy, the capacity to accomplish tasks, not "beauty"' (1998: 94).

11 As Layton notes, Gell's analysis in this case is almost archetypally structuralist, yet 'Gell's fundamental objection to the linguistic model was its reliance on structuralism' (Layton, 2003: 461).

12 A pioneering study was Fischer (1961). Hanson's (e.g. 1983) study of the relationship between Maori art style and society receives Gell's qualified approval.

13 In Arnaud's words to be 'the focus of social action and therefore invested with social agency themselves'.

14 Yolngu have used their art as a means of persuading outsiders as to the value of their way of life and establishing a basis of equivalence between their own laws and beliefs and those of the colonizers. The bark petition of 1963 was a typed statement of their rights in land and certain other demands duplicated and sent to the Australian Parliament. These statements were affixed to two sheets of bark with painted borders representing respectively the moieties Dhuwa and Yirritja into which their society is divided. The Church panels are two magnificent (if I may be excused an aesthetic judgement) 5 m high paintings on masonite, produced in 1963 by senior Yolngu artists to go either side of the altar of the new Yirrkala Church. The panels set out, in geographical relationship to each other, the main ancestral designs of the clans who occupy the region.

15 I entirely support an approach that takes advantage of the archives of images and collections of objects and 'artworks' from particular regions. I agree with Gell that formal analysis should be an integral part of anthropological method. Formal analysis may indeed uncover patterns in the data that require explanation and facilitate understanding of the art – its systematic properties and its relationship to socio-cultural context. However it is important to connect the formal analysis to the available documentary data – by including for example the temporal dimension – and then to test any hypotheses that are developed ethnographically or by using any other contextual information available about the use of the objects (see Morphy and Perkins, 2006: 323–5 for a relevant discussion).

16 The ahistorical nature of Gell's analysis is part of what Lipset criticizes in his approach (Lipset, 2005).

17 And indeed this is precisely the most important message that those who respond positively to Gell's book take away with them (e.g. Hoskins, 2006: 75). However his words are often reformulated as Hoskins does to state: 'He asserts that things are made as a form of instrumental action: Art (and other objects) is produced in order to influence the thoughts and actions of others.' Clearly such a proposition, broadened somewhat to include the performative dimension of objects, underlies most recent anthropological studies of art and material culture.

18 In a critique of the use of Gell's concept of agency by archaeologists, Johnson writes 'It is difficult to avoid the suspicion, however, that its strengths are in its rhetorical appeal to the centrality of material culture to shaping identity, rather than its coherence as an intellectual tradition' (2006: 125).

References

Arnaut, K. (2001) 'A Pragmatic Impulse in the Anthropology of Art? Alfred Gell and the Semiotics of Social Objects', *Journal des Africanistes* 71(2): 191–208.

Bowden, R. (2004) 'A Critique of Alfred Gell on Art and Agency', *Oceania* 74(4): 309–24.

Boyer, P. (1994) *The Naturalness of Religious Ideas: A Cognitive Theory of Religion.* Berkeley: University of California Press.

Campbell, S. (2002) *The Art of Kula.* London: Berg.

Errington, S. (1998) *The Death of Authentic Primitive Art and Tales of Progress.* Berkeley: University of California Press.

Fischer, J.L. (1961) 'Art Styles as Cultural Cognitive Maps', *American Anthropologist* 63(1): 79–93.

Gell, A. (1992) 'The Technology of Enchantment and the Enchantment of Technology', in J. Coote and A. Shelton (eds) *Anthropology, Art and Aesthetics*, pp. 40–67. Oxford: The Clarendon Press.

Gell, A. (1993) *Wrapping in Images: Tattooing in Polynesia.* Oxford: The Clarendon Press.

Gell, A. (1996) 'Vogel's Net: Traps as Artworks: Artworks as Traps', *Journal of Material Culture* 1(1): 15–38.

Gell, A. (1998) *Art and Agency.* Oxford: The Clarendon Press.

Guss, D. (1989) *To Weave and Sing: Art, Symbol and Narrative in the South American Rainforest.* Berkeley: University of California Press.

Hanson, A. (1983) 'When the Map is the Territory: Art in Maori Culture', in D.K. Washburn (ed.) *Structure and Cognition in Art*, pp. 74–89. Cambridge: Cambridge University Press.

Hoskins, J. (2006) 'Agency, Biography and Objects', in Christopher Tilley, Webb Keane, Susanne Küchler, and Mike Rowlands (eds) *Handbook of Material Culture*, pp. 74–84. London: Sage.

Ingold, T., ed. (1996) *Key Debates in Anthropology* (Debate: 'Aesthetics is a Cross-Cultural Category', presentations for the motion by J, Coote and H. Morphy). London: Routledge.

Johnson, M.H. (2006) 'On the Nature of Theoretical Archaeology and Archaeological Theory', *Archaeological Dialogues* 13(2): 117–32.

Layton, R. (2003) 'Art and Agency: A Reassessment', *The Journal of the Royal Anthropological Institute* 9(3): 447–64.

Lipset, D. (2005) 'Dead Canoes: The Fate of Agency in Twentieth-Century Murik Art', *Social Analysis* 49(1): 109–40.

Morphy, H (1991) *Ancestral Connections: Art and an Aboriginal System of Knowledge*. Chicago, IL: University of Chicago Press.

Morphy, H. (1992) 'From Dull to Brilliant: The Aesthetics of Spiritual Power among the Yolngu', in J. Coote and A. Shelton (eds) *Anthropology, Art and Aesthetics*, pp. 181–208. Oxford: The Clarendon Press.

Morphy, H. (2007) *Becoming Art: Exploring Cross-Cultural Categories*. Oxford: Berg.

Morphy, H. and Perkins, M. (2006) *The Anthropology of Art: A Reader*. Oxford: Blackwell.

O'Hanlon, M. (1995) 'Modernity and Graphicalization of Meaning: New Guinea Highland Shield Design in Historical Perspective', *Journal of the Royal Anthropological Institute* 1 (September): 469–92.

Price, S. (1989) *Primitive Art in Civilised Places*. Chicago, IL: University of Chicago Press.

Thomas, N. and Pinney, C., eds (2001) *Beyond Aesthetics: Art and the Technologies of Enchantment*. Oxford: Berg.

Winter, I. (2007) 'Agency Marked, Agency Ascribed: The Affective Object in Ancient Mesopotamia', in Robin Osborne and Jeremy Tanner (eds) *Art's Agency and Art History*, pp. 42–69. Oxford: Blackwell.

Chapter 32

The Blind Man's Stick (BMS) hypothesis

Lambros Malafouris

THINK OF A BLIND MAN WITH A STICK. Where does the blind man's self end and the rest of the world begin? Where do we draw, and on what basis can we draw, as Gregory Bateson asks, a delimiting line across the extended cognitive system which determines the blind man's locomotion? At the tip of the stick? At the handle of the stick? Or at some point halfway up the stick? (Bateson 1973, 318). More than four decades after Merleau-Ponty (1962), Polanyi (1966) and Bateson (1973) first raised these questions they are still with us, maybe more timely than ever if one considers the radical innovations that are taking place in the area of neuroprosthetics. For instance, Brain–Machine Interfaces (BMIs) now make it possible for a monkey or human to operate remote devices directly via neural activity (see Nicolelis 2001; 2003; Donoghue 2002). Of course, impressive as the ability to control a robotic hand by 'thought' alone might seem, it is, nonetheless, simply the most recent chapter of an old story, which archaeology knows well, and of which the first chapter was probably already written some 2.6 mya [million years ago; ed. note] with the manufacture of the first stone tools. Indeed, from an archaeological perspective the challenge that the BMS question, or in fact any other Brain–Artefact Interface, poses is even greater. One needs simply to replace the stick with any of the numerous artefacts that constitute the diverse archaeological inventory of prehistoric material culture, from the tools and marked objects of the Stone Age to the more recent symbolic or 'exographic' (Donald 1991) technologies, in order to realize that there is more to the BMS question than a mere philosophical puzzle. The problem is further complicated if one considers that for archaeology the stick is not simply a 'pathway along which differences are transmitted under transformation' (Bateson 1973, 318), but instead a *difference* in itself. The stick, to use McLuhan's formulation, is very often not the medium but the message (1964).

It may not be as obvious as it should be, but some of the most challenging questions about the emergence of human intelligence and our understanding of cultural transmission and the cognitive life of things depend on where precisely one decides, implicitly or explicitly, to draw the line between the mind and the material world and infer the direction of causality between biology and culture. Even for those of us willing to subscribe to some of the presently available relational models of embodiment recognizing that differentiations between 'inside' and 'outside' often do not apply in the context of mediated activity and material engagement, the question of the ontological status of the stick remains vague. And as long as the ontological status of the BMS remains vague it threatens not only to obscure the whole edifice of cognitive archaeology and material culture studies, but also to undermine the value and contribution of these growing research fields in the contemporary sciences of mind.

Consequently, and in order to make more clear my case in this paper, let me clarify that I will use the BMS in two major senses: on the one hand I will use the BMS as an exemplar of the Brain–Artefact Interface (BAI) – used here in the broader sense of long-term material engagement to signify the point of intersection between cognition and material culture. Secondly, I will use the BMS also as a working hypothesis stating that *the functional structure and anatomy of the human brain is a dynamic construct remodelled in detail by behaviourally important experiences which are mediated, and often constituted, by the use of material objects and artefacts which for that reason should be seen as continuous integral parts of the human cognitive architecture*. Grounded upon the general framework of the Material Engagement approach (Malafouris 2004; 2007; Renfrew 2004; 2006; 2007; Malafouris & Renfrew 2010; Malafouris 2010) the aim of the BMS hypothesis is to help us redraw the line that separates brains, bodies and things by bringing the archaeology of mind face to face with two crucial and to a large extent neglected questions: (1) The first question concerns the causal efficacy of the material world in the human cognitive system and the functional anatomy of our brain. (2) The second question pertains to the boundaries of the human cognitive system and what became known recently as the hypothesis of extended mind (Clark & Chalmers 1998): Can things, made of wood, stone and clay, really be parts of the machinery of human thought?

I start with the former question which in the case of our BMS example can be put as follows: *What does the stick do for the blind?*

Our common sense would seem to favour the idea of a cognitive agent who simply exploits a tool in order to overcome a perceptual deficiency by substituting vision with touch. To a certain extent this is precisely what happens as imaging studies indicate in the case of many blind subjects. Cortical areas normally underlying vision are recruited for other sensory modalities. Characteristic of these cross-modal plastic effects is the case of proficient Braille readers where not only do the sensorimotor representation of the reading finger become greatly developed in comparison to the representation of other fingers (Pascual-Leone *et al.* 1993; Sterr *et al.* 1998) but tactile processing is also 'rerouted' to occipital visual cortex (Sadato *et al.* 1996; 1998; Cohen *et al.* 1999). In fact, using transcranial magnetic stimulation (TMS) Pascual-Leone *et al.* (1993) were able to show that modifications in the motor cortical map associated with the reading hand in Braille readers was already manifest after only a few hours of training. Recent studies have further refined and extended these findings addressing the differences between early and late blind, and the role of tactile versus verbal/linguistic aspects of the task (for review see Merabet *et al.* 2005).

We have already touched upon the issue of sensory substitution and neural recycling, but now, and returning to our BMS example, the question to ask is the following: What about the stick? Does the stick play some causal role in the above processes of cross-modal plasticity, and if it does just what role might that be? The striking effects of sensory deprivation or lesion in one modality in the development of the remaining modalities (Bavelier & Neville 2002, 443) have been explored in detail over recent decades, but the possible role of external mediations – at the behavioural level – in bringing about and shaping the nature of these changes has received far less attention. Beyond the case of the blind, a much discussed study by Berti & Frassinetti (2000) may offer some additional insights that can prove extremely useful here. As they characteristically remark, simply holding a stick causes a remapping of far space (the space beyond reaching distance) to near space (the space within reaching distance). The significance of the above findings becomes clearer if we bear in mind the unique role which tactile perception plays in combining the 'efferent' and 'afferent' signals responsible for our sense of self. This process has been extensively investigated in attribution rubber hand experiments showing that 'tactile perception plays a major role in defining the boundary between the self and the external world' (Haggard *et al.* 2003, 173).

This brings us to our second of the previously posed questions: *Does the biological boundary of the skin apply in the case of the blind?*

Attempting to answer that question it might be useful receding into the phenomenological background of the issue, which may give us a better grasp of the relation between the blind and the stick. Seen from such a phenomenological angle it can be argued that the blind person using a stick does not sense the stick, but the presence or the absence of objects in the outside environment. Although the stick offers the actual means for this exploration it is itself forgotten. As Merleau-Ponty describes:

> The blind man's stick has ceased to be an object for him, and is no longer perceived for itself; its point has become an area of sensitivity, extending the scope and active radius of touch, and providing a parallel to sight. In the exploration of things, the length of the stick does not enter expressly as a middle term: the blind man is rather aware of it through the position of objects than of the position of objects through it. The position of things is immediately given through the extent of the reach that carries him to it, which comprises, besides the arm's reach, the stick's range of action (Merleau-Ponty 1962, 143).

The stick, as with many other examples of prosthetic 'phenomenological osmosis' (Leder 1990), becomes through time and practice incorporated and thus transparent. Tactile sensation is somehow projected onto the point of contact between the tip of the stick and the outside environment. Following what we discussed above relevant to the unique role which tactile perception plays in integrating our sense of self, this extension in the body schema could also mean that the brain treats the stick as it were a part of the body. But should we go so far as to conceive of the stick as a structural part of the blind man's living body and cognitive system?

Part of our inherent difficulty in dealing with questions of the above type stems, I believe, from the dominant representational or computational thinking that characterizes cognitive sciences, in general, and cognitive archaeology, in particular, and the major shortcomings of which I discuss extensively elsewhere (Malafouris 2004; 2007).

An easy way to overcome this conceptual problem might be by attempting to rephrase our previous question, about how to conceive of the stick as being relevant to the blind man's living body and cognitive system, using the philosophical perspective of 'active externalism' and the so-called 'parity principle': When a part of the world – like the blind man's stick in our case – 'functions as a process which, were it to go on in the head, we would have no hesitation in accepting as part of the cognitive process, then that part of the world is (for that time) part of the cognitive process' (Clark & Chalmers 1998). The implications of removing or damaging that part of the world, equals that of removing or damaging a part of the brain. The question thus can be put as follows: Are we not, by removing the blind man's stick, preventing him from seeing? Or more specifically, are we not preventing the world from touching his visual cortex? This is the point where neuroplasticity meets the extended mind and where one of the major challenges for 'neuroarchaeology' arises.

References

Bateson, G. (1973) *Steps to an Ecology of Mind*, London: Granada.

Bavelier, D. and H.J. Neville (2002) 'Cross-modal plasticity: where and how?', *Nature Reviews Neuroscience*, 3: 443–52.

Berti, A. and F. Frassinetti (2000) 'When far becomes near: remapping of space by tool-use', *Journal of Cognitive Neuroscience*, 12: 415–20.

Clark, A. and D. Chalmers (1998) 'The extended mind', *Analysis*, 58 (1): 10–23.

Cohen, L.G., R. A. Weeks, N. Sadato, P. Celnik, L. Ishii and M. Hallett (1999) 'Period of susceptibility for cross-modal plasticity in the blind', *Annals of Neurology*, 45 (4): 451–60.

Donald, M. (1991) *Origins of the Modern Mind*, Cambridge (MA): Harvard University Press.

Donoghue, J.P. (2002) 'Connecting cortex to machines: recent advances in brain interfaces', *Nature Neuroscience Supplement*, 5: 1085–88.

Haggard, P., M. Taylor-Clark and S. Kennet (2003) 'Tactile perception, cortical representation and the bodily self', *Current Biology*, 13: 170–73.

Leder, D. (1990) *The Absent Body*, Chicago (IL): University of Chicago Press.

Malafouris, L. (2004) 'The cognitive basis of material engagement: where brain, body and culture conflate' in E. DeMarrais, C. Gosden and C. Renfrew (eds), *Rethinking Materiality: the engagement of mind with the material world*, (McDonald Institute Monographs), Cambridge: McDonald Institute for Archaeological Research.

Malafouris, L. (2007) 'Before and beyond representation: towards an enactive conception of the Palaeolithic image' in C. Renfrew and I. Morley (eds), *Image and*

Imagination: a global history of figurative representation, (McDonald Institute Monographs), Cambridge: McDonald Institute for Archaeological Research.

Malafouris, L. (2010), 'Grasping the concept of number: how did the sapient mind move beyond approximation?', in C. Renfrew and I. Morley (eds) *The Archaeology of Measurement: comprehending heaven, earth and time in ancient societies*, Cambridge: Cambridge University Press.

Malafouris, L. and C. Renfrew (eds) (2010) *The Cognitive Life of Things: recasting the boundaries of the mind*, (McDonald Institute Monographs), Cambridge: McDonald Institute for Archaeological Research.

McLuhan, M. (1964) *Understanding Media: the extensions of man*, Cambridge (MA): MIT Press.

Merabet, L.B., Rizzo, J.F., Amed, A., Somers, C.D. and Pascual-Leone, A. (2005) 'What blindness can tell us about seeing again: merging neuroplasticity and neuroprostheses', *Nature Reviews Neurosicence*, 6: 71–7.

Merleau-Ponty, M., (1962) *Phenomenology of Perception*, London: Routledge.

Nicolelis, M.L.A. (2001) 'Actions from thoughts', *Nature*, 409 (18): 403–7.

Nicolelis, M.L.A. (2003) 'Brain-machine interfaces to restore motor function and probe neural circuits', *Nature Reviews Neuroscience*, 4: 417–22.

Pascual-Leone, A., A. Cammarota, E.M. Wassermann, J.P. Brasil-Neto, L.G. Cohen and M. Hallett (1993) 'Modulation of motor cortical outputs to the reading hand of braille readers', *Annals of Neurology*, 34 (1): 33–7.

Polanyi, M., (1966) *The Tacit Dimension*, New York: Routledge.

Renfrew, C. (2004) 'Towards a theory of material engagement', in E. DeMarrais, C. Gosden and C. Renfrew (eds) *Rethinking Materiality: the engagement of mind with the material world*, (McDonald Institute Monographs), Cambridge: McDonald Institute for Archaeological Research.

Renfrew, C. (2006) 'Becoming human: the archaeological challenge', *Proceedings of the British Academy*, 139: 217–38.

Renfrew, C. (2007) *Prehistory, the Making of the Human Mind*, London: Weidenfeld and Nicolson.

Sadato, N., Pascual-Leone, A., Grafman, J. *et al*, (1996) 'Activation of the primary visual cortex by Braille reading in blind subjects', *Nature*, 380: 526–8.

Sadato, N., Pascual-Leone, A., Grafman, J., Deiber, M.P., Ibanez, V. and Hallett, M. (1998) 'Neural networks for braille reading by the blind', *Brain*, 121 (7): 1213–29.

Sterr, A., Muller, M.M, Elbert, T., Rockstroh, B., Pantev, C. and Taub, E. (1998) 'Perceptual correlates of changes in cortical representation of fingers in blind multifinger Braille readers', *Journal of Neuroscience*, 18 (11): 4417–23.

Chapter 33

Making culture and weaving the world

Tim Ingold

Artefacts and organisms

In his book, *Chance and Necessity* (1972), the distinguished biochemist Jacques Monod sets out to determine the distinctiveness of living things by means of a contrast with that other class of things – apparently also endowed with properties of form and function – commonly known as artefacts. Monod invites us to imagine ourselves as the intelligent inhabitants of another planet, who are concerned to find out whether there is any evidence of artefact-producing activity back on Earth. We plan to send a spacecraft to Earth, equipped with a computer programmed to distinguish, on the basis of a range of input data, between objects that are artefacts and objects that are not. How should this program be written?

Perhaps the machine should be instructed to search for regularities of form, such as the various kinds of symmetry or the rhythmic repetition of structural elements. Since these are quite general properties of matter at the molecular level, it would have to concentrate on the macroscopic features of the objects it encountered. Even then, however, the things it could potentially register as 'artefacts' might include the Giant's Causeway, a butterfly's wings, almost every kind of sea-shell, the beehive, the head of a sunflower, and a host of other objects that – with the possible exception of the hive – we would not normally think of as artificial at all. On the other hand, the machine would discount the crumpled linen of a bed from which you have just risen after an uneasy night's sleep, and might even place the bed-making that you do at home every morning in the same category of artefact production as the bed-making that goes on in the furniture factory!

Maybe the problem arises because in programming our computer to attend only to the formal, structural properties of objects we have ignored the most salient feature of artefacts: that they have been designed for a purpose. Suppose, then, that we make up for this deficiency by instructing the machine to attend to the performance of things, that is to their capacity to function in particular ways to which they might seem peculiarly adapted rather than contingently apt (Preston, 2000). A naturally occurring stone of suitable size and shape may, in the absence of anything better, be serviceable for hammering nails into wood, but the carpenter's hammer has been specifically designed for the job, and as such would qualify as an artefact whereas the stone would not. As Monod (1972: 20) points out, however, the property of functional design is not unique to artefacts but is also shared by all living things. Parallels in this regard between human engineering and organic adaptation are legion: the wings of planes and birds, the helical arrangement of fibres in rope and of muscles in fish, the combination of arch and suspension in bridge construction and in the skeleton of the brontosaurus.[1] Our computer, registering these parallels as equivalents, would totally fail to discriminate between artefacts and life-forms.

There is only one solution to the problem, Monod concludes. That is to instruct the computer to look not just at the finished objects, but at the processes wherein they come into being: their genesis and construction. It would then note at once that of objects endowed with form and function, there is one class for which these properties result from the application to their constituent materials of forces *exterior* to the objects themselves, and another class whose properties owe nothing to the action of external forces, and everything to 'morphogenetic' interactions that are *internal* to the objects in question. The first class, then, comprises artefacts, whereas the second comprises living organisms (Monod 1972: 21). The former are 'made' by some agency that lies outside them, the latter just 'grow', entirely of their own accord.

Now let us suppose that we have successfully programmed our computer to attend to formal regularity, functional performance and morphogenesis. Amidst much popular anticipation and excitement, the craft with the computer on board is about to be despatched to Earth. Before taking up the story of what it finds there, let me pause to consider precisely what is implied about artefacts by their characterisation as things that are made rather than things that grow.

Making and growing

First of all, a distinction is assumed between form and substance, that is between the design specifications of the object and the raw materials of which it is composed. In the case of living things, it is supposed that the information specifying the design of an organism is carried in the materials of heredity, the genes, and thus that every new life-cycle is inaugurated with the injection of this specification into a physical medium. But with artefacts, this relation between form and substance is inverted. Form is applied from without, rather than unfurled from within. The very distinction between a within and a without of things, however, implies the existence of a *surface*, where solid substance meets the space of action of those forces that impinge upon it. Thus the world of substance – of brute matter – must present itself to the maker of artefacts as a surface to be transformed.

In commonsense, practical terms, this is not too hard to imagine. Many of our most familiar artefacts are (or were, before the days of synthetic materials) made of more or less solid stuff such as stone, metal, wood or clay. The very usefulness of these objects depends on their being relatively resistant to deformation. We ourselves, however, inhabit a gaseous medium – air – which, offering no such resistance, not only allows complete freedom of movement, but also transmits both light and sound. Quite apart from the obvious fact that we need air to breathe, and thus simply to stay alive, the possibilities of movement and perception (visual and aural) that air affords are crucial for any artefact-producing activity. There is, then, a pretty clear distinction between the gaseous medium that surrounds us and the solid objects that clutter our environment; moreover the patterns of reflected light off the surfaces of these objects enable us to see for what they are (Gibson 1979: 16–22).

These practical considerations, however, all too easily become confused in our thinking with speculations of a more metaphysical kind. To show why this is so, let me return to the case of the beehive whose status as an artefact – as I hinted at above – is somewhat equivocal. Surely, hives don't grow. In so far as it results from the application of exterior force to raw material, the hive would appear to be as much 'bee-made' as the human house is 'man-made'. Or is it? Musing on this question, Karl Marx famously came to the conclusion that 'what from the very first distinguishes the most incompetent architect from the best of bees, is that the architect has built a cell in his head before he constructs it in wax'. In other words, the criterion by which the house is truly artificial – and by comparison the beehive only figuratively so – is that it issues from a representation or 'mental model', which has been fashioned in the imagination of the practitioner prior to its execution in the material. We may assume that bees, by contrast, lack the powers of imagination, and have no more conception of their hives than they do of their own bodies, both of which are formed under genetic control (Ingold 1983, cf. Marx 1930: 169–170).

Here, the exteriority of the forces that shape artefacts is understood in quite another sense, in terms not of the physical separation of gaseous medium and solid substance but of the *meta*physical separation of mind and nature (Williams and Costall 2000). Unlike the forms of animals and plants, established through the evolutionary mechanism of natural selection and installed genetically at the heart of the organisms themselves (in the nucleus of every cell), the forms of artefacts are supposed to have their source within the human mind, as preconceived, intellectual solutions to particular design problems. And whereas organic growth is envisaged as a process that goes on *within* nature, and that serves to reveal its inbuilt architecture, in the making of artefacts the mind is understood to place its ideal forms upon nature. If making thus means the imposition of conceptual form on inert matter, then the surface of the artefact comes to represent much more than an interface between solid substance and gaseous medium; rather it becomes the very surface of the material world of nature as it confronts the creative human mind.

This is precisely the kind of view that lies at the back of the minds of anthropologists and archaeologists when they speak of artefacts as items of so-called 'material culture'. The last thing they mean to suggest, in resorting to this phrase, is that in the manufactured object the domains of culture and materiality somehow overlap or intermingle. For nothing about their substantive composition *per se* qualifies artefacts for inclusion within culture. The materials from which they are made – wood, stone, clay or whatever – are in any case generally available in nature. Even with objects manufactured from synthetic materials for which no naturally occurring counterparts exist, their status as items of material culture is in no way conditional upon their 'unnatural' composition. A child's toy made of plastic is no more cultural, on that account, than its wooden equivalent. It is the form of the artefact, not its substance, that is attributed to culture. This is why, in the extensive archaeological and anthropological literature on material culture, so little attention is paid to actual materials and their properties. The emphasis is almost entirely on issues of meaning and form – that is, on culture as *opposed* to materiality. Understood as a realm of discourse, meaning and value inhabiting the collective consciousness, culture is conceived to hover over the material world but not to permeate it. In this view, in short, culture and materials *do not mix*; rather, culture wraps itself around the universe of material things, shaping and transforming their outward surfaces without ever penetrating their interiority. Thus the particular surface of every artefact participates in the impenetrable surface of materiality itself as it is enveloped by the cultural imagination.

On encountering a basket

The spacecraft, having been launched from its home planet, has now arrived on Earth. The machine incorporating our sophisticated artefact-detection program rolls out onto the ground, and its computer sets to work to process the data on the first object it encounters. It is at once thrown into utter confusion. Not that it has too much difficulty with its investigations of form and function: the object is round, with a flat bottom and raised, sloping sides, rather like an upside-down truncated cone; moreover it is hollow and open at the top, which allows it to function as a container and carrying device. The problem arises when it comes to the dynamics of construction. Equipped with a time-reversal facility, our machine is able to clock back to an earlier period and to another locale, where it watches the object gradually taking shape. It wants to know whether it has grown of its own accord, or whether it has been made in the fashion of a true artefact. Let us take a look at what is actually going on.

A human being is at work here, surrounded by a quantity of fibrous material, evidently derived from the stems or leaves of certain plants. Taking a bundle of fibres, placed lengthwise alongside one another to form a kind of rope of about one centimetre in diameter, she deftly begins to turn it between her fingers to produce a flat coil, at the same time using somewhat broader fibres to wrap transversely around successive turns of the coil so as to keep it compact and prevent it from unravelling. After a while, the wrapped coil becomes recognisable as the base of the object. Then, as the work proceeds – evenly, rhythmically and repetitively – the turns of the coil are drawn tighter, so that each rises partly upon the base of its predecessor, thus forming the sides. The machine is, of course, observing the construction of a coiled basket (on this technique, see Hodges 1964: 131–132). I have the finished thing beside me as I write: it is the waste-paper basket in my study.

What is it about this mundane object that causes so much confusion? Why does its construction not seem to conform with our normal expectations of what is involved in making things? I think the reasons are threefold. The first has to do with the topology of *surface*, the second with the application of *force* and the third with the generation of *form*. In all these respects, as I shall argue, basketry appears to confound the distinction between making and growing. Of course the construction of baskets is normally described as a process of weaving. Our computer program was confounded because it tried to comprehend weaving as a modality of making. Thwarted in the attempt, it had to fall back on the default hypothesis that the basket had simply grown under its own internal dynamic, a result that seemed equally implausible. In what follows, I would like to suggest that we think of making, in reverse, as a modality of weaving. This switch of emphasis could, I believe, open up a new perspective not just on basketry in particular, but on our relationships with all the different kinds of objects in our surroundings. But it would also have the effect of softening the distinction between artefacts and living things which, as it turns out, are not so very different after all.

Surface, force and the generation of form

We have seen that making, in what for convenience I shall henceforth call the 'standard view', implies the prior presence of a surface to be transformed. Thus the flint knapper chips away at the surface of stone, the carpenter carves and chisels the surface of wood, the blacksmith hammers on the surface of molten metal, and the potter applies manual pressure to the surface of clay. But once it has been cut and prepared for weaving, the basketmaker does nothing to the surface of her fibrous material. In the process of weaving, the surface of the basket is not so much transformed as built up. Moreover, there is no simple or straightforward correspondence between the surface of the basket and the surfaces of its constituent fibres. For example, the two outer surfaces of the transverse wrapping fibres are alternately 'outside' and 'inside' so far as the surface of the basket is concerned. Indeed it is in the nature of weaving, as a technique, that it produces a peculiar kind of surface that does not, strictly speaking, have an inside and an outside at all.

In the special case of coiled basketry, there is a limited parallel with the technique of coil-building in pottery. Here the clay is first rolled out into long, thin, worm-like strips, rather analogous to the fibrous 'ropes' of the basketry coil. These strips are then wound around and around to form the base and sides of the vessel. In this case too, a surface is built up. In the process, however, the original surfaces of the coiled strips congeal into a single mass, and the final smoothing leaves no trace of the original mode of construction. But there is another difference, equally critical, which brings me to the issue of force. The potter may have to contend with the force of gravity (his material, being both heavy and pliable, is inclined to sag). But the clay does not exert any independent force. This is not the case with basketry, however, which involves the bending and interweaving of fibres that may exert a considerable resistance of their own. Indeed the basket holds together, and assumes a rigid form, precisely because of its tensile structure.[2] In short, the form of the basket is the resultant of a play of forces, both internal and external to the material that makes it up. One could say that the form unfolds within a kind of force field, in which the weaver is caught up in a reciprocal and quite muscular dialogue with the material.

This observation leads me to the final question concerning the generation of form. According to the standard view, the form pre-exists in the maker's mind, and is simply impressed upon the material. Now I do not deny that the basketmaker may begin work with a pretty clear idea of the form she wishes to create. The actual, concrete form of the basket, however, does not issue from the idea. It rather comes into being through the gradual unfolding of that field of forces set up through the active and sensuous engagement of practitioner and material. This field is neither internal to the material nor internal to the practitioner (hence external to the material); rather, it cuts across the emergent interface between them. Effectively, the form of the basket emerges through a pattern of *skilled movement*, and it is the rhythmic repetition of that movement that gives rise to the regularity of form. This point was made long ago by Franz Boas, in his classic work on *Primitive Art*.

> The basketmaker who manufactures a coiled basket, handles the fibres composing the coil in such a way that the greatest evenness of coil diameter results. . . . In making her stitches the automatic control of the left hand that lays down the coil, and of the right that pulls the binding stitches over the coil brings it about that the distances between the stitches and the strength of the pull are absolutely even so that the surface will be smooth and evenly rounded and that the stitches show a perfectly regular pattern.
>
> (Boas 1955 [1927]: 20)

Spirals in nature and art

Boas illustrates the point with a drawing. Opposite, I have placed another drawing [see original reading], this time taken from the work of the great biologist D'Arcy Wentworth Thompson, *On Growth and Form*. It depicts the shell of a certain kind of gastropod. Although both the coiled basket and the shell have a characteristic spiral form, they are spirals of different kinds: the first is an equable spiral, the second logarithmic (that is, the radius of each successive whorl increases arithmetically in the one instance, and geometrically in the other). The equable spiral, as D'Arcy Thompson explains, is characteristic of artificial forms that have been produced by mechanically bending, coiling or rolling up a given length of material, whereas the logarithmic spiral is commonly produced in nature as a result of growth by deposition, where the material is cumulatively laid down at one end whilst maintaining an overall constancy of proportion (Thompson 1961 [1917]: 178–179). Either way, however, the form appears to emerge with a certain logical inevitability from the process itself, of rolling up in the former case and laying down in the latter.

Now it is very often assumed, in the study of both organisms and artefacts, that to ask about the form of things is, in itself, to pose a question about *design*, as though the design contained a complete specification that has only to be 'written out' in the material. This assumption is central to the standard view which, as we have already seen, distinguishes between living and artificial things on the criterion of the interiority or exteriority of the design specification governing their production without questioning the premise that the resultant forms are indeed specified independently and in advance of the processes of growth or manufacture wherein they are realised. Thus it is supposed that the basic architecture of the organism is already established, as a genetic 'blueprint', from the very moment of conception; likewise the artefact is supposed to pre-exist, fully represented as a 'virtual object' in the mind, even before a finger has been lifted in its construction. In both cases the actualisation of the form is reduced to a simple matter of mechanical transcription: all the *creative* work has already been done in advance, whether by natural selection or human reason.[3]

How then, starting from this premise, might we set about accounting for the formation of spirals in nature and in art, in the shell of the gastropod and the coil of the basket? The account would likely run along the following lines: the form of the shell is internally specified in the gastropod's genetic inheritance, and revealed in its growth; the form of the basket is externally specified in the mind of the weaver, as part of a received cultural heritage, and revealed in its manufacture. Now natural selection, according to Darwinian orthodoxy, designs organisms to be adapted to their particular conditions of life, and as many scholars have suggested, a somewhat analogous process of blind variation and selective retention, operating in the arena of cultural ideas, could do likewise in designing artefacts that are well suited to their purpose. The fact that we come across spirals in the growth of living things (as in gastropods) as well as in the making of artefacts (as in basketry) may be purely fortuitous, or it may be the outcome of some kind of adaptive convergence – of natural selection and the human intellect, operating quite independently, arriving at parallel solutions to what might be, in essence, a rather similar problem of engineering design. If, to be more precise, the solution calls for a spiral of the equable type, or alternatively of the logarithmic type, then this is what we will find in the resultant forms, regardless of whether the design itself is encoded genetically or culturally. Hence by this account, the distinction between equable and logarithmic spirals would not, in itself, be relevant as an index of the organic or artefactual status of the objects concerned.

The limits of design

According to the standard view, as outlined above, form is fully explicable in terms of the design that gives rise to it. Once you have accounted for the genesis of the design you have, to all intents and purposes, explained the form. Or have you? Would it be possible, even in theory, for any design to specify the form of an organism or artefact *completely*? In his fascinating study of the design principles embodied in the construction of living organisms and manufactured artefacts, originally written as a textbook for students of engineering, Michael French speculates on the question of just how much information would be needed to specify every aspect of the form of an organism (1988: 266–267). His conclusion is that the amount would be unimaginably large, far beyond what could be coded in the DNA of any known life-form. Nor is the situation any different with artefacts. True, even the greatest achievements of human engineering are no match for the most commonplace of organisms: thus the steam locomotive, as French wryly observes, 'is simplicity itself compared with the intricacies of the buttercup' (1988: 1). But then, no human design could approach the DNA of the genome in its informational content. Once again, a complete specification would apparently lie beyond the realms of possibility. In short, the forms of both organisms and artefacts seem to be significantly underdetermined by their underlying blueprints. That being the case, French suggests, we may have to recognise that a great many features of organisms and artefacts are merely accidental, due to chance, revealing not the designs themselves but their limitations.

Though intended to shore up the argument from design against the objection that no specification can be exhaustive, this appeal to chance is a *reductio ad absurdum* that does more to highlight the poverty of the argument itself. To show why, let me turn to another example of spiral formation: the vortex of bathwater as it runs out of the plug-hole. Is the form of the vortex a matter of chance? It is certainly not dictated by the specifications of any design. You can determine whether the spiral runs clockwise or anticlockwise by setting up a current through the water with your hand; beyond that, however, the spiral appears to form of its own accord. But its formation is anything but an accident. It can, in fact, be explained in terms of well-established principles of fluid dynamics.

The example of the vortex is not my own; it is taken from the work of the biologist Brian Goodwin (1982), who uses it to say something very important about the generation of spiral forms in living organisms. In a certain species of snail, the majority of individuals have shells with a right-handed, logarithmic spiral, but in some the spiral is left-handed. It has been shown that the direction of the spiral is controlled by the products of a particular gene, just as the direction of the spiral vortex in bathwater is controlled by the intentional movement of your hand. But – and this is the crucial point – the *form* of the shell is no more the product of a genetic programme than is the form of the vortex the product of a design in your mind. There is, in short, no 'design' for the spiral of the gastropod shell. Rather, the form arises through a process of growth within what is known technically as the 'morphogenetic field' – that is, the total system of relations set up by virtue of the presence of the developing organism in its environment. And the role of genes in the morphogenetic process is not to specify the form, even incompletely, but to set the parameters – such as handedness and spiral angle – within which it unfolds (Goodwin 1982: 111).

On the growth of artefacts

Returning from the growth of organisms to the manufacture of artefacts, a parallel argument applies. Just as organic form is generated in the unfolding of the morphogenetic field, so the form of the artefact evolves within what I have called a field of forces. Both kinds of field cut across the developing interface between the object (organism or artefact) and an environment which, in the case of the artefact, critically includes its 'maker'. Where the organism engages its environment in the process of ontogenetic development, the artefact engages its maker in a pattern of skilled activity. These are truly creative engagements, in the sense that they actually *give rise* to the real-world artefactual and organic forms that we encounter, rather than serving – as the standard view would claim – to transcribe pre-existent form onto raw material. Moreover as a moment's reflection on the example of the vortex in bathwater will show, the properties of materials are directly implicated in the form-generating process. It is therefore no longer possible to sustain the distinction between form and substance that, as we have seen, is so central to the standard view of making things. Finally, the templates, measures and rules of thumb of the artisan or craftsman no more add up to a design for the artefacts he produces than do genes constitute a blueprint for the organism. Like genes, they set the parameters of the process but do not prefigure the form.[4]

All these points apply to the making of a coiled basket. Thus the equable form of the spiral base of the basket does not follow the dictates of any design; it is not imposed upon the material but arises through the work itself. Indeed the developing form acts as its own template, since each turn of the spiral is made by laying the longitudinal fibres along the edge formed by the preceding one. Now D'Arcy Thompson was of course right to point out that there is a difference between *bending* material into shape, as in basketry, and an organism's *growing* into it, as with the shell of the gastropod, and that this can lead to forms with contrasting mathematical properties. Nevertheless, if the unfolding of the morphogenetic field is described as a process of growth, would it not be fair to suggest that there is a sense in which artefacts, whose forms likewise evolve within a field of forces, 'grow' too – albeit according to different principles?

We could describe that growth as a process of *autopoiesis*, that is, the self-transformation over time of the system of relations within which an organism or artefact comes into being. Since the artisan is involved in the same system as the material with which he works, so his activity does not transform that system but is – like the growth of plants and animals – part and parcel of the system's transformation of itself. Through this autopoietic process, the temporal rhythms of life are gradually built into the structural properties of things – or as Boas put it, with regard to artefacts:

> The rhythm of time appears here translated into space. In the flaking, adzing, hammering, in the regular turning and pressing required in the making of coiled pottery, in weaving, regularity of form and rhythmic repetition of the same movement are necessarily connected.
>
> (Boas 1955 [1927]: 40)

The artefact, in short, is the crystallisation of activity within a relational field, its regularities of form embodying the regularities of movement that gave rise to it.

I would like to conclude this comparison of the coiled basket and the gastropod shell by commenting on the reasons for the remarkable durability of their respective forms. According to the standard view, since form emanates from design, the persistence of form can only be explained in terms of the stability of the underlying design specifications. In the case of the organism these specifications are genetic, in the case of the artefact they are cultural. The constancy of form is thus a function of the fidelity with which genetic or cultural information is copied from one generation to the next, combined with the effects of natural selection – or its analogue in the realm of cultural ideas – in weeding out less well adapted variants.

The argument I have proposed here, however, is just the opposite. If forms are the outcomes of dynamic, morphogenetic processes, then their stability can be understood in terms of the generative principles embedded in the material conditions of their production. For the shell the principle is one of invariant proportion; for the basket it is the principle that every increment of longitudinal extension is coupled to what has gone before by transverse attachment. Whereas the first principle, through simple iteration, will always and everywhere generate a logarithmic spiral, the second will just as reliably generate an equable one. It is these generative principles, and not the fidelity of genetic or cultural copying, that underwrite the constancy of the respective forms, and explain their persistence over immense spans of both historical and evolutionary time.

Baskets and textiles

Let me return to the computerised artefact-detection machine of our earlier 'thought experiment'. It is, we may imagine, still roaming around in search of evidence. Having first had the misfortune to encounter my waste-paper basket, the next thing it runs into is my unmade bed. What is it to make of the bed-linen? The basket, at least, had a clearly recognisable form; the linen appears to have no form at all. Of course, if the machine could only straighten out the sheets, it would immediately notice their perfect rectangular outline. But it is not programmed to do this: for if it was, if it carried an instruction to straighten out whatever it encountered, then it would naturally discover artefacts everywhere – of its own creation!

Now the sheets on my bed are instances of what we normally call textiles. The word 'textile' comes from Latin *textilis*, meaning a woven fabric, and *texere*, meaning to weave. If a textile is anything woven, and given that this applies just as well to baskets as to bed-linen, should not basketry be regarded as a *sub-division* of textiles? One answer might be that it really doesn't matter. Confronted with an object that is evidently the result of some kind of weaving process, it makes no difference whether we call it a basket or not: what matters are the properties of the object itself, and the significance it holds for those who made and use it. But if the distinction is as arbitrary and inconsequential as all that, how come that it is so deeply rooted in our thinking? For some reason, we find that to conceive of a basket as a kind of textile is somehow strange; it seems to turn our conventional understandings upside down. Why?[5]

A clue to the answer lies in our common habit of referring to woven cloth as 'material'. It would seem that in the case of textiles, the weaving process has not in itself produced a form, but only the raw substance for acts of form-making that have still to come. These acts, as in garment-making, may involve cutting out and stitching, stretching on a frame, overprinting, or other techniques, all of which involve the impression or inscription of form upon stuff that has already been woven. In basketry, by contrast, the weaving itself yields a rigid, three-dimensional form. Attempting to assimilate basketry within our overall conception of artefact-making, we are inclined to imagine that this form is somehow superimposed upon raw substance which, in this case, is identified with the original fibrous material. In short, basketry and textiles have been split apart in our thinking by the opposition between form and substance which, as we have seen, lies at the heart of the standard view of what it means to make things. Whereas weaving a basket is conceived as a kind of making, with textiles the making is understood to be secondary to, and to follow on from, the weaving. In both cases, however, the emphasis is placed squarely on the *products* – on baskets as solid forms, on cloth as material substance – at the expense of the *process* itself. There is evidence for this in the fact that in everyday usage, the notion of 'textile' is no longer anchored to weaving at all but is freely extended to any fabrics – including knitted, felted, tufted and bonded materials – so long as they can be worked up in further acts of form-making.

If we attend to the process of weaving, however, we do find a significant technical contrast. It is almost certain that, historically, basketry preceded the weaving of cloth, and there is evidence to suggest that the techniques of the latter actually developed from basketry (which, in turn, may have developed from net-making). The basketmaker's toolkit is a very simple one: even today, no more is required than a sharp knife and a heavy rod (known as a 'driving-iron') used for beating down the weave (Hodges 1964: 147). To weave cloth, however, you need one other piece of apparatus, namely a loom. This is for the simple reason that the constituent fibres of the weave exert no tensile force in themselves. The function of the loom is to keep the warp threads under tension for as long as the weaving proceeds. Once the weaving is complete and the tension removed, the cloth holds together through nothing more than the friction of its fibres. Unlike the basket, however, it cannot hold to a rigid form, for the basket, as we have seen, keeps its form only thanks to the tension exerted by its elements.

Making as a way of weaving

It is now time to return to my earlier suggestion, that we reverse our normal order of priorities and regard making as a modality of weaving, rather than the other way around. One intriguing observation points us in this direction. Our word 'loom' comes from Middle English *lome*, which originally referred to a tool or utensil of any kind. Does this not suggest that to our predecessors, at least, the surface-building activity of weaving, rather than any of those activities involving the application of force to pre-existing surfaces, somehow epitomised technical processes in general?

The notion of making, of course, defines an activity purely in terms of its capacity to yield a certain object, whereas weaving focuses on the character of the process by which that object comes into existence. To emphasise making is to regard the object as the expression of an idea; to emphasise weaving is to regard it as the embodiment of a rhythmic movement. Therefore to invert making and weaving is also to invert idea and movement, to see the movement as truly generative of the object rather than merely revelatory of an object that is already present, in an ideal, conceptual or virtual form, in advance of the process that discloses it. The more that objects are removed from the contexts of life-activity in which they are produced and used – the more they appear as static objects of disinterested contemplation (as in museums and galleries) – the more, too, the process disappears or is hidden behind the product, the finished object. Thus we are inclined to look for the meaning of the object in the idea it expresses rather than in the current of activity to which it properly and originally belongs. It is precisely this contemplative attitude that leads to the redesignation of the ordinary objects of the quotidian environment, such as my waste-paper basket, as items of 'material culture' whose significance lies not so much in their incorporation into a habitual pattern of use as in their symbolic function. In suggesting that the relation between making and weaving be overturned, my purpose is to bring these products of human activity back to life, to restore them to the processes in which they, along with their users, are absorbed.[6]

In what way, then, does weaving epitomise human technical activity? What sense does it make to say that the blacksmith in his forge, or the carpenter at his bench, in transforming the surfaces of metal and wood respectively, is actually weaving? Of course, to adopt this idiom is to interpret the notion of weaving more broadly than is customary. It does, however, help to draw attention to three points which I think are crucial to a proper understanding of technical skills.[7] First, skill is not a property of the individual human body in isolation, but of the whole system of relations constituted by the presence of the artisan in a richly structured environment. This system corresponds to what I described above, in specific reference to weaving, as a field of forces. Second, skill is not just the mechanical application of external force, but – as exemplified in weaving – involves qualities of care, judgement and dexterity (see Pye 1968: 22). This implies that whatever the practitioner does *to* things is grounded in an attentive, perceptual involvement *with* them, or in other words, that he watches and feels as he works. As the Russian neuroscientist Nicholai Bernstein wrote some fifty years ago, the essence of dexterity lies not in bodily movements themselves, but in the 'tuning of the movements to an emergent task', whose surrounding conditions are never precisely the same from one moment to the next (Bernstein 1996: 23). Third, skilled action has a narrative quality, in the sense that every movement, like every line in a story, grows rhythmically out of the one before and lays the groundwork for the next. As in weaving, to recall Boas's point, spatial structure grows out of temporal rhythm.

Weaving by birds and humans

In my preliminary discussion of the distinction between things that are made and things that grow, I showed that in the standard view, making takes place at the interface between the cultural imagination and the material world, and therefore that it is an exclusively human achievement. Bees, according to this view, do not literally 'make' their hives, since they have no conception of the task before them. The same could be said of the work of birds in constructing their nests, or of the beaver in building its dam. Unlike the products of human labour, hives, nests and dams are not generally admitted as objects of material culture. Now if weaving is understood as a modality of making, then it, too, must be uniquely human. But if on the other hand – to invert the relation – making is conceived as a modality of weaving, then there is no a priori reason why weaving should be restricted to human beings. More generally, could the qualities of skill outlined above, and which are epitomised in the activity of weaving, be attributed just as readily to the practices of non-human animals?

Perhaps the closest parallel to human weaving in the animal kingdom is furnished by the nest building of male weaverbirds, which has been investigated in a remarkable series of studies by N.E. and E.C. Collias (1984). The nest is made from long strips torn from the leaves of grasses, which are intertwined in a regular lattice formed by passing successive strips over and under, and in a direction orthogonal to, strips already laid. It is held together, and attached to the substrate, by a variety of stitches and fastenings. The bird uses its beak rather like a needle in sewing or darning; in this the trickiest part lies in threading the strip it is holding under another, transverse one so that it can then be passed over the next. The strip has to be pushed under, and through, just far enough to enable the bird to let go with its beak in order to shift its hold and pull it up on the other side. If the free end is left too short, the strip may spring back; pushed too far, it could fall to the ground. Mastering this operation calls for a good deal of practice. From an early age, weaverbirds spend much of their time manipulating all kinds of objects with their beaks, and seem to have a particular interest in poking and pulling pieces of grass leaves and similar materials through holes. In females this interest declines after about the tenth week from hatching, whereas in males it continues to increase. Experiments showed that birds deprived of opportunities to practise and suitable materials are subsequently unable to build adequate nests, or even to build at all. Indeed, fiddling about with potential nest material appears to be just as essential for the bird, in preparing itself for future building, as is the babbling of the human infant in preparing itself for speech (Collias and Collias 1984: 201, 206–207, 212, 215–220).

It is evident from the Collias's account that the abilities of the weaverbird, just like those of the human basketmaker, are developed through an active exploration of the possibilities afforded by the environment, in the choice of materials and structural supports, and of bodily capacities of movement, posture and prehension. Furthermore, what the bird acquires through practice is not a programme of instructions or a set of design specifications to be mechanically applied, but the ability to adjust its movements with exquisite precision in relation to the evolving form of its construction. As Collias and Collias report:

> In watching the numerous attempts of young male weavers to fasten initial strips of nest materials and their gradual improvement in weaving ability, it seemed to us that what every young male weaver has to learn is what in subjective terminology one would call 'judgement.'
>
> (1984: 219)

Finally, the form of the nest results from the iteration of a small number of basic movements, and from the fact that the bird stands throughout on the same spot while it weaves all around – above, below and in front – pushing out the developing shell of the main chamber as far as its beak will reach, and then tilting gradually backwards to complete the antechamber and entrance (ibid. 193, 209–210).

In brief, each of the three qualities of skill which, as I have shown, are exemplified in human weaving, is also clearly in evidence in the nest building of weaverbirds. The conventional notion that the birds' activity is due to instinct whereas humans follow the dictates of culture is clearly inadequate. The form of the nest no more follows the specifications of an innate, genetically transmitted design than does that of the coiled basket, in our earlier example, follow the specifications of an acquired, culturally transmitted one. In all likelihood the human basketmaker has an idea in mind of the final form of the construction whereas the weaverbird almost certainly does not. Yet in both cases, it is the pattern of regular movement, not the idea, that generates the form. And the fluency and dexterity of this movement is a function of skills that are developmentally incorporated into the *modus operandi* of the body – whether avian or human – through practice and experience in an environment. Such skills are fundamentally resistant to codification in the form of representations or programmes, which have then only to be executed in the material. That is why the most sophisticated computer program ever devised, as envisaged in the 'thought experiment' with which I began, could still fail to comprehend the nature of even such a mundane object as a waste-paper basket.

Conclusion

In his study of baskets and basketry among the Yekuana, a native people of southern Venezuela, David Guss observes that the master craftsman in this society, a person accredited with exceptional wisdom, 'not only weaves the world when making a basket, but in everything he does' (1989: 170). Yet this creative process of world-weaving, he suggests, is not limited to the experts. It rather engages all Yekuana people throughout their lives – albeit at a lower level of perfection – in their manufacture of the essential equipment of traditional livelihood, from canoes and graters to houses and baskets. Paradoxically, however, in translating the indigenous term by which such locally produced items are distinguished from commercially manufactured 'stuff' (such as tin cans and plastic buckets) that arrives from outside, Guss renders them as things not woven but made. Moreover the essence of making, in his view, lies in loading the object with metaphorical significance or semiotic content, such that artefacts become a mirror in which people can see reflected the fundamentals of their own culture. The symbolic capacity of artefacts, Guss insists, 'far outweighs their functional value' (1989: 70). Weaving the world, then, turns out to be a matter of 'making culture', of submitting the disorder of nature to the guidelines of traditional design.

Now the idea that in the manufacture of objects like houses, baskets and canoes, people 'weave the world', is entirely in keeping with the argument I have developed in this chapter – namely that making should be regarded as a way of weaving, and not *vice versa*. But the epistemology by which Guss converts these products of world-weaving back into 'things made', instances of the cultural transformation of nature (1989: 161), is one that I reject. It is, as I have shown, an epistemology that takes as given the separation of the cultural imagination from the material world, and thus presupposes the existence, at their interface, of a surface to be transformed. According to what I have called the standard view, the human mind is supposed to inscribe its designs upon this surface through the mechanical application of bodily force – augmented, as appropriate, by technology. I mean to suggest, to the contrary, that the forms of objects are not imposed from above but grow from the mutual involvement of people and materials in an environment. The surface of nature is thus an illusion: we work from within the world, not upon it. There are surfaces of course, but these divide states of matter, not matter from mind. And they emerge within the form-generating process, rather than pre-existing as a condition for it.

The philosopher Martin Heidegger expressed the very same point through an exploration of the notions of building and dwelling. Opposing the modernist convention that dwelling is an activity that goes on within, and is structured by, an environment that is already built, Heidegger argued that we cannot engage in any kind of building activity unless we already dwell within our surroundings. '*Only if we are capable of dwelling*', he declared, '*only then can we build*' (1971: 160, original emphasis). Now dwelling is to building, in Heidegger's terms, as weaving is to making in mine. Where making (like building) comes to an end with the completion of a work in its final form, weaving (like dwelling) continues for as long as life goes on – punctuated but not terminated by the appearance of the pieces that it successively brings into being.[8] Dwelling in the world, in short, is tantamount to the ongoing, temporal interweaving of our lives with one another and with the manifold constituents of our environment (see Ingold 1995).

The world of our experience is, indeed, continually and endlessly coming into being around us as we weave. If it has a surface, it is like the surface of the basket: it has no 'inside' or 'outside'. Mind is not above, nor nature below; rather, if we ask where mind is, it is in the weave of the surface itself. And it is within this weave that our projects of making, whatever they may be, are formulated and come to fruition. Only if we are capable of weaving, only then can we make.

Notes

1   These examples are taken from French (1988: 32–36, 117–118, 161), who provides many more. See also Steadman (1979, Chapter 2).

2   To adopt an architectural term, the coherence of the basket is based upon the principle of *tensegrity*, according to which a system can stabilise itself mechanically by distributing and balancing counteracting forces of compression and tension throughout the structure. Significantly, tensegrity structures are common to both artefacts and living organisms, and are encountered in the latter at every level from the cytoskeletal architecture of the cell to the bones, muscles, tendons and ligaments of the whole body (Ingber 1998).

3   This prioritisation of design over execution betrays a ranking of intellectual over physical labour that is one of the characteristic features of Western modernity. It divides the scientist from the technician, the engineer from the operative, the architect from the builder, and the author from the secretary.

4   In a wonderful article on the building of the great cathedral of Chartres, in the thirteenth century, David Turnbull (1993) shows that this most magnificent of human artefacts was preceded by no plan whatsoever. The building took shape gradually,

over a considerable period of time, through the labour of many groups of workers with diverse skills, whose activities were loosely co-ordinated by the use of templates, string and constructive geometry.

5   I was moved to reflect on this question by a superb exhibition, mounted in the Righton Gallery of Manchester Metropolitan University in March–April 1996. Entitled *Beyond the Bounds*, the exhibition consisted of works by artists and craftspeople that deliberately set out to explore and challenge the conventional categorical distinction between basketry and textiles. The notes accompanying the exhibition pointed out that baskets and textiles have become so separate in our thinking that we routinely fail to observe the connection between them. Wondering about the reasons for this separation eventually led me to write this paper. I would like to thank Mary Butcher, in particular, for encouraging me to do so, and participants in the 'Art, architecture and anthropology' seminar at the University of Manchester for their inspiration.

6   I do not intend by this to reinstate the time-worn opposition between practical utility and symbolic meaning. The notion of utility implied by this opposition is an impoverished one that sets up a radical division between the acting subject and the object used, and reduces skilled practice to purely mechanical relations of cause and effect. In speaking of the *absorption* of artefacts into the life-activity of their users my aim is to emphasise, to the contrary, the inseparability of persons and objects in real-life contexts of accustomed (that is, usual) practice. The usefulness of an object, then, lies not in its possession of utility but in its partaking of the *habituality* of everyday life (Gosden 1994: 11).

7   For a fuller elaboration of these points, see Ingold (1996).

8   Among the Bunu, a Yoruba-speaking people of central Nigeria, this idea is expressed in their weaving of lengths of white cloth:

> Cloths are often removed [from the loom] without cutting, accentuating the endless quality of these pieces. When eventually the unwoven warp is cut in order to use the cloth, the fringes are left, again suggesting continuity rather than the finiteness of cut and hemmed edges.
>
> (Renne 1991: 715)

References

Bernstein, N. A. 1996 'On dexterity and its development'. In M. L. Latash and M. T. Turvey (eds) *Dexterity and its Development*. Mahwah, NJ: Lawrence Erlbaum Associates.

Boas, F. 1955 *Primitive Art*. New York: Dover Publications (original 1927).

Collias, N. E. and E. C. Collias 1984 *Nest Building and Bird Behavior*. Princeton, NJ: Princeton University Press.

French, M. J. 1988 *Invention and Evolution: Design in Nature and Engineering*. Cambridge: Cambridge University Press.

Gibson, J. J. 1979 *The Ecological Approach to Visual Perception*. Boston: Houghton Mifflin.

Goodwin, B. C. 1982 'Biology without Darwinian spectacles'. *Biologist* 29: 108–112.

Gosden, C. 1994 *Social Being and Time*. Oxford: Blackwell.

Guss, D. M. 1989 *To Weave and Sing: Art, Symbol and Narrative in the South American Rain Forest*. Berkeley, CA: University of California Press.

Heidegger, M. 1971 *Poetry, Language, Thought* (trans. A. Hofstadter). New York: Harper and Row.

Hodges, H. 1964 *Artefacts: An Introduction to Early Materials and Technology*. London: John Baker.

Ingber, D. E. 1998 'The architecture of life'. *Scientific American* 278(1): 30–39.

Ingold, T. 1983 'The architect and the bee: reflections on the work of animals and men'. *Man* (N.S.) 18: 1–20.

—— 1995 'Building, dwelling, living: how animals and people make themselves at home in the world'. In M. Strathern (ed.) *Shifting Contexts*. London: Routledge.

—— 1996 'Situating action V: The history and evolution of bodily skills'. *Ecological Psychology* 8: 171–182.

Marx, K. 1930 *Capital*, Vol. I (trans. E. and C. Paul from 4th German Edition of *Das Kapital* 1890). London: Dent.

Monod, J. 1972 *Chance and Necessity* (trans. A. Wainhouse). Glasgow: Collins.

Preston, B. 2000. 'The functions of things: a philosophical perspective on material culture'. In P. Graves-Brown (ed.) *Matter, Materiality and Modern Culture*. London: Routledge.

Pye, D. 1968 *The Nature and Art of Workmanship*. Cambridge: Cambridge University Press.

Renne, E. P. 1991 'Water, spirits and plain white cloth'. *Man* (N.S.) 26: 709–722.

Steadman, P. 1979 *The Evolution of Designs: Biological Analogy in Architecture and the Applied Arts*. Cambridge: Cambridge University Press.

Thompson, D. W. 1961 *On Growth and Form*, abridged edition, ed. J. T. Bonner. Cambridge: Cambridge University Press (original 1917).

Turnbull, D. 1993 'The ad hoc collective work of building Gothic cathedrals with templates, string and geometry'. *Science, Technology and Human Values* 18: 315–340.

Williams, E. and A. Costall, 2000. 'Taking things more seriously: psychological theories of autism and the material–social divide'. In P. Graves-Brown (ed.) *Matter, Materiality and Modern Culture*. London: Routledge.

Index